Popular Culture

Popular Culture:
An Introductory Text

edited by

Jack Nachbar

and

Kevin Lause

Bowling Green State University Popular Press
Bowling Green, OH 43403

The University of Wisconsin Press
1930 Monroe Street
Madison, Wisconsin 53711

3 Henrietta Street
London WC2E 8LU, England

www.wisc.edu\wisconsinpress

7 6 5 4 3

Printed in the United States of America

Library of Congress Catalogue Card No.: 92-73539

ISBN 0-87972-571-0 (cloth)
ISBN 0-87972-572-9 (paperback)

Acknowledgments

The editors gratefully acknowledge the cooperation of the Findlay-Hancock County Public Library, Luren Dickinson, Director. Our thanks also to the members of the Bowling Green Popular Press who often had to construct this book from scraps of paper: Judy Amend, Jennifer Moore, Angie Pierce and Karen Wiechman. Wendy Woloson contributed valuable editing advice. And Pat Browne had the patience of Job.

Contents

Introduction

✌ ✌

Getting to Know Us

Getting to Know Us
An Introduction to the Study of Popular Culture: What is this Stuff that Dreams are Made of?

We Have Seen Our Culture, and It Is Us. Sort Of.

> I can't get no
> Satisfaction......
>
> You can't always get what you want,
> But if you try sometime
> You can get what you need.
>
> Two quotes from The Rolling Stones

The Rolling Stones may have been right about life, but their song would be a funeral dirge for popular culture. Popular culture is about "Satisfaction" all right, but its major concern is in ensuring that people can get what they want regardless of whether they need it or not. Not getting what you want is for monks, communists, and fans of the Cleveland Indians; getting it is why popular culture gave us credit cards.

And popular culture doesn't want you to have to sweat a lot in getting it, either. Stay on your couch and change channels, stay in your car and eat healthily, stay home alone and reach out and touch someone, stay on your Exercycle and listen to a good book. Popular culture has discovered the secret of perpetual motion in the age of relativity: stay in one place and everything will come to you. Around the world in thirty minutes—just stay tuned.

Popular culture is so easy to get because it's everywhere to be gotten—it surrounds us the way water surrounds a fish, as a transparent environment crucial to our survival. A fish looks *through* the water rather than *at* it and so do we tend to overlook the omnipresence of popular culture precisely because it is such a familiar part of our everyday environment. Consider for a moment, however, that the clothes you are wearing (mass produced, advertised, sold for profit), the mall or store you purchased them in (and the ritual of shopping which shaped the process and got you there and back), the food you eat (from restaurants or grocery store chains), the television programs which inform and entertain you (beamed to over 98% of American homes to be watched for an average of seven and a half hours each day), and the very textbook you are holding in your hands right now are *all* aspects of popular culture and you may begin to see how completely we are suspended in these popular culture seas—deep waters indeed. And just as water is necessary for the fish to survive, so popular culture has us dependent on the vast array of choices it offers for us to select from in satisfying *our* needs as well. The fact that we all get hungry and have to eat is a matter of elementary biology; the fact that American children recognize Ronald McDonald more often than any other figure except Santa Claus is a result of our popular culture and the choices we have made. We need to *understand* this culture, then, so that we can be more than a fish who just eats what's dropped into his tank, watches whatever passes by and ends up in the "big flush"—a passive part of his environment right to the finish.

Popular culture is not merely "present," however; it is also eager to please. "We know what you want..." purrs the soft, seductive voice narrating a promotional videotape for a famous shopping mall chain, and it is indeed part of popular culture's goal to find out what we want—what we think and feel and believe—and then transform its products into the image of our desires. We'll spend our hard-earned dollars to dial 1-900-POPCULT only if we can be certain that the figure on the other end of the line is a flawless reflection of an image shot through the focal point of our hearts and minds. The voice that answers our call should respond with the invitation Julia Roberts offers to Richard Gere in an early scene of the movie *Pretty Woman* (1990): When Gere asks Roberts her name she echoes popular culture's standing offer to all of us—"What would you like it to be?" Thus popular culture unlocks our hearts and then sells the key back to us.

Julia Roberts' willingness and ability to become whatever Richard Gere wanted her to be enabled her to spend "an obscene amount of money," and *Pretty Woman*'s similar skill in mirroring its audience's fantasies enabled the movie's producers to do the same. *Pretty Woman* gave Americans a materialistic fairy tale which perfectly reflected the needs of an audience immersed in the 1980s, the "decade of greed." *Pretty Woman* promises that economic and class differences are merely apparent—not real—that they can readily be overcome by a little love and a lot of money. The film taps the audiences' "champagne wishes and caviar dreams," brings the lifestyles of the rich and famous to a poor "working" girl, and makes certain that love is not sacrificed in the process—the perfect guilt-free-happily-ever-after for an audience that wanted to HAVE IT ALL, materially and emotionally. The movie kept audiences on the line to the tune of 100 million dollars at the box-office and went on to become the number one best selling video early the following year—a pretty tune indeed.

The producers of popular culture will go to great lengths to mold their products to reflect the audience beliefs and values. When the producers of *Fatal Attraction* (1987) screened an early version of their film for a test audience, the response was far from enthusiastic. Audiences were critical of the movie's original ending (in which Glen Close's Alex commits suicide to the haunting strains of *Madame Butterfly* and effectively frames Michael Douglas' Dan in the process by using a knife which has only his fingerprints on it), and registered complaints about aspects of all three of the film's major characters—Alex, Dan and Dan's wife Beth (Anne Archer). The filmmakers listened to the voice (and groans) of the people and returned to the studio to reshoot critical scenes in a manner more reflective of audience desires.

Essential to this process was the filmmakers' belief that their original film had been out of touch with the beliefs and values of mainstream America at the height of the Age of Reagan. The test audiences were "uncomfortable" with a sympathetic portrait of an independent careerwoman, and they were deeply supportive of the traditional values surrounding the sanctity of the home and protecting the nuclear family. While the early version of the movie punished Dan for his callous philandering ways—and ripped apart his home and wife in the process—the revised film highlighted Alex's villainy. Now Alex became the only careerwoman in the movie (Beth's former identity as a schoolteacher anxious to return to work was dropped), and that status was presented in a distinctly unfavorable light—Alex dresses in black leather, lives in a barren loft surrounded by burning oil drums that look like "witches caldrons," and has a "fatal attraction" for the home and family and husband she can never have. Alex proceeds to vent her frustration by attacking that world she cannot join—she pours acid on the family car, boils the family bunny, and concludes with a no-holds-barred slasher assault on the home itself. The new ending is a high noon face-off between the two opposing views of women in which the loyal wife eliminates the independent homewrecker and thus salvages home and family in the process. The final shot is of a framed photograph of the family shattered by the battle, but still intact.

The revised *Fatal Attraction* became the most notable blockbuster hit of 1987 and the "Fatal Attaction phenomenon" was the subject of seven-page cover stories in both *Time* and *People.* Susan Faludi argues that the film was an important example of the *backlash* in the "undeclared war against American women" which helped define the values and beliefs of the Reagan-era mass audience. In her book *Backlash,* Faludi demonstrates that the producers of *Fatal Attaction* managed to tap these feelings in a manner reflected by other box-office successes of the same year:

> In all four of the top-grossing films released [in 1987], women are divided into two groups—for reward or punishment. The good women are all subservient and bland housewives (*Fatal Attraction* and *The Untouchables*), babies or voiceless babes (*Three Men and a Baby* and *Beverly Hills Cop II*). The female villains are all women who fail to give up their independence, like the mannish and child-hating shrew in *Three Men and a Baby,* the hip-booted gunwoman in *Beverly Hills Cop II,* and the homicidal career woman in *Fatal Attraction.* (116)

Faludi's bestselling 1992 book demonstrates how similar themes were reflected in a vast range of popular culture—from television and magazines to fashion and politics—and reveals how shrewd and fortunate the makers of *Fatal Attraction* were in revising their film to mirror the spirit of the age.

The German word "zeitgeist" is often used to refer to this "spirit of an era"—the major beliefs and values which describe the particular outlook of a culture during a specific period of time. Many cultural analysts use the dividing yardsticks of decades to describe changing national "zeitgeists" so that the 50s become the Age of Conformity, the 60s the Age of Youth and Rebellion, the 70s the 'Me' Decade, and the 80s the Decade of Greed, for example. But what is most important for our purposes here is that we see that popular culture can become the key to formulating definitions of a "zeitgeist" and can be cited as evidence that our conclusions are sound. This reflective nature of popular culture is similar to Walt Whitman's observation that "the writers of a time hint the mottoes of its Gods" and has been expressed recently by Professor Allan Bloom:

> What each generation is can best be discovered in its relation to the permanent concerns of mankind. This in turn can best be discovered in each generation's tastes [and] amusements. . . these culture peddlers have the strongest motives for finding out the appetites of the young—so they are useful guides into the labyrinths of the spirit of the times. (19)

The study of popular culture as a reflective mirror of its audience must focus upon two aspects of this zeitgeist—the "transitory" and the "concrete." The zeitgeist which characterizes a particular era is composed of "transitory" attitudes and perspectives which last only as long as the era itself and then fade from view—perhaps to return in later times, perhaps not. But an era's zeitgeist also expresses deep-seated, highly significant "concrete" beliefs and values which transcend the specific time period and represent the fundamental character of the culture itself. Most elements of popular culture reflect both of these zeitgeist levels in important ways. *Fatal Attraction* demonstrates a Reagan Era perspective on independent, single career women, but also displays a firm reverence for the nuclear family and the sancitity of the home which characterizes American culture throughout its history; *Pretty Woman* shows its decade's delight in shopping as a transforming experience, but it also demonstrates that romantic love is capable of overcoming all obstacles in its path—a "concrete" belief demonstrated by some other "pretty women" in American culture (like Pocahantas and Scarlett O'Hara, for example). Popular culture reflects both change and stability. In other words: it tells us what we are now, what we have been in the past and where the two overlap to define what we may always be.

This "reflective" study of popular culture is guided by the *Popular Culture Formula.* This "equation" states that the popularity of a given cultural element (object, person or event) is directly proportional to the degree to which that element is reflective of audience beliefs and values. The *greater* the popularity of the cultural element—in an era and/or over time—the *more* reflective of the zeitgeist this element is likely to be. The formula assumes that audiences *choose* a specific cultural element over other alternatives because they find it attractive in its reassuring reflection of their beliefs, values and desires. Audiences 'vote' in the Nielsen Ratings for one program over another from similar motives to those that caused them to vote for Ronald Reagan over Jimmy Carter in 1986—that is, one choice is more reflective of audience convictions than the other.

When applied to American popular culture the formula suggests that we study football rather than soccer, MTV rather than opera, top-rated television programs rather than select exhibitions of modern painting, fast food restaurants with illustrated menus rather than elegant dining rooms with menus in French, etc. And, most importantly, the formula demands that we examine these cultural elements not as ends in themselves but as means of unlocking their meaning in the culture as a whole. The formula says that *Fatal Attraction* is significant not because we find its plot clever and exciting and its stars attractive or repellent but because of *why* we find the plot compelling and *why* we agree with the rewards and punishments meted out to the characters.

The popular culture formula is a valuable tool in that it both aids us in selecting cultural elements for examination and reminds us how to examine them. Too many students of popular culture end their studies with conclusions which suggest they have followed Yogi Berra's advice that "You can observe a lot just by watching" rather than heeding the formula's demand that they dig more deeply and ask *why* audiences choose one cultural element over another. The study of popular culture is a quest for meaning, not merely facts or nostalgia or entertainment.

The need and desire of the producers of popular culture to reflect audience beliefs and values in order to ensure that their product will be accepted by the masses, and the uncertainty involved in defining the precise nature of this zeitgeist at any particular time (e.g. What might have happened to their movie had the producers of *Fatal Attraction* released it in its original version?), helps to account for another important characteristic of popular culture: popular culture tends to be imitative, repetitive and conservatively resistant to change. Once producers discover a successful formula—a set of ingredients which seems to reflect audience desires—they tend to repeat it as often as it remains successful. Box-office hits (*Rocky*) produce sequels (II, III, IV, V) and imitations of their formula with slightly different characters in somewhat altered settings (*The Karate Kid*—I, II and III). Successful popular heroes (Ronald Reagan) have their sequel imitation (George Bush), and successful popular objects (Nikes) have theirs (Reeboks, L.A. Gear). The popular culture formula may usefully be broadened, therefore, to include the identification and analysis of such *trends* and patterns as well as the examination of especially popular individual examples of the successful model.

If the producers of popular culture were interested *only* in reflecting our beliefs, values and desires then the world they fashion for our satisfaction and amusement would be a soothing one indeed— a "cafeteria" of goods offered for us to pick and choose from with only our whims and convictions as a guide. The reality is more complex, however, and more often bears a stronger resemblance to a messy food fight than to an orderly cafeteria. Popular culture surrounds us not only in the comforting manner that water does a fish, but also in the way that the flesh-eating zombies encircled the besieged house in the movie *Night of the Living Dead* (1968). The *producers* of popular culture are *promoters* as well—they create a product which reflects us and will draw us to the mirror, but they also come chasing after us to instill values and beliefs likely to ensure their success. Listen, for example, to the *second* part of that mall promotional tape recorded in such a softly seductive voice: "We know what you want...AND WE WANT YOU TO WANT IT." This is the formative, "attacking" aspect of popular culture which subtly blurs the distinction between needs and wants so that while "needs" are literally biological (we've got to have these things to live) popular culture often convinces us that our "wants" are what we *need* when our needs have been satisfied (we've *got* to have these things to have a life). Popular culture does not merely reflect our hearts and minds—it manipulates them.

The clearest example of the way popular culture strives to alter our thinking in addition to reflecting it can be found in the multi-billion dollar industry of advertising, a mammoth enterprise devoted solely to calling the public's attention to needs it never knew it had. In her book *Are They Selling Her Lips?—Advertising and Identity,* Carol Moog describes advertising's encircling assault:

> Advertising shapes egos, influences our sense of self-worth. It reinforces our fears that we never have enough; we're never healthy enough, good-looking enough, or lively enough.... It feeds our wishes, profits from our illnesses, plays on our insecurities, cautions us, exhorts us, reminds us of our past and future, and encourages us to behave in ways we have never behaved before.... The best we can do...is to acknowledge and understand how it's influencing us...and then attempt to separate ourselves from the images, and act objectively. (222-23)

Advertising's "hidden persuaders" are a valuable example of the formative mode of popular culture because their intentions are so obvious—their goal is to sell us a bill of goods both literally and figuratively. But *all* popular culture instructs and molds audience beliefs to one degree or another simply because the very values being reflected are necessarily being communicated as well. The increasing violence in movies reflects an increasingly violent society and may then lead that society to become more accepting of violence—which then leads to more violent movies which then affect the society—and on and on in an endless cycle of reflection and reshaping.

Popular culture is a "Funhouse Mirror" because it both *reflects* our "image" back to us but also *alters* our image in the process of doing so. Understanding the way that popular culture exercises this dual function makes the study of it a valuable "survival manual," for we may thereby be able to exercise a greater element of control over what we believe—we may *choose* to believe something rather than merely being *led* to do so.

The basic themes of our study can be summarized by examining a term crucial to understanding both sides of the Funhouse Mirror. We can perhaps define the concept of "mindset" by illustrating it in another format—a familiar folk tale cast in a new light.

Once upon a time there was a vast unexplored mass of territory which we can term "The Land of Reality"—immense, unknown, unmapped. Three countries—each unknown to the other two—existed across the wide ocean from the land of Reality, and each decided independently to explore whatever was across the seas. The first country's exploring ship landed in the northern wastes of the land of Reality, and the intrepid explorers returned with the news that "Reality is cold, snowy, and bleak and the inhabitants share the chill nature of their environment." The second country's vessel arrived in the great center of Reality and found only water—"Reality is a land of lakes and rivers," the crew reports. The third nation finds the southern tip of the land to be "hot and humid" and the natives there to be friendly, energetic and full of entertaining festival foods and dances.

Each country now defines the entire land of Reality solely based upon the limited evidence they have experienced—Reality is cold, wet and hot. Each country is "correct," given the context of its limited experience. Each is unaware that its view is incomplete—each is *certain* it is correct in its view of Reality. And each produces objects (e.g. maps) and heroes (e.g. the crusading explorers) to express its view of Reality and to communicate it to the members of its society.

Each country has formed a "mindset"—a view of Reality based upon only limited evidence but believed to be entirely correct by those who hold it. The mindset consists of beliefs (the view of Reality) and values (the judgment or evalulation of that Reality) expressed in material forms (artifacts).

Now let us see how a mindset—once formed—comes to affect both vision and behavior.

Imagine that the King of the land of Reality becomes aware that his land has been visited by three different countries and decides to return the favor. Arriving in the first country the King finds himself placed in a house with no heating and is slightly bored by the fact that he is "entertained" by being escorted to bed before dark and given an extra blanket. Arriving at the second country he is astonished to find that he is never permitted to leave his boat! And in the third country the room he stays in is so hot that he has to sleep naked.

Each country and its inhabitants thus view this new element of Reality through the tinted lens of the culture's mindset, and that view in turn determines the actions taken and the values attached to the new phenomenon. The distorting lens has been passed along to each inhabitant so that each now shares the essential bias of the culture.

And these are precisely the characteristics which define our own mindsets as well. Our mindsets are formed by two elements: our individual experience (which makes each mindset unique) and our cultural experience (which we share with others and thus makes mindsets of those in the same culture bear a strong resemblance to each other). A mindset is like a special pair of glasses we wear whose lenses are all ground differently so as to meet our individual needs, but which are all tinted the same color—the lenses are ground by our unique experiences as individuals, the shading is provided by our culture's beliefs and values. And each of us is all too often unaware of the glasses we are wearing and thus, like each of the exploring countries, becomes convinced that only the vision of *others* needs correcting. It is so difficult to turn our glasses around to examine ourselves that we often echo Butch Cassidy's certainty in the hit movie *Butch Cassidy and the Sundance Kid* (1969) that we have "got vision—the rest of the world wears bifocals."

What is needed to examine our own glasses, of course, is simply a mirror and, as we have seen, popular culture can provide the reflection necessary to expose and highlight our cultural beliefs and values. And by reversing the process and using our trained glasses to examine popular culture to expose the beliefs and values it seeks to *instill* in our mindset, we can exercise a valuable amount of control over what we *choose* to believe; while it is inevitable that our glasses will be tinted, we can still have some say in how dark a tint we receive and how "blind" we become as a result.

Because Americans view reality through glasses tinted red, white and blue it often leads us to assume that our beliefs and values are "correct" or simply "common sense." Popular culture studies can quickly reveal our cultural biases, however, and thus enable us to *debate* what had previously been merely assumed as we come to see that each culture is "right" within the context of its own history and experience. James Fallows notes in his book *More Like Us* that Americans have always viewed the adage "a rolling stone gathers no moss" in a positive light ("If you keep on moving and being active, you will not get rusty"). A British dictionary, on the other hand, interprets the same proverb as "One who constantly changes his place of employment will not grow rich"—as a warning against the lack of perseverance, in other words (61). And the movie *Fatal Attraction* has been a resounding success in Japan—in its *original* version, reflecting as it does deeply embedded cultural beliefs about the loss of personal honor and the price that must be paid to balance the scales.

We must be careful to heed the lesson of "mindsets," therefore, and never assume that popular culture studies of the *American* mindset simply reveal that which is "obvious," "right," or "common sense." Popular culture reflects and molds beliefs and values that are so deeply embedded that their truth is assumed rather than proven. The study of popular culture brings these assumed-to-be-true beliefs and values to the surface and into the light of day—reflected in our mirrors, refracted through our lenses.

The major themes of our study of popular culture, therefore, will revolve around several important characteristics of our subject. The themes we have examined suggest that popular culture:

1) consists of artifacts (objects and people) and events (activities surrounding the objects and people).

2) reflects audience beliefs and values (it satisfies us—"We know what you want...").

3) shapes audience beliefs and values (it arouses and frustrates us—"...WE WANT YOU TO WANT IT").

4) is commercial (it is produced with the goal of making money).

5) is often imitative (of itself)—it hopes that what has worked before will work again.

6) surrounds us—it forms the fabric of our everyday lives.

While these characteristics help us study and identify popular culture, they leave open a very significant question: What *is* the stuff we are examining? What does *popular culture* mean?

The answer is that it means different things to different people—and when that happens a fight usually breaks out. It has.

The Battle Over Definitions

Popular culture and pornography have at least one thing in common: few people can define either one but everybody knows them when they see them. And some would go one step further and argue that the two share a second important characteristic as well—namely that we should be ashamed of ourselves for experiencing either one. The debate over definitions is between those who believe that popular culture is junk food for the minds of the masses (that two hundred and fifty million people can't be right) and those who believe that just because everybody likes something is no reason for us to hate it (and is probably all the *more* reason for us to pay attention to it and attempt to understand its meaning and appeal). It's the *snobs* vs. the *rest of us*, and there is more at stake than merely the meaning of a few words. Whose culture is it, anyway?

Let's begin with the part of the definition which arouses little argument. "Popular" simply refers to that which is (or has been) accepted or approved of by large numbers of people; in America, Madonna is popular, Saddam Hussein is not. In Iraq, the situation is reversed, which can tell us similar important things about the "popular" Iraqi mindset. The object of our study becomes the specific group which has made a particular cultural element "popular" by accepting or approving it.

This definition of "popular" necessarily implies an important element of *choice* as well. Because no one can choose to do otherwise, we cannot properly term "breathing" or "eating," for example, to be "popular" even though each is certainly accepted by and approved of by large groups of people. People must select a cultural artifact or event because they are voluntarily attracted to it—because they view it as an acceptable or appealing way of fulfilling a need or want—in order for it to be truly "popular" and meaningful. A "popular" culture which was coerced—forced upon a group by tyranny or biology—would tell us nothing since an offer that can't be refused isn't really an offer at all, and an "election" with only one candidate cannot be an expression of the people's voice.

It is also important to note that our definition of "popular" does not limit it to that which is *presently* accepted or approved of. "Popular" refers to the specific group which selects an artifact or event, and it does not matter whether that group consists of our neighbors or our ancestors. This definition allows us to examine the mindset of the young people who idolized The Beatles in the 1960s ("All You Need Is Love") and that of their children who compete for tickets to the latest concert tour by Guns and Roses ("Welcome to the Jungle") in the 1990s. "Popular" culture is as much about history as it is about news, as much about what we *were* as about what we *are*.

How *much* of history can be examined through the funhouse mirror of popular culture, however, *is* a matter of dispute. Some critics argue that popular culture has been around as long as there have been groups of people available to be entertained and instructed by its appeal. Chief among these "Classicists" is Ray Browne, who finds "popular culture" to be very old indeed:

> As the way of life of a people, popular culture has existed since the most primitive times, when it was simple and uncomplicated. It has obviously become more complex and sophisticated as means of communicating and ways of life have developed. (13)

Browne's perspective is especially valuable because it rescues from oblivion a vast world of daily existence which historians often ignore. If "history" is a river of infinite length upon which floats "great" men and women and their significant deeds and words, then Browne would ask us to remember the masses of people who lived along the banks of that river and produced their own culture as a reflection of their hopes and dreams, fears and fantasies. Browne enables us to examine the ways the great majority of people have lived their lives in the teeming *background* of history in the same way that most of us today play our games, listen to our stories and dream our dreams as the river of leaders and thinkers flows past. The "Classicists" include in their vision of the popular culture audience the Athenians eager to laugh at Greek plays of the comic master Aristophanes, the standing-room-only crowds which pressed into the Globe Theatre to see the latest hit by Shakespeare, and the massive Nielsen audience which made *Roseanne* the number one television program in America in 1991.

The other side of this dispute is presented by the "Modernists" who are represented notably by Russell Nye. Nye believes that popular culture is of relatively recent origin and argues that three conditions characteristic of late eighteenth-century Western Europe were necessary for its rise—masses, money and mechanics:

1) *Masses* — A *mass* culture demands the existence of a *mass* of people whose way of life it reflects and shapes. The rapid increase in population during the late eighteenth century produced the numbers, and the rise of cities gathered them together into large groups. The movement away from the countryside helped disrupt or destroy many cultural traditions and thus left a huge collection of people in need of a new culture to match their new lives.

2) *Money* — A significant portion of the new urban masses was able to profit from the Industrial Revolution to form a new middle class—a group neither peasant nor aristocrat but somewhere in between. A new class demands a new culture and just as the economy gave them the money to pursue it, so the democratic revolution helped ensure the increases in education (especially in literacy) and leisure time, which were equally necessary.

3) *Mechanics* — The "mechanics" of this new culture refer to the *means* of communicating it to the monied masses. In the late eighteenth century this meant the spread of high speed printing presses, but it can be extended at a later date to include all of the methods we associate with the mass media—radio, movies, television, etc.

Nye is valuable because he identifies an important stage in the evolution of popular culture which determined many of the characteristics we associate with it today. We have already noted that popular culture is commercial, appeals to large groups of people, and tends to be repetitive, and each trait can be traced back to the money, masses and mechanics identified by Nye. The dispute between the "Classicists" and the "Modernists" is really over the significance of the changes which took place in Western life around the eighteenth century and not over the fundamental nature of what it means to be "popular." The Classicists argue that an old culture changed while the Modernists believe that a new one was created. Both groups agree that we need to examine that which is (or has been) accepted or approved of by large groups of people; they disagree only about the additional characteristics which ought or ought not to be associated with that definition.

The dispute over the meaning of "culture" is much more basic, however. "Culture" is the focal point of a dispute between those who would decide for the rest of us what is "good" or "bad" (we can term these writers the "critics" because they evaluate, judge and label), and those who would vastly expand the definition of culture but then limit themselves to describing and analyzing their subject (we can term this group the "cameras" as they record, examine and illuminate). The conflict between these two groups has heated up in recent years as popular culture studies have been increasingly accepted in schools around the world. The critics view the encroachment with alarm—a poisonous vine creeping up the walls of their Ivory Tower—and they seek to forestall it by striking at the roots of the process—namely, at the very definition of "culture" itself.

The "Godfather of the critics" is the nineteenth-century British writer Matthew Arnold. Arnold gave the critics their rallying cry when he defined culture as "the *best* that has been thought and written" and critics have been trying to identify culture ever since. The spiritual heir to Arnold, and the chief critic of contemporary times, is Allan Bloom, whose book *The Closing of the American Mind* was (ironically) a surprise bestseller in 1987. Bloom's book is a frothing-at-the-mouth, closeminded diatribe against the "gutter phenomenon" and "voyage to the underworld" resulting from our failure to live up to Arnold's standards. Bloom picks up where Arnold left off, dismissing popular culture and producing in dictatorial tones a definition which limits culture to "the peak expression of man's creativity," "everything that is uplifting and edifying," and "that which is high, profound, (and) respectable." Bloom and his fellow critics sort things out until they produce a "canon" of classical, "timeless" works of especially high quality which they then argue need to be studied by each generation as a means of learning the everlasting truth of the ages. The fact that the critics often disagree, and thus produce canons to the left of us and canons to the right, might suggest that such lists are more reflective of the mindsets of those who draw them up than they are of any universal truth. But the critics' position remains clear even if the application of it is somewhat muddled: critics believe culture to be something which is taught rather than experienced, is mostly past and barely present, and is only a tiny number of works which have been judged to be worthy of being "canonized" as "the best."

The cameras see a great deal more in their picture of culture because they view it through a wide angle lens. These writers, influenced by the twentieth-century development of the social sciences, favor an expansive and inclusive definition of culture which allows them to examine all of the products of human work and thought produced by a given society. The cameras find their inspirational sources in the hands-on sciences of anthropology and archaeology rather than in the theoretical realms of ideology—in the field rather than the ivory tower. An anthropologist seeks to *understand* the lives of the people being studied, not to evaluate them; an archaeologist attempts to *describe* a society, not judge it. And *both* groups eagerly examine *all* bits of evidence they can find as they struggle toward their understanding and description. Both are seeking not to reveal timeless truths which somehow characterize all humankind, but rather to determine the specific truths of the single culture being examined —the mindset of a people rather than of humanity—and thus ignore restricting labels such as "good" or "bad" to look at *everything* which might be helpful in gaining understanding.

The cameras postulate a definition of "culture" which is expressed in recent times by E.D. Hirsch, who coined the term *Cultural Literacy* as the title of his 1987 bestselling foray into the hot battle over definitions. Hirsch argues that Americans share a vast range of cultural references which they use to communicate their shared beliefs and values, and in describing this "dictionary," Hirsch ignored distracting notions of "quality" to produce a list which moves effortlessly between the *canon* and the streets. Hirsch's catalog—as Robert Ray points out, "...included Saint Thomas Aquinas and Fred Astaire, Beethoven and the Beatles, Chaucer and Ty Cobb, classical music and Currier and Ives, Dante and Disney...Goethe and Grandma Moses, King Lear and King Kong..." And Hirsch himself argues that "a work may be selected because it's great or because it's just habitually *there*. The *Wizard of Oz* is in the ken of most Americans not because it is a great work but because it is a popular movie."

The battle over definitions, then, is between those who would argue that culture is *only* that which is "great" work and "good" for us, and

> ...those who...believe that worthy, enduring culture is not the possession of any single group or genre or period, who conceive of culture as neither finite nor fixed but dynamic and expansive and who [do not] believe that the moment an expressive form becomes accessible to large numbers of people it loses the criteria necessary to classify it as culture. (Ray 255)

Perhaps the dispute between the critics and the cameras can best be summarized in the following manner:

Critics decide what is "good" and then seek to determine the universal truths inherent in what they have selected.

Cameras describe what *is* and then seek to determine what function it performs and what it can tell us about the people and the culture which produced it.

If we combine our previous definition of "popular" with the camera's view of "culture" then we have a "popular culture" which refers to "the products of human work and thought which are (or have been) accepted and approved of by a large community or population." This definition ignores notions of "quality" in the culture being examined, includes the study of the culture characteristic of important subgroups within the larger mass society (e.g., we can study the meanings of the popular culture of "youth," "women," "African-Americans," etc. and not be limited to that characteristic of "America" as a whole), and embodies all of the descriptive traits we have previously identified as being associated with popular culture (Funhouse Mirror, commerciality, imitativeness).

Popular culture forms the vast majority of the artifacts and events which compose our daily lives, but it does not consist of our *entire* culture—it surrounds us but does not drown other opportunities for existence apart from it. All of us participate in at least two other kinds of culture which we need also to understand and identify as a means of illustrating several other significant characteristics of the popular culture which forms the bulk of our cultural existence.

The first alternative culture is best termed "folk culture." Folk culture refers to the products of human work and thought (culture) that have developed within a limited community and that are communicated directly from generation to generation, between "folk" who are familiar to each other. The means of communication is usually *oral*, the "author" or "creator" of the artifact or event is often *unknown* (the one communicating it being more properly termed a "spokesperson"—telling or demonstrating something which had previously been told or demonstrated to him or her), and is typically *simple* both thematically and technologically. We participate in folk culture when we learn a family recipe for baking bread from our grandmother, when a friend tells us the bloodcurdling legends surrounding the haunted house on the edge of town, and when Uncle Fred sings a song detailing the adventures of some local hero or rogue. We are all part of a "folk" as well as a member of the "masses."

It is equally important to recognize what folk culture is *not* as well. Folk culture is *not* merely the culture of the poor or uneducated, or of quaint primitives living in mountain hollows carving dulcimers and singing "Barbara Allen." Students at most universities have a rich lore of folk culture which each class (or "generation") has learned from those who have passed before and can now pass along as information concerning easy courses, good and bad instructors and weekend party rituals. Students share stories, songs, skills, legends and advice as part of a living, functioning folk culture which has nothing to do with poverty or stupidity.

The second type of culture we all experience is termed "elite culture." This category refers to the products of human work and thought produced by and for a limited number of people who have specialized interests, training or knowledge. If we restrict ourselves to elite art as our primary example of this type of culture then we can identify several other characteristics as well. The elite artist is known by the audience, and his identity is vital to understanding and appreciating his work—the artist is using his art to express his unique interpretation of the world (of society or all of reality) and the more we know about him the more meaningful his work becomes: the art attempts to be "new" and challenging. We also need to understand the aesthetic tradition in which the artist is working—the history and standards which he is attempting to meet and extend. Elite art is produced "for the ages," not for a tiny folk community or for the entertainment and diversion of the masses.

Just as folk culture is not tied to poverty or stupidity so elite culture has no necessary identification with wealth or intelligence. It requires a certain amount of interest and training to understand and appreciate a play by Shakespeare, for example, but anyone willing to read footnotes, examine the conventions of Elizabethan drama and perhaps see what a few writers have had to say about the play at hand can come to enjoy thoroughly the entire body of plays, and Will's *Collected Works* can be picked up for $10.95 at the bookstore (or free at your local library). "Elite" is specialized and limited to those interested enough to learn the specific knowledge needed, but not merely the culture of the rich and intellectual.

The *relationship* among the three types of culture is especially important in understanding the study of popular culture and the approach taken by its students. This relationship among folk, popular and elite cultures has been illustrated by Ray Browne in the following manner:

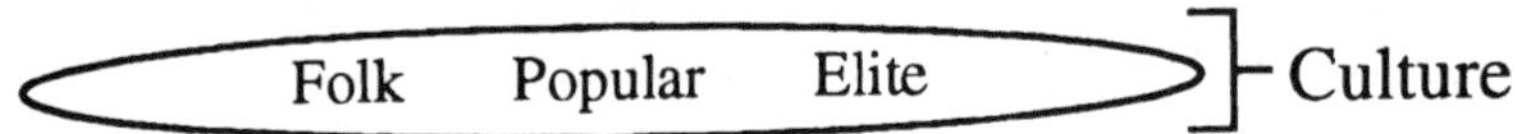

This disarmingly simple diagram actually represents several significant aspects of the way the cultures interact with us and with each other as well.

1) The relationship among the three is *nonevaluative*. The diagram places all three cultures on the same level—there is no designation of low, middle or high, and no one culture is to be considered better (or worse) than any other.

2) The shape of the representative "egg" indicates that *popular culture is the major portion* of a society's total way of life—that it surrounds us and forms the fabric of our everyday lives in a way that folk and elite culture do not.

3) The relationship among the three is *fluid*—there are no hard and fast lines separating the cultures from each other, but rather, each culture seems to 'flow' almost indefinably into its neighbor. This fluid relationship in turn has two important elements:

a) Each member of a society experiences all three types of culture. There are no lines to prevent an individual from moving freely from one cultural type to another. You might, for example, have a breakfast prepared at home by a mother who prides herself on cooking "from scratch" with family recipes, rush to a McDonald's to inhale some mass produced burgers and fries for lunch with your friends and then have dinner at a French restaurant where you must order the proper wine and know how to taste and appreciate it when it arrives.

b) A given cultural artifact or event can change culture categories over time or because of changes in its mode of presentation or audience. The role-playing fantasy game called Dungeons and Dragons provides a nice example of the fluidity of cultural identities. The game began in a small town where it was developed by a group of rabid followers and creators who invented it as they played. Few rules were written down, new players were instructed orally and through their early trial and error play, and the players manufactured their own maps, adventures, characters and relatively simple mechanisms of play. As the game developed, however, rules became increasingly complex and had to be written down and studied, several players began restricting themselves to playing the role of "dungeonmaster"—the designers and orchestrators of the game's multiple scenarios—and a language was formulated which made sense only to those interested and willing enough to learn its vocabulary (e.g., "hit points," "attack quotients," "lines-of-sight," etc.). Finally, the game was taken out of the realm of pure imagination and placed instead on a foldout board outfitted with plastic heroes and villains and marketed to the masses in K-Mart as an "easy-to-learn" quick-playing game designed to be learned and played in under two hours and—especially important—learned and played in essentially the same *way* with similar results in homes across the country. Thus, Dungeons and Dragons had "moved" from folk to elite to popular culture over time and with different audiences and changing methods of presentation. (And, of course, the game exists today in all three categories simultaneously, depending upon the context in which it is played.)

There are countless examples of this fluid relationship between and among the three cultures—our earlier use of Shakespeare as an example of this elite culture changes significantly, for example, if we consider the plays as they were produced in Elizabethan times before mass audiences in which even the illiterate "groundlings" standing in the pits could laugh at the bard's vulgar puns and marvel at the twisting plotlines putting an entertaining spin on familiar stories and contemporary events. But the primary lessons of this cultural fluidity in a society and over time are twofold. We need to examine all aspects of a cultural artifact or event to determine in which category it belongs, and we must be prepared to discover characteristics of each culture in complex interplay in any given artifact or event. The three cultures give us many rewarding questions—and remind us of how intricate our subject becomes when we examine it closely.

The chart on the following page summarizes important aspects of the three cultures by illustrating how the same cultural artifact/event (i.e. a story and storytelling) assumes a very different identity, purpose

and meaning as it functions in folk, popular and elite categories. This chart may be used in conjunction with an examination of the 1990 movie *Misery* (based upon the bestselling novel by Stephen King) as an example of how important and distinct the differences among cultures may be—as a certain author learns to his horror.

In the movie, James Caan is the bestselling author of a series of romance novels which features the continuing adventures of a plucky, put-upon heroine named Misery. While Caan has become famous as a result of his labors in the popular marketplace, he is also weary of sharing the stage with Misery and of having to follow the formulaic patterns demanded by the romance novel recipe. He wants to strike out "on his own" and write a book that has no pattern to it except the one he chooses, no character that has ever been seen before and no theme which reflects anything except his own unique outlook on life, the universe and everything. Caan is a popular author who wants to become an elite one, and he's just completed the magnum opus which will help him make the transition since this new novel is his "statement," and the latest Misery novel at his publishers kills off the burdensome heroine for good and brings the series to a close. Misery will die and an elite artist will be born: it's that simple.

Or so Caan thinks. First he must make his way back to civilization from the mountain top cabin where he has been holed up producing his serious work. Caan is so anxious to return to the amenities of modern life that he sets out down the twisting road in a hazardous snowstorm. Fishtailing around curves, it is not long before he has plowed through a toothpick guardrail and plummeted down the mountainside.

Fortunately—as happens regularly with popular authors—his audience is still around to rescue him. "I'm your number one fan," chirps his rescuer, an overeager woman played by Kathy Bates who loves Misery and adores the series' creator. Bates drags Caan back to her cabin and promises to nurse him back into writing form. This audience loves her popular author because he gives her a predictably satisfying means of escape from her daily life—she doesn't know *exactly* what will happen in Caan's latest Misery novel, of course, but she does know that it will follow the basic pattern established by others in the series, and that the tiny variations will merely supply the pleasing surprises which can enable her to become totally involved in Misery's world.

Such surprises do *not* include, however, the ending of that world. Bates reads Caan's last Misery novel and gets enraged—Caan has broken the understood contract a popular author has with his audience by violating their expectations and not reflecting their wants, needs and beliefs. And Bates hates the manuscript of Caan's elite novel too because he uses dirty words, unfamiliar ideas, and is obviously trying to disturb and mold his audience rather than reassure them. She fumes and fusses, and reflects the hostility and distance she feels from "her" author by calling him "Mr. Man."

Normally when a popular author deviates from the expected norm, the audience fights back by not buying the offending work. But drastic violations demand drastic measures, so Bates fights back with her sledgehammer and breaks Caan's legs with a few mighty swings and then chains him to a typewriter until he completes a romance novel in which Misery is somehow rescued and the series restored. Caan is living a metaphor which reflects the horror of most popular writers—they have created a monster (their audience) which demands constant feeding and attention and, when (like Dr. Frankenstein) the author/creator seeks a new mate more reflective of his individuality, his old monster won't permit him to escape its clutches. Popular authors are handcuffed to their typewriters and are punished when they write for themselves rather than for their readers.

Far from becoming the elite artist he aspired to in his mountain top retreat, poor Caan has now actually taken on characteristics of a folk artist. Caan is face-to-face with a limited audience of one who examines each new chapter the moment it is completed and passes judgment upon it. There is little room for invention, and the process is so immediate and limited (no mass copies, no advertising, no exchange of money, etc.) that Caan could almost tell the story orally to an audience which is already familiar with much of it before it ever comes out of his mouth (or his typewriter). Caan is a prisoner of shifting cultural identities as much as he is of Bates.

Eventually he escapes from the cabin, of course. But the film and novel differ as to whether he ever really escapes from his audience. The movie shows us a newly successful elite writer whose foul-mouthed masterpiece is published to critical acclaim; the novel, however, finds the central character back at the *Misery* assembly-line—grinding out romance novels to make up for the failure of his departure. King gives us a "successful" author who lives to write again (and again and again and again) but who is still crippled—providing constant escapism for his audience but allowing no escape for him.

A Whirlwind Tour of the House of Popular Culture

A major theme of our discussion thus far has been the diverse and sprawling nature of our subject matter. The artifacts and events composing popular culture include everything from clothes and cars to weddings, movie stars and bestselling get-rich-quick books. And the culture we study includes not only this vast array as it surrounds us today but also the same teeming mixture as it existed in early times as well. As chaotic as this may seem as we encounter it in our daily lives, however, there is a structure to popular culture which enables

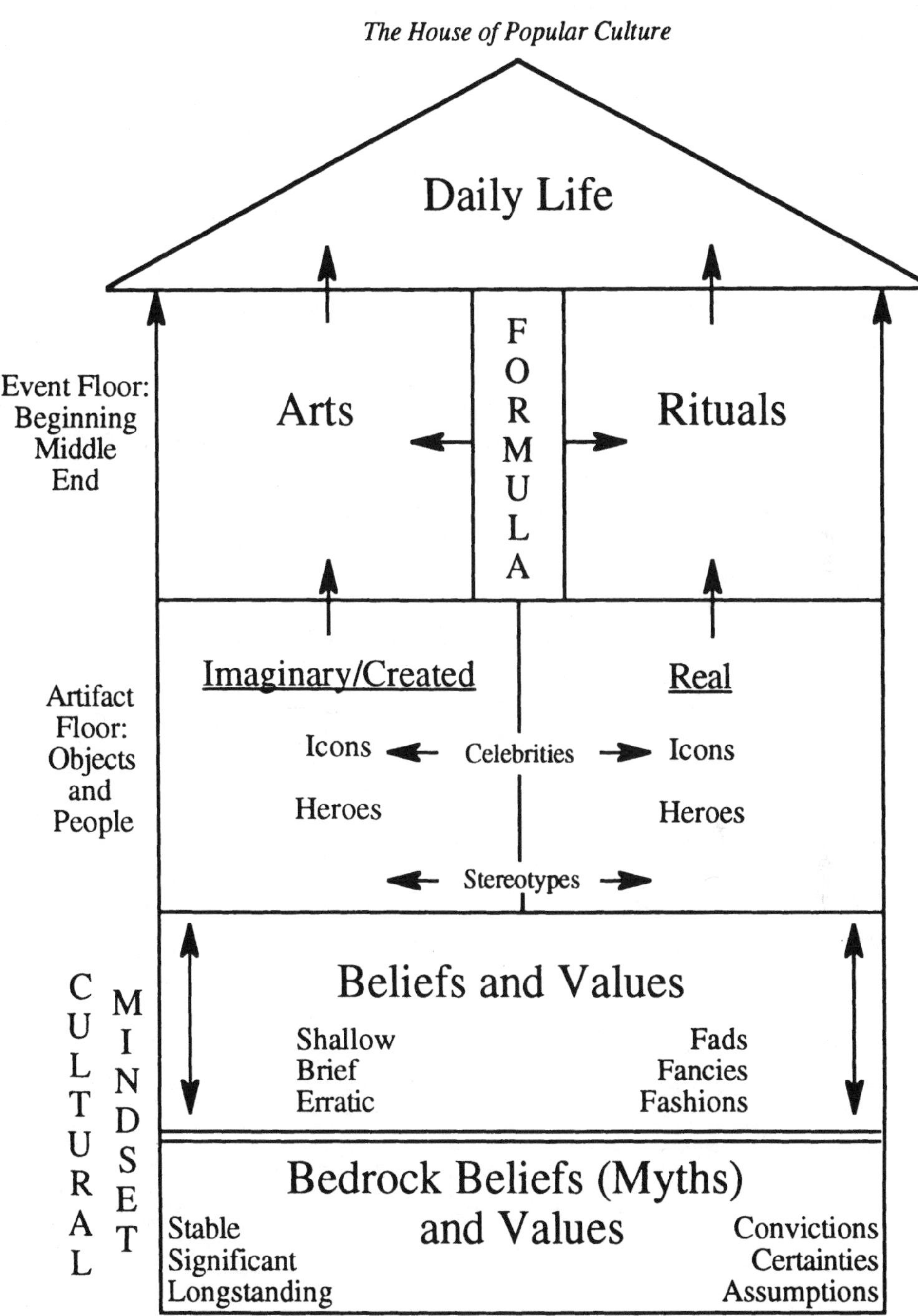
The House of Popular Culture
Daily Life
Event Floor: Beginning Middle End
Arts
FORMULA
Rituals
Artifact Floor: Objects and People
Imaginary/Created
Real
Icons
Celebrities
Icons
Heroes
Heroes
Stereotypes
CULTURAL MINDSET
Beliefs and Values
Shallow
Brief
Erratic
Fads
Fancies
Fashions
Bedrock Beliefs (Myths) and Values
Stable
Significant
Longstanding
Convictions
Certainties
Assumptions

students to explore its artifacts and events in an orderly, productive manner. This *structure* can be represented as a house with a basement and two floors, each comprised of two rooms. A quick tour of this house of popular culture at this point can help prepare us for the individual visits to the house which together comprise the rest of this book.

The house is a schematic illustration of the entire study of popular culture, in other words, and serves as a valuable introduction to the terms and relationships we will explore later. Everything may seem to come awfully fast and furious in the rapid tour which we are about to undertake, therefore, but bear in mind that we will be returning to the house many times in the pages to come. At this point it is especially important for you to keep the following points in mind as the major lessons of this overview tour:

1) All of the rooms are related to each other in important ways. Each room draws from other rooms and, in turn, provides meaning to elements of other rooms in the house. The arrows between rooms and levels reflect this vital interdependence and complex relationship.

2) The *visible* aspects of our culture (artifacts and events) are expressions of the invisible parts (our cultural mindset). We do not study in one room alone, in other words, but constantly return to the beliefs and values hidden from view in the basement to determine the meaning and significance of the contents of the rooms above ground.

The house of popular culture provides us with the tools we will use to analyze our vast subject matter, shows the relationship between and among those tools, and emphasizes that our study is *always* a search for meaning and significance as we use our tools to pry open the door leading down to the dark recesses of the cultural mindset which defines us. (Note: For purposes of this introduction our "house" will be an American one. Similar houses can be drawn for any culture, of course, but let's keep things as familiar as possible at this part.)

1) The Basement

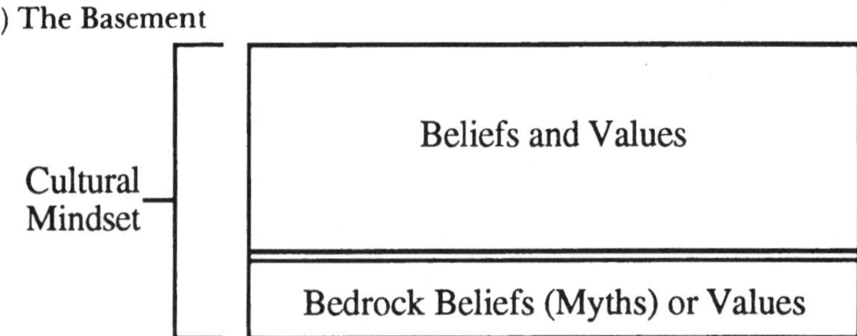

We *begin* where we must always *end*: in the basement which holds the beliefs and values forming the cultural mindset. Beliefs and values are in the basement because they are ideas which cannot be "seen" in and of themselves—they exist in the cultural mind and in the minds of the individual members of mass society. Beliefs and values closer to the surface are those which are most transitory, shallow, and faddish—e.g., the popular belief among the hippie subculture of the 60s that "drugs are good for you" has been replaced today by a highly generalized "just say no" belief. Beliefs and values deep down in the solid rock of the house's foundation can be termed "bedrock beliefs and values" because they are the most stable, longstanding and significant ones characteristic of broad components of the total population. (Recently, cultural analysts have begun to refer to the bedrock beliefs as "myths." Several of our later readings do this.) Bedrock beliefs in the American foundation include the belief in the American dream, the belief in the special mission of America as a "city on a hill," and the belief in the nuclear family as the most proper and rewarding mode of social existence—all beliefs which will be defined and explored in the next chapter (the bedrock belief in the inherent value of individual freedom will be illustrated later in this section as an example of how the entire house functions as a unit). Bedrock beliefs and values may be challenged or called into question at specific times. Certainly the Great Depression offered a powerful challenge to continued belief in the American dream, but they are present even as they are being discussed. The very fact that we do constantly explore their meanings and relationship to reality is important evidence of how significant they are to us. Popular beliefs and values are not simple and we shall see how Americans have debated and discussed the components of their mindset in an ongoing, vibrant dialogue.

Whether or not any specific belief or value is objectively true or false is, of course, an important question for each individual. But the question is irrelevant to the study of popular culture. We are concerned with determining what people *believe* to be true and with exploring the ways these beliefs are expressed and discussed. The American dream that anyone can succeed in America through hard work and a bit of good fortune may or may not be true, but the question for us to answer is whether or not it is still popularly accepted as true and what specific form this belief assumes at any given moment.

2) First Floor: Artifacts (Objects and People)

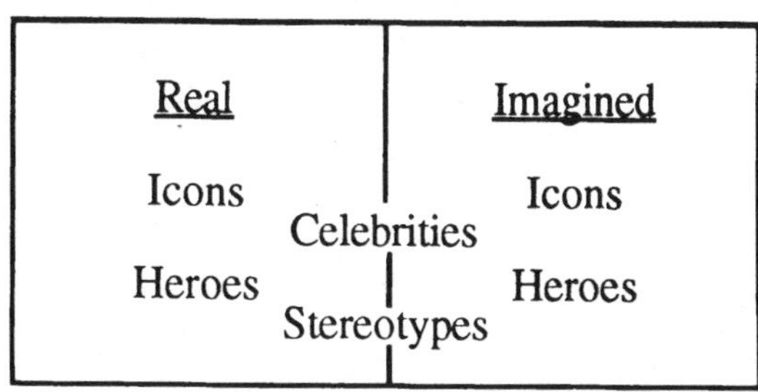

The first floor of our house contains popular artifacts—objects and people widely accepted or approved of by the masses. Artifacts are visible expressions of the beliefs and values which lie "below" in the basement.

Popular artifacts are of two types: popular objects are termed *icons,* and popular people are labeled *heroes* or *celebrities.* Each of these categories is then further subdivided into "real" and "imaginary" types depending upon whether or not the hero or icon exists in the real world—historic or present—or only within the context of some fictional creation (e.g., popular movies, television, books, etc.). Celebrities cut across the "real" and the "imaginary" because even though they actually exist in three-dimensional form—living and breathing like the rest of us—their hyped-up, fabricated star persona is often so distant from the real person as to be more properly considered a type of fiction.

A brief sampling and a more extended example of each of the four categories formed by the rooms on the first floor can help to clarify their meaning and relationship to each other:

Real Icons—cars, fast food restaurants, jeans, credit cards, American flag
Example: Skateboards
Over 10 million active skateboarders (average age: 13.8 years, sex: almost exclusively male) in America today use this "toy" as a means of expressing individual freedom, the traditional definition of male character as that forged through risky accomplishment, and as a form of youthful rebellion. Skateboarders paint the boards with specialized designs intended to reflect their individuality and, in many instances, to enhance the board's magical ability to transport the sufficiently brave and skillful rider to a special plane of existence mere mortals can never achieve, which boarders term "gleaming the cube"—"a mystical state of exalted feeling achieved by skateboarders at the top of their form." Skateboarders practice their craft by launching their iconic steeds off the steps of the very institutions which seek to control and restrict the freedom of youth—schools, churches, libraries, business establishments, etc.—and thereby rebel against such spoilsport entities by turning their own visible structures into launchpads to nirvana. Skateboarders have a magazine, *Thrasher,* devoted to their quest, spend over 300 million dollars annually on equipment alone, and have founded a National Skateboard Association devoted to developing the language, skills, and magic surrounding the icon which both expresses and forms their youthful identity. The skateboard magically transforms its rider by enabling him to demonstrate his superiority over the hardest, harshest symbol of civilization—concrete:

> "It's a freedom sport. Gliding on concrete, you feel like rolling thunder. It's a very ultimate feeling."

Can a short board with four polyurethane wheels manage all that? Only if we see it in its true form as an icon with magical powers reflective of deep beliefs and values.

Imaginary Icons—Guns in Westerns, Archie Bunker's chair, Fonzi's Black Jacket
Example: Starship Enterprise
Not merely a spaceship, the home of the *Star Trek* crew is actually a warp-speeding icon expressing in truly magical ways—faster than light travel—the American beliefs in exploration, individual freedom and America's special mission. The ship expresses the very "enterprising" notion that we should always boldly go where no man has gone before in an effort to spread the wisdom of our ways, demonstrate our power and simply find out what is out there in the spirit of the discovery and settlement of America itself. The iconic Enterprise has entered the real world as a name for the first U.S. space shuttle, and is currently extending its meaning and mission as the whooshing multicultural home of a *Next Generation* crew which is carrying America's mission into a new era more complex than its Cold War predecessor. The Enterprise continues to stand as an iconic model of America as it sees itself—pure white against the darkness of space, noble and peace seeking with the power to back its beliefs up with action, and forging forever onward to keep the frontier just slightly ahead of us.

Real Heroes—Daniel Boone, Martin Luther King, George Washington, Abraham Lincoln
Example: Charles Lindbergh

Heroes reflect the highest goals of a culture embodied in the life and image of a specific individual. Thus Charles Lindbergh, for example, became perhaps the single most popular hero of the American 1920s by flying his fragile *Spirit of St. Louis* across the Atlantic Ocean. In this first instance of such solo effort he managed to reaffirm the possibility of individual heroism at a time when the closing of the American frontier and the increasing domination of daily life by machines of all sorts (e.g., assembly line jobs) seemed to have relegated such noble deeds to the past, Lindbergh united individual freedom *with* technology to enable America to believe that both values could exist simultaneously. He was a hero for a new age who brought the best aspects of the past into the present.

Imaginary Heroes—Tarzan, Superman, Batman, Captain Kirk
Example: Dirty Harry (1971)

Clint Eastwood's movie character, Harry Callahan, expresses the American belief that justice is more important than law and that the good, skillful individual willing to risk life and career to protect society is the single best insurance we can have that no bad deed goes unpunished. Harry pursues justice in the same self-sacrificing skillful manner as Western heroes (such as the Lone Ranger), superheroes (like Batman), and private detectives (like Thomas Magnum). At a time when many Americans felt that the streets had been given over to criminals and that the law had abandoned victims to avoid infringing upon the "rights of the accused," Dirty Harry came along to rectify matters by taking matters (and a .357 Magnum) into his own hands.

Many heroes are associated with specific icons in a manner which demonstrates how all of the rooms in the house are interrelated. The Lone Ranger has his special silver-bullet gun, Thomas Edison is associated with an iconic light bulb (a symbol for the "inspiration" and inventiveness which are two of his primary heroic traits), and Charles Lindbergh has his *Spirit of St. Louis*—an iconic reminder of both the *power* of technology and the *fragility* of a scientific breakthrough which required a courageous individual to realize its potential.

If heroes can be said to represent the highest goals and ideals of a culture, then "stereotypes" are often used to encapsulate the opposite—the fears and hatreds of a popular mindset. A stereotype in and of itself is a neutral device of simplistic organization. It is a way of grouping all individual people or objects of a certain "type" into one category with a few easy-to-grasp characteristics. Negative stereotypes are often used to label groups which the mainstream culture feels threaten the status quo, like the recent negative stereotypes used in "Japan bashing" by Americans, and in "America-bashing" by the Japanese. Thus the Japanese become "robotic, soulless, ruthless, cutthroat competitors for world markets," and "all American workers are lazy and illiterate." Stereotypes are an especially useful tool in the study of popular culture, because they are direct and simple expressions of popular beliefs and values, and because they can be found in *all* areas of popular expression, both "real" and "imagined."

Celebrities, like stereotypes, cut across the division between the imaginary and the real, but for a different reason. Celebrities are real people, who, like heroes, are famous. But celebrities, unlike heroes, are dependent for their fame on a manufactured "image" of who they are. They are famous not for what they have done but how the mass media defines them. This public image may be the real person or it may be a completely created personality. Does Cher really love to hang out at Vic Tanny's and diet? Was Bubbles the chimp really Michael Jackson's only friend? Who knows? The only information most of us have about these two celebrities is what is revealed by the tabloids, gossip columns and the rest of the publicity mill that is the lifeblood of celebrityhood. What we, as students of popular culture can know for sure is that celebrities are valuable signposts of immediate cultural preoccupations. Cher, for example, reflects the late twentieth-century popular belief that thinness is a sign of inner virtue. Jackson's relationship with Bubbles suggests how we still believe the traditional story that life at the top is lonely. Both Cher and Michael Jackson reflect our culture's mania for youth and their much publicized plastic surgeries confirm for us that youth is to be pursued and preserved no matter what the cost or sacrifice.

3) Rituals

Rituals

Rituals are highly patterned symbolic events in which we all participate as a way of marking important passages in our individual lives or in society as a whole, in which we bind our culture together in a celebration of our common beliefs and values and/or in which we release tension and anxiety in a socially acceptable, "safe" manner.
Examples: Family reunions, sporting events (The World Series, Super Bowl), weddings, funerals, holidays (Halloween and "trick or treat"; Christmas and "decorating the tree" or "exchanging gifts"), etc.
Specific Example: Voting.

Voting is a popular ritual in which each election attracts over 50% of the American population, a proportion too low for an ideal democracy but a *vast* number nonetheless. Voting is patterned by strict rules, takes place at an assigned place and time, and is the focus of a wide variety of associated events taking place both before and after the occasion (e.g., campaigns, nominations, conventions, inaugurations, etc.). Voting requires a specific age qualification (and thus marks an important moment in an individual's passage into full citizenship status), and reflects basic American beliefs in individual freedom, democracy, and the innate wisdom of the "common man." Voting is such a vital ritual that achieving the right to participate has often been the central concern of cultural subgroups who recognize that participation brings with it the stamp of authenticity—of full recognition as being equal to and part of the mainstream culture. Thus, African-Americans, women, and youth have all used voting as a means of both demonstrating their equal status in the culture *and* of furthering that status by letting their special voices be heard in this powerful ritual.

Rituals build upon the rooms below by frequently integrating both heroes and icons into patterned events. In voting, for example, participants often demonstrate their preferences by wearing political buttons and, interestingly, celebrating their participation in the process itself by displaying "I voted today" stickers and signs. And, of course, a successful candidate is certainly "heroic" in his or her representation of the beliefs and values supported and expressed by a majority of voters. (Although the victorious candidate may have been less than sterling in the use of negative stereotypes to illustrate his positions in campaign ads and arouse the voters' fears of his opponent.)

4) Arts

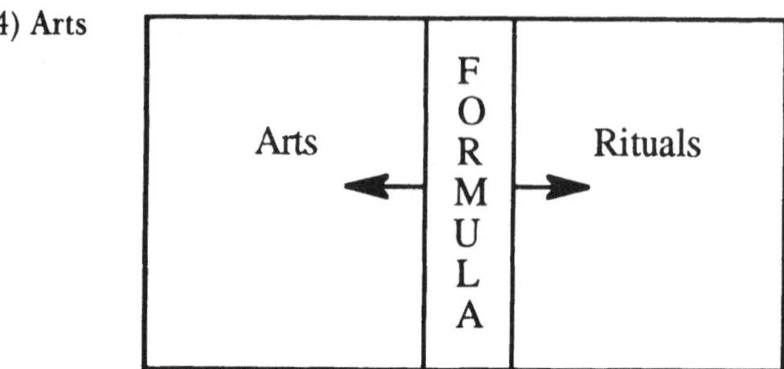

The room of popular arts is one of the largest in a house already sprawling in size. This room is so crowded as a matter of fact that critics of popular culture can almost be excused for often viewing it as the *only* room in the house for confusing popular culture with "entertainment." The arts *are* vast and diverse, however, but they do not stand isolated from the other rooms and they derive their meaning and significance from the beliefs and values in the basement of the popular mindset.

Examples: Popular magazines, movies, television, recordings, comic Books.

Our Example: To illustrate the diverse and vast nature of this room, and to demonstrate how we can begin to analyze its contents, we can take but a single category of one type of popular art and provide an abbreviated guide to its many, many subcategories.

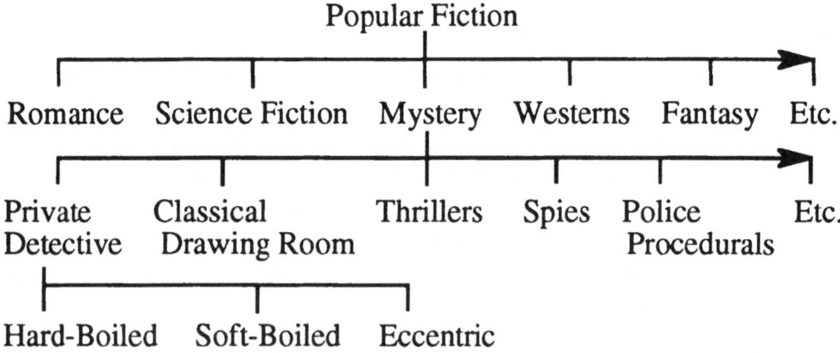

Such a breakdown illustrates another important tool of popular culture analysis as well. As we identify various categories of each art, we group them together based upon shared characteristics which are known to both the popular artist and the audience. These "formulas" are the patterns which identify each type of fiction listed above, for example, and are also the step-by-step formulaic processes which give rituals *their* order and identity (which is why the "formula" tool rests in a corridor between the arts and rituals on the floor of "events," encompassing processes with formulaic beginnings-middles-and ends). Story formulas are shared by author and audience in the way that Bates demanded specific, formulaic elements from her *Misery* romance novels *and* in the corresponding way that she insisted upon surprise and variety *within* those elements—a balance of the predictable and the inventive which we will find very characteristic of all formulas.

Many of the articles in this book discuss certain objects, heroes, and events as isolated from other popular culture elements. But it should be realized that the basis of almost all visible popular culture is popular beliefs and values and that each one of these beliefs and values is expressed in a large and complex variety of related ways. A brief examination of how one popular belief is reflected in various popular forms will illustrate this variety.

Imagine for a moment living in a society where your daily activities and long-range plans are all organized around serving the needs of that society. You work where you are told at whatever job you are assigned. Your children are not allowed to receive any education beyond what a committee determines for them. Your mate is selected for you by yet another committee. And you wear the same clothing every day, a uniform that indicates exactly what your function is within the overall running of society. To most Americans such details are repugnant, even horrible. They read like a science-fiction novel warning us about a terrifying future or like our most negative stereotypes about life within certain foreign, totalitarian countries.

The probable reason for our strong aversion to such a vision of life is a basic belief that is both accepted and cherished by almost every American—the belief in the innate value of individual, personal freedom. The bedrock belief that personal freedom is a natural right developed in the religious and social foundations of colonial America and was articulated in our two best known government documents, both written before 1800. The Declaration of Independence declares liberty an "inalienable right," and the Bill of Rights of the United States Constitution is mainly concerned with preserving the freedoms of individual citizens including freedom of speech, religion, assembly and the press. During the nineteenth and twentieth centuries this belief has been expressed again and again in various kinds of popular culture artifacts.

James Fenimore Cooper, for example, the first American best-selling novelist, created the fictional frontier hero, Natty Bumppo, in the five "Leatherstocking" novels beginning with *The Pioneers* in 1823. Natty, much like his real life model, Daniel Boone, was invariably restless in the settlements and expressed his freedom by continually choosing to move deeper into the wilderness. Cooper's character became the prototype for hundreds of frontier heroes featured in Western formula stories that appeared in magazines, books and later in radio, movies, comics, television and in national advertising campaigns. Beginning in 1933, three times a week for over twenty years and nearly 3,000 episodes, at the end of each radio show the Lone Ranger and his "trusted Indian companion, Tonto," chose to ride away from the town or ranch into the limitless freedom of the vast western landscape. "Who was that masked man?" a character always asked and the final, joyful cry of the "masked rider of the plains," "Hi Yo Silver Awaaaaay!" reminded millions of listeners that who he was was a hero of American liberty, free to be who he wanted and to go where he pleased.

A number of material objects also continually reinforce and reconfirm our belief in personal freedom. The Liberty Bell and the Statue of Liberty are the two most obvious examples. In our time, Americans have become stereotyped over the world because of our obsession with two objects—plastic credit cards and automobiles. Credit cards like VISA and Mastercard create the illusion for the possessor of financial freedom. This illusion is encouraged by advertising campaigns picturing laughing, happy people rushing from store to store or from country to country with not a financial care in the world. Cars symbolize the freedom of mobility. All we need is a full tank and, like the Lone Ranger, we are free to hit the road any time we please. Endless, fresh experiences and grand adventures are as close, the average American believes, as his or her family garage. The love of mobility symbolized by automobiles probably is the basis for a very popular American ritual—the family vacation. Although each family enjoys its own special vacation activities, in general most American families take to the road, and often more time is spent on the road than at the actual destination. It is the experience of movement itself, the free roaming across the continent that gives purpose and meaning to the family unit away from home. And, finally, within the popular arts, the title of 2 Live Crew's intentionally vulgar 1990 top selling rap album, *As Nasty As We Wanna Be,* aggressively asserts the free right of every American to say anything she/he pleases.

The examples just described show how the "house of popular culture" functions. The popular belief in the innate value of personal freedom is reinforced by each of the two rooms of visible objects, rituals and (formulaic) popular arts. From the latest ad for beer to the KOA Campground just off the freeway, our popular culture tells us endlessly that personal freedom not only exists but is an ideal of infinite value.

Furthermore, each room in the house relies on the others to maximize its message. The job of cultural reinforcement is a complex one. The automobile icon is used as an essential component of the family vacation ritual. Part of the vacation may include the reciting of formulaic stories. We move from room to room, absorbing what we need, and we combine each individual popular element until popular culture has provided us with enough signs of the validity of our society and a satisfactory definition of who and what we are.

Misconceptions About Popular Culture

In the course of introducing the study of popular culture, we have touched upon a number of the criticisms which have been levied against our subject. In each instance we have shown how the criticism simply evaporates once the misconception upon which it is based is revealed —i.e., the vast majority of critics are attacking a phantom popular culture which haunts only their house, not ours. A review of the four major misconceptions, then, will serve as both a useful summary of the nature of popular culture studies and as an elaboration of our subject as well in a new context.

Misconception Number One: Popular Culture is Simple.

While no one argues that the bulk of popular culture's artifacts and events are as intrinsically complex as many of those listed in the various "canons" of classical works, the study of this world is far more difficult and challenging than it may first appear. This can be seen in two ways:

1) Lack of distance between student and subject. Popular culture is *our* culture and it is much more difficult to achieve the perspective required for objective analysis when you are directly involved in and surrounded by the very thing you are seeking to understand. The works in a "canon" exist before critics the way that a football game is played out before the announcers who describe and analyze from on high in the broadcasting booth—the long tradition of past criticism and knowledge is spread out before them, they can "instant replay" the work as many times as necessary or desired, and they have a clear view of how all the various elements work and interact together. The student of popular culture, on the other hand, is right down on the playing field itself and is often too busy simply trying to "win" the game—to survive as an individual and to make proper choices under pressure—to be able to analyze the swirl of action, sounds, and messages which surround him/her. Even when we turn our attention to the popular culture of past times we still encounter this problem of achieving distance and perspective since much of our evidence is often tied directly to the

perceptions and experiences of those who were directly involved in the culture we are seeking to analyze. And in both past and present the students of popular culture are often the first to attempt a given analysis and therefore have nothing to guide them but their own perceptions and the framework provided by their discipline like the house of popular culture. There are no *Cliff's Notes* defining the critical consensus about the meaning of *The Simpsons.* Popular culture is widely experienced but little known—well traveled, but uncharted.

2) Complex messages are carried by popular artifacts and events. While the products of popular culture may be intrinsically "simple" in that they are imitative, predictable, and familiar, the meanings they carry are usually quite complex. Popular culture reflects and shapes the cultural mindset in a delicate dance which is itself often impossible to pin down precisely, and it magnifies the challenge of analysis by often mixing its messages in a complicated web designed to appeal to as wide an audience as possible. A persistent theme in our studies will be the way that the same cultural artifact or event can convey contradictory meanings at the very same time—the way that tractor pulls celebrate both the land *and* the machine, the individual *and* mass technology, cooperation *and* competition. Cultural mindsets are mysterious masses of truth and fiction, tradition and fad, past and present, and there is no reason to expect the popular culture which reflects such a complex mixture to be any less mysterious or complex.

We should also note that it is the very "simplicity" of popular culture artifacts and events which accounts for their usefulness in revealing cultural beliefs and values. In order to be attractive to a mass audience such popular culture elements strive to avoid anything which might confuse or unsettle potential viewers or participants like the complicating presence of an author's "unique" perspective on reality or experimental modes of presentation. Popular culture attempts to shine *directly* on the hearts and minds of its audience—and it is from those depths that it draws its meaning and complexity.

Misconception Number Two: Popular culture is trivial.

This misconception usually arises from the mistaken notion that Popular Culture consists only of *one* of our rooms in the house—that holding the wide variety of popular arts. Critics charge that the room is devoted exclusively to "entertainment" and the transitory escapist art which fades from view the moment a fickle public turns its restless attention to some other mindless distraction.

Much like the accusations of "simplicity," this misconception is based upon a confusion between the artifacts and events forming popular culture (which often are "simple" and "transitory") with the *study* of that culture (which is neither simple or "mindless entertainment"). The misconception can be countered in three ways:

1) We do not study the artifacts and events of popular culture as ends in themselves (as the fans of a TV program or film star often do, for example) but as a means of examining the underlying cultural mindset which those artifacts and events both reflect and mold.

2) Popular culture includes far more than the popular arts; it also encompasses icons, heroes, stereotypes, rituals, and, most importantly, the beliefs and values of the masses. While any single example of popular culture may (or may not) be "trivial," the culture as a whole both surrounds us and forms the great majority of our cultural experiences—a far from "trivial" entity.

3) Popular culture's seemingly trivial characteristics as imitative and repetitive actually enhance its performance of a very serious function. *Because* popular culture is familiar and accessible it serves to provide people with both a comforting escape from the weary routines and problems of daily life *and* imposes an order upon the chaos of existence as well. A popular ritual like eating out, for example, relieves us of preparing our own meals after a tiring day, enables us to escape our cares by entering a fun environment where we are served quickly and without undue fuss, and orders this part of our lives by providing familiar food prepared the same way every time.

*Misconception Number Three: Popular culture is immediate—it deals only with that which is popular right **now**.*

We already know that we can study the popular culture of past times to unlock the mindsets of people in earlier eras; and we know that we can compare past mindsets with the present in an important effort to define the most deep-seated and enduring beliefs and values which characterize a culture over time.

But there is another sense in which this misconception is in error which we have not mentioned previously. We not only study that which is immediately popular and that which has *been* popular, but also often examine that which has *never* been widely accepted or approved of. If a given cultural artifact or event is an *unsuccessful* example of a popular form then we can learn a great deal about the cultural mindset by analyzing why this specific attempt failed to attract an audience. The flip side of the popular culture formula tells us that the message carried by an unsuccessful artifact or event in an otherwise popular form is one which is quite probably not part of a cultural mindset at that particular time—a valuable bit of evidence in our attempt to determine what the masses *do* believe. On television, for example, the dramatic mystery series has been one of the most consistently popular forms—successful examples can be found in all eras, from *Dragnet* to *Columbo* to *Magnum P.I.*

In spite of this track record, however, the technically accomplished, highly publicized mystery drama program *Twin Peaks* (1990-91) never managed to attract an audience large enough for the series to be listed in the Top 50 programs of either season in its two-year run. *Twin Peaks* challenged American beliefs in the simplicity and inherent decency of small town rural life (Twin Peaks, U.S.A. was a cesspool of violence, dangerous sex, and unexplained phenomena in the woods), the fundamentally supportive and protective character of the nuclear family, and the assurance that justice will triumph through the courageous fortitude of a righteous individual even when the law has failed (investigator Dale Cooper never solved anything and ended up being possessed by the very evil forces he was attempting to destroy). The failure of *Twin Peaks* suggests that these values still have a powerful hold on the American consciousness, and the fact that successful contemporary examples of the form *uphold* these same beliefs is even more evidence for such a conclusion—*Murder, She Wrote* and *Matlock* are two recent examples of small-town folksy heroes who protect their families and solve crimes.

Misconception Number Four: Popular culture is exclusionary.

This misconception criticizes students of popular culture for examining popular artifacts and events *instead* of studying the "classics." Such critics often go so far as to claim that popular culture is an attempt to place popular works into the "canon"—to place *The Beverly Hillbillies* side-by-side of *Moby Dick* and *Oedipus Rex.*

Much like the previous misconceptions, this final one is also based upon a confusion of the artifacts and events which form the raw data of popular culture and the *study* of that data. The clarification of two points stemming from this important distinction can easily lay this charge to rest:

1) Popular culture is not evaluative. The study of popular culture is not an attempt to argue that popular artifacts are as "good" as those of a "classical canon"; popular culture says little or nothing about the quality of the materials it examines but only comments upon their meaning and significance. *The Beverly Hillbillies* is not as "good" as *Oedipus Rex* from our standpoint—it is an entirely different kind of artifact and is examined in a completely different manner. A "canon" looks for eternal truths; a popular culture student seeks evidence to define a cultural mindset.

2) Because "canon" works and "popular" works are examined in different ways and provide different answers and information, they both need to be studied. Popular culture does not seek a place in the "canon" but beside it.

A Final Word from Our Sponsor

The readings which make up the rest of this book introduce the rooms of the House of Popular Culture in greater detail and provide you with several examples of how different writers analyze artifacts in those rooms. If you want readings that will make you a better person, or show you the aesthetic perfection of great art or teach you to succeed in business without really trying, sorry. Maybe you should stop reading right now. As we have stressed all through this introduction, popular culture studies are not about any of these things, although, hopefully, studying popular culture may help you move yourself in the direction of all these things. Studying popular culture will not tell us who we ought to be. On the other hand, if you want to know more about who we really are, both good and bad, then keep reading. Popular culture is what most people choose to do most of the time. As you gaze into the funhouse mirror of popular culture you are therefore getting to know yourself and you are getting to know us, all of us.

Master mythmakers for the movies' all-time top ten hits. George Lucas and Stephen Spielberg.

Section

☞ 1 ☞

Taking Popular Culture Seriously

Introduction
Taking Popular Culture Seriously

Each of the four essays selected to introduce the serious examination of popular culture is an attempt to unlock a deeper significance or meaning from an artifact which is usually accepted at face value by the people who experience it. Kevin Lause discovers that the top ten American box-office hits are about much more than flying bicycles, sliming ghosts and Empires striking back; Marc Crispin Miller looks at an advertisement for liquor and sees a basic American drama of loneliness and longing; Jan Harold Brunvand shows that the tale you tell your friend about the babysitter you heard about who was trapped in a house with a killer upstairs may actually alert us to enemies more threatening than maniacs on the loose; and Alison Lurie finds that Dr. Seuss' fantasy beasts carry very real messages.

While each author presents an interesting analysis of his or her artifact, it is especially important at this stage of the study of popular culture to focus upon the techniques and skills applied by each writer in revealing the meanings of his or her chosen subject. What questions does each author ask as a beginning point to their analysis? What types of evidence does each offer for his or her conclusions? Can any of the various rooms in the House of Popular Culture be recognized? Try to imagine how each author's conclusions can be extended to apply to other examples of their selected artifacts. Are any of the themes Lause identifies in the top ten box-office hits also present in recent movies? Are there other advertisements which carry messages similar to Miller's liquor ad? Heard any "urban legends" lately, and thought about what they might signify?

Ultimately, it should become clear that the "serious" study of popular culture has an ironic effect: it makes popular culture more fun. It enables one to become a detective with the world's most interesting mystery to solve—the hidden mystery of a culture's beliefs and values. The clues are all around—let's begin looking at them.

Seeing What We've Said: The Top Ten American Box-Office Hits Taken Seriously

Kevin Lause

Popular culture can be very enjoyable, but is only "mindless" if we deliberately refuse to think about it. A "serious" approach to the study of popular culture should not be a sober exercise which succeeds in providing meaning only at the cost of stamping out the intrinsic pleasures of the object of its study—taking popular culture seriously means a deepening of the fun, not a destruction of it. A serious study of popular culture enriches our lives by revealing new levels of meaning and significance in the choices which form the fabric of our daily lives. If the physician's code demands that s/he "first does no harm," then the serious student of popular culture must follow a similar dictum that s/he "first doesn't deny the fun."

Taking popular culture seriously, however, does involve consideration of at least two specific levels of thought, both of which are illustrated in the essay which follows. First, Lause defines the world of popular culture in a manner which reveals the complex nature of its many interlocking components. What is especially interesting here is the way that Lause demonstrates that the elements which are often the target of elitist critics of popular culture are precisely those ingredients which give popular culture its power and function. The commercial nature of popular culture helps account for the way in which it embodies the zeitgeist of its era, while the imitative and repetitive nature of mass culture enables it to provide a soothing, reassuring familiarity to its public. In other words, Lause shows that popular culture's "crass commercialism" and "lack of creativity" are traits which enable it to embody dreams and create order out of the chaos of living.

It is the nature of these dreams and this order which Lause turns to in the second part of his essay. Once he has defined what popular culture is, he then uses the same body of popular artifacts (the Top Ten American Box-Office Hits) to reveal what it means—the second level of any serious analysis. In the course of illustrating this second level of examination, Lause also demonstrates an important point of methodology which the student of popular culture should recognize from the very beginning of his "serious" study. Lause draws upon all of the tools of popular culture analysis in his quest for understanding and thus demonstrates that the separation of "heros" from "icons," from "rituals" and "formulas" is an artificial construct adopted by this textbook purely for teaching purposes, and is not a reflection of true analysis. The deepest lesson of Lause's essay is in the technique it models as it weaves its web of definitions and meaning: the tools of popular culture are instruments which sound most true when played together to produce all the various harmonies of meaning. It takes all of the tools to build the House of Popular Culture.

"The little girl had the making of a poet in her who—being told to be sure of her meaning before she spoke—said, 'How can I know what I think till I see what I've said?' "

Graham Wallas
Art of Thought

There is nothing so unexamined as a certainty; certainties are born and certainties are made, but most of the time certainties simply are. The complex mixture of beliefs and values which forms a culture's mindset lies nestled down in a dark realm beneath the level of everyday thought and discourse—the light which it casts outward to illuminate and color the world is unable to touch itself. Thus it is that the things we are most sure of are precisely those most difficult to say and least likely to be expressed directly. Like Graham Wallas' poetic little girl we too "know" things we cannot explicitly define until we look at how we've said them. And because a culture's voice is found in the artifacts and events it produces, it is these which must be examined to find out what it is we know. Popular culture is what we're saying at any given moment, and taking it seriously means looking at it closely and carefully to help us discover what it is we're thinking. The artifacts of popular culture are the signs embedded deeply in the mindset of the times, and seeing what we've said on these can thus help us know what we believe.

Popular culture is the visible expression of our thoughts and feelings then, but it is itself "invisible" in its own way simply because its very omnipresence so often causes us to overlook it—to look through the water surrounding us rather than at it. In addition to examining the meaning of popular culture, therefore, it is necessary to begin by defining the nature of our subjects as well. Taking popular culture "seriously" means that we must understand what it *is* before moving onward to the task of determining what it is saying. We have to know *which* signs we need to examine, in other words, before deciding which destination they are leading us toward.

In the following examination of the top ten American box-office hits (as of January, 1991) we will first use the list to illustrate several defining characteristics of popular culture and then move on to see what this example of popular culture is itself defining.

I. *The Top Ten American Box-Office Hits and the Nature of Popular Culture*

The selection of this list of artifacts was guided by the popular culture formula. We can assume, in other words, that the most popular examples of a very popular art form are likely to be highly reflective of the cultural mindset of the masses and thus very useful signs of their times. The formula makes no assertions about "quality"; the movies it selects for examination may or may not be the "best" ones produced, but either judgment is irrelevant for our purposes. The formula leads us to ask *why* these films achieved such remarkable popularity, not to determine whether they "deserve" their success.

The selection of these artifacts as our raw data for study then, reflects two important elements of popular culture studies: our studies are *nonevaluative* and are *guided by application of the Popular Culture Formula.* But the list of top ten American box-office hits also illustrates several familiar characteristics of popular culture itself as well:

1) *Popular Culture Is Usually Commercial*

These movies were not made with the intention of educating, challenging or enlightening their target audience; they were produced with the intention of getting as many people into the theaters as many times as possible. Each of the movies on the list is a multi-million dollar earner in a multi-billion dollar industry, and their makers devoted all of their attentions to ensuring this *monetary* success by transforming each movie into a multi-faceted, omnipresent EVENT—a blockbuster busting our blocks off wherever we looked.

The producers of *Batman* were especially skillful at marketing their movie in this all-encompassing manner. *Batman's* studio honchos were especially worried that their expensive real-life comic book was simultaneously too dark and too foolish to achieve the popular success necessary to turn a profit. The movie created a bleak, frightening Gotham City peopled with ghoulish villains and a foolish hero—the short, balding wiseacre Michael Keaton (best known for having battled nothing more fearsome than a few household appliances in his anti-heroic role as *Mr. Mom* and for ending up in hell with a head the size of a golfball in the previous year's horror-comedy *Beetlejuice*). The marketing of *Batman* was thus of crucial importance to the movie's success and the producers directed their promotional guns at the audience's mindset in a masterpiece of manipulation. The idea of "Batman" became such an important part of every aspect of the commercial world *before* the movie was released that actually *seeing* the movie became practically inevitable—it was the only way to make certain that all that time spent thinking about it beforehand had not been wasted. And, of course, the sheer omnipresence of the Batman Idea created the overwhelming impression that the movie was somehow *already* popular and that *not* to see it would be to be left out of a cultural experience everybody else was having seemingly at every moment.

The producers saturated theaters with a brief trailer of the film which was designed to allay audience fears about Keaton's suitability by showing the actor in a muscle-costume which would have made Pee-Wee Herman look like he'd been having steroids for breakfast in the Playhouse. This "teaser" was so effective that theatre-owners reported that people were buying tickets to other movies just so they could see the *Batman* trailer as often as possible. The Batman logo—dark yet shining and gold-edged—became a central icon designed to create the impression of a movie with that same appealing mixture. And that logo was everywhere—audiences ate it up (literally) in cereals and candies, wore it on tee-shirts, hats, and rings, and saw it plastered on billboards across the country. Toys featuring the major characters and props of the movie helped pique audience interest and, more importantly, reinforced the central marketing themes emphasizing that this was what Batman looked like and this world was light and entertaining and action-filled enough to fulfill a child's fantasies—nothing too dark or fearsome or (worse yet) "artsy" here. Stars of the movie came down out of their estates in Hollywood Hills to add their celebrity lustre to the promotional efforts, and the rebellious, unpredictable, slyly grinning Jack Nicholson was especially effective in using his persona to demonstrate how accurate the movie's casting must have been to put America's quintessential laughing "bad boy" in the tailor-made role of the Joker—our king of movie rebels playing the hell out of the clown prince of crime.

The promotional efforts climaxed with the carefully planned opening of the film—on a summer weekend (when the kids are out of school, parents on vacation, and moviegoing at its seasonal peak) in over a thousand theaters nationwide. No bat-signal on night-time clouds was necessary to summon Batman—he was everywhere all at once. And had been already long before the first ticket was sold.

2) *Popular Culture Is Imitative*

The top ten box office hits illustrate this important characteristic of popular culture in four related ways:

a) *Sequels* — Six of the top ten movies are part of a popular series (*Star Wars,* and *Indiana Jones*) and *three* others spawned sequels outside the top ten list (*Ghostbusters, Jaws,* and *Batman*). The much anticipated and sought after sequel to *E.T.* has not materialized as of this writing, but *E.T.* has been a prominent and fertile source of the second example of popular culture's imitative nature because it has spawned numerous...

b) *Ripoffs and Wannabes* — movies (and other forms of popular entertainment) which seek to isolate the popular elements of a successful blockbuster and then reproduce them in slightly altered surroundings. We have *E.T.* at least partly to thank for a barrage of cute alienlike creatures invading Earth communities in the 1980s and 1990s and then palling around with a young earth person or family in an attempt to get back "home" or to find a home. *Short Circuit I* and *II* had an adorable alienlike robot (who picked up popular catch phrases and repeated them to comic effect just like *E.T.* did), *Starman* featured the Christ-like (but still cute n' funny) Jeff Bridges as an alien who brought dead deer back to life before staging his own interplanetary Immaculate Conception routine with one of "our women" and then vanishing into the starry heavens. And there was Gizmo, the furry little dear of a supernatural creature, who got wet and fed after midnight, produced a whole mess of wicked *Gremlins* — E.T.s on acid. The ripoff fever spread to television as well as a furry cat-hater alien named *Alf* who found his temporary home in American suburbia and started a successful career as an E.T. with an attitude. And a really furry Bigfoot named Harry began clogging the suburban drains of the Nuclear Family Hendersons (in a syndicated television wannabe based upon a popular movie ripoff). Popular culture really does feed on its own.

This rip-off wannabe form of commercial cannibalism is one of the most common types of imitation characterizing popular culture, and it can be found in the semi-legitimate progeny of each of the top ten movies. Thus *Batman* begat *Darkman, Jaws* spawned Big Fish (*Orca*—a ticked-off whale) and Little Fish (Piranha—mad midgets of marine life), *Indiana Jones* produced *Allan Quatermain* lurching around a backlot jungle searching for the Lost City of Gold, and *Star Wars* pumped new life into a defunct TV series and gave the *Star Trek* crew the chance to transport back to the deck of the Enterprise to embark on a new six-movie mission (leading right back to where they had been before—Planet Television and the world of *The Next Generation*).

Any outrage that we may feel at the rip-off wannabe's exploitation of the "original" hits should be tempered by the fact that movies on the top ten list are themselves examples of a different type of imitation characteristic of popular culture —viz. each is an...

c) *Imitation of Earlier Forms.*

The imitative process looks backward as well as forward—i.e., each of the six original movies in the list (*E.T., Star Wars, Jaws, Ghostbusters, Batman* and *Raiders of the Lost Ark*) not only spawned sequels and

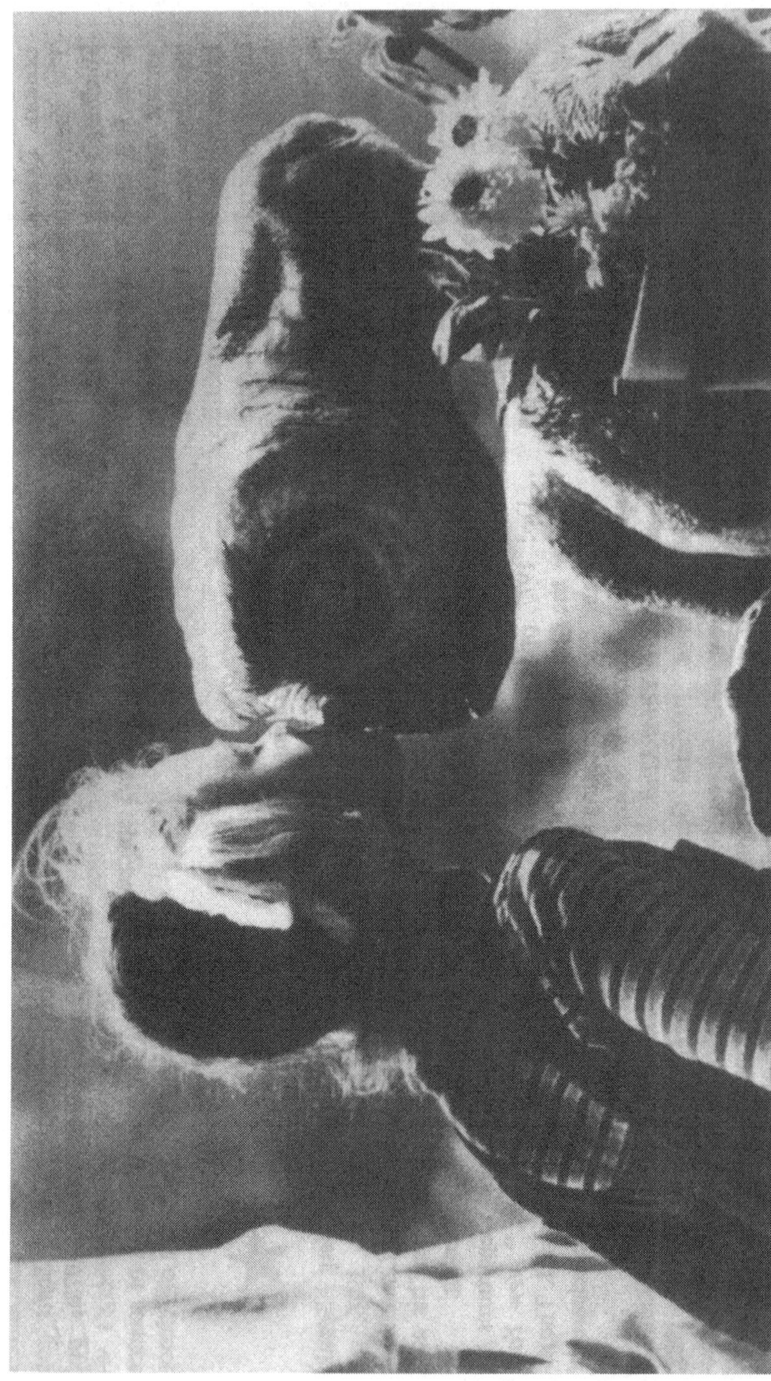

E.T.—The Extraterrestrial.

ripoffs but is also itself an example of some popular movie form of the *past.* Thus *Raiders* is a high budget version of the black and white cliffhanger serials shown in movie theaters in the 1930s and 1940s; *Jaws* is firmly in the tradition of all those rampaging giant monsters who invaded American (and Japanese) cities in the 1950s.; and *E.T.* is a simple reworking of *The Wizard of Oz*—i.e. a lost child wants to go home but is blocked by evil adults who want something the kid has. George Lucas has himself admitted that *Star Wars* is essentially a "western set in outer space" (with Han Solo as the lone gunfighter coming to the aid of the outgunned good guys) but the movie actually borrows heavily from the cliffhangers and American war movies as well—with homages to Tarzan, Wizard of Oz, and countless myths and folktales tossed in for good measure. The top ten movies are not so much unique, in other words, as they are exceedingly self-aware ("hip") repackagings of familiar forms in glossy, high-tech surroundings. In a manner which we will find demonstrated again and again in the history of popular culture, the enormous success of these movies can be attributed to their discovery of an attractive balance between old and new elements, offering audiences innovative wrinkles on top of familiar skins.

One way in which this balance may be obtained is to take familiar characters and replace them in the soils of some different media—a process which is at the heart of the fourth form of popular culture imitation:

d) *Media Makeovers*

We've already encountered this marketing hydra in the form of ripoffs and wannabes and in the saturation selling of Batman, but it is such a prevalent tool of imitation (and so diverse and often independent in its application) that it deserves to be considered in its own category. Media makeovers frequently consist of authorized imitations in other forms, for example—attempts by the producers of a successful movie to realize similar profits by adopting the characters and props to fit other products and settings. Obi Wan Lucas himself owns the rights to the Star Wars universe, for example, and his grip on the inhabitants makes Darth Vadar seem kind and gentle by comparison. *Star Wars* has shown up in comic books, breakfast cereals, fan magazines and clubs, record stores, toys (ranging from plastic models to 3-foot laser swords that glow in the dark), a series of paperback novels, board games and videogames, trading cards, candies of all sorts, etc. etc.—the Force is with us indeed—and not only in a galaxy far, far away.

3) *Popular Culture Is Escapist*

While this is most obviously true of the popular arts, it is also characteristic of most other elements of popular culture as well. Popular rituals allow us to enter a carefully ordered environment in which we can act in many ways not permitted in everyday life (e.g., as fanatical fans at a football game); popular heroes turn our focus away from what we are toward what we would like to become; and popular icons often serve to grant us new identities and powers we otherwise lack (e.g., the seductive skills magically granted to the driver of a red Corvette). This does *not* mean that popular culture is "trivial" or unimportant: escapism is serious business and a vital force in transforming mere existence into Life. Religion provides human beings a supportive world in which they can find refuge from daily (secular) life, and popular culture performs a similar function within the context of its world as well.

Six of the top ten American movies are outright fantasies (*E.T.*, the *Star Wars* series, *Batman,* and *Ghostbusters*) and the three Indiana Jones films have strong elements of the fantastic (e.g., the Ark, an underground Temple of Doom, the Holy Grail) played into a heightened romantic adventure form; *Jaws* is a straight-forward adventure tale with a mythical monster from the deep which bears a stronger resemblance to King Kong or Godzilla than it does to any known shark. None of the movies is "realistic" in plot, character, setting, or tone. Indeed, the emphasis in all ten is placed strongly upon the power of special effects to make the movies' otherwise unbelievable worlds acceptable substitutes for the world outside the theater—worlds "real" enough to escape into for two hours or so. All of the movies provide clear-cut divisions between good and evil (only the *Star Wars* series dares suggest that human beings might have tendencies to both "Forces" in the same soul—but the films raise the conflict only to demonstrate Luke's triumph of the will over the powers pulling him toward darkness), and all have happy endings in which nasty Nazis, cold-hearted scientists, and sliming spirits beat a hasty retreat while heroes celebrate. It is interesting to note in this regard that the least popular movie in the *Star Wars* triology is the middle *Empire Strikes Back* which is the one where the Dark Force confuses Luke and appears to be riding high in a cliffhanger "ending" which leaves all of our heroes in peril. The escapist hold of the top ten movies is most clearly demonstrated in the fact that their commercial success is owed significantly to the large number of repeat viewings which fueled the box office receipts. People return again and again to visit the worlds conjured up by these films—and then rent or purchase the movies on video in order to bring those worlds home with them as well.

4) *Traditional American Beliefs and Values in the Box Office Top Ten*

a) *Individual Freedom*

America was born out of a rebellion against all those who would place restrictions upon the inherent right of individuals to determine their own destinies through their own choices and actions. The earliest settlers sought a new world without the economic and religious restrictions of the old, and the American colonists gave the British their marching papers when the Crown tried to put a crimp in our free-spirited ways.

And a long, long time ago in a galaxy far, far away another group of outgunned rebels staged an uprising against their repressive, half-mad Empire leader as well. *Star Wars* and the War for the Stars and Bars are not the light years apart they might appear to be. Both feature scrappy, quick-witted and mobile rebels zipping around regimented, dull-witted storm troopers; both rebel forces called upon outside aid to further their cause; and both groups of rebels faced a crisis winter when all seemed lost until a great leader emerged to lead his ragtag forces to victory in a surprise attack. The Empire controls its troopers through fear and repression: middle manager types who question the decisions of higher-ups get the cold sweats when they flick on their video screens and Darth Vader's dark-helmeted mug shimmers on to tell them to Get With the Program. The Rebels adopt a more democratic leadership style—Han Solo is free to depart anytime he feels like it and it's only Luke's persuasive powers, his own conscience, and his hormones which cause him to decide to stay around. The conclusion of the triology is a veritable *Wizard-of-Oz*-like celebration shindig (with the midget Ewoks as Munchkins), and is also a real and symbolic wedding as well: the Princess gets hitched to Solo and thus weds her royalty to the movie's primary representative of democracy and individual freedom. Just as the victorious Washington refused offers to become "king of America," so too does Leia temper the absolution of her aristocracy (princesses and knights) with the will of the people and the right to choose (the man who has always jealously guarded his freedom to go Solo).

The same respect for individual freedom is present in *all* of the other movies in the top ten list as well. Indiana Jones thumps Nazis and mind-controlling Thuggies; Elliot defies the "authorities" to ensure E.T.'s right to return home; the Ghostbusters defy the mayor and anybody else who would stand in the way in their effort to save the city from the rampaging Stay-Puff Marshmallow Man; and Batman is the ultimate "aristocrat with a conscience" who takes orders from no one but still exercises his freedom to defend the average citizen against corrupt officials, petty criminals, and the serious Joker who would impose his twisted will through fear and violence.

The advocacy of individual freedom evident in the text of each movie is reinforced by the use of stars whose celebrity personas reflect a similar respect for this value. Bill Murray brings his Saturday Night Live irreverence to his role in *Ghostbusters*; Michael Keaton gives Batman a touch of Beetlejuice's supernatural monomania; and Harrison Ford's image as a rugged individual who goes his own way in life is highlighted by his frequent refusal to give interviews which tread on the subject of his personal life, and by the other roles he has played which share a healthy individualistic attitude—like the cop on the run from other cops in *Witness,* and the funky "liberated" businessman in *Working Girl.*

And the process has worked in reverse as well, with emblems representing individual freedom in the world of the movies crossing over into the 'real' world and bringing that association along with them. Thus the image of Elliot's bicycle soaring through the night-time sky and framed by the full moon has been adopted by Spielburg's independent company as a suitable expression of its free-spirited "Amblin" nature. And the same iconic vision continues to carry its meaning into other movies as well. The 1992 release of *Radio Flyer* featured another climactic flight *to* freedom and way *from* repression by a small boy victimized by evil adults who could find his escape only on the back of yet another magically soaring toy. The Ghostbuster's red-rimmed logo, Indiana Jones' trademark hat, and Batman's identifying symbol have all served similar roles as iconographic representation of individuality in our world as well as in their fictional birthplaces.

b) *Technology as Protector and Savior*

If necessity is truly the mother of invention then it's no wonder Americans have always valued this trait and its valuable products. An unknown, unmapped, frequently hostile New World is certainly the ultimate "necessity" Americans *had* to be shrewd and inventive about if they were to survive. American inventors are Great American heroes—Franklin, Edison—but these men are not merely Ivory Tower theorists who played around with ideas; the American inventor-hero is one who applies his big ideas to develop a technology which, in turn, is used to protect and promote other American values. Americans prize technology (and the mastermind behind it) much more for what it does than for what it is. Our real technological highpoints—the gun, the car, the telephone, the computer—are tools which protect America and promote its beliefs and ways of life.

This is one important value which Americans share with the Joker—like the Clown Prince of Crime, we too stare in awe at the Batman's technological wizardry and ask "Where does he get all those wonderful toys?" Batman *uses* his toys to preserve and protect, however, and not merely to extend his own ego the way the Joker does with his mechanisms of mayhem (e.g., disfiguring chemicals placed in cosmetics designed to make everyone share the Joker's ugly fate). And so also to the Ghostbusters.

Graduate school dropouts they may be, but it's *their* blaster-packs which send evil spirits scurrying back to the netherworld and make the Big Apple safe once again—from ghosts, anyway. And Indiana Jones gives stereotyped ignorant and posturing Third Worlders a hard-earned lesson in the equalizing powers of American technology when he calmly guns down an Arab swordsman who challenges the hero to a duel.

In *Jaws*, the squinty-eyed Captain (Robert Shaw) has contempt for the science of icthyologist college boy Richard Dreyfuss. The Captain needs a macho confrontation with the shark to feed his Moby Dick complex, and too much technology would remove the thrill and challenge of the hunt. The Captain goes too far in his egotistical rejection of science however, and soon ends up playing Jonah rather than Ahab—sliding down the shark's gullet while the fish chews up the Captain's boat for good measure. But Dreyfuss as egghead can't terminate the shark either—he's been in the laboratory too long and white sharks are not Ivory Towers. The victory is left instead to the Sheriff (Roy Scheider) who has the Captain's common-man courage and skill and also the cleverness to use technology to blow the shark into so many pieces that nothing short of a sequel could put him back together again. "Good" technology protects the small town values of Amity, the sheriff's family and loved ones, while leaving room for individual heroism as well.

The *Star Wars* trilogy provides another example of "good" vs. "bad" technology and adds another layer of meaning to the way Americans define the former. The Empire has the technological edge in their battle against the rebels—they've got a Death Star, in addition to numerous indestructible ground vehicles, and many more spaceships. But the rebels have technology which is ultimately superior finally because it is guided by the mystical "Force." Their technology has a spiritual link with their souls and the universe which strikes an ideal balance between the cold dehumanizing technological advancement of the Empire and the primitivism of the forest-dwelling Ewoks. The technology, admired by Americans, lies precisely in this middle ground between mind and heart—between culture and nature, science and religion, future and past; we believe in the force of technology *and* technology guided by the Force—a machine with a human face and personality. We believe in R2D2 and C3PO.

c) *Violence as a legitimate means of obtaining Justice outside the Law*

Americans have always sworn by the rule of law but they've always had a strong distrust of it as well. Laws are made by those with the power to write and enforce them and our earliest experiences were with English edicts which tried to tax without representation, and search and seize without warrants. America was thus born out of a rebellion which used the violence of an "illegal" war to achieve the justice which the law had denied. We've been wary of laws ever since. American popular entertainments are thus filled with private detectives who have to battle cops as often as crooks, cowboy gunfighters wanted by the law but who kill only to protect the weak, and Dirty Harry policemen who toss their badges in the river when it's time to deal with the *real* business of taking the vermin off the streets. The law in America is similar to technology. In other words it is a really nice idea, but if it gets in the way of justice (or any of the other bedrock American values) then it better move over or fall in line behind the American way of life.

All of the heroes in the *Star Wars* trilogy are rebels—outlaws by the standards of the ruling Emperor—and all are engaged in some major heavy-weight violence as a means of achieving their just due. Batman is a costumed vigilante with a hidden identity who blows up factories, knocks criminals into acid vats, zips his low-flying Batplane through city streets, and crashes through the skylight of the Gotham City Art Museum as we applaud him for each act of illegal mayhem. The Ghostbusters practice their trade in spite of the resistance offered by the mayor and his council, and in their triumph provide a succinct summary of the American love affair with violence turned toward just ends: "We came. We saw. We kicked its ass."

d) *Youth is the best period of life, and childhood in particular is a special time which needs to be protected and preserved*

As the newborn products of a New World and, later as citizens of a "great experiment," one of the world's first democracies in modern times, Americans have always quite properly perceived themselves as a young nation and have thus consistently admired the traits associated with youth as well. As a result, Americans see themselves as *innocent, energetic, rebellious, optimistic, full of good intentions,* and *idealistic.* This belief takes many forms in American life (It can be found in everything from our obsessions with dieting and plastic surgery to the way we conduct our foreign policy.), but one important variant, especially evident in the top ten movies, is the high value we place upon children and the halcyon world which is their proper environment in the garden of America.

A central component of a child's special world is formed by the family which supports, protects and loves him or her. The movies in the top ten list are especially concerned with demonstrating (and celebrating) the value and importance of childhood as it finds expression in the individual lives of children *and* as the institution of the family acts to ensure the child's emotional and physical well-being. Villains in these movies are "bad," often in direct proportion to the degree that they threaten or harm children and families, and the "good" people are either children themselves, adults protective of children, or adult-children who are struggling to resolve problems left over from childhoods scarred by bad parents or other difficulties. It has often been said that the most successful movies are those which are geared to the tastes and sensibilities of the average twelve-year-old; the top ten box office hits suggest that it helps to celebrate those traits as well.

In *Indiana Jones and the Temple of Doom,* Indy teams up with a young side-kick and together they come upon an Indian village whose arid, bleak atmosphere stands in stark contrast to the natural beauties of India which surround it. The people all shuffle around like joyless drones, as the howling wind blows dust like that of a western ghost town. What could be the cause of all this gloom—famine? Plague? No. The troubles can all be traced to one simple cause: this is the way the world looks when it has been stripped of its children. All the youth in the village have been marched off to slave away in the bowels of the earth beneath the Temple of Doom, and they have been force-fed some mystical mind control potion to prevent any resistance or rebellion: child labor and drugs have combined to rob these children of their youth. It is up to Indy to get it back for them, of course, and the final scene of the movie is a laughing and colorful paean to the restoration of a child's special world: the village is reborn, kids play in the sunlight rather than shovel in underground factories, and when adults allow themselves to get distracted by "other things" the children bring their focus right back where it belongs—on Indy and his female companion, who are just big kids at heart themselves.

Indy had his childhood problems too, however too. The young Indiana Jones was saddled with a bad dad who spent all of his time puzzling over ancient manuscripts and hustling around the world chasing after trinkets for museums. Indy needed Love and all he got was an occasional lecture and the demeaning title of "Junior." It is no wonder he "grows up" to engage in the very same sort of globe-trotting nonsense as his father as Indy's unresolved conflict with his father has placed him in perpetual competition with this stern, unforgiving parent. By the time *The Last Crusade* rolls around, the conflict is made explicit as both end up pursuing the Holy Grail—the ultimate prize in their professional lives—but both reject the goal when it is in reach because they each choose to acknowledge their love for one another instead. (Henry Jones cries at his son's apparent demise, and Indy allows the Grail to fall away from his grasp in order to pull his father to safety.) And the reward granted to each of the Joneses for finally recognizing that there is more to life than just trying to keep up with each other is perfectly in keeping with the ethic of childhood which guides these films. The characters *are* given perpetual youth and the everlasting extension of the now properly restored and loving world of childhood. Pop calls "Junior" by his real name, and Indiana exits his adventures not with a ringing "Hi-Yo Silver!" but with an equally firm (and by these movies' standards, heroic) "Yes Sir!"

Indy's problems are similar to those of Luke Skywalker and some other heroes as well. Luke is also placed in direct competition with his (*really*) "bad dad," but he also is rewarded for resolving his childhood conflict by becoming a Jedi Knight. Luke finds a substitute father in Obi Wan Kenobi, a sister in Princess Leia, and a big brother in Han. Batman, meanwhile, finds the motivating force in his career of criminal-bashing to be the perpetual re-enactment of a childhood trauma in which he was unable to save his parents from death at the hands of the Joker, and Batman's triumph in the film is not so much in the way he saves Gotham City as it is in the salvation of young Bruce Wayne's childhood. And, finally, Elliot and *E.T.* are two kids on the run from insensitive adults, and that film's soaring climax is testimony to the great value all of these films place upon the protection of a child's special world.

It is interesting to note that the heavy emphasis placed upon children and family in these movies is accompanied by a marked muting of the theme of romantic love. Romantic love *is* present in several of the films (Han and Leia, Bruce and Vicki), but these are essentially stories of children who cannot love until they resolve psychological traumas which are preventing them from entering adulthood, and about heroes who have no time for romance as long as the empire-shark-evil-priest-nazi-joker-ghost is threatening to wipe out the community. These movies are about growing up and kicking ass.

The childlike identity and violent duty of the heroes is responsible not only for relegating romantic love to the rear car of the adventure rollercoaster, but also for the regressive, "traditional" stereotype of women which characterizes most of these movies. In this universe of mayhem and tinkertoys, women exist to be loved, and to be rescued when they carelessly become prisoners of evil forces. These films may end in a clinch but the bulk of screen time is occupied with Batman freeing Vicki from the Joker, Han and Luke pulling Leia's fat out of Jabba's fire, and Indiana answering Willie's all too frequent squeals for help. Even when one of the films makes a slight bow in the direction of independent womanhood like that of Marian Ravenwood in *Raiders*, it is in response to a relationship with a man. Marian's "independence" is purely the result of her funk over having been dumped by Indy, and once the story gets rolling she is soon vulnerable and fallible like the rest of our heroines. Women in these wonderlands are not liberated—they are only rescued.

Aimed now with our understanding of the deep-seated reflective appeal of these highly successful movies, perhaps we can put this academic knowledge to practical use. Given the money and power necessary to make any movie we choose, we should have a good idea of what ingredients should be included based upon the beliefs and values which have characterized the top ten American box office hits thus far:

1) We should place a heavy emphasis upon the special world of childhood and upon the home and family which acts as its proper environment. Our hero should be male and essentially or actually a child.

2) Our hero should have a practical command of technology which enables him to protect and save the values Americans hold dear.

3) The application of technology should involve a hefty amount of violence directed toward achieving the *just* defense of American virtues in the absence of suitable assistance from the Law.

4) Our hero should demonstrate his freedom from traditional constraints through a celebration of his individuality and right to choose.

5) We need a "happy ending" in which the menace to freedom is removed and community is restored.

So we are presented with a child with repressive, insensitive parents who suddenly finds himself freed from their presence and has a high old time satisfying his every whim—"shaving," snooping in private rooms, shopping for fun—until a couple of burglars try to squelch the party. He has to use all the hardware at his command (including a VCR, toy guns, and a blowtorch) to singly and violently defend his home until his parents return and realize how much they love him—and he loves them. We are left knowing that the protected house will now be a real home and the kid will never be Home Alone. That—again.

I'll bet it would make millions of dollars, become America's highest grossing comedy of all time, and in 1992 supplant *Ghostbusters* on the Top Ten List.

What do you think?

e) *Popular Culture Is "Cultural Glue"*—binding us together in a world of shared references, meanings, characters, music, foods, and so on.

The worlds of the top ten movies have become part of our language, for example. Even people who have never seen the films recognize and use familiar phrases such as the following: "Who ya gonna call?" "Just when you thought it was safe to go back in the water," "Phone home," "May the Force be with you," and "A long time ago in a galaxy far, far away. . . ." Even the former President of the United States (himself a former inhabitant of Hollywood's escapist fantasies) borrowed the language of *Star Wars* to name his Strategic Defense Initiative in a manner he knew would be familiar and comforting to Americans.

The shared references and meanings provided by popular culture are especially important in the pluralistic American society, which lacks by definition a common religious or ethnic identity. The top ten movies are one way in which the melting pot mixes its wide variety of ingredients into a world recognizably "American." And as this American culture spreads outward, so too does the world it has fashioned—until, perhaps, the cultural glue which binds us together today becomes the unifying force of a "global village" tomorrow.

Popular culture's role as a binding, unifying force in society goes far beyond the manufacturing of catch-phrases and popular heroes. Popular culture's *nature* is to *sell* dreams and *imitate* its own success, but its *meaning* lies beneath the glittering surface in the deep-seated beliefs and values which it expresses. The top ten American box office hits tell us a great deal about popular culture, but they reveal much deeper truths about ourselves.

The Meaning of Popular Culture

In the climactic scene of *Raiders of the Lost Ark,* Indiana Jones and his "goddamn partner" Marian Ravenwood are predictably tied to a stake while the evil Nazis prepare to take a crowbar to the mystical ark. Just as one of Hitler's minions begins to lift the lid, however, Indy warns Marian not to look, and thus both our heroes are spared the effects of the lethal light show which follows.

The special effects and big budget fantasy worlds of the top ten movies often have the same effect on audiences as the ark: they reward us for "looking away" by enabling us to escape into the exciting adventures they create in such an entertaining fashion. Once we are outside the theater and safe from the distracting lights and shadows, however, it is possible to look *at* these movies and read the signs they provide as guides to deeper beliefs and values being expressed. We can use the tools provided by popular culture to identify patterns of expression—similar types of heroes engaged in similar types of quests, for example—which suggest underlying similarities in meaning as well. On a deeper level, the nosy Nazis in *Raiders* experienced the big meltdown because they tried to look at the ark without understanding its meaning and significance; the study of popular culture can help us avoid this fate by learning to look with tools more subtle and revealing than a crowbar. Our purpose here is to demonstrate that these films are revealing in ways much deeper than they are ordinarily considered to be—that they hold meanings more complex and vital than their predictable narratives and simple themes would seem to suggest. We don't *have* to look away once we've seen E.T. safely home, the Joker taking his last dance in the pale moonlight, and Indiana Jones slurping up six ounces of Immortality Juice. "The End" is only the beginning—and so is the analysis which follows.

How Much Can You Swallow?

Mark Crispin Miller

In his brief analysis of a single advertisement, Marc Crispin Miller manages to demonstrate a wide variety of the meanings and methods involved in taking popular culture seriously. Miller begins by looking at the image presented by the advertisement in a manner resembling a scientist examining an unknown species of insect on a slide in front of him. He ignores the preconceptions that would be imposed upon him by assuming that the advertisement is about the product being promoted (Miller never even mentions what the ad is "selling" until the final paragraph!), and instead looks for relationships between the figures and objects in the frame in the hope that a pattern will emerge. Everything is examined anew, and Miller draws upon the meanings offered by other elements of popular culture (e.g., a popular television series, a movie star, stereotypes of race and class) to illuminate this specific example; and he allows himself to question the very things the advertisement is asking its audience to assume*—e.g. we're supposed to "know" what the guy in the bottom corner wants and how he's managed to obtain it. Miller's essay is a marvelous example of a writer overcoming one of the major hurdles of popular culture analysis—the fact that we are all part of the very culture we are being asked to examine. Miller sees the advertisement and the audience by looking for meaning beneath the subject matter. Instead of reaching for a glass of whisky he asks himself why he may feel like doing so.*

Look what happens as a result, Miller discovers that the intended meaning of the ad (a good shot of Windsor can buy family, friends, and human warmth) is the opposite of its actual effect. This warm, cozy advertisement manipulates basic American beliefs and values to foster unease rather than serenity, fear of rejection rather than certainty of inclusion. Miller shows that the two sides of the Funhouse Mirror are very close indeed—so close that the same ad can "give" through one site by reflecting our needs and desires and take away with the others shaping those needs and desires by exacerbating them.

Reprinted by permission from the author, from *Esquire* October 1990.

Look on at those Old Friends. Could the scene be any friendlier? Fondly, in the kitchen's honeyed light, they crowd together, just like a happy family—or at least like the characters on *thirtysomething*, which, at its worst, inspired countless such dense ad-scenes of yuppie bonhomie. As all too often on that show, so here we have a cloying image of post-1960s sociability: lite chatter in a warm suburban house, where *everyone* can come to munch and kid around.

And yet, in the buttery light of this (to quote the copy) "kitchen get-together," the seeming togetherness has, in fact, strict limits. On one hand, there does seem to be a slight hint of sexual liberality among these upward movers. Although evidently married, the host and hostess—the couple working at the stove—flirt busily with other partners: The wife, a dead ringer for *thirtysomething's* Nancy, goggles responsively at the Brainy type who grins behind her, while her once-athletic mate (a Brian Dennehy look-alike) tempts that other blonde with a mouthful of what appears to be raw beef. But such "openness" is closed to some. There's that black couple placed in the background, connecting neither with the hot quartet nor with each other; and there's that sad spectator on the left—the scene's least-engaged participant, and yet its crucial figure.

Although subtly snubbed, and holding nothing in their hands (not having hands at all, in fact), the black guests are at least allowed to stand there in the same domestic space as those who wield the spoons and clink their drinks and pass the meat around—whereas that gloomy loner is shut out completely. A single (dumped? divorced? can't meet anyone?) staring at three festive couples, this odd man out is compositionally cut off from the others by that clean island unit, and also by those cornucopian heaps of bread and salad that further separate him from his only possible inamorata—that hungry-looking blonde who stands so close to him,[1] and yet ignores him, instead reaching, fascinated, for the host's hunk of meat. So exclusive is the barrier between this loner and his "friends" that he might as well be standing in the street like Stella Dallas—an ejection symbolized by the front part of the island, so like a windowsill over-shadowing a brick facade.

Small wonder, then, that our spectator looks unhappy. While the others kid around, mouths open, all set to laugh and eat (and kiss), he sits with lips compressed, sad gaze fixed on . . . what? Does he want to bolt that hunk of meat, or is he looking at it jealously, wishing that the blonde would reach for *him*? Or is he staring past the sirloin at the mother figure flirting manically with Four-eyes? Or is it Four-eyes that he's after? But this guessing game is pointless, because what matters for the advertisers is, finally, not that we crave this or that specific thing but that we feel driven, always, by the desperate need to swallow *everything*. What ads generally sell us is that neoinfantile anxiety, and *then* the endless multitude of products that are alleged to soothe it, and that never do.

While it seems to celebrate the joys of food and fellowship, this ad—like all ads—actually promotes a sense of utter deprivation. The loner has nothing but his Windsor; and if he drinks enough of it, presumably he'll have it all—for the scene glows not with a honeyed or a buttery light, in fact, but with the amber light of whisky, which also glows within the Windsor bottle placed below the picture—"One taste and you're there." This scene of sociability, the ad implies, is in this bottle and this (single) glass, available to all the lonely people in the world, as long as they never get together.

Notes

[1]She seems available not just because she's close at hand, but because of the open space above her—she's the only one without a big pot hanging over her head.

New Legends for Old

Jan Harold Brunvand

Urban legends are fascinating mixtures, indeed. Part fact (we "know" the tale is true), part fancy (well—it did not actually happen to us or to the person who told us about it—but it did *happen to the person who told the person who told us—really); part entertainment (they're creepy, spooky, humorous and amusing), part lesson (be careful or the same thing will happen to you!); part history (some happened a long time ago), part recent news (some happened in the fast food place that opened last month). Urban legends are comprised of the complex contradiction implied by their name: they are part city, part ancient village.*

Urban legends also balance lightly on the dividing line between popular culture and folk culture and thus serve to remind us that this "line" is a mobile, porous one rather than a barrier. The relationship between cultures is fluid and flexible so that precise definition is required to determine where a given cultural artifact properly belongs. An urban legend told around a campfire by someone who believes it actually happened is clearly an aspect of folk culture—but what happens when the same "legend" becomes the basis of a movie, book, or television program? And suppose that the plot of a movie or book is repeated by some other teller around a different campfire who simply changes some names, "localizes" it, and claims it actually happened? Urban legends demonstrate how time, audience, and mode of presentation can all interact to shift a given artifact across cultural boundaries.

The similarities which urban legends bear to both popular and folk cultures mean also that the questions asked about them are familiar to students of popular culture as well as to folklorists. Note especially that Brunvand begins *his essay by describing an urban legend and discussing its history and various forms, but he doesn't end there. Brunvand discerns an underlying meaning to each legend—a belief or value reflective of the audience mindset which keeps the tale alive. Like popular culture, in other words, urban legends are fun, interesting, and entertaining—but their importance lies in the meaning* beneath *the surface.*

Adapted from *The Vanishing Hitchhiker: American Urban Legends and Their Meanings.* New York: W.W. Norton & Co., Inc. 1981. Reprinted with permission.

Urban Legends as Folklore

Folklore subsists on oral tradition, but not all oral communication is folklore. The vast amounts of human interchange, from casual daily conversations to formal discussions in business or industry, law, or teaching, rarely constitute straight oral folklore. However, all such "communicative events" (as scholars dub them) are punctuated routinely by various units of traditional material that are memorable, repeatable, and that fit recurring social situations well enough to serve in place of original remarks. "Tradition" is the key idea that links together such utterances as nicknames, proverbs, greeting and leave-taking formulas, wisecracks, anecdotes, and jokes as "folklore"; indeed, these are a few of the best known "conversational genres" of American folklore. Longer and more complex folk forms—fairy tales, epics, myths, legends, or ballads, for example—may thrive only in certain special situations of oral transmission. All true folklore ultimately depends upon continued oral dissemination, usually within fairly homogeneous "folk groups," and upon the retention through time of internal patterns and motifs that become traditional in the oral exchanges. The corollary of this rule of stability in oral tradition is that all items of folklore, while retaining a fixed central core, are constantly changing as they are transmitted, so as to create countless "variants" differing in length, detail, style, and performance technique. Folklore, in short, consists of oral tradition in variants.

Urban legends belong to the subclass of folk narratives, legends, that—unlike fairy tales—are believed, or at least believable, and that—unlike myths—are set in the recent past and involve normal human beings rather than ancient gods or demigods. Legends are folk history, or rather quasi-history. As with any folk legends, urban legends gain credibility from specific details of time and place or from references to source authorities. For instance, a popular western pioneer legend often begins something like, "My great-grandmother had this strange experience when she was a young girl on a wagon train going through Wyoming when an Indian chief wanted to adopt her..." Even though hundreds of different great-grandmothers are supposed to have had the same doubtful experience (being desired by the chief because of her beautiful long blonde hair), the fact seldom reaches legend-tellers; if it does, they assume that the family lore has indeed spread far and wide. This particular popular tradition, known as "Goldilocks on the Oregon Trail," interests folklorists because of the racist implications of a dark Indian savage coveting a fair young civilized woman—this legend is familiar in the *white* folklore only—and it is of little concern that the story seems to be entirely apocryphal.

In the world of modern urban legends there is usually no geographical or generational gap between teller and event. The story is *true*; it really occurred, and recently, and always to someone else who is quite close to the narrator, or at least "a friend of a friend." Urban legends are told both in the course of casual conversations and in such special situations as campfires, slumber parties, and college dormitory bull sessions. The legends' physical settings are often close by, real, and sometimes even locally renowned for other such happenings. Though the characters in the stories are usually nameless, they are true-to-life examples of the kind of people the narrators and their audience know firsthand.

"The Boyfriend's Death"

Consider this typical version of a well-known urban legend that folklorists have named "The Boyfriend's Death," collected in 1964 (the earliest documented instance of the story) by folklorist Daniel R. Barnes from an eighteen-year-old freshman at the University of Kansas. The usual tellers of the story are adolescents, and the normal setting for the narration is a college dormitory room with fellow students sprawled on the furniture and floors.

> This happened just a few years ago out on the road that turns off 59 highway by the Holiday Inn. This couple was parked under a tree out on this road. Well, it got to be time for the girl to be back at the dorm, so she told her boyfriend that they should start back. But the car wouldn't start, so he told her to lock herself in the car and he would go down to the Holiday Inn and call for help. Well, he didn't come back and he didn't come back, and pretty soon she started hearing a scratching noise on the roof of the car. "Scratch, scratch...scratch, scratch." She got scareder and scareder, but he didn't come back. Finally, when it was almost daylight, some people came along and stopped and helped her out of the car, and she looked up and here was her boyfriend hanging from the tree, and his feet were scraping against the roof of the car. This is why the road is called "Hangman's Road."

A developing motif in "The Boyfriend's Death" is the character and role of the rescuers, who in the 1964 Kansas version are merely "some people." The standard identification later becomes "the police," authority figures whose presence lends further credence to the story. They are either called by the missing teenagers' parents, or simply appear on the scene in the morning to check the car. In a 1969 variant from Leonardtown, Maryland, the police give a warning, "Miss, please get out of the car and walk to the police car with us, but don't look back." In a version from Texas collected in 1971, set "at this lake somewhere way out in nowhere," a policeman gets an even longer line: "Young lady, we want you to get out of the car and come with us. Whatever you do, don't turn, don't turn around just keep walking, just keep going straight and don't look back at the car." The more detailed the police instructions are, the more plausible the tale seems to become. Of course the standard rule of folk-narrative plot development now applies: the taboo must be broken (or the "interdiction violated," as some scholars put it). The girl always *does* look back, like Orpheus in the underworld, and in a number of versions her hair turns white from the shock of what she sees, as in a dozen other American legends.

Urban Legends as Cultural Symbols

Legends can survive in our culture as living narrative folklore if they contain three essential elements: a strong basic story-appeal, a foundation in actual belief, and a meaningful message or "moral." That is, popular stories like "The Boyfriend's Death" are not only engrossing tales, but also "true," or at least so people think, and they teach valuable lessons. In legends the primary messages are quite clear and straightforward; often they take the form of explicit warnings or good examples of "poetic justice." Secondary messages in urban legends tend to be suggested metaphorically or symbolically: these may provide deeper criticisms of human behavior or social conditions.

People still tell legends, therefore, and other folk take time to listen to them, not only because of their inherent plot interest but because they seem to convey true, worthwhile, and relevant information, albeit partly in a subconscious mode. In other words, such stories are "news" presented to us in an attractive way, with hints of larger meanings. Without this multiple appeal few legends would get a hearing in the modern world, so filled with other distractions. Legends survive by being as lively and "factual" as the television evening news, and, like the daily news broadcasts, they tend to concern deaths, injuries, kidnappings, tragedies, and scandals.

On a literal level a story like "The Boyfriend's Death" simply warns young people to avoid situations in which they may be endangered, but at a more symbolic level the story reveals society's broader fears of people, especially women and the young, being alone and among strangers in the darkened world outside the security of their own home or car. Note that the young woman in the story (characterized by "her high-heeled shoes and evening dress") is shown as especially helpless and passive, cowering under the blanket in the car until she is rescued by men. Such themes recur in various forms in many other popular urban legends, as we shall see.

In order to be retained in a culture, any form of folklore must fill some genuine need, whether this be the need for an entertaining escape from reality, or a desire to validate by anecdotal examples some of the culture's ideals and institutions. For legends in general, a major function has always been the attempt to explain unusual and supernatural happenings in the natural world. To some degree this remains a purpose for urban legends, but their more common role nowadays seems to be to show that the prosaic contemporary scene is capable of producing shocking or amazing occurrences which may actually have happened to friends or to near-acquaintances but which are nevertheless explainable in some reasonably logical terms. On the one hand we want our factual lore to inspire awe, and at the same time we wish to have the most fantastic tales include at least the hint of a rational explanation and perhaps even a conclusion. Thus an escaped lunatic, a possibly *real* character, not a fantastic invader from outer space or Frankenstein's monster, is said to be responsible for the atrocities committed in the gruesome tales that teenagers tell. As sometimes happens in real life, the car radio gives warning, and the police get the situation back under control. (The policemen's role, in fact, becomes larger and more commanding as the story grows in oral tradition.) Only when the young lovers are still alone and scared are they vulnerable, but society's adults and guardians come to their rescue presently.

In common with brief unverified reports ("rumors"), to which they are often closely related, urban legends gratify our desire to know about and to try to understand bizarre, frightening, and potentially dangerous or embarrassing events that *may* have happened. (In rumors and legends there is always some element of doubt concerning where and when these things *did* occur.) These floating stories appeal to our morbid curiosity and satisfy our sensation-seeking minds that demand gratification through frequent infusions of new information, "sanitized" somewhat by the positive messages. Informal rumors and stories fill in the gaps left by professional news reporting, and these marvelous, though generally false, "true" tales may be said to be carrying the folk-news—along with some editorial matter from person to person even in today's highly technological world.

Growing Up Scared

People of all ages love a good scare. Early childlore is full of semi-serious spooky stories and ghastly threats, while the more sophisticated black humor of Little Willies, Bloody Marys, Dead Babies, and other cycles of sick jokes enters a bit later. Among the favorite readings at school are Edgar Allan Poe's blood-soaked tales, and favorite stories at summer camp tell of maniacal ax-murderers and deformed giants lurking in the dark forest to ambush unwary Scouts. Halloween spook houses and Hollywood horror films cater to the same wish to push the level of tolerable fright as far as possible.

The ingredients of horror fiction change little through time, but the style of such stories does develop, even in oral tradition. In their early teens young Americans apparently reject the overdramatic and unbelievable juvenile "scaries" and adopt a new lore of more plausible tales with realistic settings. That is, they begin to enjoy urban legends, especially those dealing, with "folks" like themselves—dating couples, students, and baby-sitters—who are subjected to grueling ordeals and horrible threats.

One consistent theme in these teenage horrors is that as the adolescent moves out from home into the larger world, the world's dangers may close in on him or her. Therefore, although the immediate purpose of many of these legends is to produce a good scare, they also serve to deliver a warning: Watch out! This could happen to you! Furthermore, the horror tales often contain thinly-disguised sexual themes which are, perhaps, implicit in the nature of such plot situations as parking in a lovers' lane or baby-sitting (playing house) in a strange home. These sexual elements furnish both a measure of further entertainment and definite cautionary notices about the world's actual dangers. Thus, from the teenagers' own major fears, concerns, and experiences, spring their favorite "true" oral stories.

The chief current example of this genre of urban legend—one that is even older, more popular, and more widespread than "The Boyfriend's Death"—is the one usually called "the Hook."

"The Hook"

On Tuesday, November 8, 1960, the day when Americans went to the polls to elect John F. Kennedy as their thirty-fifth president, thousands of people must have read the following letter from a teenager in the popular newspaper column written by Abigail Van Buren:

> Dear Abby: If you are interested in teenagers, you will print this story. I don't know whether it's true or not, but it doesn't matter because it served its purpose for me:
>
> A fellow and his date pulled into their favorite "lovers' lane" to listen to the radio and do a little necking. The music was interrupted by an announcer who said there was an escaped convict in the area who had served time for rape and robbery. He was described as having a hook instead of a right hand. The couple became frightened and drove away. When the boy took his girl home, he went around to open the car door for her. Then he saw—a hook on the door handle! I don't think I will ever park to make out as long as I live. I hope this does the same for other kids.
>
> Jeanette

This juicy story seems to have emerged in the late 1950s. The story of "The Hook" (or "The Hookman") really needed no national press report to give it life or credibility, because the teenage oral-tradition underground had done the job well enough long before the election day of 1960. Teenagers all over the country knew about "The Hook" by 1959, and like other modern legends the basic plot was elaborated with details and became highly localized.

One of my own students, originally from Kansas, provided this specific account of where the event supposedly occurred:

> Outside of "Mac" [McPherson, Kansas], about seven miles out towards Lindsborg, north on old highway 81 is an old road called "Hookman's Road." It's a curved road, a traditional parking spot for the kids. When I was growing up it [the legend] was popular, and that was back in the '60s, and it was old then.

Another student told a version of the story that she had heard from her baby-sitter in Albuquerque in 1960:

> ...over the radio came an announcement that a crazed killer with a hook in place of a hand had escaped from the local insane asylum. The girl got scared and begged the boy to take her home. He got mad and stepped on the gas and roared off. When they got to her house, he got out and went around to the other side of the car to let her out. There on the door handle was a bloody hook.

But these two students were told, after arriving in Salt Lake City, that it had actually occurred *here* in Memory Grove, a well-wooded city park. "Oh, no," a local student in the class insisted. "This couple was parked outside of Salt Lake City *in a mountain canyon* one night, and..." It turned out that virtually every student in the class knew the story as adapted in some way to their hometowns.

Part of the great appeal of "The Hook"—one of the most popular adolescent scare stories—must lie in the tidiness of the plot. Everything fits. On the other hand, the lack of loose ends would seem to be excellent testimony to the story's near impossibility. After all, what are the odds that a convicted criminal or crazed maniac would be fitted with a hook for a missing hand, that this same threatening figure would show up precisely when a radio warning had been broadcast of his escape, and that the couple would drive away rapidly just at the instant the hookman put his hook through the door handle? Besides, why wouldn't he try to open the door with his good hand, and how is it that the boy—furious at the interruption of their lovemaking—is still willing to go around politely to open the girl's door when they get home? Too much, too much—but it makes a great story.

In an adolescent novel titled *Dinky Hocker Shoots Smack!*, M.E. Kerr captured the way teenagers often react to such legends—with cool acceptance that it might have happened, and that's good enough:

> She told Tucker this long story about a one-armed man who was hanging around a lovers' lane in Prospect Park [Brooklyn]. There were rumors that he tried to get in the cars and carry off the girls. He banged on the windshields with his hooked wooden arm and frothed at the mouth. He only said two words: *bloody murder*; and his voice was high and hoarse.
>
> Dinky claimed this girl who went to St. Marie's was up in Prospect Park one night with a boyfriend. The girl and her boyfriend began discussing the one-armed man while they were parked. They both got frightened and decided to leave. The boy dropped the girl off at her house, and drove home. When he got out of his car, he found this hook attached to his door handle.
>
> Dinky said, 'They must have driven off just as he was about to open the door.'
>
> 'I thought you weren't interested in the bizarre, anymore,' Tucker said.
>
> 'It's a true story.'
>
> 'It's still bizarre.'

A key detail lacking in the *Dinky Hocker* version, however, is the boyfriend's frustrated anger resulting in their leaving the scene in a great hurry. Almost invariably the boy guns the motor and roars away: "...so he revs up the car and he goes torquing out of there." Or, "The boy floored the gas pedal and zoomed away," or "Her boyfriend was annoyed and the car screeched off...." While this behavior is essential to explain the sudden sharp force that tears loose the maniac's hook, it is also a reminder of the original sexual purpose of the parking, at least on the boy's part. While Linda Degh saw "the natural dread of the handicapped," and "the boy's disappointment and suddenly recognized fear as an adequate explanation for the jump start of the car," folklorist Alan Dundes disagreed, mainly because of the curtailed sex quest in the plot.

Dundes, taking a Freudian line, interpreted the hook itself as a phallic symbol which penetrates the girl's door handle (or bumps seductively against her window) but which is torn off (symbolic of castration) when the car starts abruptly. Girls who tell the story, Dundes suggests, "are not afraid of what a man lacks, but of what he has"; a date who is "all hands" may really want to "get his hooks into her." Only the girl's winding up the window or insisting upon going home at once saves her, and the date has to "pull out fast" before he begins to act like a sex maniac himself. The radio—turned on originally for soft, romantic background music—introduces instead "the consciencelike voice from society," a warning that the girl heeds and the boy usually scorns. Dundes concluded that this popular legend "reflects a very real dating practice, one which produces anxiety...particularly for girls."

"The Baby-sitter and the Man Upstairs"

Just as a lone woman may unwittingly be endangered by a hidden man while she is driving at night, a younger one may face the same hazard in a strange home. The horror legend of this version of "The

Baby-sitter and the Man Upstairs," is from a fourteen-year-old Canadian boy (1973):

There was this baby-sitter that was in Montreal baby-sitting for three children in a big house. She was watching TV when suddenly the phone rang. The children were all in bed. She picked up the phone and heard this guy on the other end laughing hysterically. She asked him what it was that he wanted, but he wouldn't answer and then hung up. She worried about it for a while, but then thought nothing more of it and went back to watching the movie.

Everything was fine until about fifteen minutes later when the phone rang again. She picked it up and heard the same voice laughing hysterically at her, and then hung up. At this point she became really worried and phoned the operator to tell her what had been happening. The operator told her to calm down and that if he called again to try and keep him on the line as long as possible and she would try to trace the call.

Again about fifteen minutes later the guy called back and laughed hysterically at her. She asked him why he was doing this, but he just kept laughing at her. He hung up and about five seconds later the operator called. She told the girl to get out of the house at once because the person who was calling was calling from the upstairs extension. She slammed down the phone and just as she was turning to leave she saw the man coming down the stairs laughing hysterically with a bloody butcher knife in his hand and meaning to kill her. She ran out onto the street but he didn't follow. She called the police and they came and caught the man, and discovered that he had murdered all the children.

The storyteller added that he had heard the story from a friend whose brother's girlfriend was the babysitter involved.

By now it should come as no surprise to learn that the same story had been collected two years earlier (1971) some 1500 miles southwest of Montreal, in Austin, Texas, and also in Bloomington, Indiana, in 1973 in a college dormitory. These three published versions are only samples from the wide distribution of the story in folk tradition. Their similarities and differences provide another classic case of folklore's variation within traditional boundaries. In all three legend texts the hour is late and the babysitter is watching television. Two of the callers make threatening statements, while one merely laughs. In all versions the man calls three times at regular intervals before the girl calls the operator, then once more afterwards. In both American texts the operator herself calls the police, and in the Indiana story she commands "Get out of the house immediately; don't go upstairs; don't do anything, just leave the house. When you get out there, there will be policemen outside and they'll take care of it." (One is reminded of the rescuers' orders not to look back at the car in "The Boyfriend's Death.") The Texas telephone operator in common with Canadian one gives the situation away by adding. "The phone call traces to the upstairs." The murder of the child or children (one, two, or three of them—no pattern) is specified in the American version: in Texas they are "chopped into little bitty pieces";

in Indiana, "torn to bits." All of the storytellers played up the spookiness of the situation—details that would be familiar to anyone who has ever baby-sat—a strange house, a television show, an unexpected phone call, frightening sounds or shocking realization at the end that the caller had been there in the house (or behind her) all the time. The technical problems of calling another telephone from an extension of the same number, or the actual procedures of call-tracing, do not seem to worry the storytellers.

Folklorist Sue Samuelson, who examined hundreds of unpublished "Man Upstairs" stories filed in American folklore archives, concluded that the telephone is the most important and emotionally-loaded item in the plot: the assailant is harassing his victim through the device that is her own favorite means of communication. Babysitting, Samuelson points out, is an important socializing experience for young women, allowing them to practice their future roles, imposed on them in a male-dominated society, as homemakers and mothers. Significantly, the threatening male figure is *upstairs*—on top of and in control of the girl—as men have traditionally been in the sexual relationship. In killing the children who were in her care, the man brings on the most catastrophic failure any mother can suffer. Another contributing factor in the story is that the babysitter herself is too intent on watching television to realize that the children are being murdered upstairs. Thus, the tale is not just another scary story, but conveys a stern admonition to young women to adhere to society's traditional values.

The Cabinet of Dr. Seuss

Alison Lurie

Dr. Seuss' recent demise means that there will be no new adventures of Gunks and Ooblecks and Hatwearing Cats, but Alison Lurie shows us that there are plenty of meanings to be found in the tales the good Dr. left behind.

Lurie's selection of the Seuss books as her popular artifact is an especially suitable choice to illustrate both the power of the Funhouse Mirror and, therefore the necessity for understanding its meaning. While the Seuss books are accurate reflections *of a large number of basic cultural beliefs and values, we also realize that their intended audience of preschool children is one which is particularly vulnerable to the* shaping *influences of popular culture as well. If we can learn to uncover the messages being conveyed by such artifacts with the same skill as Lurie exhibits, in other words, then* we *can decide whether or not the meanings being communicated are ones we desire our children to adopt. The study of popular culture is especially vital when it becomes a survival manual for responsible parenting.*

But Lurie's analysis is revealing and significant in other ways as well. The difficulty Seuss encountered in finding a publisher for his unusual stories (43 rejections!) is testimony to the resistance popular culture often demonstrates toward innovation and change (popular culture is conservative and imitative) but his eventual success is equally indicative of the way inventive forms and techniques can *and* do *finally make their way into the marketplace (where, of course, they are then copied ad infinitum—as Seuss imitated himself for over 35 years). Lurie also shows that Seuss' work represented two other common characteristics of popular culture: The Dr's books balance their inventiveness with themes and techniques familiar in the tradition of American popular humor and storytelling, and the Seuss books altered their themes and characters over time to reflect changing cultural beliefs and values.*

It is this latter evolution of Seuss' work which arouses Lurie's critical ire, but the key questions she asks which enable her to unlock the deeper meaning of these later tales are precisely the sort of nonevaluative inquiries students of popular culture need to raise in their *artifact studies*—"who *is buying this book, and* why?" *When we delve beneath the surface to search for deeper meanings in this way we will often discover that popular artifacts are like the egg that Horton hatched: What's inside bears little resemblance to what's sitting on top.*

Theodore Seuss Geisel, known to millions as Dr. Seuss, is the most popular juvenile author in America. Almost everyone under forty was brought up on his books and cartoons, and even those who didn't hear the stories read aloud or see them on TV probably met his fantastic character at school. Beginning with *The Cat in the Hat* in 1957, Seuss revolutionized the teaching of reading, managing to create innovative, crazily comic tales with a minimum vocabulary (*The Cat in the Hat* uses only 220 words). The inventive energy of these books and their relative freedom from class and race norms made middle-class suburban Dick and Jane look prissy, prejudiced and totally outdated.

What made it all the more wonderful was that Dr. Seuss's life was a classic American success story. He began as a cartoonist and advertising artist; his "Quick, Henry, the Flit!" drawings showing a citizen attacked by giant insects, half comic and half-threatening, were widely reproduced. But his first children's book, *And to Think That I Saw It on Mulberry Street*, was rejected by forty-three publishers; it was finally printed in 1937 only as a favor by a friend.

Why didn't editors see at once what a winner Seuss would be? Partly because of his artistic style, which was unabashedly cartoon-like and exaggerated in an era when children's book illustration was supposed to be pretty and realistic. Perhaps even more because of the content of his stories, especially their encouragement of wild invention and even worse, the suggestion that it might be politic to conceal one's fantasy life from one's parents. Children in the Thirties and Forties were supposed to be learning about the real world, not wasting their time on daydreams, and they were encouraged to tell their parents everything.

Marco, the hero of *And to Think That I Saw It on Mulberry Street*, is warned by his father at the start of the book to "stop telling such outlandish tales" about what he sees on the way home from school. Yet the very next day his imagination turns a horse and wagon, by gradual stages, into a full-blown parade with elephants, giraffes, a brass band, and a plane showering colored confetti—all portrayed by Seuss with immense verve and enthusiasm. Marco arrives home in a state of euphoria:

I swung 'round the corner
And dashed through the gate.

I ran up the steps
And I felt simply GREAT!
FOR I HAD A STORY THAT NO
ONE COULD BEAT!

Then he is quizzed by his father about what he has seen. His reply is evasive:

"Nothing," I said, growing red as a beet,
"But a plain horse and wagon on Mulberry Street."

The message that it is sometimes, perhaps always, best to conceal one's inner life reappears in *The Cat in the Hat.* Here "Sally and I," two children alone and bored on a rainy day, are visited by the eponymous Cat. He proceeds to totally destroy the house, causing first excitement and then panic (What will their mother say?). Finally he puts everything back in place. The Kids—and not only those in the story, but those who read it—have vicariously given full rein to their destructive impulses without guilt or consequences. When their mother returns and asks what they've been doing, there is a strong suggestion that they might not tell her:

Should we tell her about it?
Now, what SHOULD we do?
Well...
What would YOU do
If your mother asked YOU?

In these tales the children whose imagination transforms the world are abashed or secretive when confronted with possible adult disapproval. More often, however, Seuss lets fancy run free without equivocation or apology. A whole series of books from *McElligot's Pool,* (1947) through *On Beyond Zebra!* (1950) and *If I Ran the Circus* (1956), celebrates the wildest flights of fantasy. They usually begin in familiar surroundings, then move into an invented world where the scenery recalls the exotic landscapes of *Krazy Kat* comics. There, just as Seuss's Elephant-Bird, Tufted Gustard, and Spotted Atrocious defy natural history, so his buildings and roads and mountains defy gravity, seeming always to be on the verge of total collapse.

Though these stories are full of euphoric vitality, there is occasionally something uneasy and unsatisfying about them. Seuss's verbal inventions can become as shaky and overblown as the structures in his drawings. At the end of these books the elaborate language always does collapse.

Cat in the Hat.

The Grinch.

There is an abrupt return to simple diction, and a simple, realistic illustration implicitly declares that Seuss's protagonist was only fantasizing.

Innovative as he was, Seuss can also be seen as squarely in the tradition of American popular humor. His strenuous and constant energy, his delight in invention and nonsense recall the boasts and exaggerations of the nineteenth-century tall tale, with its reports of strange animals like the Snipe and the Side-Winder. Seuss brought this manner and these materials up to date for a generation raised on film and TV cartoons. And, though most of the time he addresses himself almost exclusively to children, he includes occasional jokes for adults. In *If I Ran the Zoo* (1950) for instance, the hero plans to bring a Seersucker back alive; he will also "go down to the Wilds of Nantucket / And capture a family of Lunks in a bucket." According to the illustrations, the Seersucker is a foolish, shaggy, flower-eating animal with what looks like a red bow tie, while Lunks are pale, big-eyed creatures with blond top-knots, captured with the help of beach buggies.

Parents as well as children seem to be addressed in *One Fish Two Fish Red Fish Blue Fish* (1960), in which two kids find a very large uncomfortable-looking tusked sea monster. They exult:

Look what we found
in the park
in the dark.
We will take him home.
We will call him Clark.

He will live at our house.
He will grow and grow.
Will our mother like this?
We don't know.

But Seuss is not only in favor of the free-ranging imagination: in many of his books there is a strong liberal, even anti-establishment moral. As in the classic folk tale, pride and prejudice are ridiculed, autocratic rule overturned. In *Yertle the Turtle* (1950), Mack, who is bottom turtle on the live totem pole that elevates King Yertle, objects to the system:

I know, up on top you are seeing great sights.
But down at the bottom we, too, should have rights...
Besides, we need food. We are starving!

So he burps and upsets the whole stack, turning Yertle into King of the Mud. In *Bartholomew and the Oobleck* (1949) another overreaching ruler, dissatisfied with the monotony of the weather, commands his magicians to cause something more interesting than rain or snow to fall from the sky. He gets a sticky, smelly substance which, though it appears as green, is clearly excrement ("you're sitting in oobleck up to your chin"); it does not disappear until he admits that the whole thing was his own fault.

In *Horton Hatches the Egg* (1940) and *Horton Hears a Who* (1954), a charitable and self-sacrificing elephant protects the rights of the unborn and of small nations and obscure individuals in spite of the ridicule and scorn of his friends, because "A person's a person, no matter how small." There are limits to charity in Seuss, however. Thidwick the Big-Hearted Moose (1949) allows his horns to become the refuge of an overwhelming number of immigrant animals and bugs, repeating wearily that "A host / above all must be nice to his guests." Luckily, just when he reaches the limits of his endurance and is being pursued by hunters, his antlers moult and he escapes. His guests end up stuffed and mounted on the wall of the Harvard Club, "as they *should* be."

For years Seuss's tales were hailed by experts as a wonderful way to teach children not only reading but moral values. Recently, however, a couple of them have run into opposition. Loggers in northern California recently went after *The Lorax* (1971). In this story, a greedy Once-ler and his relatives move into an area of natural beauty and proceed to chop down all the colorful Truffula Trees in order to manufacture Thneeds, which resemble unattractive hairy pink underwear. Soon the sky is choked with smog and the water with something called Gluppity-Glup. Though Seuss said the book was about conservation in general, the loggers saw it as blatant propaganda and agitated to have it banned from the school's required reading list. "Our kids are being brainwashed. We've got to stop this crap right now!" shouted their ad in the local paper, taking much the same belligerent anti-environmentalist tone as the Once-ler himself does when criticized:

I yelled at the Lorax, "Now listen here, Dad!
All you do is yap-yap and say Bad!
Bad! Bad! Bad! Well, I have my rights sir, and I'm telling you
I intend to go on doing just what I do!
And for your information, you Lorax, I'm figgering
on biggering
and biggering
and biggering
and biggering
turning MORE Trueffula Trees into
Thneeds
which everyone, EVERYONE,
EVERYONE needs!"

The *Butter Battle Book* (1984), a fable about the arms race, also provoked unfavorable comment. Like Swift's tale of the Big- and Little-Endians who went to war over how to open an egg, it begins with a meaningless difference in domestic habits. Two groups of awkward-looking flightless birds, the Yooks and the Zooks, live side by side: the Yooks eat their bread butter side up, the Zooks prefer it butter side down. They become more and more suspicious of each other, and finally a member of the Zook Border Patrol with the rather Slavic-sounding name of VanItch fires his slingshot. Escalation begins: more and more complicated weapons are developed by the Boys in the Back Room ("TOP-EST SECRET-EST. BRAIN NEST" says the sign on their door), until both sides possess the means of total destruction. Unlike most of Seuss's books, this one doesn't end reassuringly, but with the child narrator asking anxiously. "Who's going to drop it? / Will you. . . ? Or will he. . . ?" The *New York Times Book Review* considered the story "too close to contemporary international reality for comfort," while *The New Republic*, somewhat missing the point, complained that the issues between our real-life Zooks and Yooks were more important than methods of buttering bread.

Other perhaps more relevant criticisms might be made today of Seuss's work. For one thing, there is the almost total lack of female protagonists. Indeed, many of his stories have no female characters at all. *You're Only Old Once!* (1986), a cheerfully rueful tale about the medical woes of a senior citizen, which was on the best-seller list for months, is no exception. It contains one female receptionist (only her arm is visible) and one female nurse, plus a male patient, a male orderly, and twenty-one male doctors and technicians. There is also one male fish.

The typical Seuss hero is a small boy or a male animal; when little girls appear they play silent, secondary roles. The most memorable female in his entire *oeuvre* is the despicable Mayzie the lazy bird who callously traps Horton into sitting on her egg so that she can fly off to Palm Beach. Another unattractive bird, Gertrude McFuzz in *Yertle the Turtle and Other Stories*, is vain, envious, greedy, stupid, and fashion-mad. She gorges on magic berries to increase the size of her tail, and ends up unable to walk.

Seuss's little girls, unlike his boys, are not encouraged to exercise and expand their imagination very far. In "The Gunk that Got Thunk," one of the tales in *I Can Lick 30 Tigers Today!* (1969), this is made clear. The narrator relates how his little sister customarily used her "Thinker-Upper" to "think up friendly little thinks / With smiles and fuzzy fur." One day, however, she gets bored; she speeds up the process and creates a giant Gunk:

He was greenish.
Not too cleanish.
And he sort of had bad breath.

She tries to unthink him, but fails; meanwhile the Gunk gets on the phone and runs up a $300 long-distance bill describing recipes. Finally he is unthunk with the help of the narrator: who then gives his sister

Quite a talking to
About her Thinker-Upper
NOW...
She only
Thinks up fuzzy things
In the evening after supper.

Moral: Woman have weak minds; they must not be ambitious even in imagination.

Seuss's most recent book (1990) which was on the *New York Times* best-seller list for about a year, also has a male protagonist. But in other ways *Oh, the Places You'll Go!* is a departure for him. "The theme is limitless horizons and hope," Seuss, eighty-six years old, told an interviewer, and the blurb describes the book as a "joyous ode to personal fullment"; but what it really reads like is the yuppie dream—or nightmare of 1990 in cartoon form.

At the beginning of the story the standard Seuss boy hero appears in what looks like a large, clean modern city (featureless yellow buildings, wide streets, tidy plots of grass). But under this city, as an urbanite might expect, are unpleasant, dangerous things—in this case, long-necked green monsters who put their heads out of manholes. Seeing them, Seuss's hero, "too smart to go down any not-so-good street," heads "straight out of town."

At first everything goes well: he acquires an escort of four purple (Republican?) elephants, and rises in the world, joining "the high fliers / who soar to high heights," The narrative is encouraging:

You'll pass the whole gang and you'll soon take the lead.
Wherever you fly, you'll be best of the best.
Wherever you go, you will top all the rest.

In the accompanying illustration Seuss's hero is carried by a pink and yellow balloon high over fields and mountains; his competitors, in less colorful balloons, lag behind at a lower altitude.

Then comes the first disaster: the balloon is snagged by a dead tree and deflated. The boy's "gang" doesn't stop for him—as presumably he wouldn't for them—and he finds himself first in a Lurch and then in a Slump, portrayed as a dismal rocky semi-nighttime landscape with giant blue slugs draped about. Doggedly, he goes on and comes to a city full of arches and domes which looks rather Near Eastern,

where the streets are not marked.
Some windows are lighted. But mostly they're darked.

Turning aside, he continues "down long wiggled roads" toward what Seuss calls The Waiting Place. Here the sky is inky black and many discouraged-looking people and creatures are standing about:

. . . waiting, perhaps, for their Uncle Jake
or a pot to boil, or a Better Break.

For the energetic, ever-striving young American, this is a fate worse than death, and it is vigorously rejected:

NO!
That's not for you!
Somehow you'll escape all that waiting and staying.
You'll find the bright places where Boom Bands are playing.

Seuss's hero is next seen riding another purple elephant in a procession of elephants on his way to further solitary triumphs:

Oh, the places you'll go. There is fun to be done!
There are points to be scored. There are games to be won. . . .
Fame! You'll be famous as famous can be,
with the whole wide world watching you win on TV.

In the accompanying picture, some kind of fantasy football or lacrosse is being played—our hero kicking off from the back of his elephant, the other contestants on foot. But almost immediately this success is undercut:

Except when they don't
Because, sometimes, they won't.
I'm afraid that some times
you'll play lonely games too.
Games you can't win
'cause you'll play against you.

The most dangerous enemy of the celebrity is his own doubt and self hatred. The illustration shows a totally insecure-looking fantasy version of a Hollywood hillside mansion, where the protagonist is shooting baskets alone. Seuss assumes, no doubt quite properly, that in any career devoted to success, competition, and fame, "Alone will be something / you'll be quite a lot," and that often "you won't want to go on."

But his hero, of course, does go on, meeting a number of comical and/or frightening monsters.

You'll get mixed up
with many strange birds as you go...

Seuss predicts. The strange birds, who all look alike, are shown against another totally black background, some marching upward to the right with smiles, others plodding downward to the left with depressed expressions. The message here seems to be that it is a mistake to commit oneself to any organization: instead one must

Step with care
and great tact and remember that Life's
a Great Balancing Act

This is followed by the happy climax, in which Seuss's hero is even more triumphant than before:

And will you succeed?
Yes? You will, indeed!
(98 and 3/4 percent guaranteed.)
KID, YOU'LL MOVE MOUNTAINS!

This promise is depicted literally in the illustration: if we chose to take it that way, we might assume that Seuss's "kid" has become a property developer, like so many California celebrities.

In one or two of Seuss's earlier books, similar dreams of money and fame occur. Gerald McGrew, for instance, imagines that

The whole world will say "Young McGrew's made his mark.
He's built a zoo better than Noah's whole Ark!..."
"WOW!" They'll all cheer,
"What this zoo must be worth!"
(If I Ran the Zoo)

This was written in 1950, when Seuss's own imaginary zoo had just begun to make his fortune. Life wholly imitated art: his wild inventions, like those of his boy heroes—and of course in the end they are the same thing—made him fantastically rich and famous. It is difficult to estimate what Seuss's own zoo was worth: according to his publishers, over 200 million copies of his forty-two books have been sold worldwide, and many have been animated for TV.

Gerald McGrew and Seuss's other early heroes were content simply to fantasize success. *Oh, the Places You'll Go!* has a different moral. Now happiness no longer lies in exercising one's imagination, achieving independence from tyrants, or helping weaker creatures as Horton does. It is equaled with wealth, fame, and getting ahead of others. Moreover, anything less than absolute success is seen as failure—a well-known American delusion, and a very destructive one. There are also no human relationships except that of competition—unlike most of Seuss's earlier protagonists, the hero has no friends and no family.

Who is buying this book, and why? My guess is that its typical purchaser—or recipient—is aged thirty-something; has a highly paid, publicly visible job, and feels insecure because of the way things are going in the world. It is a pep talk, and meets the same need that is satisfied by those stiffly smiling economic analysts who declare on television that the present recession is a Gunk that will soon be unthunk, to be followed—On Beyond Zebra!—by even greater prosperity.

The myth of material success in a 19th-century dime novel. The virtuous Dodger comes to the rescue of the man who will help Dodger rise in the urban world of business.

Section 2

Myths

Introduction
Songs of the Unseen Road: Myths, Beliefs and Values in Popular Culture

> Oh public road—you express me better than I can express myself...
> I believe you are not all that is here.
> I believe that much unseen is also here.
>
> *Song of the Open Road*, Whitman

I. *Our Story So Far: A Brief Review*

While it is often true that "seeing is believing," it is certainly the case that what we *believe* gives shape and meaning to what we see. Popular beliefs and values are those unseen convictions about the world which form a culture's mindset and thus mold and color the way that that culture sees and interprets reality. The range of beliefs and values characteristic of a cultural mindset is as vast as the culture's history, its present circumstances, and its hopes and dreams of the future; and yet it can be as specific as the reasons which lie behind the way you have chosen to dress today and where you plan to eat tonight. Popular beliefs and values are the meanings which lie behind the artifacts and events which are their visible expressions—they are the truths which explain the facts and thus weave existence into a pattern which we can all recognize and share. A culture is the best example of St. Augustine's advice that we should seek "not to understand that [we] may believe, but believe that [we] may understand." Cultures explain things to themselves through the lens of their beliefs.

As students of popular culture, however, we need to reverse St. Augustine's command. Unlike the elements of God and religion which provided his subject matter, a culture's beliefs ought not to be taken as articles of faith—we need to understand them so that we can decide whether we choose to believe them (if we do accept them) and to be aware of what our vision entails. Popular beliefs and values do not argue the "truths" they embody and express—they *assume* them. The result is that a cultural pattern can become an entrapping web of belief if we are not careful. We need to step outside the pattern to view its separate strands and see it whole so that it may become a home built at least partly by our own thoughts and feelings rather than a prison constructed of anonymous assumptions.

While all cultural beliefs and values are important in that each contributes to the total vision of the mindset in which it is embedded, some beliefs and values are more important than others. Beliefs and values can be evaluated on two scales of measurement: the *stability* of the belief/value over time and the *significance* of the issues the belief/value shapes and defines. While many beliefs have been a part of the American mindset for hundreds of years—e.g., individual freedom, America as a land with a special destiny—others are popular for only several decades—e.g., "the Communist Bloc is an Evil Empire," "Women and African-Americans don't deserve the Right to Vote"—and still others are as short-lived as the latest fad or fashion. On the other scale of evaluation, we can identify beliefs and values which have important things to say about how Americans view their history, labor, private lives, future, and others which merely embody trivial attitudes and images surrounding many entertainments, celebrities, advertisements, and so on. A mindset is so complex and elusive by its very nature (remember that it is "visible" only in its expressions, not in and of itself) that no clear-cut division of its many interlocking beliefs and values is possible. A graph like the one below can provide a useful way of illustrating vital differences among the beliefs we will be examining and of helping us focus our attentions on those most in need of study, but remains an ideal model nonetheless.

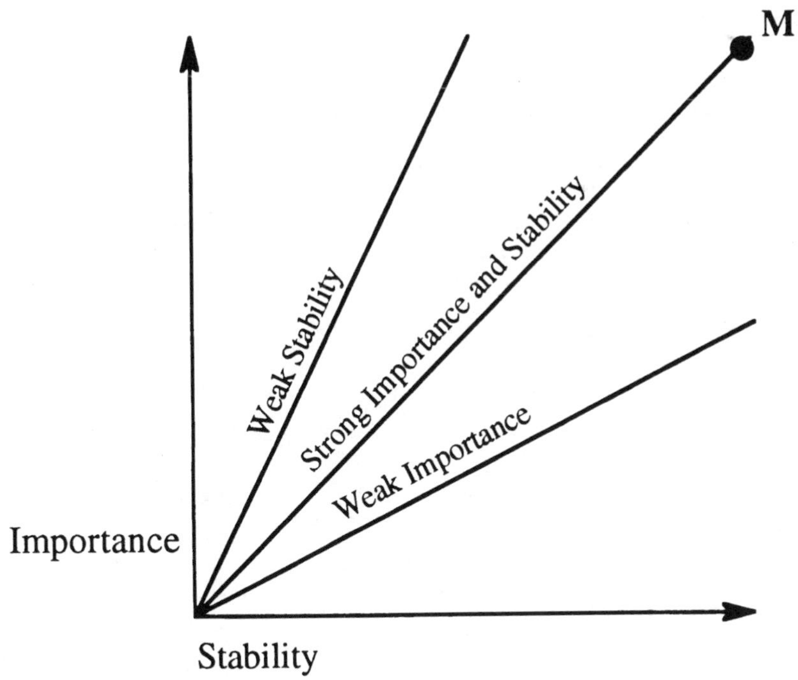

The beliefs and values which coalesce around point M are the most stable and most important ones defining the cultural mindset. They have been labeled by many popular culture scholars as "myths." We have avoided the use of this term to describe these vitally significant beliefs and values (preferring instead to call them "bedrock beliefs" or "foundation beliefs") because it often fosters the misconception in students' minds that these beliefs and values are being branded as false. The term "myth" is frequently used to describe a mistake or error which has somehow come to be accepted as true—e.g., we say that it is a "myth" that walking under a ladder brings back luck or that George Washington chopped down a cherry tree and then confessed to his father, and we mean that it is an "old wives tale" or a commonly believed falsehood. But this is not the way contemporary popular culture scholars use the term. "Myth," in the study of popular culture, says nothing about the "truth" or "falsity" of any belief or value; it says that the belief/value is significant and long lasting—vital to the mindset of the culture which holds it—and that is widely accepted as being true. The "myth of the material success" in America may sometimes be true in that some people do work hard, get a little good fortune and thereby achieve wealth, fame, and power. But in many other instances it may be false—people can do the same things and end up homeless—but the point for our purposes is that the myth is *believed* and that people make choices and take action based upon belief in the myth. Just as popular culture scholars are not interested in labeling one form of culture "better" or "worse" than another (we leave that to the critics of the Arnold/Bloom school), so also we are concerned only with describing, defining and understanding what a culture believes and values—*not* whether the culture is "wise" or "foolish," "correct" or "incorrect" in doing so (we leave that to politicians and newspaper columnists). It is an error to think that myths in popular culture have anything to do with actual truth or falsity; myths are too powerful to need facts or to allow them to get in the way.

The descriptive and analytical nature of the term "myth"—as well as several other qualities—can be seen in the definitions offered by two great popular culture scholars—Henry Nash Smith (author of *Virgin Land*) and Richard Slotkin (author of *Regeneration Through Violence, The Fatal Environment* and *The Myth of the Frontier in the Age of Industrialization*):

> *Smith:* History cannot happen—that is, men cannot engage in purposive group behavior—without images [myths] which simultaneously express collective desires and impose coherence on the infinitely varied data of experience.

Slotkin: Myths are stories, drawn from history, that have acquired through usage over many generations a symbolizing function that is central to the cultural functioning of the society that produces them....In the end myths become part of the language, as a deeply encoded set of metaphors that may contain all of the "lessons" we have learned from our history, and all of the essential elements of our world view.

While Smith uses "myth" in a manner already familiar to us from our discussion of the nature of popular culture (i.e., Smith emphasizes myth as a powerful component of the "funhouse mirror"—beliefs and values which simultaneously express and mold the people who believe them), Slotkin introduces two new aspects to our study. First, Slotkin identifies the close connection between "myth" and "history." Popular beliefs and values do not develop in some sort of timeless vacuum of cultural contemplation and musing. In most instances our myths have grown out of very real historical events and circumstances and have come to serve as expressions of the way we view that history and the "lessons" we feel it has imparted. All of the myths we have discussed thus far have been introduced and defined in terms which reflect their roots in history: the myth of individual freedom stems from Americans' flight to a New World to escape the restrictions of the Old and, later, from the birth of a new nation in rebellion against a repressive empire; the myth of violence outside the law to achieve justice evolves from the War of Independence in which violent revolution was seen as the only way to ensure the "inalienable" rights of man; the myth of youth and childhood in America is a natural outgrowth of a new world and a new nation explicitly acting out a "great experiment." Many of the myths which will be discussed later in this section will also have strong ties to history and its "teachings."

While Slotkin provides a useful and accurate interpretation of the historical nature of many myths, we need to amend his second extension of this important concept. Slotkin refers to myths as "stories" and, indeed, such a use of the term is familiar to us from Classical studies where writers refer to the myth of Hercules, or the myth of Jason and the Golden Fleece to mean tales of meaningful events and achievements usually involving gods and goddesses. In a broader sense, however, even Classical myths are essentially *narratives* which *express* deeply held, significant cultural beliefs—stories which explain nature, history and evil in the universe. To avoid confusion, therefore, we will continue to use the term "myth" to refer only to the bedrock cultural beliefs which provide the foundation of a mindset, and we will use the new term "myth-narrative" to describe the stories which express these deep-seated cultural beliefs and values. (This distinction will become clearer once you have read the essay by Charles Reich entitled "Four Morality Tales" in the readings section following this introduction.) Myth-narratives are especially important in the study of popular arts where they often exist as story formulas which achieve immense and longlasting popularity precisely because they tap continuously vital myths of the society. Thus, *Rocky* is a reworking of the "rags-to-riches" myth narrative, Westerns are myth-narrative patterns which pit elements of civilization against savages of the wilderness, and romantic comedies are often examples of a democratic myth-narrative in which love conquers barriers of class and money. Myth-narratives are stories we tell ourselves to give shape, definition and increased interest to our myths, beliefs and values.

II. *Revenge of the Nerds: Anti-Intellectualism in America*

Both the complexity and wide range of popular myths are nicely illustrated by a myth identified and defined by the historian Richard Hofstadter in his book *Anti-Intellectualism in American Life* (1963). The myth is especially interesting because instead of simply presenting the type of straightforward expression of a cultural belief we have seen in most of the other myths we have examined, this myth identifies a particular quality or trait and then analyzes it by positing a division into two categories—one of which the culture endorses, the other which it rejects or devalues. Once again, this myth has its sources in American history and in this instance evolves from a traditional American suspicion and dislike for certain types of learning, knowledge, education, stemming from the historical fact that such traits were typically characteristic of the very European, aristocratic classes. European Americans came to the New World to escape. American democratic ideals of a classless society peopled by rough hewn, "natural" citizens skilled at the practical necessities of survival and inventiveness have always stood in stark contrast to the aristocratic snobbery of European societies inhabited by the privileged few on top and the "ignorant," "illiterate" masses down in the muck below.

A simple division between "learning" and "ignorance"—or between "the smart" and "the dumb"—was certainly no solution to the dilemma of how the new American culture could posit an intellectual value without endorsing the European aristocracy with which it was associated. We didn't see ourselves as "stupid," certainly—that was the whole point. Americans had a type of intelligence perfectly suited to their circumstances and needs, *and* it was egalitarian and democratic to boot. The solution, therefore, was to heed the lesson of history and translate the distinction between "intelligence" (which is necessary, American and liked) and "intellect" (which is impractical, European and disliked).

Anti-intellectualism in America is not, therefore, a cult of ignorance and stupidity. It is *not* anti-intelligence. American mythology analyzes what it means—historically and democratically—to be "intelligent," and then develops a series of associated values which it pits against the competing world of "intellect." Thus,

Anti-Intellectualism in American Life

Intelligence	vs.	*Intellect*
American		European
practical		contemplative
thought —— action		thought ——more thought
knowledge derived from experience and books		*thought* derived from thought and experimentation books
shrewd, clever, inventive		abstract, ideological
democratic, common man, "one of us"		aristocratic, learned man "one of them"
real world		ivory tower
"professionals" (live "off ideas")		"eggheads" (live "for ideas")

Hofstadter summarizes the conflicting values by arguing that:

> ...the difference between the qualities of intelligence and intellect is more often assumed than defined [Note that this is the nature of myths—they are assumed to be true rather than proven or argued.], the context of popular usage makes it possible to extract the nub of the distinction, which seems to be almost universally understood: intelligence is...a manipulative, adjustive, unfailingly practical quality [which] works within the framework of limited but clearly stated goals, and may be quick to shear away questions of thought that do not seem to help in reaching them....Intellect, on the other hand, is the critical...and contemplative side of mind....[I]ntellect examines, ponders, wonders, theorizes, criticizes, imagines.

Intellectuals are potentially dangerous characters because they are, from this myth's point of view—so narrow-minded in their pursuit of ideas, so passionate in their love of thought, that they can easily lose sight of the "human" aspects of life. The ultimate "intellectual" is often one of those aristocratic Nazi doctors in war movies who speaks in clipped, authoritarian tones, wears tiny wire-rimmed spectacles (emblematic of his distorted vision) and coldly performs all sorts of heinous medical experiments on concentration camp victims and toughguy American prisoners of war. Intellectuals are "mind-over-body" types who fail to recognize that true human identity resides in the heart and not in the brain. In the course of analyzing the cultural mindset characteristic of "the small town mind," Conal Furay summarizes the conflict between traditional, bedrock American beliefs and those exhibited by intellectuals in precisely this head vs. heart manner:

The townsman's hostility to the intellectual rested, at last, on an intuition that his view of human nature was warped, skewed badly to the rational side, and almost wholly ignorant of the emotion side, and the organic side. Brilliant, scholarly, logical, eloquent, knowledgeable—these were the intellectuals' credentials. But they were not enough, not nearly. . .[H]e was insensitive to the fundamental subtlety of human nature.

Popular culture is filled with examples of the American hostility and suspicion directed toward intellectuals, but the myth gains expression most frequently in the form of two myth-narratives. The first (and more complex) anti-intellectual myth narrative acts out the distinctions the myth draws between "intelligence" and "intellect," and then narratively demonstrates the superiority of the former over the latter. The original version of *Star Trek* frequently examined the conflict between opposing definitions of "good" and "bad" intelligence and intellect by pitting the pointy-eared (and -headed) Spock against a crisis situation in which his "logical" response is woefully inadequate. Spock is not a completely negative stereotype of an intellectual (because he is half human, his insensitivities are excused, and due to his Vulcan heritage he is not expected to be all-American), but every time he is put in charge, things automatically take a turn for the worse. When Spock commands a small group marooned on a hostile planet, his insensitive application of the rule of logic displays a total ignorance of the true identities of the people in his command—he won't permit a dead crewman to have a proper burial, and he gets frustrated when nobody seems to understand that the deteriorating situation is merely an interesting "problem" in which physical survival is paramount, an abstract notion of duty which ignores emotional and spiritual needs. Soon the crew is plotting mutiny against their Vulcan captain, and it is only the wise and human counsel of the good Dr. McCoy that saves Spock from his own intellect.

But neither is the doctor *Star Trek*'s (or America's) intelligent ideal. "Bones" (as his nickname and profession imply) is *too* focused on the body—too emotional and headstrong in his support of heart over mind and in his dismissal of logic. Ultimately, Bones is no more flexible than Spock. His emotions blind him to truth and prevent him from being a true "intelligent leader" in the same way that Spock's relentless pursuit of logic limits him. *Star Trek*'s relegation of McCoy to a secondary position is representative of the way the myth of anti-intellectualism strives to strike the proper balance between "intellect" on the one side and a type of "ignorant emotionalism" on the other.

And the myth finds its compromised ideal in the consistently "intelligent" Captain Kirk. The Captain has enough of Bones' respect for the heart and body, but he tempers his emotions with the steely, practical, rational resolve necessary to command a spaceship (or a nation). Kirk routinely seeks the counsels of *both* Spock and McCoy and then finds a successful solution to the dilemma at hand by identifying the compromise position and carrying it out—translating thought into practical action. When Kirk has seemingly vanished for good in one episode, for example, Spock and McCoy break out a recorded message the Captain left behind to be played should he be blasted into oblivion. The recording makes explicit what the myth of anti-intellectualism has told us all along: Kirk commands Spock and McCoy to recognize that each *needs* the other—that they must reach a compromise position of practical wisdom, pragmatic and spiritual knowledge, in order to pilot the Enterprise crew to safety and be worthy exemplars of the American virtue of intelligence.

The second myth-narrative expressive of this important cultural belief is less complex but perhaps even more common than the first. While the first myth-narrative focused upon questions of leadership and judgment and was thus usually serious in tone and set in the adult world, the second myth-narrative centers upon issues of identity and self-image and therefore finds its typical setting in a younger (and comic) environment—often a high school or some other teen hangout. The narrative creates a negative stereotype of a youthful intellectual—the four-eyed, pants-hiked-up-above-the-waist, pocket full of pencils dweeb known as a "nerd"—and then pits the nerds against the "regular" kids in some form of conflict which usually favors the smugly superior nerds—a debate, science fair, examination (or even an athletic event which involves machines the nerds can construct or manipulate "scientifically"). The nerds are then either defeated by the "common man" virtues of the regular kids—persistence, intuition, cooperation, craftiness (i.e., cheating), *or* the regulars and the nerds are somehow forced to combine efforts against a common enemy to achieve a joint victory, thus proving the democratic ideal that *all* people are basically the same and can be effectively melted in the same pot.

Whatever specific version this myth-narrative assumes, however, the comic negative stereotype of the nerd still initially displays the vices we have found to be associated with intellectuals previously: the nerd is an emotional wreck who is incapable of expressing genuine feelings toward others, is obsessed with ideas and abstractions and is typically a snob whose intellect has led him to conclude falsely that he is more "worthy" than those with lower I.Q.'s. Whether or not the nerds are finally shown to be "regular folks" after all—as they were on the sitcom *Head of the Class*, for example, and (to a degree) in the *Revenge of the Nerds* movies—is ultimately immaterial since it is never their intellect which is the defining characteristic of their normality or the reason for their acceptance. It is, rather, the fact that good nerds are just as insecure, hostile to authority and in need of friendship and support as any working class, average person.

The situation comedy *Married...With Children* exhibits a strongly populist outlook which loathes all forms of pretentiousness or false superiority, and so it is not surprising that the series uses this second myth-narrative in one episode to engage in a bit of nerd-bashing. The contest in this instance concerned a test for admission to a club of intellectuals called the Alpha Club, and while the club certainly favored the nerds, the Bundy daughter Kelly (with an I.Q. midway "between an ashtray and a pickle jar") somehow managed to receive an invitation to join. Kelly is enjoying the party welcoming new "members" until her Bundy brother arrives to tell her that the Alpha Club is holding her up for a mockery by inviting her to this "Idiot Dance" in which the member who brings the stupidest date wins. Once again—because we sympathize with Kelly, of course—the nerds' worst sin is the way their snobbish intellect (all the real members of the Alpha Club are wealthy and most wear glasses; the "dates" are mostly working class and "two-eyed") breeds an insensitivity to the human feelings of others less intellectual. The nerds value the head over the heart so that the latter can be broken with impunity.

Married...With Children could turn at this point to express the more complex variant of this second myth-narrative by somehow revealing Kelly's hurt to the Alpha Club in a manner which would arouse their sympathy and awaken the human feelings hidden beneath their too thick cortical layers. This program is not heavily concerned with reconciliation and forgiveness, however, and thus opts for a straightforward ending filled with nerd-bashing—a fine example (especially judging from the audience reaction—loud applauding) of the deep-seated anti-intellectualism in America. Soon the sibling Bundys vow to redress the situation against the nerds by "destroying their superior smiles with sheer pointless violence" and gearing up to "go kick a little genius butt." The Bundys intuitively recognize that the Alpha Club has inverted the traditional democratic system in America which places the common citizen first among equals, and thus rally their fellow "average" friends with a cry to "return to the pecking order of high school" and put the intellectual back where he has always belonged in America—on the bottom.

Anti-intellectualism in America is a fascinating choice for extended study because it is very American and very complex in the manner in which it also embodies other American beliefs and values as well. Anti-intellectualism reflects the faith Americans have in common sense and immediate experience as the best guide to effective living and the virtue we find in a view of human nature which finds the soul nearer the heart than the head. Most bedrock American beliefs are similar in their complexity, but before we demonstrate this we need to provide simple definitions of their meanings and expressions.

III. *Full Houses*

While we have already defined and illustrated a number of significant American myths and beliefs, we need to provide a more formal presentation at this time so that we can draw upon the list in the more complex discussion which follows. In order to demonstrate the complexity and danger of popular mythology we need the common framework of reference outlined by the definitions and examples in the "Full Houses" in this section.

We have chosen to introduce these important American myths by placing each myth in the basement of a different house of popular culture and then filling all of the above ground rooms with artifacts and events which express the beliefs and values hidden below. We hope that this will serve not only to provide a more comprehensive definition of each myth than might be practical in purely verbal explanations, but that it will also serve as a vivid illustration of one of the most essential aspects of popular culture analysis—that the visible elements of our culture are the means by which cultural beliefs and values gain concrete form.

We should note that many other artifacts and events might have been chosen to fill the rooms of any individual house, and that any specific artifact or event may be illustrative of more than one myth or belief. The language of myth is a complex one (it has to be if it is to be able to express a culture's entire view of reality), and the range of examples and the multiple uses to which any *one* may be put are merely two aspects of its depth and richness. Think of other illustrations for each room when you can, therefore, and don't be afraid to move things from one house to another when you can justify it.

Of the ten popular traditional myths outlined here, eight of them are discussed in more detail elsewhere in the book. Two of them, however, are not. The myth of the nuclear family is a logical extension of the myth of romantic love and is at the core of nearly every politician's claims that his or her legislative agenda is the preservation of "family values." The chart itself providing examples of this important bedrock belief is hopefully self-explanatory. The other myth that is not described elsewhere is in need of the following brief discussion.

The Puritans settling in Massachusetts during the 1620s believed their new colony would be, as one of their leaders, John Winthrop, proclaimed, "as a city upon a hill," whose mission was to show the rest of the world a perfected new social order based on the Puritan interpretation of God's teachings. Not a people to be overly humble about their reasons for coming to the New Land, the Puritans saw themselves as graced instruments of a divinely ordained plan. Less than half a century later, the American colonies, including Massachusetts Bay, had already begun a process of secularization, but the notion that we are a special people with a special mission remained to become a myth deeply ingrained in the American world view. It has continuously been one stimulant for significant events in our history. During the nineteenth century, for example, great numbers of Americans believed in the concept of "manifest destiny," that the United States was destined to control the land between the two oceans and possibly all of North America. Such an assumption became an implicit reason for the great wagon train migrations to the West. And it became an explicit reason for the Mexican War of 1846-48.

In our century the myth has been linked to another basic American belief—the myth of the superiority of a democratic government. President Wilson, in announcing our entrance into World War I, said our purpose was "to make the world safe for democracy." Three generations later, during the 1980 presidential debate between Ronald Reagan and Jimmy Carter, Reagan summed up his remarks by returning to Winthrop's original Puritan optimism. America should be a "city upon a hill," Reagan said, and he promised, as most presidential candidates have, to put us on course once again toward the greatness of our special destiny. When we hear such rhetoric we may well be a bit skeptical. The continuing success of this rhetoric, however, suggests just how much the myth of a special destiny is a part of our cultural heritage. Almost exactly a decade after the Reagan-Carter debate, George Bush used the same myth to explain America's fighting the 1991 Gulf War. Citing Abraham Lincoln's statement that America is "the last best hope of mankind," Bush argued that the United States had a duty to push Iraq out of Kuwait because we were the only nation fit to do so. Once again, Bush suggested, America was a chosen nation with a destiny to fulfill. Soon after the war, Bush's approval rating soared well above 80 percent, demonstrating how effective his use of this myth had been.

House of America as a Special Nation

Myth: The United States is a nation with a special destiny and mission.

Beliefs and Values:

America is a "City on a Hill."

American democracy is the only valid social/governmental structure.

Icons:

G.I. Joe.

The American eagle.

Heroes:

Joe Louis (he whipped Nazi Max Schmeling).

Rambo.

Celebrities:

Olympic medalists who appear in product endorsements.

Stereotypes:

Negative stereotypes of "foreigners."

Positive stereotypes of Peace Corps Volunteers.

Rituals:

Pledge of Allegiance.

"Star Spangled Banner" before sporting events.

Arts:

Rocky IV (Rocky KOs a Communist).

"God Bless America" (song).

House of Anti-Intellectualism in America

Myth: The truly intelligent person translates ideas into practical solutions to real problems, lives "off" ideas instead of "for" them, and recognizes that human identity is found essentially in the heart, not the mind.

Beliefs and Values:

Experience is the best teacher.

Common sense is superior to book learning.

"If it ain't broke, don't fix it."

Heroes:

Inventors.

Ben Franklin (*Poor Richard's Almanac*).

Captain Kirk.

Celebrities:

Robert Fulghum (author of *All I Ever Needed to Know I Learned in Kindergarten*) (positive).

Howard Cosell (negative).

Stereotypes:

"Crackerbarrel Philosopher" (positive).

"Professionals" (positive).

"Nerds" (negative).

"Eggheads" (negative).

Rituals:

Trivial Pursuit.

Elections which pit common men against eggheads (Ronald Reagan vs. Jimmy "Nuclear Scientist" Carter).

Arts:

Revenge of the Nerds.

Star Trek.

House of Endless Abundance

Myth: America is a land of infinite resources. We are so wealthy and productive that we will never run out of anything we need to survive and prosper.

Beliefs and Values:

Bigger is better. New is better.
Consumerism is good—the more you buy, the better you are.
Convenience is more important than preservation.
A bad economy will always "turn around."

Icons:
Credit cards.
Christmas presents.

Heroes:
Explorers.
Santa Claus.

Celebrities:
All of them (by their very nature and number).

Rituals:
Shopping.
Trick or Treat.

Arts:
Traditional Westerns (riding off into the sunset—an infinite horizon).
Space movies (endless abundance continues with an entire universe to explore and exploit).

House of Individual Freedom

Myth: Americans have an innate right to personal freedom—the right to choose their own destinies, pursue their dreams, act in any way they see fit short of harming others or interfering with others' freedom.

Beliefs and Values:
Do your own thing—GO FOR IT.
Be yourself.
Get government off our backs.

Icons:
Statue of Liberty.
Guns.
Cars.

Celebrities:
Madonna.
Guns 'N' Roses.
Roseanne Arnold.

Stereotypes:
Rock stars.
Hippies.
Cowboys.

Rituals:
Cruising.
Voting.

Arts:

"Born to be Wild" (Steppenwolf) (song).
The Fugitive (TV Program).

House of Material Success

Myth: In America hard work leads to good fortune which in turn results in money/fame/power for the virtuous individual.

Beliefs and Values:

Ownership of personal property is a fundamental right and duty.
Poverty is a sign of laziness and vice.
America is a land of endless opportunity.
Material possessions are signs of our virtue and value as individuals.

Icons:

Big houses in the suburbs.
Rolex watches.

Heroes:

Main characters in Horatio Alger novels.
Abe Lincoln (went from a log cabin to the White House).

Celebrities:

Lottery winners.
Donald Trump.

Stereotypes:

Welfare cheats (negative).
Rich philanthropists (positive).

Rituals:

Fashion shows.
Shopping for a more expensive car.

Arts:

TV quiz shows.
Self-help bestsellers.

House of the Nuclear Family

Myth: The nuclear family (Dad, Mom, 2.5 Kids and Pet[s]) is the basic and most desirable American family unit.

Beliefs and Values:

Everybody should be married.
Divorce is a "failure."
Family values are the most valuable American values.

Icons:

Family home.
Family photograph album.
The dinner table.

Heroes:

The Huxtables.
Laura Ingalls Wilder (*Little House on the Prairie*).

Celebrities:

The Judds.
The Osmonds.

Stereotypes:
"Old maids" (negative).
The "New Male" (domesticated and sensitive) (positive).

Rituals:
Family vacations.
Family dinners.

Arts:
Family Ties (TV).
Roots.

House of Romantic Love

Myth: For each individual there is a single perfect partner who, once found, makes life complete and permanent happiness possible.

Beliefs and Values:
Love conquers all.
Sex is best in a true-love relationship.
Romantic love culminates in the unit of the nuclear family.

Icons:
Hearts.
Flowers.

Heroes:
Rick and Ilsa in *Casablanca.*
Rhett and Scarlett in *Gone with the Wind.*

Celebrities:
Prince Charles and Lady Di.
Liz Taylor and whomever.

Stereotypes:
"Old maids" (negative).
Married greatgrandparents (positive).

Rituals:
Valentine's Day.
Dating.

Arts:
Beauty and the Beast (cartoon).
Harlequin Romances.

House of Rural Simplicity

Myth: True American virtue and happiness are to be found by living close to nature on a farm or in a small town.

Beliefs and Values:
Childhood is a special time and is best lived within a rural setting.
The "good old days" were less complicated and more virtuous than

the present. (Behind this popular belief is the fact that America was less urban in the past.) Cities are places of violence, sin and corruption (except for the rural-like suburbs).

Icons:

The family farm.

Camp David (a country place where the president goes for intellectual/spiritual renewal).

Church steeples in small towns.

Heroes:

Johnny Appleseed.

Western cowboys.

Celebrities:

Country music stars.

Garrison Keillor (Lake Wobegon).

Rituals:

Farm Aid concerts.

Gardening.

Summer camp.

Arts:

City Slickers (movie).

The Waltons (TV).

House of Technology as Protector and Savior

Myth: Technology is good because it protects the other myths and helps ensure their continued validity (as long as technology doesn't threaten the other myths, it is an *essential* good).

Beliefs and Values:

Science is the servant of humankind.

"Progress is our most important product." (General Motors).

Icons:

Personal computers.

"Smart" bombs.

Heroes:

Thomas Edison.

Chuck Yeager.

Celebrities:

Astronauts.

Arthur Kent (the "Scud stud").

Stereotypes:

Robots as friendly servants (positive).

Mad scientists (negative).

Rituals:

Science fairs.

NASA launchings.

Arts:

Utopian science fiction.

James Bond movies.

House of Violence Outside the Law to Achieve Justice

Myth: The Law is made by powerful figures who—at their best—create laws to foster the common good (but often ignore or run roughshod over individuals) or—at their worst—create a legal web which protects the status quo, punishes the innocent and fosters a bureaucracy which loses justice in the details of law.

Beliefs and Values:

Americans have a right to own guns.

"A man's gotta do what a man's gotta do."

There are "moral" and "immoral" wars.

"Extremism in defense of virtue is no vice" (Barry Goldwater).

Icons:

Guns.

War toys.

Heroes:

Batman.

George Washington.

Celebrities:

Oliver North.

Bernard Goetz.

Stereotypes:

People charged with a crime who go free on a technicality (negative).

Private detectives (positive).

Rituals:

Professional wrestling.

Fourth of July.

Arts:

Superhero comics.

Star Wars.

IV. *There's More to Myth Than Meets the Eye: The Complexity of Popular Belief (Its Nature and Expression)*

The tidy picture of each myth snuggled down in its own private house can foster an image of order and simplicity which is quite at odds with the true nature of popular beliefs. Put these houses together in the same neighborhood (i.e., cultural mindset) and the complex and delightful messiness of real life begins to display itself in all its chaotic glory. Like the residents of real houses, beliefs burst out of their homes to visit each other's houses, borrow artifacts from one another, trot home with them, get in hot disputes with each other, welcome new residents who linger for a bit and then leave. The true picture of popular myths and beliefs in daily action bears as little resemblance to those isolated, frozen houses as a photograph of a military regiment lined up on display does to the blood and thunder of war. Our introduction to the individual myths has been proper and formal as we have visited and toured each house, but it is time now to move beyond simple greetings as we attempt the more complex task of fostering and understanding a *relationship* with these beliefs and values.

The complexity of popular belief can be seen both in the nature of the myths, beliefs and values themselves *and* in the way in which popular artifacts express these beliefs. We'll examine each type of complexity separately, although there is a direct relationship between them.

1. *Natural Complexity*

The complex nature of popular myths and beliefs can be seen in at least four ways:

a. Each myth has a number of associated beliefs and values.

This is illustrated in the houses themselves, so that each myth finds its place in the deepest "foundation" or "bedrock," while associated beliefs and values fill the "basement." The myth of rural simplicity, for example, supports a basement which holds American beliefs such as "the past was a simpler time," "working close to nature and the land is honest labor," "a farm or small town is the best place to raise a child," "cities are places of vice and wickedness," "land is the most valuable possession" and "animals are meant to serve man (and man to serve up animals)." The complexity of each myth in this regard can perhaps be best appreciated if it is understood that a *separate* house devoted to *each* related belief is a very real part of the cultural mindset—there are hundreds of houses in this neighborhood.

b. Each myth and its associated beliefs and values is related to at least one other myth in a symbiotic manner—that is, each related myth gives new meaning, significance and relevance to its partner(s).

A careful look at the individual houses reveals that separate myths "fit" together nicely to form complex webs of beliefs and values. Thus "rural simplicity" is usually bundled with "endless abundance" (farms and the land as both valuable in and of themselves *and* as sources of perpetual bounty). "Individual freedom" is exercised in the pursuit of "material success," "romantic love" has a great deal to do with the meaning and significance of the "nuclear family." The interlocking of different myths is indicative of the fact that they are, indeed, part of the same mindset, and this should be remembered when we examine specific artifacts and events as expressions of these myths. Most artifacts and events will embody a web of such beliefs rather than merely isolated examples.

c. Popular myths often contradict each other in important ways.

An important study of the American mindset is a book by Michael Kammen called *People of Paradox* (1972). As the title suggests, the work argues that it is precisely this complex mixture of contradictory beliefs which *is* the defining characteristic of the American worldview. Kammen notes, for example, that Americans have always believed simultaneously in the need for violence to achieve justice outside the law *and* in the virtues of peace, harmony and cooperation in both individual freedom and the good of the community, in other words. Thus:

> The Bald Eagle on the green side of your one dollar bill holds a clutch of deadly arrows in one clenched claw, and an olive branch in the other. Americans like to remind themselves, and others, that the United States emerged from a Revolution, an act of colonial self-emancipation. Nevertheless, they also like to emphasize that they stand for stability and order, balanced growth, constitutional procedures, and legitimacy. Americans like to speak the language of power and "talk tough," all the while stressing the need for a language of community and harmony. (279)

It is this same characteristic of the American mindset which Walt Whitman celebrated when he wrote: "Do I contradict myself: Very well—I contradict myself. I contain multitudes." And Whitman's pride in the complexity of the American outlook is at least partly a definition of it as well since it seems to suggest that it is the nature of a pluralistic, democratic society to be pulled simultaneously in many different directions at once. The contradictions are at the heart of an American mindset which attempts to create a nation out of a crowd of individuals—to reconcile majority rule with minority rights, the need for cooperation with the right to go one's own way, the national identity with ethnic, religious and other individual roles. The contradictions grow out of the essential conflict between "one nation indivisible" and "liberty and justice for all."

The fact that America tries to honor the group and the individual simultaneously is at the heart of our paradoxical way of thinking. Americans want to be both "pluribis" and "unum" at once—both protective family and courageous loner, happy community and free individual, unifying melting pot and diverse nation of many Nations; Americans want to be completely responsible and totally free.

While this contradiction between absolute freedom and necessary responsibility is perhaps the most important and vital conflict, there are also many other examples of myths at odds with each other in the American ethos. The myth of rural simplicity contradicts the common belief associated with American material success that cities are places of opportunity, adventure and excitement. The myth of endless abundance is at odds with the belief in conservation. The myth of material success may run counter to the belief that government should help the poor and needy; and the belief in America as policeman to the world is challenged by the value of placing America first before all others. If F. Scott Fitzgerald was correct in saying that one sign of intelligence is the ability "to hold two opposed ideas at the same time, and still retain the ability to function," then America's success as a nation is positive proof that we are powerfully "intelligent," however inconsistent.

d. *Beliefs change and evolve over time.*

Myths are the most stable and significant beliefs defining a cultural mindset, but even a myth may alter its definitions as time passes and circumstances change. The myth of endless abundance is presently undergoing drastic revision in the face of environmental problems and overpopulation, and the myth of material success has undergone at least three stages of development in its long history (see Madonna Marsden's article).

As we move nearer the surface in the houses, however, beliefs come and go with a much greater rapidity. Arthur Schlesinger, Jr., has demonstrated, for example, that there are regular *Cycles of American History* which alternate between conservative and liberal ideals in social policy and between isolationist and interventionist goals in foreign affairs. Schlesinger argues that the cycles occur at clearly timed intervals and that each brings with it an entire cluster of associated beliefs and values which are translated into political and social policy for as long as the cycle lasts. The fact that beliefs come and go, in other words, is part of the fabric, rhythm and meaning of American history.

The beliefs surrounding the identity and role of women in American society are especially noticeable examples of a recent evolution in the cultural mindset. While the movement is neither as simple nor straightforward as the examples suggest, it still does not require a great deal of supporting evidence to demonstrate that there has been a significant change between the images of housewife Donna Reed and hapless careerwoman Lucy Arnez in the 1950s to housewife Roseanne and talented newsperson Murphy Brown in the 1990s—from Alice and Trixie to *Thelma and Louise,* passive wives to *Designing Women,* from the Della Street (who typed up Perry Mason's notes and brought him coffee) to Grace VanOwen (who made and practiced her own *L.A. Law*). While Susan Faludi may be correct in identifying a pronounced "backlash" against feminism, it is highly doubtful that it will ever take us as far back as the days when an advertisement could make the claims of the one illustrated on the following page (1962) and expect to be speaking in the cultural language of the American mindset. Beliefs *do* change.

A cigarette ad from the early 1960s published in campus newspapers. Two stereotypes are obvious: women are pictured as sex objects whose only ambitions are marriage; men are seen as having a natural right to be sexual voyeurs. Both stereotypes lead to the ongoing crime of sexual harrassment.

2. *Expressive Complexity*

The complexity of popular belief does not stop at the surface of the house foundation and basement—it is mirrored in the visible rooms of artifacts and events which express the myths, beliefs and values hidden below. All four of the elements of "natural complexity" are reflected in the artifacts and events which make up the concrete aspects of our culture. The direct relationship between nature and expression is indicated in the chart below:

Natural Complexity	
1. Myths have associated beliefs.	1. An artifact or event may express both a myth and one or more of the cluster of related beliefs and values. Also, a given artifact/event will often "analyze" a given myth or belief—breaking it apart into opposing characteristics in order to define precisely what we *do* believe and dismiss or criticize what we do not (see example which follows).
2. Myths are inter-related.	2. The same artifact or event may reflect one or more interlocking myth/belief.
3. Myths/beliefs change over time.	3. Similar artifacts and events from different eras embody different myths/beliefs/values, as Donna McCrohan points out in her book *Prime Time/Our Time: America's Life and Times Through the Prism of Television*: "Watch any top-rated show. It's a mirror. Watch a rerun from an earlier decade. It's still a mirror, but it doesn't reflect what is in front of it any more. It reflects what was in front of it when it first ran in prime time. Now it's not so much a mirror as a home movie." Note, for example, the

way that TV sitcoms of different eras reflect the changing views of women and their changing beliefs/values by questioning and/or criticizing them. The Bruce Springsteen song "Born in the U.S.A." questions the reality of material success and rural simplicity in the Reagan Era ("Born down in a deadman's town/the first kick I took was when I hit the ground"); *Married...With Children* questions the reality of the myth of the nuclear family. The opening credits feature an image of green ooze dripping from the title, an ironic singing of "Love and Marriage"—cut off in mid-sentence —and the sound of jail doors slamming shut.

4. Myths/beliefs contradict each other in significant ways.	4. Artifacts occasionally function to reveal the contradiction, but more frequently produce a myth-narrative in which the incompatibility of two myths or values is buried in a resolution which allows the audience to continue holding *both* beliefs. Individual freedom and community responsibility, for example, are often reconciled in a myth-narrative which shows an independently-minded hero pursuing private goals whose achievement ends by bettering the community as well. (Dirty Harry breaks the law and tells off his more liberal superiors—but then rids the streets of vermin.)

The 1960's popular television situation comedy *The Beverly Hillbillies* provides a nice example of the two most complex expressions of popular myths and beliefs—the resolution of contradictions and the analysis of a popular myth to present its proper interpretation. *The Beverly Hillbillies* had a record of popular success in the 1960s which was every bit as impressive as that of *The Cosby Show* in the 1980s and *Cheers* in the 1990s. The program asked us to "Come and listen to the story of a man named Jed/A poor mountaineer, barely kept his family fed/And then one day he was shooting for some food/When up through the ground come a bubblin' crude/Oil, that is—Black Gold, Texas Tea." So Jed and his kin strike it rich and take off for the city (the proper home for material success and its ornaments) where they move into a Beverly Hills mansion complete with "cement pond," a pool room (with its "fancy dining table") and a doorbell ("mysterious music in the walls" after which someone always "comes knocking at the door"). The typical plot for an episode brings the naive Hillbillies into contact with some aspect of modern society (e.g., socialites, movie stars, sports heroes) and simultaneously displays the comedy of their misunderstandings and its essential common sense and human worth. The Hillbillies are not hip (and that's funny) and they're not cool (and that's *good*).

The genius of this setup is that audiences are able to experience the best of two myths which have a logical incompatability. *The Beverly Hillbillies* creates a situation in which it is possible to have all the virtues associated with rural simplicity while also enjoying all the trappings of material success. The Hillbillies are rich and poor at the same time: tied to the simple past but living in the exciting present, naive and innocent as children yet placed on equal footing with sophisticated, famous and powerful adults. The Hillbillies keep the country alive in the city and prove (by their very existence) that it is possible to be extremely rich yet *hardworking* (Granny cleans the entire mansion every day and Jethro and Ellie May always have their "chores" to do—and the entire family rises and sets with the sun), *democratic* (the Hillbillies' mansion is open to everyone—"Y'all come back now" urges the closing theme song), and *loyal* to those you have passed by on the ladder of success (the Clampetts frequently invite relatives from the Ozarks out to visit). The Clampetts may not understand how a bank works (Granny occasionally demands to see her millions in cold, hard cash) or how to play a round of golf ("Look out! Your ball's about to drop down that little hole there"), but the decent wisdom of their common sense is always vastly superior to the formal education and sophistication of the city folk. The Clampetts bring their mountains along with them and thus tower over the petty hills their wealth enables them to romp among so freely.

The Beverly Hillbillies not only invests material success with the common man's myth of rural simplicity but also analyzes the myth of material success to explain the myth's *true* meaning to the audience. The program argues that a straightforward equation of moral worth and monetary wealth is too simple an interpretation of the myth—that the American view of success is more complex than the total celebration some presentations of the myth imply. *The Beverly Hillbillies* contrasts two types of "rich people"—one good, the other bad—and thus analyzes the myth of material success to tell us what we should and should not believe. On its most basic level the series contrasts the "good" Clampetts and the "bad" Drysdales as a means of pinpointing the form of material success that should be believed and valued. The important contrasts are outlined in the chart below:

"Good" Material Success (Clampetts)	*vs.*	*"Bad" Material Success (Drysdales)*
1. Earned their wealth. (Good fortune came as a reward for hard work—Jed was out shooting for food to provide for his family when he struck oil.)		1. Inherited their wealth. (Mr. Drysdale married wealthy Mrs. Drysdale—who lives off "Daddy's" money.)
2. Continue to work hard.		2. Lazy and self-indulgent. (Mrs. Drysdale does nothing but flit around from one social occasion to another—e.g., her precious Garden Club [Drysdales grow and display flowers—Clampetts cultivate and eat food/crops]; Mr. Drysdale has a job as banker—but that is just paper pushing, not honest labor.)
3. Content with having "enough" money and very generous to those in need.		3. Greedy for more, stingy with what they have. (Mr. Drysdale is a banker who, therefore, lives off other people's money [his wife's] and he is very greedy and stingy.)

4. Democratic—friendly to all.	4. Snobby—believe and foster notions of a rigid class system—i.e., that wealth equals superiority.
5. Remember and respect those left behind on lower rungs of the ladder of success—remember the past.	5. Focus only on the present state of privilege and future success.

Individual episodes of the program deepen and enrich this analysis of material success and of other important myths and beliefs as well. When Jethro begins dating, for example, the series examines competing notions of love in terms of "good" and "bad" in much the same way that "wealth" was divided in the manner illustrated above. Other episodes similarly analyze ideas of technology, fame, European Royalty and childhood. *The Beverly Hillbillies,* like other popular artifacts and events, speak to us in a manner much more complex than a simple, straightforward expression of myths and beliefs—their expressions are full of questions, warnings, comparisons and contrasts as well. The houses are not merely our familiar, comforting homes—they are also our schools.

A healthy appreciation of the complexity of popular beliefs can help rescue a myth from propaganda, but myths are still drastic simplifications of reality—reality shaped and tinted rather than experienced whole—and thus important dangers remain.

Believing Can Be Hazardous to Your Health: The Dangers of Popular Belief

Since beliefs and values are absolutely essential if we are to function in this world (they provide the reasons for all of our activities, beyond mere biological necessities) and since beliefs are not by definition true, the mere passive acceptance of popular beliefs and values puts each of us at some personal risk. What if we accept a belief that is harmful to us? What if what we believe about reality simply is not consistent with what is obviously out there? What if others are using our reliance on beliefs and values for their purposes rather than ours? We need beliefs to provide us with a path through life, but under some circumstances, the wrong beliefs can strew that path with landmines that can blow up in our faces. These personal dangers of popular beliefs and values can be divided into two categories:

1. Exploitation

Like spoiled housecats, we all love to be "stroked." Our self-esteem is stroked whenever somebody tells us that we are correct or smart. We all want to be told that we are correct and smart. For example, if you read the record reviews in *Spin* or *Rolling Stone* and your favorite new recording gets a rave write-up, you feel great; if your favorite recording gets trashed in the review, your self-esteem has taken a shot and you, at least for a few moments, feel lousy. A similar reaction takes place in our psyches whenever others comment about any of our beliefs and values. We all want to be told that we are sensitive and brilliant. It is natural and inevitable that we feel this way.

Our desire to be intellectually stroked makes us vulnerable to being cynically used by those who would exploit our needs for popular beliefs and values. The process through which advertisers, politicians and other hucksters do this is quite simple. They attempt to convince us of the following equation:

A = B

A in this case is a popular belief or value they think we hold as true. B is whatever they are trying to get us to buy or believe. What the exploiter does is convince us that their product is identical to what we believe. Therefore, buying or believing in the "product" will fulfill us because it confirms the validity of what we already believe. Soft drinks, for example, are pleasantly sweet carbonated beverages, but the hucksters would have us believe that gulping a Pepsi confirms the American obsession with the value of youth while tossing back a livelier Dr. Pepper validates the American belief in individualism. It is almost always a lie, of course. Products may be symbols but they are rarely really what they symbolize. (Remember how President Reagan symbolized the value of the family when his real family life was in total shambles?) Yet, we so desire that what we believe be really true, that exploiters, if we are not on our guard, may successfully convince us, no matter how illogical, that one thing is really another.

2. Contradictory Confusion

A popular perfume ad on television in the 1980s featured a beautiful, obviously successful woman aggressively singing, "I can bring home the bacon/Fry it up in a pan/And never, ever let him forget he's a man." The woman and the lyrics were a perfect illustration at the time of the so-called "superwoman," a woman who could with no apparent problem combine the values of a successful career and a wife/mother. Not long after, the character of the Claire Huxtable on *The Cosby Show* provided another perfect example.

The problem with the "superwoman" ideal was not that either value was wrong, but that all too often in real life the combination did not function with the smooth success it did in the perfume ad or in *The Cosby Show*. While these images were running on TV, thousands of American women were discovering that they couldn't do it all and that after an eighteen-hour day of professional work and housework all they could do was fall asleep exhausted.

The above example illustrates the unfortunate effects that can result when competing beliefs or values combine in a conflicting combination. The result is usually anxiety, stress and unhappiness. As stated earlier, our mindset is made up of hundreds of beliefs and values, many of which we periodically revise and change. If we want to lead our lives in a harmonious pattern, the beliefs and values in our mindset should ideally compliment and mesh with each other. When they do not, the activities of our daily lives which are the result of our mindset will be pulled in directions as confusing and inconsistent as the opposing beliefs themselves.

Each of us needs occasionally to modify the beliefs and values in our mindset so that we may lead productive and satisfying lives. As the circumstances of our lives change, it is natural that our mindset will change somewhat too. The unhappy "superwoman" might need to learn, for example, that she does not have to be all things to all people at all times. Even though she believes in her duties within the nuclear family, for example, it might be useful to her state of mind to modify her beliefs about how those duties can be accomplished and about how the family might benefit if those duties are shared. We cannot always choose what we believe, of course, but a refusal to change beliefs or to modify them in the face of a changing reality is a danger that can make us ineffective, confused and miserable.

Studying popular culture artifacts and the beliefs and values they reflect is a survival tactic precisely because it can help us avoid being victimized by these dangers. We are most susceptible to the dangers in popular beliefs when we are unaware of the beliefs themselves and the fact that they are determining the conduct of our everyday lives.

Four Morality Tales

Robert Reich

The myths (or "bedrock beliefs and values") which form the core of a cultural mindset are a fascinating mixture of the simple and the complex. On the one hand, popular myths express "truths" which are so basic and fundamental to a culture's perception of its history, people, and significance that they often acquire the dogmatic simplicity of religious tenets. Popular myths are almost like "secular commandments" in this regard: Thou shalt work hard and succeed in the land of plenty; thou shalt not restrict the freedom of others or permit thy own freedom to be compromised; thou shalt find satisfaction and peace in a simple existence close to the land and nature. Myths are elemental in their direct, heartfelt expression of the "way things are and always will be."

Robert Reich's essay "Four Morality Tales" provides new names for several of the popular myths we have already encountered (so that we can easily find "material success" behind the triumphant individual, "America as a special land of destiny" at the heart of the "mob at the gates," "individual freedom" and "anti-intellectualism" fueling the rot at the top, and the "democratic ideal" helping to define what is meant by the benevolent community) and place these bedrock beliefs into the type of basic story form we have termed "myth-narrative." But they still reflect the fundamental simplicity of these myths as well. The "tales" continue to express a vision of an America in which individuals strive to succeed within the context of a helpful, supportive community and where elites need to be constantly challenged and dark foreign forces kept at bay.

There is a remarkable complexity which lies just beneath the surface of these simple truths and their storybook tales, and Reich's essay reflects this important aspect of popular myth. For one thing it should quickly

Reprinted with permission from *Tales of a New America* by Robert Reich. N.Y. Times Books (Random House) 1987.

become obvious that the tales themselves must often be in conflict with each other as the absolute beliefs and values they embody clash in the real world. The triumphant individual is acceptable until he or she seeks success at the expense of the larger society. Contradictions and compromises lend an inevitable complexity to tales which are simple only when kept apart from each other.

Reich's essay places a strong emphasis upon another type of complexity as well—one which might be termed the complexity of the empty vessel. Reich's focus here is upon the broad, loosely defined nature of popular myths (a characteristic which is emblematic of their simplicity, of course) and the way in which they can therefore be re-interpreted by each succeeding generation. Concepts of the individual, the community, and the mob, for instance, are "empty vessels" which are filled by variously colored historical waters, so that the "rot" of one era (e.g. Reagan's malevolent big government) is the benevolent community of another (e.g. FDR's big government as new deal and friend to the triumphant individual). Myths are so complex, in other words, that they are simultaneously stable and ever-changing.

Reich's essay opens at least four avenues of discussion:

1) Morality tales are basic, fundamental narrative expressions of American myths, beliefs, and values. As such they are used to give shape and meaning to a wide variety of popular artifacts and events.

2) Morality tales are often in conflict with each other as they reflect the contradictions at the heart of the American mindset.

3) Morality tales are believed to be true and therefore have a powerful effect on the choices and actions of both individuals and communities.

4) The emphasis and meaning of the tales change over time and vary with historical circumstance.

Above all, perhaps, Reich's essay reveals once again that popular culture is a very special combination of the timeless and the timely—of the past and the present—and encourages us to reject simple answers in favor of looking deeper beneath the surface where the contradictions, compromises, and the flow of history lend subtlety to our quest. The fifth "Morality Tale" might well be "the complexity at the bottom."

I

You've heard the story a hundred times, with different names, different details. George was a good man, the son of immigrants who had made their way to Marysville. They came with no money, with nothing but grim determination and hard-won freedom. Dad worked all his life in the mill; he was union, hard and proud. George was quick by nature, dogged by necessity. He studied hard at school and after school worked long and well at anything that would bring in a few dollars. George was good at sports, but he had little time for games. He had few close friends, and yet he was fair and decent with everyone and quietly kind to anybody in real trouble. He never picked a fight in his life.

But in eighth grade, when the town bully Albert Wade was slapping around the smallest kid in the class, George stepped in between them without saying a word. He let Wade throw the first punch, then put him away with one straight left, turned around and walked away.

George finished high school in 1943 and joined the army the day he graduated. Four months later he was in Europe. On the sixth day of the Normandy invasion his squad was on patrol, passing through a French orchard when a German machine-gun nest opened up from behind a stone wall, picking off the squad one by one. George broke from cover and, dodging from tree to tree, raced toward the Nazis as bullets chewed the bark and ground around him. He took out the nest with a grenade and his rifle, and he saved his buddies; but he never wore the medals they gave him, and he never talked about it much. After the war he came back to Marysville and married Kate, his childhood sweetheart. He raised three kids, and he started a little construction business, which his hard work and integrity gradually made into a big construction business. By and by, George made a lot of money. But his family continued to live modestly, and he gave generously to the local boys' club and an orphanage he founded. He was generous with his time, too, and headed the community chest. Still he kept pretty much to himself until Albert Wade inherited his father's bank, the only bank in town. Wade risked his depositors' money on shaky loans to his cronies, bought and bullied his way into power with Marysville's political leaders. When he was elected mayor the election smelled bad to everyone, but only George openly accused Wade of corruption. For six months Wade's bank refused every mortgage on houses built by George's company, and George risked everything in the showdown. But in that tense town meeting, one of the city councilmen Wade had paid off could no longer hide his shame under George's steady gaze and simple question from the back of the room. He spilled how Wade had rigged the election. Albert Wade went from city hall to county jail, and George went back to his family, his work and his quiet service to Marysville.

George's story is an American morality tale. It is a national parable, retold time and again in many different versions, about how we should live our lives in this country. George is the American Everyman. He's Gary Cooper in *High Noon.* He's Jimmy Stewart in *It's a Wonderful Life.* He's the American private eye, the frontier hero, the kid who makes good. He's George Washington and Abe Lincoln. He appears in countless political speeches, in newspaper stories, on the evening news, in Americans ballads and sermons.

Everyone has a favorite variation, but the basic theme is the same and speaks to the essence of our national self-image: Ours is a nation of humble, immigrant origins, built out of nothing and into greatness through hard work; generous to those in need, those who cannot make it on their own; a loner among nations, suspicious of foreign entanglements, but willing to stand up against tyranny; and forever vigilant against corruption and special privilege.

The American morality tale defines our understandings of who we are, and of what we want for ourselves and one another. It is the tacit *subtext* of our daily conversations about American life. It permeates *both* American conservatism and American liberalism. And—the essential point—it is a fundamentally noble, essentially life-affirming story. Much is made of the American political distinctiveness of a Constitution inspired by theory rather than by tradition. But there is a subtler yet equally profound *cultural* distinctiveness as well, a national sense of identity rooted not in history but in self-told mythology. Political scientist Carl Friedrich captured the distinction in 1935: "To be an American is an ideal, while to be a Frenchman is a fact."

This basic mythology, however integral to the American identity, is so vague as to admit of many interpretations, to present itself in multiple manifestations over time. At different times in our history, different aspects of the parable have come to the fore while others receded. Some variants of the myth are more faithful to its essence than others; some variants are more supple accommodations to current American reality than others. Our history is punctuated with wrenching national contests between competing versions of the ideal; both world wars, for example, forced us to decide whether we must love peace more or justice more. Indeed, these episodes of editing our common mythology, as painful as they may be, are themselves affirmations of the American distinctiveness.

II

George's story embodies four basic American morality tales, our core cultural parables. They are rooted in the central experiences of American history: the flight from older cultures, the rejection of central authority and aristocratic privilege, the lure of the unspoiled frontier, the struggle for harmony and justice.

1) The Mob at the Gates

The first mythic story is about tyranny and barbarism that lurk "out there." It depicts America as a beacon light of virtue in a world of darkness, a small island of freedom and democracy in a perilous sea. We are uniquely blessed, the proper model for other peoples' aspirations, the hope of the world's poor and oppressed. The parable gives voice to a corresponding fear: we must beware, lest the forces of darkness overwhelm us. Our liberties are fragile; our openness renders us vulnerable to exploitation or infection from beyond.

Hence our endless efforts to isolate ourselves from the rest of the globe, to contain evil forces beyond our borders, and to convey our lessons with missionary zeal to benighted outsiders. George fought the "good war" against the Nazis; Daniel Boone, a somewhat less savory campaign against Indians; Davy Crockett, Mexicans. The American amalgam of fear and aggressiveness toward "them out there" appears in countless fantasies of space explorers who triumph over alien creatures from beyond. It is found in Whig histories of the United States and in the anti-immigration harangues of the late nineteenth and early twentieth centuries. We heeded George Washington's warning to maintain our independence from the monarchical powers of Europe and then proceeded for more than a century to conquer, purchase or otherwise control vast territories to our west and south.

In this century Woodrow Wilson grimly rallied Americans to "defeat once and for all...the sinister forces" that rendered peace impossible; Franklin Roosevelt warned of "rotten apple" nations that spread rot to others; Dean Acheson adopted the same metaphor to describe the Communist threat to Greece and Turkey immediately after Hitler's war; to Eisenhower, South Vietnam was the first in a series of dominoes that might fall to communism; to John F. Kennedy it was "the finger in the dike," holding back the Soviet surge. The underlying lesson: We must maintain vigilance, lest dark forces overrun us.

2) The Triumphant Individual

This is the story of the little guy who works hard, takes risks, believes in himself and eventually earns wealth, fame and honor. It's the parable of the self-made man (or, more recently, woman) who bucks the odds, spurns the naysayers and shows what can be done with enough drive and guts. He's a loner and a maverick, true to himself, plain speaking, self-reliant, uncompromising in his ideals. He gets the job done.

Determination and integrity earned George his triumph. Benjamin Franklin employed a carefully conceived system of self-control (Franklin's *Autobiography* is but the first in a long line of American manuals on how to become rich through self-denial and diligence). The theme recurs in the tale of Abe Lincoln, log splitter from Illinois who goes to the White House; in the hundred or so novellas of Horatio Alger, whose heroes all rise promptly and predictably from rags to riches (not only through pluck; luck plays a part too); and in the manifold stories of American detectives and cowboys—mavericks all—who reluctantly get involved in a dangerous quest and end up with the girl, the money and the glory. It appears in the American morality tales of the underdog who eventually makes it, showing up the bosses and bullies who tried to put him down; think of *Rocky* or *Iacocca.* Regardless of the precise form, the moral is the same: With enough guts and gumption, anyone can make it on their own in America.

3) The Benevolent Community

The third parable is about the American community. It is the story of neighbors and friends rolling up their sleeves and pitching in to help one another, of self-sacrifice, community pride and patriotism. It is about Americans' essential generosity and compassion toward those in need.

The story is rooted in America's religious traditions, and its earliest formulations are found in sermons like John Winthrop's "A Model of Christian Charity," delivered on board ship in Salem Harbor just before the Puritans landed in 1630. He described the enterprise on which they were embarking in the terms of Matthew's version of the Sermon on the Mount: The new settlers would be "as a City on a Hill" whose members would "delight in each other" and be "of the same body." America began as a nation of religious communities, centered in the church and pledged to piety and charity—Shakers, Amish, Mennonite, New England Congregationalist. Biblical language and symbols continued to propel American social movements committed to enlarging membership in the benevolent community—the drive for emancipation of the slaves, women's suffrage, civil rights: "I have a dream that every valley shall be exalted, every hill and mountain shall be made low," said Martin Luther King.

The story extends beyond religion to embrace social solidarity and civic virtue. It summons images of New England villagers who meet to debate their future; of frontier settlers who help build one another's barns and gather for quilting bees; of neighbors who volunteer as fire fighters and librarians, whose generosity erects the local hospital and propels high school achievers to college; of small towns that send their boys off to fight wars for the good of all. The story celebrates America's tradition of civic improvement, philanthropy and local boosterism.

It also tells of national effort on behalf of those in need. The theme permeated Roosevelt's New Deal, Truman's Fair Deal, Johnson's Great Society: America is a single, national community, bound by a common ideal of equal opportunity and generosity toward the less fortunate. E. Pluribis Unum.

Our popular culture has echoed these sentiments. Three hundred years after John Winthrop's sermon they could be found in Robert Sherwood's plays, the novels of John Steinbeck and William Saroyan, Aaron Copland's music and Frank Capra's films. The last scene in *It's a Wonderful Life* conveys the lesson: Jimmy Stewart learns that he can count on his neighbors' generosity and goodness, just as they had always counted on him. They are bound together in common cause. The principle: We must nurture and preserve genuine community.

4) The Rot at the Top

The fourth parable is about the malevolence of powerful elites, be they wealthy aristocrats, rapacious business leaders or imperious government officials. The American parable differs subtly but profoundly from a superficially similar European mythology: The struggle is only occasionally and incidentally a matter of money or class. There are no workers pitted against capitalists at the heart of this American story. It is, rather, a tale of corruption, decadence and irresponsibility among the powerful, of conspiracy against the broader public.

This morality tale has repeatedly provoked innovation and reform. Experience with the arbitrary authority of the English Crown produced in the Founding Fathers an acute sensitivity to the possibilities of abuse of power. The result was a government premised on the Enlightenment idea that power must be constrained and limited through checks and balances and be kept firmly tied to the consent of the governed. A century later America responded to mounting concentrations of private economic power through antitrust laws, designed to diffuse such power, and later by government support for other groups—labor unions, farmers and retailers—capable of exercising countervailing power. The nation dealt with concentrations of governmental power though civil service rules that limited favoritism and through electoral reforms and limitations on campaign contributions to render politicians more accountable to the public. Government power also was held in check by periodic efforts to extend power to the states and cities, to open government decision making to greater public observation and scrutiny, to reduce the power of senior legislators and to limit the ability of the president to take action without congressional approval. Since the beginning, in sum, Americans have been suspicious of elites and anxious to circumscribe their power.

At their worst, suspicions about the Rot at the Top have expressed themselves in conspiracy theories. America has harbored a long and infamous line of rabble-rousers, from the pre-Civil War Know-Nothings and Anti-Masonic movements, through the populist agitators of the late nineteenth century, the Ku Klux Klan, Senator Joseph McCarthy and Lyndon LaRouche. They have fomented against bankers, Catholics, big corporations, blacks, Jews, foreigners, either or both major political parties and other unnamed "interests." In this version of the story, the Rot at the Top is in a great conspiracy with the Mob at the Gates to keep down the common man and allow evil forces to overrun us.

Our popular culture revels in tales of corruption in high places. At the turn of the century, muckrakers like Upton Sinclair and Ida Tarbell uncovered sordid tales of corporate malfeasance; their modern heirs (revealing CIA depredations, White House scandals and corporate transgressions) are called investigative reporters. The theme recurs in real or invented stories of honest undercover agents—Sam Spade, Serpico, Jack Nicholson in *Chinatown*—who trace the rot back to the most powerful members of the community. It's embodied by the great bullies of American fiction: Judge Thatcher of *Huckleberry Finn*, Broderick Crawford as the Huey Long-like character in *All the King's Men*, Lionel Barrymore's demonic Mr. Potter in *It's a Wonderful Life*. And in the tales of humble folk, like the Joad family of *The Grapes of Wrath*, who struggle valiantly against avaricious bankers and landowners. The moral is clear: Power corrupts, privilege perverts.

III

The four basic parables have endured throughout American history. But in each era they have been combined and conveyed in slightly different ways, emphasizing a distinct message. Variants develop, come to dominate, and eventually evolve. The evolution can be endorsed and possibly accelerated, but never dictated, by political leaders. The art of political rhetoric has been to reconfigure these stories in a manner that affirms and amplifies the changes already occurring in the way Americans tell these tales to one another. The best political tales, like any parables, are those which most elegantly and simply interpret what's happening to the average person, which render coherent the citizens' experiences of fear and shame, pride and hope.

In the early part of this century, for example, Progressive leaders merged the parables of Rot at the Top and the Triumphant Individual. The lesson was that Big Business—the trusts—blocked worthy citizens from their rightful places in society. Corruption in high places was thwarting personal initiative, stifling upward mobility for the little man. Woodrow Wilson put the matter bluntly in a speech during the 1912 presidential campaign, promising to wage "a crusade against the powers that have governed us...that have limited our development...that have determined our lives...that have set us in a straightjacket to do as they please." In his view, the struggle against the trusts would be nothing less than "a second struggle for emancipation." (For Wilson, the Mob at the Gates—the large, bellicose, prewar European states—represented a similar challenge to democratic freedoms, and required a not unrelated dispersion of power.)

By the 1930s, the parables had shifted. Now the key thematic link was between Rot at the Top and the Benevolent Community. Now the lesson was that the mutual prosperity of common people was under attack by leaders of big business and finance. In the 1936 presidential campaign, Franklin D. Roosevelt warned against the "economic royalists" who had impressed the whole of society into "royal service." "The hours men and women worked, the wages they received, the conditions of their labor...these had passed beyond the control of the people, and were imposed by this new industrial dictatorship," he warned in one speech. "The royalists of the economic order have conceded that political freedom was the business of the government, but they have maintained that economic slavery was nobody's business." What was at stake, he concluded, was the "survival of democracy."

The shift from the Progressives' emphasis on the Triumphant Individual to the New Deal's Benevolent Community was more than an oratorical device. It represented a change in Americans' understanding of social life. The Great Depression had provided a national lesson in social solidarity; nearly every American family felt the effects of poverty and insecurity. The Benevolent Community became intimately relevant as relatives and neighbors sought to help one another, as government became the insurer of last resort, and then as Americans turned together to winning Hitler's war. Roosevelt explicitly described the purpose of the New Deal as "extending to our national life the old principle of the local community." "We are determined," he said, "to make every American citizen the subject of his country's interest and concern."

In the 1980s, Ronald Reagan drew on the same parables, but they were substantially reconfigured. Repudiating Roosevelt's national community, Reagan defined the Benevolent Community as small, traditional neighborhoods in which people voluntarily helped one another, free from government interference. The Rot at the Top referred to Washington insiders, arrogant government bureaucrats and liberal intellectuals who wanted to grab power and stifle creativity. The Triumphant Individual was the business entrepreneur who started work in an attic or garage and ended up spawning an entire industry. And the Mob at the Gates comprised a wide assortment—illegal immigrants, drug traffickers, Third World debtors and revolutionaries, terrorists, greedy trading partners, and, above all, Communist aggressors—who threatened our way of life. But America would prevail. "America is back and standing tall," Reagan said in 1984. "We've begun to restore the great American values—the dignity of work, the warmth of family, the strength of neighborhood and the nourishment of human freedom."

IV

All four of our morality tales refer to a *collective* identity. They affirm a *common* destiny. Thus a fundamental theme in the American mythology is membership—inclusion and, necessarily, exclusion. In American political life, as in our sporting events and lawsuits, the pronouns of "us" and "them" contain the essential information. They signal the boundaries beyond which loyalties and commitments do not extend. We trust that others like "us" will fulfill mutual obligations that yield joint benefits. But for "them" we have only pity or disdain.

In the story of the Mob at the Gates, "they" are dangerous outsiders. Their specific identity and the quality of their menace has varied throughout our history. "They" have been, at one time or another,

American Indians, French, English, Mexicans, Southerners, European immigrants, Germans, Japanese, Chinese and Russians, to name a few. That members of these groups have on occasion done us injury is true but not essential; that the pigment of their skin is different from that of most Americans is often, but not necessarily, the case. What unites them is that, at some point, "we" have defined ourselves as definitively not like them, and our thorough repudiation of what they represent has buttressed our sense of what we stand for.

Similarly, as Triumphant Individuals we are characterized partly by contrast with who we are not. In this story, "they" are featherbedders, menial workers and time servers. They are the men in gray flannel suits who dither and grovel in the offices of large organizations, workers who mindlessly follow routine, petty bureaucrats and all the other slackers who fail to pull their own weight. That even entrepreneurial garages go dark unless the bureaucrats at the local utility keep the electricity coming may seem to suggest a more complicated story of how we get things accomplished in America, but the stirring distinction between the change master and the time server endures.

A comparable dividing line runs through our conception of the Benevolent Community. On one side of the line the governing principle is solidarity; on the other side it is altruism, even paternalism. "We" are solid citizens who ask no more than our due, who offer or accept help only in cases of unanticipated and uncontrollable calamity. "They" are *the poor*, dependent by nature and perhaps by choice. We assume, mistakenly, that they are mostly black or brown. Our sense of mercy requires that we limit their suffering; our sense of justice requires that we accompany our charity with proper discipline.

Finally, in the tale of Rot at the Top, "they" are the business tycoons, wealthy aristocrats, Washington insiders, or any other who seems to exercise unaccountable power or enjoy unearned privilege. "We" are the common people, too often robbed of true authority, unfairly dispossessed of our proper rewards, innocent victims of the venality and incompetence of self-serving elites.

Dividing the world into "us" and "them," of course, is a universal and perhaps inevitable human trait. But when the dividing line is accepted without question by all sides of the political debate, it renders our convictions about credit and blame, about the sources and solutions to our problems, sturdily resistant to evidence. This is dangerous when it undercuts the possibility of mutual responsibility and reciprocal gain. As we attribute to "them"—dangerous outsiders, lazy workers, the poor and the deviant, the scheming elites—the problems that bedevil us, we simultaneously limit our repertoire of responses to two broad categories: First, we can discipline them. By being tough and assertive, we can compel them to repent, lay down the law on acceptable behavior and punish them when they transgress. Alternatively, we can conciliate them. Through generosity, understanding and toleration we can socialize them, bring out the best in them and seduce them into changing their ways, into becoming more like us.

It is in large part this pervasive mythic division between the "us" and the "them" that explains the American propensity to squeeze the most collectively diverse and individually complex public choices into a linear array of options anchored, on the one end, by toughness and on the other, by conciliation. These are our contested principles, in issues ranging from foreign policy to welfare. Our public discourse, thus constrained, is often comfortably straightforward but perilously incomplete.

Our morality tales are increasingly at odds with the new challenges we confront. The prevailing versions have little relevance to the relationships that frame our lives—with other peoples of the earth, within our firms, toward our poor, toward our leaders. The prevailing versions do not speak of mutual obligation. They neither celebrate joint gain nor forebode reciprocal loss. Our morality tales, too long unexamined, are losing their power to inform our present. Once again we must revise and reaffirm our declaration of identity.

Culture and Continuity: Three American Myths in the Prints of Currier & Ives

Jack Nachbar

The next time you confess to a friend that you are studying "popular culture," and the friend asks you, "Huh? What's that?" (they almost always do this, as you'll see) turn the tables and ask what s/he thinks popular culture is. Chances are that your friend will quickly mention several examples of items that are popular right now. Music on the top of the charts and the movies at the local multiplex come up in nearly all of these conversations. The trouble is that even though these are common notions of what popular culture is, it is as much about the materials and beliefs of the past as it is about the present.

Jack Nachbar's article about popular myths in the nineteenth-century lithographs of the printmakers Currier and Ives might provide you with a number of examples that help explain how popular culture was a significant part of the mindset of the American past. What people choose to put on the walls of their homes helps them create an environment in which they feel comfortable and which they believe reflects their taste and values. The millions of Currier and Ives prints in the nineteenth-century homes suggests a common set of beliefs reflected in the content of these prints that makes them important popular culture artifacts.

The other important concept illustrated in the article is the idea that popular myths have continuity. Superficial beliefs can come and go. This week oat bran is good for you, next week it isn't. Myths, on the other hand, as bedrock beliefs tend to be around for a long time, sometimes hundreds of years. Thus, the Currier and Ives company has been out of the printing business for almost a century, but the three myths illustrated here are still as much with us today as when Currier and Ives were at the height of their popularity. Expressions of these

Reprinted with permission from *The Popular Culture Reader*, ed. Christopher Geist and Jack Nachbar, Bowling Green, OH: Bowling Green State University Popular Press, 1982.

myths have simply moved to new forms, from nineteenth-century living room walls to late twentieth-century television sets and stereos.

The bedrock beliefs we call myths around which different cultures are formed are invariably among the oldest beliefs of each culture. They are passed on from generation to generation, and are reaffirmed and renewed as the old share their world view with their young. In older tribal cultures priests or shaman and sometimes tribal elders initiated young people into the sacred lore of the tribe around campfires where they recited for the initiates long, magical stories, often centuries old. In the industrialized western world, especially since the coming of the mass media, the work of the priests and elders has been taken over by the creators and purveyors of widely reproduced popular culture. There is also another major difference between how tribal and mass mediated cultural beliefs are communicated.

Members of the tribe and their chosen storytellers are aware of the essential importance of their tales to their culture and usually place the telling of them within sacred ceremonies. The creators and consumers of mass produced popular culture, on the other hand, often make the products merely common props of everyday life and place no special cultural significance on them at all. Ironically, it is exactly this casual attitude toward popular culture products that makes them such excellent vehicles for the passing on of cultural traditions. If thousands, even millions, of people passively enjoy a product, that product must have an immediate, non-controversial and general appeal. In order to manufacture such appeal, the makers of popular culture, often subconsciously, build into their mass-produced creations attractive attitudes and preconceptions that usually already have long-standing acceptance in the cultural community. The types of products themselves may vary depending on public taste and changing technologies, but popular culture artifacts as a whole reveal a long continuity of key beliefs and values. Very few people are actively conscious of this transmission of cultural traditions in popular culture, yet it is there as surely as it is in the chant of the shaman and in the faces of the listeners, wide with wonder in the shadows of the campfire.

To illustrate how popular culture serves to reaffirm cultural myths over long periods of time I will briefly describe three myths most people would agree are very much present in contemporary American culture. After each description I will provide examples of the existence of this myth a century earlier in the scenes of the most popular printmakers of the nineteenth century, Currier and Ives.

Nathanial Currier began his business of printing lithographs in 1832 and by 1840 business was booming. By 1852, when John Ives joined the company, demand for Currier's prints had enabled him to open a three-story factory. On another floor the printing process itself took place. Finally, on the third floor, a dozen daughters of German immigrants hand-colored each of the prints, with individual women responsible for applying a single color and passing the print down the line. More than 7000 different prints were done in this manner by the time the company ceased production in 1898. During their period of greatest popularity, roughly from 1850 to 1880, Currier and Ives stocked as many as 3000 different prints at any one time and produced about eighty percent of the prints sold in the United States. Sales methods ranged from selling directly from their offices in New York to sending out itinerant peddlers who sold the prints in remote country districts. Prices were cheap, from twenty-five cents for a standard print to four dollars for extra-large prints, 28" x 40", carefully colored by a single artist. With prints so accessible and cheap it is little wonder that millions were sold and that Currier and Ives was the first true mass-marketer of popular visual art in the United States.

Nearly every possible subject acceptable to a middle-class audience was drawn by the numerous Currier and Ives artists. There were cartoons and still lifes, hunting and fishing scenes, scenes picturing recent fires, ship sinkings and other disasters, profiles of famous race horses and prints detailing the process of Victorian courtship. In general, these subjects fit into two broad classes—immediate events and general scenes of American life. The general scenes were those that remained in stock the longest and eventually sold the best. In presenting scenes they knew their customers would view as attractive renderings of typical events in America, Currier and Ives expressed fundamental values and beliefs most people accepted as true and approved of.

The Myth of Rural Simplicity

Articulated by Thomas Jefferson when he defined the true American as the yeoman farmer, this myth posits that true happiness and virtue are to be found by living close to the cultivated land. Television's brief history abounds with examples of highly successful shows which assume the truth of this myth from *Lassie* in the 1950s to *The Beverly Hillbillies* in the 1960s to *The Waltons* and *Little House on the Prairie* in the 1970s to *Northern Exposure* the 1990s. Other types of popular culture have arisen from this myth. The contemporary popular ritual of leaving work and camping for a vacation is based on the idea of rural simplicity and virtue, as is the common summer ritual of vegetable gardening.

The ongoing mass migration away from the industrialized cities of the north into the so-called sunbelt has been mostly a matter of going where the jobs are. An additional important factor has been faith in the myth of rural simplicity. How many of us have been told over and over that the country or the small town is a great place to bring up kids? And it is the South, after all, that has become the center in the popular imagination of a lifestyle we call "down home."

In Figure 1, *American Forest Scene,* winter in the country is pictured as a time for happy socializing rather than as a season filled with dangerous storms, isolation and cabin fever. In the center our eye is engaged by the huge pot of maple sugar over the roaring fire, the standing man leisurely whittling and the sitting group enjoying an amusing conversation. Nobody has to work hard at this "sugaring off" party and even though they are lightly dressed, no one is cold. All around this central grouping, the activities of everyone from children to old men confirm the pleasantness of the event. Figure 2, *Husking,* also deals with a party arranged around the simple necessity of rural seasonal chores. And even though it is inside a barn the picture creates the same feeling of open air friendship that *Winter in the Country* does. The man standing in the middle emphasizes that the work at hand is the primary objective. On both sides, however, work has become symbolic social play. The old man and the child on the left are united in the application of fundamental country skills. In the right a hunter has set aside his gun to woo a young woman. In this calm scene suggesting a happy camaraderie between generations and the possibility of a future new family, even the dog is peacefully at rest.

The Myth of Endless Abundance

The myth of endless abundance tells us that we possess more than we can ever use. America is a land of such overwhelming natural resources and productive potential that we will never run out of anything essential to comfort and well-being. This concept was already in the minds of the earliest settlers, such as John Smith, who wrote that the new land was blessed with such abundance that to prosper a man had to work only four hours a day. Early explorers were so convinced of this myth that an intelligent man like Ponce de Leon struggled through Florida certain that he would find a fountain of youth. Francesco Coronado roamed the Southwest believing in seven cities of gold. Later the conspicuous waste of American pioneers expressed the belief that there was an infinite supply of everything. Instead of using wood for building, forests were cleared by burning. The buffalo were annihilated largely for sport and luxury coats. In our day, the myth is still very much with us despite growing concerns about depleted energy resources. We tend, for example, to gain status by buying new things. Cars are customarily traded every two or three years not because they are worn out but because it makes us feel good to have a new one. The rise in popularity of disposable items—diapers, lighters, plates, razors, even dresses—reflects our faith that we can't ever run out of anything.

Fig. 1 *American Forest Scene: Maple Sugaring*, 1856. Artist: Fitzwilliam Tait.

Fig. 2 *Husking*, 1861. Artist: Eastman Johnson.

Cultural myths such as the myth of endless abundance are such elemental beliefs in a culture that they give rise to smaller but no less accepted concepts. Believing in endless abundance, for instance, encourages a related belief that convenience is a virtue. As a result we support gigantic companies who maintain themselves by selling appliances that will cut by a few seconds the time it takes to chop a carrot or open a can or cook a hot dog. Another related belief is that big is good. Prosperity is expressed through the purchase of a computer with more memory, even though it is not needed. And the glutton at the ice-cream shop wins a medal if he can somehow force down a super-sized sundae.

The scene in front of the farmhouse in Figure 3, *Preparing for Market,* suggests the happiness of simple rural life pictured in Figures 1 and 2. Here, however, the happiness is the result of the land's bounty. In the foreground are a duck and a turkey, both fat, and a rooster and hen with eight chicks. Behind them, produce is spread all over the yard. And at the middle, far right, a man chops at his endless supply of firewood. Even the work horses look sleek and healthy. There are so many garden crops that they cannot all be "put by." They will be sold. The huge stack of hay just to the right of the barn suggests the fertility of the tilled fields.

Fig. 3 *Preparing for Market,* 1856. Artist: Louis Maurer.

Figure 4, *The Levee—New Orleans,* suggests endless abundance in an urban environment. Unlike the leisurely atmosphere of Currier and Ives' rural scenes, this panorama of the New Orleans waterfront, despite the slacker in the right foreground, suggests intense, commercial action.

Fig. 4 *The Levee—New Orleans*, 1883. Artist: William Walker.

In the background the river is thick with steamboats with engines fired, throwing out thick clouds of smoke against a blue sky. The levee itself is loaded with goods and workers scurrying back and forth to load and unload even more. All in all, the scene suggests the boundless productive capabilities of America. Cotton, lumber, grain and tobacco will keep piling up and up and the steamboats will keep crowding the harbor to load them.

The Myth of Technology as Protector and Savior

A third important myth is the belief that technology is by definition beneficial, that nearly all problems in the present world are solvable with new inventions. The American space program is a concrete example of our fundamental faith in this myth. With only a few murmurs of dissent, billions of dollars were spent during the 1960s on the space program. Apparently most people assumed that such a remarkable technological triumph as landing on the moon inevitably would result in benefits worth the huge investment. In the 1990s, the TV networks and CNN try to outdo each other in their coverage of each new launching of the space shuttle.

In a similar fashion, the usual argument for complex new weapons systems in this country is that through the military might supplied by these weapons will come peace. Another present example of this myth is the faith most people have that technology will solve our environmental problems. Don't most of us secretly believe that we will invent machines that will repair the ozone layer? And does anyone doubt that if we ever run out of oil, clever scientists will invent a new energy source thus protecting and saving our way of life?

A belief related to the myth of technology as savior is that efficiency is always a virtue. The omnipresence of vending machines in our lives and our passive acceptance of them testify to our faith in both technology and efficiency. The popularity of cellular phones is testimony that technology can even cause us to better use the time we spend in our cars.

While both Figures 5, *The Hudson River Steamboat "St. John,"* and 6, *The "Lightning Express" Trains,* do no more than show two important nineteenth-century marvels of technology, steamboats and locomotives, both prints reveal a reverential thinking toward their subjects. The St. John in Figure 5 is drawn to look low, sleek and streamlined. Its great size is emphasized by its filling up nearly the entire length of the print, yet it hardly seems to break the placid water at all and it offers no threat to the more primitive sailboat at the far left. The two "express" trains in Figure 6 are both drawn to emphasize their speed and power. The smoke from the huge stacks is quickly left behind. And the angle on the cowcatchers creates an illusion of size and their

Fig. 5 *The Hudson River Steamboat "St. John,"* 1864. Artist: Fanny Palmer.

Fig. 6 *The "Lightning Express" Trains*, 1863.

forward thrust emphasizes speed. The trains have a clear American sky behind them but appear to be heading into a cloudy, dark night. Their headlights glare brightly forward, however, suggesting a powerful determination in the trains' journeys.

At first glance, it seems that the myth of technology as savior contradicts the myths of rural simplicity and endless abundance. High technology usually suggests cities. During the nineteenth century the technology of mass production lured millions of agrarian youth to expanding urban areas to work in factories. The efficiency of assembly production also consumed resources at an alarming rate. If such contradictions remained unresolved in our culture, the result would be a clash of opposing beliefs which in turn could lead our culture to function less securely. The famous anthropologist Claude Levi-Strauss argues that all cultures contain such contradictions of beliefs. The main purpose of myth narratives according to Levi-Strauss is to resolve these contradictions by presenting stories that "mediate" or resolve the conflict between the opposing myths. In his book *The Machine in the Garden* Leo Marx shows how literature and advertising in the nineteenth century convinced most people that manufacturing and more complex machinery would actually help America realize its ideal of rural simplicity and abundance, instead of posing a threat to them. Since that time people have for the most part assumed it to be true. We generally believe that technology provides for and protects the continuing truth of the other myths. The mass productions created by technology provide us, for example, with an endless abundance of affordable products. And, after all, don't such creations of technology as tractors and combines ease the drudgery of farm work and allow the life of leisurely communing with nature that Jefferson foresaw? Figures 7, *The Fruits of Temperance,*

Fig. 7 *The Fruits of Temperance*, 1870.

Fig. 8 *Across the Continent: "Westward the Course of Empire Takes Its Way,"* 1868. Artists: Fanny Palmer and James Ives.

and 8, *Across the Continent,* both function as myth narratives, suggesting patterns of life that harmonize technology with the other two myths.

The *Fruits of Temperance* is one of a large number of prints done by Currier and Ives illustrating the evils of drink and the virtues of abstention. The reward of avoiding the bottle, quite obviously, is an ideal domestic life. Young children scamper happily to greet their father and even the baby eagerly holds out its arms. The cottage in its country setting is a model of rural simplicity. A classic picket fence insulates it from possible harm and a vine curves around the house almost as if to protect it even further. In the background a setting sun seems to cast a halo over the entire scene. Of special interest for our purposes is the factory at the upper left of the print. Notice how instead of conflicting with the idyllic country environment, the factory, even with its belching smokestack, seems to fit into the scene perfectly. The father no doubt is employed there. The factory is thus the real provider of the quaint cottage scene in the foreground. The tones of the factory harmonize with those of the mountains in the background and it is nestled in among the mountains and trees as if it is a part of nature itself. The print suggests that the factory is part of this lovely rural scene and is a source of abundant happiness of the country family.

Across the Continent, instead of featuring the intimate scene of *The Fruits of Temperance,* presents a broad historical perspective on an epic scale. The right foreground suggests the myth of rural simplicity. Children play in front of the new public school. The men clearing the land with axes and shovels appear to be working in a healthy spirit of cooperation. The dominating image in the print is the train. Its tracks dramatically cut the picture in half. The train plays a crucial symbolic role in the scene because the composition of the picture suggests it has made possible the settling of the land and the building of the town. The train, in other words, is the catalyst for changing the landscape from a wilderness to a civilized, rural community. Unsettled land lies to the right of the train. The Indians of that land are kept away from the settlement by the train and are about to disappear in the smoke of the engine. On the left side, the train shows the way into the future. A wagon train is preparing to follow the direction of the tracks into the west. Overall the scene suggests an ecstatic confidence in the future of the United States dominated by white European-Americans made possible by the technology of the iron horse and perfected in the small town. With such a combination of technology and rural simplicity, the horizon seems doomed for the native Americans, but for the white pioneers it is limitless and infinitely promising.

The aesthetic quality of Currier and Ives lithographs has been criticized by some art historians for being crude and naive. And even to non-art experts it is evident that the subject matter of the prints was usually given greater emphasis than artistic flourishes. It is exactly because of this emphasis on subject matter that Currier and Ives' prints were able to so successfully convey to millions basic American beliefs and values. It is for this reason that Currier and Ives genuinely deserved their motto, "Printmakers to the American people." The fact that reproductions of their lithographs are still widely enjoyed suggests the enduring popularity of the scenes pictured and the continuing relevancy of the myths those scenes represent.

The American Myth of Success: Visions and Revisions

Madonna Marsden

Several recent surveys of attitudes of entering college freshmen show that the primary reason freshmen of the 1990s have decided to go to college is to make a lot of money. This goal apparently is more important than getting a meaningful job, developing moral and intellectual sophistication, becoming a better person. Some people are critical of this attitude, finding that it suggests young people are simply self-centered and greedy. As students of popular culture, however, we might well come to a different conclusion. As Madonna Marsden demonstrates in the following article, making a lot of money has been a main objective of most Americans since the seventeenth century, and making a lot of money has been seen as a sign of intelligence and goodness for almost 400 years. From Ben Franklin in the 1740s to Ross Perot in the 1990s, money means power, status and respect. Students in the 1990s are no greedier than the youth of yesterday; they are, in fact, merely following in a great American tradition.

Marsden's article, like the essay on Currier and Ives, shows us that a key American belief has long historical continuity. In addition, Marsden shows us that popular myths over a long period of time are subject to "revisions." Changing historical and cultural circumstances lead popular myths to evolve and change. A quick perusal of the self-help shelf at a local bookstore, for example, would suggest that individual success still includes earning significant wealth but also includes more personal goals with an emphasis on psychological well being. Good marriages, good sex, good health, etc. equal money as symbolic of virtue and success.

The essay also suggests that we cannot ignore popular myths, even though we may personally claim the myth does not apply to us. Many people claim that the American mania for wealth is a flaw in our cultural heritage. Perhaps they are right. But those critics who would suggest we change our greedy ways should recognize how traditional and pervasive this myth is in our culture. And they should also be aware that, as Marsden

Reprinted with permission from *The Popular Culture Reader*, 3rd Edition, Christopher Geist and Jack Nachbar, eds. Bowling Green, OH: Bowling Green State University Popular Press, 1983.

suggests, the myth takes many forms, and some of these forms (good grades in college, eating the "right" foods, sending children to "good" schools, for example) may well apply to the critics themselves. Belief in basic American myths is very difficult to avoid.

I. *The Myth*

Open almost any magazine and you'll find it—the lavish array of material objects which connote the comfort, the status and the security which are the components of The American Dream. For these are the clichés of the American good life—a chicken in every pot, a car in every garage, a place where even the person born into poverty can give a tug on his or her bootstraps and have a chance at the Presidency or a seat on the Stock Exchange. And it *has* happened here. Think of our great political and industrial heroes: Andrew Jackson, Abraham Lincoln, Andrew Carnegie, John D. Rockefeller. Though essentially simple men, they made the most of their native intelligence and natural spunk. They worked hard, rose through the ranks, and were rewarded by fame and/or fortune. And that is the American myth of success. With hard work comes achievement, and with achievement comes the material comforts of the American Dream and sometimes even great riches and a place in history.

Our mythology is not based upon invention and imagination, though it may not always be logical and is frequently heavily emotional. It is not merely the product of legend, or the result of fantasizing or wish-fulfillment, or even the effect of a primitive, prescientific mind trying to explain the ways of the world to itself (as we might be inclined to believe about the mythologies of Greece and Rome). On the contrary, our mythology derives from what is very real—our legal tradition, our history, and the biographies of our great men.

On the other hand, it would be a great mistake to say that because of this basis in reality, the American myth of success is therefore "true." We need only open the daily newspaper to find that a commitment to hard work does not always insure success. Consider, for example, the middle-aged executive "released" from his job after twenty years of devoted work for a company which suddenly decides it wants younger men. Or observe the changeovers in government personnel after an election and receive an eye-opening lesson about what kinds of allegiances America rewards.

Or consider less newsworthy cases even closer to home. An energetic and hard-working college student spends a total of seventy hours on a research paper only to receive a grade of F. Another spends a sleepless night studying for an exam only to discover that the test covers none of the materials he has so carefully perused. These and hundreds of other documented examples stand in direct contradiction to the notion that it is only the lazy who can fail here in the U.S. of A.

But in the collective American mind this does not make the myth of hard work as a prelude to success equal to a lie. On the other hand, it should not be described as a truth, either. *Myth,* as when we speak of the American myth of success, means a deeply rooted cultural belief with no implied judgement as to whether that belief is true or false. *Myth* refers only to the existence of that belief and its persistence in a culture's artistic tradition despite whatever "logical" and "well-documented" evidence which there might be to contradict it.

II. *1600-1800*

The origins of the success myth can be traced back to the days of our country's first settlement. The private diaries and journals of some of the New World's first settlers as well as their public accounts for the folks back home can quickly confirm this. For a long time, Europeans had dreamed of a "brave new world" which would offer them freedom from the oppression of a largely feudal system where a few profited from the ownership of land while the many worked the land hard and reaped only minimal fruits for their labor. And because of the unified religious tradition in Europe at the time, these longings began to shape themselves around the Biblical story of the Garden of Eden, that paradise where the first humans had been perfectly in tune because they were uncorrupted by sin and lived harmoniously with nature. Influenced by their economic and political longings as well as their Christian education, many of the first explorers and settlers of the new land sent back to Europe accounts which tended to confirm that the American continent might indeed be a New Eden.

Captain John Smith wrote of Virginia that "heaven and earth never agreed better to frame a place for man's habitation." His description of the topography made it indeed appear to be another Garden of Paradise: "The country is not mountainous nor yet so low but such pleasant plain hills and fertile valleys, one prettily crossing another, and watered so conveniently with their sweet brooks and crystal springs, as if art itself had devised them" (*A Map of Virginia,* 1612). And George Alsop promoted Maryland as a place so rich that crops grew "without chargeable and laborious manurings of the Land with Dung," watered by rains which seemed to fall "by natural instinct" (*A Character of the Province of Maryland,* 1666).

Others, however, particularly in the northern colonies, found the new land much less inviting. Those of our ancestors who landed at Plymouth Rock found the climate considerably less than ideal, the land rocky, and the Indians intimidating. Reports filtered back to Europe that the American natives were savage and hostile, "furious in their rage, and merciless where they overcome," beings who delighted "to torment men in the most bloody manner that may be; flaying some alive with the shells of fishes, cutting off the members and joints of others by piecemeal and broiling (them) on the coals" (William Bradford, *Of Plymouth Plantations,* first published in 1856). For them, America seemed much more like hell than heaven, inhabited as it was by demonic beings.

Not only those at Plymouth Plantation (who nearly starved during their first winter in America), but also the settlers in the warmer climates who found their ranks swelled by an increasing number of adventurers, vagabonds, ex-convicts and whores (lured there by the accounts of Virginia's sunshine!) suffered some second thoughts about this new "paradise." Yet both groups later came to agree that the great promise held out by America was not ease, but hard work. And the hope of freedom from want which America had to offer seemed equally as alluring as the promise of Eden.

Writing of the improved condition of life in Virginia, John Hammond noted that by paying more attention to the "planting and tending of...quantities of Corn" and caring less about "that notorious manner of life they had formerly lived and wallowed in," the Virginians began to see the benefits of their labor and to understand that there is "nothing more pleasurable than profit" (*Leah and Rachel,* 1656). Not all of those who began the Plymouth Colony lived long enough to see that first sumptuous Thanksgiving feast, but those who did could easily agree with William Woods' assessment that "the diligent hand makes rich" (*New England's Prospects,* 1634). All seemed to concur that despite the obstacles in America, the work there offered rewards impossible in the Old World, and that the condition of even the lowest in America was far superior to the plight of the average man in England. For in America, at least, a man could directly reap the fruits of his own labors on his own piece of land. No overlord was around to take most of the profits away. Even the indentured servant here could hope to find himself (as George Alsop did at the end of his four year term) with "Cattle, Hogs, and Tobacco of his own..." because, wrote Alsop, "There is no Master almost but will allow his Servant a parcel of clear ground to plant some Tobacco in for himself...." In America, all were welcome to a piece of the action.

Thus quite early in our literary tradition was born the idea that in America a hard-working man was fated not to a life of drudgery and misery, but to one of material pleasure and comfort. Here, at least, a man could escape the fate of dying in poverty, though he may have been born into it. Even those whose migration was motivated more by religious than economic reasons soon began to absorb America's promise of success into their value systems. The Puritans, influenced by the theories of John Calvin, believed that at the moment of birth everyone was predestined by a rather whimsical God for either heaven or hell. One could never know until the day of private judgement whether one was among the "elect" (those chosen for heaven) or not. But, so the logic ran, it was possible to get some hint. If one had led a virtuous and industrious earthly life, it was quite likely that one had been predestined for heaven. Whether the good, hardworking life was a cause or an effect of predestination was never made quite clear, but the appearance of industry and outward success became an important part of the Puritan ethic since these were the tickets to the good life both now and later. For men like George Alsop, hard work was a means by which a man could change his fate. For the Puritans this was not possible, but that did not make the work ethic less venerable. Industry simply confirmed the inherent fate of a just man. As a corollary, sloth became quite easy to understand. One failed in this life because one had been predestined to fail in the next life, too. Or as the "Officer Krupke" song from the musical *West Side Story* puts it, "We're deprived on account o' we're depraved."

For the Puritans, success was a spiritual matter. Material success was only an accident of a much larger goal, and the pursuit of virtue was much more important than the pursuit of the dollar. But even for those of a less religious age, material success was still accidental to the pursuit of a larger end—in this case, an ideal community. For Benjamin Franklin, an eighteenth-century Rationalist who rejected most of the beliefs of institutionalized religion, fame, fortune, and world-reknown were certainly not the means to prove to the world that he was on his way to heaven. Franklin, an avowed Deist, believed that "the most acceptable service of God was the doing good to man." And as a consequence of this belief, he devoted himself to improving the earthly life in every way that he could. He started with himself, determined "to live without committing any fault at any time" in order to be a useful citizen. Industry was one of the moral virtues Franklin most prized, and he resolved to force himself to "Lose no time; be always employ'd in something useful; cut off all unnecessary actions." (All quotations are from *The Autobiography,* c. 1771.) Franklin's life is a testimonial to the American success myth, for by his self-discipline and his industry he proved that being the fifteenth child of a poor candlemaker was no obstacle to becoming a wealthy printer, publisher, writer, inventor, and respected diplomat. The maxims that he popularized in his *Poor Richard's Almanac* (1758) have become the credo of the American cult of upward mobility: "God helps them that help themselves"; "The sleeping Fox catches no Poultry"; "Early to bed and early to rise makes a man healthy, wealthy and wise." His exhortation, "Let us then be up and doing, and doing to the purpose" became the inspiration for a later generation of Americans who found themselves impatient and unwilling to wait for future spiritual payoffs and practical-minded enough to be convinced that the combination of the Industrial Revolution and America's natural resources might indeed make a heaven out of earth.

THE GOSPEL OF WEALTH
According to Poor Richard

Industriousness

Keep thy shop and thy shop will keep thee.
Industry pays debts, while despair increaseth them.
Never leave that till tomorrow which you can do today.

Frugality

A small leak will sink a great ship.
He that goes a borrowing goes a sorrowing.
Fools make feasts and wise men eat them.

Experience

If you will not hear reason, she will surely rap your knuckles.
Experience keeps a dear school, but fools will learn in no other.

III. *1800s*

The religious tradition of the seventeenth century had attributed success to luck (some were born to succeed), while the secular eighteenth-century tradition attributed it entirely to pluck (anyone who put a mind to it could succeed). Though the two strains seemed entirely contradictory, one nineteenth-century man managed to reconcile them, and as a result, became one of the best-selling authors of all time and an American household word.

Horatio Alger, Jr. (1832-1899) is more talked about than read by contemporary Americans. But in his own time, Alger's many novels were widely consumed by a working class who had found both some job security and some leisure time thanks to the Industrial Revolution. This increased prosperity gave Americans time to dream, and Horatio Alger provided them with the subject matter when he hit upon the story formula of the poor boy who rises to riches. The very titles of his books sound like abbreviated maxims from *Poor Richard's Almanac: Strive and Succeed, Bound to Rise, Helping Himself, Forging Ahead, From Farm to Fortune.* Once again, however, it is important to emphasize that just because Alger contributed the success mythology, his works ought not to be considered idle fantasies. For in the nineteenth century, enough self-made men existed to lend credence to Alger's theme. As Alger was writing, for instance, Henry Ford was laboring for $2.50 a week polishing steam engines, George Eastman was earning $3.00 a week in an insurance office, and John D. Rockefeller was unemployed.

Though each of Alger's many novels differs in its specifics, the basic pattern of all is the same. A poor boy (who is usually an orphan) is struggling to make ends meet as a bootblack, errand-runner, or some sort of street merchant. Though the hero is almost always on one of the lower rungs of the economic ladder, his personal moral code is quite high. He is always generous, self-sacrificing, honorable and gentlemanly. He has an innate sense of self-worth and a good deal of respect for others, especially those who are in positions of authority. Alger heroes are quite frequently fatherless, and consequently must shift for themselves at an early age. Because of this, they have a mature sense of responsibility and a devotion to work as the means of preserving the family unit. They are in general the kind of good, upright boys who would make model Boy Scouts. And it is this combination of innate moral goodness and a mature devotion to diligence which pays off for them in the end.

In the process of seeking his fortune, the Alger hero must often confront an assortment of thieves and confidence men who are seeking their own fortunes in unscrupulous ways. But the hero's common sense, which seems to derive from his innate sense of what is right and wrong, always saves him from ruin, and what he might lose in material gain by taking a moral stance is always compensated for later. In *Tom Thatcher's Fortune,* for example, Tom picks up $250 at a Wall Street firm as part of an errand for his employer. On the way back to his job, he meets a con man who offers to sell him a "solid gold" watch at a very low price. Tom is tempted but his basic honesty about money and his common sense save him from closing the deal. Later on, a rich gentlemen gives the shivering Tom his overcoat, and when Tom discovers that the man has left some valuable securities in the pocket and very honestly returns them, the gentlemen gives Tom a real gold watch as a reward. Similarily, the hero of *Shifting for Himself,* unemployed because he has been falsely accused of theft, gives his last dollar to a poor flower seller who has a sick father. In his magnanimity, the young man realizes that the girl's plight is much more wretched than his own. As luck would have it, the sick man turns out to be a former employer of the hero's dead father, and he knows that the young boy has been left a substantial fortune by his father's will. It has been usurped by an unscrupulous uncle, but it can be restored. In both cases (and in almost every other Alger book), the heroes reap riches due to an accidental good turn. But the financial success they achieve is never quite accidental, because in the Alger formula, virtue is the necessary antecedent to good fortune. It alone is the spring which triggers the lucky payoff.

For Alger, then, success was definitely a combination of Puritan luck and Ben Franklin's pluck. The repetition of his unvarying literary formula through at least seventy books raised the "luck plus pluck" hypothesis almost to the validity of a scientific law. The more clinical (though still hypothetical) observations of Charles Darwin were all that was needed to actually turn this unique blend of Puritanism and Pragmatism into a scientific rationale for the ages of monopoly in American business.

Though Darwin wrote his *Origin of the Species* in 1859, it was not until the end of the Civil War that his ideas began to be widely promulgated in America. In some, Darwin inspired great fear because he undermined the Book of Genesis. No longer could humanity be seen as a special act of creation by a God who had carefully planned the universe. The creation of man was now seen as a kind of success story, an evolution from the bottom rung of life accomplished by an animal who made his way to the top not because this was his special destiny, but because he was the strongest and the fittest. Because "struggle for existence" and "survival of the fittest" were the most popular catchwords in Darwinian thought, his theories confirmed two old Puritan notions: 1) that hard work was an integral part of humanity's lot; and 2) that only "the elect" (Darwin rechristened them "the fittest") could ultimately succeed. For America's business elite, this theory served to reaffirm what Alger had implied—that for some, success was well-deserved, and that the business world was really a testing ground for the development and encouragement of an individual's personal character. In lectures and articles for the masses, the major industrialists of the time preached the gospel of self-improvement and individualism as the keys to upward mobility. Over and over again, they emphasized that success was earned only by aggression and constant work, and that one could rise only by starting very low.

Addressing students at a commercial college in Pittsburgh, Andrew Carnegie used the metaphor of a horse race to describe this struggle and said:

> I congratulate poor young men upon being born to that ancient and honorable degree which renders it necessary that they should devote themselves to hard work.... The [sons of rich men] will not trouble you much, but look out that some boys poorer, much poorer than yourselves...do not challenge you at the post and pass you at the grandstand. Look out for the boy who has to plunge into work direct from the common school and who begins by sweeping out the office. His is the probably dark horse that you had better watch. (*The Road to Business Success,* 1885)

In this same lecture, Carnegie counseled the students to cultivate practical virtues in order to advance in the race. "You all know," he said, "that there is no genuine, praiseworthy success in life if you are not honest, truthful, fair dealing." Above and beyond this, however, a man must be self-disciplined and do all things in moderation. "I beseech you avoid liquor, speculation, and indorsement [lending]," Carnegie counseled. Like Benjamin Franklin before him, Andrew Carnegie promoted temperance in all things because excess just didn't seem wise. It slowed a man down and made him less likely to succeed.

Given the influence of Darwin over him, Andrew Carnegie could not help but see life in terms of a continuing economic battle for survival that only the best could win. Both Carnegie and Alger were typical spokesmen for what the history books call the era of *rugged individualism:* an era which valued aggressive individual initiative, individual virtue, and individual goals. For in the nineteenth century, these indeed were the marks of the thoroughbred.

IV. *The Twentieth Century*

It is an ironic turn of events that the year after the death of Horatio Alger saw the birth of the United States Steel Corporation. The trend toward industrial consolidation had begun in the 1870s, and by the dawn of the twentieth century, the corporation had firmly entrenched itself as the successor to the individual entrepreneur. A study of the backgrounds of 190 of the top business executives in the first decade of the twentieth century reveals that only three percent were poor immigrants or farm boys. The average successful big businessman was profiled as white, Anglo-Saxon, Protestant, city-bred, well-educated, and from a family with high social status and a long-standing interest in business affairs (William Miller, *Men in Business* 1962). In Carnegie's race, that dark horse individualist had now become a nag. Since the odds were better than thirty-to-one that he could prove himself to be the "best" and therefore attain individual glory, the corporate structure called for yet another revision of the success myth, one which broadened the basic definition of what Americans had previously thought of as happiness.

Since the corporate mentality was essentially an update of the feudal mentality, it forever destroyed for Americans the unified dream of an ideal garden where fruit could be grown, picked, and eaten by any individual who made the effort. In fact, the whole American tradition of hard work and the struggle to the top was undermined by the two most essential features of the corporation. First, highly efficient and quick production methods made it unnecessary for people to work long hours each day, and work was therefore less of a social and cultural imperative. Between 1850 and 1950, for example, the average laborer lopped thirty hours a week off his work schedule with no loss in standard of living. Secondly, the principle of standardization which is the cardinal rule of modern business methods extended itself to employees, too, creating workers who were frequently divorced from the products they produced and the business that they did. The corporation's demand for conformity introduced the widespread use of heavy batteries of personality and preference tests to select highly "normal" people for its ranks. "Rugged individualists" were carefully screened out. Because of this, success today can only be defined by many people in terms of what they do *off* the job.

Thus though the new myth of the corporation offers the promise of material comfort and economic stability for all, it offers real profits to only a few and emotional riches to almost none. As a result, twentieth-century American success mythology fragments into a *series* of mythologies which define riches as a satisfaction of psychological rather than material needs. A scattershot look at some of the modern spokespersons for the revised myth of success will perhaps make this more clear.

One of the great best-selling books of our century is Dale Carnegie's *How to Win Friends and Influence People* (1936). It is a self-improvement handbook designed to make the reader a more pleasant and popular person by improving his or her skills in communication and human relationships. The book jacket urges: "Read it and improve your personality, secure your happiness, enhance your future and increase your income." Inside Carnegie glibly outlines "Six ways to make people like you," "Twelve ways to win people to your way of thinking," "Nine ways to change people without giving offense or arousing resentment," and "Seven rules for making your home life happier." This advice ranges from, "Become genuinely interested in other people," to, "Read a good book on the sexual side of marriage." His underlying assumption about the human condition seems to be much akin to that of Andrew Carnegie (who is no relation, incidently)—that there is a jungle out there and that most people use animal instincts in order to survive. But his solution is quite different. Rather than joining the jungle, Dale outlines ways to: first, conquer aggressive tendencies which might make one abusive and abrasive to one's fellows; and second, disarm the aggressions in others. "Smile" (rule number two of the first six) is a sure-fire way to accomplish both these things.

Just as Alger's story formula achieved credence by its constant though varied repetition, Carnegie gives his advice the posture of truth by the inclusion of testimonials made by hundreds of graduates from his very popular Institutes. The book is filled with documentations intended to show that Carnegie's principles really work. One man, for example, whose spouse had typed him as a sourpuss, forced himself to smile at her every day for two months. He found that: "This changed attitude of mine has brought more happiness in our home during these two months than there was during the last year." And at the office, this principle seems to work even better, for says this same man: "I find that smiles are bringing me dollars, many dollars every day."

How to Win Friends... is filled with testimonials such as this. Dollars may flow in by heeding Dale's advice, but it is self-assurance and congeniality which replace big bucks as the definition of success here.

The Ideal American is no longer the man who works *for* himself, but the one who works *on* himself.

And it is not just Dale Carnegie who has promoted non-material self-enrichment in this century. Over twenty years prior to the publication of *How to Win Friends...*, Russell H. Conwell, minister, writer, lawyer, schoolmaster and self-proclaimed "leader of men," had also seen that upward mobility was a concept which could be applied more broadly than just to the world of work and that the American Dream had very little to do with the land (now raped by the corporation) and everything to do with the self. In his famous lecture entitled "Acres of Diamonds" (published in book form in 1915), which he delivered nationwide, Conwell proclaimed that only plunderers seek riches in exotic places. "Your wealth is too near to you," he said. "You are looking right over it." For Conwell believed that each person had "acres of diamonds" in his or her own backyard. "The idea is that in this country of ours every man has the opportunity to make more of himself than he does in his environment, with his own skill, with his own energy, and with his own friends." Each individual was a mine of untapped physical and mental resources which the powderkeg of will power could blow open and unleash. Once this process had taken place, material riches would probably follow. But the greatest reward lay in the construction of a better self.

V. *More Recent Revisions*

From its beginnings through the early twentieth century, then, the American success myth has been orchestrated around five basic beliefs which have served as recurring motifs: 1) American democracy allows its citizens to rise above any limitations into which they may have been born; 2) hard work brings riches and physical comforts; 3) these rewards come to those who are deserving of them (virtuous), and who 4) have the drive and ambition to attain them plus 5) a modicum of good luck. Out of these motifs, authors have been able to compose their own original and unique scores which give us insights into the prevailing popular attitudes, beliefs, and values of past times. Sometimes the notes of one motif are sounded more loudly than another, and the melody of one time period may have a different rhythm than another. But the same basic motifs continue to be played and replayed well into our own time, reflecting the philosophical revisions and social revolutions which our society experiences. Success literature continues to serve as a mirror of American change.

Overcoming the limitations of one's background, for example, is a major theme in John T. Molloy's 1975 best-seller *Dress for Success*. His advice is cautious, for he acknowledges that "successful dress cannot put a boob in the board room, but incorrect dress can definitely keep an intelligent able man out." Like Dale Carnegie, Molloy is fond of numbers and offers his readers "Sixteen Ways to Look Right Without Effort," and "Sixteen Dress Rules That Always Pay Off," one of which is never to wear green. While a man's ability and ambition are definite motifs tied to Molloy's dress code, rugged individualism (at least in terms of color preferences) is not!

Michael Korda's vision of *Success* (1977) is almost a direct reversal of the ethics promoted by the Puritans and Ben Franklin. He certainly offers a new angle on riches and the elect. "People say that luxury and comfort and money are bad for the soul," writes Korda. "I don't believe it. Nothing is better for the soul than having what you want, and anybody who can become rich and comfortable and doesn't is a damned fool."

Korda's contempt for Puritanism is exceeded only by his contempt for do-gooders. He concedes that "personal success does not absolve us of our responsibility as members of the larger society, and ought not to separate us from a reasonable interest in the fate of others." But he contends that "we owe it to ourselves to enjoy life.... Why shouldn't we want to live better, drive a better car, eat caviar, enjoy ourselves as much as we can in the time we have left to us?" As far as responsibility goes, Korda argues that what might be perceived as ego and self-aggrandizement are really "desires for responsibility," and that people who seek enjoyment attain success more readily than those who approach it as an exercise in self-sacrifice. Some of Korda's maxims which would shake Ben Franklin's bones include: "Money comes first," "Greed pays off," and "Go for the jugular."

All of which is very manly advice. But the success myth has been flexible enough to adapt to women, too. During the height of American women's return to the workforce, Marabel Morgan's *The Total Woman* (1973) advised women that they need not pursue a career in order to be happy. Like Russell Conwell, Morgan believed that riches could be found closer to home. Being totally adored by one's spouse is the treasure awaiting women who follow the advice given in her book or attend the Total Woman Seminars. Her formula for creating a happy husband is as easy as measles to catch: "accept, admire, adapt, appreciate." Franklin would like the book, for it contends that if one inhibits self-interest and thinks of others, riches will follow. Dale Carnegie would like it too, for it is filled with testimony from satisfied disciples. Writes one graduate of the Total Woman course:

> [I am] in heaven—a beautiful suite overlooking the Atlantic Ocean in the heart of San Juan—new, gorgeous luggage in my closet, with the sweetest guy in the world as my companion. That course is powerful stuff! "Nothing's too good for my honey!" Bob says.

Helen Gurley Brown, former editor of *Cosmopolitan*, also emphasizes that being nice and thinking of others are important elements in the success formula for women. She would never advocate going for the jugular. "Not helping simply means you are dumb. Your head is wrong. 'Nice' girls finish first," she writes.

But she also argues that "A job...is the means by which you are going to become a Big Winner and have life's riches." Brown's *Having It All* (1982) maintains:

> Rich or poor, you have a better chance of keeping him—and keeping him *interested*—if you *belong* to something or someone besides him. Most men these days love your paycheck....

Despite the fact that Brown's success book was one of the first to specifically address itself to women, she follows the same basic formula as her male predecessors. Brown aims her book at that segment of the female population she calls "mouseburgers"—women who are not pretty, who do not have a high I.Q., are not well-educated, don't come from a good family background, and have no other noticeable assets—and tells them that it doesn't matter where they start. What does matter is *that* they start, and that they *hang in*. Deprivation can be an asset, she argues, because it creates drive. Being forced to work harder and do more than one's share brings rewards. Sounding more like a Puritan than the editor of *Cosmopolitan*, Brown counsels: "If you give, you get. If you work hard, the hard work rewards you."

But contradictory evidence abounds. In its June 17, 1991 issue, *U.S. News* reported that only three out of every 100 top executive jobs in the United States are held by women, that women earn seventy-two cents for every dollar that men earn, and that the percentage of women in the work force is actually decreasing. Figures are even lower for other minorities.

Do women and minorities have a different view of success? Or do their gender and color differences pose obstacles to sharing the beliefs of the myth? Writing in the Spring 1991 issue of Bowling Green State University's alumni magazine, a black female graduate with a 3.0 average and an admission into graduate school sounds much like her success story predecessors when she states her belief that "succeeding does require a person to be open to new challenges and to take the initiative. Nothing comes by being passive. Good things really do come to those who are willing to work hard for them." Yet *U.S. News* notes that more and more women are either lowering their goals or dropping out of the work force altogether, "because the closer they move to the top, the less certain they become that the pinnacle of the men's world is the worthiest of goals."

Eight years earlier than *U.S. News,* journalist Richard Louv noted that a different drummer had provided a new beat in the orchestra of American success. And he was nothing like Horatio Alger. Instead of marching young men and women off to large cities to find their fame and fortune, this drummer was leading them back to small town America, small-time businesses, and a down-scaled definition of success. In *America II: The Book that Captures Americans in the Act of Creating the Future* (1983), Louv notes that during the early 1980s, 600,000 new businesses were being started annually, many of them run out of a person's home or garage. The pattern in this second America, Louv claims, shows a nostalgic preference for nineteenth-century cottage industry work habits and a search for a lifestyle akin to "what Norman Rockwell painted."

Those happy housewives which Mr. Rockwell painted are just what Betty Friedan asked American women to give a second look in her 1963 best-seller *The Feminine Mystique.* This book (which is often credited as having launched the feminist movement) urged women to take their own risks and stop defining themselves by their husbands' successes. But Friedan's *The Second Stage* (1981) contends that having it all may demand a superwoman who may not really exist. It questions whether following the role models set by men is healthy and acknowledges that dressing for success is easier than changing its definition. *The Second Stage* likewise acknowledges the need for both men and women to break out of old molds and remove the "disguises" which bar them from real fulfillment. An informant (not to be confused with the disciple of the formula success book) asks:

> Do women locked in excessive reaction against female powerlessness...deny themselves certain real strengths as women, and become doubly passive and acquiescent to the excessive rigidities of masculine careerism, exchanging that despised female powerlessness for today's ever more desperate male powerlessness, under the uniform of success?

The shifts in population to smaller towns, the rise in cottage industry, and the apparent disenchantment of women with the world of work would seem to indicate that more and more Americans are once again looking for riches closer to home. Whether the trend represents a real search for a different set of values and beliefs or is merely a nostalgic looking back at beliefs we seem to have lost remains to be seen. What does seem clear is that the myth of American success is once again in flux.

Perhaps you, too, dear reader, hear the beat of a different drummer in this long orchestration of the myth of American success. If so, then why are you sitting in an uncomfortable room reading this long, boring article? Why did you pay good money to purchase this book? Do you believe that your hard work will pay off? Do you believe that a higher education is your chance to rise above the fate to which you were born

Endless Love Will Keep Us Together: The Myth of Romantic Love and Contemporary Popular Movie Love Themes

Crystal Kile

In 1936, Fred Astaire sang "The Way You Look Tonight" to his true love, Ginger Rogers in Swing Time. *Fred won Ginger and the song won an Oscar. In 1956, Gordon MacRae and Shirley Jones in* Carousel *sang a duet of "If I Loved You" and fell in love on their first date. In 1961, Richard Beymer fell in love with Natalie Wood at first sight in* West Side Story *and the two later confirmed their love in the lovely "One Hand, One Heart." Love and love songs—it's an old story. Crystal Kile writes of the connection in movie songs of the 1980s and early 1990s, but as Kile herself suggests, and as the other articles in this section of our book make clear, American myths and their expression in popular artifacts almost always have a long history.*

The myth of romantic love is probably the most common and universal myth of American popular culture. It drives the self-consciousness of our adolescence, the anxieties of our young adulthood, the traumas of our middle years and the loneliness of our old age. Our belief in the holy grail of the perfect partner is the subject matter of a majority of our songs and the central storyline of most of our movies and television shows. The belief is everywhere and the fact that about 90 percent of Americans marry at least once suggests that our faith in the belief that one true love is the key to human happiness is as strong as ever.

Kile's article shows that the myth of romantic love has ancient origins but, in the form we are most familiar with, it is a more recent belief than some of the other myths we have examined. She also shows that love songs, like so many popular artifacts, have more complicated messages than we might at first assume. Kile's method of discussion and vocabulary is somewhat more formal and academic than most of the other articles in this book. For some, this may make the reading a bit difficult. Stick with it, however. The topic is of crucial significance in the study of popular culture and Kile's analysis not only describes how the myth is present in some recent popular music, but draws interesting conclusions about how those love songs reflect ideas about sex, gender and relationships in contemporary life. You might disagree with some of her conclusions, but a careful reading might also get you thinking and discussing.

If music be the food of love, play on;
Give me excess of it, that, surfeiting
The appetite may sicken, and so die.
That strain again! it had a dying fall:
O' that it came o'er my ear like the sweet sound
That breathes upon a bank of violets,
Stealing and giving odour. Enough! no more:
'Tis not so sweet now as it was before.
O' Spirit of love! how quick and fresh art thou,
That, not withstanding thy capacity
Receivith as the sea, nought enters there,
Of what validity and pitch soe-er,
But falls into abatement and low price,
Even in a minute: so full of shapes is fancy,
That it alone is high fantastical.

Twelfth Night
William Shakespeare

People would not fall in love if they had not heard love talked about.

La Rochefoucauld

Don't threaten me with love, babe.

Bessie Smith

"You are nobody until somebody loves you," "Love makes the world go 'round." Don't you want to be in "Puppy Love," "Endless Love," "Love,-exciting-and-new," "Love,-soft-as-an-easy-chair" or "Love-the-one-you're-with"? "Don't you want somebody to love" even though, as the singers tell us, "It hurts to be in love" and "Love Stinks!"? The pervasiveness and the popularity of the theme of romantic love in Western cultural artifacts suggest that the answer is an enthusiastic and emphatic "Yes!!!!" But why?

Little girls' socialization into love begins in the nursery with Barbie brides and Disneyized versions of such tales as "Cinderella." Passing through the rigorous amorous extracurriculars of junior high and high school, expectations colored not just by the romantic experiences of parents, siblings and friends, but also by the pervasive "love offerings" of the various forms of popular culture, the importance of love and romance in our society is perhaps the lesson that adolescents of both sexes learn best. Recent surveys of college students reveal that the "romance culture" that thrives in affiliation with institutions themselves, occupies the center of college life in the minds of the majority of students—especially women. Though important in the lives of both sexes, women, even in the 1990s, remain much more dependent than men on "success" in romantic relationships as a primary source of social identity and validation of social "worth" (Holland and Eisenhardt, especially chapters 11 & 12). While the myth of romantic love means different things to men and women, our culture, especially our popular culture, teaches all of us that love promises much too much to be abandoned lightly.

Succinctly stated, the myth of romantic love in western culture decrees that one only becomes fully "self-actualized"—achieves a full, mature identity and psychic completeness—through choosing a love partner and remaining true to that partner until forces beyond one's control intervene (Harrington and Bielby 131). The search for "true love" is the most important thing in life, for the "true love" relationship promises lifelong companionship, passion and support. Even in the face of the reality of an increased divorce rate during the post-World War II period and a high rate of turnover in "serious" pre-martial and non-marital relationships, we continue to cling to this mythologically central notion that love should be forever. Few couples, even very young ones, begin a relationship, a marriage or decide to cohabitate thinking about divorce or dissolution of the relationship. Instead, we tend to think, "This could be it." To think otherwise would be to step outside the mythologized love ideal in which separation from a lover or loss of a lover is the ultimate tragedy. One of the primary reasons that the film *Ghost* struck such a nerve with movie goers is its assertion that true romantic love is indeed eternal, not just "till death do us part."

Because it is a mode of gendered social organization shrouded in the "mystical" experience of "falling" and "being in love," as inscribed and prescribed by culture myth, what we call "romantic love" is a complex cultural phenomenon. First and foremost, "love" is an emotion. When we speak of cultural myths, we usually conceptualize "myth" as a cultural belief complex based on the *fusion* of emotional and intellectual response to a given subject or cluster of historical events, a fusion that determines our attitudes towards and response to present and future situations. The myth of romantic love, while based *in* Western tradition, is based *on* the liberation of emotion for intellect. As we are initiated into the complex of cultural beliefs about adolescent and adult love relationships, we learn that love into which one "thinks" or "plots" oneself is not "true love." You cannot make a rational decision to be in love. True romantic love is an irrational state into which one falls like a ton of bricks or which strikes one like a bolt of lightening. Love chooses you, not vice versa. Furthermore, the state of "being in love" is constructed in our culture as the ultimate emotional high, the ultimate meeting of human minds and bodies, and the ultimate state of personal fulfillment and bliss. Even in the wake of the so-called sexual revolution, our culture still regards romantic love as the only truly legitimate basis for a sexual relationship outside of or within marriage.

Romantic love and all of the cultural rituals and institutions that are structured by it (e.g., dating, proms, weddings, and, ultimately, the nuclear family) seem so commonsensical and natural to us that it seems strange even to speak of a myth of romantic love. However, upon examining it more closely, the very transparency and centrality of romantic love in our culture demands just such an interrogation and demystification. "Romantic love" is a complex socially constructed ideal, one which seamlessly reproduces itself in our culture from era to era.

The Book of Love (abridged version)

Prior to the advent of cheap printing and the rise in literacy rates in European cities that attended the beginning of the Industrial Revolution, romantic love was by and large confined to elite groups in society. Historians generally agree that the "birth of romantic love" occurred during the twelfth century at the southern French court of Eleanor of Aquitaine. "Courtly love," the forerunner of "romantic love," grew out of aristocratic play on the feudal power relationship. As described by Capellanus (c. 1180), in the courtly love ritual a woman, usually married and of higher birth than the knight who courted her, took on the role of "lord," while the knight took on the role of "vassal." He declared his devotion to her, curried her favor in various small ways and did her bidding (Holland and Eisenhardt 93-94).

These "courtly" relationships were sometimes adulterous, but the vast majority remained sexually unconsummated. Sanctioned by Eleanor and perhaps even promoted by her, the ideals and rituals of courtly love spread across Europe, celebrated primarily in the ballads of wandering troubadours who rambled the countryside singing of their "romantic" longing for a particular lady fair and recounting great love stories (Holland and Eisenhardt 93-94; Solomon chapter 6). Most contemporary versions of one of the most popular stories of "courtly love," that of the Lancelot, Queen Guinevere and King Arthur "triangle," usually miss the point that while Arthur and Guinivere were man and wife, only Lancelot and Guinivere were "lovers" in the exalted and idealized "courtly" sense of the word (Solomon 56).

The preponderance of evidence in the historic and literary records of the sixteenth and seventeenth centuries indicates that "romantic love" begins to come out of the aristocratic court and into the popular mainstream during the humanist glow of the Renaissance. For example, Shakespeare brought romantic love to the popular Elizabethan stage, most memorably in *Romeo and Juliet* (c.1596). Even so, "romantic love" was not fully integrated into culture at this time. We know that in the sixteenth and seventeenth centuries, medicos, churchmen and contemporary wisdom "firmly rejected romantic passion and lust as suitable bases for marriage" (Stone 17). The aim of marriage was the maintenance or enhancement of both kin groups' social positions, and most marriages were arranged by the couples' families. It is widely speculated that Shakespeare himself married for money. Indeed, in terms of Western history, the codification of romantic love as a socially and culturally approved rationale for choice of a life-partner is a fairly recent innovation. It can be traced back only to the continental Romantic movement of the late 18th and early 19th century, and acceptance of the idea of "falling in love" and "marrying for love" was only fully accepted in much of Europe in the early twentieth century.

In early America, the New England Puritan culture of our European forbears was not on the whole as prudish or anti-sexual as popular stereotypes often suggest. Though not overly concerned with the more baroque aspects of "romantic love," Puritans regarded love and compatibility between a man and woman as a legitimate reason for marriage. Their intimate culture was based on a marriage-centered, procreative sexual ideal. Though Puritans accepted sex as natural and a comfort to both man and wife, they were not comfortable with any sort of eroticism that could conceivably be linked to paganism, idolatry or atheism. In love, as in all things Puritan, consideration of the heavenly kingdom came first. Ideal love in the domain of marriage "symbolically mirrored [the couple's] love of God" (Stone 16). Though a certain diluted Puritan influence on American love culture remained strong well into the twentieth century, the secularization of love in American culture at the end of the eighteenth and into the nineteenth century generally kept apace with the same European Romantic tendency.

When contemporary Americans think of the dominant middle-class culture of the Victorian Period, we usually think of it as an anti-sexual, repressive culture against which libertine Moderns rose up in revolt. A recent line of historical argument has even argued that the Victorians were the "True Puritans." Actually, though, as in Europe, in America, the nineteenth century is a key point of transition in the life of the myth of romantic love. The seemingly contradictory and oft-remarked-upon high "romanticism" of the Victorian era was at least in part influenced by the extension of the increased importance placed on individualism in western culture during the revolutionary and Romantic periods, and it remains rich imaginary fodder for our contemporary love ideal.

While love and sex remained for the most part antithetical during the Victorian era, it is during the nineteenth century that the institution of marriage became more secularized and based on fulfillment of one partner in the other. Even so, one must remember that though women then exercised greater control over the courtship process than they have in the twentieth century, under the eyes of the law and the churches, they were anything but equal partners in marriage. Long courtships involving an "ordeal of self disclosure" (Seidman 60) were designed to assure the middle class Victorian that he or she was affianced to a truly spiritually, morally and mentally kindred spirit. Only when a couple was so matched, according to the middle-class Victorian regime, could the "beneficent power" of sex be invigorating and uplifting (60). At the same time that the culture insisted on marriage as a control on the deleterious effects of eroticism, on "desensualization" of sex, it mandated that marriage be based on "true love" (60). Popular novels of the era such as those issuing from the "cavalier" school of Sir Walter Scott and the "American Charlotte Brontë" school of nineteenth-century women popular domestic and romance novelists such as Augusta Jane Evans, whose *St. Elmo* (1866) still ranks among the most popular novels ever published in the United States (Nye 28), advocated and perpetuated this "spiritual" romantic ideal. Perhaps more familiarly, one finds an excellent illustration of the Victorian love ideal in Louisa May Alcott's portrayal of the courtships and marriages of Meg and Amy March in *Little Women.*

In the early part of the twentieth century, the meaning and place of sex in relation to love, and therefore the meaning of love itself, began to undergo important changes. Slowly, over the first half of the century, romantic love ceased to be defined in strictly "spiritual" terms, and began to be defined in a way that made it "nearly inseparable from the erotic longings and pleasures of sex" (Seidman 4). This shift in the relationship between sex and love was due in no small part to the increased primacy of the individual in the modern world, the incursion of Freudian psychology into popular consciousness, and the heightened degree of independence from kin and homeplace, as well as increased social mobility that industrial capitalist culture increasingly afforded men, and, to a lesser degree, women. More so than in the Victorian period, "falling in love" represented the bonding of two individuals, and emphasized an increasingly sharp demarcation between the public and private spheres of our culture. Sexual attraction came to be regarded as the underpinnings of love, and thus the basis for lasting relationships (83). As our culture's euphemism of choice for sexual intercourse, "making love," indicates, physical pleasure came to be constructed as a key part of the overall transcendent emotional experience of being in love.

There is no question that from the late 1960s on, graphic, explicit representation and expressions of (hetero)sexuality have pervaded almost every corner of American society, but even at the height of the much-hyped sexual revolution of the sixties and seventies, the myth of romantic love remained central in our cultural discourse. We need only look to the movies to see that this is true. It can be argued that the texts from which the movies were derived are artifacts of the 1950s more than of the 1960s, but *West Side Story* (1961) and *Dr. Zhivago* (1965) were two of the most popular films of the decade. In *The Graduate* (1967), one of the great sixties anti-hero films, recent college graduate Benjamin Braddock is redeemed not through gratuitous sex with Mrs. Robinson, but by the love of Mrs. Robinson's daughter Elaine. In 1968 Franco Zefferelli's *Romeo and Juliet* portrayed the young couple's tragic love in such a way as to resonate with contemporary generational conflict.

Humphrey Bogart and Ingrid Bergman in the movies' most memorable celebration of the myth of romantic love, *Casablanca*. When the movie played in 1943, its love song, "As Time Goes By," was number one on the charts for more than a month.

The equally tragic *Love Story* (1971), a runaway hit based on Erich Segal's best selling novel, combined the best of the "girl-from-the-wrong-side-of-the-tracks" story and the Romeo and Juliet story into one of the great four-handkerchief movies of all times. When it aired on network television in 1972, 62% of all households watching TV in America that night were tuned in (Whetmore 176). Unlike Romeo and Juliet, Oliver's (Ryan O'Neal) and Jenny's (Ali MacGraw) love defies and overcomes the reprobation of Oliver's wealthy, patrician parents and the financial hardship that it incurs. They are becoming fairly well established in their life when Jenny falls ill and dies from a rare form of leukemia. Jenny's last words to Oliver: "Love means never having to say you're sorry." Since "Oliver's" voice-over narration frames the action of the film as an extended flashback ("What can you say about a twenty-five-year old girl who died?"), *Love Story* then becomes a story about the importance of living life to its fullest, about the importance of love to a full life, and about giving oneself over to love whenever and wherever it presents itself. True lovers know no regrets.

As fully exploring one's sexuality became an almost requisite rite of passage/duty for many middle-class Americans and was widely touted as an avenue for self-discovery in American popular culture through the seventies and early eighties, we continued to keep the ideal of romantic love alive. For example, such phenomena as the relationship pattern of pre-marital sexual monogamy nod toward romantic love. If anything, the popularity of traditional weddings, even among couples who have lived together prior to marriage, has increased during the past fifteen years. Even as popular culture representations of romantic love became increasingly sexualized during this period, sex was never wholly de-romanticized. Conversely, even with the much touted "return to romance" that has supposedly more recently accompanied the AIDS epidemic, romantic love has not become wholly de-sexualized. One need only look to the popularity of steamy "supercouple" romance storylines on soap operas or to the "Silhouette Desire" line of romance novels to see that this is the case. One need only turn on the radio or MTV.

Silly Love Songs

Top-40 love songs are intensely powerful and rich mythological nuggets. In them we find in microcosm our culture's ongoing discourse about romantic love. In the typical pop love song, the proscribed brevity of the form combines with the intense emotional affectiveness of music and the constructed emotional ultimacy of romantic love to create an almost orgasmic, ecstatic "perfect love moment" or a moment of "perfect romantic despair" over love. Even in the age of MTV when most popular love songs are packaged and sold to the listener in a highly visual format that often incorporates musical artists' performances within surreal and/or classical narrative frames, love themes from popular movies historically perform better than any other type of love song. One possible explanation for this is that these songs recall the cinematic "perfect moments" that they accompany within richly developed romantic narratives into which the listener has already projected him/herself in the eroticized context of the voyeuristic viewing ritual. The song thus resonates doubly in the "real world," and it resonates more richly on an associative level than do most songs accompanied by specially produced three-minute videos. The explicit co-option of well-loved films into music video, e.g., the use of narrative and visuals that explicitly recall *Rebel Without A Cause* in Paula Abdul's "Rush, Rush" video, as well as the casting of Keanu Reeves in the "James Dean" role, illustrate video artists' and directors' consciousness of the power of immediately recallable cinematic narratives.

Let us now turn to an examination of a series of movie-bound love songs and songs about love that topped the *Billboard* Hot 100 chart during the period 1981-1991. Individually, these songs have launched thousands of wedding receptions, themed thousands of proms and become "our song" for millions of couples. If you regularly listen to adult contemporary or soft-rock radio, chances are that you know all the words to them. Through analysis of these doubly resonant culturally inscribed texts, we can learn not only how the myth of romantic love is constructed and perpetuated in our culture, but about the ways in which the myth of romantic love is tied up in the social construction of our gendered social identities.

"Say you'll never love another, stand by me all the while"

"The Ten Commandments of Love"
The Moonglows, 1958

During the late summer and early fall of 1981, the theme for *Endless Love,* a Romeo and Julietish tale starring Brooke Shields and Martin Hewitt, topped the charts for nine consecutive weeks, becoming the bestselling single in the history of Motown records. Penned by Lionel Richie and performed by Richie and Diana Ross, it is an almost quintessentially perfect love song. A lovers' ode of absolute devotion to one another, "Endless Love" is on one level a textbook illustration of the fantasy ideal at the heart of the myth of romantic love. At the same time, though, the song hints at a paradox built into the heart of the myth of romantic love, namely, that no love can live up to it.

As they rise and fall, trade phrases and intertwine with and above the lush orchestration, Ross' and Richie's voices literally seem to make love at the same time that they sing of it. The emotional impact of the phrasing and intonations of the singers' delivery combined with the lyrics themselves creates a chimeric impression of this "endless love" as the ultimate merging of the spiritual and the physical. Following the gendered conventions of romantic love, Richie takes on the role of more experienced male lover and makes the overture: "My love, there's only you in my life, the only thing that's right." Ross answers, her voice lightly-spun, high and delicate: "My first love, you're every breath that I take, you're every step I make." Throughout the song they skillfully work trite phrases like "You will always be my endless love," "I'll hold you close in my arms, I can't resist your charms," "I'll be a fool for you," "No one can deny this love I have inside" and "Two hearts that beat as one, our lives have just begun" into a popular masterpiece. Though it would have been easy for this song to slip into absolute banality, the bittersweet-angsty edge of yearning in the intensity of emotion of

Richie's and Ross' voices lend "Endless Love" a strangely unrequieted quality. In the movie, the young lovers are forcibly separated for years by her parents after Hewitt's character accidentally burns down her family's home. They are reunited, but soon part forever of their own free wills. In the song, this "imperfection" of endless love is left unspoken, but is subtly implied.

In contrast to the abstract perfection of love celebrated and mourned in "Endless Love," the mythic aspect of romantic love celebrated in "Up Where We Belong," the love theme from *An Officer and A Gentleman* (1982) is the power of love to overcome very real adversity. Performed by Joe Cocker and Jennifer Warnes, this song lodged in the top 10 for six weeks during the late fall of 1982, spending three of those weeks at number 1, and went on to win the Academy Award for best song. There is nothing at all ephemeral or sentimental about the song's plodding verses and deliberately swelling and soaring choruses. The implication is that love is an anchor, a security bind between two people, the essence of stability.

More explicitly than in the case of "Endless Love," the lyrics of "Up Where We Belong" encapsulate the plot of the movie that it accompanies. In *An Officer and A Gentleman* a young, working-class man (Richard Gere) and woman (Debra Winger) trapped in dead-end lives try to improve their prospects for success: he by becoming a naval officer, she by latching onto him, or, initially, any naval officer, as a husband. The plot follows the ups and downs of the basic romance formula. In the triumphant climax of the film, their romance apparently over, Gere, in dress whites, in a scene similar to that he would play some eight years later with Julia Roberts at the end of *Pretty Woman*, strides into the factory in which Winger is working, takes her in his arms and carries/leads her out of the factory as "Up Where We Belong" swells in the background and they ride off into the sunset. Life is hard, Joe Cocker sings raspily, "the road is long"; but, sing Warnes and Cocker together, "love lifts us up where we belong...far from the world below, up where the clear winds blow." Their voices do not intertwine so much as reinforce one another. In the context of the movie, the song reinforces the ideal of love as a power that will allow the characters to escape painful pasts once and for all, and the idea that success and happiness are functions of love.

"Woman needs man, and man must have his mate..."

"As Time Goes By," 1931

The drama of Phil Collins' "Against All Odds," the theme for the 1984 movie of the same name, recalls that of "Up Where We Belong," but stresses more strongly the theme of romantic love and the "possession" of a woman as the source of male identity. In the film, a down-on-his-luck ex-jock (Jeff Bridges) accepts the job of tracking down an ex-teammate's girlfriend (Rachel Ward) who has fled to Mexico. In the music video, which was more popular than the movie, Phil Collins is cast strangely as the repentant lover, a man absolutely howlingly shattered by the departure of his beloved. "You're the only one who really knew me at all," he sings, "Your coming back to me is against all odds, it's the chance I've got to take." This solipsistic psychodrama of male desire and female betrayal (e.g., "I wish that I could make you turn around, Turn around and see me cry") occupied the top ten for ten weeks and rode the top of the charts for three weeks in the Spring of 1984. It was displaced from the number 1 spot by Lionel Richie's "Hello," a similar emotional statement of masculine romantic and sexual desire.

It is important to emphasize the "masculinity" of many popular love songs, especially those connected to popular movies, because all things "romantic" are so often stereotyped as feminine. The predominance of patriarchally-coded masculine address in love songs, especially those from films, presses the question of who possesses the real power in the romantic relationship. The gender relationships illustrated so transparently in movie-related love songs substantiate the argument that although the romance game is a higher stakes affair for women than for men, men still wield emotional and sexual control of the relationship. This is treated unproblematically in most popular artifacts. Phil Collins and Lionel Richie actively speak, seek love, and/or attempt to regain lost love, while contemporary popular women singers like Whitney Houston are relegated to the passive role of "[Wanting] to Dance With Somebody Who Loves Me" or "Saving All My Love For You," of waiting to be activated into love, as it were.

Even though stereotypical representations of women as nymphomaniacal temptresses, obsessive lovers, love objects or "love goddesses" are very popular in the movies and in songs, videos and television shows, there remains in our culture a significant popular taboo on women as romantic instigators. In the popular romance genre, women who are somehow "active" in the pursuit of romance are more often than not portrayed in a three-way relationship in which two women, one of whom usually fails to live up to our dominant culture's ideal of "femininity," battle one another for the love of one man. The message implied in such scenarios is clear: romantic relationships with men are to be valued over all else, especially relationships with other women. Just as in romance novels, soap operas and love songs in general, which to varying degrees flourish in an almost wholly female-centered popular subcultures, and as in fairy tales, in movie love songs, the model of traditional gender relations is upheld.

Many love songs sung by men provide an interesting counterpoint to much heterosexual male-directed pornography, the difference being that when romantic love, not sex, is foregrounded in a film or song, men's control of the relationship is depicted as flattering, reassuring or comforting rather than threatening. In John Hughes' teen-cult movie *The Breakfast Club* (1985), Judd Nelson portrays a stereotypical "bad-boy-with-a-heart-of-gold" who, over the course of a Saturday detention, tames one of the high school's "suburban Princesses" (Molly Ringwald) by insinuating himself into the role of her omnipotent, mind-gaming confessor. In a sexually and romantically ambivalent scene at the end of the movie, Ringwald's character gives him one of her diamond-stud earrings to wear. The future of their relationship is left very much up in the air, but the mark that he has left on her is very clear. As Simple Minds sings the hit "love theme" from the movie, "Don't You Forget About Me," a song that hit number one on the charts in early May 1985 and lurked in the Top Ten for eight weeks, the voice of the male singer resonates quite deliberately with the words, actions and motives of Nelson's character. "Don't you try to pretend, It's my feeling we'll win in the end/I won't harm you or touch your defenses: vanity, insecurity," he sings: "...Going to take you apart, I'll put us back together at heart." This song is an excellent example of the sort of strong, controlling patriarchal hand that our culture constructs young women to desire and accept unquestioningly. It is an example of how sex and love elide in our dominant hetersexual male culture, and in many mainstream artifacts, and of the way in which men's pursuit of women is softened by the frame of love.

This dynamic is also aptly illustrated in the 1984 "bumbling-stalker" farce, *The Woman in Red,* in which Stevie Wonder's Academy Award-winning song, "I Just Called to Say I Love You," softens the Gene Wilder character's pursuit of "the woman in red" (Kelly Le Brock). Only in such a milieu could truly dark, obsessive songs about love like "Every Breath You Take" (1983) by the Police and "The One I Love" (1987) by R.E.M. be misinterpreted as "love songs" by many listeners and as such go on to become huge hit songs and videos.

The love songs under consideration here reveal that women and men are constructed by our culture to expect very different things from romantic love, and to interpret the myth of romantic love in different ways. In the duets that we have considered thus far, love has been represented as the sublime or fortifying meeting of minds and bodies, but in both cases each voice seemed to agree unproblematically with the other on the defining importance of romantic love. Such is not the case in the two most popular movie love theme duets of the mid-late 1980s: "Almost Paradise" from *Footloose* (1984) and "(I've Had) The Time of My Life" the Academy Award winning song from the *Dirty*

Dancing (1987) soundtrack. In both of these songs, it is clear that what each partner has found is that special someone, and that the lovers' implied sexual relationship is fulfilling, but closer examination reveals that the female voices are in love with much more: that she, unlike the male voice, is in love with the magic and fantasy of romantic love itself. In "Almost Paradise," the expectations and needs of the lovers as performed by Ann Wilson and Mike Reno are reconciled to the point that both can agree that they are "knocking on heaven's door" in ecstasy, but the fit is much less comfortable in "I've Had The Time of My Life." The song invites female audiences to negotiate patriarchal restraints on female heterosexual desire by imaginatively constructing themselves in an active-passive sexual-romantic, ultimately very conservative, relationship.

Contextualized by the movie and by the video, the listener-viewer knows that the song "(I've Had) The Time of My Life" refers to a hot summer romance, not an "endless love" situation. Set in the early 1960s in a Catskills resort, *Dirty Dancing* revolves around the passionate infatuation that Baby (Jennifer Grey), a young, upper-middle-class woman, develops for the resort dance instructor, an older, highly experienced man played by Patrick Swayze. Baby's sexual initiation under the skillful touch of Swayze's character is at the heart of this movie, a big summer hit with female audiences. "(I've Had) The Time of My Life" works the same fantasy-dynamic that the plot of the movie does. For female viewer-listeners, it legitimizes a somewhat "illicit" sexual liason through not love, but by invoking the possibility of love. The voices of the lovers flirt with the notion of romance à la "Endless Love," but sing against one another in passionate challenge and reassurance. "I've been waiting so long, now I've finally found someone to stand by me," moans Bill Medley. Jennifer Warnes corroborates that, "We saw the writing on the wall as we felt this magical fantasy." Though this is a fleeting relationship, Warnes and Medley sing that "this *could* be love," and then go on to sing together that whatever the case, "they've had the time of [their] life." The song is constructed so as to imply absolute mutual consent to the brevity of the affair alluded to here, but leave the window of possibility open for the affair to work out into something more permanent. The overall effect of the song is to finesse the contradiction of love and somewhat casual sex and neatly implicate the male voice into the female-oriented mythic romantic fantasy of *Dirty Dancing*, a fantasy that remains very much within the patriarchally systemized order of gender relationships.

"I wanna love him So Bad"

The Jellybeans, 1964

How, then, do movie love songs sung by women differ from ones sung by men and from "love duets"? The only really popular examples from the time period under consideration are Madonna's "Crazy For You" from the *Vision Quest* soundtrack (1985), and Terri Nunn and Berlin's "Take My Breath Away," the love theme from *Top Gun* (1986). Both films are very male-oriented and action-oriented, and not surprisingly, especially in the case of *Top Gun,* these love themes prove snug ideological fits with the plot and themes of the movies. "Crazy For You" is a straightforward male fantasy of easy female romantic devotion and sexual surrender. Here Madonna does not play on and sweetly subvert the girl-singer, girl-group tradition as she does in the 1989 song and video, "Cherish." "I never wanted anyone like this," she sings sensuously, "You can feel it in my kiss, I'm crazy for you."

"Take My Breath Away," which won the 1986 Oscar for best song, relies much more on the sheer emotional affect of Terri Nunn's undulating voice than on simple "Crazy For You"-type lyrics. To a degree greater than that of any other song discussed here so far, the success of "Take My Breath Away" was also dependent on MTV support of the song's video, a video which pulled almost all of its visuals from the text of "Top Gun." The "Take My Breath Away" video is virtually a condensation of the film's main romance subplot which centers on the relationship between Maverick (Tom Cruise), the top gun of the title, and Charlie (Kelly McGillis), a strictly-business flight performance analyst with a Ph.D. in astrophysics.

As the film opens, Maverick and Charlie are extremely ambivalent toward one another. As the plot unfurls, the audience sees her resistance worn down by his various displays of prowess and charm. Charlie becomes more "feminine," more responsive to him. "Take My Breath Away" accompanies the painstakingly choreographed and edited consummation of their relationship. In the video as in the movie, the audience sees the characters surrender to and consume one another as Nunn sings of the fatedness of the relationship and conjures with her voice the eroticism of the perpetual constant danger that haunts the life of a warrior, an element of the movie's emotional texture celebrated in the Kenny Loggins hit "Danger Zone." To love is to overcome fear. In the lyrics it is actually a second person, her lover, who "turns to [the singer] and say[s] 'Take my breath away'," but as performed, the singer seems to make the surrender herself, to make this request of a lover. Terri Nunn's voice becomes Charlie's voice.

All of these observations take on added resonance when one considers the hyper-prevalance of phallic and sexual metaphors in *Top Gun.* The intense homosociality of the fighter pilot subculture and of the military in general is foregounded in the film in tandem with the accompanying ideal of predatory male heterosexuality. Charlie is a source of consternation within this microcosm of our dominant culture's "traditional" phallocentric ideal. She is cast not just as a love-object, but as one of the "obstacles" that Maverick must overcome on his dual quest for "Top Gun" glory and for the redemption of his father's name. Sex with Charlie, naturalized within the frame of romantic love, is a critical element in Maverick's recovery of his "manhood" following the ultimate test of his mettle, the crash-death of his best friend. Metaphorically, then, conquering fear is "conquering" the tough woman portrayed by McGillis, taking her breath away. *Top Gun* co-opts a "feminist" character and then deconstructs her using the myth of romantic love as a tool. "Take My Breath Away" takes on the resonances of the whole film and is established as part of a very one-sided, very traditional romantic relationship appropriate to the film's Reagan-era re-romanticizing of the military hero.

Post-Feminist Promises and Courtly Love Redux

Bryan Adams' "(Everything I Do) I Do It For You," the theme from *Robin Hood, Prince of Thieves* (1991) was the bestselling, most popular film-linked love song since "Endless Love," and thus is an appropriate place to begin to conclude this essay. Though it lost its Oscar bid for best song to the theme from *Beauty and the Beast*, "...I Do It For You" spent six weeks at number one during the summer and early fall of 1991. It was the most popular love song in America since iconoclastic singer-songwriter Sinead O'Connor topped the charts two summers before with her tortured and aching rendering of the Prince-penned song "Nothing Compares 2 U." While the final shots of the video that accompanied "Nothing Compares 2 U" made slight allusion to *The French Lieutenant's Woman* (1981), a film based on the John Fowles novel in which a woman commits suicide for the sake of her beloved, "...I Do It For You," like "Take My Breath Away," had the full force of visuals from a major summer movie with a major male star behind it. *Robin Hood, Prince of Thieves,* of course, had six-hundred years of lore about the vaguely "courtly" relationship of Robin and Maid Marian backing the highly romantic, non-sexual, on-screen relationship between Kevin Costner and Mary Elizabeth Mastrantonio.

As Lionel Richie did with "Endless Love," with "(Everything I Do) I Do It For You," Bryan Adams came up with an almost quintessentially perfect love song, a particularly apt power ballad that captures yet another variety of the pure essence of the myth of romantic love. More than any other song considered here, it plays explicitly on the promise of the "noble lover-saviors" archetype that is erected from early childhood as the core of the women's imaginary romantic play and later romantic fantasy life. In the video of the song, as shots of Adams and his band playing and singing in what appears to be a clearing in a medieval

English forest are intercut with heavily edited bits of especially heroic scenes from the film, "Robin Hood," Kevin Costner and Bryan Adams merge into the perfect lover.

This perfect lover is not a strong, silent Lancelot type, but a lover who tells "typical" heterosexual women viewers-listeners what they have been socialized to most want to hear from men. Ironically, since Robin is portrayed here as a dispossessed noble, the "steal-from-the-rich, give-to-the-poor" subtext of the accumulated Robin Hood legend is not foregrounded in the film. Still, it may speak especially clearly to a great number of working women of various classes and feminist stripes. In a similar way, the chaste courtliness of Robin's and Marian's relationship speaks loudly in the age of AIDS. Generous, unselfish, sensuous, brave and articulate, this Robin Hood is the fulfillment of our culture's love promise. Even though women know that the promises "Robin Hood"/ Bryan Adams sings are for the most part empty lines, in fantasy they remain very attractive, due in no small part to the fact that the woman addressed in the song is at least nominally in control of the situation. "I would fight for you, lie for you, walk the wire for you," he sings, "there's nothing I want more" than our love. Look into my heart and eyes, then look into your soul, he tells "Marian"/the listener-viewer, then you will see that we are meant for one another: I would give it all up, I would sacrifice my life for you, for our love: "Everything I do, I do it for you." If only Bryan Adams/Robin Hood could close the wage gap between men and women!

Like "Endless Love," like most of the songs that we have discussed here, "(Everything I Do) I Do It For You" quickly became overplayed and tiresome simply because it gives life in words and music to the reality of the yawing gap that exists between "ideal" *romantic* relationships as they work out in popular stories and songs and romantic *relationships* as they exist on a material day to day basis. At the same time, though, heroic songs of devotion, highly erotic songs of romantic surrender, haunting songs about the loss of love, and all of the other possible musical takes on love help insure the seamless cultural reproduction of the myth of romantic love in perpetua.

The songs and films discussed here represent but a mere drop in the great popular cultural sea of love. Limiting the topic under consideration here to select, very popular movies and movie love themes excluded a number of important issues centered on the myth of romantic love in our culture, but what we find in this limited body of texts is indeed very telling. The most cursory examination of the Top Ten charts reveals that the history of popular love songs in general—not just that of movie love songs—has been and continues to be dominated by men singing about their romantic experiences, their lovers and the ideal of romantic love, and by women who subscribe to this vision. This is a key part of the larger cultural discourse that directs and orders the social existences of women and men in our culture. Even in the 1990s women must conform to the standards of "feminine" behavior, demeanor and attractiveness prescribed by traditional modes of behavior or face social censure and marginalization. While similar standards of "lovability" do exist for men, they are nowhere near as ironclad and restrictive as those demanded of women in our culture. As Paula Kamen reports in her book *Feminist Fatale,* many young women are wary of identifying themselves as "feminist" for fear of "scaring off men." Such is the power of the myth of romantic love.

In what was indeed one of the great chart-weeks ever for the myth of romantic love, the week of May 30, 1964, the top four songs in America according to the *Billboard* Hot 100 charts were The Beatles' "Love Me Do," The Dixie Cups' "Chapel of Love," Mary Wells' "My Guy" and Ray Charles' "Love Me With All Your Heart." As this general discussion of the myth of romantic love and, more particularly, of popular movie love songs of the 1980s and early 1990s has illustrated, few really fundamental changes in our cultural love mythology have taken place since that long-ago, glorious week of radio love. If it has changed at all, the myth of romantic love has evolved in an ameboid manner to encompass and naturalize the increasing rate of divorce and remarriage, and committed non-marital relationship patterns legitimized in American society during the sexual revolution of the sixties and early-seventies and through the eighties. As the descendants of Eleanor of Aquitane and the descendants of her serfs might put it: "Plus ça change, plus reste la même."

Works Cited

Bailey, Beth L. *From Front Porch to Back Seat: Courtship in Twentieth-Century America.* Baltimore: Johns Hopkins UP, 1988.

Harrington, C. Lee and Denise D. Bielby. "The Mythology of Modern Love." *The Journal of Popular Culture.* 24(4) Spring 1991: 129-144.

Holland, Dorothy C. and Margaret A. Eisenhardt. *Educated in Romance: Women, Achievement and College Culture.* Chicago: Chicago UP, 1990.

Kamen, Paula. *Feminist Fatale: Voices from the "twentysomething" generation explore the future of the "Women's Movement."* New York: Donald I. Fine, Inc., 1991.

Nye, Russel. *The Unembarrassed Muse: The Popular Arts In America.* New York: Dial, 1970.

Seidman, Steven. *Romantic Longings: Love In America, 1830-1980.* New York: Routledge, 1991.

Solomon, Robert C. *Love: Emotion Myth and Metaphor.* Buffalo: Prometheus Books, 1990.

Stone, Lawrence. "Passionate Attachments in the West: A Historical Perspective." In *Passionate Attachments: Thinking About Love,* Willard Gaylin, M.D. and Ethel Person, M.D., eds. New York: Free, 1988: 15-26.

Whetmore, Jay. *Mediamerica: Form, Content and Consequence of Mass Communication,* 4th Edition. Belmont, CA: Wadsworth, 1991.

Whitburn, Joel. *Billboard's Top 10 Charts: A Week by Week History of the Hot 100, 1958-1968.* Menomonee Falls, WI: Record Research, Inc., 1988.

Discography

Adams, Bryan. "(Everything I Do) I Do It For You." *Robin Hood, Prince of Thieves, The Original Motion Picture Soundtrack.* PMG/Morgan Creek CS2959, 1991.

Berlin. "Take My Breath Away." *Top Gun, The Original Motion Picture Soundtrack.* CBS CS40323, 1986.

Cocker, Joe and Jennifer Warnes. "Up Where We Belong." *An Officer and A Gentlemen, The Original Motion Picture Soundtrack.* Island CD422842715, 1982.

Collins, Phil. "Against All Odds." *Against All Odds, The Original Motion Picture Soundtrack.* Atlantic CS80152-2, 1984.

Madonna. "Crazy For You." *Vison Quest, The Original Motion Picture Soundtrack.* Geffen CD2-24063, 1985.

Medley, Bill and Jennifer Warnes. "(I've Had) The Time of My Life." *Dirty Dancing, The Original Motion Picture Soundtrack.* RCA CD6408, 1987.

Reno, Mike and Ann Wilson. "Almost Paradise." *Footloose, The Original Motion Picture Soundtrack.* Columbia CD39242, 1984.

Richie, Lionel and Diana Ross. "Endless Love." *Endless Love, The Original Motion Picture Soundtrack.* Mercury CD826277-4,1981.

Simple Minds. "Don't You Forget About Me." *The Breakfast Club, The Original Motion Picture Soundtrack.* A&M CD3294, 1985.

Section

☎ 3 ☎

Icons

This cover from *Newsweek* showing how the Simpsons have become part of the national debate about the American nuclear family.

Introduction
Living in the Material World: The Meaning and Power of Popular Icons

"Strange and hard that paradox true I give,
Objects gross and the unseen soul are one."
Walt Whitman *"A Song for Occupations"*

Objects Gross and the Unseen Soul: Meaningful Objects in Popular Culture

In the opening sequence which begins the successful early 1990s TV hit, *The Simpsons,* we peer through a schoolroom window and discover a tiny forlorn figure laboring away at the blackboard. It's poor old misunderstood Bart, of course, chalking up another afternoon in detention—living out his sentence by writing out a thousand times or more a promise never to repeat his latest sin against authority (e.g. "I will not belch the Pledge of Allegiance," "I will not call my teacher 'Hot Cakes' "). Bart's trapped—stuck indoors and nearly motionless in front of a never-ending litany of words whose repressive, repetitive message has him so bushed he can't even write them in a straight line anymore—his sentences and his spirit are slumped and sliding downward. But then the school bell rings and Bart comes out of his corner a newborn face. Hopping on a skateboard which appears from nowhere (it's there when he needs it) the Bart-man swoops through the heavy double doors at the front of the building as if shot from a cannon and suddenly he's part of the day—zipping into the sky, defying the force of gravity and the grave faces which block his way, wooshing over curbs and around trees and bouncing off the tops of cars. Bart is Belleraphon on his winged horse Pegasus, the Lone Ranger raising a cloud of dust on his mighty steed Silver, Batman using his wonderful toys to crash through skylights and swing through the nighttime air.

Meanwhile, the other members of the Simpson clan are having their own love affairs with magical objects. Daughter Lisa isn't about to play the draggy beat set by her doofus band director—he's left behind impotently ticking his sagging baton as Lisa soars off down the hallway high on the bluesy improvisation of her golden saxophone; Mother Marge and toddler Maggie are at the grocery store where the endless bounty of America is displayed for their choosing, and special machines quickly total the price that everything has (even Maggie gets scanned) so that they can load up the whole haul in one fell swoop in the family station wagon to make their way home (Maggie learning to guide the powerful beast of burden by spinning her own toy steering wheel). Sadsack Homer is stuck in his adult nine-to-five detention at the local nuclear power plant until his bell rings (actually it's the grown-up's version: a whistle blowing) and he hops in the speeding car which will carry him quickly away from his working prison. Once in his car, safety-inspector Homer is completely freed from his responsibilities to anyone except himself—he tosses a glowingly radioactive ingot onto the street.

Free and individual as each Simpson is as each tools around the town in the manner of his choice, the Simpsons are still a family. Their separate paths lead them to the same place, the Simpson home. Charging into the house in a thundering, "get outta my way" stampede, the individual members pounce onto the living room couch to worship at the prime-time altar of television—the electronic hearth which is perhaps the only object powerful enough to transform Homer and Marge and Lisa and Bart and Maggie (and a rail-thin dog and scruffy cat) into *The Simpsons.*

The objects which play such an important role in the opening sequence of *The Simpsons*—Bart's skateboard, Lisa's saxophone, the grocery store where Marge shops (and Maggie learns), the cars which take Homer away from work and bring food home, and the television set which is the family's final stop (and their start)—are not merely objects. Bart's skateboard is not simply a thin plank with four wheels attached which enables him to avoid having to walk home from school; Bart's skateboard is a magical steed which lifts him out of his schoolroom cell, enables him to express his individuality and his absolute contempt for civic order and authority (to ignore sidewalks, pedestrians, signs, streets, buildings, cars) and to bind him together with all those who feel the same way he does about the repressive forces of modern society (i.e., with every other skateboarder who uses *his* precious surfboard-on-land to transcend concrete paths and to shock and amaze and annoy as many work-a-day drones as possible). Bart's skateboard is a special kind of popular object because it is one which calls forth emotional and/or intellectual meanings beyond its physical appearance or use, and because it functions to convey significant "magical powers" upon the people who use it or display it. Bart's skateboard is an icon.

Icons are three-dimensional objects (or two-dimensional images of those objects—e.g. the advertisement of a skateboard in *Thrasher* magazine can be considered an icon because it is a representative of a three-dimensional, meaningful object; Bart's skateboard can be analyzed as an icon even though it is a cartoon displayed on a television screen) which are visible, concrete embodiments of the myths, beliefs, and values which form a culture's mindset. Icons give tangible shape to invisible ideas. Skateboards for example take ideals of individual freedom, the value of mobility (in space and in identity) and the special nature of childhood, and visualizes them for the world to see. Icons, therefore, simultaneously express those ideas and provide additional evidence for their continued force and validity. Skateboards enable their riders to tell us they are free and fast and special and to prove it to us at the same time. A skateboard is a funhouse mirror on wheels.

The term "icon" stems from the Greek word for "image" and is traditionally used to refer to the religious objects developed in late medieval times in eastern Europe as a means of communicating significant beliefs and values of a faith to a largely illiterate population of believers. Traditional icons convert objects into signs that everybody can read—the same way that a traffic sign indicating a "pedestrian crossing," for example, uses a shadow figure outline against a yellow background to convey its message and warning. But traditional icons (and their popular counterparts) are more than mere "signs," however, because they express deep-seated, significant messages of faith, bind believers together in a community or belief, and impart magical powers to those who venerate the icon. A cross or crucifix, for example, is like a traffic sign in that it is a symbolic representation of an idea expressed without words; but a cross or crucifix is also an expression of religious beliefs which unites its owner with others of the same faith and magically ties the individual believer into an intimate relationship with God. A sign is just a signal; an icon is also a talisman.

Popular icons perform similar roles in the realm of secular beliefs and values. The analogy with religious icons helps us to appreciate how vital and important popular icons are in giving a tangible shape to a culture's mind set. Like traditional religious icons, popular icons are meaningful objects which unite those who believe in the icon, express the important elements of the group's beliefs and values, and impart magical powers to the iconic group. Americans are united in a culture-wide obsession with cars. For example, we identify so strongly with our automobiles that buying a car made anywhere except in the good ol' USA is often seen as an act tantamount to treason. And cars act to express our beliefs in individual freedom (everybody should be able to own one to drive wherever and whenever she/he pleases—mass transit for lemmings), material success (cars are a sign of who we are—how much money we make, how sexy we are, how responsible and hardworking), and endless abundance (enough cars for everybody and enough roads to hold them—and a limitless horizon to explore). Cars convey the magical power of mobility upward to those who own them—and help protect other important myths as well, like experiencing all the simple pleasures of a rural existence by living in the suburbs and commuting to work in the city. If cars were simply insignificant (non-iconic) objects designed solely for transportation and nothing else, then there would be no reason they couldn't all look exactly alike, be designed only for fuel efficiency and safety, and built to carry as many people as possible: a non-iconic car would be a taxicab from hell. We demand more from our automobiles because we have—as one of the readings which follows reveals—a "Driving Passion" for our magical, meaningful cars.

All icons share the three characteristics discussed above—they are all a) objects, which b) express important popular beliefs and values, and c) convey "magical" powers upon their defining group. But there are several important distinctions to be drawn among the various types of icons as well. The broadest division is between those objects which have no rule other than to express elements of a popular mindset (they are purely expressive, or **Pure** icons) and those which do something in addition to conveying beliefs (they have a function other than a symbolic one— **Functional** icons). We can also classify popular icons according to the size and nature of the group which accepts the icon and finds it meaningful. Icons which are significant only to a given individual or very small group (e.g. a family) are termed **Personal** icons; objects which have iconic significance to a small community, town, or area are called **Local** icons; and those representations of the beliefs and values of a significant cultural subgroup or of the culture as a whole are labeled **Cultural** icons. These categories cut across each other in a crosshatch fashion to produce a relationship summarized in the chart below:

	Personal	**Local**	**Cultural**
Pure	X	X	X
Functional	X	X	X

The six categories which result can be illustrated in the following manner:

1) **Pure Personal Icons**: Objects which have no function other than to symbolize a meaning important to an individual and the small group immediately surrounding him.
Examples: Tattoos (of a girlfriend/boyfriend's name); family photograph
Use for Students of Popular Culture: Minimal (audience too small) except as clues to identifying more SIGNIFICANT ICONS in the other groups (e.g. a lot of young folks getting tattoos might reflect a powerful surge of romantic love; a lot of family photographs might suggest the nuclear family is back in town).

2) **Functional Personal Icons**: Objects which have a function in addition to their symbolic meaning for an individual or small group

Examples: A baseball player's special homerun bat; a child's security blanket
Use for Us: Same as Purely Personal—i.e. look for trends/patterns. Also—often useful in understanding and revealing beliefs in an imagined setting (see "Imaginary cultural icons" below) here we can note that an examination of Indiana Jones' whip, for example, can help us understand the values of individual freedom, cunning, and skill which the movie expresses as well.

3) **Pure Local Icons**: Objects which have no function other than to symbolize a meaning or belief important to a small community or town
Examples: Statue of city founder; fraternity rocks.
Use: Accurate, straightforward, examples of mindset characterizing the community. These icons are especially useful in discovering fundamental cultural beliefs and values being translated into a local forum—e.g. that statue of Joe Founder is also reflective of American myths of individual freedom, the frontier, exploration.

4) **Functional Local Icons**: Objects which have a use in addition to their symbolic role of representing beliefs and values meaningful to a small community, group, or town.
Examples: Courthouses; community bars/taverns/nightclubs; Lovers' Lane; logos for local radio stations.
Use: Often valuable guides to the meaning and significance of local rituals as well. Also—the number and intensity of meaning associated with these icons is often an indicator of how cohesive and alive the group identity is at any given time.

5) **Pure Cultural Icons**: Objects with no function other than to symbolize significant beliefs and values meaningful to important cultural subgroups and/or to the culture as a whole.
Examples: American flag; Mount Rushmore; Statue of Liberty; Democratic Donkey and Republican Elephant; Uncle Sam.
Use: Because pure icons are developed solely for the purpose of symbolizing cultural myths, beliefs, and values they are especially useful guides to *the way a culture views itself*—the way a culture interprets its own beliefs and values. Pure icons are the closest to conscious articulations of the cultural mindset and are therefore *very* powerful, *very* obviously exploited and manipulated to bind the culture together, and *very* resonate with emotional meaning. Times of cultural stress result in these icons being replicated, displayed—and attacked. When the Supreme Court ruled that burning the American Flag is an act of political speech they explicitly recognized the iconic significance of the object: you don't merely "burn cloth," you "*say* something"—and the decision

was greeted by a hoard of American flags [tiny and large, cloth and plastic] being displayed as a means of "saying something right back").

6) Functional Cultural Icons: Objects which have a use in addition to the expression of emotional and/or intellectual meanings important to entire culture and/or to sign sub-groups within the culture.
Examples (almost endless): Cars; televisions; telephones; sunglasses; chainsaws; restaurants; videogames; blue jeans.
Use: Because functional icons are objects which are developed for a purpose other than their iconic role, there is an element of unconscious resonance and choice invested in the growth of their meaning and significance. This means that functional icons are more likely to be accurate reflections of what a cultural mindset *is* as opposed to what that mindset *thinks* it is (the latter being expressed in pure iconic forms). This is not to say that pure icons are 'false'—they are just more explicit, conscious, straightforward, permanent and consistent, and this does not mean functional icons are 'more true'—they are just more implicit, complex, likely to reflect inconsistent beliefs and values, more flexible and changing over time (as they come to reflect changes in the popular mindset), and more subtle in the exercise of their symbolizing powers. The analysis of functional cultural icons is especially rewarding, therefore, because it often enables the student of popular culture to unlock meanings and beliefs which are vitally important to the culture's identity and actions even through the culture itself makes no explicit statement of them; functional icons are mirrors that we hold up to a culture, while pure icons are like posed photographs the culture puts forth for us to see it as it wants to be seen.

Functional cultural icons have another dimension which is either lacking or relatively insignificant in local and personal forms. Functional icons receive their meaning and significance because they are used in the same (or similar) ways over a period of time—cars became emblems of individual freedom because they were marketed as such and because more and more people used them to increase personal mobility and choice —and this means that an imagined object which undergoes the same repetitive, defining process in a created, fictional environment may very well become iconic in its own realm and for its audience. Thus we can speak of "Imaginary or Fictional Cultural Icons" and use these to unlock meanings present in the created environment and, therefore, within the mindset of the audience which finds that creation appealing.

A very simple example would be the white and black hats in Westerns which were used as iconic representations of "good" and "evil"; a more complex example from the same created environment is found in the Westerns' use of the railroad train as an icon of white civilization and progress penetrating and conquering the savage wilderness. As trains came to represent cultural beliefs in exploration, movement and the frontier within the context of fictional Westerns, the meanings thus acquired fed similar associations with real trains so that railroads have often assumed similar functional iconic identities in the world of actual experience as well. This is an exceedingly complex process (and the movement is not unilateral) but what is important now is that we recognize that icons in created environments can help us in understanding the meaning and appeal of both the story form of which they are a part and of the icon's real-life counterpart. Functional cultural icons from television—objects which gain special significance and meaning through their repeated use each week—have gained such formal acceptance as important barometers of cultural myths, beliefs, values, and tastes that several have found a place in the Smithsonian Museum. Fonzie's black leather jacket (which gave him magical powers on *Happy Days* such that he merely had to snap his fingers to have every teenage girl in the vicinity swooning with lust), Archie Bunker's chair (his throne on *All in the Family*—placed smack in front of his iconic television, of course, and a visible reminder of everything Archie was and stood for—old fashioned, overstuffed, cocksure of himself in his own protected cocoon, yet warm and rumpled and comfortable all the same), and the starship *Enterprise* (*Star Trek*'s wagon train to the endless frontier) are all "imaginary icons" made real by their embodiment of issues and beliefs important to us as a culture. And thus each finds a significant place alongside The Spirit of St. Louis and the Model T—significant objects all.

The use of icons in the arts in such an important, revealing manner suggests that we should be alert to the relationships icons have with all of the other rooms in the House of Popular Culture as well. Icons express and visualize the myths, beliefs, and values in the Foundation and Basement, but they are also frequently associated with heroes (cars and Henry Ford, telephones and Alexander Graham Bell), celebrities (Michael Jackson's silver glove, Cher's tattoos), stereotypes (nerds and eyeglasses, Japanese tourists and cameras), and rituals (wedding rings, wedding cakes, wedding dresses, etc.) as well. Because icons are such tangible, concrete representations of the cultural mindset they are often a very useful place to begin the analysis of more complex expressions. The meaning of a hero or ritual or story formula can often be "unlocked" if we examine the associated icons first and then see if we can find the same beliefs and values being expressed in other ways as well.

Red, White, and Blue—Identical, Yet You: The Special Character of American Icons

As we have discussed previously in our treatment of American myths, beliefs and values there is one especially significant conflict or complexity which runs throughout the history and evolution of the American cultural mindset. Essentially, this ongoing struggle is waged between the competing ideals which lie at the heart of the Great American Experiment: Individual freedom on the one hand (with its associated values of independent movement, power and identity) vs. Democracy (with its associated stress upon group responsibilities, stability, citizenship, and majority rule). The conflict is centered around the question of how everyone can be treated exactly the *same* (Democracy) and yet permit each person to be as different and powerful as his choices and abilities enable him to become (Individual Freedom). As Phil Patton argues in his book about American icons, *Made in U.S.A.* (1992):

> There has always been a conflict between the pursuit of individual happiness and the equalizing factors of democracy. The equalization makes the magnification of the individual possible, but the pursuit of individual aggrandizement threatens democracy—that is the antiphony played out over American history.

The importance of recognizing and understanding this fundamental conflict at the heart of the American mindset cannot be overstated. It is perhaps the struggle between competing ideals of Individual freedom and Democracy which is most definitive of the American character—more vital than any expression of any single myth or belief could ever be. The "antiphony" Patton speaks of as the fundamental character of American history is also expressed in all elements of the nation's popular culture as well. We'll find heroes representing one side or the other, rituals which allow us to act out our beliefs in the contrasting ideals, and story formulas whose central purpose is to examine and resolve this great conflict. It is not at all surprising then that we should find the antiphony expressed as a characteristic of American icons as well.

American icons reflect the belief and value of democracy because they are mass produced and made equally available to all who can afford to purchase them. American icons bear the unifying stamp of the assembly line—interchangeable parts, an emphasis on quantity over quality, and identical packaging and promotion—and thus help ensure that mass consumption has the same marks of equality and fairness. But American icons are also expressions of individual freedom as well—American objects are marketed as signs of our individual identities. Here is Patton again on the unique balance between competing ideals which marks American icons throughout history:

> The irony of the American object is that it asserts the power and potential of the individual while possessing the generality of the type....To heighten the power of the individual is a very different thing from "democratizing the object." Democratizing is the means

to the end: distinguishing the individual from the uniformity of the demos and making himself wealthier or happier or more stylish than his fellows, or at least to be the first—first on the draw, first to stake his claim, first on his block with a dishwasher or color TV. To keep up with the Joneses implies Mr. Jones' initial effort to stand out.

The history of American icons is marked by a pattern in which an initial fever of democratization is gradually balanced by and an increasingly prevalent element of individuality. Cars move from the standard, identical, functional Model T's to the marketplace of different brands, colors, designs and sizes defining today's crowded consumer-oriented autoworld; skateboards move from wooden crate boards with metal wheels to the customized, stylized models of today; and blue jeans begin with no more individual definition than their name implies (they were "blue" and they were "jeans") to become the Guess Who Bugle Boy Calvin Klein wonders of individual identity they sell us today.

One way to study an American icon, therefore, is to examine the object to determine how it may express this vital conflict between the competing ideals of individual freedom and democracy. We should emphasize that not all American icons can be rewardingly analyzed from this perspective—a gun may be more important as an icon of justifiable violence or of technology as protector and savior, for example—but many can be illuminated by such study and the question is complex enough to provide us with significant leads to other angles of analysis. In the course of examining cars as an icon balancing individual freedom and democracy, for example, it is quite likely that we will also see that one aspect of that freedom is defined in the American values associated with mobility and discovery, and one aspect of that democracy is expressed in the way cars often bind families together and help maintain vital elements of rural simplicity in modern life.

The balance often achieved by American icons as they simultaneously embody conflicting ideals and beliefs is one aspect of a broader function performed by significant objects in popular culture. Popular icons—like popular culture in general—help us find order in the midst of the chaos of life, and they provide a comforting, reassuring element of familiarity and predictability in what might otherwise be a bumpy ride indeed. Alvin Toffler has written extensively about the disruptive effects—psychological and sociological—of rapid change (he's termed those disruptive effects *Future Shock*), and popular icons can help soften the blow of all the necessary chaos present in each of our individual lives and in a mass society so technological and pluralist as ours. Icons give us something concrete to hold on to, provide a visible expression of stable beliefs and values, and magically bind us together by displaying our similarities as well as our individual selves. The very characteristic which is often cited as a criticism of popular icons/culture—that of repetitiveness and imitation—is actually an important virtue, for it is the orderly familiarity of these significant objects which make the disorderly strangeness of the new bearable. Icons are anchors which permit a culture to float on the shifting currents of change—without drifting out to sea.

Asking the Right Questions: How to Study an Icon

We have seen that American icons can often be analyzed by examining their relationship to the two specific myths of individual freedom and democracy, but we've found also that as remunerative as this approach may be, there are still other approaches we can take to unlock an icon's significance. In this section we'll broaden our analytical methodology to provide as wide a variety of keys to understanding popular icons as possible with the justification that the more questions we can ask the more the meanings of an icon will reveal themselves to us.

There are essentially five groups of questions which can be asked about popular icons, and we'll examine each set of inquiries by focusing upon their applicability to a study of a great American icon—McDonald's and the Golden Arches.

We should begin by noting the importance of the icon we are about to examine. McDonald's presently employs 1 in every 15 American workers, and it has replaced the Armed Forces as the principal job training organization in the United States. Its primary spokesperson—the world's most unfunny clown, Ronald McDonald—is the second most recognizable figure among school-age children (Santa Claus is #1—but he's been around a whole lot longer), and he's number one among adults. McDonald's itself is the top fast food restaurant in the nation and is the first to establish branches in foreign lands as well. It has been estimated that going to McDonald's has replaced the tradition of the Sunday afternoon drive as a ritualistic experience binding families (and their guts) together. More families eat at McDonald's than anywhere else. McDonald's is a "functional cultural icon" then—it exists for the practical purpose of feeding a whole lot of us very quickly and represents significant beliefs and values as well. But how can we determine which beliefs and values are being symbolized?

1) *Appearance of the Icon*

We can examine the shape, color, and size of an icon for clues to its significance.

The most revealing aspects of McDonald's appearance lie in the way the restaurants are designed to promote speed and efficiency. McDonald's applies basic American techniques of mass production to food service—frying up huge numbers of hamburgers at the same time and garnishing them all simultaneously and identically (special orders do upset the folks at Mickey D's). The radical inventiveness of such a notion is apparent only when we consider the alternative "aristocratic" restaurant in which patrons are served by individual waiters and their orders prepared only when they have been suitably individualized (rare, medium, well done, etc). McDonald's limits the menu to a few items so that speed and efficiency are maximized—choice within strictly imposed parameters speeds up people who might otherwise hem and haw all night and cuts down the complexity of the assembly line process. McDonald's original design selected those putrid colors for the dining areas for exactly the same reasons they limited the menu and put conveyor belts in the back—the colors are designed to be warm and friendly for a period of about 20 minutes, when they suddenly become garish and annoying, driving squatters out into the parking lot when they might otherwise stick around nursing a Coke and clogging up the system. The restaurants reinforce their speed and efficiency with a design which associates them with another powerful icon embodying some of the same values: McDonald's are drive-thrus which welcome cars and their iconic associations as well.

We can see that the appearance of McDonald's is reflective not only of its speed and efficiency but it also carefully balances the opposing ideals of individual freedom and democracy as well. The menu allows choice within limits, the dining area is friendly for a while, and each customer is greeted and served by a friendly McDonald's drone, but then the customer has to carry his own tray and bus his own table.

The golden arches of McDonald's suggest an entrance to hamburger heaven. What's most important about the Golden Arches, however, is the mass-produced familiarity of the design and the food served therein. McDonald's is predictable—we all know what's on the menu, how much things cost, where we go to order, and what each item tastes like—and it is comforting in that predictability. McDonald's represents Americans' interest in speed, efficiency, and mobility but it also makes the dark sides of those beliefs a little lighter—a little more bearable. When our lives are messy and disorderly—when we're travelling, for example—McDonald's is around to straighten things up a bit. A McDonald's in Indianapolis is the same as a McDonald's in downtown New York and thus can bring with it some of the order and security of home. Charles Kuralt has said that "You can find your way across the country using burger joints the way a navigator uses stars" and the power of the iconic McDonald's is that of the Golden Arches it provides to replace the stars shining down on us and protect us so that even no place is like home.

2) *History of the Icon*

When did the icon first develop? What cultural circumstances helped make that development necessary and/or successful? Is the icon associated with a specific individual? Has that individual come to be representative of important myths, beliefs, and values? Where did the icon develop? (Are there specific meanings associated with the area of development?

For example, blue jeans were developed in the Old West and still carry with them Western values of ruggedness, durability, practicality, etc.)

McDonald's history is forever entwined with the fated character of its original owner, Ray Kroc. Kroc didn't invent the notion of mass produced fast food in the 1950s, but, in the great tradition of American go-getters, he knew how to recognize a good idea when he saw it and how to ride it to fortune and fame. Kroc's story is the classic myth-narrative of rags-to-riches, and McDonald's borrows its emphasis upon material success (e.g. over x billion sold, McDonald's "invades" China/Japan/Australia) from its creator. When we eat at McDonald's a little bit of success rubs off on us along with a lot of glutinous sauce: we demonstrate that we can feed ourselves and our families at reasonable prices and we become worthy participants in a tradition of "eating out" which was formerly reserved for the wealthy. After working all day for the boss who can't remember our name what better way to restore self-esteem than going where they do it all for you? We consume conspicuously (in public) and are rewarded by the good feelings we get when we're treated in a friendly, entertaining manner—Ray founded Hamburger University to train his managers in the McDonald's way so that all his restaurants would treat customers in the same special way. At McDonald's everybody is a success, just like millionaire Ray Kroc.

3) *Evolutionary Change in the Icon*

Has the meaning of the icon altered over time? Can changes in appearance be reflective of a changing iconic significance as well?

Cars are especially illustrative of this analytical tool. The "bigger is better" days of giant wings and fenders have been replaced by the compact automobile which now dominates the marketplace. Older know-how of endless abundance has been challenged with increasing force by beliefs urging conservation, and the evolution of this belief is reflected nicely in the changing appearance of our iconic cars.

The most significant change in McDonald's iconic role has also been mirrored in an ongoing alteration of its physical form. McDonald's has sought to expand its market by increasing individual freedom expressed by the restaurant. Thus, the menu has been significantly expanded and a salad bar introduced (more choices) and the architecture of various individual outlets has been altered to meld more naturally with the style characteristic of the surrounding community. Only the golden arches remain constant in some areas—reminding us that we're still in familiar, protected territory.

McDonald's has also mirrored a recent change in American beliefs about proper diet, as well. As Americans became more obsessed with their health and weight through the 1980s they began to stir up a fuss about McDonald's fatty, salt-laden, french-fried, cholesterol-rich fare. McDonald's got defensive at first (Ronald McDonald founded a house to help sick kids and McDonald's went heavy on the Olympic promotions. They seemed to be saying, "We're for good health!"), but finally knuckled under when other restaurant chains began cutting in on their action. Now we've been blessed with McLean Burgers (more expensive but chock full of non-fat filler) and those salad bars. And this same Yuppie social consciousness has been reflected in McDonald's recent elimination of styrofoam packaging and the use of recycled paper.

4) *Iconic Group*

Not all icons have an entire nation in their thrall. Many significant objects are important and symbolic to cultural sub-groups rather than the mass culture at large. We can examine icons, therefore, in terms of the demographic characteristics of their group: age, sex, class, region, etc. Skateboards are icons for young people (mostly males) and an identification of this group helps us know what to look for in the icon as well—e.g. the values and beliefs associated with teenage guys.

McDonald's has always been heavily favored by families—a decent cheap meal that still brings the whole group together in one (bright and entertaining) place. Ray Kroc loathed teenagers in his restaurants (he figured they didn't have much money and made lots of rude noises that drove away the deep pockets of middle-class families), so he attacked the problem from three angles: 1) ban jukeboxes and patrol parking lots to discourage malingerers; 2) promote McDonald's as a family restaurant (clean, quick, cheap, bonding); 3) put "good" teenagers where they belong—behind the counter at minimum wage (or less—Kroc was one of the last holdouts in the minimum wage sweepstakes, using his political leverage for years to gain exemption for minors) where fresh-faced youths could greet older customers and convey all the decent values Americans associate with youth—energy, innocence, enthusiasm and sex appeal.

5) *Exploitation of the Icon*

What do the people who are trying to sell you the icon tell you about its meaning and significance in order to make it appealing? What "magical powers" do they attach to the object? Do other groups borrow the icon and use it in different ways?

McDonald's ads emphasize all the values we've already mentioned—speed, efficiency, equality, entertainment, material success, individual freedom, familiarity and security, health consciousness, youth, energy, mobility, endless abundance (how many served?!), technology as protector and savior (new methods for cooking without fat, dirt, or individual error)—but they also show how McDonald's has sought both to expand its appeal (to the weight and health conscious, to African Americans, to older people) and identify itself with America as a nation. McDonald's is great at borrowing other icons (the Olympic torch and the icons associated with hit movies) to steal some of their mass appeal and they never forget to praise their consumers for demonstrating the good sense to choose McDonald's for their dining pleasure. One of the earliest—and most popular— McDonald's slogans urged that "You deserve a break today" and thereby patted us on the back for being diligent (we must have been working hard to "deserve" a break) and for goofing off in an entertaining, up-lifting manner.

It should be obvious from the above description that a trip to McDonald's brings on much more than high cholesterol and indigestion. Because Mickey D's is an icon, it has made us feel good by confirming a number of the things we value—thrift, cleanliness, efficiency—and a number of our most important beliefs, especially the myth of technology as savior. The golden arches have also served the "magical" function common to icons. Inside the safety of those arches we leave confusion and doubt behind. We are in a place where we are secure in the familiar. And instead of being anonymous as we often feel outside, inside the arches we are special, a specialness heightened by usually hostile young people treating us with respect and by seeing all around us the confirmation of our most basic beliefs and values.

Although McDonald's and personal computers seem to have little in common, when we look at their iconic meaning, we find them delivering much the same cultural messages. Unlike McDonald's, however, which quickly established most of its iconic meaning through dramatic growth and clever advertising, the computer in America has had to evolve gradually from a negative to a positive icon.

Power Tools for the Mind: The Computer Made American

Americans have always had a curiously ambivalent relationship with computers. On the one hand we respect and value the immense power they make available to us—their complexly woven circuitry is a paradigm of the human mind cleaned up for increased efficiency and productivity; on the other hand we fear those very same characteristics. The cold, mechanistic, completely 'logical' computer is remorseless in its pursuit of the ends for which it has been programmed and threatens to overwhelm its creator with sheer computation overload (we could be number-crunched to death). Computers are our old enemy, the emotionally barren intellectual who's more interested in theories than people, minds rather than heart—computers are nerds in a box, and we fear their skills and potential every bit as much as we are intrigued by them and desire to turn them to our own ends. More than half of all the world's computers are located in America and yet only 5 percent of Americans are able to operate one with skills higher than simple typing.

The threat of the computer is the dark power present in any form of technology which has the potential to challenge important American myths and beliefs rather than "protecting" and "saving" them. The larger the computer physically—and in the responsibility it is granted for decision*making* (rather than execution)—the more likely it is to violate vital tenets of the American mindset. Putting a computer in charge is a lot like giving the helm of the starship *Enterprise* over to Mr. Spock—human values bite the dust and things go to hell in a hurry. Computers in control are *worse* than Spock, however, since Spock is at least half human in his willingness to debate things. A computer is remorseless in moving toward fulfillment of its program so that movies, for example, often portray them as the ultimate in unstoppable forces marching toward the destruction of human beings—Jason with a keyboard and video display rather than a hockey mask. In *2001: A Space Odyssey* the initially "friendly" HAL freaks out and begins knocking off the astronauts who have placed too much of their fate in the "hands" of a computer which doesn't know its proper place. In *Colossus: The Forbin Project* the U.S.S.R. and U.S.A. each develop a super-computer which is given total control of the nation's defense system—then the two computers meet up, develop a relationship based on a language too complex for human beings to share, and soon are talking about a new race of "superior beings" (they are computer Nazies). Computers are so insensitive to human nature that they cannot accommodate the slightest element of human error—one bonehead move by man and the human race can kiss itself good-bye. In *Wargames,* a teenager's computer prank leads to the brink of nuclear war; in *Dr. Strangelove,* a crazy general initiates an invasion of the Soviet Union by American bombers which results in a computerized Doomsday Device actually destroying the planet—we are shoved over the brink; and in *Fail Safe,* the same type of scenario leads to the destruction of New York City. Computers are the stone-cold mind ticking away at the center of the mutually assured destruction time bomb. Putting computers into the command post their power and efficiency seem to demand is simply mad

The marketing of computers to Americans has always been bucking this strong current of Anti-Intellectualism and fear of dehumanizing technology, therefore, and has made a concerted effort to invest the object with an iconic significance and magical power more in keeping with basic American myths, beliefs, and values. This process can be seen in several important ways:

1) *The manipulation of counter-icons*

In the 1936 comedy classic *Modern Times,* Charlie Chaplin begins his story as a common man, victim of the dehumanizing forces of technology. His mindlessly repetitive work on the assembly line drives him insane. He can't relax in the restroom on his break without having his boss appear on a giant TV screen to bark at him to "get back to work," his lunch is "fed" to him by a computer-like contraption which almost kills him, and he ultimately ends up being eaten by a machine which sucks him up inside its gnashing gearworks—Charlie is the "little fellow" swallowed by "big tech."

IBM appropriated the Charlie figure—with all its iconic associations—and used it to identify its big machine as the opposite of that so fearsomely presented in *Modern Times*. IBM computers must be "user-friendly" if the friendly user is the ultimate common man whom we know has only had an antagonistic, competitive relationship with machines. If Charlie can trust Big Blue, then maybe computers are "protective" of individual freedom and choice afterall: Charlie uses the computer instead of being eaten by it. IBM later expanded this counter-icon process by using several characters from *MASH* to pitch IBM computers, again using characters identified with rebellion, humor, and sympathy for the little guy to assign these qualities to the machines they stood smiling over.

Apple Computers, meanwhile, developed their own counter-icon—a green medieval apple (sometimes multi-colored) with one bite taken out of it. The apple carried with it an iconic feeling of the natural world (as opposed to artificial intelligence), warmth (rather than coldness), and the missing bite suggested that the computer brought a necessary, powerful gift of knowledge somehow magically united with the world of the Garden.

2) *Computers and their Creators*

Apple Computers was founded out of a garage in Silicon Valley by Steve Jobs and Steve Wozniak and was marketed from the first as the product of these two counter-culture rebels. The two Steves took on IBM and soon Apple was the hippie, the little guy's computer pitted against the anonymous Big Blue of IBM. The most successful ad in this campaign was a silent commercial which pictured IBM as a gray, dominating Big Brother figure and the Apple forces as rebellious smashers of dour conformity and dehumanization.

The Apple people were so successful at associating their iconoclastic images with their user-friendly icon that the meanings developed began to be shared by all computers as well. The rebellious counter-culture Apple founders ultimately signed an agreement with their former Big Brother enemy to unite their systems with interchangeable software.

3) *Computers and American Myths—Computers come "Home"*

The dominating, enslaving, inflexible, "mainframe" ("Do not fold, spindle, or mutilate.") computer has been re-defined as the user-friendly "personal" computer. Computers now help individuals increase their personal freedom—allowing computers to do the boring, mechanistic jobs of record-keeping and repetitive calculations frees human beings to pursue the task for which they are uniquely suited. Computers help foster material success as well, as computer ads emphasize that good parents need to buy a computer to ensure that their children won't get left behind in school, and IBM runs endless numbers of commercials which show workers achieving and advancing by ("magically") tying into the office computer network from their homes. Computers provide an endless abundance of power and speed (the average computer owner buys a machine with far more RAM than he ever needs) and they promote an optimistic vision of a future in which people's potential is as unlimited as the combinations of letters and numbers on their keyboards. The new computer icon is not the monotone-voiced, colorless, machine-with-its-own-dark-agenda HAL; it is, rather, the compact, warmly beige, game-playing, music-making, immediately responsive, *personal* computer whose potentially cold hardware is warmed by the software which carries the message of our hearts and desires.

Computers were freed from their "intellectual" cages by being re-identified as practical instruments designed to perform tasks assigned by human beings. The personal computer combines the familiar elements of a television screen (ironically identified with entertainment and tying the viewer into the larger world outside his tiny living room) and the typewriter (an icon of communication and human message-making) into a "power tool for the mind"—an instrument which magnifies human potential (rather than the self-serving anonymous number-crunching of "intellect").

Perhaps the most representative icon associated with the computer's new image is the manipulative "mouse" which is used to enter commands into the system. As Phil Patton describes this significant symbol:

> The mouse, a device that symbolized the small computer's aims to give power to the weak, its cutesiness, its connection with moving objects, became almost universal. . . . The mouse had become more than a simple functional device; like the car or the computer itself, it was a symbol of individual power and potential, whose shape and contours should suggest speed, strength and some abstract intangible future.

It's no wonder that the favorite computer passwords used by Americans are "love" and "sex"—we've got a new passion for these magical icons of protective technology, which bring us material success, intelligence, individual freedom, and playful leisure.

For Whom the Bell Tolled

Phil Patton

The irony of the American object is that it asserts the power and potential of the individual while posessing the generality of the type.

Made in the U.S.A.

Telephones embody a magical power which enable people to "reach out and touch" someone with a loud "Hello!" and, indeed, it must have seemed in those early days that the telephone's ability to transcend space made each call as significant an event as two ships hailing one another across a vast, empty sea. The telephone line snapped forever the seemingly unbreakable tie between time and distance which had kept people's spirits as far apart as their bodies and voices happened to be. The telephone meant you could be "there" while never leaving "here" and thus opened a new world while shrinking another.

Phil Patton traces the history of the telephone in a straight-forward chronological manner, but he invests this movement with the twin meanings he argues define the nature and role of popular icons in America. On one hand, Patton argues that American icons begin with a powerful sense of "democracy" at their core. American icons are mass-produced in a manner which makes the same artifact and quality equally available to all. Once the icon's popularity has been established, however, its development continues in a direction which emphasizes individuality rather than sameness. The icon becomes increasingly adaptable and especially capable of reflecting the character, beliefs and values of its owner. In the chapter of his book devoted to the iconic development of the automobile, for example, Patton shows how the democracy of an identical Model-T in every garage moved gradually (but steadily) toward the development of a wide variety of car models from which the consumer could choose to reflect his individual freedom and identity.

Reprinted with permission from *Made in the U.S.A. The Secret Histories of the Things that Made America* by Phil Patton. NY: Grove Weidenfeld, 1991.

(America still produces many more makes and models of cars today than any other nation, even though its share of the total automobile market has declined precipitously.)

Patton's popular icons, therefore, perform an important function characteristic of many popular artifacts and events. They embody in unified form a set of conflicting myths, beliefs or values and thus enable a mass audience to experience these oppositional worlds. Patton's telephone magically transcends time and space, but its greatest power may be the way in which it enables everyone to be equal yet unique.

"Oooh, that white telephone!" marvels the waitress played by Mia Farrow in the Woody Allen film *Purple Rose of Cairo.* A small-town girl with big-screen dreams, she has never seen anything like it. Of all the things projected on the silver screen—the fine clothes, the cocktails at the Copacabana, the white piano, white curtains, glittering chromed appointments to white furniture in the luxury apartment—that white telephone is the one she most pines for. It is reminiscent of white phones in any number of black and white movies, some romances, some thrillers. In the thirties, when Woody Allen's movie is set, a white telephone was already as strange and rare as the purple rose itself, and as spiritual as a white whale.

That was because the telephone had recently been standardized. Like the Model T, the standard model 300 came in any color you wanted so long as it was black. White phones were for the rich, and the movies. The standard phone's color and shape was determined by Henry Dreyfuss Associates through exactly 2,240.5 hours of model making, testing, and refinement, of grappling with the "receiver-off-the-hook problem," and, always, of attempting to make the device lower and more compact. Dreyfuss had made the French phone—the handset combining transmitter and receiver—into the standard modern phone.

It was another classic case study of industrial design. In 1929, Dreyfuss had been one of a number of designers offered $1,000 to draw up sketches for a new phone. He turned the money down: the job could not simply be done as a piece of sculpture, he argued; it required a whole system of specifications. The company bought his argument, and Dreyfuss began extensive tests involving a thousand individuals. The 1930 model 300 became *the* telephone.

In 1946, Dreyfuss started the job all over again. Introduced in the early fifties, the model 500 had a lower, more rounded body, floating on feet, that marked a progression not unlike that from a '34 Chevrolet to a 1947. But so successful was the model 300 that the company feared some of the changes. The innovation of making the handle square in section, for instance, was considered risky: would it roll around in unskilled hands?

These phones were models of the idea of the telephone as a universal appliance, a model of the universality telephone service had finally achieved, a sculptural icon of the possibilities of phoning—the kit of connections. A 1937 Coca-Cola ad paid indirect testimony to the universality of Dreyfuss's design. Showing female hands reaching for the phone on one side, grasping the Coke bottle on the other, it was headed: "Familiar acts that mark a better way of living. You reach for the Phone...or tilt this frosty Bottle." Both objects, the copy went on, were never far from where you are, and each "means a lot." Each represented and in a sense contained the whole service and delivery system that lay behind them. The phone was a package for the telephone company.

Everyone's phone was the black phone, but the black phone was not even your phone. It was rented from the telephone company—already, by the forties, "Ma Bell," the mother of us all. That black phone was a furnishing of the weary workaday world, its shape based on the measurements of a thousand heads and hands selected as samples. It had been designed for everyone so no one could have any complaints. The same model for office and home, requiring all those man-hours of time (the exactitude of the calculations corresponded to the exactitude of the process described), the dozens of clay models, such as a car designer might use, the ergonomic or "psychophysical" studies of exact angles at which people held the phone. The existence of a single color and shape of telephone for office and home helped to break down the barriers Victorian convention had sought to erect between the sordid world of business and the genteel world of the home—and between the man's and the woman's world as well.

By 1880, Mark Twain was already noticing the change the telephone had made in social habits. Women could now be reached more directly, via the telephone, instead of by cards passed into the parlor. But the other side of it was the woman waiting by the telephone, a role that made her only more aware of her inequality, the callousness of men, and the one-sidedness of romance: "Why can't I call him?" Later, the phone figured as a means of checking in on a woman. In the fifties, the popular Nashville singer Jim Reeves wooed his love over the phone, overpowering the physical presence of his rival just as the phone and teenage girls were becoming so inseparable that AT&T unbent stylistically enough to introduce the Princess, exactly right for the purpose. Like the sewing machine and the typewriter, the telephone quickly became associated with women. They were soon adopted as switchboard operators because it was thought their voices were more pleasant, they were physically more adept at the switching process, and they were more dependable than the boys at first employed in the role.

A universal appliance implied universal service. The telephone network and the telephone company made up one communications kit, with completely interchangeable parts each of which linked you to the whole.

Among the early celebrators of the phone was Herbert Casson, who pointed out that no single phone has any value in itself and, by extension, each additional phone added to the system increases the value of each previous phone. You are not only your phone but the whole system—the reticulated possibilities of switchboards and long lines. For a nickel deposited in a pay phone, Casson enthused, you can rent a multi-million-dollar system.

The idea of the telephone network took a while to crystallize. At first, no one knew quite what to use the phone for. One early idea was to use it for broadcasting—early demonstrations featured music piped in from distant concert halls and faintly projected. It was conceived as a public device. Only later did the pattern change to one of personal conversation.

"One policy, one system, universal service," was the slogan of Theodore Vail, who, beginning around 1900, pushed the telephone into every home and business and in the process established AT&T as a *de facto* monopoly. Low basic rates and increasingly sophisticated automatic switching systems helped make this possible. Bell himself had foreseen that automating the system would "so reduce the expense that the poorest man cannot afford to be without his telephone." Compare this with Henry Ford, circa 1915, talking about the Model T. "Soon," he said, "there will be no one who cannot afford a car."

In fact, the phone took a while to become anything like universal. In 1880, there were only 60,000 phones. The takeoff did not really begin until the 1890s. From 1896 to 1899, the number doubled; from 1896 to 1906, it increased eight times. In 1910, there were 6 million phones, and by 1920, 10 million, representing one for every ten people in the United States and 70 percent of all the phones in the world.

But even in the thirties, telephone distribution was far from universal: the infamous *Literary Digest* poll of 1936, which forecast Alf Landon as the winner over FDR, whose eventual victory was a landslide, was skewed because it sampled only those people with telephones.

The white telephone was just a dream for decades. The white phone promised connection to a higher world, connections the normal standard-issue phone and the normal customer couldn't make—to, say, the world of starlets and producers ("Don't call us, we'll call you," says the agent of whom it is said in praise, "He gives good phone"). It was the symbol of the personal phone, the phone of romantic connection—who would call, what invitations?—and adjunct to the movies.

Until 1984, you could not connect any equipment not approved by the system to the system. The fact that your phone was part of the network was emphasized by the simple fact that the network owned it. Leasing phones was remunerative for the company, and few customers added up their monthly payments, but if they did, they realized that they would buy the phone many times over. Leasing was apparently originally the suggestion of a far-sighted Bell Company attorney who had previously worked for the Gordon McKay Shoe Machinery Company, which leased its sewing machines instead of selling them and charged by the number of shoes manufactured. It was McKay's sewing machine, introduced in 1862, that helped shoe the massive armies of the Union. Adding machines and computers were later marketed on the same basis. The integrity of the network was to be preserved at all costs. No alien apparatus, no strange bells, no competitive switchboards. No white phones. This not only gave the company a monopoly on lines and switching facilities but on the sale and rental of equipment. Never mind that simple connectivity standards for telephones had long ago made the black telephone as obsolete as the Model T, and phones as easy to connect as lamps to a socket.

Around the turn of the century, there were competing phone companies: the original Bell Company, a Western Union-directed series of companies, and other local competitors. The Bell system pretended to be a sort of federal system. Herbert Casson called it "a federation of self-governing companies united by a central company," and added that Vail, a sometime gentleman-farmer, had pursued this consolidation "for the same reason that he built one big comfortable barn for his Swiss cattle and his Welsh ponies, instead of half a dozen small, uncomfortable sheds." Only by constituting itself in this kind of mock federalism—local companies sharing a common long-distance network—could it escape the attacks of the trustbusters.

Surely, no good American could object to that constitutional organization; it seemed so natural. But elsewhere Casson's enthusiasm causes him to slip up and acknowledge another sort of organization that was closer to the truth. AT&T was in fact organized on a military staff system, such as General Motors would later employ. "Staff and line" at Vail's AT&T, he argued, had done for companies what Von Moltke did for armies. The phone company aspired to be a Prussian information system. In fact, the telephone system itself would eventually undercut the system that ran it—the direct staff and line control, which was better suited to the linearity of telegraph than the omnidirectional net of the phone. Calling around your boss was now possible.

The original vision of the telephone network had been there with Alexander Graham Bell. He saw it as analogous to a system of plumbing. It was to be like "a perfect network of gas-pipes and water-pipes," he wrote in 1876. But at the same time, in his mind and others, there existed the competing vision of the telephone network, as a centralized system of delivery of music, news—and, potentially, political propaganda. This last vision was what attracted Europeans, especially the always centralized French. The Europeans regarded the telephone as a public utility that should belong to the state—to the Post Office.

Americans, always uneasy with big business and central power, for a long time tolerated competition among telephone-switching systems. It took skillful public and political relations for the phone company to weed out its competitors. The process was accomplished by Vail's buying up smaller competitors, mostly between 1908 and 1913. But in 1913, when public suspicion of concentrated wealth and business power came to a head, Vail backed off and in the Kingsbury Commitment compromised with the new Democratic administration of Woodrow Wilson, agreeing not to gobble up any more independent telephone companies. He had already gotten most of them, enough to remain dominant while the others slowly withered at the end of the massive AT&T grapevine to which they had to connect the long distance, surviving as curiosities like old country stores until the forties. The arrival of long-distance wires, requiring a heavy capital investment, made duplication of resources prohibitively expensive. If ever there was a natural monopoly—conditioned by the nature of its business, and not by the tooth and claw of laissez-faire capitalism—it was long-distance telephone.

The genius of Theodore Vail lay in presenting the telephone from the mouthpiece end (from the user's viewpoint) as a network of opportunities. The key change was that of viewing the phone primarily as an outgoing instrument, a transmitter rather than a receiver. It was a simple matter of emphasis for marketing purposes. The phone as receiver was dangerous, full of fear—whether from bad news, from a stranger's abusive calls, a salesman's pitch, or a crank call. In *The Long Goodbye* (1954), Raymond Chandler speculates on the telephone's ambiguous attractions: modern man wants to be in touch, but the ringing of the phone also awakens a twinge of instinctual fear in him. "There is something compulsive about a telephone," says the private eye Marlowe. "The gadget-ridden man of our age loves it, loathes it, and is afraid of it. But he always treats it with respect...The telephone is a fetish." The phone as receiver inspired that fear and respect. But the phone as transmitter emphasized its power and potential—it reinforced universality.

It was the personal power of the telephone, requiring no special training, no office, no third-party sender, that distinguished it. This power was the focus of the company's appeal. In his wonderful letter of indignation to Hartford's gas company in 1891, Mark Twain fumed and cursed about an interruption in service, concluding: "Haven't you a telephone?"—so, that is, I can chew you out more directly, make you squirm, and receive immediate satisfaction? Advertisements beginning in the late twenties featured the powerful modern man in his office as a figure to be admired. Buy our insurance, car, or mouthwash, the appeal went, and you will share the power of this captain of industry. Advertising historian Roland Marchand calls this image "the master of all he sees" image. And the key icon of this picture, the man's scepter of power, his mode of transmitting his control out into the industrial landscape he surveys, was the telephone.

There was some truth to this depiction of the phone as the power lever of modern business. The arrival of the telephone, for instance, helped build the stock exchange—and to facilitate stock manipulation. Edward Harriman, the railroad magnate, was famous for having telephones everywhere he went—in all his houses, in his office, in his private railcar. Accused of being slave to the telephone, all he is said to have replied is: "Not at all; I am its master." His multiple phones were his weapons against the Morgans and Hills. Herbert Casson could barely contain himself: "What the brush is to the artist, what the chisel is to the sculptor, the telephone was to Harriman. He built his fortune on it."

Grover Cleveland put the first phone into the White House—and generally answered it himself. McKinley's "front porch" campaign of 1896, in which the candidate seemed to hold himself above the fray, was in fact the first telephone campaign. While the candidate posed on the white porch sipping lemonade with his neighbors in Canton, Ohio, while William Jennings Bryan crisscrossed the country recapitulating his "Cross of Gold" speech, boss Mark Hanna in the backroom was dunning big corporate contributions and organizing the McKinley campaign by phone.

It was not until the 1960s, however, that our presidents, beginning with John F. Kennedy, were commonly shown on the phone in power positions; before that, direct contact was preferred. Talking on an item anyone possessed seemed to diminish the presidential power. But the publicizing of the hotline, the red phone, in sixties movies—such as *Dr. Strangelove* and *Fail-Safe*—enhanced its iconic power. An acknowledgment of the global reach of power, it was the desktop version of *Air Force One*. If the white phone expressed the power of romance, the red phone expressed the romance of power.

Only after the black phone had begun to be the universal standard did the white phone take on its special meanings. In 1928, a Bell vice president named Arthur W. Page illustrated the significance of the black phone when he urged the company to expand its market by emphasizing comfort and convenience. The wealthy could afford extra phones, Page argued. One way the comfort and convenience factor would be expressed was by phones of various colors and shapes. This stood in contrast to sheer necessity, basic service, as expressed by the single black phone. "Give the public what they *desire*," he argued. Already, Kodak had begun offering cameras in colors, and the Model T was in the process of being succeeded by the Model A, available not just in black but in Duco paints of red and blue and yellow. Why, Page asked, did AT&T sell only "one black desk set, a hand set, a wallset, and one of those black buttoned inter-communication systems"?

Ford, Page noted, "made one little black instrument, too, and it did just what ours did: when it got started, it went fine, and so did ours. But, you know, Henry has recently come to the point where he realized he had to make a change and I think now that he has made a lady out of Lizzie, we might dress up these children of the Bell System."

Ford had sold basic transportation, but now people wanted more. Page argued that people wanted more than basic telephone, too. His efforts were only partially adopted. AT&T had no General Motors to compete against. Some advertisements were run on Page's suggested themes. They spoke of the convenience of "enough telephones properly placed" to "prevent annoying delays when one is preparing for bridge, travel or the theater." But the color of the phones did not change—until the 1950s. Color came to phones in extension phones, in décor colors, for extra rooms. Bell now was fearful of a saturated market. It began to offer a few colors, and it replaced the stern black with beige as the most common color of standard issue.

By the 1980s, with the breakup of AT&T, customers could own their phones. New phones appeared in virtually every shape—footballs, cartoon cats and mice, white elephants and white whales. A thousand shapes bloomed. There are phones shaped like Porsches, phones shaped like women's shoes, phones shaped like a set of lips (courtesy of the original by Man Ray), phones shaped like piles of Tyco children's blocks. The "Classique," a "Classic French rotary phone in ivory with gold-tone accents," intones a recent catalogue, is "Perfect for the Boudoir!" It is the great white phone, straight from Hollywood.

Today, however, that still may not be good enough. What the customer really aspires to is a phone so powerful it is completely freed from the network, to the incorporation of the power of the network and its transcendence, entirely inside the individual instrument. In another Woody Allen film, *Play It Again Sam,* the joke is on the Hollywood producer who spews out a list of the telephone numbers at which he can be reached. He must always be in touch, reachable, reeling off a series of numbers that describe the sequence of his daily locations.

This was before the car phone, which would surely have solved his problem, or the briefcase cellular phone. The phone booth, dating back to 1889, first fulfilled this function. It developed from a huge kiosk for the wealthy (early booths in Bell offices were used to showcase long-distance service) to common utilities. The booth became office and tepee for the Times Square con men A.J. Leibling called "telephone booth Indians." Today, the phone booth, softly emitting its light across the empty prairie behind the roadside, or offering a bell jar of privacy in the midst of the noise of Grand Central Terminal, is an icon of individuality—and loneliness.

It represented the beginning of the process of disassociating phone from place that culminated in the portable phone, soon to be shrunk to the size of Dick Tracy's wrist radio—a private ear for private investigation. The absolutely unconnected phone was a sign of prestige. The car phone was so much a status symbol that by the mid-1980s pimps had taken to installing them—or putting on dummy phone antennas if they couldn't afford them. The cordless phone was as much an anomaly as the white phone. The mobile phone was another version of Moby phone, the mystic and magic white phone of infinite possibility.

Cordless phones were boosted by the prime-time soap operas, like *Dallas.* J.R. Ewing, sitting at breakfast on the patio of Dallas's South Fork, carries out his connivances in comfort, using a cordless phone. Like the distant tones lent by Speakerphones, this device offers the convenience of power, never far from command, with the tycoon letting his fingers do the walking all over his enemies and competitors.

The telephone figures as the *deus ex machina* in many plays and movies of the period when it was just becoming universal. The ring offstage is as compelling a reason to move characters in and out as any backstage alarum. The ring of the phone can be either a welcome or a sinister intrusion—possible harbinger of bad news or threats. (The first telephone exchange had been developed as a sideline by a burglar alarm company.)

In *Sorry, Wrong Number,* the 1948 adaptation of Lucille Fletcher's radio play, the action centers on calls made through the single white telephone of the bedridden heroine. The film opens with a view of switchboard operators at work, over which flashes the premise: "In the tangled network of a great city the telephone is the unseen link between a million lives. It is the servant of our common needs—the confidant of our inmost secrets...life and happiness wait upon its ring...and horror...and loneliness...and *death*!!!" The phone is the film's *deus ex machina.*

Dial M for Murder, the play Alfred Hitchcock brought to the big screen, asserts that the phone magnifies the individual to the extent that he can make his impact felt in two places at once—in the theater lobby, secure with his alibi, and, via his human and electrical agent, back home, killing his wife.

The power of the telephone system as a whole could only be demonstrated by the criminal. The phone hacker and the blue box of the 1970s demonstrated not only that the system was the solution but that all its mysteries had solutions. You could, if you knew what you were doing, break into the great computer that was the phone system and call the Kremlin. A computer was an aid in dealing with a computer; MIT hackers used the school PDP-1 for this in the mid-sixties. So did the Matthew Broderick character in *War Games*; he found he could start World War III with a computer, a modem and a phone call. He had the power of the red phone in his simple black phone.

"Phone phreaking" was a preview of hackers invading big computers. Their motive, said one phone phreak, quoted in Ron Rosenbaum's 1971 *Esquire* article, was that "the phone company is a System, a computer is a System...The phone company is nothing but a computer." Some managed to steal, but most simply wanted to exercise power by sabotage, infecting other computers with destructive virus programs or destroying stored information. The phone invaders enjoyed simply hearing the clicks that signaled they had switched their way from Dayton to Dakar. One blind phone phreak would literally feel his way through switching systems, courtesy of tours the company allowed him to take. One game involved making connections that circled the globe.

Part of the attraction was power—power as proven by its destructive potential. "Captain Crunch," another of the phone phreaks Rosenbaum interviewed, and among the most famous, claimed he could "busy up" the nation's phone system with three callers. "Captain Crunch" was a man named John Draper, who took his name from the cereal in which he found a toy whistle that exactly replicated the 2,600-cycle frequency critical to hacking the phone system. (AT&T had slipped up, printing the frequencies used in its long-distance switching system in the *Bell System Technical Notes*, a publication avidly read by all true phone phreaks.)

Draper became a member of the famous Homebrew Computer Club and a friend of Steve Jobs and Steve Wozniak, the founders of Apple Computer, who were inspired by Rosenbaum's article and later by Draper himself to make blue boxes they sold to Berkeley students. Wozniak once called the Vatican using such a box, pretending to be Henry Kissinger. He nearly managed to have the Pope himself called to the line. Draper spent time trying to tap into the Defense Department's ARPANET computer connection system. And when Jobs and Wozniak hired him to design a phone interface for their Apple II computer, he created basically a blue box on a computer board. The outlaw skills of "hacking" the phone system formed the basis of computer hacking. Hacking at last made the single phone the instrument of tremendous power the phone company had all those years proclaimed it to be.

The Malling of America

William Severini Kowinski

At some point in the early 1920s the productive capacity of the industrialized United States exceeded our need for goods. Quite simply, we were geared up to manufacture things faster than what we already owned wore out. As a result, to keep the American economy running smoothly and to keep employment high, it became necessary for Americans to buy goods they didn't really need. Earlier in our history, a belief related to the myth of material success was the belief that it was virtuous to be thrifty. Careful saving was a sign of a person's integrity. In the new economy that developed in the 1920s, however, thrift was no longer a virtue that served the best interests of a nation that had to keep spending if it was to remain prosperous. As a result people were encouraged to quit saving and to start spending. There was a huge increase in mass advertising and, for the first time in our history, buying material goods on credit became common in American homes. People were taught to not only spend for what they did not actually need, but to spend beyond their immediate ability to pay. The result of this important change in the American mindset was a modern myth—the myth of material consumption.

Basically, the myth of material consumption tells us that the buying and possession of material goods is an outward, physical sign of inner goodness and the value of the person possessing the goods. Shopping thus becomes a virtuous ritual, even though what we buy may be a relatively worthless gadget like a salad shooter. And owning new things reconfirms our status in society. We therefore feel compelled to buy a new car even though our old one is still running fine. Or we rush to clothing stores every fall to buy a new wardrobe even though there may be clothes in our closet we bought last year but haven't even worn yet. Evidence of our national belief in this myth is everywhere from bumper

Excerpted from: *The Malling of America: An Inside Look at the Great Consumer Paradise* by William Severini Kowinski, N.Y.: William Morrow and Co., Inc., 1985.

stickers that instruct us to "Shop till you drop," to the weekend urban ritual of rushing from garage sale to garage sale. It is even present in the consumptive habits of rioters who loot appliance stores first and foremost and who haul away anything they can carry irrespective of whether or not they will really use it. On a more acceptable social level, what icon of the myth of material consumption is more common these days than the credit card? So pervasive is the myth and this symbol that the ads tell us, "Don't leave home without it." We must be ready every minute of every day to express through a purchase our allegiance to this bedrock belief.

Since the late 1950s, as William Severini Kowinski demonstrates in the following article, the main icon representing the myth of material consumption in this country has been the enclosed shopping mall. Severini shows us how malls are constructed and presented to us to provide fantasies of consumption. The controlled space and temperature provide a utopian enclosure in which the shopping experience adds to the perfection of the perfect place. And the community-like environment makes shopping seem like old-fashioned Americana.

The myth of material consumption is present in a number of the other popular artifacts discussed in this book. Astute readers will find it in Barbie Dolls, the thinness stereotype and even in Harlequin Romances where the purchased environments and trendy clothes of the main characters are always described in great detail. In fact, the myth is so much with us, that as you read this article you might think about grabbing your credit card, racing to a bookstore at your nearest mall and buying several extra copies of this book. It will make you a better person. We promise.

The Mall as Theatre

When the Greengate Mall was devoid of people and movement, I could take note of the architecture; I could look at the mall simply as space, and try to see what had been done with that space. I looked at its size and scale. It felt comfortable, intelligible, not overwhelmingly large but big enough to be a bit mysterious, to warrant walking around and exploring. I saw the wide shiny courts, the gleaming silver escalator ending in the kind of tile you associate with the outside in a plaza or a sunny path around a garden. There was a staircase, too; it looked like a staircase that should be inside a building, even a house, yet its wide landings overlooked a broad square and two rows of storefronts along an indoor street. All the elements that didn't seem to belong together were here, nevertheless, in a kind of harmony, with a strange feeling—perhaps inevitable in the emptiness of night—of magic.

Then suddenly I knew why, or anyway I started to find my way to why. My next perceptual jolt was the sudden realization that this space was special, that it could break so many rules and preconceptions because it was completely separated from the rest of the world. It was its own world, pulled out of time and space, but not only by windowless walls and a roof, or by the neutral zone of the parking lot between it and the highway, the asphalt moat around the magic castle. It was *enclosed* in an even more profound sense—and certainly more than other mere buildings—because all these elements, and others, psychologically separated it from the outside and created the special domain within its embrace. It *meant* to be its own special world with its own rules and reality. That was the first and most essential secret of the shopping mall.

Its space is also special because it is *protected.* The mall banishes outside threats of disruption and distraction: No cars are allowed in the mall, no traffic, noise, or fumes. The natural world can't even intrude; there's no rain or snow, heat or cold, no seasonal changes—not even gathering clouds to cause concern. This space is protected so that people will not be distracted or feel threatened; they'll relax and open themselves to the environment, and trust it. That must be part of the reason why very little is allowed in the mall that is larger, faster, or more powerful than a person.

The mall is also *controlled* space. This essential element is clearly implied in the official definition of a shopping center that I read in a publication of the Urban Land Institute, an organization that works closely with the mall industry. The operative part of that definition is: "a group of architecturally unified commercial establishments built on a site which is planned, developed, owned and managed as an operating unit. . . ." Unity, preplanning, single and centralized management (and Harry's rules) are the instruments by which the mall creates its special conditions, by which it controls the environment created by enclosure and protection.

The process begins with the mall's careful design: The developer selects what goes into it, from concrete to conceptual statement, from tenants to trees. Then the process continues in the day-by-day management: the control of temperature, lighting, merchandise, and events.

The mall's special space is achieved by enclosure, protection, and control. Those are its secrets, the keys to the kingdom, the whole mall game. Within the environment established by those elements, a mall can contain five department stores or none, one level or six; it can be a brand-new building or deposit itself in the shell of an old one; it can thrive in Alaska or Hawaii, in the desert or on the beach; it can put in skating rinks and roller coasters and historical markers; it can be as small as a garage or as big as a country, and it will still be a mall.

These are also the elements that make the mall an extremely efficient and effective selling machine—but that is a subject for the daytime. At night the mall reveals other implications that contribute to its selling success; but they are also intriguing to consider on their own. For when you have a space that you have separated from the outside world, and the ability to create your own world inside, governed by your own rules, what you have is the ability to make magic. You've got yourself a house of fantasy.

For after all, isn't this sense of separated, protected privileged space common to the special worlds of history and myth, from the castles and walled cities of medieval Europe and the Forbidden City of China to the enchanted wood, the city in the sky or under the sea, the Shangri-La in the mystic mountains of fantasy? These are the necessary conditions for magic places apart from the ordinary world: through the looking glass, up the beanstalk, down the rabbit hole, off to the Emerald City. Such magic places may also be separated by time (whether places that time forgot or places in the far future or the distant past accessible only by time travel) and by a combination of time and space (as in the *Star Wars* saga—"long, long ago in a galaxy far, far away . . ."). So it is no wonder the mall is full of themes and suggestions of the past and an intergalactic future.

But of course the mall is not completely inaccessible from the real world—in fact, it's convenient, with plenty of free parking. It is instead a special space within the usual world where the imagination is given strong suggestions for fantasy. And there is a model for that kind of environment.

I saw that, too, on this night in the empty mall, as I stood at the second-level railing and looked down into center court. I saw the white pools of light, the areas of relative darkness, the symmetrical aisles and gleaming escalator, the bracketed store facades, the sudden strangeness of live trees and plants indoors. It was as if I were standing on a balcony, looking down on a stage, waiting for the show to begin.

That was it. This is theatrical space. The mall is a theater. At Greengate the theatrical element is fairly explicit. Over the center court are a series of arches—a subtle proscenium—lined with double rows of white lights in marquee array. These lights also surround the cupola over the landing of the center stairs, and are incorporated into the design of many mall stores. In comparison to downtown, the stores are brighter and glitzier; even the banks, staid and sturdy on Main Street, are sprightly and open at the mall. On Halloween, the vice-presidents and loan officers dress up as ghouls and goblins, and on the mall's Country and Western Days the tellers wear cowboy hats. The mall environment is itself a magic theater—trees grow out of the tiled floor! Plants flourish without sun or rain!

But even before the theatrical effects, the conditions for theater are set by design and management. For a space to be a theater, the outside rules of time and space must be banished. The mall keeps out such reference points—not only its windowless enclosure but its very uniformity (one mall resembling another) means it could be anywhere. It is placeless. Many malls banish all sense of time by eliminating clocks, and although Greengate has a large but unobtrusively decorative clock about center court, it neutralizes time by controlling light and sound—morning, noon, and night, they are the same. The mall doesn't allow the appearance of aging—the stores are forever new in an environment that is forever now. It is timeless.

The mall is kept squeaky clean, the stores bright, the fountains gushing, the greenery fresh—or at least those are management's goals. The effect is one of almost unreal perfection. Moreover, this continuous, flowing environment with no reference to the outside—this sense of a special world—permits a kind of unity of experience within an effortless enclosure that is something like the classical theater's unities of time, place and action. It's all here, now. The mall concentrates the drama, suspends disbelief.

For theater, after all, is largely a matter of light and darkness. The mall at night suggests this most strongly. The idea is to darken all distractions and to focus attention with light. For the mall, the process begins with excluding the outside in order to concentrate on what is happening inside. To do that, the basic environment must be created and maintained. The audience must not be distracted; it must be lulled into receptivity by a comfortable, sweet neutrality.

Then comes the shaping of what is in the spotlight, what's on the stage. For once the mall's space is enclosed, protected, and controlled, it can be further designed to create almost any fantasy within it. Like a theater in which *King Lear* might be followed the next night by *Camelot* and the next by the Jacksons in concert, the mall is a Never-Never-Land that says let's pretend. What is pretended can be virtually anything. The mall is, in a word, malleable, and that becomes another key to its success.

There are essential differences between theater and the mall, too; between the kind and intent of the fantasies created in each. But the similarities were fascinating as I gazed out over the mall: silent and still, with its dramatic lighting, its props and staging, and the costumed mannequins in store windows. It looked like a stage anticipating the play, a movie set on down-time, waiting to be brought alive.

Mousekatecture on Main Street

So much for the theater—what is the show? Greengate Mall looks like a set for many potential plays, movies, and television shows—a little *Our Town*, a bit of *High Noon*, a touch of *Star Wars*, a piazza from

Fellini thrown into an atmosphere out of *Ozzie and Harriet,* as well as a little of *The Twilight Zone* (or maybe a lot). But what is the central image that pulls all these other images together?

Pondering this problem at home, I happened on help. I saw a tiny wire-service story in the local paper, not much more than a filler in a page of advertisements. It was about how shopping malls were becoming community centers. By now that wasn't news to me, except perhaps that it was happening elsewhere and to an impressive extent. The article quoted a few mall industry people, a public relations director or two, and one writer. His name was Ralph Keyes, and the quote selected was from his book, *We, the Lonely People.* "Malls aren't part of the community," he wrote. "They are the community."

That was a pretty strong statement. Keyes evidently also saw something special in malls, something that made them more than shopping centers. I got in touch with Ralph Keyes, and it turned out that although his interest in malls began when he was a reporter for *Newsday* on Long Island, he now lived across the state of Pennsylvania from me, near Allentown. He was kind enough to send me a copy of his book and an earlier article he'd done on teenagers at Walt Whitman Mall on Long Island.

He also put me in touch with Richard Francaviglia, a young professor of geography at University of Texas, Arlington. Geography is one of the old disciplines (like landscape architecture) that studies such new phenomena as the organization of cities and the nature of theme parks, phenomena that have escaped or transcended traditional academic categories. Even so, as Francaviglia told me in a letter, he had a tough time getting his academic colleagues to take malls seriously. When he read one of his papers on malls at a Popular Culture Association convention in Chicago, "I nearly started a riot," his letter said. "Quite literally, scholars were yelling back and forth at each other—and me. It was all very stimulating, but while we were arguing, 20 million people were shopping in malls and generally enjoying themselves."

What Francaviglia apparently wanted to know was *why*? Why were all those people at malls? What were the malls doing to attract them? In two articles for scholarly journals that he sent me, he came up with some ingenious answers.

Two of the now conventional observations about the mall are that because it has become such a community center, it is "the new Main Street," and, because of the bright array of consumer products, it is a "Disneyland for adults." Francaviglia not only demonstrated deeper meaning in each of these ideas, he showed how they were connected. In the process he answered my question: What is the central image that brings all the mall theatrics together?

Francaviglia began by analyzing "Main Street U.S.A.," the centerpiece of Disneyland and Disney World, the world-famous amusement parks. These parks are, it should be noted, commercial environments that are preplanned, enclosed, protected, and controlled (and therefore might just as well be called "shopping malls for kids").

Francaviglia was interested in how Walt Disney took the popular mythology about small towns and created a brilliant but artificial design for Main Street U.S.A. Francaviglia began by pointing out that there are two basic kinds of Main Street in the real America. The most common kind is the Main Street that is not only the principal business district but also the "main drag"—the road that leads through town. Essentially this Main Street is both for pedestrians conducting business and social affairs, and for cars and trucks passing through. This, in fact, is the kind of Main Street that Greensburg's is—it's part of Route 66, the principal north-south artery, and has a substantial amount of truck traffic rumbling along it for that reason.

The other and much less frequently encountered type is the Main Street that has only one way in and out; the other end of it leads to a town square or village green. So the destination of cars on this Main Street has to be Main Street itself. As Francaviglia pointed out, this is the kind of Main Street most often portrayed in movies and on television, especially when the purpose is to evoke small-town nostalgia. The reasons for that are obvious: This kind of Main Street is quieter and more peaceful; it doesn't have the roar of traffic crashing through town on its way from somewhere to somewhere else. The town square itself makes it even more peaceful, pedestrian-oriented, and probably prettier.

But Disney took this second and rarer kind of Main Street and did it one better. He put town plazas at both ends, enclosing it completely. Furthermore, cars and trucks were banned altogether from Disney's Main Street, and as Francaviglia noted, such clearly enclosed space creates a strong, if mostly unconscious, psychological confidence that no car *could* even be on this street. It is a toy street, a fantasy, a Main Street of dreams.

So Disney, who had already outdone inventors who merely try to build a better mousetrap by inventing a better mouse—the sweet, lovable, suburban-head-of-household Mickey Mouse—now evoked small-town nostalgia by building a better Main Street. He based Main Street U.S.A. on the Main Street of Marceline, Missouri, as it was when he was a boy growing up there. But besides enclosing it, he encased it in the mistiness of memory. Part of Disney's genius was his ability to make fantasies concrete, and he did this with Main Street U.S.A. by improving on reality.

Marceline's Main Street had been (in Francaviglia's words) ". . . rutted and rilled and horse manure helped turn it into a soupy quagmire in wet weather. . . . Gaunt telephone poles with many cross arms, rather than trees, bordered the sidewalks." But Disney's Main Street U.S.A. was lined with shapely trees, and not only the occasional horse droppings but everything else was cleaned up immediately, to keep this street as pristine as any gold-paved avenue of paradise.

There were also no sleazy bars, dingy luncheonettes, seedy pool halls, or dirty jail cells arrayed along Disney's Main Street. There were only pleasant, clean, colorful, and nostalgic small-town stores which seemed to shimmer with remembered magic.

Disney employed another device to achieve his effects which I found particularly intriguing. The buildings along Main Street U.S.A. are not only better than life, they are smaller; according to Francaviglia, they are five-eighths the size of actual stores on real streets. This scaling-down appeals psychologically to both children and adults; children find the smaller spaces more comfortable and comprehensible—more their size—while the adults, as Francaviglia writes, "are reminded of trips back to childhood haunts; everything is much smaller than one remembers."

Francaviglia goes on to make the connection with the enclosed shopping mall. The rows of stores are set up as on a street, but the street of the mall is also clearly enclosed. Except for auto shows, a car in the mall is unthinkable, and the mall's street is bounded by plazas or courts. Francaviglia claims that so-called pedestrian malls in real downtowns that are created by blocking off real streets never really succeed in subliminally convincing customers that they are safe from traffic. But the mall does, because its street is obviously—theatrically—enclosed and artificial.

Like Disney's street, the shopping mall plans and carries out a consistent design so that the mall's street looks unified, quaint yet familiar. The mall also excludes the rougher elements of real downtowns—no dives or pool halls here—and like the Disney versions, the stores are smaller than stores on town streets.

So the resemblance goes beyond enclosure, protection, and control. It struck me that the basic image the mall delivers—what this stage was set up to be—is a simplified, cleaned-up, Disneyfied fantasy version of Main Street U.S.A. Francaviglia doesn't claim that mall designers copied directly from Disney, but mall people that I met all praised the Disney parks. Still, it's worth noting that Disneyland and the first enclosed malls were being built at about the same time.

Suddenly it seems so obvious, and all too ironic: The "new Main Street" for Greensburg was not just a metaphor for the mall as the major retail and community center of town. It was literally true: The mall was the new "Main Street."

The mall not only acted like a Main Street, it was designed to be one. But not the real one—an archetypal Main Street, designed to fulfill wishes and longings and to allay fears; it was meant to embody a dream and keep out the nightmares. So Greengate Mall's Main Street was an idealization of Greensburg's Main Street, with just the right touch of obvious artificiality to make it permanently extraordinary. It was also cleaner, dryer, more comfortable, more convenient, better scaled and designed for walking, apparently safer, brighter—and in the final irony, more nostalgically reminiscent of small-town Main Street life. The mall was Old-fashioned Bargain Day every day of every year.

The Retail Drama and the Management of Fantasy

Alte Faust, promotional director for Tysons Corner Center in Virginia, personally dyed baby elephants pink for the mall's Christmas parade. Her job, she told a reporter, was "show business."

I was beginning to search out articles written about malls and to peruse some of the trade publications produced for mall industry people. I was surprised by how many trade magazines there were. *National Mall Monitor, Shopping Center World, Shopping Center Age,* and *Shopping Centers Today*, the monthly newspaper published by the International Council of Shopping Centers, itself one of the largest trade organizations in America. This was the mall industry talking to itself, and I was intrigued by the abundance of theatrical images.

The theatrical aspect is pretty obvious in the plethora of promotions these magazines described: Rock-a-thons for crippled children, Ben Franklin birthday kite-flying competitions, spaghetti-eating contests, bluegrass jamborees, hypnotists, and petting zoos. The Hudson Valley Vagabond Puppets presented *The Silly Jellyfish* at The Market in Manhattan's Citicorp Center, while the Spruce Up for Spring Program at Paramus Park in New Jersey included tennis and golf clinics and home improvement shows.

The show business analogies went beyond promotions. Obviously the mall industry itself considered malls to be theaters of a sort, but since these were the people putting on the show, they could talk about their intent. What exactly is the production all about? The mall industry's answer is: The Retail Drama.

"The Retail Drama" is a term actually used in these trade magazines to describe what the mall is doing. The ultimate goal of everything in the mall is to persuade customers to buy. This fantasy world is managed in order to orchestrate The Retail Drama, and the roar of the cash drawer is its ultimate music.

The Retail Drama is a responsibility of the mall itself, not just of the stores, because the mall provides the basic environment that can attract customers, keep them shopping, and bring them back again.

"Customers shop centers rather than stores," Robert Bearson, managing director of a business consulting firm, warned readers of *Shopping Center World*. "Loyalty is developed to your center."

Besides maintaining a comfortable and subtly exciting environment with the splash of fountains and the lilt of Muzak, the mall preplans The Retail Drama through the selection of its stores and services. This selection is called "the tenant mix" and it is considered crucial to the success of the show. Because of its importance, not every store that wants to get into a particular mall always does, nor do tenants always get the particular location in the mall they might want. Big department stores can quite often cut their own deals, but malls increasingly try to shape an overall image, or at least skew their tenant mix to their target customers.

An ad I saw said it perfectly: PERL-MACK'S LONNIE CLINE IS "CASTING" HIS NEXT EPIC! the headline screamed, but it wasn't in *Variety*—it was in *Shopping Centers Today*. The epic that was being cast was Southwest Plaza, a major mall in Colorado. According to the ad, "Lonnie has already cast Sears, Wards, the Denver, May and Joslins to star in Perl-Mack's next box office smash." The ad featured a picture of Lonnie in a director's chair.

For a mall like Greengate, the tenant mix is more likely to be balanced for breadth, with something for everybody. Greengate is a bread-and-butter kind of mall, serving a mostly middle-class and working middle-class market with a basic array of stores and services, and it is conscious of being a community center. Greengate is where Florence Henderson and the Walton family are supposed to go for shoes and sheets, pantyhose and lunch boxes.

Westmoreland Mall—like many malls that go into the area that already has one—is a little more specialized. Its decor is flashier and its tenant mix is slanted toward younger and more affluent customers. This is where the law partners and television news anchors, along with the local versions of John Travolta and Victoria Principal are supposed to shop for tailored suits, designer dresses, the latest in cosmetics, expensive exercise outfits, and video cassettes.

The tenant mix of each of these malls also reflects the geographic and demographic characteristics of their chief customers: Greengate, west of Greensburg, gets much of its clientele from the more working-class towns of Jeannette and Irwin to the west; Westmoreland, east of Greensburg, goes after a more affluent customer in Ligonier in the Laurel Highlands, which was for years the summer home territory of the industrial magnate families of Pittsburgh. Both malls draw from the appropriate groups within Greensburg itself. This division is not simply assumed, either; both malls began with detailed marketing studies, and update them frequently. Both malls also hedge their bets with stores of different appeal. Greengate has Horne's, one of the better Pittsburgh department stores; Westmoreland has Sears.

The tenant mix also has to do with the internal drama of the mall, so the malls strive for variety and completeness too. They also go for the hot trends in mall outlets (the latest retail stores, like computer stores in the early eighties, and the latest fast-food fads) both to keep on top of the market and to promote a sense of novelty and excitement.

Much of The Retail Drama is up to the stores themselves—their merchandise and displays, their management and customer relations. But the mall management continues to organize and prod and keep the show moving; it takes care of the basic environment, encourages tenants to merchandise effectively and aggressively, puts together advertising campaigns and themes, and sponsors special events in the form of mall promotions. Some of these promotions are simple crowd-gatherers; some try to attract a special crowd (families to the school art shows, women to see the soap opera stars); others have a direct merchandising goal, such as mall-wide sales. From Bozos to blood banks, the mall provides all manner of pleasing sideshows and carefully calibrated special audience attractions to lure the customers to the mall, keep them there, and implant the idea in their heads that they had a great time and ought to come back soon.

Other techniques of The Retail Drama are concerned with creating a maximum buying frenzy while the customers are treading the courts. In the Retail Drama, it seems, the customers are not only the audience; they are the action and the actors. The mall environment itself gives them the script. All the mall's a stage, and they are but players in it.

Apparently it's very consciously done. Another advertisement in a mall trade magazine says it all in one visual image: a drawing of a pair of nyloned legs, a woman's sleek foot sheathed in a smart high-heeled shoe, but around her tender ankle is a steel band connected to a ball and chain. The legend with the picture says simply, "The Captivated Shopper." The copy (advertising the Shopco Company, a developer based in New York City) begins: "Getting CAPTIVATED shoppers is not simply a matter of luck, but rather a science."

The people who practice this science are the mall's management, and I saw them at work as they created their most important moment of the year. Christmas at the mall.

Greengate was known throughout western Pennsylvania for its elaborate Christmas displays, which saturated the entire mall and turned it into a single Christmas fantasy. Greengate had spent some $50,000 on decorations over the years, resulting in a grab bag of holiday images. The train that children rode around center court, for example, was called the Sugar Plum Express, and there the kids could (according to the sign at its entrance) "learn the true meaning of Christmas from the Wizard of Oz." But this year all the decorations were going to be new, and all tied into one Christmas theme: the story of the Nutcracker.

"This is the first time we've done a completely coordinated theme," said Karen Kozemchak, who, in her mid-twenties, was Greengate's director of marketing, advertising and promotion.

Neighbors in Never-Never Land

America has always cherished the small town, at least as an ideal. It is where the mythic constituents of the American character were to be found: simplicity, idealism, decency, and a down-to-earth intelligence. Our heroes were supposed to spring from its soil, nurtured by the intimacy of its streets and the deep moral lessons and perhaps magical strength derived from closeness to nature. It was the place for the young to dream before they went into the larger world to achieve; it was also where old dreamers returned, to pass on their dreams. "As Thornton Wilder's *Our Town* reminded us," John Updike writes, "small-town people think a lot about the universe (as opposed to city people, who think about one another)." Even today, Americans routinely tell pollsters that the small town is the ideal place to live, and in a sense many have tried to get back to it, in suburbia.

But the small town is almost impossible to find now. The highway, the mall, and television—which, in Updike's words, "imposed on every home a degraded sophistication"—became only the most recent and most effective agents of its destruction. Still, the dream of the small town remains, and these same postwar phenomena have appropriated it for their own purposes, sometimes perverting it in the process.

In the last decade, television advertising has refined its ability to manipulate viewers, going so far as to use research on the hemispheres of the human brain to isolate the elements it can use to bypass the brain's logic and make a direct connection with the emotions. That's one reason there is so much small-town imagery in commercials: The small-town dream has powerful emotional appeal. The ads tap the same elements the malls do: the small-town virtues on a small scale, familiarity and security. But some of these ads go further; they ingeniously substitute the Highway for the Hometown as the place where small-town relationships exist.

Consider the ads that contrast the friendliness and quality to be found at national chain outlets with the sleaziness and sloppiness of small-time independents, usually depicted as shiftless rubes and rude incompetents. These commercials turn the assumption of small-town community on its head: It is now the anonymous chain that "cares about you" and offers personal service, not a business from your own town run by somebody who knows you personally. Such ads respond to the facts: Most Americans live in large cities or suburbs, and see small towns only as they are passing through. They are accustomed to dealing with strangers, so when they search for a shock absorber or a motel room, they crave the security of a known chain where there are "no surprises."

So now TV advertises "your hometown Pizza Hut," although about the only thing hometown about it is that there is probably one on the highway near where you live, pretty much like every other one in the country. Even the idea of a pizza "hut" is neutralizing; not only is it devoid of ethnic content (unless you're thinking Polynesian), it doesn't even make sense.

The highway chain outlets with the dependability supposedly guaranteed by national advertising and centralized management, and the carefully designed imagery of nostalgia, friendliness, and personal service, make up what Ralph Keyes has called our "National Hometown," and it is just about the only kind of hometown we have left. Television may be the disembodied bedrock of the National Hometown, but the mall is its greatest physical manifestation.

When I was growing up, there was still a living downtown not yet completely replaced by the National Hometown. It was a mostly dying organism by then, but there was yet a discernable cycle of change: Some things got old, some aged gracefully and usefully, and some decayed. Some were replaced by something new. But most of what was new wasn't happening in town anymore, so this openness to uncontrolled change became a kind of tragic flaw. The Main Street of Greensburg was not enclosed or protected, and so without the infusion of the new, it simply got old and empty. It wasn't a street that began at a castle and ended in a village square. It had dirty, noisy trucks adding to the heat of summer or splashing slush in the winter.

It had its inconveniences, but what I remember best about growing up mall-less in Greensburg is the weather, and how it related to the world of the town and added its character to my experiences there. As an adolescent, I played off my moods against the wind and rain and sunshine, the contours of clouds and the colors of the sky, the part of every day ruled by the stars, and the months made by the moon. I saw it where my life took me, including Main Street. Weather changed and it was worth watching, as were the cycles of day and night and the seasons. The gradations of weather and time taught me something about the gradations and complexities of emotions.

An irony of my return was that I had to escape the staginess of the city, the blotting out of the sky by buildings and high electric lights, I wanted again those reassuring glimpses of the moon and stars through a window, the feel of a bright sky widening my eyes. I found those sensations again—but I also found my hometownspeople flocking to enclosures isolated from their hills and trees and as separated from nature and weather as any city street.

You don't learn much about cycles and changes in the mall, except perhaps for the nearly secret way one store replaces another. There is no reference to the triumphs or disasters of history, unless you count Presidents' Day sales. It is unchanging, ideal, and neutral, except that everything is linked to commerce. It becomes as addictive as junk food—pretty soon we can't accept any environment unless it has shopping. The absence of weather—of anything larger than the mall itself and its commerce—intensifies the shopping experience until it assumes a disproportionate importance. The mall is the universe! There's no relief, no contrast, no cosmic *caveats*; just the mall.

The mall's neutrality is in some ways democratic; nowhere else, at least before the mall came, was absolutely any style clothing appropriate for everything and at every time of the day. The mall, being everything, is nothing in particular. Still, there is the sense in which the artificial dream world of the mall is like an artificial flower: It will never die because it was never alive.

Probably the mall-goer wants it just that way. After all, nobody goes to the mall to be depressed, or even to learn anything; certainly not to face reality. The real world is too troubled, and even the small town sees that, not only on television but in the hospitals, the divorce courts, the shelters for battered women, the drug and alcohol rehab programs, the child abuse agencies, the welfare office, the Unemployment Compensation lines; in the homes that need repair, the cars that need to be replaced, or with the children whose college education promises to cost a small and nonexistent fortune. It's better to escape to a place where, in the parlance of the eighties, everything is "positive." The real world drives the mall-goers inside, where they are sold a superficial dream. They go looking for novelty but they want to be protected, passively embraced, brought home.

Still, even before the mall, Greensburg was not an idyllic place to be young. In many ways it was a classically crushing small-town environment. I yearned for a wider world. In particular, growing up there in the 1950s and 1960s was hardly ideal. It wasn't Clark Kent's Smallville of the twenties—it was too large a place and too late in history for that. But as prosperity took hold, the new ideas and materialism were adamantly resisted at the same time that every new gadget and fast-food invention was excitedly embraced. Then, when the degraded styles associated with the sixties finally became financially profitable, they, too, were eagerly accepted.

The typical blandness and provinciality of a small town were in some ways made even worse by industrial prosperity. As long as anyone put in the hours and played the game, attainment of the American Dream was apparently automatic. Taking risks to achieve a special dream was considered foolhardy. The dreamer was called conceited. There was little incentive to learn for the sake of learning, to think and feel more subtly and appreciate more deeply, to speak and move through life more gracefully, or act more compassionately. Those who tried to connect with that kind of wider world faced the censure of the certain. For all the new stuff and styles the malls brought, they didn't change this.

Now that the willingness to punch a time clock no longer guarantees a life of two cars and a new house filled with microwave ovens and color TVs, some Greensburg people are in shock. Their certainty has been taken from them, along with their work and earning power. You can see them sometimes, dazed, angry, and exhausted, sitting in the malls—the castles of the middle-class kingdom that has used and callously abandoned them.

By the 1960s, there were few places left for the young to be together informally or to be alone in pleasant and evocative circumstances, as there would be when the malls came. But even if its golden age could be recaptured, few Greensburgers of any age would really want to go back to the old small-town Main Street. By now it would be far too dull. Out at the mall they can have it both ways, for the mall's Main Street—the Highway Comfort Culture in the guise of the small town—has brought the brightness inside and scaled it down to the slow gait of people on the ground rather than to fast glances from speeding metal on the highway. Here the fantasy is savored and walked around in. It's the consumer Garden of Eden in the postwar paradise.

Besides, people come to the malls from towns and suburban tracts as far as fifty miles away. They don't have to know each other—they know what to expect. They will come together in this timeless, placeless space that's always colorful, clean, spacious, comforting, always new, always the same. Good malls make good neighbors, and they are neighbors here, in Never-Never Land.

"Seen Through Rose-Tinted Glasses" The Barbie Doll in American Society

Marilyn Ferris Motz

She has the face of an angel, the body of Jamie Lee Curtis, the IQ of a lettuce leaf, but she's a real doll.

Pop Catalog

While students of popular culture acknowledge the "molding" powers of popular artifacts and events, there is little doubt that the primary focus of our studies is usually placed upon the reflective side of the "funhouse mirror." Perhaps this is in reaction to the strident criticisms offered by elite critics who rail against the pernicious influence of popular culture, or perhaps it is simply a result of our intense interest in revealing and understanding the cultural mindset finding expression in this mass culture. Whatever the cause, however, we need to be careful to recognize that the reflective and formative functions are finally inseparable from each other—that a given artifact or event inculcates a message at the very same time that it carries it.

This balance—and the need to ensure that the formative "educative" powers of popular culture do not go unnoted—is especially important when the object of our analysis appeals to an audience composed primarily of children. Children are both more likely to be influenced by the hidden messages defining a popular artifact and less likely to have a worldview reflected by their culture. While an adult audience may have its pre-existing beliefs and values reinforced and expressed by the culture it chooses, children are more often passive recipients of messages designed and promoted by adult producers.

Motz's essay detailing the beliefs and values embodied in the Barbie Doll is imbued with an especially serious tone which aptly indicates the importance of such messages when our children play with (dress up) and hug these dolls. Motz suggests that the "magical power" of

This essay in different form was published in *The Popular Culture Reader*, 3rd Edition, Christopher Geist and Jack Nachbar, eds. Bowling Green, OH: Bowling Green State University Press, 1983.

this icon may well rest in its transformation of each new generation into women who can only inhabit the very same world of endless consumerism, fanatical desire for an impossible-to-realize body image, and female subservience as their mothers. Motz draws upon all aspects of iconic Barbie—the doll's appearance, history, audience, and evolution—to demonstrate how Barbie's central meanings have both remained the same while her wardrobe has changed with the times to communicate these messages to new generations.

The voluptuous, plastic Barbie doll is an object familiar to almost every American. Probably the most popular doll ever produced, Barbie, at thirty-something, is already raising her second generation of children. She has appeared in countless newspaper and magazine stories and cartoons and has even entered into our everyday speech.

Barbie has become an icon. Much more than a mere toy, she has come to represent much of what we, as Americans, most admire and dislike about ourselves. She embodies our love/hate relationship with our consumption-oriented society. As a model for feminine behavior, Barbie is curiously outdated. Perhaps she was an anachronism even at the time she was invented in the late 1950s. Yet she functions as an icon because she represents so well the widespread values of modern American society, devoting herself to the pursuit of happiness through leisure and material goods. Elizabeth and Stewart Ewen have defined fashion as a language of "social dialogue in which desires are expressed, and symbolically met" (233). This is the language that Barbie speaks, and she translates it for female children, teaching them the skills by which their future success will be measured: purchase of the proper high-status goods, popularity with their peers, creation of the correct personal appearance, and the visible achievement of "fun" through appropriate leisure activities.

Barbie has served as a symbolic focus for debate over desirable cultural norms in general and over ideal behavior and appearance for women in particular. She has come under attack from both ends of the political spectrum for portraying women as hedonistic sex objects. Writers in such diverse publications as *Ms.*, *Christian Century* and *The Saturday Evening Post* have expressed concern about the values represented by the doll. Writing in the feminist magazine *Ms.* in 1979, Jane Leavy describes the Barbie doll as "a stereotype made flesh—Well, vinyl, anyway," retaining "the shape and sensibility of the year she was born, 1959," while teaching girls to be "sex objects and consumers." An editorial commentary in *Christian Century* in 1981 describes a surprisingly similar conservative outcry against the doll:

Oldsters will remember how Christians blasted Barbie for hedonism and materialism. A woman of leisure, she embodied little of the work ethic. What is more, her skimpy bikinis and sheer negligees were called the garb of the seducer. What is most, the seduced has an evident live-in friend named Ken, who with her must have consulted Planned Parenthood: she never became great with child.

The *Saturday Evening Post* in 1964 articulated the concern many Americans felt even then about the influence of the Barbie doll. William K. Zinsser writes sarcastically that Barbie truly "is a person of sensitivity and taste, a fit model for American girlhood, which sees projected in her—in her lavish clothes, coiffures and activities—its dream of the ideal life." Zinsser goes on to discuss the extent to which the Barbie doll may reveal some unpleasant truths about our society. "With its emphasis on possession and its worship of appearances, it is modern America in miniature—a tiny parody of our pursuit of the beautiful, the material and the trivial" (72-73).

By the 1980s, when her early owners had reached adulthood, Barbie had attracted adult fans as well as critics. Adult collectors, male and female, have amassed comprehensive and valuable collections of Barbie dolls, clothes and accessories. They have joined to form a Barbie doll collectors' association, and one California woman has opened her collection to the public as a Barbie museum.[1] Several laudatory pictorial histories of Barbie have been published, ranging from price guides for collectors to Billy Boy's lavishly illustrated oversize *Barbie: Her Life and Times*. The latter was produced in conjunction with an exhibit of clothes specially designed for Barbie by many of the world's leading dress designers, including Yves St. Laurent and Bill Blass, to celebrate Barbie's twenty-fifth birthday. Tiffany was commissioned to create a sterling silver Barbie doll, and Mayor Ed Koch proclaimed Fifth Avenue "Barbie Boulevard" in honor of the occasion (Robins 108). Billy Boy, who assembled the exhibit with the financial support of Mattel, writes of his childhood fascination with Barbie: "Growing up with Wilma Flintstone, Betty Rubble, Lucy, Patty Duke, and a myriad of other pop heroines, I knew that when Barbie entered my life it was going to be a *long* relationship! She was the perfect one. The goddess long awaited. The endless search was over. My interest in fashion and sociology undoubtedly stems from this early encounter." The opening of the show featured "a series of life-sized Barbie environments that represented the current collection of Barbie theme dolls. The entertainment included two-story-high Barbie cutouts, smoke machines, a breakaway wall of TV monitors, holograms of Martians, an animated video of Barbie and the Rockers debuting 'Born with a Mike in my Hand,' and six models dressed as Barbie, including one that glowed in the dark" (Boy 9-10). Also for Barbie's twenty-fifth birthday, the Indiana State Museum created an exhibition, curated by Susan Dickey, on the history of the Barbie doll and its surrounding paraphernalia. Although the show itself examined both positive and negative cultural aspects of the doll, it drew an enthusiastic response from Barbie fans and collectors, many of whom traveled hundreds of miles to see the exhibit. Countless newspapers and magazines, including *Newsweek,* ran stories in 1989 about Barbie's thirtieth birthday, which Mattel celebrated and publicized with a black-tie Valentine's Day party in New York City (Kantrowitz 59).

Barbie has become available as an immediately recognized image of contemporary American society and as such is now frequently used by artists who want to comment (usually negatively) on the attitudes Barbie has come to represent. Andy Warhol included Barbie in the pantheon of images of American popular culture depicted in his art, and the doll has appeared in numerous cartoons and comic strips. A recent film based on the life of Karen Carpenter (who died of anorexia) used a Barbie doll to play the leading role, and a 1965 John Cleese photo comic strip, "Christopher's Punctured Romance" (in *Help!* magazine) depicts the infatuation a bored middle-aged man experiences for his daughter's Barbie doll.[2] The cover of the September 1991 issue of *National Lampoon* pokes fun at the artificial perfection of the Barbie doll's bustline. Silversmith Carol Green creates silver jewelry reminiscent of Barbie accessories: Barbie is so ubiquitous that even the shapes of characteristic accessories, such as her shoes, are readily recognizable. Barbie has become a visual symbol for consumption of material goods, attention to physical appearance, voyeuristic sexuality, and a lifestyle focused on personal pleasure. In the postmodern aesthetic characterized by pastiche, the blurring of the line between elite and popular culture, and the frequent referencing of earlier styles and symbols, however, the distinction between nostalgia and parody becomes blurred. Indeed Barbie's treatment by artists and the media reflects a common ambivalence about cultural values and gender roles. Graffiti artist Keith Haring created two "glowing baby" tee-shirts for the fashion exhibit celebrating Barbie's twenty-fifth birthday: his trademark design symbolizing nuclear holocaust had become fashion chic (Boy 184).

The doll itself has changed in response to changing cultural values. A *Hi and Lois* cartoon suggests Barbie has grown from Prom Queen to career woman. In the 1980s Mattel directed some of its marketing strategy to mothers who themselves played with Barbie dolls and who were concerned that Barbie provide a career-oriented role model for their daughters. In the 1980s Barbie acquired outfits for working as an airline pilot, doctor, astronaut, reporter and business executive, as well as for working out in the gym. On military bases, she was sold in uniforms for the Armed Forces, and during the Gulf War, Mattel announced plans to market these dolls to the general public as well. An ad for the astronaut Barbie, produced in 1986, reads:

> Not so long ago, you played with Barbie and dreamed of becoming all Barbie was. A Career woman. A trendsetter. A sweetheart to someone special.
>
> A mother now, you hold those dreams doubly dear—for you, and your daughter. And Barbie is still the doll to dream on. To grow on.
>
> Bring Barbie into your little girl's life. Because when a girl has dreams, she can do anything. Right, Barbie?

In 1991 Mattel introduced a line of African American dolls. Shani, whose name is Swahili for "marvelous," wears clothes that reflect her African heritage. In contrast to earlier black dolls in the Barbie line, Shani has African American friends, Asha and Nichelle. After conducting focus groups with mothers and daughters, Mattel decided to create the line of dolls with diverse skin tones, facial features, and hair color to represent the diversity of the African American population.

Most American women who are today in their twenties or thirties grew up with Barbie, and if newspaper columns are any indication, many view the doll as a factor (positive or negative) in their own psychological development. A columnist for the *Toledo Blade* described her childhood envy of a playmate whose more affluent parents could afford to buy her numerous Barbie dolls and outfits, while another woman, writing in the *Cleveland Plain Dealer*, discusses how her mother's prohibition of the doll as too large-breasted led to her negative feelings about the female body.[3] Such articles, written by former Barbie owners, reflect a more complicated response to the doll than evidenced in the critiques of earlier decades. Adult women react to the doll on the basis of childhood memories, adult assessments of the current doll's attributes, awareness of the doll as a cultural symbol, and, for many, experiences with their own daughters. For the past three decades the Barbie doll has played an important and complex role in the socialization of American women.

Barbie was first manufactured by Mattel in 1959, and, in an industry in which most products quickly come and go, Barbie's longevity is unique. Ruth Handler claims to have created Barbie after observing her own daughter, after whom the doll is named, cutting out clothes for her paper dolls. She set out to design a three-dimensional fashion doll. Despite the initial skepticism expressed by buyers about a doll with the figure of a mature woman, Barbie rapidly became a success ("It's Not the Doll" 51; Zinsser "Barbie" 73). Mattel sold nearly 112 million Barbie dolls between 1958 and 1978 (Leavy 102). By 1981, Barbie's sales had increased to nearly 8 million dolls per year, or 70 to 72 percent of the fashion doll industry, according to Mattel (Walsh 2). By 1988, Mattel sold over 20 million Barbie dolls per year (Robins 124). The popularity of the

Barbie doll led to many imitations, including Miss Sergio Valente, Brooke and Jordache. Barbie remains the star, however, and is the only one of these dolls to achieve national recognition as a cultural icon.

With each early Barbie doll came a small booklet picturing and describing each of Barbie's outfits. The young owner of a Barbie doll could contemplate at leisure the choice between the floor length black lamé "Solo in the Spotlight," complete with microphone, or "Candy Striper Volunteer," with food tray and uniform. Since most outfits sold for no more than three or four dollars, she could even buy the clothes with her allowance. It requires little skill in arithmetic to see that the dolls, which cost only about three dollars, quickly could amass quite an expensive array of clothes. Mattel provided an unending supply of variations on the basic Barbie and Ken, including "Barbie Twist and Turn" who could be bent into various poses, "Barbie Color and Curl" whose hair could be colored and styled, "Talking Barbie" (some of whom spoke Spanish), "Malibu Barbie" with a suntan, "Hispanic Barbie" with darker skin and black hair, and an African American Barbie. For those who tired of the original Ken, Mattel created a long-haired "Malibu Ken," who came quipped with a razor to "shave" the beard drawn on with a special pencil. Barbie's entourage of friends and relatives is extensive. In addition to her boyfriend, Ken, and girlfriend, Midge, Barbie has had a younger sister, Skipper, sibling twins, Tutti and Todd, and numerous friends, as well as a horse, a dog with puppies and a kitten.[4] Many girls own several Barbies, as well as her friends and relatives.

Like any successful brand-name product, Barbie's image is carefully presented and nurtured by marketing and public relations departments. By 1964, Mattel employed twenty-five press agents and forty-five advertising executives in addition to "personal secretaries" who answered the thousands of letters Barbie received each month. Fifteen people were hired to run the Barbie Fan Club, which attracted half a million members and published a bimonthly Barbie magazine with 100,000 subscribers (Zinsser, "Barbie" 73). Mattel also created a Barbie "Queen of the Prom" game and authorized other products with the Barbie insignia. In the 1980s the Barbie Fan Club was revived. For five dollars, which can be applied toward the purchase of certain Barbie outfits, a girl (with her Barbie doll in hand) can attend meetings of her local Barbie Fan Club and receive a poster, magazine and other products. Barbie, of course, also is advertised in magazines and on television. In 1987, Mattel sponsored a contest to select a real-life Barbie to perform as "Rocker Barbie" at Universal Studios (Robin 120).

Over the years, Mattel has created a personality for Barbie. Through the choice of accessories produced for the doll, the images of Barbie in advertisements and on doll clothing and accessory packages, and the depiction of Barbie in books, comic books, baseball-type trading cards,

The cover of a Barbie coloring book with an emphasis on leisure and fun.

coloring books, sticker books and records, Mattel has developed Barbie as a distinct character. Children commenting on Barbie in a panel discussion in conjunction with the Indiana State Museum Barbie exhibit suggested that although they realized that Barbie did not really exist as a living person they viewed her as a fictional character with a specific personality. She is helpful, pleasant, cheerful and concerned about other people and the environment. In the 1970s, Barbie and her friends could be heard on a series of records. Barbie sings:

> Standing on the edge of time
> I can see I want to be
> In a place where good things happening
> Good things follow me.
>
> I'm happy I'm Barbie
> The feelings growing in me,
> Take time and we'll make
> Our own time being free.[5]

A 1983 Barbie sticker album copyrighted by Mattel describes Barbie:

> As beautiful as any model, she is also an excellent sportswoman. In fact, Barbie is seen as a typical young lady of the twentieth century, who knows how to appreciate beautiful things and, at the same time, live life to the fullest. To most girls, she appears as the ideal elder sister who manages to do all those wonderful things that they can only dream of. With her fashionable wardrobe and constant journeys to exciting places all over the world, the adventures of Barbie offer a glimpse of what they might achieve one day. If Barbie has a message at all for us, it is to ignore the gloomy outlook of others and concentrate on all those carefree days of youth. Whatever lies in store will come sooner or later. If you stay close to your friend Barbie, life will always be seen through rose-tinted glasses.

Most owners of Barbie dolls are girls between the ages of three and eleven years of age. A Mattel survey shows that by the late 1960s, the median age for Barbie doll play had dropped from age ten to age six (Rakstis 30). Younger children find it difficult to manipulate the relatively small dolls, although Mattel created "My First Barbie," that ostensibly was easier for young children to handle and dress. Although some boys admit to playing with Ken, or even Barbie, Barbie doll play seems to be confined largely to girls.

Like all small figures and models, Barbie, at 11 1/2 inches high, has the appeal of the miniature. Most people are fascinated with objects re-created on a smaller scale, whether they are model airplanes, electric trains, dollhouse furnishings, or doll clothes. Miniatures give us a sense of control over our environment, a factor that is particularly important for children, to whom the real world is several sizes too large. In playing with a Barbie doll, a girl can control the action, can be omnipotent in a miniature world of her own creation.

When a girl plays with a baby doll, she becomes in her fantasy the doll's mother. She talks directly to the doll, entering into the play as an actor in her own right. When playing with a Barbie doll, on the other hand, the girl usually "becomes" Barbie. She manipulates Barbie, Ken and the other dolls, speaking for them and moving them around a miniature environment in which she herself cannot participate. Through the Barbie doll, then, a pre-adolescent can engage in role-playing activities. She can imitate adult female behavior, dress and speech and can participate vicariously in dating and other social activities, thus allaying some of her anxieties by practicing the way she will act in various situations. In consultation with the friends with whom she plays, a girl can establish the limits of acceptable behavior for a young woman and explore the possibilities and consequences of exceeding those limits.

The girl playing with a Barbie doll can envision herself with a mature female body. "Growing-Up Skipper," first produced in 1975, grew taller and developed small breasts when her arms were rotated, focusing attention on the bodily changes associated with puberty. Of course, until the end of puberty, girls do not know the ultimate size and shape their bodies will assume, factors they realize will affect the way others will view and treat them. Perhaps Barbie dolls assuage girls' curiosity over the appearance of the adult female body, of which many have only limited knowledge, and allay anxiety over their own impending bodily development.

Through Barbie's interaction with Ken, girls also can explore their anxieties about future relationships with men. Even the least attractive and least popular girl can achieve, by "becoming" Barbie, instant popularity in a fantasy world. No matter how clumsy or impoverished she is in real life, she can ride a horse or lounge by the side of the pool in a world undisturbed by the presence of parents or other authority figures. The creator of the Barbie doll, Ruth Handler, claims that "these dolls become an extension of the girls. Through the doll each child dreams of what she would like to be" (Zinsser, "Barbie" 73). If Barbie does enable a girl to dream "of what she would like to be," then what dreams and goals does the doll encourage? With this question, some of the negative aspects of the Barbie doll emerge.

The clothes and other objects in Barbie's world lead the girl playing with Barbie to stress Barbie's leisure activities and emphasize the importance of physical appearance. The shape of the doll, its clothes and the focus on dating activities present sexual attractiveness as a key to popularity and therefore to happiness. Finally, Barbie is a consumer. She demands product after product, and the packaging and advertising imply that Barbie, as well as her owner, can be made happy if only she wears the right clothes and owns the right products. Barbie conveys the message that, as the saying goes, a woman can never be too rich or too thin. The Barbie doll did not create these attitudes. Nor will the doll insidiously instill these values in girls whose total upbringing emphasizes other factors. An individual girl can, of course, create with her own doll any sort of behavior and activities she chooses. Still, the products available for the doll tend to direct play along certain lines. Barbie represents an image, and a rather unflattering one, of American women. It is the extent to which this image fits our existing cultural expectations that explains the popularity of the Barbie doll.

In physical appearance, Barbie's resemblance to a real woman is vague. Standing 11 1/2 inches tall, the original Barbie measured 5 1/4 x 3 x 4 3/4 inches. Translating these measurements into human terms, if Barbie stood five feet nine inches tall, her bust measurement would be 33 inches, her waist a meager 18 inches and her hips only 28 1/2 inches. In comparison, one beauty contest organizer assessed the average measurements of beauty contest winners who are 5 feet 6 inches tall as 36 x 25 x 35 (Boyd 1). Barbie's arms are extremely thin and her hands disproportionately small. Her legs are much too long and her tiny feet are permanently molded in a position suitable for wearing high-heeled shoes. This not only forces Barbie into a peculiar position when skiing, ice skating, riding horseback or wearing bedroom slippers, but also increases the already extraordinary length of her legs. While the Barbie doll at first glance appears to be large-busted, this is true only in comparison to the unrealistic thinness of other areas of her anatomy. Barbie's breasts, however, defy the force of gravity, jutting out unsupported at a 45 degree angle from her chest.

Does Barbie affect the body-image of girls as they approach adolescence? Do some girls consciously or unconsciously expect to attain Barbie's anatomically impossible proportions? Does Barbie represent an ideal of beauty that leads thousands of young women to starve themselves, suffering from eating disorders such as anorexia nervosa and bulimia, in a futile attempt to achieve a Barbie-like thinness that they view as the normal shape of the female body? Barbie probably is proportioned as she is to enable her to wear clothing without looking overly bulky. Since miniature figures usually are clothed in fabrics of normal thickness, the figure itself must be molded to thinner than normal proportions to compensate for the relative thickness of the fabric and seams. Yet regardless of the rationale for Barbie's proportions, she remains a significant model of adult femininity for pre-adolescent girls who are in the process of forming their own body images and expectations. Furthermore, since the vast majority of Barbie dolls have been white, and until the 1990s even black Barbie dolls differed only in skin tone, the ideal of feminine beauty presented was that of a white woman.

Mattel spokesperson Candace Irving notes that, "We don't make our toys for feminists, we make them for kids. And little girls love to comb hair and play with clothes and pretend what they're going to be

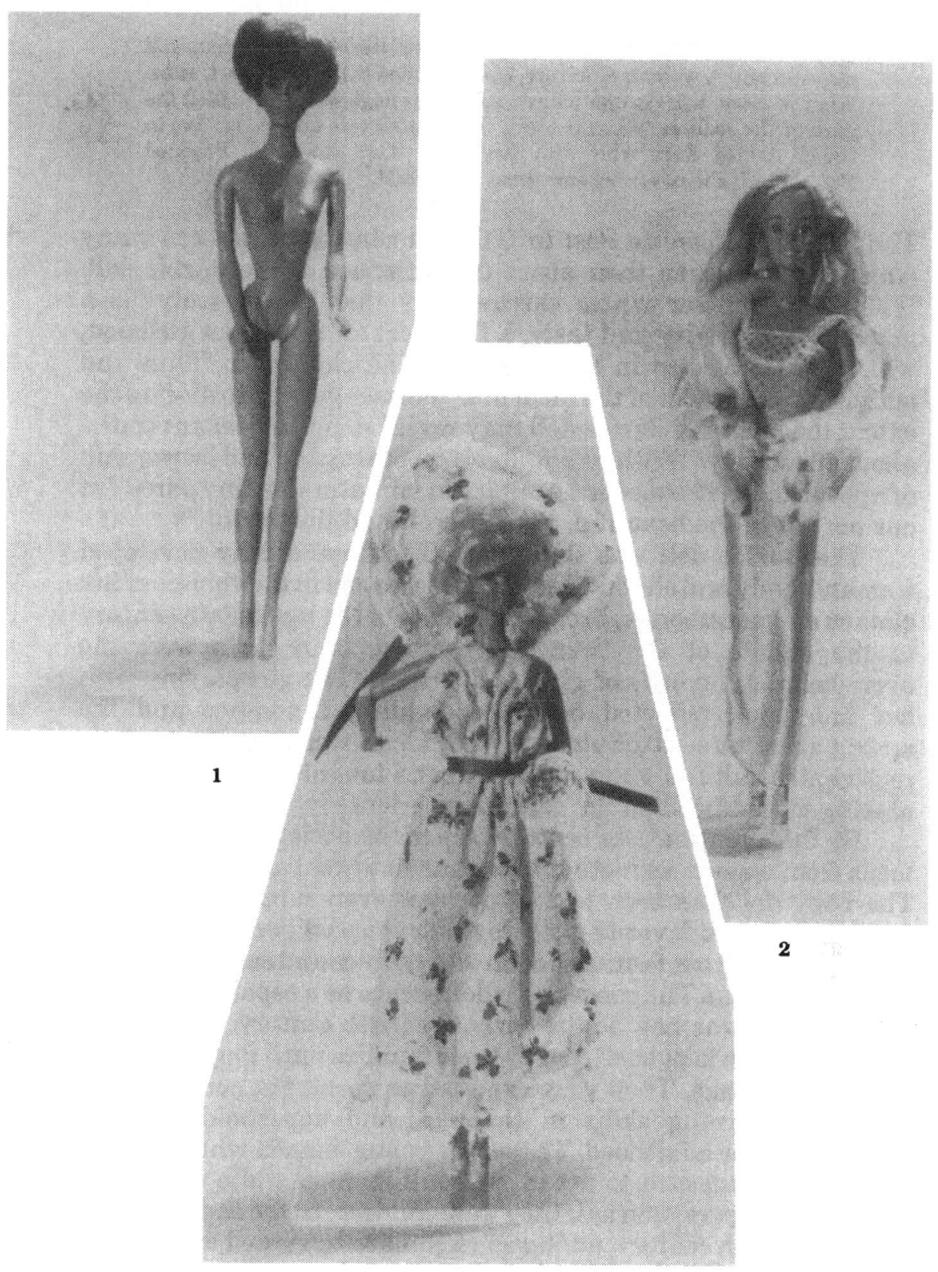

1. Barbie, c.1962.
2. "Pink and Pretty Barbie," c.1983. Doll courtesy of Meghan Marsden.
3. "Fashion Barbie," c.1979, in hand-made dress and hat. Doll courtesy of Sascha Geist.

like when they get to be teenagers" (Noll 13). Mattel conducts focus groups of children and mothers to gauge their responses to proposed Barbie items, and the company adjusts its production decisions accordingly. Clearly, the doll represents a young child's view of the adult world. To some extent this may literally be true. To a child looking up, adults' legs would appear elongated and women's busts might appear to project horizontally.[6] Children's own art work typically depicts the human body (and other subject matter) in a stylized way, with some features exaggerated and others eliminated. This effect appears in many toys and seems to fit with children's perceptions of the world around them. Similarly, the bright colors of Barbie's wardrobe reflect children's tastes: the colors and styles of Barbie's clothing are closer to those of girls' clothes than to those of adult women's clothes. Given the doll's lasting popularity, it is probably safe to assume that Barbie satisfies the needs and desires of large numbers of girls. What is difficult to determine is the extent to which girls playing with Barbie recognize her as a fantasy creation unlike any real women, or conversely, the extent to which they view her as a realistic role model.

Most children recognize that some toys and stories are not intended to represent a realistic image of the world but instead to create a fantasy environment. This is the case with traditional fairy tales as well as modern cartoons, superheroes, etc. When toys are close enough to reality to be plausible, however, as is the case with most dolls, many young children have difficulty determining whether they represent realistic or fantasy appearances and lifestyles. The extent to which a child makes this distinction is influenced in part by the attitude of the child's parents toward the toy and the extent to which other aspects of the child's view of the world (such as personal observation, television, other toys, books, etc.) support or contradict the image of reality presented by the toy.

The impact of toys on children is complex and controversial. It is easy to see that toys often reflect or recreate the adult world and therefore express adult cultural values. One of the ways children learn how to act in a particular society is through role-playing—in other words, through acting out in their play the behavior and attitudes they observe in the adult world or which are described to them by adults, other children, or the mass media (Barthes 53-55). Through this type of play, children can imagine themselves to be adults: they can try out in fantasy various situations and roles. In doing this, they are developing their own self-images and building goals and expectations for their future lives. Thus toys, which often encourage specific forms of role-playing, not only reflect adult values and behavior but also ensure that those values and behavior patterns are passed on to the next generation. But the process is not quite that simple: individual children may play with the same toys and yet grow up with very different attitudes and behavior patterns. Toys are only a small factor in a child's perception of the world. Each child's unique personality and environment may lead her to unique interpretations of a particular toy regardless of the intentions of the manufacturer or the opinions held by adults.

Parents limit and direct children's play scenarios; playmates partially determine the nature of dramatic play; and the values the child develops through other sources (family, school, religion, television) influence the way she will interact with a doll. While some children may be influenced heavily by the play scenarios encouraged by the clothing and accessories marketed by Mattel and the depiction of the character of Barbie created through *Barbie* magazine and other sources, other children may create their own idiosyncratic Barbie personas and use the doll in play scenarios independent of commercial accessories (making clothes for Barbie and using her in conjunction with blocks, for example). One doll exhibited at the Indiana State Museum Barbie exhibition, for instance, wore homemade maternity clothes over a pillow attached to her abdomen with velcro. A clinic specializing in helping children adjust to the results of limb amputations uses Barbie dolls specially fitted with prostheses to assist its young patients in dealing with their new body images (Gellene 4). Doubtless many children use the dolls to act out scenarios relevant to their own lives. Some children even use toys in a subversive way—for instance, turning Barbie into a witch or dismembering the doll—to express their rejection, at least temporarily, of the values Barbie is intended to represent.

Children will also view the vast array of items consumed by Barbie in different lights according to their own economic situations. To some girls, Barbie may seem to live a lifestyle not very different from those of their own families, while to others she may represent a lifestyle either to be resented or dismissed as unattainable or to be desired as a goal in their own lives. Mattel's 1980s advertising slogan, "You can be anything you want to be. Right, Barbie?" not only plays on women's increased life choices but also suggests that Barbie may represent a form of imaginative escape to girls dissatisfied with their own situations in real life. Candace Irving, manager of marketing and public relations for Mattel, claimed that "Barbie is every little girl. She is the person they are working out how to become. She is very personal to every little girl who plays with her, representing their fantasies of what they'll be as a teenager or an adult" (Robins 5). Although this statement may have been intended to allay criticism of the doll as a purveyor of negative values, individual children probably do view Barbie differently. Twelve-year old Nicole Alexander, commenting on Barbie at the Indiana State Museum Barbie exhibition, noted: "She's on Easy Street. She's always sitting around and looking pretty, and that's basically it. But some girls can't be glamorous and pretty. It really doesn't matter whether you're beautiful on the outside. You have to be beautiful on the inside" (Garlock 15). Given the paucity of data currently available, discussions of the impact of playing with Barbie can only be suggestive rather than conclusive.

What can be stated with confidence is that the Barbie doll revolutionized the doll industry and formed a substantial part of the childhood play environment experienced by the majority of American women under forty-five years of age. Barbie has become a cultural icon recognized by almost all Americans. She represents values common in late twentieth-century America and assists girls in assimilating those values as their own. While individual families and girls may reject or modify these values, the message conveyed by the doll continues to resonate with a majority of Americans: the keys to happiness are an attractive physical appearance, popularity, the accumulation of material goods, and the enjoyment of leisure time. The Barbie doll encourages girls to view as desirable those values and behavior patterns which support an economy in which the women's primary function is that of consumer and a social structure in which her key role is to be attractive to men.

From the middle of the nineteenth century to the middle of the twentieth century, when innocence, maternal instinct, and domesticity were highly valued in women, baby dolls were the overwhelming favorite of girls and parents. The girl playing with her baby doll reflected both the childlike innocence and the maternal nature attributed to the ideal woman. These dolls represented cultural values to adults and taught them to children, placing motherhood as the central experience in a woman's life (Motz). By the late twentieth century, American society had shifted its focus from woman as mother to woman as sexual and social being. The baby doll has been joined, perhaps even supplanted, by the fashion doll as a favorite girls' toy. The Barbie doll was the first doll to have a fully developed woman's body, and she outdoes her predecessors in the volume of her clothes and accessories. For the past twenty-five years girls have acted out fantasies of an adolescence and early adulthood without children. The concept of adolescence as a separate phase in the life cycle was new to the early twentieth century. Before that time, girls were kept sheltered by their families until they reached a marriageable age. They were expected to spend the period of late childhood learning skills in childcare and household tasks in preparation for adulthood. Those few young women who attended college were expected to act in an adult manner while remaining under close supervision as if they were children. In the early decades of the twentieth century, adolescence came to be viewed as a unique period of life. For the first time young adults were perceived as "teenagers," whose behavior differed from that expected of either children or adults. They became, indeed, a privileged class, largely free from the responsibilities of adulthood, yet also free of the restraints and control exercised over children.

In the affluent 1950s, these teenagers became a highly visible portion of society, with their rock music, transistor radios, bobby sox and hot rods. Adolescence developed a culture of its own and the teenage girl became a star of the social scene. Unrestrained by chaperones, and not yet burdened with children and housework, she kept all her options open. For the only time in her life, she could control her own actions as well as the actions of the men who admired her. It is no wonder that she appeared to many of those older as well as younger than herself to lead an ideal life. Adolescence was anticipated with longing, remembered with nostalgia. To many Americans, the teenage girl represented the epitome of feminine attractiveness. The greatest compliment one could pay a mature woman was to tell her she looked "just like a teenager." The early Barbie doll, following this trend, baby-sat, attended the prom, was a cheerleader, and participated in other aspects of adolescent life. Parents, many of whom had seen their own adolescence clouded or cut short by World War II, encouraged their sons and daughters, like Barbie, to enjoy their teenage years. Indeed, the affluent, carefree teenager represented the new prosperity and leisure of the post-war years.

Barbie seems to have grown older along with the rest of the post-war "baby boom" generation. She attended college in the 1970s and now lives alone (or with Ken) in her own house or townhouse. The high school activities have disappeared. By the 1980s Americans had replaced the teenage beach party idol with the athletic, independent woman in her late twenties or even early thirties, and Barbie has kept pace. Like many of the baby boom generation, Barbie is enjoying the life of the affluent single, or married but childless, woman. Barbie presents, in a concrete image, adult society as seen by the children of America. For if Barbie had failed to appear "real" to American girls, her popularity would have ended years ago.

While the overall impression of the Barbie doll is of a sexually mature body, Barbie presents a smoothed-over version of the female anatomy, clearly designed to titillate rather than to provide sexual gratification to herself or to Ken. Indeed, Barbie projects a sexual come-on while remaining virginal (a virginity ensured by Ken's total lack of sexual equipment). One look at the original Barbie's face reveals that she was not a warm, understanding, intelligent partner but a cool, controlled, perhaps even manipulative lady. Thus what might appear to be a sexually suggestive doll, as critics at first feared, is in actuality a model of self-control, using her sexuality to attract men while ensuring that her relationships would remain safely platonic. Far from being a sex goddess, Barbie was the epitome of the unapproachable woman. It is interesting that in the late 1960s, when standards of sexual behavior relaxed and make-up and clothing emphasized the natural look, Mattel gave Barbie a new face. The newer Barbie has a more friendly, open expression, with a hint of a smile, and her lip and eye make-up is muted. In 1971, as assertiveness in women became desirable, Barbie's coy glance to the side was replaced with the more direct look of pupils staring straight ahead.

Much of the cultural significance of the Barbie doll arises not from the doll itself but from its many clothes and accessories. At the time the Barbie doll was created, many parents hailed the doll as a model of wholesome teenage behavior and appearance. Barbie clearly scorned the world of gang members, known as "greasers" or "hoods," wearing black leather jackets. Barbie was affluent, well-groomed, socially conservative. Her choice of outfits in the 1960s included "Country Club Dance," "Debutante Party" and "Sorority Meeting." During the late 1960s and early 1970s, Barbie may also have allayed new fears about daughters growing up to be "hippies," political radicals or recreational drug users. Barbie conforms to the status quo; she is the All-American girl. Ruth Handler, creator of the doll, was quoted in 1964 as saying that:

> parents thank us for the educational values in the world of Barbie....They say that they could never get their daughters well groomed before—get them out of slacks or blue jeans and into a dress, get them to scrub their necks and wash their hair. Well, that's where Barbie comes in. The doll has clean hair and a clean face, and she dresses fashionably, and she wears gloves and shoes that match. (Zinsser 73)

Barbie's appearance, as well as the many accessories that accompany her, follow traditional standards of feminine behavior and appearance, standards that, as Mrs. Handler's comments suggest, were already becoming outdated by the time the doll became popular. Early Barbie costumes included those of a ballerina, a nurse, an airline stewardess and a nightclub singer, as well as an apron with rolling pin and pot holder and a wedding dress. The sixty-four outfits sold for Barbie in 1963 included only one "Career Girl" suit, and few of the outfits produced would be even remotely appropriate to wear in an office. Most of Barbie's accessories even today focus on fashion, glamour and leisure. In the 1970s "Miss America" Barbies were produced. Barbie has had a modeling studio, clothing and record stores, and a beauty shop in which to have her hair styled.

Mattel claims that Barbie's theater, created in 1964, was of educational value (Zinsser 73). However, the costumes provided by Mattel indicate that what was being taught was submissive behavior for women. "Arabian Nights" included an Aladdin's lamp along with costumes for Barbie and Ken. It is unclear whether Barbie was intended to be a genie or a member of Ken's harem! "Cinderella" included two dresses. One consisted of rags for Barbie to wear until Ken, dressed as "The Prince," came to the rescue, after which she could don the formal ball gown. As "Guinevere," Barbie could await the arrival of Ken, now literally a knight in shining armor in his "King Arthur" costume, complete with helmet, sword and shield. Finally, dressed as "Red Riding Hood," Barbie could encounter the "Wolf," presumably played by Ken, for whom a grey plush hooded mask with red tongue was provided.

As an icon, Barbie not only reflects traditional, outdated roles for women; she and Ken also represent, in exaggerated form, characteristics of American society as a whole. Through playing with these dolls, children learn to act out in miniature the way they see adults behave in real life and in the media. The dolls themselves and the accessories provided for them direct this play, teaching children to consume and conform, to seek fun and popularity above all else.

Thorstein Veblen wrote in 1899 that America had become a nation of "conspicuous consumers." We buy objects, he wrote, not because we need them but because we want others to know we can afford them. We want our consumption to be conspicuous or obvious to others. The more useless the object, the more it reflects the excess wealth the owner can afford to waste. In the days before designer labels, Veblen wrote that changing fashions represent an opportunity for the affluent to show that they can afford to waste money by disposing of usable clothing and replacing it with new, faddish styles that will in turn be discarded after a few years or even months of wear (Veblen 60-131).

Sociologist David Riesman wrote in 1950 that Americans have become consumers whose social status is determined not only by what they can afford to buy but also by the degree to which their taste in objects of consumption conforms to that of their peers. Taste, in other words, becomes a matter of assessing the popularity of an item with others rather than judging on the basis of one's personal preference. Children, according to Riesman, undergo a process of "taste socialization," of learning to determine "with skill and sensitivity the probable tastes of the others" and then to adopt these tastes as their own. Riesman writes that "today the future occupation of all moppets is to be skilled consumers" (94, 96, 101). This skill lies not in selecting durable or useful products but in selecting popular, socially acceptable products that indicate the owner's conformity to standards of taste and knowledge of current fashion.

The Barbie doll teaches a child to conform to fashion in her consumption. She learns that each activity requires appropriate attire and that outfits that may at first glance appear to be interchangeable are slightly different from one another. In the real world, what seems to be a vast array of merchandise actually is a large collection of similar products. The consumer must make marginal distinctions between nearly identical products, many of which have different status values. The child playing with a Barbie doll learns to detect these nuances. Barbie's clothes, for instance, come in three lines: a budget line, a medium-priced line, and a designer line. Consumption itself becomes an activity to be practiced. From 1959 to 1964, Mattel produced a "Suburban Shopper" outfit. In 1976 the "Fashion Plaza" appeared on the market. This store consisted of four departments connected by a moving escalator. As mass-produced clothing made fashion accessible to all classes of Americans, the Barbie doll was one of the means by which girls learned to make the subtle fashion distinctions that would guarantee the proper personal appearances.

Barbie must also keep pace with all the newest fashion and leisure trends. Barbie's pony tail of 1959 gave way to a Jackie Kennedy style "Bubble-cut" in the early 1960s and to long straight hair in the 1970s. "Ken-A-Go-Go" of the 1960s had a Beatle wig, guitar and microphone, while the "Now Look Ken" of the 1970s had shoulder-length hair and wore a leisure suit (Leavy 102). In the early 1970s Ken grew a detachable beard. In 1971 Mattel provided Barbie and Ken with a motorized stage on which to dance in their fringed clothes, while Barbie's athletic activities, limited to skiing, skating, fishing, skydiving and tennis in the 1960s, expanded to include backpacking, jogging, bicycling, gymnastics and sailing in the 1970s. On the shelves in the early 1980s were Western outfits, designer jeans, and Rocker Barbie dressed in neon colors and playing an electric guitar. In 1992 a rollerblade Barbie was introduced.

Barbie clearly is, and always has been, a conspicuous consumer. Aside from her lavish wardrobe, Barbie has several houses complete with furnishings, a Ferrari and a '57 Chevy. She has at various times owned a yacht and several other boats as well as a painted van called the "Beach Bus." Through Barbie, families who cannot afford such luxury items in real life can compete in miniature. In her early years, Barbie owned a genuine mink coat. In the ultimate display of uselessness, Barbie's dog once owned a corduroy velvet jacket, net tutu, hat, sunglasses and earmuffs. Barbie's creators deny that Barbie's life is devoted to consumption. "These things shouldn't be thought of as possessions," according to Ruth Handler. "They are props that enable a child to get into play situations" (Zinsser 73). Whether possessions or props, however,

Conspicuous consumption. Barbie and her Ferrari.

the objects furnished with the Barbie doll help create play situations, and those situations focus on consumption and leisure.

A perusal of the shelves of Barbie paraphernalia in the Midwest Toys "R" Us store reveals not a single item of clothing suitable for an executive office. Mattel did produce a doctor's outfit (1973) and astronaut suit (1965 and 1986) for Barbie, but the clothes failed to sell. According to Mattel's marketing manager, "We only kept the doctor's uniform in the line as long as we did because public relations begged us to give them something they could point to as progress" in avoiding stereotyped roles for women (Leavy 102). In the 1960s, Mattel produced "all the elegant accessories" for the patio, including a telephone, television, radio, fashion magazines and a photograph of Barbie and Ken (Zinsser 72). The "Busy Barbie," created in 1972, had hands that could grasp objects and came equipped with a telephone, television, record player, "soda set" with two glasses and a tray, and a travel case. Apparently Barbie kept busy only with leisure activities; she seems unable to grasp a book or a pen. When Barbie went to college in the 1970s, her "campus" consisted only of a dormitory room, soda shop (with phone booth), football stadium and drive-in movie! (Zinsser 72). In the 1980s, Barbie traveled in her camper, rode her horse, played with her dog and cat, swam in her pool and lounged in her bubble bath (both with real water).

The Barbie doll of the 1980s presents a curiously mixed message. The astronaut Barbie wore a pink space suit with puffed sleeves. The executive Barbie wore a hot pink suit and a broad-brimmed straw hat, and she carried a pink briefcase in which to keep her gold credit card. Lest girls think Barbie is all work and no play, the jacket could be removed, the pink and white spectator pumps replaced with high-heeled sandals, and the skirt reversed to form a spangled and frilly evening dress. Barbie may try her hand at high-status occupations, but her appearance does not suggest competence and professionalism. In a story in *Barbie* magazine (Summer 1985) Barbie is a journalist reporting on lost treasure in the Yucatan. She spends her time "catching some rays" and listening to music, however, while her dog discovers the lost treasure. Barbie is appropriately rewarded with a guest spot on a television talk show! Although Barbie is shown in a professional occupation and even has her own computer, her success is attributed to good luck rather than her own (nonexistent) efforts. She reaps the rewards of success without having had to work for it; indeed, it is her passivity and pleasure-seeking (could we even say laziness) that allows her dog to discover the gold. Even at work, Barbie leads a life of leisure.

Veblen wrote that America, unlike Europe, lacked a hereditary aristocracy of families that were able to live on the interest produced by inherited wealth. In America, Veblen wrote, even the wealthiest men were self-made capitalists who earned their own livings. Since these men were too busy to enjoy leisure and spend money themselves, they delegated these tasks to their wives and daughters. By supporting a wife and daughters who earned no money but spent lavishly, a man could prove his financial success to his neighbors. Therefore, according to Veblen, affluent women were forced into the role of consumers, establishing the social status of the family by the clothes and other items they bought and the leisure activities in which they engaged (Veblen 44-131).

Fashions of the time, such as long skirts, immobilized women, making it difficult for them to perform physical labor, while ideals of beauty that included soft pale hands and faces precluded manual work or outdoor activities for upper-class women. To confer status, Veblen writes, clothing "should not only be expensive, but it should also make plain to all observers that the wearer is not engaged in any kind of productive employment." According to Veblen, "the dress of women goes even farther than that of men in the way of demonstrating the wearer's abstinence from productive labor." The high heel, he notes, "makes any, even the simplest and most necessary manual work extremely difficult," and thus is a constant reminder that the woman is "the economic dependent of the man—that, perhaps in a highly idealized sense, she still is the man's chattel" (Veblen 120-21, 129).

Not only is Barbie a conspicuous consumer who lives a life of leisure; standing as she does, on her toes, she is as immobilized as the nineteenth-century woman that Veblen described. Indeed, Veblen writes that in societies in which women are expected to confer status on their husbands and fathers through their display of leisure activities, "the ideal requires delicate and diminutive hands and feet and a slender waist. These features, together with the other, related faults of structure that commonly go with them, go to show that the person so affected is incapable of useful effort and must therefore be supported in idleness by her owner. She is useless and expensive, and she is consequently valuable as evidence of [high status]." Consequently, Veblen continues, "women take thought to alter their persons, so as to conform more nearly to the requirements of the instructed taste of the time," while men learn to "find the resulting artificially induced pathological features attractive" (Veblen 80). With her miniscule hands, feet and waist, Barbie presents just such a model of feminine beauty. Indeed her 33 x 18 x 28 figure is similar to those of women who were laced into corsets in the nineteenth century. Perhaps in modern American society, when few women are willing or able to model such ostentatious consumption and leisure, the doll itself provides the ritual family display of female uselessness.

Sociologist C. Wright Mills wrote in 1951 that men as well as women had begun to establish a sense of identity based on leisure activities, measuring their social status by the cars, boats or swimming pools they could afford to buy. Mills wrote that in an industrialized and urban society, people could no longer be known by their achievements, their traits of character or their family heritage. Instead, they established their status through visible leisure and consumption of objects. Hence the suburban lifestyle with its emphasis on leisure activities arose. Mills wrote that by the 1950s success was no longer expected to result from skill or hard work. One would succeed on the basis of personality and on the ability to make friends and get along with one's peers. One of the most popular books of the decade, *The Power of Positive Thinking*, provided guidelines to achieving business success through personality and social contacts. Personality, according to Mills, replaced character as a primary measure of one's worth. A pleasant smile, a well-groomed appearance, self-control and conformity replaced honesty, integrity and hard work as means to success in business and in personal life. The most valued traits became the "ability to get along with people and work co-operatively with them, ability to meet and talk to people easily, and attractiveness in appearance." Our cultural heroes, according to Mills, were no longer business or political achievers, but "those successful in entertainment, leisure, and consumption" (Mills 183-86, 236, 263-64).

Barbie clearly expects to achieve success on the basis of her social skills. In order to win "Queen of the Prom," a Barbie board game produced in 1961 and 1962, a contestant had to be crowned Prom Queen, a feat accomplished by getting a date with a popular boy, buying an appropriate prom dress, and being elected president of a school club. In the 1960s the Barbie doll could be either a cheerleader or a drum majorette. She had special outfits not only for sports activities but also for "a lunch date, an after-five date, a Friday night date, Saturday Matinee, theater date, golden evening" and a masquerade party. Of the sixty-four outfits available for Barbie in 1963, seventeen were evening clothes" (Zinsser, "Most" 72-75).

Barbie's world consisted of numerous friends, many of whom are no longer produced. By joining the Barbie Fan Club a girl could, in the 1970s, receive a poster signed by all the members of Barbie's social circle with such sentiments as "Be good, Ken," "Your friend Barbie," "To my friend, Skipper," "With love, Francie," and "Do Your Thing, P.J." The pictures on the boxes that house Barbie's pool and other accessories show Barbie happily involved with her friends. One collector estimated that Barbie's entourage has included at one time or another fifty-two different friends, relatives and pets, including celebrities like Debbie Boone (Walsh 2E). Describing contemporary American society in 1950, Riesman wrote that "making good becomes almost equivalent to making friends, or at any rate the right kind of friends." When popularity, or acceptance by one's peers, becomes the primary goal in life, then "people and friendships are viewed as the greatest of all consumables; the peer group is itself a main object of consumption" (Riesman 66, 102). With the creation of Barbie and her friends, Mattel enabled children to buy themselves an entire peer group, to "collect friends" quite literally.

Despite changes in the lives and expectations of real women, Barbie remains essentially the woman described by Veblen in the 1890s, excluded from the world of work with its attendant sense of achievement, forced to live a life based on leisure activities, personal appearance, the accumulation of possessions and the search for popularity. While large numbers of women reject this role, Barbie embraces it. The Barbie doll serves as an icon that symbolically conveys to children and adults the measures of success in modern America: wealth, beauty, popularity and leisure.

Notes

[1]In 1988, the Barbie Fan Club had 8500 chapters. Evelyn Burkhalter's Barbie Hall of Fame is located in Palo Alto, California. Cynthia Robins, *Barbie: Thirty Years of America's Doll* (Chicago: Contemporary Pooles, 1989) 124, 128.

[2]Kim Johnson, *The First 200 Years of Monty Python* (New York: St. Martin's, 1989) 33-43. I would like to thank Allyn Wilkinson for bringing this source to my attention.

[3]Ann Fisher, "Some Barbies had everything," *Toledo Magazine, Toledo Blade* 12-18 Feb. 1989: 23; Jeanne Marie Laskas, "Barbie (What a doll)," *The Plain Dealer Magazine, Cleveland Plain Dealer* 14 May 1989: 6-14. See also Robin Abcarium, "Barbie: Role model vs. fashion model," *Detroit Free Press* 8 March 1990 and Sandra Cisneros, "Barbie-Q," *Woman Hollering Creek* (New York: Random, 1991) 14-16.

[4]For description and photographs of Barbie dolls and accessories see Sibyl DeWein and Joan Ashabraner, *The Collectors Encyclopedia of Barbie Dolls and Collectibles* (Paducah, KY: Collector Books, 1977).

[5]"I'm Happy I'm Barbie," Mattel Inc. 1152, 1970 (7"/45 rpm), Music Library, Bowling Green State University.

[6]Art historian Timothy Motz made this observation.

[7]Roland Barthes elaborates on this point in *Mythologies* (New York: Hill and Wang, 1957—trans. 1972) 53-55.

Works Cited

Abcarian, Robin. "Barbie: Role Model vs. Fashion Model," *Detroit Free Press* 8 March 1990.

Barthes, Roland. *Mythologies*. New York: Hill and Wang, 1957—trans. 1972.

Boy, Billy. *Barbie!: Her Life and Times and The New Theatre of Fashion*. New York: Crown, 1987.

Boyd, L.M. "Checking Up." *Toledo Blade* 12 March 1983 (Peach Section): 1.

Cisneros, Sandra. "Barbie-Q" *Woman Hollering Creek*. New York: Random, 1991.

DeWein, Sibyl and Joan Ashabraner. *The Collectors Encyclopedia of Barbie Dolls and Collectibles*. Paducah, KY: Collector Books, 1977.

Ewen, Stuart and Elizabeth Ewen. *Channels of Desire: Mass Images and The Shaping of American Consciousness*. New York: McGraw-Hill, 1982.

Fisher, Ann. "Some Barbies Had Everything." *Toledo Magazine, Toledo Blade* 12-18 Feb. 1989.

Garlock, Karen. "Pink and Pretty Plastic." *The Enquirer Magazine, Cincinnati Enquirer* 24 March 1985.

Gellene, Denise. "Forever Young." *Los Angeles Times* 29 Jan. 1989.

"It's Not the Doll, It's the Clothes." *Business Week* 16 Dec. 1961.

Johnson, Kim. *The First 200 Years of Monty Python*. New York: St. Martin's, 1989.

Kantrowitz, Barbara. "Hot Date: Barbie and G.I. Joe." *Newsweek* 20 Feb. 1989.

Laskas, Jeanne Marie. "Barbie (What a Doll)." *The Plain Dealer Magazine, Cleveland Plain Dealer* 14 May 1989.

Leavy, Jane. "Is There a Barbie Doll in Your Past?" *Ms.* Sept. 1979.

Marty, Martin. "Baby in Toyland." *Christian Century* 23 Dec. 1981.

Mills, C. Wright. *White Collar: The American Middle Classes*. New York: Oxford UP, 1951.

Motz, Marilyn, "Maternal Virgin: The Girl and her Doll in Nineteenth Century America." *Objects of Special Devotion*. Ray Browne, ed. Bowling Green, OH: BGSU Popular Press, 1982.

Noll, Nancy. "Barbie: A Legend at 25." *Capital Magazine, Columbus Dispatch* 20 May 1984.

Riesman, David, Nathan Glazer and Reual Denney. *The Lonely Crowd: A Study of the Changing American Character*. Garden City, NY: Doubleday Anchor, 1950.

Rakstis, Ted. "Debate in the Doll House." *Today's Health* Dec. 1970.

Robins, Cynthia. *Barbie: Thirty Years of America's Doll*. Chicago: Contemporary Pooles, 1989.

Veblen, Thorstein. *The Theory of the Leisure Class*. 1899. New York: Mentor, 1953.

Walsh, Mary T. "Barbie Still Means Big Business." *Ashbury Park Press* 13 Sept. 1981: Sec. E, 2.

Zinsser, William K. "Barbie is a Million Dollar Doll." *Saturday Evening Post* 12 Dec. 1964: 72-73.

_____"The Most Popular Doll in Town." *Life* 23 August 1963.

Section
❁ 4 ❁

Stereotypes

Introduction
Breaking the Mold:
The Meaning and Significance of Stereotypes in Popular Culture

You See One King, You've Seen Them All: Defining Stereotypes

When the King of the Land of Reality whom we met in the Introduction arrived home after visiting the countries of his three trading partners, he was quite angry. All of the marvelous variety present in his land and in his people had been lost on his narrow-minded hosts. Each country had used a small number of characteristics to describe the inhabitants of the King's massive and variegated land—assuming that all Reality dwellers were cold fish, hot tamales or sons of the sea. The more he thought about it, the madder he became. He wondered if he could sue due to prejudicial treatment. The King's attorney checked a few case references and returned with the following verdict: the countries perceived reality and its inhabitants incorrectly, causing them to act foolishly and insensitively. But there was no cause for a lawsuit over the situation because there was no evidence of their intent to do harm. The countries had simply defined Reality dwellers in a limited manner which enabled each to plan their reception in an organized and (so they thought) appropriate way.

The King was upset with his trading partners because they had diminished him by treating him like a *stereotype*. His experience can provide us with an illustration of several important characteristics of this term:

1) A stereotype is a standardized conception or image of a specific group of people or objects. Stereotypes are "mental cookie cutters"—they force a simple pattern upon a complex mass and assign a limited number of characteristics to all members of a group. While we commonly use the term as it is applied to human beings, it is quite possible to stereotype objects as well. The King's trading partners stereotyped both the Land of Reality and Reality dwellers. In popular culture we can examine both types of stereotypes so that we often find people stereotyped around characteristics of *age* ("All teenagers love rock and roll and have no respect for their elders."), *sex* ("Men want just one thing from a

woman."), *race* ("All Japanese look and think alike."), *religion* ("All Catholics love the Pope more than their country."), *vocation* ("All lawyers are greedy weasels.") and *nationality* ("All Germans are Nazi warmongers."). Objects can be stereotyped around characteristics of *places* ("All cities are corrupt and sinful." "Small towns are safe and clean." "In England it rains all the time.") and *things* ("All American cars are cheaply and ineptly made." "A good house has a large lawn, big garage, and at least two bathrooms."). Because objects are studied more rewardingly as icons, however, we will use stereotypes primarily as a tool to examine popular beliefs and values about people.

2) The standardized conception is held in common by the members of a group. Popular stereotypes are images which are shared by those who hold a common cultural mindset—they are the way a culture, or significant sub-group within that culture, defines and labels a specific group of people. The three trading partners of Reality held stereotypical views of their visitor's land and people which were shared by most of the inhabitants of each country, and these stereotypes told the King something important about the way in which his land and people were being viewed and defined by different cultures. All of us have many narrow images of people, places, or things which are unique to our personal outlook, but these are of interest only to psychologists and our immediate family and friends, not to students of popular culture. Our goal is to define the cultural rather than individual mindset, so we therefore must search and examine wide social patterns of thought and behavior, not their exceptions.

3) Stereotypes are direct expressions of beliefs and values. A stereotype is a valuable tool in the analysis of popular culture because once the stereotype has been identified and defined, it automatically provides us with an important and revealing expression of otherwise hidden beliefs and values. This means that stereotypes are especially useful in tracing the evolution of popular thought—the way in which the beliefs and values associated with specific groups change over time. American attitudes toward Russians, for example, can be easily marked by the changing nature of the popular stereotype associated with them—from WWII ("fur-hatted vodka drinking comrades-in-arms") to Cold War ("Godless communists in an Evil Empire") to the break-up of the Soviet Union ("poor, hungry victims of a disorganized and self-defeating socialist system").

The Uses of Stereotypes

Stereotyping is a natural function of the human/cultural mind and is therefore morally neutral in and of itself. A culture, however, endorses moral or immoral actions based upon the beliefs and assumptions implicit in the simplifying stereotype.

The King couldn't sue his trading partners for their insensitive stereotyping because the countries had each simply done what every culture does—seek to simplify a complex Reality so that it can better determine how best to act in any given circumstance. What matters to us in evaluating and studying a specific stereotype is what type of actions result from belief in the stereotype and to what degree the stereotype is accurate. The stereotypes held by Reality's trading partners were essentially harmless as they roused no negative feelings toward the King, and he was actually even treated with respect. Stereotypes might actually have been quite helpful to each nation: suppose, for example, that country A had received a visitor from Northern Reality—then the stereotype of Reality dwellers would have a greater degree of accuracy and would have been a valuable tool in helping country A plan appropriate activities for their visitor, being relatively certain he or she was comfortable as well.

Stereotyping is such a natural human function and is so common that it occasionally functions in a useful way. For one thing, it is sometimes valuable to create classifications of individuals. The term "freshman" on college campuses brings to mind a popular image of a rather naive newcomer who is not familiar with both the social and intellectual life of a campus. Of course, many freshmen don't fit this narrow picture. Nevertheless, the stereotype of the freshman serves the purpose of encouraging professors to construct introductory courses for those with no experience in the subject matter and it also encourages campus social organizations like fraternities and sororities to sponsor group activities planned especially for campus newcomers.

A second useful function of stereotypes is in the use of what can be termed "countertypes." A countertype is a positive stereotype (one which arouses "good" emotions and associates a group of people with socially approved characteristics) which evolves as an attempt to replace or "counter" a negative stereotype which has been applied previously to a specific group of people. Negative stereotypes of African Americans were attacked by countertypes in the 1960s and 1970s in movies such as *Guess Who's Coming to Dinner* and *Shaft,* both of which featured strong, dynamic, intelligent black males. The process continues today with the positive portrayal of "Bumpies" (Black Upwardly Mobile Professionals) on television programs such as *The Cosby Show* and *L.A. Law.* The negative stereotype of "Women as Helpless Victims" has been challenged in recent years as well with countertypes on television ranging from the tough cops of *Cagney and Lacy* to the headstrong, independent *Murphy Brown.* And the negative view of Southern males as racist rednecks has been reworked through countertypes promoted in advertisements for the new South—television programs like *Evening Shade, Designing Women,* and *Matlock,* and the massively popular songs of country superstar Garth Brooks. Countertypes are important reflections (and shapers) of popular beliefs and values, but at least two characteristics need to be emphasized lest we permit good intentions to blind us to their real meaning and nature:

1) Countertypes are still stereotypes, and this means that they are still oversimplified views of the group being stereotyped. Many African Americans came to resent the "Sidney Poitier" stereotype of the black male which was a ubiquitous countertype in movies of the late 1960s and early 1970s, for example, because it seemed to imply that blacks were now simply slaves to another image promoted by white middle-class society—a different stereotype to be sure, but a stereotype nonetheless. The Poitier-countertype was often interpreted to be nothing more than a racist command for black males to clean up their acts, cut their hair, learn to speak English clearly and "properly," and pursue professional goals. Black males labeled the Poitier-countertype with their own definition of the stereotype—an Oreo (Black on the outside, white at heart)—and argued that it meant only that blacks who were "better" than whites at the white man's game were "acceptable." A countertype, in other words, cannot be accepted at face value any more than the negative stereotype it is seeking to replace or meliorate.

2) Countertypes are often merely surface correctives—scratch an intended countertype and you will often discover an old stereotype lurking underneath. The Poitier-black male is one example of this characteristic as well. In addition to being too simple and entrapping, it is also possible to view this countertype as nothing more than the old "self-made black man pulling himself up by his own bootstraps" image which characterized the efforts of turn-of-the-century African American conservatives such as Booker T. Washington, who sought to improve the lives of blacks without upsetting the fundamental balance of power in white-black relationships. This quality of countertypes is present in many other examples as well: beneath the "independent career-woman" there is often just a lonely dame who wants to get married; beneath the responsible teenager (Doctor Doogie Howser) there's just a kid with a need for strong parental guidance and love; and beneath the humorous, well-intentioned nice guy *L.A. Law*yers there's still a greedy weasel lurking ready to pursue a case for his own ends or compromise a client to protect the well-being of the firm. Perhaps the major lesson countertypes can impart to us is that stereotypes are very difficult to alter.

Stereotypes have a third useful function as well: as conventional characters in popular stories. Stereotyped characters allow the storyteller the luxury of not having to slow down to explain the motivations of every minor character in the story. This permits the author to get on with the plot itself and to concentrate on suspense and action. In a Western we don't need to know the inner psychology of the bad guy. It's enough to know he is a murderous rustler, for example. What we really want to see or read about is the gunfight in the dusty streets at sundown.

Even though stereotypes are useful conventions in popular storytelling, this does not mean that we can ignore them as examples of significant cultural beliefs and values. Stereotypes in imaginary, created worlds are often valuable indicators of attitudes and feelings which are very real—beliefs and values held quite deeply and sincerely by the audience, not merely by the author. If our "murderous cattle rustler" also happens to be Mexican, for example (and we can find quite a large number of popular Westerns in which the stereotyped villains are similarly characterized), then it's quite possible that the cultural mindset holds certain negative views of our neighbors south of the border. We don't need to know anything much about the villain in *Die Hard*, either—the fact that he is a scummy death-dealing terrorist is enough to explain why he wants to take an entire building hostage and endanger Bruce Willis' wife. But it is interesting, to say the least, that the villain is also German, that the reason Willis' wife has left him and begun to use her maiden name is because her company has been purchased by Japanese businessmen who do not appreciate employees whose loyalties are divided between home and office, and that the press and incompetent police heads battle Willis as much as the terrorists. As one critic has written of the beliefs and values expressed in the movie:

> [*Die Hard*] panders to the blue-collar American's worst fears and resentments—foreigners are not to be trusted, feminism has destroyed the fabric of the American family, coke-sniffing yuppies have all the good jobs; bureaucrats are incompetent fools, the media is inherently evil....The Japanese are seen to be building huge, vulgar monuments to themselves on American Soil, and they have driven a wedge between a good American cop and his wife, who has been forced to conceal her marriage to get ahead in the invaders' game. Commanding officers and the FBI are characterized as totally incompetent, egotistical imbeciles who pay no attention to the dedicated rank and file and send them to their doom with impunity. Where the media is concerned, it is suggested that all anchormen are pompous, ignorant jerks, and all street reporters are calculating, ambitious vampires who care nothing for the people about whom they report.

The point for our purposes is that all of these vital, significant cultural beliefs and values—characteristics reflected in public opinion polls and national elections and letters to the editor and social policy—are all expressed through the simple use of stereotypes in a created setting, and the manipulation of these stereotypes results in a movie which is—even by the standards of the critic quoted above—"well made [and] exciting." The stereotypes are exceedingly useful, in other words, but perhaps even more meaningful.

Being a Thing: Two Dangers of Stereotypes

The actions taken or facilitated by cultural stereotypes are not often so benign or neutral as may have been suggested thus far. Stereotypes are frequently negative, and because a culture bases its actions upon beliefs and values which characterize the cultural mindset, negative stereotypes can be associated with actions of an exceedingly negative, harmful nature—ugly emotions and even worse behavior.

The American civil rights movements of the 1950s and 1960s dramatically demonstrated to the world that non-white American ethnic groups, in being considered inferior human beings by a large proportion of the white majority, had also suffered through centuries of horrible social and economic victimization. Conversely, the narrow view of whites as a group of racist exploiters, termed "honkies" by some non-whites during the last quarter century, had led to a hardening of racial resentments by both groups. It is clearer now than it once was that the oversimplification of characteristics of any race of people into a narrow, negative stereotype can have tragic consequences. Black Americans were enslaved through three-quarters of a century during which the United States Constitution guaranteed basic human rights. Characterizations of Orientals in popular books and movies of the 1920s and 1930s as vicious, rat-like sneaks, part of a world-wide "yellow peril," may have unconsciously been one reason why more than 100,000 Japanese Americans were incarcerated in American concentration camps during the Second World War and might even have strongly contributed to the causes that led to the outbreak of that war. Germans, believing Jews to be pollutants of the Aryan master race, stood by passively while the Nazis systematically butchered six million men, women and children.

A second danger of stereotyping is not quite as obvious as these actions because it is often the result of popular stereotypes which are neutral or even somewhat positive in nature. Yet this danger is responsible for a great deal of frustration and unhappiness. Essentially, this second danger results from the fact that stereotypes are not merely *descriptions* of the way a culture views a specific group of people, but are also often prescriptions as well—thumbnail sketches of how a group of people is perceived and how members of that group perceive themselves. Stereotyping is, as we have seen, a natural ordering function of the human and social mind: stereotypes make reality easier to deal with because they simplify the complexities that make people unique, and this simplification reflects important beliefs and values as well. These two characteristics combined mean that a society has two powerful motives to encourage people to "live up to their stereotypes": to encourage them to act like the images a culture already has of them (popular culture is conservative) and to thereby fulfill their proper social roles. In other words, stereotypes encourage people to internalize a cultural image, as their goal—a task which may be convenient for the culture (and especially for the power structure status quo) but this proves to be both impossible and damaging to the individuals being asked to mold themselves in such a narrow manner.

As human beings, each of us has a seemingly infinite number of choices about what kind of person we want to be. In fact, most of us choose to be several kinds of persons—efficient at the office, sloppy around the house, formal with our boss, loose and vulgar with our friends, warm and loving with our parents—we enjoy wearing different personalities for different occasions. If we accept someone else's stereotyped image of what we *ought* to be, even if the image is a positive one, we sadly, perhaps even tragically, limit the choices that are such a wonderful part of our humanity, and confine ourselves to being narrow and standardized. We become less human and more like robots. Jane Caputi and Susan Nance's essay on the current national stereotype of the attractive woman being pencil-thin and the fads that accompany this stereotype dramatically illustrates this danger. As Caputi and Nance argue, for the woman who comes to fully embrace this stereotype as valid and adopts it for herself, the symbol of her robotization is the self-destructive *anorexia-nervosa,* and if accepted fanatically enough, it is the ultimate symbol of dehumanization and death.

The dangers of this kind of "internalized stereotype" are magnified by the ways in which advertisers exploit the fears engendered in individuals who have embarked on the futile task of attempting to squeeze themselves into one of society's cookie cutters. Women who come to accept the Barbie-doll image of themselves, for example, can be easily convinced to spend bundles on the latest fashions, exercise equipment, and breast implants. And men who "decide" that the heroic G.I. Joe is just the role they yearn to play are easily manipulated into foxholes, fighter jets, and post-traumatic stress syndrome—"being all you can be" does *not* mean holding yourself to the models manufactured by Hasbro Toys and cultural stereotypes. Molds can produce only two things: perfect dolls and scarred human beings.

Four Characteristics of Stereotypes

The term stereotype initially referred to a printing stamp which was used to make multiple copies from a single model or mold, but the great journalist and commentator Walter Lippmann adopted the term in his 1922 book *Public Opinion* as a means of describing the way society set about categorizing people—"stamping" human beings with a set of characteristics—as well. In his pioneering work, Lippmann identified four aspects of stereotypes. A brief look at them will serve as a summary of this valuable popular cultural tool. Lippmann argued that stereotypes are:

1) Simple: certainly more simple than reality, but also often capable of being summarized in only two to three sentences.

2) Acquired Secondhand: people acquire (and absorb) stereotypes from cultural mediators rather than from their own direct experience with the groups being stereotyped. The culture "distills" reality and then expresses its beliefs and values in stereotypical images which convince audiences of the "truth" of the stereotype by placing it in a carefully controlled context in which there is a measure of truth to the image. Of course women *can and should be and are* thin and beautiful—there's Barbie! There's the *Sports Illustrated* swimsuit issue, and Jane Fonda's exercise tape is number one on the charts.

3) Erroneous: *all* stereotypes are false. Some are less false than others, and (more importantly) some are less harmful than others. But all are rendered false by their very nature. They are attempts to claim that each individual human being in a certain group shares a set of common qualities. Since an individual is different from all other individuals by definition, stereotypes are a logical impossibility. Even countertypes are false when they are presented as the "new" truth about a group and escape this label only when they are presented as possibilities rather than actualities.

4) Resistant to change: during the last twenty-five years the difficulties with racial and gender inequalities in American life have alerted most people to the tragic consequences lurking in beliefs about popular stereotypes. Yet, even after more than a quarter of a century, old stereotypes still stubbornly color our perceptions. During 1992, for example, two sensational rape trials dominated the headlines in the popular press: William Kennedy Smith was tried and found innocent of raping Patricia Bowman, and boxer Mike Tyson was convicted of raping Dessiree Washington. In both cases, stereotypes assumed by both the prosecution and the defense dominated the public images of both the accusers and the accused. Smith was pictured as a typical rich kid, selfish and spoiled. Bowman was characterized by the defense as an unescorted woman in a bar and therefore obviously looking for quick sex. Tyson was seen as a black ghetto male, violent and sexually uncontrolled, while the defense argued that Washington fit the ancient role of the attractive black woman—sexually "hot" and promiscuous. The student of popular culture can only guess how these nasty uses of negative stereotypes may have influenced the outcome of each of the trials.

Despite the fact that stereotyping is a natural method of classification and despite the fact that stereotyping has some useful functions under certain circumstances, all too often stereotypes are the festering rot in the American mindset. It is not very pleasant to study them and it is even less pleasant to study their horrific effects. But study them we must. Common stereotypes directly reflect our beliefs, and like other more pleasant beliefs, we must understand them if we are to understand ourselves.

The VALS Typology

Arnold Mitchell

Stereotypes are commonly thought of as having two outstanding characteristics—they are usually negative and they most often categorize a cultural sub-group which is somehow "different" from the rest of us. Arnold Mitchell counters both of these preconceptions in the following essay in which he defines and discusses nine stereotypes which are either neutral or positive in the traits they assign and are directed toward classifying mass society as a whole rather than its powerless fringe. "The Vals Typology" stereotypes all of us and does so with a statistical rigor which is more purely descriptive—more "truthful" (although not completely so) than we may have thought possible.

Since Mitchell's book was published in 1983, the powerful forces of Madison Avenue (New York City's—and America's—"Ad Alley") have branded his insights "psychographics" (i.e. a means of classifying or stereotyping groups in mainstream society according to emotional, psychological characteristics—needs and wants—rather than physical or geographical traits) and have used them to create advertisements which target products to appeal to each specific group. By identifying the emotional need and/or desire of a group and then producing an ad which "suggests" that purchasing and using a specific product will fill that psychological gulf, Ad Alley can sell things much more effectively than it ever could by simply emphasizing boring qualities like "utility" or "price." How much more seductive an ad can be if it makes you certain that your next purchase will help you "belong," make you more "societally conscious," or enable you to "emulate" the rich and famous!

What this means for students of popular culture is that their studies can once again be seen to provide them with a "survival manual" for life in the 1990s. If Ad Alley (or any powerfully manipulative group) knows and understands more about you—and your culture's myths, beliefs and values—than you know and understand about yourself and your cultural mindset, then that group can use its insights to control your

A longer version of this essay originally was the first chapter of *The Nine American Lifestyles: Who We Are and Where We're Going* by Arnold Mitchell. NY: Warner Books, 1983.

actions, limit your choices, and (not incidentally) exploit you in the process. Understanding the psychographic approach and the way it is defined in the identification and use of popular stereotypes can enable you to "break the code" of an advertisement and determine for yourself *whether or not the promise being made is "real stuff" or merely "nonsense." Does drinking a Pepsi really make you as hip as Ray Charles? Is your next car actually your ticket to true love and exciting adventure? Will a computer make you smarter and ensure your ability to compete on an equal plane? Identifying the stereotype to which others think you belong can enable you to take an important step toward defining your own identity through what you are rather than by what you buy.*

More than anything else, we are what we believe, what we dream, what we value. For the most part we try to mold our lives to make our beliefs and dreams come true. And in our attempts to reach our goals, we test ourselves again and again in diverse ways, and in doing so we grow. With this growth comes change, so that new goals emerge, and in support of these new goals come new beliefs, new dreams, and new constellations of values. Some unusual people grow and change many times throughout their lives. Others change hardly at all with the decades. Most experience one or two periods when what is most important, most compelling, most beautiful shifts from one comprehensive pattern to another. These are the times when a person's values change—and lifestyles are transformed.

The values and lifestyle (VALS) typology that is the subject of this essay incorporates the above concepts. In addition it rests upon data obtained in a major mail survey conducted by VALS in 1980. The survey asked over 800 specific questions on a great range of topics. Sample size exceeded 1,600. Respondents constituted a national probability sample of Americans aged eighteen or over living in the forty-eight contiguous states. Statistical analysis of survey results quantified and enriched the basic concepts of the VALS typology and enabled us to provide detailed quantitative and human portraits of the VALS types, together with their activities and consumption patterns.

Need-Driven Groups

At the lowest levels of the lifestyles typology come the Need-Driven groups, called Survivors and Sustainers. The two groups are very different, but they share the burden of being poverty-stricken, so that their lives are driven by need. The luxury of choice in many economic matters is a relative rarity. This means, in effect, that they are less able to express their values in everyday living in the contemporary American society than are more affluent people. This overwhelming fact shows up dramatically in the activity and consumption patterns of the Need-

Drivens: Their poverty forces them into patterns that deviate greatly from national averages, and the greater the poverty, the larger the deviations. One might say, then, that the Need-Drivens are, from an economic perspective, a values-based group more in the sense of denial of values than of expression of them. But happily there are many exceptions. Thus, many Need-Drivens occasionally splurge—accounting, for example, for many color TVs and splendid automobiles in "poor" neighborhoods. More significantly, many activities—such as gardening or baking—and virtually all the emotional and spiritual aspects of life do not involve appreciable income, and in these the Need-Drivens are as able as others to find rewards and self-expression.

Survivors

Located at the foot of the lifestyles typology, the nation's 6 million Survivors are the least favored segment of the population. Terrible poverty marks them. Only 22 percent of Survivor households made over $5,000 per year in 1979, and none made over $7,500. And the direction is down. Very few Survivors experienced improved finances in the 1977-1980 period, and only about 12 percent expected to be able to keep up with inflation in the years ahead. Many are old—the median age is sixty-six. Many are ill, without the energy to fend for themselves. Most are poorly educated—over a third haven't gone beyond eighth grade, and half have not graduated from high school—and hence find it difficult to take advantage of whatever opportunities come their way to better their positions. Not surprisingly, Survivors tend to be despairing, depressed, withdrawn, mistrustful and rebellious about their situation. They lack self-confidence and find little satisfaction in any aspect of their lives. Their focus is on the elemental need of survival and security; the aim is less to get ahead than not to slip backward. For many, existence has shriveled to the bleak reality of the moment and the fantasy world of television. As a group, Survivors are traditional, conservative and conventional. Of all the segments of the U.S. population, they are the most likely to think things are changing too fast.

There appear to be at least two rather distinct classes of Survivors. One consists largely of those ensnared in the culture of poverty. Generation after generation are born, live, and die in unchanging, paralyzing poverty. Few expect to escape, and even fewer do, for the experience of these people shows there is little reason to put out the enormous mental and social effort of trying to move upward through classic means—education, work, leadership. Those who do achieve financial success usually choose other channels, such as athletics, or drugs, or various rackets that can pay off hugely. The proportion of minorities in this class of Survivors is very high. Most live in urban ghettoes and some in rural backwaters of the South. In general, minority group

Survivors are younger than other Survivors, probably less well educated, and certainly farthest (but not wholly) removed from the trends and ideas that power the society.

The other class of the Survivor is less likely to have been born into the predicament; rather, through bad luck, lack of enterprise, or the onslaughts of old age, they have slipped back into the Survivor lifestyle, after following most of a lifetime spent as a Sustainer or Belonger. This, the largest group of Survivors, tends to be older than the other and is more likely to be white, to be in better touch with the events of the world, and to have larger resources, especially a home. Some live in city slums and ghettoes, but many inhabit the aging frame houses of small towns or the porches and shuttered rooms of old folks' homes.

For most of these people, the years of ambition and achievement have passed. Life has become a waiting game. Television is their main entertainment. Their homes are filled with mementoes of the past. Most are retired, and at least 80 percent are widows. They lead lives full of echoes, for most of their friends are dead or have moved to places unknown.

Sustainers

Sustainers are angry, distrustful, rebellious, anxious, combative people who often feel left out of things—but, unlike Survivors, they have not given up hope. Their life problem is less merely to survive than to secure and sustain hard-earned gains and, if possible, to move ahead to a better life. They live at the edge of poverty, probably with erratic incomes, for over a fourth are looking for work or work only part-time. Average income of Sustainers in 1979 was about $11,000, with only 22 percent exceeding $15,000. Few get much satisfaction from their jobs, which are heavily skewed to machine, manual and service occupations. It is not surprising to find that Sustainers are the least satisfied of any lifestyle group with their financial status and the most anxious to get ahead economically.

Sustainers have the largest families despite the fact that over 25 percent are divorced, separated, or living together unmarried. They contain the highest fraction of minorities—13 percent are of Hispanic origin and 21 percent are black. More than any other group Sustainers see themselves as having low social status. Only a relative handful have gone beyond high school. They rank second lowest of the lifestyle segments in self-evaluation of overall happiness.

Mistrust of the system goes deep. Sustainers have less confidence in elected officials and corporate leaders than any other group. They are least likely to think products are getting better or safer or that labeling is improving. More than any other group they think the energy crisis is imaginary. They also rank high in thinking things are changing too fast.

Despite all this, Sustainers see themselves as financially expert—probably a reflection of their adroitness in stretching a dollar and, perhaps, their ability to operate in the so-called underground economy. Over 80 percent look forward to better things. And many support some contemporary social trends—for example, unmarried sex and legalization of marijuana. At the same time, deep insecurities seem evident in the high need Sustainers express to have social status and to feel part of a group.

There appear to be several distinct types of Sustainers. First is the street-smart operator of urban slums and ghettoes, where much organized and disorganized crime originates. Sometimes of minority descent, these Sustainers know the ropes of the illicit economy—dope, liquor, gambling, prostitution, and the like. Extreme violence, threats, payoffs, and gang agreements are common.

Far more common and less dramatic is the crafty Sustainer, who makes ends meet through barter, side jobs done for cash, and, sometimes, adroit manipulation of the welfare systems. This variety of Sustainer is likely to be other than the hard-crime type, less systematic, less urbanized, less exclusively male. They may think of themselves as taking advantage of a system that asks for it, but they do not see themselves as criminals.

A very different kind of Sustainer is found in the impoverished family struggling to keep going on minimal wages supplemented sometimes by food stamps, sometimes welfare. The lone mother, divorced or separated, with several children is frequently a Sustainer. So, too, are members of the family whose wage earners are frequently unemployed or whose income is minimal. Because they are subject to intense ups and downs financially, these people often consider that they're in the grip of temporary hard times, and they promise themselves the revved-up muscle car and the new TV as soon as the corner has been turned.

A final type of Sustainer, less common today than early in the century, is the recent immigrant trying to make a go of it in a new world. Without much English, without appropriate skills, without sophistication, sometimes without real friends or family, this individual finds that only substandard jobs are available. But these are enterprising, hard-working, ambitious people with faith in the system and drive sufficient to keep striving. Many of them will not escape from the Sustainer pattern, but their children may do so, driven by the conviction that here indeed is the land of opportunity.

Outer-Directed Groups

The Outer-Directeds make up middle America. It is a huge category, including about two-thirds of the adult population, or well over 100 million people. It is also highly diverse, consisting of three distinct lifestyles we call Belongers, Emulators and Achievers. Belongers, at about 57 million adults, are the largest group in the typology. They are followed in size by Achievers at about 35 million, and about 16 million Emulators.

The common denominator of these three groups is what we call Outer-Direction. Outer-directed people respond intensely to signals, real or fancied, from others. They conduct themselves in accord with what they think others will think. Since "out there" is paramount, this tends to create ways of life geared to the visible, tangible and materialistic.

Attributes shared (especially by Belongers and Achievers) include a sense that most people are honest, a lack of rebelliousness, a sense of being "with it," conventional behavior, and insistence that the family is the most important thing in their lives.

Belongers

Belongers typify what is generally regarded as middle-class America. Traditional, conforming, conservative, "moral," nonexperimental, family-oriented, Belongers are a mighty force for stability in a world of tumbling change. As a group, Belongers prefer the status quo if not the ways of yesteryear. Old-fashioned values still shine bright: patriotism, home and family, sentimentality. These are people who above all cherish shared institutions such as the family, church, and loyalty to nation, job, and old associations.

The key drive of Belongers is to fit in, not to stand out. Their world is well posted, and they follow the rules. About 95 percent are white. Most are middle-aged or older and have middle incomes and middle levels of education. Women, largely housewives, predominate; in fact, 30 percent are housewives, the highest fraction of any values group. Belongers tend to live in small towns or the open country and to shun big cities. They are not much interested in sophistication or intellectual affairs. All the evidence suggests that Belongers lead contented, happy lives and are relatively little vexed by the stresses and mercurial events that swirl around them.

Belonging as a lifestyle in the United States is almost always associated with the "middle middle" class. Belongers are the people for whom soap operas and romance magazines are created to fill their emotional needs. The needs of Belongers reflect the fact that many were exposed to much rejection or ridicule in their formative years, resulting in an excessive need for acceptance. Family mores were usually conventional; as children Belongers often were criticized for unusual ideas or punished for experimental actions (which often were called "bad" or, worse, "deviant"). Dependency and conformity were cultivated in family life through reward and punishment. The usual message was that the parents (or the church) knew what was right.

People brought up this way tend to be puritanical, conventional, dependent, sentimental, nostalgic, mass-oriented, outer-directed, xenophobic. Most Belongers have exceptionally strong matriarchal feelings because the first belonging relationship for most people is with their mothers, and mothers provide the classic image of the most unselfish, forgiving, nurturing, belonging symbol.

Belongers see safety in numbers; they think it is important to be an insider; alikeness, togetherness, and agreement are important measures. But closeness with others tends to be quite formalized; open emotionalism and sensuality are embarrassing. Tolerance for ambiguity is low. They feel the system should reward "virtue." They prefer to follow rather than to lead; to avoid hostility they will accept the lowest common denominator. They are threatened by the aberrant. Adherence to tradition and the status quo is essential. "Should" and "ought" are dominant words.

Belonging of this sort has the strength and virtue of providing a reference point, a sense of stability and often tradition, a set of agreed-upon rules, a charted road, a nest. At the same time, unalloyed belonging tends to exclude unaccustomed ways and in that sense is prejudiced, authoritarian, and closed. The Belonger thus tends to be accepting and following within the group and rejecting of anything outside it. Group interests and concerns come first; the individual tends to be suppressed. The world the Belonger feels most comfortable in is a well-posted, well-lighted place whose outer limits are in view at all times.

Belongers are easily the most old-fashioned and traditional of the VALS groups. This stance is taken against a background of much happiness and intermediate levels of satisfaction and trust in people. Although they are not particularly affluent and their financial progress is not above average, Belongers are satisfied with their situation. Generally they seem a contented, unambitious group. Traditional values emerge clearly in their opposition to "women's liberation," moral and sexual freedom, and rights for blacks. Belongers feel strongly that obedience is a prime virtue in children and that the military deserves much confidence. They tend, relatively, to abstain from alcohol; they are heavy TV watchers. This description is to a degree overdrawn, yet it captures the sense of the Belonger seeking security through avoidance of surprise, comfort through being surrounded by the familiar, and happiness through acceptance by the group.

Emulators

The outer-directed world of the Emulator is totally different from that of Belongers. Emulators are intensely striving people, seeking to be like those they consider richer and more successful than they are—that is, Achievers. They are more influenced by the values of others, than any other lifestyle group. Whether man or woman, they tend to be ambitious, competitive, ostentatious, unsubtle, "macho." They are also hard-working, supportive of contemporary social trends, and fairly successful. Despite a relatively young median age of twenty-seven, Emulator households in 1979 had an average income of over $18,000. But they are spenders and tend to be in debt. The problem for Emulators is that they do not really understand the values and lifestyle of those they emulate. Nor are their life patterns very similar. The important area of occupation illustrates the mismatch: 29 percent of Achievers hold professional or technical jobs, but only 9 percent of Emulators do; 17 percent of Achievers are managers or administrators vs. 6 percent of Emulators.

Emulators are more likely than any other group to have attended technical school. Unusually large numbers have one or two years of college but have not graduated. Self-assessed social class is strongly skewed to the low side, although the Sustainer pattern is more extreme. On the other hand, educational patterns of the fathers of Emulators are surprisingly high—higher, in fact, than those of Survivors, Sustainers, or Belongers, even when age differences are taken into account. Our data provide some support for the hypothesis that the Emulator stage is a key resting place for many upwardly mobile members of minority groups. Blacks and Hispanics both are materially overrepresented in the group, but not as much as they are among Sustainers. Despite this, Emulators appear to include many raised in favored circumstances but who, for one reason or another, have conjured up ambitions inappropriate for their achievements and perhaps for their abilities. Although many surely sense this—witness their anger at and mistrust of "the Establishment"—they seem unable, or unwilling, to realign their goals.

The information that Emulators have about Achievers tends to be secondhand—from movies, romanticized magazines, gossip columns. The result, naturally, is that they experience much rejection, inevitably generating a pervasive sense of anger, mistrust of individuals, and little faith that "the system" will give them a break. Emulators wind up with a poor self-image: for example, only 5 percent (vs. 41 percent for Achievers) regard themselves as upper-class; many often feel left out of things; they are below average in considering the inner self more important than fame or power; they rank next to lowest (after Survivors) in their self-confidence; they are unable to get much satisfaction from job or friends; their levels of confidence in institutional leaders are low, and they distrust information coming from institutional sources. It comes as no surprise to find that Emulators rank near the bottom of the lifestyle groups in overall self-ratings of happiness.

Although Emulators are probably the most upwardly ambitious of the lifestyle groups, it appears likely that most of them will not make it to Achiever status. One reason is that their blind upward striving seems to force many into leading lives of deception—lives filled with acts calculated to mislead others. Hence Emulators tend to be "operators" and to embrace conspicuous consumption, follow the voguish fashion, and spend only where it shows. This profoundly secondhand or imitative lifestyle accounts for the extraordinary lack of differentiation of Emulator activity and consumption patterns from those of other lifestyles. Thus Emulators seem in some sense to lead hollow lives—solid in appearance on the outside, empty inside.

Achievers

Achievers are at the top—at the pinnacle of Outer-Direction. They are the driving and driven people who have built "the system" and are now at the helm. Including almost one-fourth of the adult population, they are a diverse, gifted, hard-working, self-reliant, successful, and happy group.

Achievers come in many shapes and forms. The ambitious, competitive, effective corporate executive is one familiar type. But there is also the skilled professional—lawyer, doctor, scientist—the adroit politician, the money-oriented athlete or entertainer, and the artist whose goal is fame and "the big life." Then there is the vicarious Achiever—the individual who expresses his or her achievement needs through others as much as through personal attainment.

To some, Achievers typify the stereotype of the wealthy, successful American. To social critics, Achievers represent the Establishment. But more than anything else Achievers have learned to live the comfortable, affluent, affable, outer-directed life, and in so doing they have set the standard for much of the nation.

In things material Achievers are far in the vanguard among the life-style groups. Average household income in 1979 exceeded $31,000; over 20 percent were self-employed, and two and one-half times as many Achievers as any other VALS group held managerial or administrative jobs. Almost half had total household assets of over $100,000 in 1979, compared with 31 percent for the next highest lifestyle group. Life appears to be comfortable: almost half of Achievers live in the suburbs, 87 percent own their own homes, and they top the lifestyle groups in recent financial improvement.

Importantly, this success enables Achievers to feel good about themselves: 94 percent rate themselves as "very happy." They lead all groups in trusting people, in considering themselves upper-class, in having self-confidence, in not feeling rebellious or left out of things, and in supporting many national issues, such as encouraging industry growth, spending on the military, and supporting U.S. involvement in world affairs. They are more satisfied with their financial situation than any other group. They feel that products are getting better and safer. They support technology and go for the "new and improved" product. Achievers are staunchly Republican and conservative. Politically they do not want radical change. After all, much of the culture is of their making; they are on top, and radical change might shake them off.

The demographics of Achievers show them to have a mean age in the early forties, but with a wide spread. Over 95 percent are Caucasian and only 2 percent black. A third are college graduates, and many went on to attend graduate school. Contrary to popular impression, the evidence is that they are more happily married (that is, with fewer broken marriages) than any group other than Belongers. It is clear from data on their fathers' educational attainment that Achievers tend to be self-made people. Regionally they are a bit underrepresented in the South and overrepresented in the West.

No doubt because they are leaders, Achievers tend to be conservative, not only politically, but socially as well. Only Belongers rate themselves as more conservative in their general behavior. Specifically, they are far down the list in support of such issues as sex between unmarried people, working women also being good mothers, legalization of marijuana, or air pollution as a world danger. But they are not full of resentments. Indeed, Achievers show their psychological maturity by their success in bringing their ambitions into good alignment with reality.

Inner-Directed Groups

The Inner-Directeds are so named because the principal driving forces of their lives are internal, not external. That is, what is most important is what is "in here," not what is "out there." This extends to attitudes toward job, personal relationships, spiritual matters, and the satisfactions to be derived from everyday pursuits. Inner growth—sometimes sought through the great Western religions or analytic techniques, but often through transcendental meditation, yoga, Zen, or other Eastern spiritual practice— is central to many of the Inner-Directeds. Most seek intense involvement in whatever they are doing; the secondhand and vicarious are anathema. Their sensitivity to their own feelings enables them to be sensitive to others and to events around them. Many are active in social movements such as consumerism, conservation, or environmentalism, while others express their concerns more privately in artistic pursuits. As a group the Inner-Directeds are highly self-reliant and notably indifferent to social status. Money is of relatively little concern to them. They are powerfully supportive of such modern trends as women working, sex between unmarried people, or legalization of marijuana. They tend to be self-expressive, individualistic, concerned with people, impassioned, diverse, complex.

Most Inner-Directeds have excellent educations and hold good jobs, often of a professional or technical nature. Except for the most youthful among them, incomes average around $25,000 per year. Politically, the Inner-Directeds are heavily independent.

Essentially all Inner-Directeds were raised in the predominantly outer-directed society of the United States—especially in Achiever families. As children and adolescents they learned and internalized outer-directed parental and societal values, but at some point, usually in mid or late adolescence, Outer Directedness began to seem less than the way to live a lifetime. Their family affluence was such that money and materialism no longer had to dominate existence as it has for almost everyone else in industrial societies. Relieved of incessant economic pressures, prosperous parents tended to raise their children permissively, perhaps thinking thus to improve upon their own upbringing. A natural effect was to emphasize noneconomic aspects of life, and this aspect became the focus of many of the most socially favored youths of the 1960s and 1970s. In dramatic distinction to strictly raised Belonger children, the offspring of most Achiever families were freed (if not invited) to reject the economic values of the society. And so, in a sense as a result of the success of the U.S. economic system, a new class of lifestyles was born—lifestyles focused on the inner world rather than the external world of tangibles. Inner-Direction, of course, has always been part of the American romantic tradition—witness Emerson and Thoreau—but until the past twenty years it has been confined to a relative few. Today it is a mass movement. And it is assuredly one of the most significant sociological phenomena of the post-World War II period, although it is remarkably little noted in these terms.

We have identified three inner-directed lifestyles, which we call I-Am-Me, Experiential, and Societally Conscious. Emerging as a major tend in the early and mid-1960s (when the first big wave of the postwar generation was reaching age eighteen), Inner-Direction has now reached major proportions. Survey results for 1980 indicate that about 20 percent of American adults are now more Inner-Directed than Outer-Directed or Need-Driven. This amounts to over 30 million individuals, the majority of whom are in their twenties or thirties with their years of greatest influence as citizens, parents, and consumers still ahead of them.

I-Am-Mes[1]

This is a stage of tumultuous transition from an outer-directed way of life to Inner-Direction. It is usually short-lived—no more than a few years—and marked by spectacular emotional ups and downs and sidewise veerings. It is a stage of much anxiety brought on by fear of losing the old and uncertainty concerning the new. As a frantic result, I-Am-Mes are both contrite and aggressive, demure and exhibitionistic, self-effacing and narcissistic, conforming and wildly innovative. To give the appearance of solidity and direction, they have developed whims of iron.

The immediate shift is usually from the comfortable, established, well-defined, deeply outer-directed lifestyle of Achiever parents to the evanescent, fanciful, mercurial, flighty styles of I-Am-Me peers and contemporaries. The change is powered by both love and hate, admiration and disgust, envy and resentment of outer-directed ways of life. The stage thus is not only I-Am-Me but also I-Am-Not-You. Clearly it is a time full of confusions, contradictions, uncertainties, excesses, and protean changes. But the style also involves genuine inventiveness, for the shift from the outer to the inner dimension often brings with it the discovery of new interests and new interior rewards that redirect life goals. It is this aspect of the I-Am-Me lifestyle that is of central significance, not the accompanying flamboyance expressed through conspicuous dress, spectacular behavior, or the famed insolence of the modern teenager toward parents.

The picture we have, then, is of youths raised in favored circumstances seeking out—often ungraciously and noisily, to be sure—a new way of life for themselves. Average age is about twenty-one, and almost none are over thirty. The majority are students, and only a few have been married. Many still live with their parents and identify strongly with them—a fact that complicates their sense of personal identity. Interestingly, in 1980 only 36 percent of I-Am-Mes were found to be female, in contrast to a majority of women ten or fifteen years earlier. Because the I-Am-Mes learned to understand Outer-Direction as children and adolescents, they can afford to leave it behind as adults. The evidence is that the new way of life, once found, is a permanent change. The I-Am-Mes of ten and more years ago retain the essence of their old values. But the I-Am-Mes of the 1980s appear in many ways to be less extreme than the I-Am-Mes of yesterday.

As a lifestyle, the I-Am-Me mode is expressed more through activities and demographics than through attitudes. Indeed, many I-Am-Mes appear not to have thought in great depth about many societal issues, but they have no problem in being and acting. Their actions mark them as energetic, enthusiastic, daring, and seeking the new. Intellectual and cultural activities attract them as well as social pursuits and physically demanding games. Overall, in fact, I-Am-Mes display the most distinctive activity patterns of any group in the values typology save the Survivors. I-Am-Mes represent the zippy, high-energy, enthusiastic end of the lifestyle spectrum, Survivors the withdrawn, despairing, weary end.

Experientials

Next in the typology of American values and lifestyles come the Experientials, the name deriving from the fact that above all these people seek direct, vivid experience. For some what matters most is deep personal involvement in ideas or issues, for others it is intense hedonism; for some it is the challenge and excitement of great physical exertion, like rock climbing; for many the quest of inner explorations is all-important; for a few the core of existence is a lifestyle of voluntary simplicity—what Emerson called "plain living and high thinking." For most of the Experientials life at one moment is a noisy parade and at the next a journey, often touched with the mystic, through the silent inner domains of thought, feeling, and spirit. For them, the secondhand, the inhibited, the unfeeling is not living. Action and interaction with people, events, and ideas—pure and strong—is the essence of life.

Most such people passed a few years earlier through the chaotic exhibitionistic I-Am-Me stage. A few years hence many will extend their perspectives to the society—perhaps even the globe—and become more activist and mission-oriented. But for now it is not things that count, but emotion. The intangible and evanescent is likely to loom larger than the plain and visible. Experientials tend to be artistic people attuned to subtlety and nuance.

Experientials are youthful—mostly in their late twenties—excellently educated and with incomes averaging between $23,000 and $24,000 annually. Many hold technical and professional jobs. They are happy, self-assured, well-adjusted people with faith in the trustworthiness of others and great assurance that they are on top of things. They tend to be liberal politically and highly supportive of such phenomena as the women's movement, unmarried sex, legalization of marijuana, conservation, consumer movements, and limits to industrial growth. Many are intensely opposed to spending on military armaments (for they are part of the "Vietnam generation") and have little faith in institutional leaders.

Most Experientials have a deep sense of the natural and a belief in the innate rightness of nature. As a result they prefer natural products to the synthetic; almost as much as Belongers, they like to grow their own flowers and vegetables. Many preserve their own food or shop in organic food stores. Many have much faith in holistic medicine. It is they who do most of the rock climbing and backpacking. It is they who love above all to get out away from it all, where the signs of civilization are few.

Finally, one of the powerful forces in the lives of most Experientials is a feel for the mystic. Usually this is not connected with the formal Western religions, but is more likely to reflect personal insight and perhaps the study of Zen, Yoga, and the *Tao Te Ching* or other ancient Eastern works. For some Experientials, marijuana and other drugs play an important role in mystic experience; for others the way lies through transcendental meditation; for still others self-hypnosis or learned deep introspection works best.

The Experientials tend to be happy individuals, not because they don't have their depressions and frustrations, but because they feel they are growing and changing and any day may bring a fresh new insight—a peak experience—to illuminate all that has gone before. In its way, the Experiential phase is an untroubled time, not in the sense of being motionless (it is far from that), but in the sense that most of what happens is considered self-induced and is welcomed as one more step on the very long road of life—a road that many of the Experientials think may, in fact, be eternal.

From the psychological standpoint the Experiential lifestyle is much less self-centered than I-Am-Me, is concerned with a broader range of issues, is more participative, is more self-assured. Experientials are notably self-reliant, whereas I-Am-Mes, being in transition to Inner-Direction, are more dependent on peer support and social status for their self-image. The Experientials appear quite able to risk a wide range of inner-exploration techniques. They have begun to leave their flamboyance and aggressively conspicuous behavior and are moving on to more spiritual, intellectual, and artistic preoccupations.

Societally Conscious

The focus of the inner-directed drives of some 13 million Americans is not rejection of other lifestyles (as in the I-Am-Mes) or intense personal experience (as in the Experientials) but concern with societal issues, trends, and events.

The range of concerns and the styles of dealing with them are great. Consumer issues are foremost for some people, who become leaders or supporters of movements concerned with such issues as pricing, additives, labeling, and advertising. Other individuals concentrate on conservation; their concerns range from national lands to energy, packaging, and a host of practices regarded as wasteful. Other concerns are with issues of product safety, environmental pollution, protection of wildlife. Stylistically the Societally Conscious range from aggressive political antagonism, to the more muted collaborative resistance of networks with a common interest, to withdrawals to lives of voluntary simplicity.

As a group the Societally Conscious are successful, influential, mature. They are, in a sense, the inner-directed equivalent of outer-directed Achievers, but they differ attitudinally in fundamental ways. Most Societally Conscious people share some key beliefs: that humanity should live in harmony with nature and not try to dominate it; that nature has its own wisdom; that small is usually beautiful; that this truly is one world; that nonmaterial aspects of life are in some sense "higher" than the material; that each person can, and should, help remedy societal problems; that outer simplicity often goes with inner richness; that simplicity may be the most powerful lifestyle of the future.

Few of the Societally Conscious live fully the life of voluntary simplicity, but all act on at least some aspect of it (although, of course, they are not the only ones who do). Thus, for example, they may ride a bicycle or drive an economy car, insulate their home or install solar heating, eat only foods grown without pesticides or prepared without additives.

As a group the Societally Conscious are a sophisticated and politically effective lot. At an average age of almost forty, they have arrived at positions of influence in their jobs and communities. An extraordinary 39 percent have attended graduate school and, even more extraordinary, 59 percent hold professional or technical jobs. Average income in 1979 exceeded $27,000. These outward trapping of success combine with a consistent attitudinal pattern to create a high degree of political activism. Most try to lead lives that conserve, protect, heal. Their confidence in outer-directed leadership is minimal. They have returned unsatisfactory products or complained to a store more than any other group. They are much worried about air pollution, support more spending to protect the environment, believe industrial growth should be limited, and feel more than most that military spending is too high. Societally conscious people place a high importance on energy conservation in the home—more than any other group they have looked into solar heating—and, again leading the groups, they believe the energy crisis is real.

The fact—and action—of societal awareness is of course the psychological hallmark of this lifestyle. Although numbering only 8 or 9 percent of the adult population (but rapidly expanding), the Societally Conscious have had, and are having, a very substantial political and corporate impact on the country.

Combined Outer- and Inner-Directed Group

Integrateds

Maturity, balance, and a sense of what is "fitting" are prime characteristics of the Integrateds. These are people who have put together the decisiveness of Outer-Direction with the penetration of Inner-Direction. To these rare individuals Outer-Direction and Inner-Direction are equally good, powerful, useful, and needed; the two styles are simply different, each appropriate in its own place. Psychologically mature, the Integrateds have an unusual ability to weigh consequences, to consider subtlety along with flamboyance, to see the small within the large and the potential within what has gone wrong.

These qualities of mind and spirit enable Integrateds, we think, often to pluck the best from opposing views and combine them into a solution that subsumes both perspectives. Abraham Lincoln—surely an Integrated human being in his later years—was able to do this in trying to mend the wounds of the Civil War.

Such people elude the common ways, hence are recognized less by exterior measures than are members of the other categories. Most of us know some few people who seem to have a kind of inner completeness, a kind of deep-core certainty, that commands respect, admiration, sometimes awe, and not infrequently love. These are people one truly trusts and seeks to be like. These are people who seem to have more wisdom than the rest of us. Very likely these people are Integrateds.

Because of the elusiveness of the Integrated lifestyle, we have not yet been able to identify Integrateds on the basis of the demographic and attitudinal items we have used to categorize the other eight lifestyle groups. One reason is that there are not many people who have attained a truly integrated outlook on life. Our estimate for the fraction of American adults that qualify is 2 percent. If this correct, our main survey should have included thirty-three Integrateds—not a large enough number to identify with confidence.

Our sense is that Integrated people adapt easily to most conventions and mores but are powerfully mission-oriented on matters about which they feel strongly. They are people able to lead when action is required and able to follow when that seems appropriate. They usually possess a deep sense of what is fitting and appropriate. They tend to be open, self-assured, self-expressive, keenly aware of nuance and shadings, and often possessed of a world perspective. Our guess is that they are able to do their best, to be satisfied with the result, and to move on to what is next. We would expect them to be quick with laughter and generous with tears, to have found ways to meld work and play, to combine close relationships with people with the drive to accomplish (rather than visibly achieve). We think they are both makers and movers, observers and creators—people who believe in themselves and in what they are doing.

We would expect most Integrateds to be people of middle or upper-middle years, many of whom have lived decades as successful Achievers or Societally Conscious. They find it wise or necessary to move from those ways of life to the integrated pattern usually as a result of changing basic values as to what is important. A smaller but particularly interesting group probably consists of much younger people, in their thirties or even twenties, who have had the good luck, the means, and the gifts to find themselves early in life.

Reflecting Achievers and the Societally Conscious, we would expect Integrateds to be slightly more male than female, generally married, heavily Caucasian, very well educated, working in well-paying occupations, with average incomes of $30,000 or more. They probably would be less conservative than Achievers and less liberal than the societally Conscious.

Notes

[1]We use the colloquial phrase as more appropriate despite the command of grammar that this be I-Am-I!

From the Plantation to *Bel-Air*: A Brief History of Black Stereotypes

Christopher D. Geist and Angela M.S. Nelson

Christopher Geist and Angela Nelson use a chronological overview in the following article to examine the evolution of several stereotyped images of African Americans long present in the popular culture of European Americans. Going back to sixteenth-century Europe, they trace black stereotypes into the plantation slave experience and into that very popular nineteenth-century entertainment, the minstrel show. Their purpose is to discover the cultural origins of these well-known and long-lived racial stereotypes and to suggest how and why these images are still being incorporated into more recent popular art forms. Geist and Nelson's essay suggests how deeply ingrained black stereotypes really are in American popular culture and in the consciousness of white Americans.

On any particular evening, turn on some cable television channels that feature old movies or recent television series reruns. Note the uncritical use of black stereotypes and how the stories you are watching include them so casually that it is obvious the makers of these stories never expected us to question those images. Being sensitive to how these negative images permeate our entertainments provides us with a valuable perspective on why, almost 130 years after the abolition of slavery in the United States, we are still so far from dissolving the racial divisions of income, education and opportunity in this country. Racism is the great American tragedy and part of its life blood are the images discussed in this essay.

With the possible exceptions of Native Americans and women, no other group in the United States has been linked so consistently with stereotyped presentation in the popular and folk arts than African

This essay in different form was published in *The Popular Culture Reader*, 3rd Edition, Christopher Geist and Jack Nachbar, eds. Bowling Green, OH: Bowling Green State University Popular Press, 1983. Reprinted with permission.

Americans. "Sambo," "Mammy," "Jim Crow," "Zip Coon," "Uncle Tom" and others have been used in crude racial jokes, in popular literature (both children's and adults'), in song lyrics, in films, in advertising campaigns, in folktales, on radio and television, and as trademarks. Since the days before the Civil War whites have developed their perceptions of black people and their culture through reference to stereotypes.

Stereotypes are great levelers. Simply speaking, a stereotype develops, exaggerates, and exploits one or two attributes of a given group or class of people and applies those attributes to *all* members of that group or class without any distinction. The irony lies in the reality that they are based in part on truth. For instance, a common stereotype is that all tall black males play basketball. Even though this is not true for the entire group, there are in fact a disproportionate number of tall black males playing basketball and other popular American sports like football.

Stereotypes pare down and simplify reality; too many variations would complicate and confuse. Their purpose is to set a group apart from the mainstream. To endow that group with too much variety in appearance or actions might well make them too real, too human. Furthermore, distinguishing among them would require more effort on the part of the observer. In the case of African American stereotyping in popular culture, the creators were white writers, actors, illustrators, and so forth. These creators, often white males, had little or no direct contact with blacks. Seen from a distance, it was obvious that blacks were different. First, and most obviously, blacks were set apart by physical characteristics, primarily their skin color. A white ethnic has the opportunity, at least through his/her children, to escape any derisive ethnic stereotype associated with his/her background. In the course of a few generations, perhaps even one, a German immigrant family might alter its name (say from Braun to Brown) and blend inconspicuously into the mythical melting pot. That same family could, of course, decide to maintain its heritage and discover a sense of pride in its ethnic origins. Either way, there is a choice which is generally not available to blacks. Though blacks may choose to celebrate their African heritage, whites often feel threatened and puzzled by such displays. In the 1960s when the "Black Pride" movement gained momentum it also gained a revolutionary aura. The same phenomenon more recently occurred somewhat with the rise of rap music as more white teenagers and young adults listened to rap and as more rappers explored the distortions of African history in their lyrics.

Fear of the unknown often contributes to the creation of stereotypes. When European whites were first establishing contacts with blacks in the 1500s, they knew very little about the culture and civilization of Africa. Early explorers and traders returned from the "Dark Continent" with fantastic stories of strange beasts. Among those newly discovered marvels of nature was the black man-ape with "large Breasts, thick Lips and broad Nostrils" (Jordan 8). Direct contact with blacks was not a part of the experience of most Europeans. Thus, from the earliest periods, white men and women relied on a relatively small number of observers who wrote travel accounts which tended to focus on the facets of African life and culture which were most unlike those of European cultures. They felt free to invent details, to fabricate amusing anecdotes, and to rely on hearsay. Bizarre tales (most of them incapable of being substantiated) soon began to circulate which linked blacks with magic, bestiality, and cannibalism.

Perceiving their own lighter pigmentation as "normal," Europeans attempted to account for the "abnormal" darker pigmentation of Africans. Some blamed the Africans' darker skin color on the effects of the intense, equatorial sun. Those who adhered to this theory believed that blacks who were transported to the more temperate areas of the world would soon be "cured" and would return to "normal" color. Another theory linked the skin color of Africans with Biblical and Talmudic curse. Ham had committed the sin of looking on his drunken, naked father, Noah, and was told that this indiscretion would cause his descendants to be "ugly and dark skinned." Furthermore, in the Biblical version of the tale, Ham and his progeny would forever be "servants of servants" (Jordan 17-18; Genesis Ch. 9 and 10). This phrase would have obvious utility later in the defense of slavery in the United States.

Curiously enough, the true source of any white fear of Africans may be rooted even more deeply than in superficial concerns such as physical characteristics and the European culture ignorance of African civilization. Winthrop D. Jordan, in his monumental study of white racism, *White Over Black*, has suggested that there was a long history of English aversion to blackness. The *Oxford English Dictionary*, notes Jordan, provides the following definition of "black" *prior to the sixteenth century*:

> Deeply stained with dirt; soiled, dirty, foul...Having dark or deadly purposes, malignant; pertaining to or involving death, deadly; baneful, disastrous, sinister...Foul, iniquitous, atrocious, horrible, wicked...Indicating disgrace, censure, liability to punishment, etc. (Jordan 7)

Jordan goes on to say that the color "black" had already become "the handmaid and symbol of baseness and evil, a sign of danger and repulsion" *before* Africans and Englishmen came into contact (Jordan 7). Shakespeare and other Elizabethan artists used black to symbolize evil and danger. Black is also associated with evil and uncleanliness in the folklore of many European countries. Even today we resort to the color black to symbolize mourning, while on the other hand associating the "purity" of white with such positive symbolic rites as baptism and the wedding. Long-held, unconscious cultural meanings associated with their skin color has helped insure that blacks are stereotyped as base and inferior.

In the early history of slavery in the United States, many of the most enduring black stereotypes were developed. Though the formation of these caricatures undoubtedly drew upon the earlier experiences of the Europeans, there is ample evidence to suggest that various stereotypes grew out of the American slavery experience itself. Some slaves, for example, may have indeed "shuffled," acted ignorantly, and moved slowly as a ruse to fool their masters, thus developing into the Sambo stereotype: "Indolent, faithful, humorous, loyal, dishonest, superstitious, improvident, and musical, Sambo was inevitably a clown and congenially docile" (Blassingame 34). Sambo put on the mask of ignorance and incompetence, and, if the master was convinced that Sambo's act was real, then he could not expect too much around the plantation from this supposedly dumb slave.

Sambo became one of the most enduring and popular of the black stereotypes. It is fairly easy to see why this image would appeal to white masters. Sambo's mindless frolicking, his intense loyalty to his master, and his childlike need for protection and guidance were just the proper traits the planters needed to justify the institutionalization of slavery. Sambo was basically a happy child. Given freedom of choice he would not work a single minute of his life. He would dance, fiddle, and spend his hours in wanton idleness. Sambo needed his master as much as his master needed him. To enslave another race requires some justification. The Sambo stereotype, coupled with the "Curse of Ham" and other Biblical passages, helped to provide that justification. Besides, all whites, whether slaveholders or not, could and did look upon all blacks as inferior. Thus, no matter how poor, no matter how ignorant white slaveowners might be, they could always see in Sambo someone beneath themselves.[1]

In addition to Sambo, every plantation had its fat, jolly, motherly cook—or so we have been taught through the popular arts. Remember Hattie McDaniel as Mammy in *Gone With The Wind*? These happy-go-lucky mammies took care of the children, prepared the sumptuous plantation banquets, despised "poor white trash," and loved "Ol' Massa" and his family more deeply than anything else in the world. Mammy was so loyal that she would reject a chance of freedom just to remain with her white family. More than likely Mammy lived with Uncle Tom, an older slave who had served the master competently and faithfully for many years. Now old Uncle Tom just lazed around the plantation, worked a bit at light tasks, and generally entertained Ol' Massa and others with tall tales and fiddling. He was now enjoying a life of ease which the master provided as a reward for his past service—a slave's retirement. He had virtually no worries, for the kindly master provided for his every need. Contented, Old Uncle Tom was a stereotype which helped reinforce the planter's assertion that slavery was a necessary institution which benefitted the slaves.

Another stereotype which developed on the plantations of the Old South was nothing like Mammy and was almost the reverse of Sambo. This stereotype, "Nat," the dangerous, rebellious black man, terrorized whites. He was probably a necessary creation to remind white slaveholders that, in spite of gentle, amazing Sambo, some slaves could be dangerous. Though historians have shown that there were relatively few major slave rebellions in the United States (none of them successful) (Aptheker), a few bloody uprisings such as one led by Gabriel Prosser in 1800 and another by Nat Turner in 1831 struck fear in the hearts of whites. Nat Turner and his band had slain over fifty whites before their rebellion was contained. These seemingly random incidents helped to convince the slaveholders and their non-slaveholding neighbors that lurking behind Sambo's broad grin and "Yassa, Massa" personality was a potentially dangerous revolutionary.

The successful slave rebellion in Haiti in the 1790s also helped to persuade whites that slaves could be devious and dangerous. Mysterious acts of covert defiance around the plantation strengthened the stereotype of the black man as rebel. Tools and heavy equipment seemed to break down at critical times. Food disappeared from the master's larder. Clumsy slaves "accidentally" ruined a portion of the crops or seriously injured a valuable animal. Sure, they grinned back in Sambo-like puzzlement at such bad luck, but wasn't Nat really behind all those shining teeth?

Yet, an even more potent white fear helped to shape white images of blacks. Since the earliest contacts between European explorers and Africans, African views on sexuality were seen by whites as wanton, uncontrollable, and insatiable. In white folklore black men were envisioned as lustful beasts who posed an ever-present threat to white women, while black women were characterized as willing temptresses. Such beliefs, however inaccurate, have had a powerful and pervasive influence on race relations in the United States. One of our most enduring cultural taboos is that which prohibits interracial sexuality.

Scores of white writers, both before and after the Civil War, continually condemned the supposed "bastardization" of the white race should intermixture occur. Such tracts reinforced old folk beliefs which suggested that black men continually and unashamedly lusted after white women. The Nat stereotype came to represent this vision, and white fear of slave rebellion was based in good measure on the assumption that many enslaved black men would be drawn to rebellion largely because of the opportunity to rape white women. This assumption by white males in America caused countless lynchings of black men immediately following Emancipation up through to the 1960s. Even though the history of American slave uprisings indicates that sexual attacks on women were the exception rather than the rule, stereotyping based on white misconceptions and fear of black sexuality persisted (Aptheker 298-299).

The diffusion of these and other black stereotypes through popular culture has a long and disturbing history. Perhaps the single most important influence was the nineteenth-century minstrel show. From about 1820 to 1880, minstrelsy was the most popular form of theatrical entertainment in the United States and to the world, America's unique contributions to the theatrical stage (Southern 91). Minstrelsy had its origins in the years following the War of 1812 when traveling "African delineators," or "Ethiopian minstrels," began to perform songs and dances which they originally drew from authentic black sources. These performers were primarily white males who blacked their faces with burnt cork and applied white make-up around their eyes and mouth to give themselves a wide-eyed, grinning Sambo look. Ethiopian minstrelsy was a conscious imitation of the black man's songs, dances, and humor by white performers in blackface (Southern 228). It was on the minstrel stage that many Americans of the nineteenth-century received their only impressions of black culture. It was from the minstrel stage that black stereotypes would enter (sometimes with very little change) into advertising, film, radio, and television.

The Sambo stereotype developed into two basic types of slave impersonations. In a rural plantation setting he was an ignorant, slow-moving, slow-thinking, and slow-talking, fun-loving buffoon named "Jim Crow." In an urban setting he was portrayed as the dandy city slave in the latest flashy clothing who boasted of his exploits among the ladies (Southern 89; Lemon 102). This second "impersonation" became known as "Zip Coon." Zip Coon was overly pretentious, a womanizer, and just as lazy as his rural cousin, Jim Crow. The difference was that Zip Coon, a Northern black stereotype, was totally unequipped to deal with urban life. He could not hold a job, he did not understand the urban north, and he could never succeed on his own. He was foolish, tended toward exaggerated speech inflections and malapropisms, and walked with a ridiculous strut.

Another typical presentation of the minstrels was that of Mammy. One "Ethiopian song" characterized her as follows:

> She'd joked wid de old folks and play wid de child
> She's cry wid de surrowing, laugh wid de gay;
> Tend on de sick bed, and join in de play
> De fust at de funeral, wedding or birth
> De killer ob trouble and maker ob mirth
> She spoke her mindly freely, was plain as de day
> But never hurt any by what she might say
> If she once made a promise, it neber was broke. (Toll 79)

Mammy was a truly lovable, jolly old slave who demonstrated by her life and actions that slaves could be happy and content. Old Uncle Toms were also sentimentalized on the minstrel stage. In addition, Harriet Beecher Stowe's nineteenth-century bestselling novel, *Uncle Tom's Cabin* (1852) permanently etched the personality of Uncle Toms as saintly dedicated and contented blacks who, though mercilessly treated by their masters, knew the role assigned to them by white society and forgave their torturers' sins. Sam Lucas (Milady) was the first black man to play the title role in the stage version of Uncle Tom's Cabin in 1878 (Southern 237).

Always and in every conceivable manner white minstrels portrayed African Americans in gross stereotypes. So strongly were these portrayals accepted that when black men began to enter minstrelsy after the Civil War, they were forced, to a certain extent, to adopt the same conventions like blacking up their (already darker hued) faces with burnt cork (Southern 200-01). Even though it may be difficult to comprehend why talented black men would voluntarily humiliate themselves, it must be understood first that minstrelsy offered African Americans a measure of financial security and also it was the sole route to the theater and concert world for the majority of them (Southern 234).

Robert C. Toll, whose *Blacking Up* is the finest book on minstrelsy, has described the manner in which white minstrels depicted blacks:

> Minstrel blacks did not have hair, they had "wool"; they were "bleating black sheep," and their children were "darky cubs." They had bulging eyeballs, flat, wide noses, gaping mouths with long, dangling lower lips, and gigantic feet with elongated, even flapping heels. At times, minstrels even claimed that Negroes had to have their hair filed, not cut....(67)

White minstrels also lampooned the diet, dress, and beliefs of African American slaves. They portrayed blacks as lovers of music and dance. In short, minstrelsy helped to popularize all the major conventions which have made up the various black stereotypes in other popular arts. Again, it is important to note that these stereotypes were created by whites for a predominantly white audience.

By the 1880s the popularity of the minstrel show was fading, but not the stereotypes. Other popular culture phenomena continued and extended the traditions begun on the minstrel stage. Late in the century the emerging advertising industry adapted black stereotypes to help fix product and brand names in the public consciousness. Companies began to distribute little cards with humorous sayings and cartoons which were accompanied by a pitch for some household product; baseball cards originated in this fashion. Among the most popular of these cards were those which depicted comic images of black people, usually embodying some form of Uncle Tom, Mammy, or Sambo stereotypes.

Because of the association of black Americans with the culture of cotton, products made from this staple crop such as thread and cloth were advertised on cards showing black men and women picking, baling, or processing the fluffy harvest. Other products as diverse as stove polish, baking powder, breakfast cereal, bath soap, and spices also drew heavily on stereotypical representations. The illustrations almost always featured black people with enormous lips, bulging eyes, excessively kinky hair, and wide-tooth grins. The activities depicted ranged from the predictable to the absurd. In the former category were cards illustrating the work of black servants: cooking, sewing or caring for white children. One of the most ridiculous cards portrayed a smiling mammy rocking a black child in a cradle fashioned from a watermelon (Harris 92-96). In addition to advertising cards, postcards also depicted African Americans in stereotypical situations. For example, some postcards showed small black children up in a tree branch having apparently barely escaped the capture of a large alligator.

After the demise of minstrelsy, a new musical form called "coon songs" became popular with the American public. Coon songs were early, syncopated, ragtime songs which primarily characterized black men as womanizers and black women as sultry and seductive. Coon songs with titles such as "Coal Black Rose," "The Coon's Eye," "By the Watermelon Vine," and "At A Darktown Cake Walk" used lyrics which portrayed black people as strutting, eating 'possum and watermelon, addicted to flashy clothing, superstitious, and generally incompetent in any activity which did not involve dancing or playing the drums. Although the majority of coon songs were written by white men, the most popular coon song from about 1896 to 1900 was entitled "All Coons Look Alike to Me" written by the black minstrel Ernest Hogan (Southern; Lemons). Although these songs perpetuated stereotypes of African Americans, for some black musicians coon songs were just another vehicle for the continuation of the African aesthetic of improvisation.

Black stereotypes were also found in popular theater and popular literature during the mid- to late nineteenth-century. Joel Chandler Harris' 1881 work, *Uncle Remus, His Songs and Sayings,* while generally sympathetic to black southerners and devoid of obvious racial slurs, depicted black life and culture in terms of stereotypes. The supposed narrator of Harris' tales, which he had collected from several informants, was a kindly old black man who resembled Uncle Tom. As a modern critic noted, Uncle Remus "...is a superannuated freeman, who sits in the sun making fish baskets of white-oak splits, mixing herbs for allin's, and talking to the little [white] boy in the cool of the evening ...Uncle Remus symbolizes the Negro who accepts life rather than revolt against it" (Fishwick 75).

A collection of representative advertising cards from the late nineteenth century.

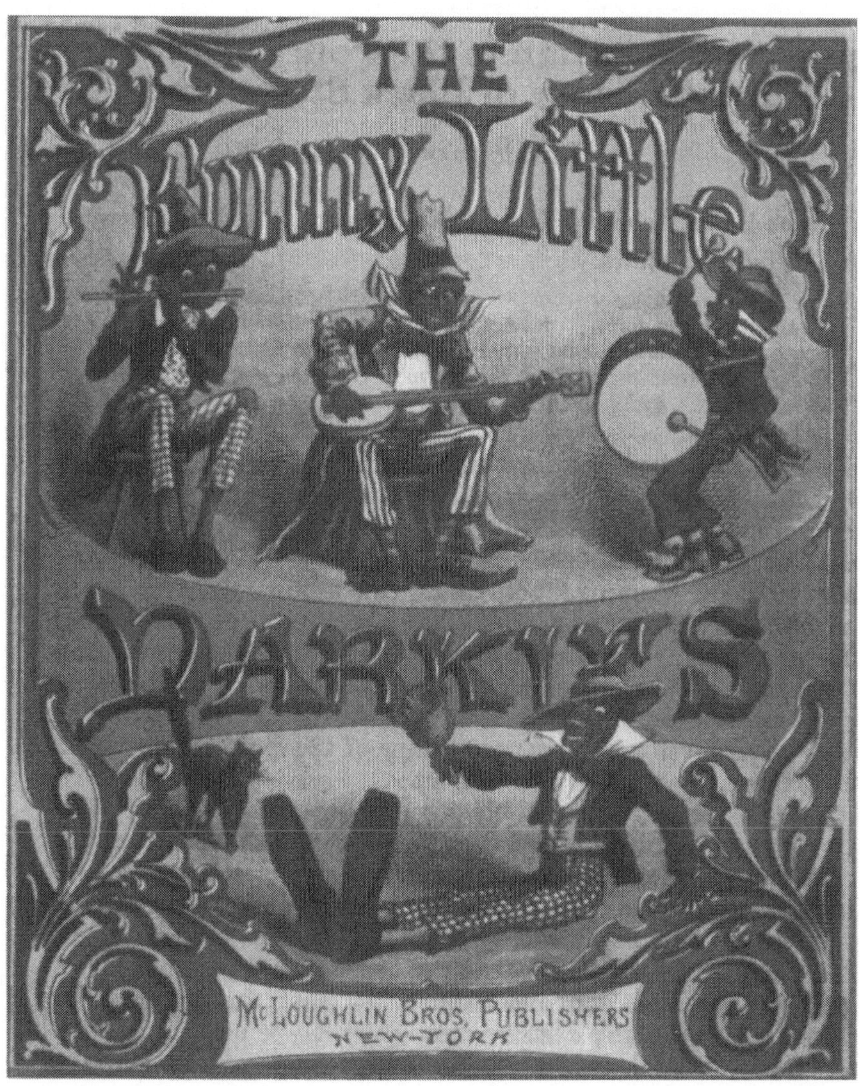

An early song sheet featuring some of the minstrel stereotypes.

Perhaps even more popular was *In Ole Virginia* (1887), a collection of short stories by Thomas Nelson Page. Set on antebellum plantations, Page's stories portrayed the pre-Civil War South as an idyllic Garden of Eden. The black characters were devoted creatures, simple and docile in personality, whose greatest pleasures in life were derived from serving their white masters. The South of Harris and Page was a never-never land of racial harmony with happy and contented black people.

Other popular entertainments ignored Mammy, Uncle Tom, and Sambo while focusing on the more threatening aspects of black stereotypes. For example, "miscegenation plays" were fairly popular on the American stage at the turn of the century. Such plays as *The Real Widow Brown* depicted devious black women who "passed for white" and tricked unsuspecting white men into marriage. Even more frightening to whites were such works of fiction as *The Clansman*, the 1905 best selling novel by Thomas Dixon, Jr. This racial diatribe, which was the basis for D.W. Griffith's important 1915 film epic, *Birth of a Nation,* not only depicted black politicians as corrupt and inept, but utilized white fears and misconceptions of black sexuality. In the Dixon and Griffith products, black men were portrayed as violent, sexual savages who derived particular satisfaction in lusting after white women.[2]

Since 1900 virtually all media have tended to rely on stereotypes whenever African Americans are portrayed. Early film images of blacks were quite similar to those found on the minstrel stage. In fact, many "blacks" in early American films were actually white actors in blackface make-up. Black actor Stephin Fetchit (Lincoln T. Perry) came to epitomize the Sambo stereotype in American films. Other black thespians, from gifted tapdancer Bill "Bojangles" Robinson to the great singer and entertainer Lena Horne, frequently had to play supporting roles in white films, roles which offered little more than an opportunity to enact stereotyped background characters. It was not until the 1950s that films with major black characters could be sold to white moviegoers.

In many of these major films, Sidney Poitier was one of the deserving and inoffensive black actors whose mannerisms promised an easy integration of blacks into American mainstream society.[3] In what Thomas Cripps calls the "age of Poitier" from 1950 to 1967, Poitier's characters were like Stephin Fetchit's, "giving and open, even in the face of white hostility; unlike Fetchit [however,] he stood apart—cool, reserved, and possessed of superior skills which the whites in the plot would soon need in order to avoid an awful fate" (Cripps 28). While performing in the role of racial ambassador, Poitier and other "laid back" actors like Harry Belafonte and Sammy Davis, Jr., eschewed sexual liasions as though avoiding the possible igniting of white sexual anxieties.

Under the aura of Poitier's controlled and reserved characters, a new stereotype emerged by 1971. Actors such as Jim Brown (the ex-football star), Richard Roundtree, and Raymond St. Jacques were cast as "Superspade," a new image which emerged in such films as *Shaft, If He Hollers Let Him Go,* and *Superfly*. Although these "blaxploitation films" certainly did not look back to the Sambo image and were produced primarily for black audiences, they were stereotypical nevertheless. Daniel J. Leab, whose *From Sambo to Superspade* is a good overview of the history of blacks in film, had this to say about the "Superspade" films:

> [They] were filled with sadistic brutality, sleazy sex, venomous racial slurs, and the argot of the streets. Social commentary of any sort was kept to a minimum. Superspade was a violent man who lived a violent life in pursuit of black women, white sex, quick money, easy success, cheap "pot," and other pleasures. (Leab 254)

Our nineteenth-century forebears would undoubtedly recognize Superspade as an unusual cross between Nat Turner and Zip Coon.

There are, of course, hundreds of other examples of the manner in which the traditional black stereotypes have been embraced by the creators of twentieth-century popular art and culture. In advertising there is Aunt Jemima, the kindly mammy who sells so many pancakes. Uncle Tom is a close relative of Uncle Ben, who offers us rice. In the music industry some of the "coon songs" became widely popular records. Two particularly racist examples, "All Coons Look Alike to Me" and "If the Man in the Moon Were a Coon," were especially popular and were heard regularly on the radio well into the 1940s. Enormously successful popular literature such as *Gone With The Wind* (1936) and *Mandingo* (1957) popularized the traditional stereotypes even more than had been the case in earlier works. Even children's literature, with such publications as long-in-print *Ten Little Nigger Boys,* helped to inculcate the familiar images. In confrontation with these traditional stereotypes, some black artists during the Black Arts Movement of the 1960s and 1970s reinterpreted these popularized symbols. For example, Murray N. DePillars took the same Aunt Jemima/Mammy stereotype in his pen and ink drawing *Aunt Jemima* and portrayed her on a pancake and waffle mix box as she really was: "a very angry women who may still be in the white lady's kitchen, but on very different terms—shorter, more reasonable working hours, familiarity, if allowed, and social security (Klotman 172, 174).

One of the most successful and long-running radio programs (1927-1960) of all time was *Amos 'n' Andy*. In minstrel tradition, its creators and stars were white actors Freeman Gosden and Charles Correll. Bumbling Andy and his scheming pal, George "Kingfish" Stevens, both resembled Zip Coon. *Amos 'n' Andy* also featured such characters as the slow, bumbling and lazy janitor known as "Lightnin'" and the inept and marginally corrupt lawyer, Algonquin J. Calhoun. The series was produced for television in the early 1950s, and although black performers were featured, the series continued to rely almost entirely upon the stereotypical presentation of black life and culture. Protests by the National Association for the Advancement of Colored People (NAACP) eventually forced it off the TV screen, but reruns continued on local stations until 1966 (MacDonald 26-33).

Another situation comedy featuring a stereotypical character was *The Beulah Show*. Beulah debuted on ABC TV on October 3, 1950. Its first star was Ethel Waters. "Beulah," who originated as a supporting role on radio's *Fibber McGee and Molly* program in 1944, was a Mammy-figure who was employed by the middle class Henderson family. Although Beulah worked hard to solve the problems of her employers, like *Amos 'n' Andy,* the NAACP also caused the withdrawal of *Beulah* from network syndication in 1953 (MacDonald 28).

In the 1970s, American television turned to black stereotypes in a variety of situations. In some cases, the old, negative images endured. This was certainly the case with the comedic series *Good Times,* in which "J.J.," the character portrayed by Jimmie Walker, was clearly a derivative of the minstrel's Zip Coon. Also, Walker's early 1980s creation, the scheming and jiving "Valentine" of the military comedy *At Ease,* occasionally lapsed into the same stereotype. Bud Yorkin and Norman Lear's *Sanford and Son* and *The Jeffersons* both featured "Sapphire-like" loud-mouthed black female characters: Florence the maid played by Marla Gibbs and Louise Jefferson (Isabel Sanford) both of *The Jeffersons*; and Aunt Esther (LaWanda Page) of *Sanford and Son.* In dramatic television presentations, however, there has been a conscious effort to lay the old stereotypes aside to favor more realistic portrayals. The highly acclaimed mini-series *Roots* (1977) not only eschewed the traditional stereotypes, but presented strong, intelligent black characters who clearly possessed a sense of their own dignity and self-worth.

The 1980s brought with it positive signs that traditional black stereotypes were being replaced in popular culture with more sophisticated images. Several television series cast black actors in significant supporting roles which varied considerably from the usual stereotypes. Such characters included detective Washington and officer Hill in the award-winning police drama *Hill Street Blues, Barney Miller's* Detective Harris and Benson, the sharp-witted butler created by actor Robert Guillame in *Soap* and later in a series of his own. Using satire as their weapon, some black comedians, most notably Richard Pryor and ex-*Saturday Night Live* star Eddie Murphy, confronted the traditional stereotypes head on. Murphy, for example, lampooned the image of urban black men as sleazy thieves and dope addicts in his "Mr. Robinson's Neighborhood" sketches, which are thinly disguised satires of a popular

PBS children's program. The debut of *The Cosby Show* in 1984, featuring a strong family with loving parents who were successful, upper middle class professionals, also began a trend of more positive portrayals of African Americans.

1990 ushered in Keenan Ivory Wayans' sketch comedy *In Living Color* and Will Smith's *Fresh Prince of Bel-Air.* In the vein of Pryor and Murphy, Wayans had earlier displayed a considerable amount of control over traditional black stereotypes in his blaxploitation film parody *I'm Gonna Git You Sucka* (1988). His *In Living Color* continued in this direction but also with a youthful, black, hip hop aesthetic of improvisation, truth-telling, and satire. NBC's *Fresh Prince of Bel-Air* starred rapper Will "The Fresh Prince" Smith. *Fresh Prince,* about a Philadelphia street teenager transplanted to the home of his aunt in Bel-Air, California, lampooned urban black street culture and the reactions to it of the white and black middle class. *Fresh Prince* and *In Living Color,* though still relying on stereotypical roles, mocked African American and mainstream culture while, at the same time, affirming and celebrating "blackness."

But even with these recent developments, the point remains that traditional negative black stereotypes still exist and are still used in the popular arts. Even though many have been toned down and even though media artists are now consciously limiting their frequency, there is no doubt that the use of these images continues to influence the state of racial and ethnic relations in the United States. Too many white Americans still obtain their most important impressions of black Americans through such misrepresentations. Thus, the study of black stereotypes remains an important area for the student of American popular culture. The more we understand about the impact of these images and their history, the more we will be able to understand about the state of our multi-racial and ethnic culture into the 21st century.

Notes

[1]Edmund S. Morgan has even argued that slaveholders actively promoted racial animosity, partially through stereotypes, in order to insure that slaves and poor whites would not combine to oppose the privileged planter class. See his *American Slavery, American Freedom: The Ordeal of Colonial Virginia* New York: W.W. Norton and Company, Inc., 1975. See also William H. Cohn, "Popular Culture and Social History," *Journal of Popular Culture,* XI (Summer, 1977): 167-179.

[2]For excellent discussions of *Birth of a Nation* and *The Clansman* see Jack Temple Kirby, *Media-Made Dixie* (Baton Rouge: Louisiana State UP, 1978, 1-22, and Edward D.C. Campbell, Jr., *The Celluloid South* (Knoxville: U of Tennessee P, 1981), 3-32 and *passim.*

[5]Some of the finest studies of black stereotypes in recent years have dealt with American films. The best of these is Thomas Cripps, *Slow Fade to Black* New York: Oxford UP, 1977. See also Cripps' article "The Dark Spot in the Kaleidoscope: Black Images in American Film," 28, in Randall M. Miller, editor., *The Kaleidoscopic Lens: How Hollywood Views Ethnic Groups* (Englewood, NJ: Jerome S. Ozer, 1980).

Works Cited

Aptheker, Herbert. *American Negro Slave Revolts.* New York: International Publishers, 1943.

Blassingham, John W. *The Slave Community: Plantation Life in the Anti-Bellum South.* New York: Oxford UP, 1972.

Campbell, Edward D.C., Jr. *The Celluloid South.* Knoxville: U of Tennessee P, 1981.

Cohn, William H. "Popular Culture and Social History." *Journal of Popular Culture.* XI: 1 (Summer 1977).

Cripps, Thomas, *Slow Fade to Black,* New York: Oxford UP, 1977.

_____ "The Dark Spot in the Kaleidoscope: Black Images in American Film," in Randall M. Miller, ed., *The Kaleidoscope Lens: How Hollywood Views Ethnic Groups.* Englewood Cliffs: James S. Ozer, 1980.

Fishwick, Marshall W., "Uncle Remus vs. John Henry: Folk Tension," in Marshall Fishwick, ed., *Remus, Rastus and Revolution.* Bowling Green, Ohio: Popular Press, 1973.

Jordan, Winthrop D. *White Over Black: American Attitudes toward the Negro,* 1550-1812. New York: W.W. Norton and Co., Inc., 1977.

Kirby, Jack Temple. *Media-Made Dixie.* Baton Rouge: Louisiana State UP, 1978.

Klotman, Phyllis Rauch. *Humanities Through the Black Experience.* Dubuque, Iowa: Kendall/Hunt Publishing, 1977.

Leab, Daniel J. *From Sambo to Superspade.* Boston: Houghton Mifflin Company, 1975.

Lemons, J. Stanley. "Black Stereotype as Reflected in Popular Culture, 1880-1920." *American Quarterly* 29.1 (Spring 1977).

MacDonald, J. Fred. *Black and White TV.* Chicago: Nelson-Hall Publishers, 1983.

Morgan, Edmund S. *American Slavery, American Freedom: The Ordeal of Colonial Virginia.* New York: W.W. Norton and Company, Inc., 1975.

Southern, Eileen. *The Music of Black Americans: A History,* 2nd ed. New York: Norton, 1983.

Toll, Robert C. *Blacking Up: The Minstrel Show in Nineteenth-Century America.* New York: Oxford UP, 1974.

Yellow Devil Doctors and Opium Dens: The Yellow Peril Stereotype in Mass Media Entertainment

Gary Hoppenstand

Stereotypes are always false beliefs. Since they tell us that certain groups of individuals are all identical, by definition they are a lie. Whether they are true or not, however, like other commonly accepted beliefs, stereotypes lead people to action. In the case of negative stereotypes, the actions that people are led to by these beliefs are invariably negative as well. Nowhere in American history is this more dramatically illustrated than in the development of the anti-Asian American Yellow Peril stereotype in this country during the first half of the 1940s. As Gary Hoppenstand details in the following essay, a century of the popular portrayal of Asians as sneaky, treacherous sub-humans led in 1942 to the roundup of 120,000 Japanese, 80,000 of whom were full American citizens, and the placing of them in "internment camps," for the duration of World War II. The reason given for depriving these Americans of their constitutional rights was the fear of espionage. In 1983, however, a national commission reported that the real reason was racism. There was never any evidence that espionage was imminent. Negative stereotypes had trained our national leaders to simply assume that the Japanese would try to destroy us from within.

Hoppenstand suggests that the core of the Yellow Peril stereotype was economic. Lest we assume that in the 1990s we are more enlightened on this issue, consider the orchestrated "Japan bashing" led by American automobile manufacturers. Once again, Asians are portrayed as a threat to our national well being. Once again, they are portrayed as heartless financial imperialists. And, quite simply, as in the 19th century, once again the reason is simply economics. When our jobs or businesses feel threatened, it becomes easy to hate. Usually this hate manifests itself

This essay in slightly different form was published in ***The Popular Culture Reader***, 3rd Edition, Christopher Geist and Jack Nachbar, eds. Bowling Green, OH: Bowling Green State University Popular Press, 1983. Reprinted with permission.

in negative stereotypes. And thus instead of rationally solving economic problems, we are left with the seamy pleasures of irrational hatred based on a lie.

"Men call me Erlik Khan, which signifies Lord of the Dead. I am...a direct descendant of Genghis Khan, the great conqueror...."

"The Lord of the Dead" by R.E. Howard

The Stereotype

People are continually in the process of negotiating reality during the course of their daily lives. This negotiated construction results, in part, from there being too much information for the limited capacity of the human mind to process, and, in part, from the need or desire for us to establish a mental grip on the flow of reality. As reasoning thinkers we employ many "tools" in the construction of our reality. We invent stereotypes to assist in the processing and categorization of reality information. Stereotyping is that method of defining an entire group of people according to a particular characteristic or set of characteristics shared by that group. As part of our reality construction process, stereotyping aids in the definition of our beliefs, the implementation of our rituals, and the creation of our literary formulas. The human mind, unable or unwilling to grasp all of the particulars of a given form or situation, "streamlines" that form or situation so that it remains simple enough for the sophisticated or unsophisticated mind to comprehend.

Stereotypes function in highly formulaic story forms to 1) keep the action of the story moving, 2) detail character sketches without wasting time on unnecessary descriptions, and 3) create heroes and villains who are simply motivated, for good or for evil, and emotionally charged. The potential danger of stereotyping stems from this third characteristic of the term. Just as heroes are written in popular stories so that we readers love them, villains are written so that we despise them. The inability to distinguish the stereotype from the original article, the inability to sift the fictionalized "streamlining" of characteristics from the complex and dynamic "real thing," the inability to objectify the stereotype and remain emotionally detached from it, can all result in the permanent incorporation of that stereotype into the stereotyper's structure of negotiated reality.

An examination into the history of the "yellow peril" stereotype's incorporation into our national mindset and the resulting popular formulas illustrates what happens when a nation's people permanently include a stereotype in their belief system and then act upon it.

To begin, imagine that you are living in America during the spring months of the year 1913—that "innocent" Edwardian era when our country was still polishing the gilt off what Mark Twain called "the Gilded Age" and some four years before our involvement in the First World War. You come from a comfortable, mid-western, middle-class family, which allows you the time and affords you the means by which you can entertain yourself. Deciding that you want a "good read," you visit the local drugstore or newsstand and purchase a current issue of *Collier's Weekly*, a popular magazine of the time. Sitting at home in a comfortable easy chair, you thumb through the issue and, discovering a story written by Sax Rohmer, you begin to read....Instantly you are transported to the world of London's Chinatown district, Limehouse, that vile place of billowing gray fog and twisting dark city streets, populated by "rat-raced" Orientals and ruled by that master yellow fiend himself, Fu-Manchu:

> Imagine a person, tall, lean and feline, high-shouldered with a brow like Shakespeare and a face like Satan, a close-shaven skull, and long, magnetic eyes of the true cat-green. Invest him with all the cruel cunning of an entire Eastern race, accumulated in one giant intellect, with all the resources, if you will, of a wealthy government—which, however, already has denied all knowledge of his existence. Imagine that awful being, and you have a mental picture of Dr. Fu-Manchu, the yellow peril incarnate in one man. (Rohmer 17)

Thus is the villain of Rohmer's fiction described by Nayland Smith, Rohmer's stalwart British hero who is full of pluck and who is the last hope of the white race. Petrie, the narrator of the story and Smith's assistant, gulps down a peg of brandy and collapses in his easychair after listening to Smith's description of Fu-Manchu. And you, sitting in your own chair (in that comfortable middle-class America of 1913) shudder at the thought of the "yellow peril" as you turn the page to read the next chapter....

Rohmer's cycle of stories about Nayland Smith and Fu-Manchu, first published in *Collier's Weekly*, were later collected and published by McBride, Nast and Co., in September 1913 under the American title *The Insidious Dr. Fu-Manchu.* Over the years, more than forty different hardcover and paperback editions were published of that single title alone in Britain and America. Recognizing the potential commercial success of a series based on the "yellow peril incarnate," Sax Rohmer wrote twelve more books about the "Devil Doctor," and the bulk of his other fiction (which totaled over fifty titles) concerned itself in one form or another with the conflict between the morally pure West and the mysterious, seductively evil East. Rohmer became one of the most successful authors ever to write about the yellow peril, influencing nearly all types of subsequent entertainment media, and the yellow peril stereotype that he helped to develop was to become one of the most frequently used negative stereotypes in our popular culture.

Historical Development

The yellow peril was the fear held by Western society—in particular British and American societies—that Orientals would one day unite and conquer the world. Chinese, Japanese, Mongols and other Orientals, as part of the yellow peril, were continually being utilized as villains of popular formulas. Described primarily by animal metaphors, the agents of the yellow peril were depicted as being the predators of Western society. They were often portrayed as beasts (wolves, rats, vultures and the like), the sort of animals that are strong, crafty, savage...and malevolent. Their hunger for world domination—for destruction of the Anglo-American and his civilization—was only matched by their hunger for the Anglo-American woman. Thus, in issue after issue of the most lurid and melodramatic dime novels and pulp magazines, and in episode after episode of the most sensational movies and comic strips, feral, rat-faced Chinese lusted after virginal white women. The threat of rape, the rape of white society, dominated the action of the yellow formula. The British or American hero, during the course of his battle against the yellow peril, overcame numerous traps and obstacles in order to save his civilization and the primary symbol of that civilization: the white woman. Stories featuring the yellow peril were arguments for racial purity. Certainly, the potential union of the Oriental and white implied, at best, a form of beastly sodomy, and, at worst, a Satanic marriage. The yellow peril stereotype easily became incorporated into Christian mythology, and the Oriental assumed the role of the devil or demon. The Oriental rape of the white woman signified a spiritual damnation for the woman, and at the larger level, white society. A favorite convention of the yellow peril featured the lone white woman surrounded by a horde of Chinese bent on debauchment. She holds them at bay with a revolver, and that revolver has only a single bullet left. Seeing that her situation is hopeless, she points the barrel of the gun to her temple...

The threat of the yellow peril in popular stories was powerful and difficult to eliminate. Thus, even though the blue-eyed, blond hero thwarted countless attempts by Oriental masterminds for world conquest, and even though the hero saved the white heroine innumerable times from "a fate worse than death," the threat of the yellow peril was never destroyed. Thousands of cruel Chink or Jap or Mongol killers lined the dirty streets of their Limehouse and Chinatown ghettos, armed with hatchets and knives (the favorite weapons of the yellow peril), awaiting the word from their inhuman leaders to begin a new round of pillage, rape and killing. Needless to say, prejudice and discrimination were by-products of the yellow peril stereotype in our entertainment. They constructed a reality in which it was defensible for white Americans to discriminate against Oriental Americans in various crisis situations.

The development of the yellow peril stereotype in American culture began even before the Chinese Coolie emigration to the American West Coast during the 1850s. Its origins can be traced back to the initial contacts between the European and Chinese cultures. In nearly all pre-medieval European mythologies there existed the belief that to the west lay a paradise or Eden where people lived in bliss and where society, according to Plato and Homer, was a virtual Utopia (Billington 1-28). Prior to the discovery of the Americas, this paradise was thought to reside in the lands of China, which, in part, explains why European explorers and merchants were so anxious to develop travel routes across the Atlantic. Christopher Columbus, upon his discovery of the New World, thought that he had uncovered a passage to the Orient. Later European explorers, realizing that what Columbus had discovered was a new land mass between the European continent and Asia, endeavored to locate a Northwest Passage to the Indies, which they never did but which nonetheless facilitated the exploration of America. As Europeans began to trade with China, they realized that Chinese craftsmanship was superior to theirs, and as Europeans began to estimate the "wealth" of the Orient, they became jealous of it. This jealousy manifested itself in religious terms. To the medieval and Renaissance European Christian, China was a land of heathen barbarians. It was the role of the good European Christian to either convert these barbarians or destroy them. The medieval Crusades, and later the Chinese/European missionaries were motivated by this religious militarism. Upon the structure of economic, religious and cultural jealousy, the yellow peril stereotype had its early foundations.

As the British imported Chinese workers to Singapore around 1823, they instigated the credit-ticket system, in which brokers of a particular labor market in Singapore or Penang would advance money to recruits in China, who would then solicit workers from the different villages of the Kwantung province. The workers' passage to Singapore would be paid by the recruits with the understanding that the fare would be reimbursed from the workers' labor upon arrival in the Peninsula settlements. The credit-ticket system was quite successful, so much so that the Chinese, traveling to Singapore in great numbers, created severe resource competition in the region. They also presented demographic problems for British (and other European) city managers in that they emigrated faster than the city could house or feed them. Thus, the first characteristic of the yellow peril stereotype—the belief that Orientals are part of a great, undifferentiated horde that robs non-Orientals of economic resources—began to evolve.

Following the allure of the California gold fields during the 1850s, the Chinese developed their own ethnic communities within large West Coast ports. The largest Chinatown district blossomed in San Francisco. Great merchant families gained control of these various Chinatown ghettos, and they acted with hostility, indifference or secrecy towards non-Oriental government officials. The next element, then, of the yellow peril stereotype became entrenched in the Anglo-American mindset: the belief that Orientals are schemers and that their plots involved something dreadful for white society.

The Chinese merchant families adopted the credit-ticket system in America, adding their own particular modifications including the loan system, where Chinese emigrants, upon arrival in America, would not only owe the amount of the fare to their sponsor; they would owe an additional interest as well. The interest on the credit-ticket often kept the Chinese emigrants indebted to their sponsors over a long period of time. The Chinese merchant families were then invested with a great deal of money and labor, and they subsequently sought to vie for greater power with one another. Assassins (or high-binders) were trained, and Tong wars broke out. Hence, another component of the yellow peril stereotype entered the American belief system: the notion that Orientals are blood-thirsty killers who possess a low regard for human life.

With the advent of the railroad industry in America during the 1850s, the opportunity arose for even greater Chinese emigration to the West Coast. The Irish, an emigrant labor force that had proved useful in the construction of rail systems in the East, initially began construction of the west coast railroads. But soon it was evident to railroad management that an ever larger labor force would be needed to help complete that construction. At first Chinese laborers were imported from the Chinatown ghettos of San Francisco and other west coast cities, and it became quickly apparent (to non-Oriental workers and management alike) that the Chinese worked harder, longer and for less pay than did any other group. The credit-ticket system was reintroduced by American railroad businessmen, and tremendous numbers of new Chinese emigrated to the West Coast. Between the years 1852 and 1875, it was estimated that some 200,000 Chinese emigrated to the U.S.; most of those arrived in this country via the credit-ticket system. The white labor forces, witnessing the influx of this cheap, admirably efficient emigrant labor group, became resentful of the Chinese since the Chinese were taking jobs away from their own workers. They feared that the Chinese, if not stopped in time, would soon assume all labor positions, and thus the belief that Orientals would conquer the white man's world if left unchecked was added to the yellow peril stereotype.

The Yellow Peril in Popular Story Formulas

The first entertainment mass medium in America to adopt the yellow peril stereotype was the dime novel. During the first twenty years of the dime novel's production (1860 to 1880), the Western was one of the most popular story formulas. The most-often encountered villain of the Western dime novel was the savage Indian, but just as the Western was being replaced in popularity by the detective dime novel (from 1880 to 1900), the savage Indian was being supplanted by the yellow peril stereotype. By the mid-1880s, when such detective dime novel series as *New York Detective Library, Old Sleuth Library, Old Cap Collier* and *Secret Service* were at their respective publishing heights, the various aspects of the yellow peril stereotype were being disseminated among a relatively wide audience. Literally, hundreds of garishly illustrated, and even more garishly written, dime novels were published sporting such titles as *The Bradys and the Yellow Crooks*; or, *The Chase for the Chinese Diamonds* or *The Opium Den Detective*; or *The Stranglers of New York*. The world of the yellow peril, as portrayed by the dime novel, was the Chinatown district of a big city in which decent, honest white folk never ventured. It was described as "No Man's Land," a place where the police held no power. It was an evil land populated with "hatchet-men" and scarlet Chinese "vamps." The opium den, that site of exotic opium water pipes where cheap dreams and even cheaper death could be bought by anyone who had the money, became the predominant locale where the yellow peril hatched their schemes. Chinatown and the opium den, because of the dime novel's influence, framed a symbol of warning to every Anglo-American who wanted to "experiment" in foreign Oriental cultures, suggesting that such an experimentation could result in drug-induced madness or a hatchet in the back.

Sax Rohmer's contribution to the yellow peril stereotype had a profound effect on popular entertainment media. Rohmer's unique addition to the stereotype was the creation of the evil Oriental mastermind—a brilliant, powerful character who plots the destruction of Western civilization, who commands the resources of Western science and Eastern magic, and who governs an army of devoted assassins. The pulp magazines were later to borrow Rohmer's Oriental mastermind, re-tailor him a bit and employ him as one of the most popular villains of the medium.

Dozens of hero pulp titles, including *The Phantom Detective, Secret Agent X, The Spider, G-8 and His Battle Aces, Operator 5, Doc Savage* and *The Shadow* contributed their own legion of Oriental masterminds. This species of villain became so well liked in the pulps, two magazine titles were created by Popular Publications (one of the major pulp magazine publishers) that solely featured Oriental masterminds: *The Mysterious Wu Fang* (six issues published from September 1935 through March 1936) and *Dr. Yen Sin* (three issues published from May 1935 through September 1936). Strongly patterned after Rohmer's Fu-Manchu series, Wu Fang utilizes a swarm of deadly insects, poisonous snakes and venemous spiders, as well as an army of assassins in his vile plans for world domination, and he is opposed in each issue by U.S. Federal Agent Val Kildare and his assistant, Jerry Hazzard. Dr. Yen Sin, known as the "Invisible Peril" as well as the yellow peril, is so nasty that it requires all the efforts of hero Michael Traile—"The Man Who Never Slept"—to keep Yen Sin in check.

October 1934 introduced Milton Caniff's adventure comic strip, *Terry and the Pirates* in which Terry—"a wide awake American boy"—experiences slam-bang adventure in the then exotic lands of China (Goulart 130). Caniff's comic strip accomplished two things in reference to the yellow peril stereotype. It created a female version of the Oriental mastermind called Dragon Lady, and it offered an example of the comic strip's special version of the yellow peril. Recalling how he created the character of the Dragon Lady, Caniff says: "[The Dragon Lady is] one who combines all the best features of past mustache twirlers with the lure of the handsome wench..." (Goulart 131). What Caniff did with his insertion of the Dragon Lady into the strip was to personify the image of the Oriental prostitute first introduced in American culture some fifty years earlier in the dime novels, augmenting previous elements of the male Oriental mastermind. Caniff's Dragon Lady became so prevalent in our culture that she included herself in our language vernacular, permanently etching the character itself in our national mindset. As the strip entered the Second World War, Caniff narrowed the yellow peril to the Japanese, and then, in the best propaganda tradition of this country, he differentiated the "good guy" Orientals (our Chinese allies) from the "bad guy" Orientals. The yellow peril stereotype proved to be as flexible as it was persistent.

Other comic strips of the 1920s, 1930s and 1940s hallmarked the yellow peril, and like Caniff's *Terry and the Pirates,* documented a narrowing image of the stereotype through World War II. Buck Rogers—that unfortunate hero who is trapped in an abandoned mine shortly after World War I and put into a state of suspended animation by radioactive gas, and who later awakes in the world of the Twenty-Fifth Century—combats the armies of the Red Mongols. The Red Mongols have conquered America in the future and rule it by the technology of their evil science, which included great flying battlecraft and disintegrator rays. Buck dedicates his life to the overthrow of the cruel Mongol overlords and the reversal of the actualized yellow peril. Alex Raymond's science fantasy comic strip *Flash Gordon* pits the virile, fair-haired Flash against the hosts of Ming the Merciless, Emperor of the Universe. Gordon—a world renowned polo player and graduate of Yale—and Flash's girlfriend, Dale Arden, are abducted by Dr. Zarkov aboard

The Mysterious Wu Fang was one of two pulp magazine series devoted exclusively to the Oriental mastermind. This time, the helpless white woman is about to be hanged and dropped into a pit of deadly snakes and lizards.

his spaceship and transported to the planet Mongo where they begin a series of adventures battling the evil powers of Ming. Unlike the dime novels or the pulps, the science fiction comic strips presented a bleak future world in which the Oriental agents of the yellow peril have achieved their goal of world domination. These strips acted as a genuine social warning for the Anglo-American and suggested that the yellow peril should never be ignored, lest the future be lost. Later, these two comic strips were produced as successful movie serials by Hollywood, and thus reached audiences far greater than any preceding entertainment medium. The yellow peril had invaded the movies.

Through the 1930s the Oriental received a mixed reception in Hollywood. On one hand, dozens of serial film were produced that featured Chinese or Japanese heroes, like the Charlie Chan and Mr. Moto movies. On the other hand, the Oriental mastermind continued to be durable villain material in adventure and science fiction films. In addition to the Flash Gordon serials (including *Perils From the Planet Mongo* [1936], *Spaceship to the Unknown* [1936], *Purple Death From Outer Space* [1940], etc.) starring Buster Crabbe, two other well known yellow peril film adventures were *The Mask of Fu-Manchu* (1932) featuring horror actor Boris Karloff as Rohmer's "Devil Doctor," and *Gunga Din* (1939), starring Cary Grant and Douglas Fairbanks, Jr., which described the vile goings on of the fanatic and deadly Cult of Kali in its attempt to destroy British rule in India. As the comic strips centered on the Japanese menace during World War II to the exclusion of other Oriental groups, Hollywood cranked up its powerful anti-Japanese propaganda machines, as well, and produced dozens of war films. The Japanese villains in these efforts were lacking any redeeming social values. They were beasts who launched a sneak attack on Pearl Harbor and who killed blue-eyed American boys. They deserved nothing better than swift symbolic death. Naturally, American popular film contributed its part to the war effort by stereotyping the Japanese as the yellow peril.

Part of that flexibility of the yellow peril stereotype was demonstrated in the publication of Ian Fleming's novel *Dr. No*, in 1958, as part of his James Bond series. Like his literary ancestor, Fu-Manchu, Dr. No was a rather unpleasant fellow:

> I loved the death and destruction of people and things [says Dr. No to Bond]. I became adept in the technique of criminality—if you wish to call it that...I was smuggled to the United States. I settled in New York. I had been given a letter of introduction, in code, to one of the most powerful Tongs in America—the Hip Sings...In due course, at the age of thirty, I was made the equivalent of the treasurer. The treasury contained over a million dollars. I coveted this money. Then began the great Tong Wars of the late 'twenties. The two great New York Tongs, my own, the Hip Sings, and our rival, the On Le Ongs, joined in combat. Over the weeks, hundreds on both sides were killed

Horror actor Boris Karloff portraying Dr. Fu-Manchu in the film, *The Mask of Fu-Manchu* (1932). Note the curious mixture of science and alchemy paraphernalia surrounding the Devil Doctor.

and their houses and properties burned to the ground. It was a time of torture and murder and arson in which I joined with delight.... (Fleming 162-163)

Dr. No, after saying that he stole the Tong's money, and was nearly killed by the Tongs for the theft, vows to Bond that he will employ the money to "extend his power to the outside world." Needless to say, he is stopped in his efforts by the sophisticated British secret agent. Fleming's novel, which was later to become the first in a long and commercially successful series of movie adaptations, incorporated past formulaic elements of the yellow peril stereotype that both honors the popular formulas of the past and updates the stereotype by placing it in a setting of international political intrigue.

Following Fleming's example, espionage and detective television programs of the 1960s and 1970s featured a host of new yellow peril villains. As the stereotype adapted itself during World War II to reflect American fears of the Japanese, it re-adapted itself during the Cold War years of the 1950s and highlighted the Communist Chinese evildoer, instead of the Japanese monster (who was by this time a valued commercial ally). Television programs, as well as movies, found the Communist Chinese to be popular villains with American audiences. For example, Robert Culp and Bill Cosby, the tennis-pro secret-agent heroes of *I Spy* (broadcast during the 1960s), dedicate their efforts against the evil political designs of the Communist Chinese in episode after episode, while the head of the "super police force" in *Hawaii Five-O*, Steve McGarrett (Jack Lord) encounters as his first great criminal adversary, Wo Fat, a devious agent of the Communist Chinese government. Again reflecting the then current state of American societal fears, this new brand of Oriental world conquerors possessed a definite Marxist flavor.

A Negative Result of A Negative Stereotype

After the Japanese bombing of Pearl Harbor on Sunday, December 7, 1941, the entire yellow peril stereotype, which had previously existed in American popular entertainment, became narrowly incorporated in our nation's war propaganda. The Japanese fit all the elements of the stereotype: a racial jealousy that the Japanese had caught the American navy unprepared; a fear that the Japanese would lust after the American controlled Pacific empire; and a belief that the Japanese, because of their sneak attack on Pearl, were bloodthirsty killers, schemers and world conquerors. What the Japanese had not counted on in their war against America was the presence of the yellow peril stereotype in our culture, a stereotype that enabled this country to whip itself into a war fever quickly. Thus, the barriers between the stereotype and prejudice and discrimination were soon torn down, and the fiction of the stereotype, as it then appeared in American comic books, pulp magazines, movies and radio, became intimately intertwined with the fact of America's war with Japan, and the two became as one in our nation's mindset.

One of the by-products of this country's inability to distinguish the yellow peril stereotype from the implicit reality of the situation was the implementation of Executive Order 9066 which called for the evacuation of all "enemy aliens" from the western half of the coastal states and the southern third of Arizona. More than 100,000 Japanese Americans were "relocated" into ten holding camps. Many of these Japanese Americans were stripped of their property and land holdings, even though two-thirds of them were American citizens. General John DeWitt, the person who saw to the transportation of the Japanese Americans to the camps, explained his philosophy thus:

> In the war in which we are now engaged racial affinities are not served by migration. The Japanese race is an enemy race and while many second and third generation born on United States soil, possessed of United States citizenship, had become "Americanized" the racial strains are undiluted.

Hearst paper sportswriter Henry McLemore reflected national sentiment when he wrote:

> I am for the immediate removal of every Japanese on the West Coast to a point deep in the interior. I don't mean a nice part of the interior either. Herd 'em up, pack 'em off and give 'em the inside room in the badlands. Let 'em be pinched, hurt, hungry and dead up against it. . . . Personally, I hate the Japanese. And that goes for all of them.

DeWitt's and McLemore's notorious examples of non-logic certainly indicated that the yellow peril stereotype was accepted at that time as truth. Even evidence to the contrary could not deter a belief in the yellow peril. DeWitt continued to explain in his recommendation to the Secretary of War (dated February 14, 1942) that even though no subversive enemy action had been undertaken by the Japanese Americans: "The very fact that no sabotage has taken place to date is a disturbing and confirming indication that such action will be taken. . . ."

It was race prejudice, motivated by the notion of the yellow peril, which prompted Earl Warren, who was then Governor of California, to say:

> I want to say that the consensus of opinion among the law-enforcement officers of this state is that there is more potential danger among the group of Japanese who are born in this country than from the alien Japanese who were born in Japan.

Protesting the mass Japanese evacuations, the national president of the Japanese American Citizens League stated:

> Never in the thousands of years of human history has a group of citizens been branded on so wholesale a scale as being treacherous to the land in which they live....We question the motives and patriotism of men and leaders who intentionally fan racial animosity and hatred....But we are going into exile as our duty to our country only because the President and the military commander of this area have deemed it a necessity. We are gladly cooperating because this is one way of showing that our protestations of loyalty are sincere.

To this day, no military evidence has ever been produced that linked Japanese Americans to any "fifth column" group.

Describing his own personal experience in an internment camp, Congressional Representative and Japanese American Norman Y. Mineta—in an article entitled "An American Tragedy: The Internment of Japanese-Americans During World War II" published in the May, 1984 issue of *USA Today*—states that soon after February 19, 1942 (when President Franklin Roosevelt signed into law Executive Order 9066 which authorized an "imprison-by-background policy") his family was quickly displaced from their home, imprisoned for six months at an "Assembly Center" located at the Santa Anita Racetrack in southern California, and then finally transported under armed guard from California to a camp in Wyoming. Mineta writes:

> I spent two years living in that camp. Indeed, the word "camp" was and is a euphemism. Some governmental officials said that the internment was being conducted for the protection of those who were being interned. However, our "camp" in Heart Mountain was surrounded with barbed wire, and the army guards in the watch-towers pointed their machine guns in at us and not out towards the cold, barren land which surrounded us. Those guards were preventing escape, rather than attack—and we were living in a prison, not a congenial camp.

John Hersey, in an article entitled "Behind Barbed Wire" published in the September 11, 1988 issue of *The New York Times Magazine,* states that after Roosevelt's re-election: "all evacuees who passed loyalty reviews could, at last, go home." But Hersey goes on to say that when Japanese-American detainees returned home, they were often met with hostility; their homes were seized for unpaid back taxes and their possessions were stolen. They also had difficulty finding jobs and were frequently greeted with signs proclaiming: "No Japs Wanted." The movie *Come See the Paradise* (1990), directed by Alan Parker, is Hollywood's version of this turbulent moment in American history, and it provides a fairly accurate portrayal of the blind racial hatred directed towards the Japanese American during World War II.

Nearly fifty years later, the October 11, 1990 Washington *Post* reported that the U.S. Government had finally begun enacting the terms of the 1988 Civil Liberties Act, which provided an official apology to the more than 60,000 surviving Japanese Americans who were detained during

World War II. In addition to a letter of apology signed by President Bush, the U.S. government provided an estimated 1.25 billion dollar cash settlement to those Japanese Americans who were incarcerated. Thus, an attempt at redressing a past wrong had been initiated by the government, a wrong committed, in part, because of the underlying efficacy of the yellow peril stereotype that was historically so pervasive in American culture.

In the 1990s the yellow peril stereotype finds itself still firmly embedded in our national mindset, and for virtually the same reasons that saw its creation in the 1800s. American television commercials berate Japanese producers of automobiles and other mass produced goods. "Japan-bashing" has entered the everyday speech of the millions of Americans and is, for the most part, passively accepted. Why? Because the Japanese often produce better products than their American counterparts. The green-eyed serpent of economic resource jealously continues to raise its ugly head, though this time the evil doctors and yellow fiends reside in the auto plant rather than the opium den.

Works Cited

Billington, Ray. *Land of Savagery, Land of Promise*. New York: Norton, 1981.

Fleming, Ian. *Dr. No*. New York: Berkley Books, 1982.

Goulart, Ron. *The Adventure Decade*. New Rochelle: Arlington, 1975.

Rohmer, Sax [Arthur Henry Sarsfield Ward]. *The Insidious Dr. Fu-Manchu*. New York: Pyramid Books, 1961.

One Size Does *Not* Fit All: Being Beautiful, Thin and Female in America

Jane Caputi with Susan Nance

One of the main dangers of stereotypes is that if the stereotype is some sort of ideal, we may voluntarily sacrifice part of our individual identity to become this ideal image. Since stereotypes take away all individual differences to create a uniform type, they are always untrue. Thus, if a person gives up his or her unique selfhood to become a stereotype, that person has sacrificed his or her singular selfhood for a lie. At best, doing this will make us anonymous. At worst, as Jane Caputi and Susan Nance argue in the following analysis of the thinness stereotype, doing this may cost us both our identities and our lives.

Caputi and Nance show us the pervasiveness of the popular belief in the stereotype that thinness, especially in women, means intelligence and beauty. In doing this they employ most of the methods for the analysis of popular stereotypes. They provide multiple examples from a variety of sources. They provide helpful historical background, even going back a thousand years to Chinese culture for parallel patterns of the stereotype. They cite data to prove just how common and influential the stereotype is. And, finally, they discuss the social implications of believing in the stereotype, in this case dangerous implications indeed.

Chances are that no matter what you read in this article and no matter how convinced you may be that what it says is true, during the next couple of years, whether you are a man or a woman, you will go on a diet. You will suffer and then soon after, gain at least all of the weight back again. This is the statistical pattern that a vast number of American adults experience regularly. (Most Europeans and Africans think we are nuts in this mania.) Thus we experience the power of popular beliefs, especially beliefs in stereotypes, first hand. Despite scientific evidence, despite medical advice, despite the negative effects on our

This essay in slightly different form was published in *The Popular Culture Reader*, 3rd Edition, Christopher Geist and Jack Nachbar, eds. Bowling Green, OH: Bowling Green State University Popular Press, 1983. Reprinted with permission.

individuality, despite our continuous failure, despite all common sense, we go ahead and diet anyway. Popular beliefs are above logic and, above all, they move us to action.

In the past few seasons, they [the writers on *Growing Pains*] have been insensitive in making her character [Carol Seaver] look fat even though she wasn't in real life. Her TV brothers were always making belittling fat jokes about her. The worst Carol-bashing took place in an episode in which Carol was exercising in her room and the floor beneath her collapsed. Of course, everyone blamed her weight for the accident.

(Duane Eklof, in a letter to *TV Guide*, Feb. 17, 1992)

"I told her it looked like she was going too far with the weight thing."

(Joanna Kerns, actress who played Tracey Gold's mother on *Growing Pains*)

"We teased her in a friendly way when she got thin, but then she went over the edge."

(Alan Thicke, actor who played Tracey's father, a psychiatrist, quoted in Rosen, *People*, Feb. 17, 1992: 94-5).

Tracey Gold, a young actress on the rather aptly-named television family sit-com, *Growing Pains,* is but the latest of a long line of dancers, models, actresses and athletes to "go public" with her story of anorexia and bulimia. First diagnosed with anorexia at the age of twelve, Tracey was treated and apparently "cured" by four months of psychiatric therapy. In the midst of her success, seven years later, she began compulsive dieting again.

I was made fun of by a casting agent. If I were a different person, it probably would have rolled off my back. But I have the kind of personality where I will let these kinds of comments affect me. I've always wanted to please people. (Rosen 94)

By the time Tracey's mother noticed her body without the oversized sweaters which she affected, the 5'3" actress weighed 90 pounds. Like the more than seven million other young women who suffer from eating disorders, Tracey Gold's desire to please others resulted in her self-imposed starvation. Tracey was persuaded to leave the show and to work on her recovery.

In contemporary America, not only sex appeal, but beauty, success, intelligence, morality, health and likability are just some of the qualities that are put to the scales. For example, one study of college admission rates found that overweight girls have only one-third the chance of being admitted to prestigious colleges as slim girls with identical records (Mayer 91). In college, as everywhere else, only one female body type is socially valued—the trim line, slender-all, maxithin, or Virginia slim. Even our consumer products display the desired form for the cult of the thin that has invaded every facet of the culture. The thin ideal is visually preached not only by commodities, but by celebrity images, fashion models and rituals such as beauty contests. It is acted out for us by "weight saints" such as Jane Fonda and Richard Simmons. It is prescribed by best-selling diet and work-out books, women's magazines and TV shows, and shamed into us by the unfunny jokes of family and friends or the unfriendly, but trendy, advice of health professionals.

It might at first appear that all this worry about weight revolves simply around concern with the fit and healthy body, but this would be as foolish as presuming that the sun revolves around the earth. Although the bottom-line argument for thinness and dieting is that being overweight constitutes some grave health hazard, this is increasingly being shown up as false. Being 25-30 percent above your optimum weight can contribute to diabetes, gall bladder or cardiac problems, but for the majority who are only a few pounds over the standard, this is by no means the case. Actually, the latest studies have shown a greater longevity for those who are slightly padded. The Metropolitan Life Insurance Co., the organization responsible for those intimidating height and weight charts, has revised its recommendations for healthy proportions, upping the allowed weights by thirteen pounds in some instances ("Keep Your Double Chins Up," *Newsweek*, March 14, 1983: 65). Recent evidence has also suggested that each individual has some natural "setpoint" weight around which their body naturally fluctuates. That is why most of those who do manage to lose weight through dieting invariably "fail" and return to their original weight. It also indicates that those who achieve thinness through constant dieting do so at the high risk of permanent physical and mental stress, actually sacrificing health for the fashionably thin image (Bennet and Gurin).

First and foremost, thinness is a fashion. Fat and thin are shifting standards (as are those for ugliness and beauty) and have been differently defined in every human culture. Furthermore, fat and thin have to do with fascism as well as fashion, with politics as well as aesthetics. Thinness is primarily an ideal of female beauty but such beauty is neither value free nor culturally anonymous. We must always ask to whom it is pleasing and why, how wide the defined range of beauty or how narrow and if, in fact, that range admits only one, idealized type. In Nazi Germany, for example, the stereotypic blue-eyed blonde was the fashion dictate for purely ideological reasons. That, of course, was a racist and genocidal system in which, "Outward appearance was always stressed as a sign of the correct racial soul" (Mosse). Yet how qualitatively different is that attitude from the one in modern America whereby outward appearance is taken to be an infallible indicator of one's sexual, racial or economic desirability?

Although slenderness is only a look, an image presumably of beauty, it is frankly a narrow stereotype that functions as a badge or token for an accompanying ideology. In America, thinness is a socially recognized sign, for class status, sexuality, grace, discipline and "being good," whereas *fat* is now a categorical derogative for those stigmatized as stupid, sick, self-indulgent, neurotic, lazy, sad, bad and invariably ugly.[1] All such associations, images and prejudices have coalesced into a modern image of good looks, physical size and social consequences—a body of culturally specific beliefs that both reflect and reinforce the sexual, racial and economic politics of the time.

The Fair Sex

Why does a beautiful girl need an I.Q. to say I do?

20th century popular song[2]

The stereotype of female slenderness is a sub-set of a much larger stereotype of women and beauty. Thus, before specifically analyzing the modern fashion of thinness, we first should give some attention to cultural conceptions and functions of beauty.

No one is born with an innate sense of what constitutes good looks; rather, we learn and internalize cultural standards through a general process of socialization. Furthermore, the traits we are taught to either esteem or scorn are often rooted in narrow prejudices. When Black Liberation in the 1960s first coined the slogan, "Black is beautiful," it was a reaction against decades of racist conditioning that black features were in and of themselves displeasing. For example, in August 1968, *The Thunderbolt,* an extremist anti-black newspaper, stated quite baldly, "most white men are not attracted to Negro women because they are ugly" (Stember 20). One of the most effective methods of transmitting racist attitudes is to fuse some racial traits with ugliness (brown skin, big lips, kinky hair) and to exalt others as the epitome of earthly beauty (white skin, blonde hair, blue eyes). Moreover, we are then judged not only by how well we ourselves fit the culturally approved standards, but also by how much we have accepted these as our own, even if they negate our actual physical selves and self-interests.

A Stanford-Binet I.Q. test from 1960 makes all of this abundantly clear. Drawings of two women illustrate one of the test questions which reads, "Which is prettier?" The figure on the left has styled hair; her face shows evidence of make-up. Perhaps most significantly, her eyes are cast downward and to the side. The figure on the right, however, presents a totally different aspect and mood. Her hair is coarse and unattended; even worse, facial hair can be seen on her cheeks. Her nose is large as are her lips. She looks directly into the eyes of her beholders.

"Which" (we might also consider the use of the inanimate pronoun) then, "is prettier?" Any who do not wish to make their intelligence suspect would necessarily choose the figure on the left. Yet how fair is such a test? What does this question really measure—our intelligence or our internalization of a cultural bias? Also, is its function not only to test, but also to teach us that very cultural bias?

This simple set of images effectively conveys some basics of sexism and racism as they are intertwined with the larger cultural stereotyping of beauty.

1) *Women are the pretty sex*: It is hardly likely that this question could be sexually reversed and that there be drawings of two men with the same query, "Which is prettier?" Even if we substituted the word *handsome* the situation would remain absurd. In our culture, looks are not supposed to be a primary concern of men. Handsomeness might be a side-effect of masculinity, but it is certainly not a necessary or definitive attribute. Prettiness and the primacy of appearance are, however, considered to be eminently feminine traits. In 1852, *Godey's Lady's Book* (a combination *Cosmopolitan/Good Housekeeping* for the 19th century) offered this dictum, "It is a women's business to be

"Which is prettier"? (Stanford-Binet, 1960

A test question from an I.Q. test.

beautiful" (Banner), i.e. her occupation, preoccupation and sexual obligation. Although such an association of women and beauty may at first appear to be complimentary, its ramifications are actually far from flattering.

In return for this "compliment," women are expected to relinquish their claims to vast fields of human endeavor. The first of these is intelligence and creativity. Rather than create great works of art, women are expected to regard themselves as works of art, to sculpt their bodies, develop their breasts, and paint their faces as aesthetic expression. Furthermore, the negative correlation of beauty to brains is everywhere propagandized. Oscar Wilde once flattered his own sex by noting, "No woman is a genius; women are a decorative sex." Rooted in this belief about female beauty is the stereotype not only of the dumb blonde, but also the companion belief in the general intellectual inferiority of women.

The second field that must be surrendered is worldly power. Whereas women's sexual charm is centrally located in their physicality, men's chief allure emanates from their work, achievement, wealth and social station, essentially from their *power*. Henry Kissinger, then Secretary of State, was once asked about the nature of his attractiveness to and escorting of some of the renowned beauties of the late 1960s. "Power is the ultimate aphrodisiac," he responded.

Finally, the stereotype of feminine beauty designates women as sex objects, not only in the eyes of the men who behold them, but also in their own eyes. Fashion thus becomes a social master and the female body, and all that is considered to be wrong or ugly about it, becomes a woman's enemy and obsession for life. Although fashion purportedly exists because women are inherently so beautiful, its actual implication is that without submitting to its standards, treatments, and rituals, most women would be hopelessly fat, hairy, aged and ugly. Such standards have come more and more to include medical "intervention." In a new and dangerous trend, breast augmentation and implant surgeries have reached new heights. Encouraged by a self-serving medical specialty, almost two million women have had silicone implants; only recently have studies and statistics begun to accumulate the data which cites the dangers. Moreover, one of the most insidious manipulations of women's fears and insecurities about their bodies took its form when the American Society of Plastic and Reconstructive Surgeons, in testimony before the FDA, stated: "There is a substantial and enlarging body of medical information and opinion to the effect that these *deformities* (small breasts) are really a disease." Thus, what is natural in a woman's body is transformed by male size preference, in collaboration with a $500 million-a-year implant business, into the disease of "micromastia." It becomes another reflection of fashion for which there is now a "cure," a final decision to re-create oneself according to external guidelines (Ehreneich

88). It is really only the made-up woman, concocted in cultural stereotypes and imagery, who is considered to be the "true" beauty.

2) *Submission is beautiful and feminine beauty is submissive*: Marabel Morgan wrote in her best-seller, *The Total Woman*, "It is only when a woman surrenders her life to her husband, reveres and worships him, and is willing to serve him, that she becomes really beautiful to him" (Morgan 96). Beauty here is unmistakably in the eye of the beholder and that eye is one of an overseer.

In the imagery of the I.Q. test, it is crucial to note that the prettier picture has cast her eyes demurely to the side while the fearsome woman gives a direct and unwavering gaze. This is a classic instance of body language. Averted eyes signify submission. A component of feminine prettiness and desirability is a willingness to submit. Such principles are then coded into the stereotypes that say that men must be older, taller, larger, stronger and more experienced than women, and that women must be younger, smaller, thinner, weaker and more naive than the men they accompany.

3) *The image of the beautiful woman functions as an icon or symbol for the beliefs and values of the core culture*: Today's culture worships itself in its myth of physical perfection as dramatized by celebrities, fashion models, sports heroes and movie stars. These types are the modern equivalent of more traditional, action-oriented heroes. But the *look* of such figures in this image-ruled world is as critical to analyze as were the *deeds* of the former types. Film theorist Bela Balazs has commented:

> The physical incarnation of the hero or heroine is beauty of a kind which exactly expresses the ideologies and aspirations of those who admire it. We must learn to read beauty as we have learned to read the face. (284)

We have seen that racism can be discerned in both the absence of any truly celebrated images of colored beauty and in the ceaseless procession of clone-like, blue-eyed blondes from Farrah Fawcett and Cheryl Ladd to Cheryl Tiegs and Christie Brinkley. This type is celebrated because it represents an idealized racial and sexual symbol. That is also why those particular looks are stereotyped and finally perceived by nearly all to actually *be* beautiful.

And what of our Stanford-Binet illustrations? The pretty woman shares with supermodels Tiegs and Brinkley those regular and clearly white features. Her ugly counterpart, however, is just as clearly of an unspecified, but (because of the association with ugliness) strongly disfavored ethnic origin; her nose, lips and hairiness all point in that unmistakably racist direction. Furthermore, what would we find were we able to view these figures from the neck down? Undoubtedly, our pretty model would be somewhat shapelessly slim and trim while the

A deliberately distorted advertisement photograph, elongating the already slim model.

ugly would fall somewhere into that wide range of the hopelessly and unfashionably fat. The thin ideal is as much an ideological symbol as blond hair or certain facial features. What then are the ideologies and aspirations it reveals and how can we learn to read the "beautiful" body along with the "beautiful" face?

The Fashionable Woman

Although not everyone in the urban west suffers from anorexia, a social dimension of the problem can also be suggested. While it was once fashionable to be as plump and "well-discovered" as ladies in paintings by Titian and Renoir, we have seen a shift towards an ideal of thinness as exemplified in the art of Klimt and Schiele and in fashion models such as Twiggy and Veruschka. This change in socially accepted style has been so complete that it is necessary to pause and remind ourselves that in other societies and historical periods girls who looked like Twiggy would have had to resign themselves to camouflage or to staying at home. (Polhemus 22-3)

In ideal cultural form, men become heroes; in ideal cultural form, women appear as models. Art historian John Berger has written that how a woman appears to others, especially men, is of crucial importance for what is normally thought of as the success or failure of her life. He states, "Men act and women appear. Men look at women. Women watch themselves being looked at. This determines not only most relations between men and women, but also the relation of women to themselves" (46-7). In response to this situational surveillance, women do tend to cultivate themselves as objects of the male gaze. They watch themselves in mirrors, watch other women to see how they compare, and finally, following fashion, they watch their weight.

All the researchers agree; fear of fat is primarily a female concern. Even though the incidence of obesity is not always higher among women and in some age brackets is actually lower than in men, the generic dieter, anorexic and bulimic are all female. At any given time, nearly 50 percent of all American women are on a diet of some kind of another; moreover, 80 percent rate themselves as unhappy with their present weight. Dieting is an obsession not only among adult women, but has assumed the dimensions of an initiation rite for teenage girls. One study found that 60 percent of all girls between the ages of ten and thirteen had already been on a diet; 80 percent of all American girls have dieted by the time they reach eighteen.[3] It has often been disparagingly remarked that were it to become fashionable for women to be plump tomorrow all diets would be immediately abandoned and women would begin to stuff themselves like geese. That may be superficially true, but the meaning can be all too easily misconstrued. Such an observation does not really attest to some simple foolishness of women. Rather, it indicates the immense weight of social pressure on women to submit to the dictates of fashion.

Indubitably, women are the fashionable sex. Yet, although easily overlooked, the word *fashion* is not only or even primarily a noun or adjective. It is also a verb and it is the verb form that reveals its character. As a verb, *fashion* means "to make; shape; form; mold; contrive." Hence, the fashionable woman is literally the one who can be bent, stretched, shrunk or even beaten into the requirements of the prevailing mode. Fashion often seems freely chosen, but oppression can be made to look consensual, torture pleasurable. Marilyn Frye tells us that:

> The root of the word "oppression" is the element "press." *The press of the crowd; pressed into military service; to press a pair of pants...* Presses are used to mold things or flatten them or reduce them in bulk, sometimes to reduce them by squeezing out the gasses or liquids in them. Something pressed is something caught between or among forces and barriers which are so related to each other that jointly they restrain, restrict or prevent the thing's motion or mobility. Mold. Immobilize. Reduce. (54)

For nine centuries in China (ending only with the 1949 revolution) female footbinding was the mandatory and definitive beauty ritual for women. Only those peasants who had to work were spared this practice which left the less fortunate, but truly fashionable women with three inch putrescent stubs that were useless for walking, let along running or dancing. The doctored feet leaked pus, reeked of rotten flesh, and had to be kept wrapped and hidden in bandages. Nevertheless these ceremonial wounds were fetishized as the supreme expression of beauty and given such deceptive names as "lotus" feet (Daly 1978).

Western civilization has by no means been free of such customs. As Helene Roberts has pointed out, tight-lacing of a corset produced the mandatory hourglass figure for 19th century American women. Yet at the same time it interfered with the oxygen supply and frequently caused hazardous compression of the vital organs and displacement of the ribs. The corset not only constrained a woman's figure, but also her movements and lifestyle. Thus bound, she could never engage in any strenuous activities. Her movements restricted, she was "naturally" confined to the domestic sphere. As Roberts argues, such dress actually molded not only the body of the wearer, but also her consciousness:

> Dress projected the message to the observer that the wearer was willing to conform to the submissive...pattern, but dress also helped to mold the behavior of the woman to that pattern.

The diet is the logical descendent of rituals such as foot binding and corseting. Its purpose, equally, is to fashion the body of the subject to the culturally dictated standard and, like those prior rites, dieting and the general cult of slimness have as great a molding effect on the *psyche* of the dieter as on her *physique*. Such effects include a distorted self-image, anxiety, self-hatred and a self-destructiveness that can even lead to disease and death.

A women who stands 5'5" and weighs 150 or even 140 pounds might consider herself something of a monster. Yet she is really far less of a human anomaly than that international sensation of 1966-67, fashion model Twiggy. Dr. Hilde Bruch, an expert on eating disorders, reminds us that:

> ...as a malnourished waif, "Twiggy" (5'7", 92 lbs.), was held up as a model for thousands of normally developing adolescents. It made them concentrate their mental energies on achieving a similar starved appearance even at the sacrifice of their health. (*Eating Disorders* 19)

The Twiggy image not only transmitted a drastically new look, but simultaneously scrambled the perceptions of all those who received it. With Twiggy as the new standard, the whole scale of thin through fat was down-shifted. Those healthy women who clearly did not look anything like Twiggy were bumped up into the fat zone and were seen that way, not only by others, but by themselves. It has been shown that men don't start to worry about their weight until they are at least thirty-five pounds over the national average, but women think of themselves as *fat* if they are fifteen or twenty pounds over their culture's desire (Chernin 62).

Seeing yourself as fatter than you really are is actually a characteristic symptom of anorexia nervosa, a disease Bruch defines as the "relentless pursuit of excessive thinness" (*The Golden Cage* ix). Extremely rare before 1960, it has now gotten seriously out of control. A PBS *Nova* program broadcast on March 22, 1983 reported that one out of every hundred girls in America was developing the disease, and that up to twenty-one percent of these die from starvation or related complications. Eight years later, the disorders of anorexia nervosa and bulimia have become classified by the Surgeon-General of the United States as an epidemic. A 1990 NCAA survey of athletic programs at 801 schools in the U.S. states that 64 percent of their athletes reported at least one incident of an eating disorder within the previous two years (*Women's Sports and Fitness* 22).

At least one precedent for this collaboration between disease and fashion was set in 19th century America. The reigning feminine stereotype at that time was that of a flower-like, ethereal, almost tubercular creature. Historian Lois Banner has written:

> So powerful was the desire for delicacy that it became fashionable to appear ill, according to contemporary observers. Abba Gould Wilson contended that "the ill are studiously copied as models of female attractiveness." (51)

Although this notion of the ill being used as models of female beauty sounds bizarre, this is actually quite similar to the contemporary situation. One writer on eating disorders reserved a small section of her book to those whom she termed "vocational anorexics," those who must appear thin in order to perform their jobs—dancers, fashion models, and actresses (Cauwels 108-9). (The ballet dancer Gelsey Kirkland, however, lost the starring role in *The Turning Point* because—at 87 pounds—she was too weak to perform and *too* thin for the film aesthetics [Rosen 98].) Yet these are the very women who function as role models for young women. Not only is their professional thinness achieved through the artifice of constant dieting, but the photos in which they appear are themselves masterworks of illusion, literally trick photography. One model who participated in an ad for designer jeans related that the jeans she had to wear were actually two sizes too small. Nevertheless, three people were enlisted to force her into them. Then, unable to move, she had to be lowered to the floor like a board. The finished picture, nonetheless, seemed to be an effortless illustration of what we should all aspire to look like in designer jeans.

One of the characteristic symptoms of anorexia nervosa is the inability to realistically gauge one's own body size and image. When these girls, often weighing as little as 70 pounds, look into the mirror they continue to see themselves as too fat, still not thin enough for the marketplace. It is not improbable that this psychic and symptomatic distortion is causally connected to the conventional distortions and glamour of fashion imagery. Moreover, this style of "thinking anorexically" affects almost all nominally healthy women to some degree. Rare indeed is the woman who is not convinced that she would look far better minus a few pounds of flesh, the woman who has never dieted, the one who is not always aware of her weight and body image or one who can refrain from agonizing on this theme in the company of like-minded cultists.

Starving oneself through anorexia is admittedly an extreme form of self-hatred, but normal dieting itself can induce similar alienations. The dieter not only despises her fat image, but constantly aware of her body, its appetites and their denial, experiences her own body as an enemy presence, one that must be defeated, stifled, shut up and reduced. Self-loathing often reaches such an extreme that many women have expressed their desire to just cut away the offending flesh—the protruding or merely curved stomach, the supposed glut of buttocks, the seemingly excessive thighs. The obsession with slenderness has caused many to seek out those very mutilations, and a new line of cosmetic surgeons has emerged to enable anyone who can afford it to act out those very fantasies and desires. So-called cosmetic mutilations are external; other varieties are internal. Of those 5,000 people who annually have their intestines removed to block absorption of nutrition, 80 percent are women (Chernin 62). The relatively new technique of liposuction actually vacuums away the offensive fat, disposing of it entirely or reinserting some of it into other body sites.

Finally, in pursuit of the unrealistic and patently unreachable stereotype of slenderness, most women achieve only an unremitting sense of failure. Studies have consistently demonstrated that 98 percent of those who lose weight by dieting gain it all back within a year. Worse yet, 90 percent of those who have "successfully" dieted gain back more than they ever lost in the first place. Thus, in a bizarre reversal, the widespread practice of dieting itself may be responsible for much of the added weight upon Americans (Chernin 29-30).

Ninety Pound Weaklings

Two years ago I won the President's Physical Fitness Award. I was 5 feet and 103 lbs. The boys at school said I was "built" and my parents worried that physically I was too mature for my age. Before I left for summer camp, my boyfriend and father joked about my "padded" hips. For the first time, I considered dieting...That fall I stopped eating. (Shaughn Reiss, recovering anorexic, in Rosen 94)

Fashionable customs such as foot binding or corseting not only reshaped the female body, but crippled and constrained it in the process, thus female beauty could be found in a useless three-inch foot, or a breathless, sixteen-inch waist. Then, the finished or fashioned body could be used to confirm the stereotype of women as the "weaker" sex. In this regard, dieting manifestly continues that tradition.

The relation between women and fashion has traditionally been one of dominance and submission. If the basic purpose of fashion is to make women "beautiful," i.e. pleasing to men, it may well be that the constantly shifting styles—be they thinness or roundness, long skirts or short—are themselves secondary. What is primary is a common symbolic denominator of *submission.* Submission, weakness and inferiority are the background attraction factors in female fashion and it is these factors that imbue any style with its fundamental sex appeal. Recently, slenderness has come into its own as a mass style with a similar strategem and effect.

In the late 1960s, a body of research on the social implications of dieting pointed to a marked sexual difference in attitudes toward body weight and size. Girls consistently perceived themselves as fatter than they actually were and chose dieting as their favorite method of trying to lose weight. Boys, on the other hand, not only tended to diet far less frequently than girls, but usually expressed a desire to *gain* weight and to be larger in all dimensions. Girls, however, wanted "to be smaller in almost all dimensions and to lose weight" (Dwyer et al.). Here we reach the symbolic message center of the slenderness style and stereotype. We can express it this simply: in this culture men are encouraged to gain or win and women are encouraged to lose, men to increase and women to reduce.

Even in our afraid-of-weight era, a larger physical size still communicates strength, solidity and power. Contemporary slang designates important matters as "heavy." Important people are said to "carry more weight," to have some "weight to throw around." Those who are inconsequential are "lightweights" who can be easily "blown off." Such notions cannot be separated from sexual stereotypes. Thinness and dieting are part of a comprehensive process of female minimization and diminishment. Almost all elements of feminine charm conspire to produce this effect—the demure, downcast eyes, the carefully modulated voice, tiny graceful movements, a neat and contained appearance, etc. But no contemporary stereotype has been so relentless as slenderness, no ritual so effective as the diet which actually reduces the physical boundaries of the female, striking particularly hard during those crucial, formative and initiatory rites of adolescence.

In *The Silent Language*, Edward T. Hall states quite simply that "space speaks" (162). The fact that women now ritually inhibit their appetites and reduce their bodily dimensions means that they literally take up even less space than before and, as always, less space than men. No wonder that the creator of the Miller Lite beer commercials, one of the most successful ad campaigns on television, stresses that his commercials never mention *dieting*. Instead they concentrate on evoking a rough, macho atmosphere and promote beer as "less filling" because dieting is for women ("Rich, Thin and Beautiful," ABC, April 10, 1983). Of course, those people who fill up less space are perceived to be less intimidating and powerful. You can be sure that when a *Cosmopolitan* cover (Feb. 1983) exhorts its readers to be "Bigger and Firmer," it is referring not to their self-image or decisiveness, but to their busts.

The writer-producer-director of the first film to deal specifically with eating disorders (*The Famine Within*, 1990), Katherine Gilday, stated in an interview:

> I'm...interested in the way that our North American culture values the idea of control of the body over nature to such an extent that we're terrified at the thought of letting appetite go. If we let appetite go, it's going to be this overwhelming force. The idea that the body might have its own regulatory system means that your control is illusory—the whole culture seems to have a lot of trouble with that. I was particularly interested in the way that women's bodies so often bear the burden of these fears about loss of control. (*Cineaste* 39)

Along these lines, Kim Chernin has argued that dieting is a specifically female ritual because in a sexist culture men are basically allowed to eat, to literally and symbolically satisfy their appetites and pleasures. Women, however, must learn to limit themselves and their desires; they are urged to deny their urges, to refuse pleasure and to limit their appetites, be they for food or for more abstract gratifications. Chernin further proposes that the current obsession with female slenderness is a cultural response to feminism, a reaction provoked by male fear of a burgeoning female power, not waistline (96-110). Before dismissing such an approach, remember that we are not talking only about the obviously obese, but also about an artificial and unhealthy ideal of thinness imposed upon normal-sized women.

Some might object here and point to what *Time* magazine a decade ago proclaimed as a "new ideal of beauty," a female strength and fitness (72-77). Yet the classification of strength as a fashion or ideal of beauty weakens it intolerably by putting it back into the cage of that most sacrosanct feminine stereotype—the obligation to appearance. Although often heralded under the banner of health, strength or cardiac control, the true mission of the female dieter or work-out artist is almost invariably a very feminine concern with beauty.

A close reading of that bestselling phenomenon—*Jane Fonda's Workout Book*—exposes that all too familiar and flabby motivation. Although some cheers are directed toward getting strong, sound nutrition and the hazards of environmental pollution, Fonda's rationalizations and confessions reveal the traditional femininity behind her approach: looks are still the number one issue. For example, her preoccupation with working out dates from an intimidating moment in *California Suite* when she had to appear in a bikini. A few years later, her commitment would receive renewed vigor when *On Golden Pond* required a similar scene. And that film itself was so irritating because of Fonda's *image* of strength was so clearly belied by the weakness of her character. One critic observed, "As *On Golden Pond's* Chelsea, Fonda sure looked like a dynamic, physically strong woman, but she had the emotional strength of a whiny nine-year-old" (Hoffman 15-18). Obviously, this was strength for strut, not substance.

In the introduction to the *Workout,* Fonda admits that like so many women she had been guilty of abusing her body—binging, purging, and crashing in order to achieve "an imposed ideal of beauty." In a later interview, Fonda said that she had been bulimic from the age of 12 to 35, and often vomited as often as 20 times each day (Rosen 97). She further confesses, "I myself had played an unwitting role as a movie star and sex symbol in perpetrating the stereotypes that affected women all over the world" (Fonda 20). But where exactly is the big change?

Fonda is still doing exactly what she gets paid for—setting stereotypic standards, performing as a movie star, a professional beauty dispensing her secrets (for a price) to the ordinary who hope (mostly in vain) that some of her glamour will rub off on them. Above all she is a *female* star (could anyone seriously consider a *Peter Fonda's Workout Book*?) and a sex symbol whose most recent acceptance of those standards finds its expression in her recent silicone breast implantations. Women worked out with Jane in the 1980s and 1990s like they cut their hair for Farrah in the 1970s. An ad in *Cosmopolitan* tells it exactly like it is: "Jane Fonda's Workout has shaped thousands of beautiful women. Let it make YOU the most beautiful ever." This ad is wedged in with all the other sleazy black and white one-pagers for breast developers, diet pills and Shrink Wrap reduction systems. As these ads indicate, the Fonda book is generically the same; finally, it is equally insulting for the new thin and strong ideal is actually a very old one, not only of traditional femininity, but also of class privilege, conspicuous display and conspicuous leisure. The workout is primarily a form of pretend work for those who do not need to labor to survive.

The Consumer Society

In this era, when inflation has assumed alarming proportions and the threat of nuclear war has become a serious danger, when violent crime is on the increase and unemployment a persistent social fact, five hundred people are asked by the pollsters what they fear most in the world and one hundred and ninety of them answer that their greatest fear is "getting fat."

Kim Chernin

I won't even lick a postage stamp—one never knows about calories.

Esther, an anorexic

In the nineteenth century the wealthy proclaimed themselves to the world with conspicuous consumption—opulent display in both their persons and their possessions. The situation has shifted in this century. A vast gulf still exists between rich and poor but in America at least, most people can get enough to eat. Moreover, junk food, fast food and cheap food is always more fattening. In order to distinguish themselves from the lower classes, the rich have taken to spending enormous amounts of time and money to remain "in shape," i.e., thin. In one study, researchers showed that while only 5 percent of upper-class women in Manhattan were overweight, fully 30 percent of lower-class women were. Such discrepancies cannot be attributed to some racial or ethnic factor, because among people who moved up the class ladder only 12 percent remained overweight (Beler 261-2). In America, as they say, you can never be too rich or too thin.

Just as white people can relish getting a tan because they really don't have to be colored in a racist society, so can comparatively rich people exalt thinness because they really don't have to starve. Most of the world's population does not get enough to eat while 25 percent systematically overeat. If all the available food calories for any given day were distributed evenly among the world, we would each get about two hundred. Everyone would starve. That is not because the earth cannot support its population, but because equitably feeding the world is neither a priority nor even a goal. Five times as many agricultural resources in the form of land, water, energy and fertilizer are used to provide for a North American than for the average Indian, Nigerian or Columbian (Brown et al. 219-30). Not only do Americans consume more, the quality of their food in the form of meat, milk and eggs is also much higher. An individual in an underdeveloped country consumes a share of roughly 400 lbs. of grain directly per year, while individuals in the developed countries feed 800 lbs. of an annual 1,000.-lb share to the stock so that they can eat beef. Twenty pounds of vegetable protein are lost in the production of each pound of beef (of which each American consumes a yearly average of 116 lbs.). This expensive eating habit provides the body with far more protein than it can absorb and, when measured in with the meat-eating of other developed nations, results in the loss of 18 million tons of protein, enough to make up 90 percent of the protein deficit in the entire world (Pines 77).[4]

It has been pointed out that it has become literally an American patriotic duty *to consume* (Wright et al. 226-37). Yet we over-consume and waste not only food, but all of the natural resources—oil, gas, electricity, water and space as well as technology, leisure and luxury. In order for the West to realize its "ideals" of abundance, the rest of the world must be relatively deprived. It is fully ironic that Twiggy first hit her stride in the fashionable West approximately coincident with the international sensation of mass starvation in Biafra. As pictures of each phenomenon flooded our consciousness, it would not have been too difficult to understand this style's symbolic undercurrent of pain, guilt and even death—a subliminal message undoubtedly intuited and internalized by each subsequent anorexic.

One anorexic confessed:

> I feel guilty when I eat anything, especially high-calorie food. I feel naughty, low, base, repulsed by myself after I eat. I feel like I overeat if I eat normally. (Bruch, *Golden Cage* 85)

The new disease of anorexia and its fatalities are sacrificial or scapegoat deaths for the self-proclaimed consumer society. We all speak of "being good" when we stick to our diets and "being bad" or naughty when we ritually "pig out." Yet the issue of food and who eats what in the modern world is truly one that is fraught with morality, guilt and anxiety—those emotions that anorexics ritually dramatize for us all. While the world starves, the rich countries have invented a fashion of artificial thinness. We buy food that is deliberately empty of calories—all the *lite* products, the Nutrasweet chewing gums and sodas—billion-dollar industries against a backdrop of death in the third world.

The world's death toll from starvation must also be seen as ritualistic and even requisite in order for the West to maintain its glutted standard of life. We fetishize the consumption of food and despise its resultant fat because it so obviously demonstrates our gluttony for the goods of the world. We contain any shame, concern and morality by giving lip service to slenderness, watching our weights, and making mostly women—again being used as the showpieces and symbols of the core culture—mimic the effects of starvation in their bodies. But this is pure glamour and show. There is little evidence that the core culture wishes in any way to restrict its appetites. The show of leanness is finally both hypocritical and absurd.

In an interesting footnote to these issues, reports in the 1990s are surfacing of an anti-dieting movement, both within women's ranks and in those of the medical profession. Recent N.I.H. (National Institutes of Health) studies have confirmed that diets simply do not work and may, indeed, be detrimental to good health. Anti-dieting advocates argue that eating in accordance to one's *natural appetites*, consumption of healthy foods, regular exercise and, specifically, acceptance of and making peace with one's own body, will result in weight stability and well-being. Recognition that most weight issues are societal and value-laden is resulting in a growing number of women who are rejecting this traditional means of self-punishment. Demonstrations are reported at which women are trashing scales and carrying banners with such messages as "Scales Are For Fish, Not For Women." Those in the vanguard of weight loss professionals directly challenge the practices of conservative, traditional medicine. They say that:

> The medical establishment's drumbeat, blaming excess weight for health problems, is one way that medicine and the $37 billion diet industry keep dieters, who are overwhelmingly female, on weight-loss regimes.... "There are no studies proving that weight causes disease; the predilection to certain diseases could well cause the extra weight...." (O'Neill 1, 21)

For women accustomed to the punishment and deprivations of traditional weight-loss diets, to the pain and loss of self-esteem inherent in the irrational and artificial standards of "thin is beautiful," this change in perception can be extremely politicizing. The growing awareness of how deeply one's life has been affected by the failure to meet these external standards (and of the arbitrary nature of the standards themselves) must inevitably lead to a positive self-consciousness and a freedom from the confinement of this artificial beauty trap.

Notes

[1]Interestingly, members of NAAFA (National Association to Advance Fat Acceptance) have chosen to claim the word "fat" as opposed to "overweight," stating that the latter assumes the actuality of an *ideal* "over" which one is judged to be.

[2]This line is cited in Una Stannard "The Mask of Beauty," *Women in Sexist Society*, Vivian Gornick and Barbara K. Moran, eds. New York: Basic Books; reprinted by Signet, 1972. 187-203.

[3]For statistics on women and weight control see *Newsweek*, March 7, 1983: 59.

[4]We are indebted to Kriemhild Ornelas for these sources and the use of her unpublished paper, "Development of Western Countries as a Model for Underdeveloped Countries," 1977.

Works Cited

Balazs, Bela. *Theory of Film*. New York: Dover, 1970.

Banner, Lois. *American Beauty*. New York: Knopf, 1983.

Beler, Anne Scott. *Fat & Thin: A Natural History of Obesity*. New York: Farrar, Strauss and Giroux, 1977.

Bennet, William, and Joel Gurin. *The Dieter's Dilemma*. New York: Basic Books, 1983.

Berger, John. *Ways of Seeing*. London: the BBC and Penguin Books, 1972.

Brown, Lester, and Erik Eckholm. "The Changing Face of Food Scarcity." *Food for People Not for Profit*. Catherine Lerza and Michael Jacobson, eds. New York: Basic Books, 1975.

Bruch, Hilde. *Eating Disorders: Obesity, Anorexia Nervosa and the Person Within*. New York: Basic Books, 1973.

_____ *The Golden Cage: The Enigma of Anorexia Nervosa*. New York: Vintage, 1979.

Cauwels, Janice M. *Bulimia*. New York: Doubleday, 1983.

Chernin, Kim. *The Obsession: Reflections of the Tyranny of Slenderness*. New York: Harper and Row, 1981.

Corliss, Richard. "The New Ideal of Beauty." *Time* 30 Aug. 1982.

Daly, Mary. *Gyn/Ecology: The Metaethics of Radical Feminism*. Boston: Beacon, 1978.

Dwyer, Johanna T., Jacob J. Feldman and Jean Mayer. "The Social Psychology of Dieting." *Journal of Health and Social Behavior* 2 (1970).

Ehrenreich, Barbara. "Stamping Out A Dread Scourge." *Time* 17 Feb. 1992.

"Fat Chance in a Thin World." *Nova*. PBS: 22 March 1983.

Fonda, Jane. *Jane Fonda's Workout Book*. New York: Simon and Schuster, 1981.

Frye, Marilyn. "Oppression." *Race, Class & Gender*. Paula S. Rothenberg, ed. New

York: St. Martin's, 1992.

Hall, Edward T. *The Silent Language.* New York: Anchor Books, 1973.

Hoffman, Jan. "The Exercist: Jane Fonda Redistributes the Fat of the Land." *Village Voice* 9 Nov. 1982.

"Keep Your Double Chins Up." *Newsweek* 14 March 1983.

Lucia, Cynthia. *Cineaste* 18. 4.

Mayer, Jean. *Overweight: Causes, Cost and Control.* Englewood Cliffs, N.J.: Prentice-Hall, 1968.

Morgan, Marabel. *The Total Woman.* New York: Pocket Books, 1975.

Mosse, George L. *Nazi Culture.* New York: Grosset and Dunlop, 1966.

O'Neill, Molly. "A Growing Movement Fights Diets Instead of Fat." *New York Times* 12 April 1992.

Pines, Maya. "Breaking the Meat Habit." *Food for People Not for Profit.* Catherine Lerza and Michael Jacobson, eds. New York: Basic Books, 1975.

Polhemus, Ted. "Introduction." *The Body Reader: Social Aspects of the Human Body.* New York: Pantheon Books, 1978.

Reiss, Shaugn. "Each Hunger Pain Delighted Me." *Ms.* Aug. 1976.

"Rich, Thin and Beautiful." ABC: 10 April 1983.

Roberts, Helene. "Submission, Masochism and Narcissism: Three Aspects of Women's Role as Reflected in Dress." *Women's Lives: Perspectives on Progress and Change.* Virginia Lee Lissier and Joyce Wolstredt, eds. Newark, DE: University of Delaware, 1977.

Rosen, Marjorie. "A Terrible Hunger." *People* 17 Feb. 1992.

Stember, Charles Herbert. *Sexual Racism.* New York: Harper and Row, 1976.

TV Guide. 19 Feb. 1992.

Wright, David E., and Robert E. Snow. "Consumption as Ritual in the High Technology Society." *Rituals and Ceremonies in Popular Culture.* Ray B. Browne, ed. Bowling Green, OH: Popular Press, 1980.

Women's Sports and Fitness. 13.8 Dec. 1991.

Instant Guide to Popular Heroes

	Citizen-Hero	Rogue-Hero	Citizen-Celebrity	Rogue-Celebrity
Adulating Group	mainstream/mass	significant sub-group (age, sex, race)	mainstream/mass	subgroup (often bound together by their attraction to the celebrity)
Means of Adulation	holidays, parades, associated icons of national significance (coins, monuments, etc.)	pilgrimmages to birthplace (and especially death/ grave site)	awards (Lifetime Achievement, Kennedy Center)	fan magazines, fan clubs, fame
Role	defends and embodies significant mainstream myths, beliefs and values (especially those associated with democracy and community)	embodies spirit of individual freedom and rebellion	helps mainstream culture validate itself by celebrating domestic values and reaffirming the American myth of success	role model for subgroup
Use to Students	key to how a culture views itself and wants to be viewed by others -- goals define cultural hegemony	enables us to identify important cultural conflicts (defines what culture is rather than what it strives to be)	measure cultural self-satisfaction, "happpiness"	enables us to identify and define fads and temporary lifestyle conflicts
Time/ Stability	longlasting	longlasting	lifetime	brief (as long as they are famous)
Known For	achievements in promoting and defending cultural values	living fast and dying young	ability to stay famous	embodiment of current taste, temporary cultural mindset
"Reality"	real person or fictional character	real person or fictional character	real person/ imaginary-invented persona through a role: image	real person/ imaginary-invented persona through a role: image
Inter-relationships	often portrayed by citizen-celebrity	(1) often portrayed by rogue-celebrity (2) may become a citizen-hero with change in cultural zeigeist	often "borrows" characteristics from celebrity-hero with whom he/she is associated	(1) often "borrows" characteristics from rogue-hero with whom he/she is associated (2) may become citizen-celebrity if fame lasts long enough
Abilities	especially gifted	especially energetic	especially comforting	especially famous
Examples	Susan B. Anthony Martin Luther King, Jr. Charles Lindbergh Lone Ranger Superman	Muhammed Ali James Dean Dirty Harry (young) Elvis Thelma and Louise	Katharine Hepburn Gregory Peck Sidney Poitier Jimmy Stewart	Ice-T Madonna Luke Perry Axl Rose Roseanne

Section ☆ 5 ☆

Heroes

Look! Up in the Sky!
(And Right Next Door): Popular Heroes in America

Getting bitten by a radioactive spider while attending an experimental demonstration for his high school science class was both the best and the worst thing that ever happened to the bespectacled Peter Parker. On the one hand, the arachnidian ambrosia that now coursed through his veins as a result of the sting gave him lots of impressive special abilities: the proportionate strength of a spider (which can hold many times its own weight), a tingling "spider sense" which warned him of unseen dangers, extraordinary reflexes and the ability to clamber up the walls of buildings and rooms were only some of his new found "insectiskills." All that remained for Peter to do was to create a red and black costume, *apply* a few of those nerdy science talents to develop an artificial webmaking device, and he was ready to begin a new life as the spectacular Spider-Man.

Peter Parker may be a bookworm and a veritable social outcast, but he realizes that his super-powered talent can be profitable. The money he imagines earning tossing fat guys out of the wrestling ring and doing tricks and stunts on national television will help him repay his Uncle Ben and Aunt May for giving him a home. Peter gets so excited about the big checks he is going to start picking up that when a burglar runs by him in the hallways of the TV studio, super-powered Spidey just lets the guy escape—why bother to get involved?

Oops. Peter returns home that night with an already failed career. He's got no money since the studio can't make out a valid check "payable to Spider-Man," and the network won't pay off in cash without knowing his real name. Peter also discovers that Uncle Ben has been killed as the result of an encounter with—that's right—the same burglar Peter had allowed to run past him at the network. Out of his terrible anguish, however, comes the lesson that would guide his life from this point onward: "With great power there must also come—great responsibility." And thus it is that Spider-Man, Opening Act gives way to Spider-Man, Superhero.

Inspiring? You bet! But things don't change all that much for poor Peter. Bookworm Parker is still picked on by bullies and given the cold shoulder by women. And even when he grows up a bit and gets a girlfriend and a job he's still beset by all the cares of everyday life—a rival in love, a boss who underpays him (and loathes Spider-Man to boot), and a sickly Aunt May who's always just one tiny step away from the grave. Peter even gets the flu when he's got a super-villain to battle and gets rejected by the women in his life when he has to break dates so he can risk his life to save the world.

But Peter continues to do his best in meeting the demands of his two identities. As Spider-Man, he jokes his way through each pitched battle with the forces of evil and strives to save his city from falling prey to the villains' clutches; as Peter Parker he pursues personal happiness, courts true-love, and struggles to pay the rent. In paying equal attention to both roles, he becomes "your friendly neighborhood Spider-Man." He thus is emblematic of the true American Hero in that he is simultaneously *better* than each of us (super-powered, super-dedicated, super-courageous, and witty) and yet *one* of us (an average person who gets up early, works hard, and comes home tired only to stay awake worrying about money, love and security). American heroes are up in the sky for us to point at and admire, but they are also right next door so we can share with them a cup of coffee and a heartache.

Popular American heroes are common men and women who rise to great heights of achievement—from log cabin to white house, from bookworm to superhero—and thus demonstrate to us both their own special abilities and characteristics and their continued ties to the masses. The implication is, of course, that each of us is capable of achieving similar goals—anybody born in America can grow up to become president of the United States of America. But it is also true that heroes must not rise so high that they imperil the very values which produced them and which they have sworn to protect. We've seen this conflict before—it's the familiar "individual freedom vs. democracy" debate that helped define icons, for example—and here American heroes help resolve it by embodying both values at the same time: achievement and humble origins, power and humility, special skills and ordinary problems. American heroes are not aristocrats, King Arthurs, or demigods we can only stand back and admire; American heroes are men like Abe Lincoln (who walked miles to school but ended up saving the Union), Teddy Roosevelt (who liked to fish and hunt but also charged up San Juan Hill right into the White House), and Thomas Edison (who said that "genius is 99 percent perspiration" and yet had the extra one percent that gave us the light bulb and phonograph as well). American heroes demonstrate *modesty*, arise *from commonplace* origins, and engage in *everyday activities* and events.

Popular heroes are real or imaginary people who represent for the members of a culture the ideals of that culture. They are human icons representing as individuals the most admirable person a culture is capable of producing. Odysseus, with his combination of great physical strength and cunning wits thus represents the ideal human qualities revered by the ancient Greeks. The first legendary American hero was Daniel Boone, who came to represent virtues of which Americans were particularly fond: skills in the wild, bravery, a strong commitment to assist in the civilizing of a new land, and, as described in the discussion of beliefs and values, the valued American belief in the innate right to personal freedom. Such heroes as Odysseus and Boone provide a valuable function for the other, less talented, members of a culture. First, they provide us with concrete images of what we all can strive to become. They stand and beckon to us from the pinnacles of the mountain we all try to climb. Second, heroes represent a perfected member of a culture who is a source of pride to that culture because it is the culture itself that has produced such perfection.

While all heroes have certain characteristics in common, it is especially important for the student of popular culture to understand the differences between two broad categories of heroes. Since each group is often representative of its own set of beliefs and values each is useful in its own and illuminates different aspects of the cultural mindset. Each also differs from the other in the emphasis it places upon one or the other of the competing value of "democracy" and individual freedom. *Citizen-heroes* are those men and women who embody myths associated with mainstream America—the traditional values of the community and the nation. *Rogue-heroes* by contrast, are representative of the beliefs and values associated with individual freedom—with the need to challenge the mainstream when its powerful currents threaten to wash away minority rights in favor of majority rules. We will examine each heroic category separately so that we can better define and detail the differences between them.

Heads on Mountains, Money, and Mail: Citizen-heroes in America

Three main conditions must be present for a person to attain the status of a citizen-hero. The first condition is that the person must be exceptionally gifted in some way. Professional athletes, for example, have become heroes in the twentieth century because we can read about and witness their extraordinary physical skills. Television sets all over the country were tuned to Henry Aaron, April 8, 1974, as he belted his 715th homer that beat Ruth's record. Within a few minutes Aaron had become a national hero. Charles Lindberg was a skilled pilot. Robert E. Lee was a military strategist. Thomas Edison was a great inventor. Annie

Oakley was a great shot with a rifle. And imaginary persons striving for status as citizen-heroes must be similarly skilled. Over the course of three movies spent battling the Empire in an attempt to restore Princess Leia to her throne and establish good government, Luke Skywalker becomes a Jedi Knight capable of besting the powerful Darth Vadar in fancy laserplay; Batman pumps iron and practices his acrobatics until he is capable of eliminating crooks and murderers with impunity; and Spider-Man has all those amazing arachnid abilities that enable him to leap short buildings in a single bound and climb right up over ones a little taller.

American citizen-heroes George Washington and Abraham Lincoln illustrate the second necessary condition for heroic status: the hero must possess qualities the culture values highly. Historically, George Washington seems to have been a man with gifts as a military and political strategist. What we remember most affectionately about Washington, however, is two other qualities, both of them immortalized through legends. The famous telling of the truth after little George chopped down his father's cherry tree never happened, but it illustrates a prized American quality—telling the truth. Since Americans prize individualism as a virtue, it has always been our belief that a person should have nothing to hide. Therefore, George's telling the truth testifies to his dignity as an individual.

The other legendary event, the terrible winter at Valley Forge, exemplifies the American virtue of perseverance, of sticking to something no matter how hard until the job is done. (This of course links Washington to a major myth already discussed—the myth of success.) Lincoln, as his nickname "Honest Abe" clearly shows, is also admired as a teller of the truth. Another Lincoln nickname, "the Great Heart," illustrates another admired quality Lincoln is said to have had in great measure—compassion for the unfortunate. Just as we applaud a Horatio Alger boy who gives his last nickel to a starving chum, Lincoln is still praised for his plans to gently welcome the South back into the Union. The admired qualities of citizen-heroes are essentially those we associate with being "good citizens," including honesty, integrity, understanding of those less fortunate, participation in community activities and striving for achievement of community goals. Even Washington's "individualism," for example, is demonstrated by an action which reflects his respect for authority and responsibility—a confession of wrongful rebellion in chopping down the cherry tree rather than a protest in favor of his individual right to do as he pleased.

The third necessity for the citizen-hero is his duty to the mainstream culture itself. Citizen-heroes must be defenders of the community, they must put their gifts and qualities to work so that the culture is preserved and made prosperous. It is the third necessity that has made the soldier such a popular hero type throughout history. England has its St. George, France its Joan of Arc, and South America its Simon Bolivar. In the United States, men like Washington, Andrew Jackson, Teddy Roosevelt and Dwight Eisenhower have attained heroic status through military feats and have used this status as springboards to the presidency. It is of some interest to note that the last two American wars in Korea and Viet Nam have produced few heroes. In earlier wars Americans felt their way of life was directly threatened or their quest for territory justifiable. Military heroes naturally resulted because it was clear that soldiers were either protecting or spreading the American way of life. Asia, on the other hand, is far away, and the ideological basis for fighting in Korea and Viet Nam was so ambiguous that the military connection with preservation of prosperity was tenuous. The resultant mixed feelings about these wars created a national mood unreceptive to soldier heroes.

Ex-president and eternally second-rate movie actor Ronald Reagan is a good example of a man many Americans consider to be the most significant citizen-hero of recent times. Reagan rose from modest beginnings (a small town boyhood in heart-of-America Illinois) to be swept into the White House on the flood tides of two victories. Even as holder of the nation's highest office, Reagan maintained a disarming modesty (his frequent use of self-depreciating humor, for example) and engaged in the types of ordinary, everyday activities (riding horses at his ranch, cheering on superstar athletes in the World Series and SuperBowl, napping during boring cabinet meetings and social occasions) which demonstrated that he was very much a regular human being just like the friendly folks who elected him. "Dutch" Reagan—one of us—but Leader of the Free World as well.

Reagan had a gift which was rendered special by the historical context in which he rose to power. In an era in which politics and entertainment were simultaneously united and controlled by the electronic media, Ronald Reagan was "The Great Communicator." Reagan put his acting experience and his folksy image to powerful use so that he used the media without being touched in return. He delivered his message directly to the hearts of the American people so that they heard exactly what he wanted them to hear and saw precisely what he wanted them to see. While Jimmy Carter was boring us with statistics and his drawling messages of "sacrifice" and "malaise," while Walter Mondale whined that the one thing he could promise us was that he would increase our taxes, Ronald Reagan was looking right at us with a twinkle in his eye, an innocent smile on his face, and a rich confident tone in his voice as he reassured us that it was "Morning in America" once again. While other leaders were defeated and used by the media, Reagan grabbed hold of the electronic beast and tamed it by becoming a better performer than he had ever been at Warner Brothers. Reagan had the magical gift of being able to manipulate the media while remaining immune from its attempts to affect him—everything tossed at him just slid right off the "Teflon President."

Reagan possessed a number of qualities greatly admired by mainstream American culture, but two in particular have been repeatedly cited as reasons for his immense popularity—eternal optimism and eternal youth. Reagan believed that the critics of America—environmentalists, civil rights organizations, advocates for the homeless, Congressional Democrats—were all a bunch of cynical bureaucrats. If critics cried that we were polluting the atmosphere with fossil fuels, for example, President Reagan would just point out that trees—the environmentalists' leafy friends—were the major polluters on the planet; if nuclear scientists and disarmament freaks complained about the folly of "mutually assured destruction" then the President would simply crank up a Star Wars Defense Initiative that would zap invading missiles out of the sky with an accuracy that would turn earth into the biggest videogame in the Universe.

Reagan ground Jimmy Carter into peanut butter in the 1980 election by posing one simple question to the American people, "Are you better off now than you were four years ago?" The answer had to be "No" of course, but the real message was in the implication that something must be terribly wrong if this was true—things are simply supposed to get better and better in America. Meanwhile, Reagan was not only ebullient with easy answers and cheerful messages but also seemed to be getting magically younger as well—an emblem of eternal youth in the world's young nation. Reagan was the oldest man (73) ever elected President, but he looked and acted youthful. "Ronnie" had a head full of hair and a full load of steam—not even the assassination attempt by John Hinckley could slow down our president for more than a few days of well-deserved rest. While doctors were tending to him, Dutch was passing humorous quips to them ("Please tell me you're Republicans," "Send me to L.A. where I can see the air I'm breathing"). Reagan had the humor, optimism, youth, rugged individualism, and common man qualities which have been shared by a long line of citizen-heroes in America.

Reagan also applied his skills to defend his/our way of life. The President "liberated" Grenada, combatted wicked terrorists, and packed the Supreme Court with even more conservative justice. Above all, however, Reagan has been associated with two major attempts to recapture the idyllic past to which he so often referred in his speeches: Reagan played hardball with the "Evil Empire" and (according to this heroic view of the president) caused the godless Communist regime to crumble. Reagan waged a war of "deregulation" on the domestic front which was intended to restore individual freedom by making big government a little smaller. Reagan made the world safe for democracy and the United States safe for cablevision companies to charge whatever they could get. Freedom reigned.

The fact that the era since Reagan left office has been marked by a drastic reassessment of Reagan's status as citizen-hero (e.g. the Iran-Contra Hearings, the *Acting President, The Role of A Lifetime*, etc.) is reflective of the fact that citizen-heroes in general seem to be somewhat of an endangered species. We are a more cynical nation (polls show that most of us have no heroes and most of us distrust nearly everyone in a position of leadership), and the all-seeing eye of the media does tend to emphasize the flaws of those aspiring heroes rather than their positive qualities. It may be, however, that citizen-heroes merely seem to be diminishing in number because of the proliferation of two other kinds of famous popular people—the celebrity (who will be examined in a later section of this introduction) and a second type of hero who (as Public Enemy's rap song says) "don't appear on no stamps."

Live Fast, Die Young, and Leave a Beautiful Corpse: The Rogue-Hero in America

A rogue-hero—real or imaginary—is one whose primary characteristics are an *exceptional vitality* and an assertion of a radical *individual freedom* over the communal democratic values associated with the cultural mainstream. Rogue-heroes do live fast, die young, and (sometimes) leave a beautiful corpse, and in the course of doing so they act out the fundamental American fantasy of absolute personal freedom in a land of infinite frontiers, endless roads and limits set only by what the human body can withstand before collapsing. A rogue-hero believes in Steppenwolf's dictum that you should "fire all of your guns at once and explode into space."

In the story of *Zorba, the Greek* the central character tells of an encounter he once had with a very old man. The old man was dutifully and painstakingly planting an almond tree outside his small village and Zorba was astounded at the man's waste of time. Why, Zorba wanted to know, would you plant a tree you couldn't possibly hope to ever see grown, whose bounty you could never share? The old man struggled to his feet, stomped down the dirt about his tree, and answered, "I live each day as though I will never die." And Zorba replied, "Ah—I live each moment as though I will die the next!" The old man was a citizen-hero in the making, while Zorba is all rogue—do it here, do it now, just do it.

Because their vitality and freedom usually place them in opposition to the mainstream and its forces of authority and conformity, rogue-heroes often represent sub-groups within the culture which feel similarly alienated from the larger community. Rogue-heroes are thus a valuable tool in aiding the student of popular culture in studying significant cultural conflicts: the struggles and mind sets of youth, African-Americans (and other ethnic groups), women, gays, blue collar workers, and other groups are represented by a long line of rogue-heroes who defend the sub-group rather than the mainstream culture.

Rogue-heroes are often (but not always) outlaws—Jesse James, John Dillinger, Thelma and Louise, Smoky and the Bandit—but they are always outrageous. They create a useful category because of the conflicts they embody, but also because they explain the great fascination this type of individual has always held for Americans. Americans admire their citizen-heroes and carve their faces into stone and metal, but Americans *love* their rogues and put them into the more intimate realms of movies, music, and memory with an intensity generally lacking in presentations of citizen-heroes. James Dean, Jimi Hendrix, Dirty Harry, Rosa Parks, Janis Joplin, Sam Spade, Malcolm X, Hell's Angels, Charlie Parker, Jack Kerouac: the names themselves make the heart beat faster.

Citizen-heroes defend the culture and represent us in much the way pure icons do—as emblems of the way we see ourselves and want others to see us. Rogue-heroes are closer to regular icons in that their symbolism is generated by our strong feelings about them. Citizen-heroes make life and culture possible, but rogue-heroes make it exciting and fun.

The various characteristics associated with citizen- and rogue-heroes are summarized in the chart at the beginning of the chapter. In addition to classifying a given individual in this manner, however, there are several other questions we can ask in an attempt to unlock and reveal the myths, beliefs, and values associated with a specific hero.

Who is that Masked Man?: How to Study a Popular Hero

There are at least nine inquiries we can make as we attempt to determine the cultural meaning and significance of a hero. We should preface this list, however, by noting that this process of study is not a rigid, inflexible procedure and we should not demand simple, clearcut answers as a result. A given individual may share qualities of citizens and rogues, (e.g. a rogue-hero like Han Solo ends up defending his culture and embodying skills the mainstream greatly admires), and many heroes serve as "heroic mediators" in that they simultaneously embody conflicting or even contradictory beliefs and values. Heroic mediators enable us to believe both myths/values because they "prove" they are actually compatible. Thus Jed Clampett can be poor and rich at the same time, Spider-Man a freedom-loving outcast and yet good crime-fighting citizen, and Thelma and Louise a pair of gun-toting women on the run and yet simultaneously appreciative of good-looking, good-loving men, as well. We'll find heroic mediators many times in the pages to follow, but one way of discovering them and understanding the beliefs and values they represent is by using the following questions:

1) Are there important *myth-narratives* associated with the hero? Do the stories have a common theme or message?

We've already mentioned George Washington and the cherry tree, of course, but many more modern heroes have similarly revealing myth-narratives associated with their lives and heroic deeds. When Muhammad Ali (then Cassius Clay) returned from the Rome Olympics in 1960, he was refused service in a restaurant in his hometown of Louisville. The myth-narrative says that Ali left the restaurant, walked to the nearest bridge, and dropped his precious Gold Medal (which he had not removed from around his neck since it had been placed there by the Rome officials) into the river's depths. The story tells us that Muhammad Ali—rogue-hero and black activist war protestor—was inside Cassius Clay waiting to be born. Disposing of his medal told the white world that African-Americans could not be appeased by an occasional pat on the head—meals were more important than medals, equality a greater fight than any boxing match.

2) What is the *cultural context* of the hero's life and heroic deeds? How does the hero represent his/her era?

Here we are asking how a hero seems to embody the specific cultural zeitgeist of the hero's lifetime. Heroes help to shape their times, of course, but the times also help produce the heroes that are needed. Thus Ronald Reagan's deregulation of business made him the perfect hero for the greedy decade of the 1980s, Charles Lindbergh's lone flight made him the man who embodied the 1920's need for individual feats of daring in a technological age, and Muhammad Ali's brash braggadocio was the perfect 1960s symbol of an African-American underclass developing the spirit of Black Pride.

3) Are there *notable quotations* by or about the hero? What do these suggest about the hero's significance and/or meaning?

Muhammad Ali is often quoted as saying "No Viet Cong ever called me nigger" and "I ain't got no quarrel with no Viet Congs," and both reflect his status as a rogue-hero defying the forces of mainstream America and asserting his individual right to choose his enemies and to define them as those who oppose his race, not his country.

4) What *group* idolizes the hero? Does the group represent some specific cultural belief or value which they then find embodied in or defended by the heroic individual?

Muhammad Ali was a hero of two of the most significant cultural sub-groups of the 1960s and 1970s in America—youth and African-Americans. When Ali refused induction into the Armed Forces on the grounds of his Black Muslim religious convictions, he simultaneously expressed the African-American desire to assert individual pride and power, and he captured the spirit of youthful rebellion in an age of war protests and draft card burnings as well.

5) What images of the hero are especially common? How is the hero represented visually?

When it was finally decided that Elvis Presley deserved his own postage stamp, a new controversy immediately erupted over which image of the King should be reproduced—the young "Jailhouse Rock" Elvis or the older "In the Ghetto" King. The battle appeared to be about pure cosmetics but it actually reflected a very significant issue in the realm of popular heroes: the recognition that images (as icons) carry important messages means that the way we visualize our heroes must embody the beliefs and values we associate with them. In this instance, Elvis was such a powerful and meaningful heroic force for three decades of American life that he came to embody traits associated with both rogue-heroes and citizen-heroes—he was a hard-rockin', immensely gifted, vital performer who outraged Ed Sullivan and mainstream America in the 1950s, but then went on to serve in the Army, become a Hollywood superstar, and live in a mansion built from his own hard work and ambition. Which one was he, then? A rocking rogue or consumer citizen or, perhaps, transcendent over both? The image finally selected tells us how the culture of the 1990s "views" him both literally and figuratively.

6) Are there important icons associated with the hero? What are they and what meanings (beliefs and values) do they embody?

The Lone Ranger has a silver gun which shot silver bullets—emblematic of both his special skill (as an accurate, magical marksman) and of the fact that he recognized the immense value of human life—those bullets were to be used wisely and economically. The Lone Ranger fired skillfully to disarm—not kill indiscriminately. His gun and bullets help tell us that.

7) How is the hero "*better than us*" and yet "*one of us*"? What are the aspects of his/her life and character which represent his/her modesty, everyday concerns and activities, and commonplace origins?

American heroes are idolized and respected—but not worshipped. What ties the hero to the community/sub-culture and makes the ideal she/he embodies a reachable one?

8) Are there specific villains associated with the hero? Does the hero have an enemy who frequently challenges him/her?

The values and beliefs embodied by a representative, repeated villain are often antithetical to those embodied by the hero and thus give us an accurate key to determine our hero's meaning as well. Certainly England embodied many of the aristocratic values which George Washington challenged with his belief in representative democracy; Lex Luthor demonstrates how power can be turned to selfish ends rather than the public service evinced by our hero Superman; and Joe Frazier battled Muhammad Ali three times in the ring and for an entire decade outside the arena as he continued to represent a more mainstream view of the black role in America. He called Ali "Clay," emphasized his own hard work and closed-mouth dedication to the profession, and was the favorite of many white fans and conservative blacks.

9) Does the hero still have the same meaning for us today as she/he did for the people of his/her own era?

Myths, beliefs, and values evolve over time and they thus provide an ever-changing lens through which we view and interpret our heroes. We've already seen that Elvis passed from rogue to citizen as he changed but often the same movement occurs because the culture moves as well.

Muhammad Ali began as a rogue-hero representing a vital individual freedom pitted against a monolithic white middle class establishment Stripped of his title and cast into exile, he nonetheless returned to win the heavyweight crown two more times. But the period of enforced inactivity had cost him dearly—his skills had diminished so much that he had to absorb a horrendous amount of punishment during his second career—punishment which certainly contributed to the debilitating Parkinson's Syndrome afflicting him today.

With the cultural consensus that the Vietnam War and racism are both now best regarded as unfortunate errors or sins, however, Ali has been transformed from the rebellious rogue to the respected citizen. More importantly, however, Ali's savior-like reenactment of rise-exile-return has been reimagined as a sacrifice of almost Biblical proportions. Muhammad Ali—the brash, energetic, quicksilver mind, body, and heart—has been replaced by the whispering ghost of a hero who symbolically "died for our sins." Our pursuit of an unjust war, our maintenance of an unequal, racist society stripped him of his title and voice, Muhammad Ali's biggest fight was outside the ring—and he won it, he paid the price, and we honor him for it with network television specials and endless awards. Ali is a special hero because he made us worthy enough to be proud of him.

The Meaning of Our Stars is in Ourselves: The Significance of Celebrities in America

Each year teenagers across the United States are asked to name the person in the public eye whom they most admire. The results are published in the World Almanac as "The Heroes of Young America." The winner for each of the twelve years we think of as the "1980s" is listed below:

The Heroes of Young America 1980-1991

Burt Reynolds (1980)	Bill Cosby (1986)
Burt Reynolds (1981)	Tom Cruise (1987)
Alan Alda (1982)	Eddie Murphy (1988)
Sylvester Stallone (1983)	Michael Jordan (1989)
Michael Jackson (1984)	Paula Abdul (1990)
Eddie Murphy (1985)	H. Norman Schwarzkopf (1991)

The list is interesting in many ways (the oddly disproportionate number of African-Americans in a poll of white teenagers, the presence of only a single woman) but for our purposes here its outstanding characteristic is that no one person mentioned is a true "hero" at all. Only General Schwarzkopf can lay claim to any significant accomplishment (crushing an outmanned, outgunned, browbeaten Iraqi military) and even the General has pretty much dropped from view since the parades have stopped. Even if we consider Schwarzkopf a "hero," we are still left with a list of eleven people who are exceedingly well known, have obviously served as important role models for young Americans, and yet have not accomplished the great deeds or evinced the truly special qualities needed for heroic status. We are left, in other words, with a list of celebrities. Celebrities are real people who are made and kept famous by the news media, who through the media perpetuate a created image of themselves and who principally embody momentary—but often intense—cultural preoccupations. If we return to the graph of beliefs we examined in Chapter 2, then we can see that celebrities fall at a point which marks beliefs which are *usually* unstable and (relatively) insignificant.

Celebrities such as Cher and Michael Jackson reflect our contemporary concern with plastic surgery and diet as means of maintaining eternal youth, and Don Henley and his movement to save Walden Pond from real estate moguls reflects our environmental consciousness of the moment. But Cher and Michael Jackson also embody the myth of material success and the myth of individual freedom, and Don Henley's quest also reflects the myth of rural simplicity, all highly significant aspects of our cultural mindset.

We still must be careful, therefore, not to underestimate the meaning and significance of this very special group of popular people. While celebrities are famous primarily and simply for being famous, they may still embody very important myths, beliefs, and values for the time they are with us. The chart above, therefore, represents the way that celebrities are *usually* treated (often deservedly so), but the student of popular culture must recognize that the transitory nature of a specific celebrity does not mean that the celebrity represents only minor beliefs and values or that the more important myths and beliefs associated with the famous person vanishes when the celebrity does. What usually happens is that the deeper associative values simply find themselves being expressed by a new celebrity whose outward appearance is different (and therefore embodies new cultural concerns of the moment) but has essentially the same mythic contents. Celebrities consist of interchangeable parts—mass produced embodiments of transitory tastes and long-standing myths and beliefs.

This means that we can classify celebrities in much the same way that we categorize heroes, placing those who represent mainstream, community values in the category of "citizen-celebrities" and those who embody the beliefs associated with individual freedom and cultural sub-groups under the heading of "rogue-celebrities." The differences between the two types of celebrities are summarized in the chart which concludes this introduction to "famous people," but two points require elaboration here:

1) Citizen-celebrities are notable primarily for the way they make the mainstream "feel good" about itself by reassuring the audience that traditional beliefs and values are still around, and that there is a comforting continuity in the midst of eternal change. Whether it is Jimmy Stewart drawling out one of his old college cheers on *The Tonight Show* or Bill Cosby nursing a cigar and reminding us that fatherhood, middle-age and nostalgia are the bittersweet centers of life, the citizen-celebrity tells us everything is all right now and the only reason to worry is if your television shorts out and you have to find this kind of reassurance in your own life.

Rogue-celebrities, on the other hand, are notable for the way they make *cultural sub-groups* "feel good" about themselves. Rogue-heroes serve as role models (in dress, speech, behavior, etc.) for people who are at odds with mainstream culture, and they do so with an exceptional vitality and energy. Rogue-celebrities do not rebel against traditional, community values with anything like the intensity expressed by their rogue-heroic counterparts. Rogue-heroes are interested primarily in their mission of individual freedom—they seek often to change society—but rogue-celebrities are concerned mainly with staying famous. Their rebellion is a means to this end, not the larger social one of justice or change in social policy/structure. The difference is between Malcolm X (rogue-hero) and Eddie Murphy (rogue-celebrity), Gloria Steinem (r-h) and Madonna (r-c), Ralph Nader (r-h) and Kevin Costner (r-c) between putting your life on the line and merely signing on the dotted line.

2) All celebrities are chimeras—half real, half imaginary. A celebrity is a real person, of course, but in the public eye the celebrity is transformed into a created image which is every bit as imaginary—removed from the celebrity's private life and identity—as any movie or television role. The celebrity as "real" person is interesting to us only as aspects of his or her life reflect or enhance the celebrity's image—i.e. the way he/

she is defined in the media. It is this image which is the embodiment of myths, beliefs, and values—the image which provides a highly visible role model for fans and audience. Guests on *The Tonight Show* prepare their answers to the host's questions in advance, highly paid publicists attend magazine interviews of their celebrity clients to help control the tone and substance of the meeting, and celebrities consider only those movie and television roles which they feel are "right" for them—those which are consistent with the carefully crafted and maintained image.

This is especially significant for students of popular culture because it focuses our attention upon the aspect of the celebrity most likely to explain the celebrity's meaning (instead of allowing us to get lost in trying to uncover the "real" Cher, for example, which is a matter for a biographer or psychologist not a cultural analyst), and it enables us to examine the roles played by actor-celebrities as a key to defining this image. There is very often a relationship between image and role so that celebrities "play" the same image both on screen and on the *Tonight Show* couch, and the characteristics and meanings associated with the roles thus become associated with the celebrity as well. Clint Eastwood is not Dirty Harry, of course, but his long-standing association with the character means that we can analyze Harry (a rogue-hero) as a clue to defining the meaning of Clint Eastwood (with his image as a rogue-celebrity). Who is it, after all, that is speaking to us in those familiar stern, breathy tones to remind us not to damage our National Parks—Clint Eastwood or Dirty Harry?

This close relationship between image and role—between the meaning of the celebrity and the meaning of the parts he/she plays—may account for the classification of the twelve celebrities on the annual polls as "Heroes," and mean that while the labeling is mistaken, it is not completely false. Teenagers (like the rest of us) simply confuse the celebrity with the roles they play and thus confuse image with reality. While we cannot be certain, it is probable that most respondents were at least partially honoring Dr. Huxtable by way of praising Bill Cosby, Axel Foley through Eddie Murphy, *Top Gun* flying ace Tom Cruise, Hawkeye Pierce's Alan Alda, Smokey's Burt Reynolds, etc. And we can thus legitimately conclude that the myths, beliefs, and values associated with these characters—heroes each and every one—are vital elements in defining the cultural significance of the celebrities who feed on their image-making power.

Another reason for this supposed confusion is the possibility that 1980s teens weren't confused at all. According to a 1991 survey of American opinions, *The Day America Told the Truth*, 70 percent of all Americans believe this country no longer has any real, living heroes. We live in an era in which imaginary heroes have seemingly replaced genuine heroes and in which celebrities, through their domination of the media, have invaded our present culture and crowded out the heroes. Celebrities dominate the realm of famous people.

Enquiring Minds Want to Know:
Why We Are Presently So Obsessed with Celebrities

In the 1990s, and for the last twenty years, celebrities have dominated the mass media. From the tabloids in the grocery story checkout line, to *People* on the magazine rack, to the endless talk shows on television, to the gossip column in the newspapers, celebrity images flood our collective consciousness dozens of times a day. Reasonable people not familiar with contemporary American life must surely wonder why. Why should we be so enthralled with the personal lives of people whose main quality is being well known? What difference does it make if Prince Charles and Princess Di are unhappy? Celebrities, for all practical purposes, cease to exist when their faces stop appearing on the covers of magazines. They permanently effect nothing. They come, they go. It seems crazy that millions of us tune in to *Entertainment Tonight* regularly just to see photos of these trivial people. Yet, we do tune in and tomorrow we'll buy *People*. The following are six reasons why, despite all common sense, celebrities are so dominant in our own times:

1) Celebrities fill the gap left by our skepticism about real heroes. As mentioned earlier, a majority of us apparently believe there are no longer any real heroes. At the same time, society needs images of people to provide visible models that we can imitate or symbolic examples of what to avoid. Celebrities have rushed in to fill the need for these models left by our disillusionment with real heroes. Malcom X, a genuine rogue-hero is thus replaced in the 1990s by Ice-T, a rogue-celebrity.

2) Celebrities reflect a contemporary cultural environment dominated by the mass media. Since we live in a nation in which our perceptions of reality are derived mainly from mass-produced images, there is a kind of logic to our interest in people whose creation and life-blood proceeds from television, movies and magazines. *Stars*, as mass-produced images, simply reflect our current, mass-mediated reality.

3) Celebrities provide our society with a cultural glue. We come from diverse backgrounds in this nation made up almost entirely of recent immigrants. Stars give us all something in common. We all know about them and can communicate our interest in them as the events in their lives pervade our shared pool of knowledge. We become unified by our mutual knowledge of the star's image.

4) Celebrities gain our admiration by reflecting our own desire to be popular. Many of us live within huge social structures that seem to make us anonymous. We sit in classrooms with hundreds of other students who dress just like us. Later we may work for a huge corporation where, once again, everybody dresses the same and only our immediate

superior knows what we do. In this kind of environment we naturally cry out to be known, to be noticed. Under these circumstances, celebrities become heroic. They are recognized for the very magnification of their personalities. Stars have achieved the personal recognition we all crave. Teddy Kennedy may be little more than an alcoholic lout in the pages of *The National Enquirer*, but at least we all know his name, and for this he has our begrudging admiration.

5) Celebrities are up-to-date models for quickly changing consumer lifestyles. Check out Michael Jordan for the right shoes. See photos of Cher for the latest in tattoos. Switch on the MTV stars for the hippest dance craze. We want to be recognized as individuals, but we also want to fit in, to be accepted. When the stars appear in the media, they wear the latest fashions and display the newest fads. They become immediate behavior models. We look to them for guidance through all the consumer choices available to us in the world of mass production. Stars are our surest role models as we express our belief in the myth of material consumption.

6) Celebrities verify that the meaning of life is to be found in our simpler world of home, family, work, etc. Even though stars tend to be models of how to act and what to buy, the intense scrutiny of their personal lives by the media almost always shows them to be unhappy, confused and beset by tragedy. They are, in other words, despite the glamor and fame, worse off than us. The media would have us believe that Eddie Murphy is smothered by his entourage, that every European princess is doomed to a life without real love, and that Liz Taylor is invariably at death's door. Compared to celebrities, our personal lives are trouble-free. Our lives may be relatively unimportant, but compared to the miserable existences of the stars, they are more stable and predictable. Celebrities allow us to validate our own lives by providing us with dramatically unpleasant alternatives.

Given the above six reasons for celebrity veneration, perhaps our obsession with the famous isn't so excessive after all. In the tangled world of popular culture, celebrities provide us with signposts for personal and social identity. Heroes also do this in a more admirable manner. But in an era of diminishing belief in heroes, celebrities fulfill our need for images of people who can help us define who we are and how we are supposed to behave.

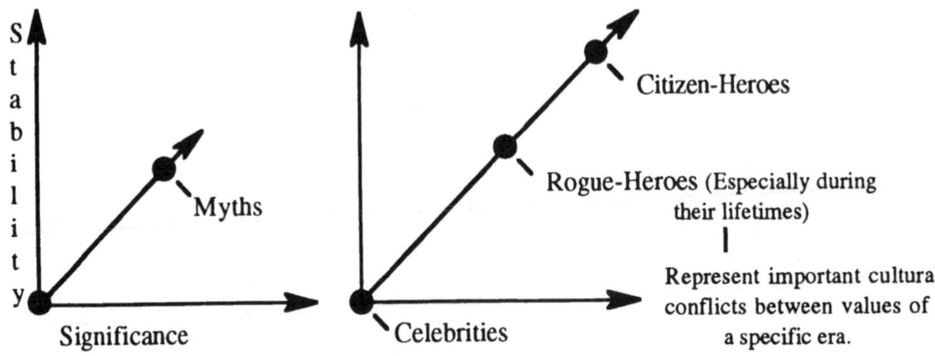

This graph represents the way in which celebrities, rogue-heroes and citizen-heroes have traditionally been viewed, and the significance each usually carries. Keep in mind that this is a very generalized representation meant only as a guide. It does not account for all possible characteristics of the types presented in the diagram, nor does it include every type of popular personality.

What Makes Superman So Darned American?

Gary Engle

...Science-Fiction Writer Harlan Ellison has estimated that there are only five fictional creations known in practically every part of the earth: Tarzan, Sherlock Holmes, Mickey Mouse, Robin Hood, and Superman.

Time Magazine *14 March 1988: 68*

One of the principal delights encountered in the study of popular culture takes place when an application of "The Popular Culture Formula" leads us to examine an artifact for important meaning and significance which might otherwise have been taken at face value. The Formula guides the student of popular culture to question and ponder many of the very things which unenlightened critics dismiss as "mindless entertainment" or "low art." We *know that if millions of people are drawn to a popular television program or moved to leave their homes to pay for the right to dream together in a darkened movie theater offering the latest box-office hit, then there must be messages in these seductive artifacts which can tell us much more about our culture than simply that the world would be a trifle more boring and mundane in their absence. Discovering the deeper meanings in a bit of "chewing gum for the masses" is much like being a great detective in a classical whodunit—we can see clues that others overlook, and can thus shed light on mysteries that leave others to worry and fret only about who the next victim will be.*

*Comic books are perfect examples of the type of popular artifact which is so often only condemned and rarely analyzed. Yet comic books attract an avid audience of millions every month (the circulation of one leading comic book alone—*The Uncanny X-Men*—is nearly 500,000 each month) and have been continuously popular for over 50 years. And who*

Reprinted with permission from *Superman at Fifty: The Persistence of a Legend,* Dennis Dooley and Gary Engle, eds. Cleveland, OH: Octavia Press, 1987.

can argue with the popular significance of a single hero who is (in the words of Time *magazine) "an institution [with] a half-century of crime-busting adventures in* Action Comics *and* Superman Comics *(as well as in some 250 newspapers), 13 years of radio shows, three novels, 17 animated cartoons, two movie serials of 15 installments each, a TV series of 104 episodes, a second animated-cartoon series of 69 parts, a Broadway musical and five feature films...not to mention...a plunder of spin-offs and by-products: T-shirts, rings, bedsheets." Superman is a hero—a super-hero—whose red, white and blue presence is woven into the fabric of our daily lives and nighttime fantasies; he doesn't merely rescue us from the latest (imaginary) alien threat but also gives* us *a type of x-ray vision which reveals our (very real) myths, beliefs and values.*

Robert Reich would not be surprised at any of this. He could easily argue, for example, that the story of Superman embodies aspects of all four of the "morality tales" he claims are at the heart of the American mindset. As Gary Engle demonstrates (from a slightly different perspective) in the following essay, Superman is a triumphant individual who arrives in a New World and strives to succeed and who contributes by his every action to the vision of a benevolent community which unites (behind its hero, of course) to beat back The Mob at the Gates and eliminate The Rot at the Top. Another author has labeled Superman "a flag with a human face," and the deft manner in which our hero weaves together the central tenets of Reich's Morality Tales would seem to support his status as the red, white and blue embodiment of how America chooses to present itself to the world.

Engle's essay illustrates another vital aspect of American heroes which helps them resonate with long-lasting significance. American heroes often embody contradictory traits or qualities—both sets of which are important to Americans—which enable us to believe wholeheartedly in what might otherwise be contradictory ideas and beliefs. From Engle's perspective the unification of Clark Kent and Superman in the same heroic being enables audiences to resolve the conflict in their own lives and history between the need to assimilate and conform (expressed in the conservative repression of goodguy Clark) and the opposing need to maintain and flaunt an individual, immigrant identity (expressed in the highflying, open-faced heroism of superguy Superman). While Engle's article was written before the current debate over the values of the melting pot vs. those of a multicultural, "politically correct" ideal, his insights into Superman's meaning and appeal suggest that Superman is even more relevant in the present climate, in which the opposing tendencies he embodies are engaged in a hot and vocal war. The scholars who search fruitlessly for answers in the "classics" might actually find a resolution to their dilemma if they simply were to look toward the path of one of America's most popular super heroes.

Superman, I've always thought, is an angel. I base this assumption on the fact that all the fathers of the church up until Aquinas thought that angels had bodies, if only "spiritual or ethereal bodies" (Platonic philosophy permitted only God to be Pure Spirit). It has always seemed reasonable to me that on other planets the evolutionary process is further along and has therefore come much closer to developing angels than we have. Probably the angel stories found in all of the world's religions are traces of the work in our world of Superman and his relatives. Who is to say I'm wrong?

Andrew M. Greeley, best-selling author and social commentator

When I was young I spent a lot of time arguing with myself about who would win in a fight between John Wayne and Superman. On days when I wore my cowboy hat and cap guns, I knew the Duke would win because of his pronounced superiority in the all-important matter of swagger. There were days, though, when a frayed army blanket tied cape-fashion around my neck signalled a young man's need to believe there could be no end to the potency of his being. Then the Man of Steel was the odds-on favorite to knock the Duke for a cosmic loop. My greatest childhood problem was that the question could never be resolved because no such battle could ever take place. I mean, how would a fight start between the only two Americans who never started anything, who always fought only to defend their rights and the American way?

Now that I'm older and able to look with reason on the mysteries of childhood, I've finally resolved the dilemma. John Wayne was the best older brother any kid could ever hope to have, but he was no Superman.

Superman is *the* great American hero. We are a nation rich with legendary figures. But among the Davy Crocketts and Paul Bunyans and Mike Finks and Pecos Bills and all the rest who speak for various regional identities in the pantheon of American folklore, only Superman achieves truly mythic stature, interweaving a pattern of beliefs, literary conventions and cultural traditions of the American people more powerfully and more accessibly than any other cultural symbol of the 20th century, perhaps of any period in our history.

The core of the American myth in *Superman* consists of a few basic facts that remain unchanged throughout the infinitely varied ways in which the myth is told—facts with which everyone is familiar, however marginal their knowledge of the story. Superman is an orphan rocketed to Earth when his native planet Krypton explodes; he lands near Smallville and is adopted by Jonathon and Martha Kent, who inculcate in him their American middle-class ethic; as an adult he migrates to Metropolis where he defends America—no, the world! no, the Universe!—from all evil and harm while playing a romantic game in which, as Clark Kent, he hopelessly pursues Lois Lane, who hopelessly pursues Superman, who remains aloof until such time as Lois proves worthy of him by falling in love with his feigned identity as a weakling. That's it. Every narrative thread in the mythology, each one of the thousands of plots in the 50-year stream of comics and films and TV shows, all the tales involving the demigods of the Superman pantheon—Superboy, Supergirl, even Krypto the superdog—every single one reinforces by never contradicting this basic set of facts. That's the myth, and that's where one looks to understand America.

It is impossible to imagine Superman being as popular as he is and speaking as deeply to the American character were he not an immigrant and an orphan. Immigration, of course, is the overwhelming fact in American history. Except for the Indians, all Americans have an immediate sense of their origins elsewhere. No nation on Earth has so deeply embedded in its social consciousness the imagery of passage from one social identity to another: the Mayflower of the New England separatists, the slave ships from Africa and the subsequent underground railroads toward freedom in the North, the sailing ships and steamers running shuttles across two oceans in the 19th century, the freedom airlifts in the 20th. Somehow the picture just isn't complete without Superman's rocketship.

Like the peoples of the nation whose values he defends, Superman is an alien, but not just any alien. He's the consummate and totally uncompromised alien, an immigrant whose visible difference from the norm is underscored by his decision to wear a costume of bold primary colors so tight as to be his very skin. Moreover, Superman the alien is real. He stands out among the host of comic book characters (Batman is a good example) for whom the superhero role is like a mask assumed when needed, a costume worn over their real identities as normal Americans. Superman's powers—strength, mobility, X-ray vision and the like—are the comic-book equivalents of ethnic characteristics, and they protect and preserve the vitality of the foster community in which he lives in the same way that immigrant ethnicity has sustained American culture linguistically, artistically, economically, politically and spiritually. The myth of *Superman* asserts with total confidence and a childlike innocence the value of the immigrant in American culture.

From this nation's beginnings Americans have looked for ways of coming to terms with the immigrant experience. This is why, for example, so much of American literature and popular culture deals with the theme of dislocation, generally focused in characters devoted or doomed to constant physical movement. Daniel Boone became an American legend in part as a result of apocryphal stories that he moved every time his neighbors got close enough for him to see the smoke of their cabin fires. James Fenimore Cooper's Natty Bumppo spent the five long novels of the Leatherstocking saga drifting ever westward, like the pioneers who

The great American hero. Also an angel, a secular Messiah and the ideal American immigrant.

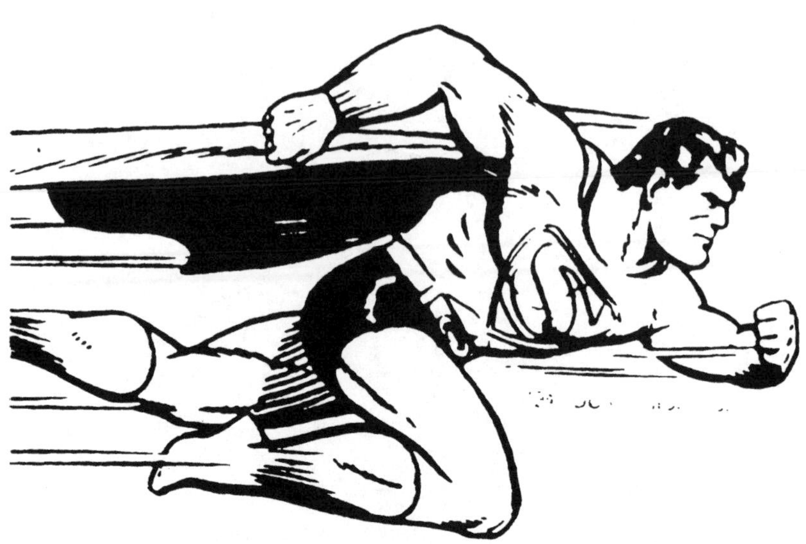

The Man of Steel in flight. Mobility as an "integral part of America's dreamwork."

were his spiritual offspring, from the Mohawk valley of upstate New York to the Great Plains where he died. Huck Finn sailed through the moral heart of America on a raft. Melville's Ishmael, Wister's Virginian, Shane, Gatsby, the entire Lost Generation, Steinbeck's Okies, Little Orphan Annie, a thousand fiddlefooted cowboy heroes of dime novels and films and television—all in motion, searching for the American dream or stubbornly refusing to give up their innocence by growing old, all symptomatic of a national sense of rootlessness stemming from an identity founded on the experience of immigration.

Individual mobility is an integral part of America's dreamwork. Is it any wonder, then, that our greatest hero can take to the air at will? Superman's ability to fly does more than place him in a tradition of mythic figures going back to the Greek messenger god Hermes or Zetes the flying Argonaut. It makes him an exemplar in the American dream. Take away a young man's wheels and you take away his manhood. Jack Kerouac and Charles Kurault go on the road; William Least Heat Moon looks for himself in a van exploring the veins of America in its system of blue highways; legions of grey-haired retirees turn Air Stream trailers and Winnebagos into proof positive that you can, in the end, take it with you. On a human scale, the American need to keep moving suggests a neurotic aimlessness under the surface of adventure. But take the human restraints off, let Superman fly unencumbered when and wherever he will, and the meaning of mobility in the American consciousness begins to reveal itself. Superman's incredible speed allows him to be as close to everywhere at once as it is physically possible to be. Displacement is, therefore, impossible. His sense of self is not dispersed by his life's migration but rather enhanced by all the universe that he is able to occupy. What American, whether an immigrant in spirit or in fact, could resist the appeal of one with such an ironclad immunity to the anxiety of dislocation?

In America, physical dislocation serves as a symbol of social and psychological movement. When our immigrant ancestors arrived on America's shores they hit the ground running, some to homestead on the Great Plains, others to claw their way up the socio-economic ladder in coastal ghettos. Upward mobility, westward migration, Sunbelt relocation—the wisdom in America is that people don't, can't, mustn't end up where they begin. This belief has the moral force of religious doctrine. Thus the American identity is ordered around the psychological experience of forsaking or losing the past for the opportunity of reinventing oneself in the future. This makes the orphan a potent symbol of the American character. Orphans aren't merely free to reinvent themselves. They are obliged to do so.

When Superman reinvents himself, he becomes the bumbling Clark Kent, a figure as immobile as Superman is mobile, as weak as his alter ego is strong. Over the years commentators have been fond of stressing how Clark Kent provides an illusory image of wimpiness onto which children can project their insecurities about their own potential (and, hopefully, equally illusory) weaknesses. But I think the role of Clark Kent is far more complex than that.

During my childhood, Kent contributed nothing to my love for the Man of Steel. If left to contemplate him for too long, I found myself changing from cape back into cowboy hat and guns. John Wayne, at least, was no sissy that I could ever see. Of course, in all the Westerns that the Duke came to stand for in my mind, there were elements that left me as confused as the paradox between Kent and Superman. For example, I could never seem to figure out why cowboys so often fell in love when there were obviously better options: horses to ride, guns to shoot, outlaws to chase and savages to kill. Even on the days when I became John Wayne, I could fall victim to a never-articulated anxiety about the potential for poor judgment in my cowboy heroes. Then, I generally drifted back into a worship of Superman. With him, at least, the mysterious communion of opposites was honest and on the surface of things.

What disturbed me as a child is what I now think makes the myth of *Superman* so appealing to an immigrant sensibility. The shape-shifting between Clark Kent and Superman is the means by which this mid-20th-century, urban story—like the pastoral 19-century Western before it—addresses in dramatic terms the theme of cultural assimilation.

At its most basic level, the Western was an imaginative record of the American experience of westward migration and settlement. By bringing the forces of civilization and savagery together on a mythical frontier, the Western addressed the problem of conflict between apparently mutually exclusive identities and explored options for negotiating between them. In terms that a boy could comprehend, the myth explored the dilemma of assimilation—marry the school marm and start wearing Eastern clothes or saddle up and drift further westward with the boys.

The Western was never a myth of stark moral simplicity. Pioneers fled civilization by migrating west, but their purpose in the wilderness was to rebuild civilization. So civilization was both good and bad, what Americans fled from and journeyed toward. A similar moral ambiguity rested at the heart of the wilderness. It was an Eden in which innocence could be achieved through spiritual rebirth, but it was also the anarchic force that most directly threatened the civilized values America wanted to impose on the frontier. So the dilemma arose: in negotiating between civilization and the wilderness, between the old order and the new, between the identity the pioneers carried with them from wherever they came and the identity they sought to invent, Americans faced an impossible choice. Either they pushed into the New World wilderness and forsook the ideals that motivated them or they clung to their origins and polluted Eden.

The myth of the Western responded to this dilemma by inventing the idea of the frontier in which civilized ideals embodied in the institutions of family, church, law and education are revitalized by the virtues of savagery: independence, self-reliance, personal honor, sympathy with nature and ethical uses of violence. In effect, the mythical frontier represented an attempt to embody the perfect degree of assimilation in which both the old and the new identities came together, if not in a single self-image, then at least in idealized relationships, like the symbolic marriage of reformed cowboy and displaced school marm that ended Owen Wister's prototypical *The Virginian*, or the mystical masculine bonding between representatives of an ascendant and a vanishing America—Natty Bumppo and Chingachgook, the Lone Ranger and Tonto. On the Western frontier, both the old and new identities equally mattered.

As powerful a myth as the Western was, however, there were certain limits to its ability to speak directly to an increasingly common 20th-century immigrant sensibility. First, it was pastoral. Its imagery of dusty frontier towns and breathtaking mountainous desolation spoke most affectingly to those who conceived of the American dream in terms of the 19th-century immigrant experience of rural settlement. As the 20th century wore on, more immigrants were, like Superman, moving from rural or small-town backgrounds to metropolitan environments. Moreover, the Western was historical, often elegiacally so. Underlying the air of celebration in even the most epic and romantic of Westerns—the films of John Ford, say, in which John Wayne stood tall for all that any good American boy could ever want to be—was an awareness that the frontier was less a place than a state of mind represented in historical terms by a fleeting moment glimpsed imperfectly in the rapid wave of westward migration and settlement. Implicitly, then, whatever balance of past and future identities the frontier could offer was itself tenuous or illusory.

Twentieth-century immigrants, particularly the Eastern European Jews who came to America after 1880 and who settled in the industrial and mercantile centers of the Northeast—cities like Cleveland where Jerry Siegel and Joe Shuster grew up and created Superman—could be entertained by the Western, but they developed a separate literary tradition that addressed the theme of assimilation in terms closer to their personal experience. In this tradition issues were clear cut: Clinging to an Old World identity meant isolation in ghettos, confrontation with a prejudiced mainstream culture, second-class social status and impoverishment. On the other hand, forsaking the past in favor of total absorption into the mainstream, while it could result in socio-economic progress, meant a loss of the religious, linguistic, even culinary traditions that provided a foundation for psychological well-being. Such loss was particularly tragic for the Jews because of the fundamental role played by history in Jewish culture.

Writers who worked in this tradition—Abraham Cahan, Daniel Fuchs, Henry Roth and Delmore Schwarz, among others—generally found little reason to view the experience of assimilation with joy or optimism. Typical of the tradition was Cahan's early novel *Yekl*, on which Joan Micklin Silver's film *Hester Street* was based. A young married couple, Jake and Gitl, clash over his need to be absorbed as quickly as possible into the American mainstream and her obsessive preservation of their Russian-Jewish heritage. In symbolic terms, their confrontation is as simple as their choice of headgear—a derby for him, a babushka for her. That the story ends with their divorce even in the context of their gradual movement toward mutual understanding of one another's point of view, suggests the divisive nature of the pressures at work in the immigrant communities.

Where the pressures were perhaps most keenly felt was in the schools. Educational theory of the period stressed the benefits of rapid assimilation. In the first decades of this century, for example, New York schools flatly rejected bilingual education—a common response to the plight of non-English speaking immigrants even today—and there were conscientious efforts to indoctrinate the children of immigrants with American values, often at the expense of traditions within the ethnic community. What resulted was a generational rift in which children were openly embarrassed by and even contemptuous of their parents' values, setting a pattern in American life in which second-generation immigrants migrate psychologically if not physically from their parents, leaving it up to the third generation and beyond to rediscover their ethnic roots.

Under such circumstances, finding a believable and inspiring balance between the old identity and the new, like that implicit in the myth of the frontier, was next to impossible. The images and characters that did emerge from the immigrant communities were often comic. Seen over and over in the fiction and popular theater of the day was the figure of the *yiddische Yankee*, a jingoistic optimist who spoke heavily accented American slang, talked baseball like an addict without understanding the game and dressed like a Broadway dandy on a budget—in short, one who didn't understand America well enough to distinguish between image and substance and who paid for the mistake by becoming the butt of a style of comedy bordering on pathos. So engrained was this stereotype in popular culture that it echoes today in TV situation comedy.

What was true for Jews was true for other ethnic groups as well. Irish, German, Italian, Slav—each had the image in popular culture of a half-assimilated American. Some were comic, others not. But none confirmed wholeheartedly the American dream. A case in point is George McManus' long-running comic strip *Bringing Up Father*, about an Irish-American bricklayer who wins the Irish sweepstakes. His sudden and fabulous wealth is the realization of the American dream. The energy of the strip, however, arises out of his failure to wear his new identity well. While his wife makes a fool of herself slavishly following fashion and aping the forms of high culture, he longs for the freedom to put aside his ascot and morning coat, go unshaven, put his feet up on the furniture, smoke cigars or sneak out to the old neighborhood for cards with the boys or bar meals of corned beef and cabbage. The clear moral of the strip has been from the beginning that the reward of pursuing the American dream is a longing for what one loses in the process.

Throughout American popular culture between 1880 and the second world war the story was the same. Ox-like Swedish farmers, German brewers, Jewish merchants, corrupt Irish ward healers, Italian gangsters—there was a parade of images that reflected in terms often comic, sometimes tragic, the humiliation, pain and cultural insecurity of people in a state of transition. Even in the comics, a medium intimately connected with immigrant culture, there simply was no image that presented a blending of identities in the assimilation process in a way that stressed pride, self-confidence, integrity and psychological well-being. None, that is, until Superman.

The brilliant stroke in the conception of Superman—the *sina qua non* that makes the whole myth work—is the fact that he has two identities. The myth simply wouldn't work without Clark Kent, mild-mannered newspaper reporter and later, as the myth evolved, bland TV newsman. Adopting the white-bread image of a wimp is first and foremost a moral act for the Man of Steel. He does it to protect his parents from nefarious sorts who might use them to gain an edge over the powerful alien. Moreover, Kent adds to Superman's powers the moral guidance of a Smallville upbringing. It is Jonathan Kent, fans remember, who instructs the alien that his powers must always be used for good. Thus does the myth add a mainstream white Anglo-Saxon Protestant ingredient to the American stew. Clark Kent is the clearest stereotype of a self-effacing, hesitant, doubting, middle-class weakling ever invented. He is the epitome of visible invisibility, someone whose extraordinary ordinariness makes him disappear in a crowd. In a phrase, he is the consummate figure of total cultural assimilation, and significantly, he is not real. Implicit in this is the notion that mainstream cultural norms, however useful, are illusions.

Though a disguise, Kent is necessary for the myth to work. This uniquely American hero has two identities, one based on where he comes from in life's journey, one on where he is going. One is real, one an illusion, and both are necessary for the myth of balance in the assimilation process to be complete. Superman's powers make the hero capable of saving humanity; Kent's total immersion in the American heartland makes him want to do it. The result is an improvement on the Western: an optimistic myth of assimilation but with an urban, technocratic setting.

One must never underestimate the importance to a myth of the most minute elements which do not change over time and by which we recognize the story. Take Superman's cape, for example. When Joe Shuster inked the first Superman stories, in the early 1930s when he was still a student at Cleveland's Glenville High School, Superman was strictly beefcake in tights, looking more like a circus acrobat than the ultimate Man of Steel. By June of 1938 when *Action Comics* no. 1 was issued, the image had been altered to include a cape, ostensibly to make flight easier to render in the pictures. But it wasn't the cape of Victorian melodrama and adventure fiction, the kind worn with a clasp around the neck. In fact, one is hard-pressed to find any precedent in popular culture for the kind of cape Superman wears. His emerges in a seamless line from either side of the front yoke of his tunic. It is a veritable growth from behind his pectorals and hangs, when he stands at ease, in a line that doesn't so much drape his shoulders as stand apart from them and echo their curve, like an angel's wings.

In light of this graphic detail, it seems hardly coincidental that Superman's real, Kryptonic name is Kal-El, an apparent neologism by George Lowther, the author who novelized the comic strip in 1942. In Hebrew, *el* can be both root and affix. As a root, it is the masculine singular word for God. Angels in Hebrew mythology are called *benei Elohim* (literally, sons of the Gods), or *Elyonim* (higher beings). As an affix, *el* is most often translated as "of God," as in the plenitude of Old Testament given names: Ishma-el, Dani-el, Ezeki-el, Samu-el, etc. It is also a common form for named angels in most Semitic mythologies: Israf-el, Aza-el, Uri-el, Yo-el, Rapha-el, Gabri-el and—the one perhaps most like Superman—Micha-el, the warrior angel and Satan's principal adversary.

The morpheme *Kal* bears a linguistic relation to two Hebrew roots. The first, *kal*, means "with lightness" or "swiftness" (faster than a speeding bullet in Hebrew?). It also bears a connection to the root *hal*, where *h* is the guttural *ch* of *chutzpah*. *Hal* translates roughly as "everything" or "all." *Kal-el*, then, can be read as "all that is God," or perhaps more in the spirit of the myth of *Superman*, "all that God is." And while we're at it, *Kent* is a form of the Hebrew *kana*. In its *k-n-t* form, the word appears in the Bible, meaning "I have found a son."

I'm suggesting that *Superman* raises the American immigrant experience to the level of religious myth. And why not? He's not just some immigrant from across the waters like all our ancestors, but a real alien, an extraterrestrial, a visitor from heaven if you will, which fact lends an element of the supernatural to the myth. America has no national religious icons nor any pilgrimage shrines. The idea of a patron saint is ludicrous in a nation whose Founding Fathers wrote into the founding documents the fundamental if not eternal separation of church and state. America, though, is pretty much as religious as other industrialized countries. It's just that our tradition of religious diversity precludes the nation's religious character from being embodied in objects or persons recognizably religious, for such are immediately identified by their attachment to specific sectarian traditions and thus contradict the eclecticism of the American religious spirit.

In America, cultural icons that manage to tap the national religious spirit are of necessity secular on the surface and sufficiently generalized to incorporate the diversity of American religious traditions. Superman doesn't have to be seen as an angel to be appreciated, but in the absence of a tradition of national religious iconography, he can serve as a safe, nonsectarian focus for essentially religious sentiments, particularly among the young.

In the last analysis, Superman is like nothing so much as an American boy's fantasy of a messiah. He is the male, heroic match for the Statue of Liberty, come like an immigrant from heaven to deliver humankind by sacrificing himself in the service of others. He protects the weak and defends truth and justice and all other moral virtues inherent in the Judeo-Christian tradition, remaining ever vigilant and ever chaste. What purer or stronger vision could there possibly be for a child? Now that I put my mind to it, I see that John Wayne never had a chance.

Henry Ford:
Symbol of an Age

Roderick Nash

For most of us living in the 1990s, the name Henry Ford means little more than the man who started one of the "Big Three" car companies in Detroit. He is not a hero for us because we know little about his life and because his image does not call forth in our minds any notable beliefs or values. He is just a name out of American history. This present indifference to Henry Ford was not always the case, however. In the following essay Roderick Nash demonstrates how three quarters of a century ago the still active Ford was such a commanding presence in American culture that for the decade of the 1920s, perhaps more than any other single individual, Ford was a "symbol of an age."

For millions of people in the 1920s, Ford represented all the admirable characteristics of the citizen-hero. He rose to great heights and was acquainted with presidents and kings. Yet he came from humble, agrarian origins and had become successful in the best Horatio Alger tradition of American self-reliance. He had notable skills. In the 1920s, a time when President Coolidge announced, "The business of America is business," Ford had perfected the assembly-line method of production and had built a great industrial company.

Ford also represented traditional cultural virtues. While being practical, efficient and forward-looking, he also espoused old-fashioned, rural perspectives. Finally, Ford was perceived as a defender of American values. In his writings he declared that "History is more or less the bunk," thereby becoming a proponent of American progress. At the same time, however, Ford spent millions on publications advocating traditional agrarian values and on collecting artifacts from the past and showing them to the public in his Henry Ford Museum and Greenfield Village.

Reprinted by permission of the author from *The Nervous Generation: American Thought 1917-1930*. Chicago: Ivan R. Dee, 1990.

As you read Nash's essay, note how he uses most of the nine ways of studying a popular hero. Nash uses some methods, such as notable quotations, more than others, of course, but virtually all the methods are employed. His article can serve, therefore, as not only to show an example of a citizen-hero, but as a model of how the student of popular culture can study one.

Few names were better known to Americans from 1917 to 1930 than that of Henry Ford. Whether one read his publications,[1] or followed his headline-making public life, or merely drove the car his company manufactured, Ford was inescapable in the twenties. Indeed it is possible to think of these years as the automobile age and Henry Ford as its czar. The flivver, along with the flask and the flapper, seemed to represent the 1920s in the minds of its people as well as its historians.

Cars symbolized change. They upset familiar patterns of living, working, recreating, even thinking. Much of the roar of the twenties came from the internal combustion engine. While providing portable bedrooms in which to enjoy the decade's alleged sexual freedom, cars also assisted gangsters and bootleggers in getting away. The image of two of them in every garage helped elect a President in 1928. The rise of widespread use of the automobile, in a word, contributed significantly to setting the twenties apart. And Henry Ford, calling machinery the "new Messiah" (as he did in 1929), seemed to herald the new era.

Beneath the surface, however, such generalizations ring hollow. Neither Ford nor the twenties merited the cliches with which each has been so frequently discussed. In the case of the man, both old and new mingled in his mind. On the one hand Ford was a builder and bulwark of the modern, mechanized nation; on the other he devoted a remarkable amount of effort and expense to sustaining old-fashioned America. In fact, the nostalgic, backward-looking Henry Ford repeatedly deplored the very conditions that Ford the revolutionary industrialist did so much to bring about. This ambivalence did not signify a lack of values so much as a superfluity. His faith was strong if bigoted and contradictory. His prescriptions for America were clear if simple-minded. He seemed to the masses to demonstrate that there could be change without disruption, and in so doing he eased the twenties' tensions. The "average citizen," editorialized the *New Republic* in 1923, "sees Ford as a sort of enlarged crayon portrait of himself; the man able to fulfill his own suppressed desires, who has achieved enormous riches, fame and power without departing from the pioneer-and-homespun tradition." In this nervous clinging to old values even while undermining them Ford was indeed a "crayon portrait" of his age.

But was Ford typical of the twenties? Can he really be said to symbolize the age? He was, after all, in his middle fifties when the decade began. However, a great many Americans were also middle-aged in the 1920s, far more in fact than the twenty-year old collegians who have hitherto characterized these years. And at one point even a group of college students ranked Ford as the third greatest figure of all time, behind Napoleon and Jesus Christ.

The Dearborn, Michigan, into which Henry Ford was born in 1863 was a small farming community only a generation removed from the frontier. Both sides of the Ford family had agrarian backgrounds, and the children grew up on the farm. Henry's formal education began and ended in the Scotch Settlement School which he attended for eight years. The staple of his academic diet was the McGuffey reader with its moral-coated language lessons. When Ford left school to become an apprentice mechanic in Detroit, he also left the farm. But the farm never left Henry. Agrarian ideas and values shaped his thought even as he became an industrial king.

The 1880s for Ford were a time of aimlessness, his only real interest being in tinkering with watches and other engines. In 1892 he joined the Edison Company in Detroit as an engineer. During his spare time he struggled with the problem of building a gasoline engine compact enough to power a moving vehicle. By 1896 Ford had his automobile. Soon he had it doing ninety miles per hour! It required seven years more, however, for him to secure the necessary financial and administrative backing to launch the Ford Motor Company. The rest was pure Horatio Alger.

The first Model T appeared in 1908, and it soon made good Ford's boast that he could build a car for the masses. Six thousand sold the first year. Six years later, after the introduction of assembly line production, the figure was 248,000. From May to December 1920 almost 700,000 Model Ts rolled out of the Ford plants. The total for 1921 was one million. In 1923 57 per cent of all cars manufactured in the United States were Fords. Three years later the Ford Motor Company produced its thirteen millionth car. From the perspective of efficient production the Ford organization was also something of a miracle. In 1913 it required twelve hours to make a car. The following year, after the introduction of the assembly line techniques, the figure dropped to ninety-three minutes. In 1920 Ford achieved his long-time dream of building one car for every minute of the working day. And still he was unsatisfied. On October 31, 1925, the Ford Motor Company manufactured 9,109 Model Ts, one every ten seconds. This was the high point, and competition was rising to challenge Ford's preeminence, but by the end of the twenties Henry Ford was a legend, a folk hero, and reputedly the richest man who ever lived. Transcending the role of automobile manufacturer, he had become an international symbol of the new industrialism. The Germans coined a word to describe the revolutionary mass production techniques: *Fordismus*. At home Ford's popularity reached the point where he could be seriously considered a presidential possibility for the election of 1924.

Fortunately for the historian of his thought, if not always for himself, Henry Ford had a propensity for forthrightly stating his opinions on a wide variety of subjects outside his field of competence. He also had the money to publish and otherwise implement his ideas. The resulting intellectual portrait was that of a mind steeped in traditional Americanism. For Ford agrarian simplicity, McGuffey morality, and Algerian determination were sacred objects. Nationalism was writ large over all Ford did, and America was great because of its heritage of freedom, fairness and hard, honest work. Ford's confidence in the beneficence of old-fashioned virtues verged on the fanatical. The "spirit of 76," equal opportunity democracy, rugged individualism, the home and motherhood were Ford's touchstones of reality. He deified pioneer ethics and values. "More men are beaten than fail," he declared in 1928. "It is not wisdom they need, or money, or brilliance, or pull, but just plain gristle and bone." A decade earlier "Mr. Ford's Page" in the *Dearborn Independent* stated that "one of the great things about the American people is that they are pioneers." This idea led easily to American messianism. "No one can contemplate the nation to which we belong," the editorial continued, "without realizing the distinctive prophetic character of its obvious mission to the world. We are pioneers. We are pathfinders. We are the road-builders. We are the guides, the vanguards of Humanity."

The tension in Henry Ford's thought between old and new, between a belief in progress and a tendency to nostalgia, is dramatically illustrated in his attitude toward farming and farmers. On the one hand he believed farm life to be a ceaseless round of inefficient drudgery. Indeed, he had abundant personal evidence, remarking at one point, "I have traveled ten thousand miles behind a plow. I hated the grueling grind of farm work." With the incentive of sparing others this painful experience, Ford addressed himself to the problem of industrializing agriculture. The farmer, in Ford's opinion, should become a technician and a businessman. Tractors (Ford's, of course) should replace horses. Mechanization would make it possible to produce in twenty-five working days what formerly required an entire year. Fences would come down and vast economies of scale take place. Ford's modern farmer would not even need to live on his farm but instead could commute from a city home. To give substance to these ideals Ford bought and operated with astonishing success a nine-thousand-acre farm near Dearborn.

Still Ford, the "Father of Modern Agriculture," as he has been dubbed, was only part of the man. He also retained a strong streak of old-fashioned, horse-and-buggy agrarianism. Farming, from this standpoint, was more than a challenge in production; it was a moral act. Constantly in the twenties, even while he was helping make it possible, Ford branded the modern city a "pestiferous growth." He delighted in contrasting the "unnatural," "twisted," and "cooped up" lives of city-dwellers with the "wholesome" life of "independence" and "sterling honesty" that the farm environment offered. In Ford's view the importance of cities in the nation's development had been greatly exaggerated. Early in the 1920s the *Dearborn Independent* editorialized: "when we all stand up and sing, 'My Country 'Tis of Thee,' we seldom think of the cities. Indeed, in that old national hymn there are no references to the city at all. It sings of rocks and rivers and hills—the great American Out-of-Doors. And that is really The Country. That is, the country is THE Country. The real United States lies outside the cities."

As such a manifesto suggests, a bias toward nature and rural conditions was an important element in Henry Ford's thought. "What children and adults need," he told one reporter, "is a chance to breathe God's fresh air and to stretch their legs and have a little garden in the soil." This ideal led Ford to choose small towns instead of cities as the sites of his factories. "Turning back to village industry," as Ford put it in 1926, would enable people to reestablish a sense of community—with nature and with men—that urbanization had destroyed. Ford believed that cities were doomed as Americans discovered the advantages of country life.

Ford's enthusiasm for nature did not stop with ruralism. From 1914 to 1924 he sought a more complete escape from civilization on a series of camping trips with Thomas A. Edison. John Burroughs, the naturalist, and Harvey Firestone, the tire king, also participated. Although the equipment these self-styled vagabonds took into the woods was far from primitive, they apparently shared a genuine love of the outdoors. In the words of Burroughs, they "cheerfully endure wet, cold, smoke, mosquitoes, black flies, and sleepless nights, just to touch naked reality once more." Ford had a special fondness for birds. With typical exuberance he had five hundred birdhouses built on his Michigan farm, including one with seventy-six apartments which he called, appropriately, a "bird hotel." There were also electric heaters and electric brooders for Ford's fortunate birds. The whole production mixed technology and nature in a way that symbolized Ford's ambivalence. When he could not camp or visit his aviary, Ford liked to read about the natural world. Indeed he preferred the works of Emerson, Thoreau, and Burroughs to the Bible. Ford so admired Burroughs' variety of natural history that even before becoming acquainted with him he sent him a new Ford car.

As for roads and automobiles, Ford saw them not as a threat to natural conditions but rather as a way for the average American to come into contact with nature. The machine and the garden were not incompatible. "I will build a motor car for the great multitude...," Ford boasted, "so low in price that no man...will be unable to own one—and enjoy with his family the blessings of hours of pleasure in God's great open spaces." In *My Life and Work* of 1923 Ford again confronted the tension between nature and modern civilization. He declared that he did not agree with those who saw mechanization leading to a "cold, metallic sort of world in which great factories will drive away the trees, the flowers, the birds and the green fields." According to Ford, "unless we know more about machines and their use...we cannot have the time to enjoy the trees and the birds, and the flowers, and the green fields." Such reconciliations only partially covered Ford's nervousness about the mechanized, urbanized future. Contradictions persisted in this thinking. The same man who envisaged fenceless bonanza farms could say, "I love to walk across country and jump fences." The lover of trees could state in utmost seriousness, "better wood can be made than is grown."

Ford's attitude toward history has been subject to wide misunderstanding. The principal source of confusion is a statement Ford made in 1919 at the trial resulting from his libel suit against the *Chicago Tribune.* "History," he declared, "is more or less the bunk. It is tradition. We don't want tradition. We want to live in the present, and the only history that is worth a tinker's dam is the history we make today." On another occasion he admitted that he "wouldn't give a nickel for all the history in the world." Complementing this sentiment is Ford's reputation as a forward-looking inventor and revolutionary industrialist unsatisfied with the old processes. Here seems a man fully at home in the alleged new era of the 1920s. But in fact Ford idolized the past. His "history...is bunk" remark came in response to a question about ancient history and Napoleon Bonaparte and had reference to written history. For history itself—what actually happened in his nation's past and its tangible evidence—Ford had only praise.

The most obvious evidence of Ford's enthusiasm for history was his collector's instinct. He began with that bastion of his own youth, the McGuffey readers. Sending agents out to scour the countryside and putting aside considerations of cost, Ford owned by 1925 one of the few complete collections of the many McGuffey editions. Hoping to share his treasures with his contemporaries, Ford had five thousand copies of *Old Favorites from the McGuffey Readers* printed in 1926. The book contained such classic stories as "Try, Try Again" and "The Hare and the Tortoise." It dispensed an ideal of individualism and self-reliance at the same time that Ford's assembly lines were making men cogs in an impersonal machine.

From books Ford turned to things, and during the 1920s amassed a remarkable collection of American antiques. He bought so widely and so aggressively that he became a major factor in prices in the antique market. Everything was fair game. Lamps and dolls, bells and grandfather clocks made their way to Dearborn. Size was no problem. Ford gathered enough machines to show the evolution of the threshing operation from 1849 to the 1920s. Another exhibit traced the development of wagons in America. Eventually the entire heterogeneous collection went into the Edison Museum at Dearborn, a pretentious building designed to resemble, simultaneously, Independence Hall, Congress Hall, and the old City Hall of Philadelphia. Ford delighted in showing visitors around the five-acre layout. Asked on one occasion why he collected, Ford replied, "so that they will not be lost to America." Later, on the same tour, Ford played a few bars on an antique organ and observed, "that takes me back to my boyhood days. They were beautiful days."

This sentiment undoubtedly figured in Ford's 1920 decision to restore his boyhood home. Everything had to be exactly as he remembered it. Furniture, china, and rugs were rehabilitated or reconstructed. Ford even used archeological techniques to recover artifacts around the family homestead. The ground was dug to a depth of six feet and the silverware, wheels, and other equipment used by his parents in the 1860s were recovered. In 1922 Ford purchased the Wayside Inn at Sudbury, Massachusetts, to preserve it from destruction. Celebrated by the poet Henry Wadsworth Longfellow, the old inn appealed to Ford as a symbol of pioneer days. He opened it for the public's edification in 1924. But a new highway ran too near. Roaring cars disturbed the horse-and-buggy atmosphere. So, turning against the age he helped create, Ford had the state highway rerouted around the shrine at a cost of $250,000. He also bought and restored the schoolhouse in Sudbury alleged to be the site where Mary and her little lamb gamboled. Naturally the shop of the "Village Blacksmith," also in Sudbury, had to be included in Ford's antique empire.

Beginning in 1926 with the construction of Greenfield Village near Dearborn, Ford embarked on a career of large-scale historical restoration. This time not a building but a whole community was the object of his attention. Greenfield, named after the Michigan hamlet in which Ford's mother grew up, was a monument to his agrarianism as well as his reverence for the past. "I am trying in a small way," Ford explained with unwarranted modesty, "to help America take a step...toward the saner and sweeter idea of life that prevailed in pre-war days." Greenfield Village had gravel roads, gas street lamps, a grassy common, and an old-fashioned country store. The automobile mogul permitted only horse-

A young Henry Ford at the beginning of his fabulous success.

drawn vehicles on the premises. The genius of assembly line mass production engaged a glass blower, blacksmith, and cobbler to practice their obsolete crafts in the traditional manner. Ford dispatched his agents to seek out, purchase, and transport to Greenfield the cottages of Walt Whitman, Noah Webster, and Patrick Henry. In time they even secured the crowning glory: the log cabin in which William Holmes McGuffey had been born and raised.

History, then, was not "bunk" to Henry Ford. The speed of change seemed to increase proportionately his desire to retain contact with the past. As Ford declared in 1928, a year before completing Greenfield Village, "improvements have been coming so quickly that the past is being lost to the rising generation." To counter this tendency Ford labored to put history into a form "where it may be seen and felt." But values and attitudes were also on display. Ford looked back with nostalgia to the pioneer ethic. With it, he believed, the nation had been sound, wholesome, happy, and secure. "The Old Ways," as the *Dearborn Independent* declared, "Were Good."

Ambivalence is the key to the mind of Henry Ford. He was both old and new; he looked both forward and backward. Confidently progressive as he was in some respects, he remained nervous about new ways. The more conditions changed, the more the nostalgic Ford groped for the security of traditional values and institutions. He was not lost; on the contrary, he had too many gods, at least for consistency. But Ford was popular, indeed a national deity, in the twenties even if his senatorial and presidential bids fell short. As a plain, honest, old-fashioned billionaire, a technological genius who loved to move into the future without losing the values of the past.

Note

[1]In all probability Henry Ford did not actually write the numerous books, pamphlets, and articles associated with his name and attributed to him in this chapter. He was not a literary man; his critics even alleged he could not read. But Ford could pay people to express his opinions for him, and there is no reason to think that the ideas these writers recorded were not those of their employer.

The Rap on Rap

David Samuels

For anyone interested in relating the meaning of popular heroes, including rogue-heroes to the audiences who venerate those heroes, it is obviously necessary to determine just who that audience is. Most popular culture artifacts, including heroes, do not appeal to everyone. A majority of popular materials appeal mainly to large subgroups of American society. What a hero means to a culture depends on the cultural group that embraces the hero. Sometimes determining who the hero worshippers are is less obvious that we might think.

The main audience for rock and roll has traditionally been young people just breaking away from the domination of parents and teachers. Rock music itself began in the 1950s as a rebellion against the stifling lifestyles of adults. It is hardly surprising, therefore, that rock stars have been the most visible rogue-heroes in America during the second half of the twentieth century. From the censoring of the lower half of Elvis' body on the Ed Sullivan television show in the mid-fifties to the arrest of Doors lead singer Jim Morrison in the late sixties to the police harassment of punk rockers in the late seventies to religious protests against heavy metal band in the eighties, older people have fought against rock performers for their non-conformist music and lifetyles, and young people have loved these performers for exactly the same reasons. In the late 1980s and early 1990s, the most visible anti-social music is rap performed by the most visible rogue-heroes (at least in the public images record companies sell to us), the gangster rappers.

In 1992, rappers Sister Souljah and Ice-T were condemned by the democratic and republican presidential candidates, respectively, making rogue-heroes out of both of them. In inner Los Angeles this was a cause of resentment. But in white suburbs all over America, young, white males rushed out to buy their albums.

A slightly longer version of this essay appeared in *The New Republic*, Nov. 11, 1991.

It is natural to assume that the natural fans of gangster rappers are young, urban, African Americans. Most rap performers are black males and the lyrics of most outlaw rap deals in harshly explicit language with the sexual, social and legal problems of inner-city black men and adolescents. It is surprising to discover in David Samuels' essay that a majority of the buyers of outlaw rap albums are young, suburban whites. Many writers about rappers and their music claim gangster rappers express the authentic rage of the disenfranchised African-American homeboy, furious about having no prospects for the future except exclusion from the American dream and the likelihood of an early death. In some cases, these writers are undoubtedly correct. But Samuels' identification of the main buyers of rap in the affluent white community forces us to view gangster rappers in dramatically different ways.

During the summer of 1991, Soundscan, a computerized scanning system, changed *Billboard* magazine's method of counting record sales in the United States. Replacing a haphazard system that relied on big-city record stores, Soundscan measured the number of records sold nationally by *scanning the bar codes at chain store cash registers.* Within weeks the number of computed record sales leapt, as demographics shifted from minority-focused urban centers to white, suburban, middle-class malls. So it was that America awoke on June 22, 1991, to find that its favorite record was not *Out of Time,* by aging college-boy rockers R.E.M., but *Niggaz4life,* a musical celebration of gang rape and other violence by N.W.A., or Niggers With Attitude, a rap group from the Los Angeles ghetto of Compton whose records had never before risen above No. 27 on the Billboard charts.

From *Niggaz4life* to *Boyz N the Hood,* young black men committing acts of violence were available that summer in a wide variety of entertainment formats. Of these none was more popular than rap. And none has received quite the level of critical attention and concern. Writers on the left have long viewed rap as the heartbeat of urban America, its authors, in Arthur Kempton's words, "the pre-eminent young dramaturgists in the clamorous theater of the street." On the right, this assumption has been shared, but greeted with predictable disdain.

Neither side of the debate has been prepared, however, to confront what the entertainment industry's receipts from that summer prove beyond doubt: although rap is still proportionally more popular among blacks, its primary audience is white and lives in the suburbs. And the history of rap's degeneration from insurgent black street music to mainstream pop points to another dispiriting conclusion: the more rappers were packaged as violent black criminals, the bigger their white audiences became.

If the racial makeup of rap's audience has been largely misunderstood, so have the origins of its authors. Since the early 1980s a tightly knit group of mostly young, middle-class, black New Yorkers, in close concert with white record producers, executives, and publicists, has been making rap music for an audience that industry executives concede is primarily composed of white suburban males. Building upon a *form* pioneered by lower-class black artists in New York between 1975 and 1983, despite an effective boycott of the music by both black and white radio that continues to this day, they created the most influential pop music of the 1980s. Rap's appeal to whites rested in its evocation of an age-old image of blackness: a foreign, sexually charged, and criminal underworld against which the norms of white society are defined, and, by extension, through which they may be defied. It was the truth of this latter proposition that rap would test in its journey into the mainstream.

"Hip-hop," the music behind the lyrics, which are "rapped," is a form of sonic bricolage with roots in "toasting," a style of making music by speaking over records. (For simplicity, I'll use the term "rap" interchangeably with "hip-hop" throughout this article.) Toasting first took hold in Jamaica in the mid-1960s, a response, legend has it, to the limited availability of expensive Western instruments and the concurrent proliferation of cheap R&B instrumental singles on Memphis-based labels such as Stax-Volt. Cool Dj Herc, a Jamaican who settled in the South Bronx, is widely credited with having brought toasting to New York City. Rap spread quickly through New York's poor black neighborhoods in the mid-and late 1970s. Jams were held in local playgrounds, parks, and community centers, in the South and North Bronx, Brooklyn, and Harlem.

Although much is made of rap as a kind of urban streetgeist, early rap had a more basic function: dance music. Bill Stephney, considered by many to be the smartest man in the rap business, recalls the first time he heard hip-hop: "The point wasn't rapping, it was rhythm, DJs cutting records left and right, taking the big drum break from Led Zeppelin's 'When the Levee Breaks,' mixing it together with 'Ring My Bell,' then with a Bob James Mardi Gras jazz record and some James Brown. You'd have 2,000 kids in any community center in New York, moving back and forth, back and forth, like some kind of tribal war dance, you might say. It was the rapper's role to match this intensity rhythmically. No one knew what he was saying. He was just rocking the mike."

Rap quickly spread from New York to Philadelphia, Chicago, Boston, and other cities with substantial black populations. Its popularity was sustained by the ease with which it could be made. The music on early rap records sounded like the black music of the day: funk or, more often, disco. Performers were unsophisticated about image and presentation, tending toward gold lamé jumpsuits and Jericurls, a second-rate appropriation of the stylings of funk musicians like George Clinton and Bootsy Collins.

The first rap record to make it big was "Rapper's Delight," released in *1979* by the Sugar Hill Gang, an ad hoc all-star team drawn from three New York groups on Sylvia and Joey Robinson's Sugar Hill label. Thanks to Sylvia Robinson's soul music and background, the first thirty seconds of "Rapper's Delight" were indistinguishable from the disco records of the day: light guitars, high-hat drumming, and hand-claps over a deep funk bass line. What followed will be immediately familiar to anyone who was young in New York City that summer:

I said, "By the way, baby, what's your name?"
She said, "I go by the name Lois Lane
And you can be my boyfriend you surely can
Just let me quit my boyfriend, he's called Superman."

Like disco music and jumpsuits, the social commentaries of early rappers like Grandmaster Flash and Mellie Mel were for the most part transparent attempts to sell records to whites by any means necessary. Songs like "White Lines" (with its anti-dug theme) and "The Message" (about ghetto life) had the desired effect, drawing fulsome praise from white rock critics, raised on the protest ballads of Bob Dylan and Phil Ochs. The reaction on the street was somewhat less favorable. "The Message" is a case in point. "People hated that record," recalls Russell Simmons, president of Def Jam Records. "I remember the Junebug, a famous DJ of the time, was playing it up at the Fever, and Ronnie DJ put a pistol to his head and said, "Take the record off and break it or I'll blow your...head off.' The whole club stopped until he broke that record and put it in the garbage."

It was not until 1984 that rap broke through to a mass white audience. The first group to do so was Run-DMC, with the release of its debut album, Run-DMC, and with King of Rock one year later. These albums blazed the trail that rap would travel into the musical mainstream. Bill Adler, a former rock critic and rap's best known publicist, explains: "They were the first group that came on stage as if they had just come off the street corner. But unlike the first generation of rappers, they were solidly middle class. Both of Run's parents were college-educated. DMC was a good Catholic schoolkid, a mama's boy. Neither of them was deprived and neither of them ever ran with a gang, but on stage they became the biggest, baddest, streetest guys in the world." When Run-DMC covered the Aerosmith classic "Walk This Way," the resulting video made it onto MTV, and the record went gold.

Rap's new mass audience was in large part the brainchild of Rick Rubin, a Jewish punk rocker from suburban Long Island who produced the music behind many of rap's biggest acts. Like many New Yorkers his age, Rick grew up listening to Mr. Magic's Rap Attack, a rap radio show on WHBI. In 1983, at the age of 19, Rubin founded Def Jam Records in his NYU dorm room. (Simmons bought part of Def Jam in 1984 and took full control of the company in 1989.) Rubin's next group, the Beastie Boys, was a white punk rock band whose transformation into a rap group pointed rap's way into the future. The Beasties' first album, *Licensed to Ill,* backed by airplay of its anthemic frat-party single "You've Got to Fight for Your Right to Party," became the first rap record to sell a million copies.

The appearance of white groups in a black musical form has historically prefigured the mainstreaming of the form, the growth of the white audience, and the resulting dominance of white performers. With rap, however, this process took an unexpected turn: white demand indeed began to determine the direction of the genre, but what it wanted was music more defiantly black. The result was Public Enemy, produced and marketed by Rubin, the next group significantly to broaden rap's appeal to young whites.

Public Enemy's now familiar mélange of polemic and dance music was formed not on inner-city streets but in the suburban Long Island towns in which the group's members grew up. The children of successful black middle-class professionals, they gave voice to the feeling that, despite progress toward equality, blacks still did not quite belong in white America. They complained of unequal treatment by the police, of never quite overcoming the color of their skin: "We were suburban college kids doing what we were supposed to do, but we were always made to feel like something else," explains Stephney, the group's executive producer.

Public Enemy's abrasive and highly politicized style made it a fast favorite of the white avant-garde, much like the English punk rock band The Clash ten years before. Public Enemy's music, produced by the Shocklee brothers Hank and Keith, was faster, harder, and more abrasive than the rap of the day, music that moved behind the vocals like a full-scale band. But the root of Public Enemy's success was a highly charged theater of race in which white listeners became guilty eavesdroppers on the putative private conversation of the inner city. Chuck D denounced his enemies (the media, some radio stations), proclaimed himself "Public Enemy #1," and praised Louis Farrakhan in stentorian tones, flanked onstage by black-clad security guards from the Nation of Islam, the S1WS, led by Chuck's political mentor, Professor Griff. Flavor Flav, Chuck's homeboy sidekick, parodied street style: oversize sunglasses,

Ice-T.

baseball cap cocked to one side, a clock the size of a silver plate draped around his neck, going off on wild verbal riffs that often meant nothing at all.

The closer rap moved to the white mainstream, the more it became like rock 'n' roll, a celebration of posturing over rhythm. The back catalogs of artists like James Brown and George Clinton were relentlessly plundered for catchy hooks, then overlaid with dance beats and social commentary. Public Enemy's single "Fight the Power" was the biggest college hit of 1989:

'Cause I'm black and I'm proud
I'm ready and hyped, plus I'm amped
Most of my heroes don't appear on no stamps
Sample a look back, you look and find
Nothing but rednecks for 400 years if you check.

After the release of "Fight the Power," Professor Griff made a series of anti-Semitic remarks in an interview with *The Washington Times*. Griff was subsequently asked to leave the group, for what Chuck D termed errors in judgment. Although these errors were lambasted in editorials across the country, they do not seem to have affected Public Enemy's credibility with its young white fans.

Public Enemy's theatrical black nationalism and sophisticated noise ushered in what is fast coming to be seen as rap's golden age, a heady mix of art, music, and politics. Between 1988 and 1989 a host of innovative acts broke into the mainstream. KRS-One, now a regular on the Ivy League lecture circuit, grew up poor, living on the streets of the South Bronx until he met a New York City social worker, Scott La Rock, later murdered in a drive-by shooting. Together they formed BDP, Boogie Down Productions, recording for the Jive label on RCA. Although songs like "My Philosophy" and "Love's Gonna Get 'Cha (Material Love)" were clever and self-critical, BDP's roots remained firmly planted in the guns-and-posturing of the mainstream rap ghetto.

The ease with which rap can create such aural cartoons, says Hank Shocklee, lies at the very heart of its appeal as entertainment: "Whites have always liked black music," he explains. "That part is hardly new. The difference with rap was that the imagery of black artists, for the first time, reached the level of black music. The sheer number of words in a rap song allows for the creation of full characters impossible in R&B. Rappers became like superheroes. Captain America or the Fantastic Four."

By 1988 the conscious manipulation of racial stereotypes had become rap's leading edge, a trend best exemplified by the rise to stardom of Schoolly D, a Philadelphia rapper on the Jive label who sold more than half a million records with little mainstream notice. It was not that the media had never heard of Schoolly D: white critics and fans, for the first time, were simply at a loss for words. His voice, fierce and deeply textured, could alone frighten listeners. He used it as a rhythmic device that made no concessions to pop-song form, talking evenly about smoking crack and using women for sex, proclaiming his blackness, accusing other rappers of not being black enough. What Schoolly D meant by blackness was abundantly clear. Schoolly D was a misogynist and a thug. If listening to Public Enemy was like eavesdropping on a conversation, Schoolly D was like getting mugged. This, aficionados agreed, was what they had been waiting for: a rapper from whom you would flee in abject terror if you saw him walking toward you late at night.

It remained for N.W.A., a more conventional group of rappers from Los Angeles, to adapt Schoolly D's stylistic advance for the mass white market with its first album-length release, *Straight Out of Compton*, in 1989. The much-quoted rap from the album, "...the Police," was the target of an FBI warning to police departments across the country, and a constant presence at certain college parties, white and black:

They have the authority to kill the minority...
A young nigger on the warpath
And when I'm finished, it's gonna be a bloodbath
Of cops, dying in L.A.

Other songs spoke of trading oral sex for crack and shooting strangers for fun. After the release of *Straight Out of Compton*, N.W.A.'s lead rapper and chief lyricist, Ice Cube, left the group. Billing himself as "the nigger you love to hate," Ice Cube released a solo album, *Amerikkka's Most Wanted*, which gleefully pushed the limits of rap's ability to give offense. One verse ran:

I'm thinking to myself, "why did I b... her?"
Now I'm in the closet, looking for the hanger.

But what made *Amerikkka's Most Wanted* so shocking to so many record buyers was the title track's violation of rap's most iron-clad taboo—black on white violence:

It's time you take a trip to the suburbs.
Let 'em see a nigger invasion
Point blank, on a Caucasian.

Ice Cube took his act to the big screen in *Boyz N the Hood* (1991), drawing rave reviews for his portrayal of a young black drug dealer whose life of crime leads him to an untimely end. The crime-doesn't-pay message, an inheritance from the grade-B gangster film, is the stock-in-trade of another L.A. rapper-turned-actor, Ice-T of *New Jack City* (1990) fame, a favorite of socially conscious rock critics. Tacking unhappy endings onto glorifications of drug dealing and gang warfare, Ice-T offers all the thrills of the form while alleviating any guilt listeners may have felt about consuming drive-by shootings along with their popcorn.

Ice Cube.

It was in this spirit that "Yo! MTV Raps" debuted in 1989 as the first national broadcast forum for rap music. The videos were often poorly produced, but the music and visual presence of stars like KRS-One, LL Cool J, and Chuck D proved enormously compelling, rocketing "Yo!" to the top of the MTV ratings. On weekends bands were interviewed and videos introduced by Fab Five Freddie: hip young white professionals watched his shows to keep up with urban black slang and fashion. Younger viewers rushed home from school on weekdays to catch ex-

Beastie Boys DJ Dr. Dre, a sweatsuit-clad mountain of a man, well over 300 pounds, and Ed Lover, who evolved a unique brand of homeboy Laurel and Hardy mixed with occasional social comment.

With "Yo! MTV Raps," rap became for the first time the music of choice in the white suburbs of middle America. From the beginning says Doug Herzog, MTV's vice president for programming the show's audience was primarily white male, suburban, and between the ages of 16 and 24, a demographic profile that "Yo!"'s success helped set in stone. For its daytime audience, MTV spawned an ethnic rainbow of well-scrubbed pop rappers from MC Hammer to Vanilla Ice to Gerardo, a Hispanic actor turned rap star. For "Yo" itself rap became more overtly politicized as it expanded its audience. Sound bites from the speeches of Malcolm X and Martin Luther King became de-rigueur introductions to formulaic assaults on white America mixed with hymns to gang violence and crude sexual caricature.

Holding such polyglot records together is what Village Voice critic Nelson George has labeled "ghettocentrism," a style-driven cult of blackness defined by crude stereotypes. P.R. releases, like a recent one for Los Angeles rapper DJ Quik, take special care to mention artists' police records, often enhanced to provide extra street credibility. When Def Jam star Slick Rick was arrested for attempted homicide, Def Jam incorporated the arrest into its publicity campaign for Rick's new album, bartering exclusive rights to the story to *Vanity Fair* in exchange for the promise of a lengthy profile. Muslim groups such as Brand Nubian proclaim their hatred for white devils, especially those who plot to poison black babies. That Brand Nubian believes the things said on its records is unlikely: the group seems to get along quite well with its white Jewish publicist, Beth Jacobson of Electra Records. Anti-white, and, in this case, anti-Semitic, rhymes are a shorthand way of defining one's opposition to the mainstream. Racism is reduced to fashion, by the rappers who use it and by the white audiences to whom such images appeal. What is significant here are not so much the intentions of artist and audience as a dynamic in which anti-Semitic slurs and black criminality correspond to "authenticity," and "authenticity" sells records.

The selling of this kind of authenticity to a young white audience is the stock-in-trade of *The Source,* a full-color monthly magazine devoted exclusively to rap music, founded by Jon Shecter while still an undergraduate at Harvard. Shecter is what is known in the rap business as a Young Black Teenager. He *wears* a Brooklyn Dodgers baseball cap, like Spike Lee, and a Source T-Shirt. As editor of *The Source,* Shecter has become a necessary quote for stories about rap in *Time* and other national magazines.

An upper-middle-class white, Shecter has come in for his share of criticism. "There's no place for me to say anything," Shecter responds. "Given what I'm doing, my viewpoint has to be that whatever comes of the black community, the hip-hop community which is the black community, is the right thing. I know my place. The only way in which criticism can be raised is on a personal level, because the way that things are set-up, with the white-controlled media, prevents sincere back-and-forth discussion from taking place." The latest venture in hip-hop marketing, a magazine planned by Time Warner, will also be edited by a young white, Jonathan van Meter, a former *Conde Nast* editor.

Sister Souljah

In part because of young whites like Shecter and van Meter, rap's influence on the street continues to decline. "You put out a record by Big Daddy Kane," Rubin says, "and then put out the same record by a pop performer like Janet Jackson. Not only will the Janet Jackson record sell ten times more copies, it will also be the cool record to play in clubs." Stephney agrees: "Kids in my neighborhood pump dance hall reggae on their systems all night long, because that's where the rhythm is.... People complain about how white kids stole black culture. The truth of the matter is that no one can steal a culture." Whatever its continuing significance in the realm of racial politics, rap's hour as innovative popular music has come and gone. Rap forfeited whatever claim it may have had to particularity by acquiring a mainstream white audience whose tastes increasingly determined the nature of the form. What whites wanted was not music, but black music, which as a result stopped really being either.

White fascination with rap sprang from a particular kind of cultural tourism pioneered by the Jazz Age novelist Carl Van Vechten. Van Vechten's 1926, best seller *Nigger Heaven* imagined a masculine, criminal, yet friendly black ghetto world that functioned, for Van Vechten and for his readers, as a refuge from white middle-class boredom. In *Really the Blues,* the white jazzman Mezz Mezzrow went one step further, claiming that his own life among black people in Harlem had physically transformed him into a member of the Negro race, whose unique sensibility he had now come to share. By inverting the moral values attached to contemporary racial stereotypes, Van Vechten and Mezzrow at once appealed to and sought to undermine the prevailing racial order. Both men, it should be stressed, conducted their tours in person.

The moral inversion of racist stereotypes as entertainment has lost whatever transformative power it may arguably have had fifty years ago. MC Serch of 3rd Bass, a white rap traditionalist, with short-cropped hair and thick-rimmed Buddy Holly glasses, formed his style in the uptown hip-hop clubs like the L.Q. in the early 1980s. "Ten or eleven years ago," he remarks, "when I was wearing my permanent-press Lee's with a beige campus shirt and matching Adidas sneakers, kids I went to school with were calling me a 'wigger,' 'black wanna-be,' all kinds of racist names. Now those same kids are driving Jeeps with MCM leather interiors and pumping Public Enemy."

The ways in which rap has been consumed and popularized speak not of cross-cultural understanding, musical or otherwise, but of a voyeurism and tolerance of racism in which black and white are both complicit. "Both the rappers and their white fans affect and commodify their own visions of street culture," argues Henry Louis Gates Jr. of Harvard University, "like buying Navajo blankets at a reservation road-stop. A lot of what you see in rap is the guilt of the black middle class about its economic success, its inability to put forth a culture of its own. Instead they do the worst possible thing, falling back on fantasies of street life. In turn, white college students with impeccable gender credentials buy nasty sex lyrics under the cover of getting at some kind of authentic black experience."

Gates goes on to make the more worrying point: "What is potentially very dangerous about this is the feeling that by buying records they have made some kind of valid social commitment." Where the assimilation of black street culture by whites once required a degree of human contact between the races, the street is now available at the flick of a cable channel—to black and white middle class alike. "People want to consume and they want to consume easy," Hank Shocklee says. "If you're a suburban white kid and you want to find out what life is like for a black city teenager, you buy a record by N.W.A. It's like going to an amusement park and getting on a roller coaster ride—records are safe, they're controlled fear, and you always have the choice of turning it off. That's why nobody ever takes a train up to 125th Street and gets out and starts walking around. Because then you're not in control anymore: it's a whole other ball game." This kind of consumption—of racist stereotypes, of brutality toward women, or even of uplifting tributes to Dr. Martin Luther King—is of a particularly corrupting kind. The values it instills and reflects find their ultimate expression in the ease with which we watch young black men killing each other: in movies, on records, and on the streets of cities and towns across the country.

The Wretched of the Hearth: The Undainty Feminism of Roseanne Arnold

Barbara Ehrenreich

It has been said that the face of feminism in the 1990s has two sides to it—both staring in the same direction, perhaps, but with perspectives radically divergent as the upturned grin and downturned sadness of the masks of Comedy and Tragedy. On the one side there is the determined, athletic and fit, upscale and articulate image of the careerwoman—the face of a Murphy Brown; on the other side there is the contrasting image of the downscale and working class, overweight and undereducated image of the working mother—of a Roseanne Arnold/ Connor. The former doesn't have to worry about achieving success but only about dealing with its consequences, while the latter is far too preoccupied with simple survival to worry about "making it big." Murphy Brown receives most of the accolades and official attention (she has been singled out by both Emmy Award and Dan Quayle in equally notable contexts), but she is, after all, the highly visible voice of the already visible and articulate—the pulpit for those who are already being heard and seen. Roseanne Arnold/Connor, on the other hand, has never been nominated for television's highest award and is quite probably not the image the Murphy Brown branch of the feminist tree would choose to define the movement in the 1990s. Roseanne is the voice for millions who have no other means of expression and is, therefore, an especially powerful example of the way in which popular culture can provide a vehicle for the expression of beliefs and values which lie churning just beneath the surface of mass consciousness.

Barbara Ehrenreich defines and illuminates the meaning of the Roseanne phenomenon, and in doing so provides a fine example of how useful and revealing the concept of "celebrity" can be as a means of uncovering the beliefs and values defining specific eras and groups. Ehrenreich's essay portrays Roseanne Arnold in a manner which we would

This essay in slightly different form appeared in *The New Republic* 2 April 1990. Reprinted by permission of the author.

argue labels the star a "rogue celebrity"—i.e., someone whose associated beliefs and values are contrary to the mainstream and are expressive of the thoughts and feelings of a cultural sub-group which is in opposition to the controlling masses and elites. What is especially remarkable about Ehrenreich's portrait is the way in which she uses a concept which is often considered to be at home only in cheap tabloids and glitzy television talk shows (i.e. "Celebrityhood") to demonstrate that Roseanne Arnold's massive popular appeal is representative of a complex web of conflicts which incorporate sex, class, education and even weight control into a powerfully resonant, meaningful protest. Ehrenreich's essay shows that celebrityhood can embody the same sorts of contradictory meanings as the other tools of popular culture analysis (note her complex examination of Roseanne's ambivalent view of the nuclear family, for example), and also illustrates the way in which celebrity (Roseanne Arnold) and heroine (Roseanne Connor) overlap and reinforce each other's meaning. "Roseanne" is a star whose light twinkles for millions each Tuesday evening—but Ehrenreich lets us see the darkness that surrounds the star as well.

In the second half of the eighties, when American conservatism had reached its masochistic zenith with the re-election of Ronald Reagan, when women's liberation had been replaced by the more delicate sensibility known as post-feminism, when everyone was a yuppie and the heartiest word of endorsement in our vocabulary was "appropriate," there was yet this one paradox: our favorite TV personages were a liberal black man and a left-wing white feminist. Cosby could be explained as a representative of America's officially pro-family mood, but Roseanne is a trickier case. Her idea of humor is to look down on her sleeping family in the eponymous sitcom and muse, "Mmmm, I wonder where we could find an all-night taxidermist."

If zeitgeist were destiny, Roseanne would never have happened. Only a few years ago, we learn from her autobiography, Roseanne Arnold was just your run-of-the-mill radical feminist mother-of-three, writing poems involving the Great Goddess, denouncing all known feminist leaders as sellout trash, and praying for the sixties to be born again in a female body. Since the entertainment media do not normally cast about for fat, loud-mouthed feminists to promote to super-stardom, we must assume that Roseanne has something to say that many millions of people have been waiting to hear. Like this, upon being told of a woman who stabbed her husband thirty-seven times: "I admire her restraint."

Roseanne is the neglected underside of the eighties, bringing together its great themes of poverty, obesity and defiance. The overside is handled well enough by Candice Bergen ("Murphy Brown") and Madonna, who exist to remind us that talented women who work out are bound to become fabulously successful. Roseanne works a whole different beat, both in her sitcom and in the movie *She-Devil*, portraying the hopeless underclass of the female sex: polyester-clad, overweight occupants of the slow track; fast-food waitresses, factory workers, housewives, members of the invisible pink-collar army; the despised, the jilted, the underpaid.

But Arnold—and this may be her most appealing feature—is never a victim. In the sitcom, she is an overworked mother who is tormented by her bosses at such locales as Wellman Plastics (where she works the assembly line) and Chicken Divine (a fast-food spot). But Roseanne Connor, her sitcom character, has, as we say in the blue-collar suburbs, a mouth on her. When the cute but obnoxious boss at Wellman calls the workers together and announces, "I have something to tell you," Roseanne yells out, "What? That you feel you're a woman trapped in a man's body?" In *She-Devil*, where Arnold is unfortunately shorn of her trademark deadpan snarl, revenge must take more concrete forms: she organizes an army of the wretched of the earth—nursing home patients and clerical workers—to destroy her errant husband and drive the slender, beautiful, rich-and-famous Other Woman dotty.

At some point, the women's studies profession is bound to look up from its deconstructions and "re-thinkings" and notice Roseanne. They will then observe, in article and lecture form, that Arnold's radicalism is distributed over the two axes of gender and class. This is probably as good an approach as any. Arnold's identity is first of all female—her autobiography is titled *My Life As a Woman*—but her female struggles are located in the least telegenic and most frequently overlooked of social strata—the white, blue-collar working class. In anticipation of Roseannology, let us begin with Arnold's contribution to the sociology of social class, and then take up her impressive achievements in the area of what could be called feminist theory.

"Roseanne" the sitcom, which was inspired by Arnold the stand-up comic, is a radical departure simply for featuring blue-collar Americans—and for depicting them as something other than half-witted greasers and low-life louts. The working class does not usually get much of a role in the American entertainment spectacle. In the seventies mumbling, muscular blue-collar males (*Rocky, The Deer Hunter, Saturday Night Fever*) enjoyed a brief modishness on the screen, while Archie Bunker, the consummate blue-collar bigot, raved away on the tube. But even these grossly stereotyped images vanished in the eighties, as the spectacle narrowed in on the brie-and-chardonnay class. Other than "Roseanne," I can find only one sitcom that deals consistently with the sub-yuppie condition: "Married...with children," a relentlessly nasty portrayal of a shoe salesman and his cognitively disabled family members. There may even be others, but sociological zeal has not sufficed to get me past the opening sequences of "Major Dad," "Full House," or "Doogie Howser."

Not that "Roseanne" is free of class stereotyping. The Connors must bear part of the psychic burden imposed on all working-class people by their economic and occupational betters; they inhabit a zone of glad-handed gemeinschaft, evocative, now and then, of the stock wedding scene (*The Godfather, The Deer Hunter, Working Girl*) that routinely signifies lost old-world values. They indulge in a manic physicality that would be unthinkable among the more controlled and genteel Huxtables. They maintain a traditional, low-fiber diet of white bread and macaroni. They are not above a fart joke.

Still, in "Roseanne" I am willing to forgive the stereotypes as markers designed to remind us of where we are: in the home of a construction worker and his minimum-wage wife. Without the reminders, we might not be aware of how thoroughly the deeper prejudices of the professional class are being challenged. Roseanne's fictional husband Dan (played by the irresistibly cuddly John Goodman) drinks domestic beer and dedicates Sundays to football; but far from being a Bunkeresque boor, he looks to this feminist like the fabled "sensitive man" we have all been pining for. He treats his rotund wife like a sex goddess. He picks up on small cues signaling emotional distress. He helps with homework. And when Roseanne works overtime, he cooks, cleans, and rides herd on the kids without any of the piteous whining we have come to expect from upscale males in their rare, and lavishly documented encounters with soiled Pampers.

Roseanne Connor has her own way of defying the stereotypes. Variously employed as a fast-food operative, a factory worker, a bartender and a telephone salesperson, her real dream is to be a writer. When her twelve-year-old daughter Darlene (brilliantly played by Sara Gilbert) balks at a poetry-writing assignment, Roseanne gives her a little talking-to involving Sylvia Plath: "She inspired quite a few women, including *moi*." In another episode, a middle-aged friend thanks Roseanne for inspiring her to dump her chauvinist husband and go to college. We have come a long way from the dithering, cowering Edith Bunker.

Most of the time the Connors do the usual sitcom things. They have the little domestic misunderstandings that can be patched up in twenty-four minutes with wisecracks and a round of hugs. But "Roseanne" carries working-class verisimilitude into a new and previously taboo dimension—the workplace. In the world of employment, Roseanne knows exactly where she stands: "All the good power jobs are taken. Vanna turns the letters, Leona's got hotels, Margaret's running England...'Course she's not doing a very good job...."

And in the workplace as well as the kitchen, Roseanne knows how to dish it out. A friend of mine, herself a denizen of the low-wage end of the work force, claims to have seen an episode in which Roseanne led an occupational health and safety battle at Wellman Plastics. I missed that one, but I have seen her, on more than one occasion, reduce the boss's ego to rubble. At Chicken Divine, for example, she is ordered to work weekends—an impossibility for a working mother—by an officious teenage boss who confides that he doesn't like working weekends either. In a sequence that could have been crafted by Michael Moore, Roseanne responds: "Well, that's real good 'cause you never do. You sit in your office like a little Napoleon making up schedules and screwing up people's lives." To which he says, "That's what they pay me for. And you are paid to follow my orders." Blah, blah, blah. To which she says, staring at him for a long time and then observing with an evil smile: "You know, you got a little prize hanging out of your nose there."

The class conflict continues on other fronts. In one episode, Roseanne arrives late for an appointment with Darlene's history teacher, because she has been forced to work overtime at Wellman. The teacher, who is leaning against her desk stretching her quadriceps when Roseanne arrives, wants to postpone the appointment because she has a date to play squash. When Roseanne insists, the teacher tells her that Darlene has been barking in class, "like a dog." This she follows with some psychobabble—on emotional problems and dysfunctional families—that would leave most mothers, whatever their social class, clutched with guilt. Not Roseanne, who calmly informs the yuppie snit that, in the Connor household, everybody barks like dogs.

Now this is the kind of class-militant populism that the Democrats, most of them anyway, never seem to get right; up with the little gal; down with the snotty, the pretentious, and the overly paid. At least part of the appeal of "Roseanne" is that it ratifies the resentments of the underdog majority. But this being a sitcom, and Arnold being a pacifist, the class-anger never gets too nasty. Even the most loathsome bosses turn out to be human, and in some cases pathetically needy. Rather than hating the bad guys, we end up feeling better about ourselves, which is the function of all good and humanistic humor anyway.

According to high conservative theory, the leftish cast to a show like "Roseanne" must reflect the media manipulations of the alleged "liberal elite." But the politics of "Roseanne"—including its feminist side, which we will get to in a minute—reflects nothing so much as the decidedly un-elite politics of Arnold herself. On the Larry King show, Arnold said that she prefers the term "working class" to "blue collar" because (and I paraphrase) it reminds us of the existence of class, a reality that Americans are all too disposed to forget. In her autobiography, right up front in the preface, she tells us that it is a "book about the women's movement. . .a book about the left."

Roseanne, My Life As a Woman traces her journey from alienation to political commitment. It must stand as another one of Arnold's commanding oddities. Where you would expect a standard rags-to-riches story, you find a sort of rags-to-revolution tale; more an intellectual and spiritual memoir than the usual chronicle of fearsome obstacles and lucky breaks. She was born the paradigmatic outsider, a Jew in Mormon Utah, a low-income Jew at that. Within the Mormon culture, she was the "Other" (her own term), the "designated Heathen", in school Christmas pageants, always being reminded that "had we been in a Communist country, I would never have been allowed to express my religion, because 'dissent' is not tolerated there." At home she was loved and encouraged, but the emotional density of the Holocaust-haunted Barr family eventually proved too much for her. After a breakdown and several months of hospitalization, she ran away, at nineteen, to find the sixties, or what was left of them in 1971.

Her hippie phase left Arnold with some proto-politics of the peace-and-love variety, three children, and an erratic wage-earner for a husband. It was in this condition that she wandered into the Woman to Woman bookstore on Colfax Avenue in Denver, where she discovered the Movement. Arnold seems to have required very little in the way of consciousness-raising. With one gigantic "click," she jumped right in, joined the collective, and was soon occupied giving "seminars on racism, classism, anti-Semitism, pornography, and taking power." If this seems like a rather sudden leap to political leadership, I can attest from my own experience with venues like Woman to Woman that it happens every day.

But even within the ecumenical embrace of feminism, Arnold remained the Outsider. "We did not agree anymore," she tells us of her collective, "with Betty Friedan, Gloria Steinem, or party politics within the women's movement," which she believes has turned into "a professional, careerist women's thing." When she found her "voice," it spoke in a new tone of working-class existentialism: "I began to speak as a working-class woman who is a mother, a woman who no longer believed in change, progress, growth, or hope." It was this special brand of proletarian feminism that inspired her stand-up comic routine. "I am talking about organizing working-class women and mothers," she tells us, and her comic persona was her way of going about it.

Middle-class feminism has long admitted the possibility of a working-class variant, but the general expectation has been that it would be a diluted version of the "real," or middle-class, thing. According to the conventional wisdom, working-class women would have no truck with the more anti-male aspects of feminism, and would be repelled by the least insult to the nuclear family. They would be comfortable only with the bread-and-butter issues of pay equity, child care, and parental leave. They would be culturally conservative, sensible, dull.

But we had not met Arnold. Her stand-up routine was at first almost too vulgar and castrating for Denver's Comedy Works. I wish *Roseanne: My Life As a Woman* gave more examples of her early, Denver-era, stand-up style, but the videotape "Roseanne" (made later in a Los Angeles club) may be a fair representation. On it she promotes a product called "Fem-Rage," designed to overcome female conditioning during that "one day of the month when you're free to be yourself," and leaves her female fans with the memorable question: "Ever put those maxi-pads on adhesive side up?"

In "Roseanne," the sitcom, however, Arnold has been considerably tamed. No longer standing bravely, and one must admit massively, alone with the microphone, she comes to us now embedded in the family: overwhelmed by domestic detail, surrounded by children too young for R-rated language, padding back and forth between stove, refrigerator, and kitchen table. Some of the edge is off here. There are no four-letter words, no menstruation jokes; and Roseanne's male-baiting barbs just bounce off her lovable Dan. Still, what better place for the feminist comic than in a family sitcom? Feminist theory, after all, cut its teeth on the critique of the family. Arnold continues the process—leaving huge gaping holes where there was sweetness and piety.

All family sitcoms, of course, teach us that wise-cracks and swift put-downs are the preferred modes of affectionate discourse. But Roseanne takes the genre a step further—over the edge, some may say. In the era of big weddings and sudden man shortages, she describes marriage as "a life sentence, without parole." And in the era of the biological clock and the petted yuppie midlife baby, she can tell Darlene to get a fork out of the drawer and "stick it through your tongue." Or she can say, when Dan asks "Are we missing an off-spring?" at breakfast, "Yeah, Where do you think I got the bacon?"

It is Arnold's narrow-eyed cynicism about the family, even more than her class consciousness, that gives "Roseanne" its special frisson. Archie Bunker got our attention by telling us that we (blacks, Jews, "ethnics," WASPs, etc.) don't really like each other. Arnold's message is that even within the family we don't much like each other. We love each other (who else do we have?); but The Family, with its impacted emotions, its lopsided division of labor, and its ancient system of age-graded humiliations, just doesn't work. Or rather, it doesn't work unless the contradictions are smoothed out with irony and the hostilities are periodically blown off as humor. Coming from mom, rather than from a jaded teenager or a bystander dad, this is scary news indeed.

So Arnold's theoretical outlook is, in the best left-feminist tradition, dialectical. On the one hand, she presents the family as a zone of intimacy and support, well worth defending against the forces of capitalism, which drive both mothers and fathers out of the home, scratching around for paychecks. On the other hand, the family is hardly a haven, especially for its grown-up females. It is marred from within by—among other things—the patriarchal division of leisure, which makes dad and the kids the "consumers" of mom's cooking, cleaning, nurturing, and (increasingly) her earnings. Mom's job is to keep the whole thing together—to see that the mortgage payments are made, to fend off the viperish teenagers, to find the missing green sock—but mom is no longer interested in being a human sacrifice on the altar of "pro-family values." She's been down to the feminist bookstore; she's been reading Sylvia Plath.

This is a bleak and radical vision. Not given to didacticism, Arnold offers no programmatic ways out. Surely, we are led to conclude, pay equity would help, along with child care, and so on. But Arnold leaves us hankering for a quality of change that goes beyond mere reform: for a world in which even the lowliest among us—the hash-slinger, the sock-finder, the factory hand—will be recognized as the poet she truly is.

Maybe this is just too radical. The tabloids have taken to stalking Arnold as if she were an unsightly blot on the electronic landscape of our collective dreams. *The New York Times* devoted a quarter of a page to some upscale writer's prissy musings on Roseanne. "Was I just being squeamish" for disliking Arnold, she asks herself: "a goody-two shoes suburban feminist who was used to her icons being chic and sugar-coated instead of this gum-chewing, male-bashing...working-class mama with a big mouth?" No, apparently, she is not squeamish. Arnold is just too, well, unfeminine.

We know what Arnold would say to that, and exactly how she would say it. Yeah, she's crude, but so are the realities of pain and exploitation she seeks to remind us of. If middle-class feminism can't claim Roseanne, maybe it's gotten a little too dainty for its own good. We have a long tradition of tough-talking females behind us, after all, including that other great working-class spokesperson, Mary "Mother" Jones, who once advised the troops, "Whatever you do, *don't* be ladylike."

Norman Rockwell's famous 1943 painting, "Freedom from Want," celebrating Thanksgiving, an American "Rite of Unity."

Section

❄ 6 ❄

Rituals

Introduction
All Together Now:
Popular Rituals in America

Ceremonies are the signposts of our lives. Birthdays are marked by ice cream, cake, presents and parties. We are welcomed to early adulthood by driver's tests, dances and graduation exercises. Later (usually) come weddings, celebrations of the birth of our children, anniversary parties, retirement dinners and, finally, our final ceremony, a funeral. In between these signposts we participate in or observe a continuous string of ceremonial activities which give us pleasure or provide us with personal and social identity. We play board games like checkers or Monopoly and card games like poker or bridge. We learn the rules of dating behavior.

We are taught skills by our parents such as cooking, ironing, how to fish and how to fix a car. With our friends we play double-dutch jump rope or sharpen our verbal skills by playing the dozens. We learn how to play sports and we enjoy seeing "Our" teams play. We have Fourth of July picnics, Thanksgiving dinners and we go on family vacations. We exchange phone calls or write letters to friends far away. We go to circuses, parades, fairs and carnivals.

Life without ceremonies such as these is unthinkable. To be human is to participate in rituals. It is no wonder that as we climb out of the first floor of the house of popular culture, where we examined three-dimensional objects (things or people we can *see*) up to the next room, popular events (things we *do*), we enter a room of the house that is absolutely essential to our human psychological and emotional well-being.

Rites and Wrongs: Patterns of Popular Rituals

Rituals, or rites (the terms are used interchangeably here), are formal and elaborately repeated sets of actions. A ritual, in essence, must be a special activity that has a number of repeated parts. Some rituals are personal ones. Baseball great Wade Boggs, for example, does a little dance, scratching the dirt in front of each foot with the spikes on his other foot, as he waits in the on-deck circle before he hits. He has done this ceremony since his Little League days and he believes it makes him a better hitter. Many of us have elaborate personal rituals with which we start our day or get ready for bed. They help us prepare for the unknown events of the day or face our vulnerability as we sleep. If we do these mindlessly they are merely habits (such as when basketball star Michael Jordan sticks out his tongue as he drives to the basket) but if, as in the case of Wade Boggs, we do them on purpose at preordained moments, they fit our definition of rituals. In most cases, however, we participate in ritual activities with others. Rituals tend to be communal activities by their nature. It is when rituals are public in nature and known and participated in by large numbers of people that we include them in the house of popular culture.

When we hear the term public ritual, probably the first things that pop into most of our heads are religious ceremonies of various types. "Ritual" is associated with worship in churches, synagogues, mosques or temples. The reasons for religious worship vary widely, of course, depending on the religion and the specific ceremony. Praise of the deity being worshipped is one common component. Another common element is the comfort and security participating in the ritual provides the worshipers. We exist in a world where, no matter how much we plan out our lives, we have minimal control over what happens to us. Fate rules the roost. At any moment we may have an accident or catch a virus that will annihilate us. Or we may win a lottery and be rich. Good or bad happens to us all the time and these things are out of our control. (The fact that violence in the United States is the single biggest cause of adolescent death is a scary confirmation of this point.) Religious worship provides relief from the anxieties caused by our vulnerable state of existence in three ways: it allows us to re-express our beliefs in a relationship between humans and the deity in which humans are important in the universe. It gives us access to divine power by providing a way for us to communicate directly with our deity. This access provides us with a feeling of control over our fate. And, third, the fact that we know the structure of the repeated ritual and we participate in the known ceremony gives us the security of the known and the comfort of participating in a predictable event.

Secular (non-religious) popular rituals provide some of the same emotional needs as religious rituals, specifically a parallel comfort and security of participating in an elaborately repeated set of actions. Religious rituals are more profound than secular rituals; after all, they reflect our beliefs about not just our nation or ourselves, but the deepest core of reality itself. Nevertheless, secular rituals do provide us with a sense of inner well-being which, if less profound than provided by religious rituals, is still substantive and important. In order to provide us with this well-being, most secular popular rituals share several key elements.

1) Popular rituals use elements from the other rooms in the house of popular culture. Quarterbacks are heroes in football games. Clowns are stereotypes in circuses. Caps and gowns are icons in graduation ceremonies. The material objects in the lower rooms of the house are

all employed in the ritual precisely because they are, as popular items, already known to us.

2) Popular rituals are formulaic. Like the popular arts described in the next section of this book, the heart of the meaning of popular rituals is their repetitiousness. As fans of baseball, for example, we may enjoy discussing the minute unique details of an individual game. But as students of popular culture we mainly study these overall structures of the game because we know that it is the repeatable aspects of baseball or any other popular ritual that provide us with the comfort and satisfaction of being part of the familiar and predictable.

3) Popular rituals are usually performed in special places. Anthropologists speak of "sacred" and "profane" spaces. Profane space is where our normal living activities take place. Sacred space, the place of popular and religious rituals, are places meant to take us away from day-to-day activities and to provide an atmosphere to get the maximum value from the ceremony. The sacred space itself becomes known and therefore part of what comforts us. Athletic stadiums are sacred spaces if we use the term in this context. Sometimes we turn profane space into sacred space for special ritual activity. We decorate for high school proms or we hang crepe paper to celebrate someone's birthday. At rock concerts, the space is made special by the colored effects and mainly by turning up the volume to an extraordinary level. All of these places allow us to escape for a short period of time the chaos of our everyday lives, to go to a place where we experience the pleasure of ordered familiarity. Added emphasis on this escapist element of popular rituals is provided by a majority of the popular rituals themselves, which are intentionally entertaining in nature.

4) Popular rituals verify popular beliefs and values. They are therefore, like all the other elements in the house, part of the popular culture funhouse mirror. Rodeos, for example, celebrate the triumph of European Americans over the untamed Western frontier just as do Western formula stories as described later by Thomas Schatz. Circuses are wonderful, glossy fun and part of that fun is confirming for us our belief that humans are at the pinnacle of nature. Lion tamers control gigantic killer beasts and trapeze flyers conquer height and distance. Beauty pageants (many argue this is unfortunate) celebrate our beliefs in stereotypes of feminine beauty. The sending of greeting cards, a very common ritual in America, sometimes verifies the myth of romantic love (especially on the ritualistic Valentine's Day) or at the least our value in human community spread over great distances. Because popular rituals, like the other elements of popular culture, reflect mostly beliefs and values we already have, this becomes another way in which the ritual gives us the comfort of the familiar. Thus once again in our survey of why and how to study popular culture, piecing through the surface

elements of popular rituals to discover their hidden meanings becomes the key process in studying them.

Acting Up, Acting Out and Just Watching: Six Types of Popular Rituals

The following divisions of popular rituals into six distinct types hopefully will be a handy way for you to discover functions and meanings inside them. However, you should understand that these divisions are mainly for purposes of study. In the real world such clear divisions among popular rituals do not exist. Most specific rituals contain elements of more than one general type of ritual. This will be seen in the next part of this introduction in our discussion of Christmas. In the meantime, here are six categories of popular rituals, each with their own ways of giving us the security of the known.

1) *Rites of passage.* We understandably feel insecure when we pass from one important stage of our lives to another. Going from childhood through puberty, from being single to being married, from employment to retirement and from life to death can be tough on us and on those around us. Rites of passage are rituals whose main purpose is to help us and those we know accept our changed stage of life. For this reason these rites involve both the central participant(s) and witnesses. Most religious and ethnic groups recognize the importance of this type of ritual and have formal ceremonies marking each stage of life. To celebrate puberty, for example, many Christian denominations have confirmation; Jews initiate thirteen-year-old boys into adulthood through the *bar mitzvah* ceremony; Mexican Americans use the lovely *quinceanera* rite to usher fifteen-year-old girls into their womanhood. Secular popular coming-of-age rituals include the senior prom and graduation, the ritual activities surrounding getting a driver's license (lessons, the test, the first time out alone with the family car, etc.), and, in some peer groups, initiating friends into drinking beer.

Usually, rites of passage have three distinct stages: the threshold stage (anthropologists refer to this as the liminal stage and the initiates as liminals) before the actual ceremony; the transition stage which includes the most formal part of the ritual; and the celebration stage in which the community joyfully celebrates the initiate's entrance into his or her new stage of life. Weddings provide a clear instance of this threefold process. The high point of the endlessly detailed threshold phase are the bridal shower and bachelor party rituals. The emphasis in bridal showers, according to folklorist Christopher Geist, is on practical gifts, domestic games and pleasant conversation about topics that interest the exclusively women guests. Sexual jokes, especially jokes about male sexuality, are also quite common and help the bride-to-be be accepted into her upcoming role as a fully sexual adult.

Bachelor parties are much rawer fun. There is much drinking, plenty of sexual humor, probably about the bride, and possibly other sexual activity such as stag movies or strippers, demeaning comments about the end of the groom's freedom and intentionally impractical, gag gifts. The purpose of the party is obviously to preserve the groom's essentially male identity. Each rite is sexist in defining the upcoming public role of the initiates in terms of traditional stereotypes. The transition stage of weddings is obviously the wedding ceremony itself. The celebration stage is mainly the reception in which the community welcomes the new stage of life of the married couple with food, drink and dancing. Also part of this stage is the honeymoon, which includes the bride and groom appearing as a married couple in a new public place. It is interesting to note that a celebration stage occurs in a rite of passage as sad as a funeral. After the funeral itself, the friends and neighbors of the family of the deceased gather at the family home for food, drink and words of consolation. Thus, the community accepts the family back into the community without the deceased member.

2) *Rites of Unity*. There is an inevitable tension between individuals and the groups they join. Individuals have their own personal desires while groups demand that we squelch our personal wishes for the greater good of the group. Hence, almost all formal groups, and many informal ones have ceremonies celebrating the unity and value of each group. Some rites such as military basic training, and fraternity and sorority initiations (which all are also rites of passage) even build humiliation of individuals into their rites of unity to insure the preservation of group loyalty. Rites of unity thus preserve group unity against the possible chaos of individual self-interest. These are probably the most common popular rituals. They include everything from Boy Scout troop meetings to professional sports, from community festivals to high school band candy sales. Dating is also a notable popular rite of unity. In a prescribed set of activities that include talking, touching and selecting other popular rituals to attend, each of the pair decides if and how they may want to be unified with their partner.

3) *Rites of Season*. The change from one part of the year to another reminds us that we have little control over our environment. Consequently, seasonal change is a cause of anxiety and fear for the future. For this reason, ceremonies which publicly celebrate the change of seasons have evolved over long periods. These public celebrations ease our fears and allow us to begin the new season with confidence. The secular aspects of Easter, for example, help us move from the inactivity of winter to the more energetic lifestyle of spring. Easter brings us Easter baskets and the Easter bunny. Both the decorated eggs and

the bunny itself are fertility symbols. These Easter icons herald the rebirth of life that comes with spring. Other icons like Easter lilies and new clothes also symbolize rebirth. Other popular rites of season in America are Halloween, Christmas, Labor Day, Ground-hog Day and May Day.

4) *Rites of Reversal.* Society continually tell us what to do. Obey your teachers; hold down the noise; keep off the grass; don't park in handicapped zones. The list of dos and don'ts seems continuous and endless. Sometimes don't you want to toss all the rules overboard and just run wild? Most people need to do this once in a while. Most cultures seem to understand the urge of people to act nuts occasionally. And they recognize that this urge is a potential threat to public stability. The culture therefore sets aside certain times and places and allows certain normally forbidden activities to take place. In this way, the culture maintains a semblance of control over this natural urge of its individual members and once the rather harmless fun is over, the members, their anti-social energies exhausted, can go back to behaving themselves again.

Rites of reversal are present in most cultures and some can be traced back hundreds of years. Perhaps the most famous European rite of reversal was the medieval Feast of Fools (featured in Victory Hugo's novel *The Hunchback of Notre Dame*) where commoners were allowed to publicly mock bishops and priests, local members of the aristocracy and even royalty. Normally such activities would have resulted in prison and, possibly, torture. Some current rites of reversal popular in the United States include New Year's Eve (drunken disorder), Mardi Gras (costumed revelers running amuck in the streets of New Orleans), demolition derbies (intentionally wrecking cars instead of driving carefully) and, of course, our feast of fools, April Fool's Day, when it is permissible—even good—to pull nasty stunts on friends and colleagues, no matter what their social status.

The key to studying rites of reversal is to analyze exactly what is being reversed. Since rites of reversal lampoon what is normally a positive element in society, to understand in depth the source of the reversal is to focus in on shared popular values.

5) *Rites of Displacement.* There are certain times when we may feel that certain cherished beliefs, myths and values are threatened by sociocultural forces over which we have no control. During such times our fears of losing our values and beliefs are displaced by certain rituals which serve to reinforce our traditional moral and intellectual perspectives, thereby suggesting to us that we have nothing to fear. Rites of displacement are never this exclusively. They are normally other types of rituals which become rites of displacement in times of special stress. Moviegoing during the Depression 1930s, for example, served such a purpose. Normally moviegoing is a rite of spectacle, or if it is part of a date, a rite of unity. During the Depression, however, the destitute

could pay fifteen cents and sit in a theater to see glamorous people leading thrilling lives and living happily ever after. In Woody Allen's movie about how this rite does its therapeutic work, *The Purple Rose of Cairo* (1985), Mia Farrow plays a 1930s wife of a brutish, unemployed laborer who gambles away Mia's meager salary and beats her. She finds her only refuge in daily moviegoing. The ritual is so essential to her that one day she sees the characters on the screen come to actual life. Other rites of displacement are patriotic rallies during wartime. Such nationalistic activities are normally simple rites of national unity. In wartime patriotic rallies take on the additional burden of showing us that our way of life will indeed be preserved and that the enemy will not destroy what we believe in and value.

6) *Rites of Spectacle.* Circuses, parades, automobile thrill shows, fair midways, ice shows, professional wrestling, fashion shows, burlesque, the World Series and the Super Bowl. What all of these rituals have in common is that most of those attending are passive spectators rather than participants (imagine the horrors if everyone jumped into a car at an auto thrill show) and they do obviously fit the other five of popular rituals. Their main appeal on surface is also entertainment. When we attend or watch them on television we are dazzled by thrills, chills and in the case of wrestling, gigantic fat guys in skimpy trunks. Simple diversion seems to be their main purpose. But don't be fooled. These spectacles are enjoyed by millions. Part of the fun of these rituals is, as with other popular rituals, at a deeper level than their surface glitz; they powerfully reinforce cultural beliefs and values. Those thrill shows, for example, are related to the myth of technology as savior. Even professional wrestling informs us about our beliefs in certain stereotypes, as they validate our faith in American justice. Some rites of spectacle are related to the other five types of rituals. We can see this in parades which are sometimes community rites of unity. For the most part, however, we are better off not trying to force these rituals into fitting the patterns of the other five. Study these in and of themselves.

Taken together, these six types of popular rituals provide us with an affirmative personal identity within the boundaries of our culture. They give us the security of a repeated set of physical actions and they tell us over and over again that what we believe is right and good. The ancients so instinctively believed in the power of rituals that they said even the stars and the planets danced. It is little wonder, then, that popular rituals play such a continuous role in the lives of all of us.

The celebration of Christmas is most obviously a Christian ritual celebrating the birth of the Redeemer. Nobody is sure just when Jesus was born, however. Biblical scholars disagree on dates between January and May. Practically no one argues for December. Most scholars agree that December 25 was chosen so that an all-important Christian birth could replace the pre-Christian Roman birthday of the sun which by the Julian calendar fell on December 25, also the date of the winter solstice. Christmas in a more secular sense may be seen, then, as a winter solstice ritual that has parallels in numerous other religions and cultures. It is from this perspective that we will briefly examine it here.

The main icon used in the Christmas ritual is light. Participants put lights on their Christmas trees and decorate the outside of their homes with lights. Many put lights in the windows of their houses and candles are usually burned during meals. These lights are appropriate as icons because Christmas is mainly a rite of season that in the midst of the dead of winter celebrates the human hope for the renewal of life in the return of the light. The winter solstice is the shortest day of the year. In the Gregorian calendar, December 25 is about the first day it becomes noticeable that days are getting longer again. The light is returning and revelers celebrate its return by putting a couple of more strings of lights on their trees. The bringing in of tree boughs and the Christmas tree itself is also symbolic of the renewal of the life-force in the dead of winter. Evergreens are living things and life is given to houses where they are used as decorations.

Christmas is also an important family rite of unity. Millions of people travel long distances to be with their families during this holiday when they wouldn't conceive of making such a trip at any other time of the year. The home itself is the sacred space for the family ritual with its bright decorations. The ceremonial high point of the rite of unity is Christmas dinner (note how often food and drink play a part in rites of unity), where the serving year after year of almost all the same types of foods makes each member of the family feel at home and secure.

Upon occasion, Christmas incorporates the other ritual types as well. A rite of passage may occur, for example, when a child is allowed for the first time to pass out the gifts, suggesting he or she has reached a new level of responsibility. Rites of reversal occasionally take place at office Christmas parties where too many cups of holiday cheer may break down in embarrassing ways the normal distance between managers and their underlings. A small rite of displacement happens when food baskets are distributed to the needy. This lessens fears about poverty and creates in the givers the warm confidence that in America people have enough to eat. Finally, if we extend the celebration of Christmas to its traditional twelve days, we can include a ritual of spectacle—viewing the Rose Bowl parade on New Year's day. The floats each with their thousands of live flowers are yet another reminder of our faith of the return of life from winter's deathly darkness.

Besides valuing the return of the light, Christmas reaffirms other important American values and beliefs. The multi-national origins of Christmas icons, for example, express our belief in America as a land of opportunity for all. Manger scenes come from Italy. The Christmas tree originated in Germany. The customs of hanging Christmas stockings and hanging mistletoe come from England. Poinsettia plants originated in Central America and Mexico. And Saint Nicholas, the original model for the jolly old elf himself originated in the City of Myra in Asia Minor. Another popular belief confirmed by the Christmas ritual is the value of being a good neighbor. Writing and mailing all those Christmas cards shows that you care about others. Receiving cards gives the receiver the comfort of knowing that others care about the receiver. A third belief reflected in the Christmas ritual is the belief in the myth of material consumption. Holiday shopping is a national passion. While giving presents may be a sign of our generosity, the often desperate process of looking for gifts and buying them reflects our belief that buying goods is a sign of our worth as human beings. So tied is Christmas with this myth that one half the consumer goods sold in the United States are purchased between Thanksgiving and Christmas Eve.

Icons are the most visible of the tools of studying popular culture, but stereotypes and heroes also make an appearance. Part of the shopping desperation many people experience comes from a longing to live up to the stereotype of the good parent. And the stereotype of the child as a sweet innocent is never stronger than it is at Christmas. The main secular hero of the season is undoubtedly Santa Claus. Santa, with his tubby belly and his bright red suit, comes out of the dead zone of the North Pole as a vibrant sign of robust life. In the best democratic spirit he gives presents to every good child. And his sack never is empty. Like America, Santa is endlessly abundant. Best of all, the heroic self is a perfect model of the virtue of generosity. Santa gives freely, with no expectation of getting anything in return. Santa is the perfect model for all the service organizations in America dedicated to helping others.

Overall, the secular elements of the ritual of Christmas provide a rich and varied series of enjoyable experiences with family members and friends. Sometimes the pace of these experiences causes us much stress, but that is hardly the fault of the ritual itself. Below the surface, the varied aspects of Christmas reflect a surprisingly broad variety of traditional American beliefs and values.

Getting it Rite:
How to Study Popular Rituals

You probably have noticed by now that the key to studying the artifacts of popular culture is asking the right questions. The same is true for studying popular rituals. Asking and answering the right questions will help us unlock the deeper meanings of repeated sets of actions. Unfortunately, because rituals utilize most of the other tools of popular culture, the list of questions that need to be asked about popular rituals is longer than the questions we have so far asked about the other tools. For each different ritual, some questions will suggest more meaning than others. You should probably ask all of the following questions and then concentrate on those that produce interesting answers.

I. *General Questions About the Overall Ritual*

A. *Who* enjoys and participates in this ritual? (This will tell you who the ritual appeals to. Further study can then be directed toward *why* the ritual is satisfying to this specific group of people.)

1. Ethnic groups?
2. Male or female?
3. Social or taste level?
4. Economic level?
5. Age levels?

B. What *type* of popular ritual are you examining? (It is a good idea to settle this question right at the beginning of your examination of the ritual but sometimes it cannot be answered until you've answered some of the other questions first.)

When you answer this question, you usually partially answer the question of what is the *purpose* of the ritual.

C. What is the *history* of the ritual? (Often the hardest part of the study of a ritual. The information is sometimes difficult to find and sometimes the history turns out to be of only minor significance.)

1. When did the ritual begin?
2. When was it most popular?
3. How and in what ways and when did the ritual change in any significant way?

II. *Questions About the Specific Elements of the Ritual*

A. Descriptive questions.

1. Where does the ritual occur? (room, town, park, etc.)
2. What special preparations are made for the ritual ahead of time, if any?
3. Is there a special time for the ritual to be held? A special day?
4. Is there a leader in the ritual? If so, how is that leadership made visible?

5. Do certain participants in the ritual have certain specific roles? (bringing cakes, giving away the bride, making the first toast, tossing out the first ball, etc.)

6. Is the ritual recorded? (photos, newspaper announcements, ads, etc.)

7. Exactly what happens during each of the three important parts of most rituals?

a. Preparation
b. Core ceremony (the heart of the ritual)
c. Release (post-ceremony activities)

8. What icons are part of the ritual?

a. Special clothing or uniforms
b. Special food or drink
c. Special "tools" (hockey sticks, dishes, etc.)
d. Pure icons (rings, flowers, etc.)

9. Why did the observers attend the ritual? Social obligation? Patriotism? Fun? (This may be very hard to determine.)

B. Analysis Questions

1. What are the *symbolic* implications of the materials studied in the descriptive questions?

a. Symbolic meaning of the *objects* (icons) used in the ritual?
b. Symbolic meaning of the *actions* within the ritual?
c. Symbolic meaning of the *active participants* in the ritual?

2. In what ways are the celebration of the ritual similar or different from other rituals of the same general type?

3. Are any elements of the ritual *analogous* or traceable to other past or present sacred or secular rituals? (Examples: Is putting on a football uniform like a knight putting on his armor? Does the youthful ritual of sharing a pizza have anything important in common with the taking of communion in Christian worship ceremonies?)

Although analogies can be enlightening, remember that they do not constitute proof of an actual relationship.

4. Is there any evidence to suggest the effects the ritual had on the community? If so, what? What were the effects?

III. *Based on all the conclusions gathered from the above questions, what beliefs and values of the participants in and/or observers of the ritual are suggested by the ritual you are studying?*

Family Reunion

Jean Fields

Rituals (or rites) of unity unite us at all levels of group identity. Fourth of July fireworks, all about 10:00 PM on the Fourth, unite millions of us in a national celebration of our place within a unique nation. Homecomings at high schools and colleges are supposed to unite generations of students in a renewal of loyalty to the school. On a more personal and intimate level than these two large-scale rituals are the large number of ritual ceremonies that validate a person's family life and the status of each person's place with the family structure. On a basic level, the nightly family dinner brings together the diverse members of the household for a few minutes, as they freely share food and drink, and the individual events experienced by each family member are integrated into the general family unit. When this ritual is working correctly, we leave the dinner table with our stomachs comfortably full and our psyches comfortably secure. Once again, we know we have a place at the table and we know what that place is.

Jean Fields' description and meditation on a recent family reunion she attended in the mountains of West Virginia shows us a ritual for extended families. Family reunions are a popular summertime ritual in the United States. Families from diverse ethnic backgrounds with members from almost every economic class perform this ritual at least every few years. The specifics of these outdoor celebrations of extended family unity vary with each family and tend to be passed on from generation to generation. They are therefore folk culture, for the most part. So many families have reunions, however, that the general concept of them and the numbers of people who participate in them places them within the category of popular culture.

Reprinted with permission from *The Popular Culture Reader*, 3rd Edition, Christopher Geist and Jack Nachbar, eds. Bowling Green, OH: Bowling Green State University Popular Press, 1983.

Most of us, of course, are aware of the delicate nature of family rituals. Too often they have the opposite effect of their intended purposes of providing the security of unifying us with other members of our families. Family vacations, for example, sometimes produce only car sickness, vicious fights that proceed mainly from boredom, and tired, screaming parents. Family dinners may on any particular evening degenerate into arguments, insults and punishments. Fields' very personal reminiscence, however, reminds us that family rituals, like other rites of unity, actually do provide us with crucial psychic security when they work as they are supposed to. Outsiders are welcomed back, food is prepared together and shared, and stories and traditions are passed on from the old to the young. At its best, a family ritual truly can be a "circle of love."

Our family Bible contains a note which reads: "June 10 1872 Fields and Barefoot reunion, 77 came." We still have reunions every other year on the "home" farm at the confluence of Kelly's Creek and the Kanawha River. We are Appalachians who have lived in the mountains of West Virginia since the 18th century. History books state that bands of Scotch and Irish landed in Virginia to find the Piedmont occupied and so settled at the foot of the Appalachian Mountains. But by a treaty with the Indians, the British agreed to pull all settlers back to the Piedmont by 1728. Instead the farmers fled to the nearly inaccessible mountains. When immigration began again, it flowed south to the rich lands of Kentucky and Tennessee and north to Ohio and Pennsylvania, leaving the mountain people isolated and forgotten. The differences of the mountain people result from this historical fact. We are clannish; we have a sense of belonging to a particular place. Because of our isolation, many of the frontier values and practices survive to this day. My family is no exception.

Our reunion is ritualized around preparing, serving and eating "vittles" with blood kin. Food is still a sign of hospitality and affection in the mountains. To offer food means: "Welcome, you are my friend; we will sit down together and share whatever we have with you." The variety and abundance of traditional food, traditionally prepared and eaten by the family is the equivalent of a kinship rite filled with affection and uncritical acceptance. In addition, it initiates the younger members into the history of the family.

The preparation of the food is very important. For example, the oldest men and the youngest children always prepare the smoked meat together. After World War I my great-grandfather cleaned out six steel drums, cut hinged doors near the bottom and bored holes in the lids. These are now rolled out. The children bring arm-loads of hickory branches while the old men show them how to cut them into shavings and start smoldering fires in the bottom of the drums. Next, wires are suspended from the lids and the children are shown how to attach hams and turkeys to them. Now the lids are replaced and soon the field is redolent with hickory smoke and the smell of meat. At night around a campfire, the old men tell the children stories of the coal mines, hunting and fishing trips, and of course ghost stories. I stood in the dark and listened to the familiar story of the headless dog who haunted his cruel master. My small niece, shivering, crawled into my lap, just as I had crawled, delightfully frightened, into my mother's lap as a child. That made me very happy. Suddenly, we were not so different after all, despite the differences in our ages. We both loved feeding the fires with hickory shavings, smelling the meat, anticipating how good it would taste, and we both loved the same ghost story.

Catfish are an important food at the reunion and they are caught fresh from the river. Since all the children want to help with the fishing, we make them draw straws. This year two seven-year-old inexperienced fishermen and two nine-year-old experienced fishermen won. Three adults accompanied them. We started at dusk, a Coleman lantern tied to the stern and the end of the trotline secured to a stout maple. A trotline is a heavy fishing line approximately one hundred feet long, with hooks suspended on lines every foot. The end of the line is tied to a heavy rock which acts as an anchor. Slowly the boat is rowed directly across the river, while the nine-year-olds put a piece of salt pork on each hook and drop it into the river. At the end of the line, the rock is tossed overboard, and everyone returns to shore and the campfire of the meat-smokers. The children were excited (no one bothers to sleep much at the reunion), and couldn't wait to run the line for the first time. They listened bugeyed as we told them the same tales we had been told about gigantic catfish that wouldn't fit in a bathtub, the number and length of those caught in past years. They listened just as I had listened as a child, as my parents and their parents before them had listened. At 3 a.m. we ran the line the first time. They were white faced, incoherent with excitement. As the bluecats began to break the surface, shouts of "Look how big he is," and "Don't let him hook you with his whiskers," rang across the water. In the dark it could have been 1872 or 1912 or....

The high point of the reunion for me comes at the beginning of the dinner. Long tables have already been covered with sheets and spread with food. Then the oldest man in the clan moves to the front. In one hand he holds a Bible and in the other arm he holds the youngest baby. Great uncle John Fields was ninety-four years old and he held his great-great-grandchild Joseph as he gave the blessing. He spoke simply and eloquently, with a strong hill accent asking no favors, simply thanking the Lord. I am not a religious person nor have I much interest in ancestors; when a West Virginian speaks of ancestors he is usually referring to

Game Day U.S.A

The South - Willie Morris
The Midwest - Frank Conroy
The West - Richard Hoffer

Vince Lombard: never really thought about winning; his trip was not losing.
Hunter S. Thompson

According to the 1991 The Whole Pop Catalogue *gunfighter Bat Masterson called it "a brutal and savage slugging match between two reckless opposing crowds"; bare-knuckle heavyweight champ John L. Sullivan witnessed the carnage that marked the sport in the 1909 college season (27 players killed and hundreds of others seriously injured) and branded it "murder"; and even today statistics reveal that "more women report physical abuse from spouses and boyfriends during the Super Bowl than at any other time of the year." The uniquely American game of football is perhaps most "American" in the way in which it reflects the violence which is such a long-standing, defining element of the national character, but the widespread and intense popularity of the sport is remarkable nonetheless. There are very few ritualistic spectacles so broad based—so unifying—in their appeal as to be able to produce the unforgettable image which marked one* Monday Night Football *contest when Ronald Reagan looped a long arm around John Lennon in the broadcast booth and traded pigskin enthusiasms which transcended their generational, political and cultural differences. Football brings together what politics, age and geography may divide; cheering individuals unite in a "human wave" which surges round a stadium with such force that it is felt in the living rooms of those watching at home regardless of whether the house is California Ranch or New England Colonial or Southern Mansion.*

Reprinted by permission from the authors, from *Game Day U.S.A.* Charlottesville, VA: Eastman Kodak and Thommason Grant, Inc., 1990.

The authors of the following essays share an enthusiasm and love for the sport of football and all of them emphasize the game's unifying character—the way in which the sport makes each of them feel a part of something larger and grander than their individual lives and petty private concerns. Like most popular rituals, football is a complex web which ties together many of the elements of popular culture into a series of symbolic actions and events: heroes (coaches and players), icons (pennants and mascots), important associated rituals (pep rallies and marching bands at half time), and clearly defined stereotypes which provide roles for everyone ("fans" and "cheerleaders"). All work together to produce that special combination of "uninhibited spontaneity" and careful orchestration which lies at the heart of popular ritual in mass society

While the three authors share the central ritualistic experience which defines the unifying spectacle of football, we miss an important point of these essays if we focus exclusively upon the elements which they have in common. The surface structure of the ritual is remarkably similar in all areas of the country—the same rules of the game apply, bands march at all half time ceremonies, coaches rage at referees and fans at both—but the meaning *being expressed through this structure varies significantly indeed. Long-lasting and vital popular rituals must be sufficiently flexible to adapt themselves to the peculiar needs and wants of a wide range of participating groups. (All weddings have certain meanings in common, for example, but there remains a vast difference among ceremonies in different classes, regions, religions, ages and races.) The authors here seem to suggest that football is more varied in its ritualistic meaning than the striking similarity of its rules and ceremonies suggests.*

The deeper lesson of these essays, then, is that the student of popular culture always needs to look beneath the surface of a popular ritual (or of any element of his subject matter) in order to understand its significance and meaning. If we stop at the surface level of facts and appearances then we will be as lost as the great Midwestern coaches "Woody and Bo," who journeyed to California and the Rose Bowl year after year and were almost always defeated because they could not recognize that while the rules were the same, the ritual had changed.

The South

This is a tale not of one Game Day but two, because each was deeply enmeshed in the other.

It begins with the Ole Miss-Vanderbilt game of October 28, 1989, in Oxford, Mississippi. It was Ole Miss Homecoming, one of those

Southern autumn days touched with the airy bittersweet languor of the past and memory and childhood. . .and football.

Ole Miss is small by measure with other state universities, with 10,000 students—roughly the same population as the town—who are suffused with the flamboyant élan of their contemporaries everywhere. In moments there is a palpable, affecting sophistication to its stunningly beautiful campus in the rolling rural woodlands of the South.

On this homecoming day, one might recall Thomas Wolfe's only slightly fictional Pulpit Hill, patterned after the Chapel Hill of many years ago in *Look Homeward Angel*: "There was still a good flavor of the wilderness about the place—one felt its remoteness, its isolated charm. It seemed to Eugene like a provincial outpost of great Rome: the wilderness crept up to it like a beast."

Two hours before the kickoff, the young men of the Ole Miss team, led by coach Billy "Dog" Brewer, walked single file through the Grove, a huge old verdant circle only a stone's throw from the stadium, as avid tailgaters applauded. From the distance the band played "From Dixie with Love," a blended rendition of "Dixie" and "The Battle Hymn of the Republic." As the mighty sounds wafted across this wooded terrain, little girls in the school's Harvard red and Yale blue tossed and leapt, and miniature quarterbacks in replica jerseys threw footballs to incipient Rebel wide receivers. The adults were drinking, and everywhere was the ineffable cachet of fried chicken and barbecue. On one lengthy table draped with a vintage Delta tablecloth were eight-branch silver candelabra with red tapers and mounds of food on matching silver trays. On another was a substantial arrangement of flowers flowing out of an Ole Miss football helmet—lacy white fragile baby's breath and red carnations.

The stadium itself, surrounded by young magnolias, was cozy and contained, and much removed from the mega-stadiums of the SEC behemoths Alabama, Tennessee, Georgia, LSU and Florida. Its grassy turf had seen Bruiser Kinnard, Charlie Conerly, Barney Pool, Jake Gibbs and Squirrel Griffin, Gene Hickerson, Archie Manning and Gentle Ben Williams.

There were 34,500 in attendance on this afternoon, including a smattering of Vandy partisans down from Tennessee in their bright gold colors matching the golden patina of this day. The *New York Times* would report of what was to follow: "The game blends into the dense history of a school that has often played out the richest and darkest passions of the region."

There is a special flavor, a texture, to Deep Southern collegiate football, and this was best expressed years ago by Marino Casem, the long-time coach at Alcorn University:

In the East college football is a cultural exercise. On the West Coast it is a tourist attraction.

In the Midwest it is cannibalism. But in the Deep South it is religion, and Saturday is the holy day.

There was indeed a religiosity to this mingling crowd in the moments before game time. In the south end zone a loyalist group perennially regarded as The Rowdies, a perfervid cadre consisting of professors, bartenders, writers and reprobates, shouted epithets at the visitors down from their cerebral Nashville halls: "Down with the Eggheads! Stomp the Existentialists!" A Yankee reporter, surveying this end zone phalanx, asked one of its number, Dean Faulkner Wells, niece of the hometown bard, why she supported Ole Miss football. With a succinctness uncharacteristic of the Faulkner Breed, she replied: "Continuity."

The record of the Ole Miss team at this juncture was five wins, two losses. They were hobbled with injuries. At one point the entire starting defensive backfield was down, including football and academic all-America safety Todd Sandroni, who today was playing on one good leg. The Rebels' largest margin of victory had been seven points. They had upset Florida on the road by four while gaining only 128 offensive yards. They had defeated Georgia on a touchdown pass with 31 seconds to go in this stadium, and Tulane on another pass in New Orleans with four seconds remaining. It was a funny, gritty ball club, small and hurt in the mighty SEC, a ball club people could not help but love.

There was 6:57 left in the first quarter when it happened.

Vandy faced third and goal from the Ole Miss 12 in a scoreless game, Quarterback John Gromos faded for the pass. Brad Gaines, the 210-pound fullback, caught it on the two.

Roy Lee "Chucky" Mullins, 175-pound Ole Miss cornerback, suddenly raced across the field, leapt high, and tackled the receiver, forcing him to drop the football. The resounding thud could be heard for yards around. Cheers rolled across the stadium. But Mullins lay prone on the field, and when he did not move a fateful quiet descended.

"I couldn't get off the sideline." Ole Miss coach Dog Brewer would later recall. "In all the years I've been coaching, it's the first time I haven't gone on the field when there was a serious injury. I couldn't go. I thought the kid was dead. No matter how long I coach, I'll always remember how he came flying through the air and made that hit—the thud of it."

The silent throng watched as the trainers and doctors cut Mullins' face mask away and strapped him to a wooden board. It took more than 10 horrible minutes. They carried him to the opposite sidelines, and the ambulance slowly wound its way out of the stadium toward the hospital. The scene would not easily be obliterated.

The rest of the first half seemed bitter anticlimax. The flat, listless Ole Miss team fell behind 10-0. Chucky Mullins' injury likewise cast an ominous pall over the homecoming rituals of halftime, the Ole Miss beauties in evening dresses, the playing of the Alma Mater.

How to explain such human moments? Ole Miss came out in the third quarter on fire, then erupted in the fourth. Trailing 17-16. Ole Miss took over on its own 21 with 9:18 remaining. Halfback Tyrone Ashley carried twice for 13 yards, then quarterback John Darnell hit tight end Rick Gebbia of Long Island ("our own Yankee") for 49 yards to the Commodore 17. On the ensuing play, Ashley broke free for the winning touchdown with 7:18 left. The game ended 24-17.

In the locker room the Ole Miss players were choked up over their fallen teammate. There was no celebration.

Sometime in the second half Chucky Mullins had been flown to Memphis, 75 miles away. The small hospital in Oxford could do little but stabilize his condition. He lay now in neurosurgery intensive care in the Baptist Memorial Hospital.

He was paralyzed from the neck down. The injury was serious, with little likelihood that he would ever recover. The attending doctors would call it one of the most dramatic injuries they had ever seen, likening the impact that crushed his back to the crushing of an empty can. The vertebrae had exploded; there was nothing left. On the Monday after homecoming, four surgeons performed a three-hour operation using wire and a bone graft from Chucky's pelvis to fuse the shattered vertebrae. He would remain a quadraplegic.

The mood of the university, the town and the state in the following days was of grief and sadness. Ole Miss dedicated the rest of the season to him.

In 1987 Chucky Mullins, a 17-year-old from the tiny town of Russellville, in northeast Alabama, came to Ole Miss, one of many poor young blacks signed each year by the Rebels. When he was recruited and given an athletic scholarship, he did not have the money to get to Oxford. His mother had died when he was six, and his father not long after that. He was raised by a legal guardian, a young man who suffered from a debilitating lung disease. In his senior year in high school, Chucky was the football captain, and his team won the state championship. Both Auburn and Alabama considered him too small and slow, and he wanted to go to Ole Miss.

He was Dog Brewer's kind of athlete: "He was lanky, always clapping, having fun, what we call a 'glue' player, not that fast or big, but the kind that holds a team together. What you saw him wearing was damn near what he owned. But to see him, you'd think he was a millionaire."

Chucky's best friend on the Ole Miss was a white freshman named Trea Southerland. After Chucky's operation in Memphis two days after the Vandy game, he came out of the anesthesia whispering Southerland's name. "Chucky added a lot to other people's lives." Southerland said.

"and I know that if desire and character make a difference, he'll find a way to bear this."

A chance photograph before the Vanderbilt homecoming game had caught a pristine moment. Coach Brewer and Mullins are standing together in the north end zone, not far from where Chucky would soon be hurt, the coach's arm around number 38's waist as the two of them lead the team onto the field. It was a gesture of symbolic affinity: Brewer was also from a poor family and a broken home, attending Ole Miss in its glory days as a "step slow" ball player. "When you love the game, it has a hold on you." Dog says of Mullins, but it is an autobiographical confession too. "I kind of saw myself in him. The only way out for both of us was football."

Ole Miss was matched the next Saturday against the Bayou Bengals of LSU. For the first time since 1961, the tumultuous and historic rivalry would be played in Oxford.

Within hours of Chucky Mullins' injury a trust fund had been started for him. LSU collected donations at its Purple-Gold basketball game in Baton Rouge. The University of Delaware shut down a football practice an hour early for a prayer session. Calls from coaches—and the White House—came from all over America. Coach Bill Curry of Alabama collected donations from his players. "Statistics tell us," Curry said, "that football is a very safe game when you're talking about catastrophic injuries. Ankles? Knees? Fingers? No, it's not safe. But not one time in a billion do you see the kind of injury that happened to Chucky Mullins."

Mike Archer, the LSU coach, visited Chucky in the hospital Friday night before the Saturday game. "I can understand how this affected their team," he said "I almost broke down with tears when I visited with him. It hurts to see a strong, healthy kid like that, so young."

Shortly before the game, seven young white Ole Miss men in the final for "Colonel Reb," the campus' highest accolade, withdrew from the election and swung the honor to Mullins.

The LSU match would be one of the most dramatic moments in Ole Miss sports annals. The Rebel players wore number 38 on their helmets. The largest crowd in the history of the little stadium, 42,354, turned out for the contest. Hundreds of Ole Miss students volunteered to pass buckets during the game for the trust fund. More than $240,000 would be collected at this game, five times more than the goal.

Chucky Mullins was listening to the radio in the intensive care unit in Memphis. Just prior to the kickoff there was a prayer for his welfare.

The Vandy victory the previous Saturday had given 6-2 Ole Miss an opportunity at the SEC title and a chance at its first Sugar Bowl since 1970. Yet devastation struck the Rebels early, and it was obvious that they were taut with emotion—fumbles, incomplete passes, penalties. LSU quarterback Tom Hodson was magnificent, and the Tigers jumped to a swift 21-0 lead. The score was 35-10 late in the third period, and the LSU depth was showing.

Then, suddenly, as they had all year against adversity, the Rebels, outweighed and outmanned at nearly every position, crippled by injury and despair, came alive in the final quarter. Quarterback Darnell's formerly errant passes began to click, and slashing runs by sophomores Randy Baldwin and Tyrone Ashley left gaping holes in the Louisiana phalanx. The Rebel players were yelling to each other after each big play "This one's for Chucky! We're gonna do it!"

The score was now LSU 35. Ole Miss 30. The Rebels were driving from their own territory as the game ebbed away. A burnt orange sun was descending behind the Vaught-Hemingway Stadium, and the air was eerie with the early dark. The entire assemblage was on its feet, and the partisan fans were stomping in unison, filling the afternoon with the pandemonium of fealty.

Twenty-five seconds remained now, and the Rebels had first and 10 on the LSU 30. Quarterback Darrell, injured five plays before, limped back onto the field. An uncommon hush descended, and a member of the south End Zone Rowdies fell out of a lower row of the bleachers.

As the play unfolded, Darrell hobbled back into the pocket. The nimble wide receiver, Willie Green, streaked toward the south end zone, covered only by cornerback Jimmy Young, four inches shorter. It took only seconds. The ball was in flight now, suspended it seemed for the briefest eternity etched against the waning hour, as Willie Green leapt high, arms outraised in one quick pirouette of hope.

The pass came up two feet short: The Bayou Bengals defender, high in the air with Green, intercepted in the end zone, then fell lovingly to the turf, ball in breast.

If the Rebels had scored, they would have led 36-35 with 20 seconds left. Going for and making the two-point conversion, they would have achieved a symbolic 38, the number they wore on their helmets for their stricken teammate.

Yet life often does not work that way. A great sporting event indeed emulates life, its ecstasies and sorrows, its gallantries and failures, and its time running out, the time that runs out in Dixie autumn twilights for all of us who wish life to give us feeling and victory and hope against old mortality. The Bayou Bengals intercepted, twenty seconds left. Only the love remained, and the possibility.

The Midwest

The people who live here call it The Heartland—that agricultural region of the Midwest that includes Iowa, Nebraska, Kansas and vast stretches west of the Mississippi—and in many ways the name seems apt.

Certainly the national interest in sports can be seen here in its purest form, as an expression of regional pride, as a *celebration* of the power and beauty of youth. Not youth in the abstract, but in the actual sons and daughters of farmers, bank managers, teachers, combine operators, lawyers, real estate brokers, fertilizer salesman, auto mechanics, chiropractors and everybody else who lives here. Sports here are bound to family and community. They are not Roman rituals imposed from above to divert the populace. Their heady energy bubbles up from below as a distillation of the liveliness and vigor of the people themselves.

It is a journalistic truism to say that the most passionate fans are found in those communities with the most trouble—the once-great but now decaying and confused cities of New York, Detroit, Los Angeles—as people cling to whatever thread they can grasp of a social fabric that is coming apart. Perhaps that passion has a dark side. Football riots in England as an expression of despair, frustration and economic hopelessness. Fist fights and belligerent drunkenness at Yankee Stadium in a city torn by racism. Certainly it can have a dark side. But in The Heartland the fans seem truly to come together, to infect each other with their enthusiasm and hope, much as they might, in a very different way, in church. There doesn't seem to be a great deal of pain in the stands out there. Elation, disappointment, but all of it in scale somehow. All of it against the background of an enormous, open-ended, everybody-welcome public celebration. A party, in short. It's supposed to be fun, and it is.

Iowa City, a university town whose population increases 25 percent the day before a game and 50 percent on the day itself. Thousands of cars, pickup trucks, vans and Winnebagos converging from all directions on Kinnick Stadium. Route 90, Route 380, Route 6, and every country road bringing people in from all over the state. From 30 miles away. From 300 miles away. Eighteen hundred and seventy-three motel rooms on the Coraville strip! Welcome to the Home of the Hawkeyes! Go Hawks!

People show the colors, and the colors are yellow and black—the yellow of corn, perhaps, and the black of the deepest and richest topsoil on the face of the planet. Yellow and black banners and pennants, yellow and black jackets, sweatshirts, running suits, socks and sweaters, decals and bumper stickers. Yellow and black banners in the shop windows and restaurants all over town, with the logo of a hawk, whose fierce gaze suggests swiftness and single-mindedness. The hawk is a powerful symbol in this kind of open country, where on any given afternoon you might see one gliding high over the fields and gently rolling hills, imperious and free in the air, patrolling its vast domain. The hawk, and the eye of the hawk, which can spot a mouse from 500 yards.

Yellow and black are the colors of the eye of the hawk. Even the buses in Iowa City are yellow and black. The truck stop out by the interstate highway is called the Hawk-I. The whole town is decked out. Everybody gets into the act. This is us! the colors seem to say. Here we are, by God!

On game day the visitors are everywhere, Most people don't even bother to try to park near Kinnick, where the lots are bound to be full, or where you can pay an enterprising householder 10 bucks for a piece of his front yard. Paying 10 bucks to park rubs Iowans the wrong way, tantamount to lighting up a cigar with a flaming bill. (Actually, $10 goes a long way in Iowa. A case of Rhinelander, a perfectly good underadvertised beer imported from Wisconsin, sells at the Econo Foods for $6.48. It moves particularly well on football weekends.)

Vehicles cluster up at different places around lunchtime. A large group from Cedar Rapids is over in City Park taking advantage of the public barbecue pits, the benches and tables where they set out spreads of potato salad, corn dogs, pickled eggs, chips and homemade cakes and pies. People eat from paper plates and clean up after themselves. Ten or 12 families from Davenport traditionally gather in the university parking lot beside the river, tailgates down, the kids busy feeding the ducks. Farmers from North Johnson County join up in the old practice field near Manville Heights.

After lunch people lock up their cars and start drifting toward the stadium, converging from all points of the compass, ambling over the river on the bridges and footbridges (even the old railroad bridge), strolling along the streets and paths into the thickening crowd. Pre-game announcements from the PA system can be heard echoing in the crisp air. Band music floats like invisible smoke. A walk into emotion, because the closer you get to the field, the more charged the atmosphere.

By the time people get inside they are pumped. They look around at their fellow Iowans and a sense of well-being overcomes them. This is it! This is the day, the time and the place, and here we are together and powerful. Soon we will roar, and it will be strong enough to raise the hairs on the back of your hand. It will be deep enough to be heard a mile away, and it will arch over everything like a hawk in the sky.

In The Heartland some things remain relatively simple: the pleasures of coming together: the confirming power of common ritual; the affirmation of decency and fair play, of self-respect and hard work. It's all still here, tacit and modest most of the time, but truly celebrated on game day. The spirit of the people lifts every action, and every action lifts the people.

The West

When you grow up in Ohio, the idea of a football game played in full, unchecked sunshine beneath fluttering palms on New Year's Day is an act of faith. There is no possible reality to it, but conditioned by ritual, you believe it nonetheless. The Ohio wind whistles outside your door, perhaps piling drifts of snow against it in the growing darkness. And in the Rose Bowl, a shirt-sleeved crowd watches a football game beneath full unchecked sunshine. You make a resolution: That's where you'll go.

How many midwesterners have been thus converted? There is no telling, although the popular history is that the Rose Bowl activities, parade and game, were conceived as just the kind of extravagant flyer, a complicated land promotion, to draw shivering masses to Pasadena, a town that was itself a Midwest invention (the dominating Gamble family was of Cincinnati). How could the game work otherwise? And with TV taking the place of the postcard, the concept became even more convincing blue skies behind the San Gabriel mountains, the wealth of climate and scenery promising equal returns in opportunity and experience.

In the decade since I arrived from Ohio, I do not remember the Rose Bowl stinting in that illusion. It may have rained New Year's morning. Perhaps as recently as the day before, the San Gabriels were fouled by a cloud of pollutants. The traffic to and from was certainly nightmarish. But by game time, as some rightfully wary team from the Midwest began testing the stadium floor, the conditions of sunshine and clarity and order were inevitably restored. A pre-game show might reveal the fans sprawled on the grassy arroyo floor, framed by hillsides of bougainvillea. Back in Ohio, a young boy would lean forward in disbelief.

I cannot tell you who played that first game I attended a decade ago. What I remember is a terrific and violent shaking that reached me high in the press box. It was as if the 100,000 shirt-sleeved fans had suddenly begun pounding their feet the way high school kids will do on wooden bleachers. It was an earthquake, my first. A decade later an earthquake would visit a California game site with far more tragic results. But this one was considered strictly for its entertainment value, and it was my definite impression that the crowd was more thrilled than frightened by this pre-game show. (This impression was certainly validated sometime later when a nearby theme park incorporated the sensation into a ride.) A parade, a football game, an earthquake. A pretty good day all in all.

For a certain personality this type of experience—one attraction piled onto another—was more threatening than satisfying. I'm thinking of my fellow midwesterners, the ones who came to visit but would never stay. I guess I'm thinking of men like Woody and Bo, and the boys they molded, arriving reluctant but determined. The evidence is, they hated it. The Big Ten teams remain conservative, both in their football and in their lifestyle, and the flamboyance of the West was an affront. The West Coast teams passed wildly, for one thing. A UCLA coach who has been winning regularly with ordinary (that is, Big Ten style) offenses switched to a throwing game simply because the press and fans demanded more excitement for their entertainment dollar. More than that, there wasn't a pre-game event the West Coast boys wouldn't attend. Yet every year, the teams arriving generally on Christmas day, Bo or Woody would declaim these extravagances and announce a new and lower threshold of distractions. No Disneyland. No Beef Bowl. Or no press.

They generally lost anyway, their degree of futility given a comic edge by a coach's temper tantrum. Even when Woody punched a photographer, or Bo became especially vitriolic, it was possible to be sympathetic. What possible chance did they have in a land of earthquakes, bougainvillea and theme parks? In the West, hard work was not only not enough, it may have been irrelevant. Variety of experience was the point for all the pioneers here. For goodness sakes, a coach discarded a perfectly good offense because it bored the team's fans.

Do you really wonder why they hated it here? The Rose Bowl seemed to enforce every mid-westerner's worst stereotype of California. The next Rose Bowl game I attended was Michigan-USC. There were no natural disasters, except from Bo's point of view. Late in the game, on another gorgeous afternoon, Trojan tailback Charles White, who would later wither in Cleveland as a pro (this works both ways), scored the winning touchdown without he encumbrance of a football. Bo was properly apoplectic. The Trojan coach could barely stifle his amusement. It seemed like he scored, and illusion goes a long way in these parts. You can imagine the midwesterners returning home and explaining this to their neighbors: I tell you, it's a fantasy factory out there—even their football is staged for effect.

In those 10 years, of course, the Big Ten teams won a few games. Even Bo, whose career was otherwise exemplary except for postseason play, managed to avoid a shutout. But they were always outsiders, distrustful and resentful. They couldn't wait to go back to Ann Arbor or Columbus, where college football was the proper focus of a community, where there was no competition for the fan's imagination, where matters were exactly as they seemed, where hard work counted more than style.

Bo's last game as a head coach came, fittingly enough, in the Rose bowl. Even in Southern California there seemed to be some support for a Michigan victory, just because it conformed to Hollywood's standards for a happy ending: Gruff coach finally leaves game a winner, hoisted by his players above an unforgiving turf. You know how it came out, though. And if there's a scene that will stay with me, it's Bo violently protesting an official's call, getting tangled up with some wires and falling to the ground, his clipboard held high. The sheer fury of his protest allowed some dignity to an otherwise childish temper tantrum. But it seemed to me he went out pretty much the way he came in: He never did get it.

Leaving the Rose Bowl that day, I was amused to find it had begun to drizzle. The skies were darkening, and the traffic was typically terrible. Of course, the cameras had long since been turned off, and a picture postcard of sunny skies and fluttering palm trees remained unspoiled in many imaginations deep in the heartland. I thought for sure there had to be a boy back in Ohio, his head filled to bursting with this fantasy, resolving to come here, where anything but big Ten football was possible. Come on.

Halloween: Rite of Season, Rite of Passage

Jack Santino

Next to Christmas, with all those fancy packages and that long school vacation, probably the favorite day for kids is Halloween. Dressing up, gathering a bucket of candy, pulling pranks on neighbors you don't like—what could be better? Thanksgiving is only a dinner to a kid. And the treats in an Easter basket are meager compared with the bagful of booty from Halloween. In his discussion of the origins and traditions of the Halloween ritual in the following article, Jack Santino demonstrates that the satisfying pleasures of celebrating October 31 each year also include ritual elements that go beyond dressing up and getting candy.

Santino points out that Halloween rituals perform multiple functions and in fact fulfill most of the purposes of popular rituals described in the introduction to this section. They celebrate the harvest, initiate us into new stages of our lives, and unify us first with parents and then with friends. Halloween is also a rite of reversal. Doing "tricks" on October 31 allows us to exercise our urge for anti-social mischief while most of society is willing to look the other way during this single night each year. On a more primal level, the ancient origins of these ritual activities perhaps appeals to our unconscious past. When we go out into the night filled with strange creatures, we reconnect with ceremonies thousands of years old, ceremonies hundreds of years older than Islam and Christianity.

When you finish Santino's essay, test his generalizations against your own Halloween experiences. Has Halloween been as important in your life as he says it is for millions of people? Has it performed the ritual functions for you that he says it should? These types of questions should be asked of all the articles in this book. The ideas being put forth will never seem valid unless you can verify them to a certain degree in your own experience. Remembering your Halloween experiences is a good place to begin this process because, if Santino is right, Halloween is a night that has provided you with some of your most special memories.

When I was a child in the late 1950s growing up in Boston, Halloween was, without a doubt, one of the best days—or should I say nights?—of the year. Literally, it is the eve of All Saints' Day, November 1 in the calendar of the Roman Catholic Church. But to many revelers, young trick-or-treaters and adolescent pranksters when I was a kid, and even moreso today, there is little connection between Halloween on the evening of October 31 and the Christian feast the following day. Rather, the celebration is often thought to be secular, sometimes even described as pagan, in the sense of having religious overtones that have nothing to do with Christianity. Such a view is historically correct. Halloween embodies the persistence of ancient, pre-Christian and non-Christian beliefs and practices carried through to the eve of the 21st century, partially because the ancient festivals were Christianized.

The steadily increasing popularity of Halloween among many different groups of people of many different religious backgrounds points to the fact that the symbols we associate with that festival, such as pumpkins and jack-o-lanterns and games such as bobbing for apples, relate more to the time of year in which it is celebrated than to its position on the Christian calendar. Apples, nuts, pumpkins and corn are all in season in late October, and a great deal of Halloween symbolism involves these seasonal harvest items. In addition, a good deal of Halloween imagery, such as ghosts and skeletons, points to death and the supernatural. In order to understand how Halloween came to combine these two different strands of symbolism—organic images of harvest and supernatural images of death and the otherworld—and why we celebrate it the way we do today, we must first understand something of its history.

Although Halloween has changed a great deal over the centuries, a predecessor of our contemporary goblin gathering is found in an ancient Celtic festival called Samhain (pronounced "Sahwin"). The Celts were an ancient race who once lived in most areas of Europe. Eventually, however, they settled mainly in the British Isles and Northern France. The Celts are the ancestors of today's Irish, Scottish and Welsh peoples. Samhain was the New Year's Day of the Celts, which they celebrated on November 1. It was also a day of the dead, a time when it was believed that the souls of those who had died during the previous year were allowed access through the world of the living to the land of the dead, a time when spirits were believed to be wandering the earth. The festival also related to the season: by Samhain, the crops would be harvested and animals brought in from the distant fields.

It was both the first day of the new year and the first day of winter. As a point of transition in the annual calendar, a great many beliefs and rituals were associated with the day. It was believed that the gates that separated the worlds of the living and the dead, of this world and the world of spirits, were opened, the barriers between this world and the next were down, and the souls of those who had died during the year were allowed entry to the otherworld. Bonfires were lit on Samhain, some say to light the way for the spirits, others say to keep them away from peoples' homes. With the belief in the wandering spirits of the dead came the customs of preparing offerings of special foods as a goodwill bribe to the possibly threatening apparitions and of dressing as these spirits and as other wild creatures as a way of taking and enjoying these foods. These customs were associated with Samhain since before recorded history and were widely practiced in ancient Ireland, which was converted to Christianity (by St. Patrick, among others) in the early centuries of this millenium, a.d. 300-400. With conversion came a reinterpretation of the local religion and its calendrical celebrations, due in large part to a successful strategy of the Christian missionaries.

The Catholic church, when sending missionaries to convert native peoples, encouraged the redefinition of traditional customs into Christian terms and concepts. Thus, in a.d. 601 Pope Gregory I instructed his priests that if a group of people worshipped a tree, rather than cut the tree down, the priests were to leave it standing and consecrate it to Christ. The people should be instructed to gather regularly at the same site, Gregory wrote, but it should be explained to them that they were no longer worshipping the tree, but rather Christ in whose name the tree was consecrated. In such a way the early church adapted and accommodated the traditional religious beliefs and practices of those peoples it sought to convert to Christianity. Many of the festivals and holidays we enjoy throughout the year round today have resulted from this policy and were derived in some part from already existing festivals and celebrations. Halloween is no exception. November 1 was declared All Saints' Day; later, November 2 was proclaimed All Souls' Day.

The celebration of Samhain began on the sundown prior to November 1. A number of traditional beliefs and customs associated with it, most notably the belief in that night as the time of the wandering dead, the practice of leaving offerings of food and drink to masked and costumed revelers and the lighting of bonfires continued to be practiced by the Christianized Celts on October 31, known to Christendom as the Eve of All Saints, or the Eve of All Hallows, or Hallow Even. It is the glossing of the name "Hallow Even" that has given us the name Hallowe'en. November 1, All Saints' Day, is a day set aside on the church calendar to pay honor to all the saints who do not otherwise have a feast day reserved for them. In around a.d. 900, the church recognized that All Saints' Day had not supplanted the pre-Christian customs, so in an attempt to get closer to the original intent of the ancient Celtic festival, declared November 2 as All Souls' Day. This day is in recognition of the souls of all the faithful departed who have died but have not yet entered heaven. It is obviously much closer in spirit to the Celtic Samhain than is All Saints' Day.

Through its missionaries, the church also redefined the beliefs along with the rituals and practices of the peoples it converted. The spirits of Samhain, once thought to be wild and powerful, were now said to be something even worse: evil. The church taught that the gods and goddesses and other spiritual beings of traditional religions were deceptions caused by the devil. That is, the spirits that people had experienced were real, but they were not really gods or goddesses. The church taught that these spirits were manifestations of Satan, the Prince of Liars, who misled people to the worship of false idols. Threatening, frightening monsters joined the traditional imagery of Halloween. Thus, the customs associated with Hallow Eve included representations of ghosts and human skeletons—symbols of the dead—and also of the devil and other supposedly malevolent creatures, such as witches. In more recent times, dark, evil characters such as Dracula and Frankenstein's monster, and even more recently, Freddy Krueger and other mass murderers of the movies seem appropriate on Halloween.

Actually, the Celtic Samhain, while it provides a backdrop for the contemporary American Halloween, is by no means the only precursor of it. Trick-or-treating, as such, seems to have begun in this country in the 1930s, but there were many earlier customs involving begging worldwide that could have influenced the American custom. Shakespeare mentions children reciting rhymes in return for money on St. Valentine's Day, for instance, and adults wearing costumes perform a very old traditional play from house to house at Christmastime in Newfoundland. In Ireland young people go "hunting the wren" on the day after Christmas, St. Stephen's Day, also known as Boxing Day. This involves chanting a rhyme from door to door in return for a gift. Also, the practice of playing tricks on people, which we associate with Halloween today, was done in some parts of the United States in the past on the First of May and the Fourth of July. So the customs that we associate with Halloween are not the same everywhere you go, and they have not always been the same.

The observance of the Eve of All Hallows has flourished in the Christian era, despite the efforts of the Christian church to channel people's attention toward the holy day of All Saints' and All Souls' Days. All Hallows Eve was celebrated in some parts of the North American continent since the colonial days. By the middle of the twentieth century during my trick-or-treat years, Halloween had become largely a non-religious children's holiday in which tiny folks in scary outfits snapped up bagfuls of goodies in an orgy of socially sanctioned greed. More recently, however, Halloween has exploded in the United States. Adults have begun celebrating it in such great numbers that it can no longer

Pumpkins and a decorated Jack-O-Lantern. Ancient icons from Western Europe adapted for America's rite of season.

be considered the exclusive domain of children. If we are to judge by the masquerade parties, the decorated houses and yards, the campus festivities and the urban street celebrations all around the country, it appears that today Halloween is also very much an adult celebration. In this regard, it has come full circle. In each costumed adult of the 1990s, deep down there lurks the spirit of the pre-Christian Celts.

Halloween as Rite of Seasonal Passage

In celebrations the world over, we find contrasting images of death and life. Certain American holidays, such as Halloween, overtly feature symbols of death and of evil, such as skulls, skeletons, witches and devils. Others, such as Christmas, prominently feature images of birth, such as the nativity of Jesus. In general, holidays of spring, anywhere from February to May, are dominated by images of rebirth and renewal (eggs, rabbits, flowers and so forth) while those of the fall and the early winter emphasize death, the harvest and other images of the darker side of life. As the seasons change, the holidays of midwinter reflect this transition with symbols of new light, such as candles.

Many of our holidays reflect the seasons in which they occur. Winter snow is almost always depicted as part of Christmas iconography, even in places such as Southern California or Florida, where snow rarely falls. People even put cotton batting around crèches to suggest snow, even though there would not have been snow at the actual Nativity in Bethlehem. Likewise, Halloween features images of harvest that reflect the autumn, with Halloween icons such as pumpkins and apples and the corn shocks which decorate front porches and yards. Early mentions of Halloween in the 17th and 18th century United States refer to it as a calendrical marker, as a day by which certain chores, agricultural or pastoral, must be done and preparations for winter begun. In the 19th century, most accounts of Halloween mention traditional pranks associated with the day, such as putting logs in a roadway or overturning outhouses. Games such as bobbing for apples, or suspending an apple from the ceiling by a string and trying to take a bite out of it without touching it with your hands also became popular in the 19th century.

Certain games that were said to predict one's future spouse also gained popularity in the 19th century Halloween festivities. For instance, it was said that if you peeled an apple in one long, continuous peel, then tossed it over your shoulder it would spell out the initials of your future spouse. Another game was played with nuts. Two nuts representing a couple would be placed near a fire in the hearth. If the two burned slowly and evenly, that meant a long and happy relationship for the couple. But if the nuts snapped and exploded, the relationship was doomed. This game was so popular that Halloween was often called Nutcrack Night. The foods that were eaten also reflected this dual quality of the natural and the supernatural. A favorite Halloween dish was apple pie, for instance. Embedded in the pie would be a small coin, a ring, perhaps also a thimble. If you found the ring in your piece of pie, it meant you would be married. The thimble meant you would remain single. The coin meant you would be wealthy. So the pie was made from apples, which were in season, and contained within it the ability to predict the future, if only in a playful way.

Most of these games, beliefs and customs were brought to America by the Irish, who immigrated to the United States in large numbers throughout the 19th century. Pumpkins, however, were introduced to the British colonists—the Pilgrims—by Native American Indians. Pumpkins did not grow in Ireland or Great Britain. The English and Irish settlers knew folktales of a wandering spirit named Jack O'Lantern. Jack was a blacksmith who bragged that he was the greatest craftsperson in the world. When he died, he was not allowed into Heaven, because of his pride. So he went to the gates of Hell, but the devil would not let him in. As the gates were closing behind him, he scooped up a burning lump of coal in the turnip he was eating. From that day on, he has wandered the earth, not good enough for Heaven nor evil enough for Hell. He carries the turnip lantern to light his way, known forever as Jack of the Lantern, or Jack O'Lantern. In Ireland, people carve out turnips on Halloween, but these vegetables are different than the type of turnips we are familiar with in the United States. They are much larger. The pumpkin, one of the primary symbols of Halloween, is American in origin.

As the New Year's Day of the ancient Celts, the festival of Samhain was a kind of rite of passage, in this case from the old year to the new. Festivals and celebrations very often celebrate points of transition; our New Year's Eve parties are focused on the precise moment—midnight—when the old year ends and the new one begins. Today Halloween serves more as a celebration of autumn, although it still has some of the feel of seasonal passage. After Halloween, the following November days rapidly grow shorter, greyer and colder as winter approaches.

Halloween as a Rite of Passage of the Life Cycle

Across America, we do not celebrate Halloween in any one way. What one does on or around Halloween varies, depending on such factors as age, place of residence (rural, urban or suburban), region of the country, ethnicity and even associational group. Going from house to house trick-or-treating, for instance, may not be done in rural areas where homes are separated by great distances. Halloween activities also vary according to a person's age. The idea of the rite of passage is particularly appropriate to the more celebrations that we enjoy throughout our lives in which individuals are made the center of the ceremony. Birthday parties, for instance, mark the transition from one year to the next. We have rituals at birth that welcome infants into the world, such as naming ceremonies, christenings and baptisms. Weddings are rituals that take us from being single to being married, and we certainly surround death with wakes, funerals and other rituals. Throughout life, we have a great many rituals, festivals and celebrations that mark, in one way or another, transitions from one stage of life to the next. Others of these would include commencement ceremonies and graduation parties, quinceanera parties, bar and bat mitzvahs, confirmations, the bris and retirement parties. In a less formal way, Halloween activities can also act as rites of passage for children and for the entire life-cycle.

For instance, as I review my own life, I see the following: as a young child, I was escorted on my trick-or-treating adventures by members of my immediate family, either a parent or an older sister. As I got a little older, perhaps about ten years of age, I began to trick-or-treat with a group of pals from my street. When I reached early adolescence, about twelve or thirteen, I continued to go out with a group of friends on Halloween, but the friends were buddies from school, the territory we walked was larger, and we no longer rang doorbells to ask for (or demand) treats. Instead, we made mischief, soaping the occasional car window or throwing the occasional egg.

Halloween activities waned somewhat for me through high school, but in college, Halloween meant a masquerade party. Masquerades and costume parties continued to be my major Halloween activity through graduate school. When I moved to Washington, D.C. to begin my career, I began to notice the growth in urban Halloween parades. In cities all over the country, and in college towns as well, Halloween had become a night of dressing up and partying in the streets for adults of all ages. In Washington, D.C., Georgetown is the scene of the street festivities. Perhaps the most famous such parades and parties are in San Francisco and New York's Greenwich Village. In addition to the public processions, I also noticed a rise in the number of homes that were decorated for Halloween, often elaborately, to an extent that rivaled even Christmas. Whole families were now involving themselves in this autumn festival.

I now have three children. My involvement in Halloween has changed again. I have taught my children how to carve a jack-o-lantern, as I fondly remember my father teaching me. Now my wife and I provide the treats instead of begging for them. Times have changed, however. Unlike when I was a child, some parents today don costumes themselves to accompany their children on their rounds; many people handing out the treats also wear costumes and wait to receive the children at their doors. And although some folks turn their homes into haunted houses and invite the children inside to see the spooky sights and to have a donut and a spot of cider before they go on the next visit, Halloween is very much celebrated outdoors. As an adult, I am now aware that much of the fun of the evening is sensual: being surrounded by flickering candlelight on a street full of colorful, costumed creatures, tasting the treats, with a soundtrack provided by the crispy autumn leaves crunching underfoot.

The point of all this reminiscing is that the customs of Halloween vary according to age. From shy begging, to nasty tricks, to drunken parties to parental nurturing, we all do different things at different ages. To an extent, these different activities mark different stages of life. Trick-or-treating with one's friends rather than a family guardian was, I personally felt, a sign of growing up. So was the time at which I ceased to wear a costume for trick-or-treating and began simply to indulge in pranks in my everyday clothes. Certainly, dealing with Halloween as a parent was a major transition for me. College students frequently express nostalgia and regret over the fact that they are too old to participate in Halloween in the ways they did as children. My sense of this is that these activities are each associated with a particular age-group. Leaving aside one set of Halloween activities and embracing another reflects a movement from one stage of life to another and are informal rites of passage. This explains the sense of loss as well as gain, because to move to a new stage of life brings to mind the awareness that one does not go back. So Halloween, and to greater and lesser extents, other holidays as well, can function as rites of passage of the life cycle, as we take on one set of customary activities and leave another behind.

From the early Christian missionaries who sought to demonize the Celtic deities to those religious groups who would do away with it today, Halloween has always had its formal persecutors. However, Halloween continues to be celebrated, not as a marginal survival of an otherwise dead tradition, but as a thriving, contemporary, post-industrial festival. Its symbolism is powerful and its customs are elastic enough to appeal broadly to groups of different ages, national origins, sexual orientations and regional backgrounds. Despite the economic commercialization of the customary activities of costuming and dispensing treats, it is an unofficial celebration. No day off is given for Halloween, no federal decree is proclaimed establishing it as a national holiday; it is not a "red letter day" on the calendar. People simply do it. Halloween is manifested throughout all aspects of our society. As society has changed, so has the celebration, but predictions of its demise a few decades ago have proven wrong. Despite the fact that it is not officially a holiday, Halloween has become one of the most important and widely-celebrated festivals on our calendar.

LOVE STORIES OF THE WEST

WESTERN

25¢

ROMANCES

MARCH

Section

✍ 7 ✍

Formulas

Introduction
Would You Repeat That—Please!: The Meaningful Delights of Formula in the Popular Arts

...the marvelous thing about Westerns is that they're all the same movie. This gives a director unlimited freedom.

Jean Renoir

She can't be dead! Misery Chastain CANNOT BE DEAD! You Lie. I thought you were good, but you are not good. You are just a lying old dirty birdie.

#1 Fan, Annie Wilkes, to Author Paul Sheldon (upon discovering that Paul's latest Misery romance novel ends the series by killing the heroine)

Standing Room Only: The Crowded Room of the Popular Arts

Americans devote a larger portion of their income to entertainment than do the inhabitants of any other nation on the planet. We own more television sets, take longer and more diverse vacations, produce more movies, plays, records, magazines and books, watch and play more games and sports and, generally speaking, make it our business to have a enjoyable time of it. Welcome to America—land of entertainment. What this means to students of popular culture is that we are presented with a remarkable bulk and diversity of material stored in the vast room of the popular arts on the top floor of the house of popular culture. The older, more familiar and conservative realm of the print media alone includes the wide array of books, magazines and newspapers produced each year, each week, each day. And when we add the rapid and fluid elements disseminated by the electronic media—music, movies, television, radio—we are confronted with a mass of material so large it virtually defies cataloguing, let alone careful study and analysis. The popular arts are so ubiquitous that there is a separate, extensive segment of them today which is devoted entirely to providing entertainment by covering entertainment. *People* magazine, the paper tabloids, *TV Guide* (the 3rd largest circulating magazine in America), television's *Entertainment Tonight* and Entertainment Network, dozens of talk shows, MTV's Music News, all are examples of a concentrated (if futile) effort by the entertainment industry to impose order on itself and to communicate that order to a public which might otherwise be overwhelmed by the diverse entertainments clamoring for the public's attention, leisure time and disposable income. While audiences in the 1950s watched television with little knowledge of the ratings or the precise popularity of individual programs (they knew far more about the Nelsons than the Nielsens) and went to movies without paying much (if any) attention to the weekend box-office statistics, their 1990s counterparts have CNN's *Showbiz Today* to update them on the previous week's most and least watched TV programs, and *USA Today* to tell them how they are feeling about the latest box-office hit. Americans today think about fun nearly as much as they devote their time and attention to having fun. The self-referential climate created by the nearly obsessive focus upon the behind-the-scenes facts of the entertainment universe has fostered an audience with more knowledge about its amusements than any past public but not one which has any greater understanding. The weekend box office receipts, latest Billboard Charts, television ratings and even the "big thumbs" of Siskel and Ebert in their exclusive balcony are no substitute for the analysis and insight provided by the study of popular culture.

One method of approaching studying the popular arts has already been suggested in previous sections of this text. We can apply the popular culture equation ("the greater the popularity of an artifact or event, the more likely it is to be reflective of popular myths, beliefs and values") and simply select the most successful elements of the popular arts for individual analysis. The problem with this, however, is that such an approach ignores the vast majority of popular works, tends to focus upon the immediate present (what is popular right now) to the exclusion of past data and restricts our evidential base to the specific mass audience participating in a specific entertainment artifact or event. Most importantly, this item-by-item approach involves a great deal of speculation, which severely limits both its reliability and validity. (A movie or television program is rarely; if ever, released at a different time for a new audience, which would provide a subject for comparison, and further, there are many elements which may account for the popularity of a specific popular artifact or event. Its connection to the zeitgeist is only one possibility.) We need a method of analysis which enables us to examine a wide range of the vast array of popular entertainments in an orderly manner which will also ensure the highest possible validity for our conclusions by extending our evidential base over both time and the widest possible audience. The analytical tool developed by popular culture theorists is implicit in the nature of popular culture itself. We have emphasized on several occasions that popular culture is repetitive and imitative in its attempt to ensure continued commercial success. Sometimes this repetition takes the form of immediate imitation—a popular movie spawns sequels and spin-offs for example. But in a deeper, more illuminating sense, the repetition is one of "form" rather than of strict duplication. Sequels and spin-offs imitate a popular artifact in a slavish attempt to capture the same audience. But the "original," which inspires such duplication, is itself usually an example of a type of movie which has proven to be popular over a long period of time. Popular artists, in other words, recognize that there are certain formulas which have developed in the history of popular entertainment that serve as reliable recipes for success. While the five movies nominated for the 1992 Best Picture Oscar can all be expected to produce specific imitations, it is far more useful to note that each is itself an example of a popular formula which is already familiar to audiences and liked by them as well. *Bugsy* is a "gangster" movie like *The Godfather, Bonnie and Clyde* and *Goodfellas; Beauty and the Beast* is a romance similar to *Pretty Woman, Ghost; Prince of Tides* is a family melodrama reminiscent of *On Golden Pond* and *Terms of Endearment; JFK* is a political thriller following *All the President's Men, The Manchurian Candidate*; and winner *Silence of the Lambs* is a cop-crime movie like *The Untouchables* and *Lethal Weapon*.

The particular variant of the cop-crime movie illustrated by *Silence of the Lambs* includes such a formulaic elements as: a *hero/heroine* who is a competent (but not extraordinarily gifted or powerful) cop called upon to confront a *villain* who is especially threatening and evil; a plot which involves action and often death or injury of someone close to the hero/heroine at the hands of the villain; and a final confrontation between hero and villain in which the hero emerges triumphant but also changed in some important manner. Audiences know this formula, like this formula, and expect certain things to take place in movies which typify the formula, and popular artists strive to fulfill the public's expectations.

The study of the popular arts, then, is centered around an attempt to identify and define the elements which a large number of popular artifacts and events share, and which can thus be assumed to help account for their popularity. When we have identified and detailed the specific formula which unites many artifacts and events and which a vast number of audiences have found consistently appealing over a long period of time, then we can begin to speculate about the myths, beliefs and values which each formula embodies and to reach conclusions which are based upon an evidential base that is far more extensive than a similar focus upon a specific work can ever hope to provide. While the concept of a formula can be applied to any of the popular arts ("The Rap on Rap," which is in the rituals readings, is an example of how formula is used to analyze popular music) we will restrict ourselves to examples of popular story formulas in the discussion from this point onward. Popular story formulas, sometimes termed "genres," are more commonly familiar and enduring. All story formulas share certain elements which help define the overall pattern as a formula creating specific audience expectations which the popular artist must meet to produce a successful result. There are obligations which must be satisfied, and there are components of story formula which we can analyze to determine the meanings beneath the formula's success.

Rules of the Game: The Structure of Story Formulas

A popular formula is a created product (often a story) that is generally repeatable and is therefore familiar to both the creator (of the specific formulaic work) and to the audience. Audiences experience an example of a specific formula more in terms of their implicit knowledge of the formula itself than with reference to the real world or a unique artifact or event. One of the earliest (and most perceptive) genre critics was Robert Warshow who, in a ground-breaking study of popular culture titled *The Immediate Experience* (1962), observed that this aspect of audience response meant that "it is only in the ultimate sense that the type appeals to the audience's experience of reality; much more immediately, it appeals to the previous experience of the type itself; it creates its own field of reference." An audience judges a Western or a Detective drama not by the degree to which it reflects an actual historical era, event or personality type (We know that policework in contemporary America is not actually the way Danny Glover and Mel Gibson experience it in *Lethal Weapon* movies), but by the degree to which it satisfies our expectations of certain formulaic elements. While we attend a non-genre film (such as *A Passage to India, My Left Foot, The Last Emperor*) with the hope that it will be a largely surprising, unique experience which will attempt to instruct and or change us with new knowledge, unfamiliar characters and challenging insights, we seek out genre entertainments largely for the opposite kind of experience—the predictable excitements and titillations offered by the comfortingly familiar worlds we have contentedly visited on so many previous occasions.

A popular story formula consists of two broad categories of elements, which can be termed *conventions* and *inventions.* A single formula convention is one familiar building block of the genre and a combination of conventions serve to define the genre's framework—i.e. conventions are the elements which each specific example of a genre shares with every other specific example. Conventions in turn can be grouped into six separate subcategories which serve to delineate the type of common element being examined and shared. We will examine each of these subcategories and draw upon several popular genres to illustrate how these familiar elements can be combined to produce a popular story formula. In each instance we will cite at least one example from the classical Detective Formula, a formula which reached its peak of popularity in England during the 1920s and 1930s but which has evidenced a remarkable staying power and flexibility in that it remains popular today in many media (films, television, print) on both sides of the ocean and has given us the indelible character of the Great Detective, from Sherlock Holmes and Hercule Poirot to Lt. Columbo and Jessica Fletcher. The Classical Detective Genre is so clearly defined and consistently popular that most people are familiar with its basic devices—the isolated setting, the murder and its attendant mysterious clues, the final gathering of the suspects—even though many have never actually read or seen a specific example of the formula in its entirety. The Classical Detective Genre perfectly embodies the half-conscious familiarity which audiences possess with regard to most genres—a familiarity which is rarely articulated, usually far more extensive than consciously realized, and often recognized by the audience only when its assumed expectations are violated.

Genre conventions are classified in the following categories:

1) *Plot*—the familiar pattern by which the storyline of a genre develops; the stages of action and resolution which move the narrative from beginning to end.

The traditional Horror Genre, for example, often follows a plotline marked by the following stages of development: 1) the establishment of a "normal world"—dull, boring, conformist but also seemingly safe and secure; 2) Violation of the normal world by a monster; 3) unsuccessful attempts to defeat the monster (often marked by an initial difficulty in convincing normal people to believe in the monster's existence); 4) attacks by the monster leading to suspense, terror and death; 5) defeat of the monster through death or exile; 6) a "revised" normal world—reality forever changed by new recognition of the darkness in humanity and the precious fragility of existence.

The Classical Detective Genre also has a 6-stage plotline and is defined in the following manner: 1) introduction of the Great Detective, 2) crime (almost always a murder) with mysterious clues; 3) investigation (interviewing witnesses and suspects); 4) announcement of the solution; 5) gathering of the suspects and explanation of the solution; 6) capture and removal of the criminal. The fact that the Classical Detective Genre centers upon a mysterious crime which is presented as a puzzle and that it also derives its principal appeal by establishing a content between the Great Detective and the audience in achieving the solution to this puzzling crime helps solidify the formula in a manner which is not always characteristic of other genres which have more complex goals. If a Classical Mystery tale is to play fair with the audience, in other words, then it must closely follow the stages outlined above. However, a deeper and more varied genre (such as the Western, for example) may have several conventional plotlines from which to choose. It is important to remember that when identifying and explaining genre conventions that all conventions are guidelines rather than absolute regulations.

2) *Motifs*—the individual building blocks of each plot stage; smaller stories (with beginnings, middles and ends) which work together to drive the overall plot from start to finish.

While most plot stages are present in one form or another in nearly every example of a given genre, motifs provide the creator with a wide variety of familiar scenes and conflicts from which to choose in realizing each stage of the plot. In the Western, for example, motifs range from violent scenes establishing the rough nature of the wilderness to domestic events which help demonstrate the virtues of civilization. The Western is such a well-developed, familiar genre that many of its motifs can be effectively parodied with the creators' assurance that audiences will recognize the familiar conventions being reversed or subverted. *Blazing Saddles*, for example, is an entire movie intended as a parody of the traditional, accepted, familiar Western format.

The Classical Detective Genre is marked by a wide variety of motifs—from the detective's initial demonstration of skill (like Sherlock Holmes' knowing precisely what Dr. Watson is thinking) to the false solution (often presented by a competing policeman who has been on the case). Two motifs in particular are especially important in helping identify both the appeal and the significance of the genre—the "roving finger" of Suspicion and the "red herring." As the detective proceeds in his investigation, he gathers additional clues and information regarding the crime that makes it appear as though each character in the story could have done the dastardly deed. The roving finger tends to indict an entire society, to present a world in which everyone is guilty and no one is saved. The detective's solution, therefore, identifies a single person responsible for all the evil which has taken place and allays the audience's fear that everyone is to blame. The evil-doer is removed from the greater society neatly and efficiently, and thus the embodiment of the darkness of humanity is expelled to restore the ideal world.

The roving finger is animated by a motif often referred to as the "red herring." (This term derives from the practice of early animal rights activists who used to drag the ground with fish before foxhunts in an attempt to confuse the dogs and send the hunters astray while the fox made his escape.) Classical mystery writers use the same technique to mislead the audience about the guilty party. In her classic *And Then There Were None*, for example, Agatha Christie leads the readers to restrict their suspicions to a steadily dwindling number of suspects as, one by one the ten characters all meet their deaths. Christie's red herring, however, lies in leading us to believe that all deaths are equal—that because some characters meet undeniable ends in a rigid pattern (revolving around the nursery rhyme "Ten Little Indians") that all the characters must as well. The solution reveals that some deaths are more certain than others and that our initial assumptions have led us far away from the solution. Christie's red herrings serve as diversions to lead the readers away from discovering the truth.

3) *Setting*—the formula's time and place of action.

In his book *Hollywood Genres*, Thomas Schatz identified two broad classifications of genre settings which are useful in determining how each formula's setting functions to present the story's meaning and conflicts. Schatz argues that certain genres (which he terms Genres of Social Order) present a setting whose nature is undetermined—it is being violently contested between the forces of savagery and darkness on the one hand and those of civilization and lightness on the other. Genres of Social Order (such as Western, Horror and Detective formulas) give us settings which are battlegrounds upon which the forces of evil vie with the characters who are most like us for control. Schatz argues that the conflict is decided in such instances by a hero who borrows qualities from each of the opposing forces but who places his skills on the side of progress, civilization and justice. Examples of this are the lone gunfighter defending the hapless town against an invasion of outlaws, the dropout hard-boiled detective rescuing an innocent from the web of corruption which threatens to swallow them both and the young hero who believes in the monster and is thus able to confront and destroy it.

Genres of Social Integration, however, take place in a setting which has already had its defining characteristics clearly established and are now unchallenged—a civilized social environment which operates smoothly according to its won codes and mores. These genres (including musicals, romantic comedies, family melodramas) do not place the society in peril, as Genres of Social Order do, but detail the actions and choices of a "doubled hero" (i.e., a couple) as they struggle to adapt their individual characters and goals to the established social milieu. Genres of Integration are marked by discussion rather than violence, negotiations rather than ultimatums, marriages rather than gunfights. The value of Schatz's scheme is that it alerts us to a crucial aspect of a genre's lasting appeal—that formulas are essentially ritualistic reenactments of fundamental social conflicts both within the society (Integration) and between opposing philosophies seeking to define the society in the making (order). Audiences respond to a genre not solely (or even primarily) because they enjoy seeing the same story repeatedly re-enacted but because they find the genre's resolution of one or more fundamental social conflicts to be both revealing (as the conflict is raised and explored) and reassuring (as the conflict is resolved at story's end). Schatz's distinction between integrated settings and contested settings is merely the beginning of this deeper study of genre's meaning and appeal, but it is worth noting here both as a preface to our discussion below and as a caution against viewing genre conventions as simplistic surface structures applicable only to "mindless entertainment."

The primary characteristic of the setting in the classical detective genre makes it one of Social Order in which the nature of the society itself is being violently contested. In this case a murderer has broken one of the most basic of social laws as innocents are swept up in the crime and ensuing investigation, risking being implicated by the roving finger of suspicion. The setting establishes the background to this allegorical conflict by creating an isolating set of circumstances—the English country manor house cut off from the rest of the world by a raging storm, the luxury cruise liner traveling slowly across the seas, miles from any port, the Orient Express stalled on the tracks by a blizzard in the middle of nowhere—within which a tiny number of characters are gathered to enact their grand drama of murder, investigation and expulsion. The critic David Lehman describes the essence of such settings as:

> ...a sense of an island remoteness from which there is 'no escape' is what all the whodunit's classic settings have in common. It's as true of the exclusive prep school, the antique university town, the provincial vicarage and the titled estate where the weekend guests try their hand at amateur theatricals. In each case the setting is an implicit celebration of limits, order and rules even though—or because—the plot involves a violation of that order and those rules. Therefore, any self-enclosed community with a firm social hierarchy and enough local color to make it an object of nostalgic desire will serve.... In the murder mystery in its purest forms, the assembled suspects inhabit a world out of time, measuring out their lives in cups of sherry and glasses of port. Everyone knows his place; each must be conscious of his assigned role in the local scheme of things...[L]ife seems blissful and murder an incongruity, as in Paul McGuire's *A Funeral in Eden* (1938) which is set in a tropical but suitably anglicized Pacific isle. McGuire's title says it all.

In a classical mystery story, therefore, what is true more or less for all genres is made quite explicit: the setting is the society (and its defining mores, values and patterns of behavior) and the conflict around which the story revolves is thus about fundamental cultural issues, not merely stale plot devices.

4) *Characters*—In a story formula "characters" generally fall into one of two broad categories: the hero (or heroic couple) in the instance of Genres of Social Integration—e.g. romances, musicals, and everybody else (usually a set of well-established supporting stereotypes).

The hero is the character who animates, embodies and resolves the basic conflict of values which is at the heart of the specific genre. The Western hero, for example, often finds himself caught between opposing forces of the wilderness and civilization, sharing characteristics of each (he can be a highly skilled killer capable of triumphing in the savage wilderness, but only applies his deadly skills in pursuit of civilized justice, honor and protection of the innocent), and he is at the center of a specific conflict between the two ethics, which he violently resolves in favor of civilization. The hero in the Horror genre is similarly suspended between opposing worlds, in this instance between the normal existence of the conformist masses and the exciting and dangerous world of monsters and madmen, which both fascinates and repels him. The actions and motivations of the hero can often be used as a clue to the deeper thematic meanings associated with the specific genre and with genres as a class of popular entertainment for a certain culture (so that, for example, the general observation that American genre heroes are so often lone men of violent action is a way of identifying a significant number of myths, beliefs and values which help define American culture.) Genres exist in a highly charged world in which basic, important, fundamental social values are both at risk and at play. As the central character responsible for arousing, driving and resolving this deeply symbolic conflict, the hero's importance stems from *what* rather than *who* he is and from the motivations of his actions, rather than the actions themselves.

The Classical Detective hero is a combination of opposing characteristics which embody the values the genre is both examining and supporting. Fundamentally the Great Detective is a person of exceptional intellect (capable of understanding the meanings of clues which are puzzling to all other observers); but who is also poetic artist and (above all) exceedingly eccentric. George Grella accurately describes the primary qualities associated with this hero:

> They generally possess a physical appearance as distinctive as Holmes' hawklike profile—they may be either very tall or very short, very fat or very thin, or they may affect unusual attire. They are usually pronounced eccentrics, enjoying odd hobbies, interests or lifestyles and frequently overindulging in...the vices of eating, drinking, smoking and boasting...Whatever his particular mode of detection, the sleuth is blessed with a penetrating observation, highly developed logical powers, wide knowledge and a brilliantly synthetic imagination.

This special set of characteristics associated with the Great Detective renders him a hero who exemplifies the values and skills of reason and also enables him to approach the solution of the crime at hand as an external puzzle rather than as an emotional or highly personalized quest for justice. The Great Detective is detached from the horror and dark consequences of the crime and approaches it merely as an interesting problem worthy of exercising his powerful intellect and unique skills.

The Great Detective is rendered all the more heroic because he is usually associated with a secondary character (known as the "Watson" stereotype) who relates the detective's adventures with suitable awe and admiration. The detective's abilities and character are also highlighted by contrast to two other significant characters in the genre—the victim and the murderer. The victim in the classical whodunit is typically an unlikable, often evil character who largely deserves what he gets—he's preventing the marriage of two lovebirds, is planning to re-write his will to leave his vast fortune to his pet cat, is blackmailing a business associate, or is just too abrasively overbearing and boorish to evoke our sympathies. The death of the victim, therefore, ignites a complex situation in which nearly everyone present has a motive for committing the crime even when actually innocent. This situation calls for a special mind to rectify things properly. The murderer, on the other hand, is crafty enough to use this set of circumstances to his own advantage, committing crime so clever that suspicion falls on every person except himself (thereby rendering him the "least likely suspect"). The murderer, therefore, is a worthy opponent for our hero, and the Great Detective's triumph is rendered all the more remarkable because of his so formidable enemy.

Basil Rathbone and Nigel Bruce as the famous Sherlock Holmes and Dr. John Watson.

5) *Theme*—the deeper meaning and/or significance of the genre; the specific myths, beliefs and values the genre is exploring and expressing. All stories share certain highly generalized themes—good triumphing over evil, love rewarded, justice achieved—but these are too generalized to provide a relevant discussion of the thematic basis of any specific genre. What is important for the student of popular culture is the precise way in which a culture's genres *define* these generalized values. What Americans mean by "good" and "evil," what kind of love should be "rewarded" and what it means to call for justice in the resolution of a specific conflict are all called into question. A culture's popular

story formulas reflect and communicate that specific culture's myths beliefs and values in a manner very similar to the way in which specific artifacts and events have been shown to do so in the previous sections of this text devoted to icons, sterotypes, rituals, etc. A genre is an especially powerful and deep example of this type of "funhouse mirror," however, because each genre is a distillation of the elements common to hundreds of individual works and is generally accepted and approved of over long periods of time. A genre is a framework. Its conventional characters, plots and settings are formed through a longstanding, ongoing communication with its audience so that it achieves consistent popularity precisely because it raises and expresses myths, beliefs and values which that audience finds relevant and meaningful, not simply because the genre tells age-old, crosscultual tales of "good vs. evil." Any meaningful discussion of a genre must attempt to place the formula firmly within its "cultural context"—to define its themes and associated conventions in terms of the specific manner in which they reflect the time, place and ideological environment within which the genre has achieved and maintained popularity.

The Classical Detective Genre, for example, obviously expresses such universal themes as good triumphing over evil, crime and punishment, but its significance lies in the cultural context of 1920/1930 England and the dreams and values of that specific postwar environment. Britain in 1920 was a society forever changed by the recent Great War, and as John Paterson and George Grella explain in the book *Dimensions of Detective Fiction*, the Classical Detective Genre developed as the perfect entertainment to provide a soothing answer to the contemporary crisis in values:

> In the age of the Boom, the Great Depression, flappers and gangsterism, and the Fascist Solution, it recalls the sober gentility and crude optimism of an earlier and more complacent generation; it asserts the triumph of a social order and decorum that have all but passed away...Just as the Elizabethans often found solace in rigidly conventional, peaceful, and essentially unreal literary forms, so too the twentieth-century Briton apparently longed for the aristocratic aura, knowable universe, and unerring truth-teller of the detective novel when poverty threatened the established social order, when the cosmos had lost its infinite meaning, and when the Big Lie drowned out all attempts at truth. Dreaming of luxury, longing for stability, desiring the security of formal rigidity, readers of all classes turned toward the detective story, where significant truth lurked behind the arrangement of cigars in an ashtray, where a timeless society re-established its innocence anew, where nubility triumphed over senility, where a wizard disposed of the bad parent, the impostor, the parvenu, the outsider, and bestowed his magical blessings on decent young women and deserving young men. (102)

The Classical Detective Genre presented its audience with a social world which mirrored its own surroundings. It also placed that world in danger by violating one of its most vital laws, and, perhaps more significantly, by passing a roving finger of suspicion which seemed to indict everyone. Finally, it then released all such fears and tensions by explaining the mysterious in terms of the logical, and social quilt in terms of individual evil (which was then banished from the Garden.) In a pattern which we will see to be characteristic of many genres, the Classical Detective Genre uses the body of its narrative to challenge and question the status quo—to express conflicting ideals and goals—and uses its resolution to celebrate a restoration of that status quo which thereby reassures the audience that its culture's myths, beliefs and values are secure.

Genres explore timeless themes in a timely manner, expressing universal conflicts in culturally specific terms.

6) *Props*—material objects which have acquired emotional and/or intellectual meaning as a result of their repeated use in a story formula over time. Props are icons in an imaginary context which, nonetheless, embody very real meanings. So real, as a matter of fact, that props often come to affect the way a culture views and values the objects' real-life counterparts—some of America's fascination with guns is no doubt directly due to the important iconic role played by guns as props in the Western. The Western is an endless source of icons which serve to embody the values which that genre explores. Items associated with the Western hero's costume (a white hat for example, or the rugged but highly stylized dress which enables him to function equally well in savage and civilized worlds), his environment (his intimate relationship with his horse, for example, and the way he moves freely between town and forest/desert), and weaponry (his mastery of the Colt Peacemaker) all carry iconic meanings which transcend their merely practical functions.

The Classical detective often has similarly reasonant objects associated with him as well. Thus Sherlock Holmes has a trio of icons which effectively embody the great detective's most important heroic traits: a special pipe (reflecting his logical, dispassionate, contemplative powers), his deerstalker hat (showing that he's a hunter) and his violin (embodying his soulful artistic temperament). In a similar fashion, we find Holmes to be at home in an iconic setting (221B Baker Street places him in the heart of London while he can also remain—in a highly eccentric fashion—detached from it) filled with items which have been borrowed by other writers in the genre and have thus also acquired an iconic significance of their own, such as magnifying glasses, chemistry sets and guns.

The use of special items as icons and props reflects another very important lesson about formulas. The complexity of a formula is such that we can and must use all of the other rooms in the house of popular culture as "tools" to help unlock a formula's meaning. All genres have heroes, stereotypes, icons and ritualistic scenes (labeled "motifs"), and when they are translated into movies and television they also frequently have associated celebrities as well (Basil Rathbone as Sherlock Holmes, John Wayne and Clint Eastwood as essential Western Heroes, etc.)

The essence of any genre lies in its repetitive, familiar nature in the conventions which are recognized by both creator and audience. But no formula could maintain its popularity if each example was identical to every sample of the form. Audiences demand the comforting fulfillment of certain conventional expectations, but also need to be surprised as well. There must be a balance between conventions and, the other principal defining element of formulas, *inventions*. Inventions are the special twists which a creator applies to formulaic conventions in an effort to keep the formula fresh and interesting—to "intensify the expected experience without fundamentally altering it" (Warshow). The balance between conventions and inventions in any specific example of a formula must be such as to provide the audience with the security of expectations fulfilled while also providing pleasurable risks associated with the unfamiliar and surprising.

Inventions serve a second important purpose as well. As a formula evolves over time it must present its conventions in a manner which continues to reflect changing cultural beliefs and values. A Western which continues to portray Indians as raging savages, for example, would have little chance of acceptance in the emergent multicultural nation which bestowed seven Oscars on *Dances with Wolves,* a movie featuring the Sioux dispensing their natural wisdom.

Inventions can provide a twist or surprising turn to any convention of content or form. The Classical Detective formula especially fosters inventive plots in order to provide the reader with a baffling puzzle to solve in competition with the great detective. Agatha Christie was very adept at taking a specific convention and then exploiting the audience's familiarity with it to distract them from the mystery's solution. If, for example, we always seem to feel that the roving finger of suspicion has indicted everyone, then it would be effective to fashion a mystery in which that turns out to be precisely the case—everybody did it in *Murder On The Orient Express.* If certain characters are conventionally immune from suspicion—e.g. the great detective, the butler—then an effective invention would make this type of least likely suspect actually guilty, such as the Watson-like narrator of Christie's *The Murder of Roger Akroyd,* who turns out to be the murderer.

The gasps of outrage which greeted this latter invention reflects the fact that creators must be careful not to be too inventive lest they fail to fulfill their central responsibility of providing the "expected experience" the audience demands. *Ackroyd* is now regarded as a classic because Christie balanced her one startling invention by placing it within a novel which was very conventional in every other aspect. It included an eccentric, brilliant great detective, a closed circle of suspects, a baffling crime. Above all, Christie fulfilled her contract with her audience by "playing fair" with them in her presentation of the murder and clues, so that a careful reader could reasonably identify the narrator as the murderer by following evidence which finally points only in that direction. Stephen King's character, novelist Paul Sheldon, on the other hand, attempted an "invention" in his romance which upset the necessary balance between conventions and inventions, and found only *Misery* as a result. Inventions need to reflect and surprise an audience, not shatter and shock.

Recipes For Reflection: The Importance of Popular Formulas

In the course of detailing the conventional framework and inventive twists which drive a genre over time, we have already discussed many of the "deeper" meanings of this important tool of popular culture analysis. This concluding section therefore, is intended as a summary and extension of concepts which have already been introduced, but which require additional clarification and illustration. John G. Cawelti, in his book *Adventure, Mystery and Romance*, has identified four central cultural functions performed by popular formulas. His observations provide an appropriate framework for concluding our discussion:

1) Popular formulas provide a ready-made means of shaping popular entertainment. The longstanding popularity of specific genres enables creators to produce works which have a high probability of achieving commercial success, and it provides audiences with a type of escapist entertainment which effectively meets and balances two basic human needs: security and risk. The predictability of formulaic entertainment—the implied assurance that the hero will triumph over the threat to social order—provides a foundation of security within which audiences can then "safely" give themselves over to the exciting, titillating "symbols of danger, uncertainty, violence and sex" (Cawelti) which permeate formulaic entertainment. A popular formula mimics a roller coaster ride by depicting this vital balance between security and risk, enabling us to enjoy a frightening, shocking experience full of dramatic twists and sudden drops, with the assurance that we will ultimately find a predictable outcome at journey's end.

2) Popular formulas reaffirm the existing cultural values and beliefs by providing a means to demonstrate their utility and importance within a familiar framework. Thus, Westerns conjure up a world in which fundamental American values of individual freedom, violent administration of justice outside the law and the democratic community are all magically realized and celebrated. The Classical Detective genre performs a similar service with regard to the ordered, aristocratic, class-

obsessed society which its audience found so attractive and romances reaffirm a culture's views of love, courtship and the proper relationship between men and women. The foundation of all popular formulas is, therefore, the very same body of cultural myths, beliefs and values which forms the foundation and meaning of every artifact and event in the House of Popular Culture

3) Popular formulas "enable the audience to explore in fantasy the boundary between the permitted and the forbidden" (Cawelti). Popular formulas almost always end by reaffirming the social status quo, but the very security created by this promised resolution enables a formula to devote the body of its story to raising questions about, and even criticizing, the very order it will ultimately support. The Western hero's need for individual freedom (and the Western genre's celebration of that freedom as essentially heroic) conflicts with the communal, cooperative needs of the civilized community, which is reaffirmed in the story's resolution. A Western hero often exercises his individual freedom (and the violent skills which express it) by choosing to promote the very same community values which cannot accommodate him unless he compromises that freedom. The Western hero cannot settle down without foregoing the most significant aspects of his character which render him a "hero" in the first place. Therefore, in the classic resolution he must "ride off into the sunset" to follow the frontier westward even as his own choices and actions are responsible for establishing the civilization from which he is exiled.

This pattern of criticism-reaffirmation is found in many genres. The Horror genre illustrates the staid boredom of normality and the seductive appeal of the darkness on the edge of town, and yet ends by returning the hero and heroine to the protective arms of the very community they had grown weary of earlier. Romantic comedies are resolved with marriage, but spend the major portion of their time celebrating the raucous and humorous individuality of each lover; soap operas entrance and titillate their audiences with dramatic violations of conventional morality and behavior, but then resolve each plotline with a reaffirmation of those very same mores; and science fiction often condemns science and reason by demonstrating their role in the creation of a monster/bomb/invasion and yet resolves the conflict by displaying the triumph of these same qualities in overcoming the very threat they have created. Formulas are complex, revealing artifacts indeed—excitingly capable of identifying and expressing cultural tensions while promoting lasting cultural beliefs and values.

4) A popular formula helps incorporate and communicate changes in cultural myths, beliefs and values. As a culture alters its mindset over time so the formulas it uses to express those beliefs change as the formulas both reflect and change the audience mindset. The Horror genre has

evolved from defining evil as a monstrous "Other" to one which is less capable of any rational explanation at all (see Walter Evans' essay and the introduction which precedes it), and the Western has moved from an early celebration of civilization to a view which is far more harshly critical of the corruption and vice which seem to accompany the closing of the frontier. Television's situation comedies have evolved from idealized 1950s portraits of the nuclear family at home in the suburbs and "fathers who knew best" to Murphy Brown who relinquishes the idea of a "traditional" family and chooses to become a single parent. A group of tart-tongued "designing women" form a familial support group which requires no men at all, and the nuclear family, when it is portrayed on television, is very often black (*Cosby*) or blue-collar and bordering on the dysfunctional (*Roseanne*).

The essays and introductions which follow will illustrate all of these vital functions of popular formulas as we demonstrate the delicate balance between conventions and intentions, the reciprocal relationship between creator and audience in their shared knowledge and expectations, the criticism of a social order which is finally reaffirmed, the safe risks providing both security and excitement and the evolution of cultural beliefs and values within a context of unchanging myth. Formulas derive their appeal from a predictable sameness—and their ongoing interest from their surprising depth and creative excitement.

Works Cited

Cawelti, John G. *Adventure, Mystery, and Romance.* Chicago: U of Chicago P, 1976.

Grella, George. "Murder and Manners: The Formal Detective Novel." *Dimensions of Detective Fiction.* Larry N. Landrum, et al, eds. Bowling Green, OH: Popular Press, 1976: 37-57.

Warshow, Robert. *The Immediate Experience.* Garden City, NY: Doubleday, 1962.

The Western

Thomas Schatz

John G. Cawelti, in his book The Six-Gun Mystique, *says that the classic Western story celebrates America's "epic moment" and that every time we read or see a Western we once again experience the equivalent of a "Fourth of July celebration." What Cawelti means is that the basic Western story formula tells in a positive way what most white Americans believe is the essence of American history. The story of how the civilized fought the forces of savagery to make a good new land began on the east coast and concluded in the deserts and mountains and plains of the great West. Westerns, as Thomas Schatz describes them in the following essay, are therefore "foundation rituals," repeating endlessly the last great triumph of settlers over the hostile wilderness.*

The Western story as described by Schatz is the most popular American action story of the twentieth century. At the height of their popularity in the late 1950s, there were 30 Westerns on prime-time television and they comprised seven of the top ten shows in the ratings. In addition, Western novels comprised about ten percent of the fiction sold in the United States and about thirty Western features each year were appearing in American movie theaters.

Since the late 1950s, the popularity of Westerns has gradually declined so that in the 1990s most students claim they don't like them. During this same period Westerns have also evolved to meet the changing perceptions of their audience. As Schatz demonstrates, Westerns have become more complicated than the simple celebrations of Western expansionism they tended to be forty years ago. As people learn that a part of nineteenth-century Western history also included runaway, exploitative capitalism, the near extermination of Native Americans and harsh indifference to the hardships experienced by women, Western stories have changed to reflect these unpleasant revelations about our past. Questions about personal honor and about social responsibility now dominate the few Westerns being written or filmed in the 1990s. Older

Adapted from *Hollywood Genres*, NY: Random House, 1981. Reprinted with permission.

Westerns were, in Schatz's words, our "idealized past." Many newer Westerns still thrill us with shootouts, hard riding and great pictures of an awesome landscape. There are still good guys and bad guys. But, in a more sober age, Westerns will never again be such "ideal" versions of the American past.

"This is the West, Sir. When the legend becomes fact, print the legend."
Newspaper editor in *The Man Who Shot Liberty Valance*

The Western is without question the richest and most enduring genre of Hollywood's repertoire. Its concise heroic story and elemental visual appeal render it the most flexible of narrative formulas, and its life span has been as long and varied as Hollywood's own. In fact, the Western genre and the American cinema evolved concurrently, generating the basic framework for Hollywood's studio production system. We might look to Edwin S. Porter's *The Great Train Robbery* in 1903 as the birth not only of the movie Western but of the commercial narrative film in America.

The origins of the Western formula predated the cinema, of course. Its genealogy encompassed colonial folk music, Indian captivity tales, James Fenimore Cooper's *Leather-Stocking Tales,* nineteenth-century pulp romances, and a variety of other cultural forms. These earlier forms began to develop the story of the American West as popular mythology.

The significance and impact of the Western as America's foundation ritual have been articulated most clearly and effectively in the cinema—the medium of twentieth-century technology and urbanization. And it was also in the cinema that the Western could reach a mass audience which actively participated in the gradual refinement and evolution of its narrative formula.

The Landscape of the West

The Western depicts a world of precarious balance in which the forces of civilization and savagery are locked in a struggle for supremacy. As America's foundation ritual, the Western projects a formalized vision of the nation's infinite possibilities and limitless vistas, thus serving to "naturalize" the policies of westward expansion and Manifest Destiny. It is interesting in this regard that we as a culture have found the story of the settlement of the "New World" beyond the Alleghenies and the Mississippi even more compelling than the development of the colonies or the Revolutionary War itself. Ironically, the single most evocative location for Western filmmaking and perhaps the genre's most familiar icon (after the image of John Wayne) is Arizona's Monument Valley, where awesome stone formations reach up to the gods but the desolate soil around them is scarcely suitable for the rural-agricultural bounty which provided America's socioeconomic foundation. The fact is, of course, that Hollywood's version of the Old West has as little to do with agriculture—although it has much to do with rural values—as it does with history. The landscape with its broad expanses and isolated communities was transformed on celluloid into a familiar iconographic arena where civilized met savage in an interminable mythic contest.

The Western's essential conflict between civilization and savagery is expressed in a variety of oppositions: East versus West, garden versus desert, America versus Europe, social order versus anarchy, individual versus community, town versus wilderness, cowboy versus Indian, schoolmarm versus dancehall girl, and so on. Its historical period of reference is the years following the Civil War and reaching into the early twentieth century, when the western United States, that precivilized locale, was establishing codes of law and order as a basis for contemporary social conditions. The opening of virtually any Western "cues" us in to these oppositions: cowboys pausing on a hillside during a cattle drive to gaze at the isolated community in the distance (*My Darling Clementine*, 1946); a lone cowboy, who after riding into a pastoral valley, is accused by an anxious homesteader of gunslinging for land-hungry local ranchers (*Shane*, 1953); a rider on a mountainside watching railroad workers blast a tunnel above him and outlaws rob a stagecoach below (*Johnny Guitar*, 1954); the distant cry of a locomotive whistle and a shot of a black, serpentine machine winding toward us through the open plains as the steam from its engine fills the screen (*The Man Who Shot Liberty Valance*, 1962).

John Ford's Stagecoach

Even as early as Ford's 1939 film, *Stagecoach*, these oppositions are presented concisely and effectively. Ford's film marks the debut of Monument Valley in the Western genre, a fitting arena for the most engaging and thematically complex of all prewar Westerns.

The film opens with a shot of Monument Valley, framed typically beneath a sky which takes up most of the screen. Eventually we hear two riders approaching from across the desert and then see them coming toward us. As the riders near the camera, Ford cuts from this vast, panoramic scene to the exterior of a cavalry camp, and the horizon is suddenly cluttered with tents, flagstaffs, and soldiers. The riders gallop into the camp, dismount, and rush into the post. In the next shot, a group of uniformed men huddle around a telegraph machine. Just before the lines go dead, the telegraph emits a single coded word: "Geronimo."

The stage enters the awesome landscape of Monument Valley in *Stagecoach* (1939).

This sequence not only sets the thematic and visual tone for Ford's film with economy of action and in striking visual terms, but also reflects the basic cultural and physical conflicts which traditionally have characterized the Western form. In Hollywood's version the West is a vast wilderness dotted with occasional oases—frontier towns, cavalry posts, isolated campsites, and so forth—which are linked with one another and with the civilized East by the railroad, the stagecoach, the telegraph: society's tentacles of progress. Each oasis is a virtual society in microcosm, plagued by conflicts both with the external, threatening wilderness and also with the anarchic or socially corrupt members of its own community. Ford's stagecoach, for example, is journeying to Lordsburg (what better name for an oasis of order in a vast wasteland?) through hostile Indian country. Its passengers must contend not only with Indian attacks but also with the conflicts which divide the group itself. The stagecoach carries a righteous sheriff, a cowardly driver, an alcoholic doctor, an embezzling bank executive, a whiskey drummer, a gold-hearted prostitute, a genteel gambler, an Eastern-bred lady, and the hero, an escaped convict bent upon avenging his brother's murder and, simultaneously, his own wrongful imprisonment.

In this film, as in the Western generally, the conflicts within the community reflect and intensify those between the community and its savage surroundings. The dramatic intensity in *Stagecoach* only marginally relates to the disposition of the hero, whose antisocial status (as a convict) is not basic to his character but results from society's lack of effective order and justice. Wayne portrays the Ringo Kid as a naive, moral man of the earth who takes upon himself the task of righting that social and moral imbalance. He is also a living manifestation of the Western's basic conflicts. Like the sheriff who bends the law to suit the situation, the banker who steals from his own bank, the kindly whore, or the timid moralizer who sells whiskey, Ringo must find his own way through an environment of contrary and ambiguous demands.

The appeal of the stagecoach's passengers derives from their ambiguous social status. Often they are on the periphery of the community and somehow at odds with its value system. Perhaps the most significant conflict in the Western is the community's demand for order through cooperation and compromise versus the physical environment's demand for rugged individualism....coupled with a survival-of-the-fittest mentality. In *Stagecoach,* each of the three central figures—Ringo, Doc Boone (Thomas Mitchell), and Dallas (Claire Trevor)—is an outcast who has violated society's precepts in order to survive: Ringo is an accused murderer and escaped convict sworn to take the law into his own hands, while Doc Boone has turned to alcohol and Dallas to prostitution to survive on the frontier.

We are introduced to Dallas and Doc Boone as they are being driven out of town by the Ladies' Law and Order League, a group of puritanical, civic-minded women dedicated to upholding community standards. This scene is played for both comic and dramatic effect, but it does establish conformity and Victorian moralizing as elements of a well-ordered society. This initial view of the community's repressive and depersonalizing demands eventually is qualified by the film's resolution, however. Ringo and Dallas finally are allowed by the sheriff to flee to Ringo's ranch across the border. As the two ride away to begin a new life together the camera lingers on Doc Boone, ever the philosopher, who muses, "Well, they're saved from the blessings of civilization." Beneath his veneer of cynicism, however, is an optimistic vision: the uncivilized outlaw-hero and a woman practicing society's oldest profession have been united and go off to seek the promise of the American West's new world.

The Changing Vision of the West

The gradual fading of this optimistic vision, more than anything else, characterized the evolution of the Western genre. As the formula was refined through repetition, both the frontier community and its moralistic standard-bearers are depicted in increasingly complex, ambiguous, and unflattering terms. The Western hero, in his physical allegiance to the environment and his moral commitment to civilization, embodies this ambiguity. As such he tends to generate conflict through his very existence. He is a man of action and of few words, with an unspoken code of honor that commits him to the vulnerable Western community and at the same time motivates him to remain distinctly apart from it. As the genre develops, the Westerner's role as promoter of civilization seems to become almost coincidental. Eventually, his moral code emerges as an end in itself.

The stability of the westerner's character—his "style," as it were—doesn't really evolve with the genre. Instead, it is gradually redefined by the community he protects. Both the hero and the community establish their values and world view through their relationship with the savage milieu, but as the community becomes more civilized and thus more institutionalized, capitalistic, and corrupt, it gradually loses touch with the natural world from which it sprang. Because the Westerner exists on the periphery of both the community and the wilderness, he never loses touch with either world. His mediating function between them becomes increasingly complex and demanding as the society becomes more insulated and self-serving.

Actually, the image of the classic Westerner who mediates the natural and cultural environments while remaining distinct from each does not emerge as a mainstream convention until the mid-40s. In earlier films, the narrative conflicts were usually resolved with the suggestion that the Westerner might settle down within the community which his inclination toward violence and gunplay has enabled him to protect. The promise of marriage between Ringo and Dallas is indicative of this tendency, although their shared outlaw status and their eventual flight to Mexico undercut any simplistic reading of the film's prosocial resolution. A typical example of this tendency is William Wyler's 1940 film, *The Westerner*. In this film, the hero, Cole Hardin (Gary Cooper), mediates a violent confrontation between anarchic cattlemen and defenseless, idealistic homesteaders. These distinct communities are depicted in two narrative movements. The first shows Hardin's arrival and near lynching in a lawless cattle town run by the outrageous Judge Roy Bean (Walter Brennan), the self-appointed "law west of the Pecos." The second follows the hero's gradual assimilation into the community of homesteaders and his courtship of the farmer's daughter, Jane Ellen (Doris Davenport).

Bean's and Jane Ellen's worlds are locked in the familiar cattleman-homesteader struggle for control of the land, and Hardin is the only character who can function effectively in both worlds. Thus Wyler's film (from Jo Swerling's script) develops the classic configuration of the anarchic world of Male Savagery pitted against the civilized world of Woman and Home. The heroic Westerner, again, is poised between the two. Throughout the first half of the film, in which the competing ideologies are established, this configuration remains in perfect balance. Eventually, however, Hardin is won over by the woman-domesticator and turns against Bean, throwing off the film's narrative equilibrium. After Hardin prevails against Bean in a climactic gunfight, the Westerner is able to settle down with Jane Ellen in "the promised land."

Nothing could be more damaging to the hero's image, of course. He has compromised his self-styled, renegade world view by acquiescing to civilization's emasculating and depersonalizing demands. The earlier silent Westerns and their later low-budget counterparts had understood the logic of sending the Westerner "into the sunset" after the requisite showdown, thereby sustaining the genre's prosocial function while reaffirming the hero's essential individuality. Perhaps it was John Ford's experience with silent Westerns that motivated him to temper the marital and communal values of *Stagecoach's* resolution, or perhaps it was his intuitive understanding of what made the Western genre work. But certainly the ambiguous ending of Ford's film renders it decidedly more effective than most of the Westerns of its day. It was not actually until World War II and the ensuing post-war productions, though, that the Western hero and his particular role within the Western milieu would be radically reconsidered along the lines previously established in *Stagecoach*.

Shane: *The Initiate-Hero and the Integration of Opposites*

Shane filtered through the consciousness of a young boy (Brandon De Wilde as Joey Starrett), and much of the film's clarity of vision and idealized simplicity derives from his naive perspective. The actions of the principal characters, the setting of a lush green valley, even the distant Rocky Mountains, attain a dreamlike quality under George Stevens' direction and Loyal Grigg's cinematography.

The film opens with Shane (Alan Ladd) riding into the pastoral valley where ranchers and homesteaders are feuding. (As in *The Westerner*, "open range" and fenced-in farmland manifest the genre's nature/culture opposition.) Shane is a man with a mysterious past who hangs up his guns to become a farm laborer for Joe Starrett (Van Heflin), the spokesman for the homesteaders in their conflict with the villanous Ryker brothers.

The film is a virtual ballet of oppositions, all perceived from Joey's viewpoint. These oppositions become a series of options for him—and us—that he must negotiate in order to attain social maturity. The following diagram summarizes these oppositions.

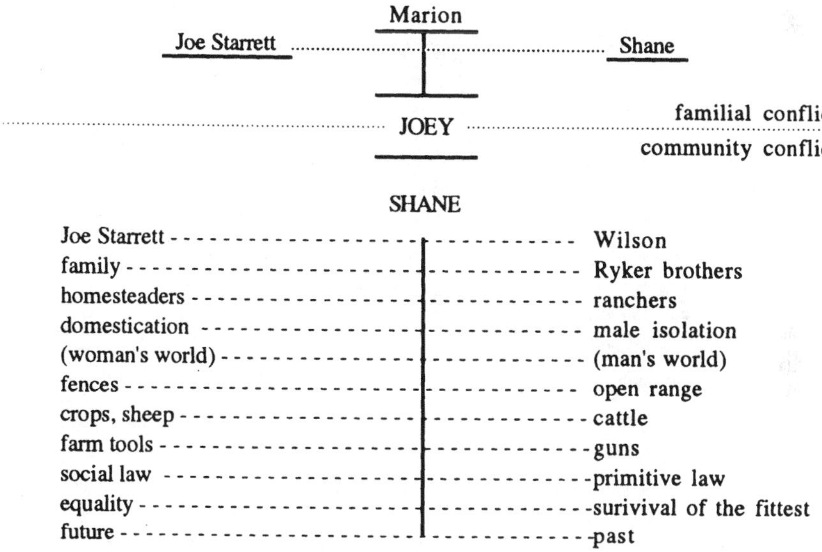

Marion

Joe Starrett .... Shane

JOEY .... familial conflicts / community conflicts

SHANE

Joe Starrett	Wilson
family	Ryker brothers
homesteaders	ranchers
domestication	male isolation
(woman's world)	(man's world)
fences	open range
crops, sheep	cattle
farm tools	guns
social law	primitive law
equality	surivival of the fittest
future	past

Not only does this diagram indicate the elaborate *doubling* in the narrative, but it also points up the hero's mediation of both the rancher-homesteader conflicts and the boy's confused notions of his ideal father figure. Although Starrett is the bravest and most capable of the homesteaders—and the only one respected and feared by the ranchers—he is basically a farmer of rural sensibilities and simple values. Starrett is clearly no match for Shane in either Joey's or his wife's (Jean Arthur) eyes, although the family proves strong enough to withstand the interloper's influence. By the end of the film, Marion's attraction to Shane

Shane (1953). The living legend and the initiate-hero.

complements her son's, although her family and her role as mother-domesticator remain her first concerns. In accord with her son's (and the genre's) sexual naiveté, the thought of Shane's and Marion's romantic entanglement is only a frustrating impossibility. Among Joey's parting cries to Shane as he rides away at the film's end is, "Mother wants you."

This sexual-familial conflict is, however, tangential to the film's central opposition between fenced land and open range. Nevertheless, it does reaffirm Shane's commitment to the values of home and family rather than those of power and capital. During the course of the film, Shane offers his services to the other farmers, but he is never really accepted because of his past and his stoic, detached manner. The cattlemen, who are generally seen drinking in the local saloon or else out harassing "sodbusters," show more respect for Shane than do the farmers, and attempt to recruit him at higher pay. Shane refuses, so the Rykers bring in Wilson (Jack Palance), a *doppelganger* from Shane's gunfighting past. Here, as in many genre films involving a violent, nomadic hero, the only real difference between the protagonist (Shane) and his antagonistic double (Wilson) has to do with their respective attitudes about social order and the value of human life.

The film ends with Shane knocking Starrett out with his pistol after a fierce fist-fight. He knows he must face Wilson and the Rykers alone. Joey follows Shane to town to watch the confrontation in the deserted saloon. Shane prevails against the men but is wounded, and he rides off into the mountains as Joey's calls echo after him. Those mountains, which like Shane's mysterious, violent past had remained in the background throughout the film, emerge now as his Olympus, as the Westerner's mythic realm beyond the reality of dirt farms and ramshackle towns.

But while Shane's heroic stature is affirmed, there is still a shade of ambiguity which tempers that stature. Just before the gunfight in the darkened saloon, Shane suggests to Ryker that "his days are numbered." "What about you, gunfighter?" asks Ryker. "The difference is, I know it," replies Shane, who then turns to the black-clad Wilson. The two simply stare at one another before the exchange of ritual dialogue that will initiate the gunfight. As in an earlier scene when the two had met and silently circled each other, a mutual understanding and respect is implicit in the look they exchange in addition to the promise of a violent, uncompromising confrontation. After the gunfight Shane tells Joey that "There's no living with the killing," but it's clear enough from the relationship established between Shane and Wilson that there's no living without it either. They purposefully end their days in a fashion that they could control and that we in the audience come to expect.

As these various examples indicate, the Westerner is motivated to further the cause of civilization by his own personal code of honor, which seems to be existentially derived. Often this code leads him to an act of vengeance. The vengeful hero is different from the classic Westerner in that his past—either his entire past or an isolated incident—is of immediate concern and provides him with a clear sense of mission. But he does share with the classic hero his characteristic function: he is an isolated, psychologically static man of personal integrity who acts because society is too weak to do so. And it is these actions that finally enforce social order but necessitate his departure from the community he has saved. In *Stagecoach, Winchester 73 (1950), The Searchers (1956), One-Eyed Jacks (1961), Nevada Smith (1966),* and countless other revenge Westerns, the hero rids society of a menace, but in so doing, he reaffirms his own basic incompatibility with the community's values.

The Changing Hero: The "Psychological" and "Professional" Westerns

As an element of our national mythology, the Western represents American culture, explaining its present in terms of its past and virtually redefining the past to accommodate the present. The image of the Western community in Hollywood movies tends to reflect our own beliefs and preoccupations, and the Western's evolution as a genre results both from the continual reworking of its own rules of construction and expression and also from the changing beliefs and attitudes of contemporary American society.

As American audiences after World War II became saturated with the classic Western formula and also more hardbitten about sociopolitical realities, the image of the Western community changed accordingly, redefining the hero's motivation and his sense of mission. Hence the "psychological" Westerns of the late 1940s and the 1950s that traced the Westerner's neuroses (and eventual psychoses) stemming from his growing incompatibility with civilization as well as the cumulative weight of society's unreasonable expectations.

One of the more notable examples of this development is Fred Zinneman's *High Noon,* in which a local lawman (Gary Cooper) awaits the arrival of outlaws bent on avenging his having sent their leader to prison. The wait for the arrival of the outlaws provides the dramatic tension in the film, which is heightened by the fact that the townspeople ignore or evade Cooper's appeals for assistance. After he and his Quaker wife (Grace Kelly), a woman committed to nonviolence for religious reasons, finally confront and dispose of the outlaws, Cooper throws his badge into the dirt and leaves the community to fend for itself.

Howard Hawks' *Rio Bravo* (1958), supposedly a belated answer to Zinneman's "knee-jerk liberalism," describes a similar situation in an even more claustrophobic and helpless community. From Hawks'

John Wayne and Jimmy Stewart in *The Shootist* (1976).

typically machismo perspective, however, the local lawman (John Wayne, with deputies Dean Martin, Walter Brennan, and Ricky Nelson) continually rejects offers of aid from the frightened citizenry, insisting, "This is no job for amateurs." Wayne and his cohorts prevail, and thus both the heroes and the community emerge with integrity intact. While *High Noon* and *Rio Bravo* each project substantially different views of the community and its redeemer-hero, both underscore the hero's incompatibility with the community. Ultimately, it is the hero's professional integrity and sense of responsibility to his job as lawman which induce him to act as an agent of social order.

The "professional" Western was, in fact, Hollywood's own answer to the psychological Western, much as Hawks' film had answered Zinneman's. In general, the psychological Western poses the question: how can the morally upright, socially autonomous Westerner continue to defend a repressive, institutionalized, cowardly, and thankless community without going crazy? The professional Western answers this question in one of two ways. The Westerner either works for pay and sells his special talents to the community that must evaluate his work on it own terms or else he becomes an outlaw.

The prospect of the classic, morally upright Westerner turning from his self-styled code of honor is closely related to the changing view of society in the Western. As the community's notion of law and order progressively squeezes out those rugged individualists who made such order possible, the Westerners turn to each other and to the outlaws they had previously opposed. At this point, the "honor among thieves" that the Westerner can find with other lawless types is preferable to buckling under to the community's emasculating demands.

Consequently, many recent Westerns incorporate a group that is led by an aging but still charismatic hero figure and whose demand of payment, either as professional killers or as outlaws, undercuts the classic Westerner's moral code. Thus the professional Westerns of the past three decades, most notably *Rio Bravo, The Magnificent Seven, The Professionals, El Dorado, the Wild Bunch, True Grit, Butch Cassidy and the Sundance Kid, The Cowboys, The Great Northfield Minnesota Raid, The Culpepper Cattle Company, and The Missouri Breaks.*

Gone in these films is the isolated, heroic cowboy with no visible means of support whose moral vision and spiritual values set him apart from—and essentially above—the community he defends. Now he is cynical, self-conscious, and even "incorporated"; these traits render him increasingly unheroic, more like one of us. Still, despite his gradual descent from heroic demigod (superior in many ways to nature as well as to other men) in early Westerns to a psychologically more complex and generally more sympathetic character, the Westerner does maintain distinct traces of his isolated sense of honor. He strikes a romantic pose even in the face of extinction.

Sam Peckinpah's *The Wild Bunch* (1969), for example, describes the exploits of an outlaw collective (William Holden, Ernest Borgnine, Warren Oates, Edmund O'Brien, Ben Johnson, et al.) in their sustained rampage through the American Southwest and in Mexico just before the outbreak of World War I. Whereas the outlaw collective violates with equal disregard the laws of God, man, and nature, the real villain of the piece is progress. Big business, typified by the banks and the railroad, force the Bunch out of the United States and into a confrontation with a corrupt Mexican bandit army. When one of their own group is captured and tortured by the Mexican bandits (whose leader has given up his horse for an automobile and is doing business with German warmongers), the Bunch undertakes a final, suicidal act of heroism—something that is very much in America's "national interest." In one of the most spectacular showdowns ever filmed, the Wild Bunch and the bandit army destroy each other in a quick-cut, slow-motion dream of blood and death.

Sam Peckinpah has understood and articulated, perhaps better than any Western filmmaker since John Ford, the concept of the Westerner who has outlived his role and his milieu. Particularly in *Ride the High Country* (1962), *Major Dundee* (1964), *The Wild Bunch* (1969), and *The Ballad of Cable Hogue* (1970), Peckinpah evokes a strong sense of irony and nostalgia in his presentation of a cast of aging heroic misfits. His men are hopelessly—and even tragically—at odds with the inexorable flow of history. The most evocative of these films is *Ride the High Country*, made in the same year as Ford's *The Man Who Shot Liberty Valance*. (Both films express regret over the passing of the Old West and its values.) The film stars Randolph Scott and Joel McCrae, two familiar cowboys from countless '40s and '50s Westerns, who are now reduced to tending bar and sharpshooting in a Wild West show. The opening sequence in *Ride the High Country* immediately establishes the hero's displacement in the new West and shows what he must do to contend with it. McCrae (as Steven Judd) arrives in town having given up his bartending job to guard a mine shipment, happy to return to the type of work which had sustained him through his more productive years. The town itself is modern, with automobiles, policemen, and even a Wild West show, where Judd finds his former deputy, Gil Westrum (Randolph Scott), reduced to a sideshow attraction. This opening sequence not only pits the old West against the new, but it also sets up an opposition between McCrae/Judd and Scott/Westrum. The former has retained his idealistic desire to continue as an agent of social order; the latter manifests a pragmatic willingness to make a profit off his former lawman status. Judd recruits Westrum to help him with the mine shipment, although Westrum agrees only because he assumes he'll eventually grab it for himself. Judd's reactionary idealism and Westrum's self-serving adaptability provide the central conflict throughout the film. This split is intensified by the presence of an initiate-hero (Ron Starr as Heck Longtree) who must decide between the two opposing world views. The initiate ultimately rejects Westrum's scheme to rob the shipment, and Westrum himself finally elects to join Judd and Longtree in a climactic showdown with another band of outlaws. The flexible, practical Westrum and the initiate Longtree survive the gunfight, but Judd falls, mortally wounded.

The film's closing shot is an over-the-shoulder, point-of-view shot from ground level, where we gaze with the dying Judd at the "high country" in the distance. As in the closing sequence in *Shane* (although this film is much bleaker in its outlook), the Westerner's status is reaffirmed in mythic proportions. However, instead of riding into the mountains as Shane had done, into the timeless terrain beyond the reach of civilization, Judd must be satisfied with only a dying glimpse of them.

Our Idealized Past: The Western

The Western, like the gangster and hardboiled detective genres, grudgingly recognized the inevitability of social progress as well as the individual sacrifice involved in society's progression. But despite the inexorable flow of civilization and history and its necessary transformation of the Western hero—or perhaps because of it—his heroic stature persists. The values associated with his individual character and posture are as important to us, the audience, as is the social order he provides. The violent resolution and departure of the Westerner at film's end, whether into the sunset or into the grave, not only ensure social order but also perpetuate the stoic self-reliance and willful violence embodied by the Westerner. Revisionist historians may insist that men like Wyatt Earp and Billy Bonney were hardly the heroic paragons that Hollywood movies have made them, but that is precisely the point of the genre film's mythic capacity. These films do not celebrate the past itself, but rather our contemporary idealized version of the past, which forms the foundation and serves as the model for our present attitudes and values.

Television Soap Opera: "Incest, Bigamy, and Fatal Disease"

Charles Derry

Soap operas have been a significant part of the world of popular entertainment in nearly all times and places. If we interpret the genre in the broadest possible way as a "serialized dramatic presentation of the emotional concerns and events of everyday life—with a moral" then we could easily include the literary works of Dickens, for example, whose long novels were actually published in installment fashion in nineteenth-century British popular magazines. We would also have no trouble identifying the conventions which mark today's adventures of young and restless dreamers and schemers in the more gentle, genteel events detailed "up the block and down the street" of early radio's Vic and Sade.

Soap operas offer an especially popular example of the essential conservatism of mass culture and, specifically, of popular formulas. They detail the "scandalous" actions of common folk who skirt around the boundaries of correct, socially acceptable behavior and whose radical doings enable the audience to experience vicariously the delights (and tingling fears) of rebellion in the kitchen, of revolution in the town square. And yet for all of their salacious surface characteristics—the affairs, blackmailings, murders plotted and carried through—the final determining force in the soap opera formula is embodied in the Community which finally judges and executes those who "go too far." The vixen of the kitchen is finally forced to give way to the good mother who watches all her children—and the soaps—with a cautionary "tsk tsk" on her lips and a glint in her eye.

Charles Derry does a fine job of identifying the formal conventions of soap operas—the plots, settings, characters and themes which provide the framework of the formula.

This article originally appeared in *The Journal of the University Film and Video Association*, Winter 1983, copyrighted by the author. This version is edited from the complete, revised version which appeared, by permission of the author, in *American Television Genres*, edited by Stuart M. Kaminsky, Chicago: Nelson-Hall, 1985.

To analyze soap opera is a difficult task, since one must first overcome the cultural prejudice against the genre. This prejudice is reflected even in the genre's name. The word *soap* is associated with these shows because originally they were used to sell soap and housekeeping products, as they still are. There is, therefore, irony and derision incorporated in the word. One cannot help but wonder why these shows came to be named for the products they sold. We do not refer to sports as beer or shaving shows, nor to the Saturday morning cartoons as breakfast food shows, nor to police shows like "The F.B.I." as automobile dramas. Associating these shows with the word *soap* implies that the genre is simply a vehicle to sell soap and, in and of itself, lacks any inherent meaning or value. Such an attitude indicates a prejudice in that it accuses one genre, the soap opera, of being what all television shows must be to their producers—that is, a means of selling a product.

More insidious is the male chauvinism in this attitude: the "soap" label binds these shows to that which our society has held to be unimportant: "women's work." This false association promotes the misguided, sexist premises that soap opera belongs exclusively to women and that the genre, therefore, reflects a sentimental, escapist, and/or hysterical sensibility. Studies of soap opera audiences have shown that the majority are women, in part because women have historically tended to be home in the afternoon, when these programs are run; however, of the male television population at home in the afternoon, basically similar percentages are watching. High numbers of policemen, second-shift factory workers, and college students watch the soap opera as well—a fact that should effectively destroy the myth that their audiences are exclusively composed of unliberated housewives.

A sustained examination of soap opera reveals a sensibility that is nowhere Pollyanna-ish or simplistic but often ambiguous and ideologically progressive. The word *soap* further ties in to the genre's subversive subtext. There is an ironic symbiosis between the genre's "unwholesome" content, which deals with socially dirty or taboo concepts, and the commercials, which deal with the superficial cleaning of surfaces. In this sense, the term *soap* redeems the program material by symbolically cleansing it. If Westerns are titled thus because they deal with the West, and detective shows titled thus because they deal with detectives, could our society really accept a genre entitled "Incest, Bigamy, and Fatal Disease"?

Like *soap*, the word *opera* tends to be derisive and ironic. Opera is high art which stylizes human emotional experience, while these programs are low art.

Opera is popularly disliked but respected, while television soap opera is popularly liked but disrespected. Thus, opera and, by extension, its audience are validated, while television soap opera and its audience are not.

The *opera* appellation is nonironically relevant, however, in the way that the television soap opera, like its higher-art counterpart, is predicated upon extensive stylization of human emotional experience. Thus, *soap* and *opera* both describe and ridicule the form. This cultural rejection of soap opera creates a situation of guilt for the viewers, who generally apologize for their pleasure. It is no wonder that soap opera producers and writers often call their product "daytime drama" to avoid such prejudicial baggage....

Soap operas reject the traditionally structured plot, whereby a character is embroiled in a conflict that leads to an integrated series of crises and one concluding climax. Stories in soap opera move more with the haphazardness of life. Conflicts may develop quickly and then suddenly be suspended (in soap opera parlance, be "put on the back burner"); characters' problems may be solved haphazardly without a climax; a character may dominate the narrative and then suddenly become irrelevant. Sometimes a major event (such as a storm or a revealed secret) can, without warning, change everything. Other times, a main character, perhaps even one around whom an entire show is built, can suddenly die, and the narrative can simply and cruelly continue on—a shocking resilience relating to the real-life situation in which we all inevitably consider ourselves the focus of the primary narrative and find it difficult to conceive of a world going on without us. That some of these phenomena are caused, inevitably, by the exigencies of performers' contracts and ratings does not mitigate the basic, inescapable resemblances between soap opera and life: In both, things just keep happening....

A good example of this unconventional narrative can be found in "All My Children," which dealt with the story of innocent Mary Kennicott, all-American girl, and her marriage to upstanding Dr. Jeff Martin, all-American boy. The problem began when Mary started to suffer dizzy spells. Although blood tests initially proved negative, the spells did not go away, and ultimately, the test indicated a problem with Mary's blood cells. At least a year of episodes chronicled—albeit torturously slowly, on the back burner—Mary's health problem. The experienced viewer knew—indeed, at Mary's final fainting spell—that it was only a matter of time before the diagnosis would come in as... leukemia, and the story would jump to the front burner. One day, when Mary was at home and the audience was expecting the definitive lab results that would finally catapult the story to its inevitable hospital stay, pain, remission, remorse, regret, pregnancy, miscarriage, loss, and life-and-death struggle, an escaped convict broke into Mary's house and killed her. The leukemia story, so carefully set up, was itself aborted by the intruder who seemed almost outside the control of the writers themselves. In what other genre—other than life itself—is the precipitous removal of main characters such a seminal organizing principle? Thus the continuing nature

When the millions of fans of soaps aren't tuned in, they keep up with magazines and newspaper features.

of soap operas allows them to deal with the very capriciousness of existence.

....To understand exactly how soap opera is organized, it is useful to divide the genre into its component parts—focusing on temporal structures, spatial structures, themes, plots, and character types.

Temporal Structures

The temporal components of soap operas are extremely complex, in that contradictory time schemes can coexist. First there is what can be termed a *Landmark Time*: that is, the episode broadcast on Thanksgiving is generally represented as Thanksgiving, as is the Christmas episode Christmas. Landmark Time is complicated by the intrusion of *Extended Time*, whereby one day of soap opera story can be extended into a week or more of half-hour or hour episodes. Once on "General Hospital," preceding the murder of Phil Brewer, the show's chief villain for over ten years, one day of soap opera story took close to two months of episodes, and the hour including his murder took two weeks. Thus, it is possible for a soap opera to present a year of Landmark Time between Christmas episodes, even though, in Extended Time, the soap opera—in those approximately 250 episodes of story—presents only two or three weeks....

Soap opera time is also made more complicated by certain story events which are allowed their own idiosyncratic time schemes. For instance, although a woman may conceive on a November episode, she may not give birth until almost two years of episodes later; although the term of her pregnancy represents nine months, by the time of her delivery she may have actually passed two Christmas episodes pregnant (although by the same token, those episodes may have only represented four or five months of Extended Time). If pregnancy seems to take more time, early childhood growth seems to take less. If a soap opera girl is born, say, on a January episode, it is not at all surprising that on the episode broadcast exactly two years later, she (with the help of a different performer) may celebrate her fourth or fifth birthday. Similarly, a child may advance to teenage status in a matter of six or seven years. The benefit of this rapid growth is that once a child reaches the teens, she or he is qualified for sexual/romantic/familial problems; subsequently, children in soap opera grow so fast that members of different generations tend to be near contemporaries, and relatively young women tend to be grandparents even while continuing to have children of their own. Since prepubescent children tend not to be able to have soap-operatic problems, it is for these ages that the mortality rate is the highest. If a soap opera child can survive these years, she or he is lucky indeed: more often than not, survival can be attributed to the mercy and acumen of writers who will send the child into a upstairs room or boarding school for a few years or so, to be rescued at a useful older age when it is narratively convenient and not inordinately farfetched to do so....

Spatial Structures

The spatial component of virtually every soap opera operates primarily within the context of a specific city—generally Smalltown, U.S.A. "All My Children" takes place in Pine Valley; "Another World" in Bay City; "General Hospital" in Port Charles; "Mary Hartman, Mary Hartman" in Fernwood; "Days of Our Lives" in Salem; and "As the World Turns" in Oakdale.... Fictional soap opera cities are often given elaborate geographical identities. Pine Valley, for instance, is close enough to commute to New York City by train; two of its neighbor cities include Center City (which is where the prostitutes live) and Llanview, Pennsylvania, the base of operations for "One Life to Live." The proximity of Llanview, Pennsylvania (as well as its creation by Agnes Nixon, the writer-producer of "All My Children"), allows the soap operatic worlds of these two series to connect and enables characters to occasionally move from one show (and city) to the other—as attorney Paul Martin of "All My Children" did once for the murder trial of Vicki Riley of "One Life to Live," and a second time, years later, for the murder trial of Vicki's husband, Clint Buchanan.

The stability of the usual setting contrasts with the turbulence of the characters' personal lives. Soap opera towns are comprised of designer boutiques, designer hospitals, well-appointed homes in a variety of tasteful/conventional styles, and plenty of opportunities to accidentally run into your enemies at the health club/art gallery/free clinic/disco.

The incursion of political corruption or crime becomes therefore all the more horrifying. The mythically beleaguered down of Monticello, locale of "The Edge of Night," must deal with the seemingly unending horrors inflicted by psychotic killers and organized-crime chieftains; Llanview has had already to deal with its first massage parlor as well as with left-wing terrorism; the New York City of "Ryan's Hope" is riddled through and through with mob control, nursing home scandals, and political shenanigans. The most recurrent example of corruption in these programs is prostitution. Perhaps the title "The Edge of Night" provides the most apt metaphor: the nearness of darkness and decay to communities that appear to be light and forthright. If this metaphor emphasizes the corruption of our society, the metaphoric title of "The Secret Storm" emphasizes the corruption and obsessions of the individual.

The emphasis on the individual psyche in soap operas is reflected in the emphasis on the world of the indoors. Certainly the enclosed spaces of the soap opera contribute to a sense of entrapment, allowing the characters to contemplate, discuss, and act upon their guilty desires. Given this emphasis on interiors, it is not surprising that the soap opera has developed a stable of specific interiors—each of which serves a metaphorical function that allows the genre to deal with one or more of its themes.

Among the most important of these interiors is *The Hospital*, which is always, no matter how small a town, one of the most modern in the country, with the latest multi-million-dollar technological equipment. Its staff, however, includes only a few surgeons who are talented enough to do emergency surgery, a situation that inevitably causes problems when an emergency occurs while a surgeon has a broken arm or is temporarily psychologically paralyzed. The interior allows the genre to deal with the theme of life and death: patients hovering on the edges of existence, guilt-ridden, contemplative, their own destinies about to be sealed as ever-widening circles of cause and effect engulf the other characters and their world. Many soap operas emphasize the hospital almost exclusively—an emphasis reflected in titles such as "The Nurses," "The Doctors," and "General Hospital." Indeed, there is no afternoon soap opera that does not include a hospital in a more or less prominent position.

The Court Room serves the genre as a locale where characters can deal with right and wrong, guilt and innocence. Inevitably, a major story will build to a murder and then culminate in a dramatic trial in which culpability will be attributed. Guilt in soap operas is complex: generally, whenever a murder is committed, most of the characters are psychologically guilty of having at least wished the evil deed. Uncovering the actual murderer—who is often psychologically innocent—is quite difficult. Significantly, the use of the courtroom does not reflect the genre's faith in social justice or the American political system. On the contrary, the soap opera suggests that justice cannot be organized by a social agency but only, on occasion, by a capricious fate. The government frequently puts the wrong party on trial, just as the jury almost always finds the innocent person guilty....

The Newspaper Office and The TV Studio function as a place for the dissemination of information or gossip, thus documenting the dynamic by which the attitudes and sensibilities of the soap opera community are formed. There is or was a newspaper office in "Peyton Place," "Somerset," "One Life to Live," and "The Edge of Night," among others. There is or was a television studio in "Ryan's Hope," "One Life to Live," "General Hospital," and "All My Children." Many of soap opera's most attractive characters are involved in the media search for truth: the late Joe Riley, editor extraordinaire of "One Life to Live," for instance, or Jack Fenelli, hard-hitting columnist of "Ryan's Hope." Of all the soap operas, "Mary Hartman, Mary Hartman" took fullest advantage of these themes, making obsessive fun of media targets as varied as Dinah Shore, David Susskind, cinema vérité, the eleven o'clock news, the television talk show, the radio call-in program, and investigative reporting—in the process lambasting the media's role in programming us to bourgeois tastes and attitudes. "Mary Hartman, Mary Hartman" is in contrast, of course, to the more conventional soap opera, which often presents media as having an almost mystical relationship with truth and discovery.

The Restaurant or Nightclub allows the genre to deal with the process of socialization. In these locations people meet, glances are exchanged, trysts are arranged, coincidences occur, secrets are overheard, and rumors are begun. If the soap opera generally eschews exteriors, it is the nightclub that provides an interior to which the characters can journey in search of human contact or social reinforcement. Not surprisingly, encounters are frequently disastrous....

Lastly, *The Private Home* provides the setting for the most personal obsessions of the individual: the ambitions, dreams, guilts, and sexual pleasures that originate here, only to affect/contaminate/transform the entire community. Until the last few years, the emphasis has been on the sitting or living room: sipping coffee or tea, characters would talk to each other about their problems. More recently, however, the bedroom has increasingly become a major focus: no longer do we only hear characters talking about their sexual/romantic exploits, we witness them (albeit tastefully, with careful ellipses and only marginal nudity)....

Conventional Themes

The third component of soap opera, the thematic, is best approached through a trichotomous organization: 1) the breaking of taboos, 2) the basic horrific and random destiny, which organizes the universe and all of our lives, and 3) the twin mysteries of birth and death, which confront and confound us at every turn.

In *Totem and Taboo*, Freud discusses one of the most basic taboos: the prohibition against having sexual intercourse with members of forbidden totem clans. Just what constitutes a taboo varies among cultures, but soap operas most frequently present a dominant female character who breaks the taboos defined by the status quo—either consciously or as a result of subconscious urges she can neither understand nor control. Invariably, this female is one of the most popular characters on the program. Although she may be committing acts society would regard as destructive, our attitude towards her is ambivalent and rather sympathetic. She does what others refrain from because they fear the social disruption and personal tragedy that may result from breaking the taboo.

After undergoing two miserable marriages, unhappy, doomed Erica on "All My Children" finally finds a man whom she loves and who loves her;

we empathize with her determination to marry him, although we are taken aback at the revelation—discovered but not believed by Erica until the last moment—that the man she intends to marry is actually a long-lost half-brother. Narrowly escaping that taboo, Erica's fixation on her dead father leads her next to an erotic obsession with Nick Davis, the older man who had been the best friend of Erica's own mother as well as the father of one of Erica's own ex-husbands. Incestuous and pseudo-incestuous relationships like these are common....

Anyone who violates a taboo and challenges society can then become taboo and infect others. Erica on "All My Children," for instance, has at times been avoided like the plague by almost everyone in Pine Valley. Occasionally "All My Children" will present an episode comprised of good-intentioned Erica making calls on a variety of characters, all of whose lives she obliviously leaves in shambles.

The contagion of the taboo breaker is itself a kind of punishment which ensures that taboo-breaking is not condoned. Although we may wish that the taboo breaker be punished, our response is complex, because we spend so much time in secret empathy that our hope is eventually replaced by a dread of the inevitable outcome. Often sins and deceit will so compound themselves in the course of several years of a soap opera narrative that no punishment could ever redress the broken taboos. The genre rejects any simple concepts of justice and rarely punishes the taboo breaker at the moment of his or her most arrogant act. What happens more frequently is that circumstances begin to change the behavior of the taboo breaker—who is not punished until her or his life has already begun to become more conventional. Thus, when the punishment arrives, there is the overwhelming sense that it is no longer fair. Even worse, the punishment often destroys the former taboo breaker, who becomes contaminated once again.

A recent example of this can be found in Karen Wolek's adventures on "One Life to Live." Karen began as the archetypal evil woman. Mean and pretty toward her sister, Jenny, an ex-nun, the ex-con Karen schemed herself into marriage with a respectable doctor and then promptly became a nymphomaniac and a prostitute. Her sordid life climaxed with a hit-and-run accident which left a little boy dead and at least three lives shattered. The virtuous heroine Vicki came to Karen's aid and helped Karen change her ways; just as Karen was almost completely transformed, fate intervened again and put Vicki on trial for murder. Only Karen's testimony could help clear her; it was, dramatically, during cross-examination that Karen's overwhelming guilt was expiated in a remarkable courtroom scene in which Karen, in a selfless attempt to save Vicki, allowed herself to be broken down, hysterically confessing her nymphomania, prostitution, and manslaughter to a shocked town. So completely destroyed and humiliated was Karen that the audience could not help but feel guilty for having ever wished Karen's sins to be revealed. Karen spent the subsequent year of the story undergoing more trials, redeemed by her suffering and assimilated back into Llanview society only when she was victimized and raped by her taboo-breaking brother-in-law.

If villainous women like Karen are often redeemed (if temporarily), villainous men are often simply expelled from the soap opera community. Sometimes they are killed—which results in a trial and untold misery for the other characters; other times they merely go away—to Argentina or somewhere, coming back periodically to do more damage when the plot requires stirring. In the last few years, however, there have been a variety of villainous men, who, in their own neurotic ways, break taboos, are redeemed, and break taboos again—much like the villainous women....

Soap operas do not, however, as is sometimes claimed, deal simplistically with the idea of sin being followed inexorably by punishment. Although it is true that taboo breakers are generally punished, it is also true that those who do not break taboos are also generally punished—though for what? If many plots revolve around an individual transgressing society's rules, just as many revolve around a conventional individual buffeted by an essentially horrific destiny. A good person will be struck by a train and develop amnesia (Donna Beck Tyler on "All My Children"); a doctor, on the verge of announcing the solution to a mystery, will suddenly have a heart attack and die (Dr. Peter Taylor on "General Hospital); a virtuous heroine will be viciously killed by thugs (Mary Ryan on "Ryan's Hope"). The innocent, you see, suffer also.

Indeed, perhaps the most important aspect of soap opera is the way the genre reflects some of our most profound fears: that is, that the universe is hostile, that fate conspires against us, that every life leads inevitably to death. If our belief in God or a plan allows that hubris will be punished by nemesis, our skepticism regarding God's goodness allows that innocence will also be punished. No one stays happy.... Our empathy with the taboo breaker stems directly from this cynicism: if one cannot count on just rewards, why should one accept moral constraints? Why not pursue fulfillment according to one's own selfish instincts?

So obsessively willed is selfish Erica on "All My Children" that every one of her successful plots represents a minor victory over the chaotic and malevolent destiny. It is this emphasis on *destiny* that is responsible for the major mode of irony that the soap opera so clearly expresses. Two examples will suffice. The first ten years of "General Hospital" revolved around the doomed love affair between Dr. Steve Hardy and Audrey March. A variety of problems kept them irrevocably apart, love-torn and unhappy. When finally, after a decade of episodes, a nonchalant conversation turned suddenly into a mutual declaration of love, Dr. Hardy (goodness personified) announced to Audrey, "We're going to live happily ever after," and bounded ecstatically out of the room, whereupon he promptly fell down a flight of stairs and became critically injured. Only soap opera could get away with that kind of blatantly ironic and bleak juxtaposition. Likewise, a character may cause misery for others even though she or he is not, strictly speaking, a taboo breaker. A good example of this is Jennie, the virtuous ex-nun from "One Life to Live," whom fate seems to take an extra pleasure in torturing. Pursued at various times by at least four different men, Jennie saw the first die in a fall during an argument in which he was trying to convince others that he wasn't corrupting her; the second guiltily give up his romantic obsession with Jennie when his jealous wife committed suicide; the third become a rapist, a corporate criminal, and possibly a murderer; and the fourth institutionalize his jealous-crazed wife and then himself die in a horrible automobile accident while trying to prevent Jennie from hearing a life-shattering secret. Jennie is a kind of taboo but not a taboo breaker: suffering, smiling, blameless, innocent, beloved—but with fate dooming her and those around her to cosmic unhappiness.

Accompanying soap opera's emphasis on taboos and fate is the genre's obsession with the twin mysteries of birth and death. Women in soap opera are always obsessed with pregnancy: will they deliver safely? Time is most extended during the nine months in which the woman carries her child; has there ever been even one soap opera pregnancy that did not include a hospital stay after a near miscarriage? If it is the mother who is given the responsibility of childbirth (always portrayed as dangerous, traumatic, but wished for), it is the father who is given the responsibility for the actual genesis of life—but which man?

Paternity is soap opera's most critical and often unknowable issue. Little Phil Tyler's father on "All My Children" is not Chuck Tyler but actually Phil Brent; similarly, Phil Brent's own father is not Ted Brent but Nick Davis. Little Brian Kendall's father on "One Life to Live" is not Paul Kendall but actually Tony Harris; similarly, Tony's father is actually the multimillionaire Victor Lord, whose name Tony finally adopts. Soap operas can be seen as a search for paternity, an exploration of the meaning of the man/woman union in the face of their different physiological relationship to the procreative function. It is not at all uncommon for a soap opera to reveal or alter a paternity long after a child's birth. Although "General Hospital" began in 1963, only several years ago was Dr. Steve Hardy revealed to be the father of Dr. Jeff Webber....

The soap opera emphasis on the pre-birth state and the attendant concerns of miscarriage, still birth, and abortion are balanced by the genre's emphasis on the pre-death state of semiconsciousness and coma and the attendant concerns of mercy killing and suicide. At what point does an individual really die? Soap opera characters constantly fall into critical comas, as they linger for months of episodes in semiconscious states. And yet even when a character does die, this finality is attenuated by the fact that, as often as not, he or she comes back! In soap opera you can never count on a character's death—particularly if you haven't seen the body in the casket. And even if you have (for instance, Marco Dane in "One Life to Live"), it's possible that the individual may return (you see, the real corpse was Mario Dane, Marco's twin brother, invented specifically by the writers to allow Marco's complex return)....

As with procreation, the ambiguity regarding mortality tends to be more often reserved for men. It is almost as if man's mobility, unhampered by pregnancy and its complications, inherently allows him the facility to transcend physical limits more easily. Women are invariably victims of this ambiguity, forced into accidental bigamy upon the return of their presumed-dead spouses. Ironically, both these birth and death concerns tend to put women in the victim position, a circumstance that understandably promotes feminist analysis of the genre.

Conventional Plots

In the service of the thematic organizations articulated above, the soap opera enlists a variety of conventional plots. They are described below:

Love Confronted by Obstacles

Soap operas thrive on the love affair that cannot be consummated. Perhaps the best example—certainly the most drawn out—is the story of Phil and Tara on "All My Children." Although they loved each other as far back as high school, their marriage plans fell through when Phil left town after he developed amnesia upon the discovery of his real parentage. In the meantime, Tara becomes involved with Phil's best friend Chuck and indeed would have married him had he not, in the middle of the ceremony, gone into kidney failure. While Chuck recuperated, the returned Phil, himself recovered, reestablished his relationship with Tara. As Tara decided to break it off with Chuck, Phil was unexpectedly drafted. A snowstorm on the eve of Phil's departure overseas prevented their elopement, so Tara and Phil married themselves in a makeshift ceremony. Just as Chuck had recovered enough to allow Tara to tell him the truth about her relationship with Phil, word came that Phil had been killed in Vietnam. Tara decided to go through with the wedding to Chuck—because now she was carrying Phil's child, who needed a father. Surprisingly, miraculously, Phil came back from Vietnam—not really dead—and figured out, after more than a year, that Tara's child was really his, but not before he married Erica out of desperation and loneliness. Remembering how Phil reacted to the revelation of his own paternity, Tara was too afraid to disrupt her own marriage and reveal her son's actual paternity—even though she still loved Phil. By the time Phil divorced Erica, Tara was finally psychologically ready to leave Chuck. Just as she was about to tell Chuck that she wanted to marry her one great love, Chuck went into kidney failure—again postponing the inevitable. By the time Chuck was sufficiently recovered to be told of Tara's and Phil's intentions, Phil's son, who did not yet know who his real father was, had begun opposing his mother's divorce and developing psychosomatic asthma attacks which were successfully preventing his parents' union. When Tara and Phil finally did get together—many obstacles later—Phil was transferred to Washington, where he promptly went on a secret mission and was reported killed. Tara moved back to Pine Valley, where she was cautiously being comforted by Chuck, who had since himself remarried....

The Slow and Drawn-Out Death

Shall the plugs be pulled? Can one die in dignity? Occasionally, when a romance does manage to succeed against all obstacles, and more problems that will pit them against one another, the only solution is to give one of the characters an incurable disease. This is precisely what happened to Linc Tyler and the late Kitty Shea on "All My Children." So popular was this story that the actress who played Kitty was resurrected as Kitty's long-lost twin sister Kelly, who then proceeded to fall in love with Linc Tyler herself.

The Sudden and Unexpected Accident or Illness

This device seems always to work as a reminder that fate can intercede at any moment and dramatically, in one bold stroke, change everything. Examples include Brian's accident on "One Life to Live" or Mary Ryan's death on "Ryan's Hope."

Personal Tensions That Erupt into a Murder and a Trial

This plot is used periodically by almost every soap opera. Examples include the murder of Eddie Dorrance on "All My Children" and the murder of Marco (or was it Mario?) on "One Life to Live."

The Intrusion of a Psychotic Killer

When events are not complex enough in themselves, the writers can introduce a psychotic killer. In "Ryan's Hope," for instance, there was Kenneth Castle, who terrorized Faith Coleridge before pushing her father off a roof.

The Appearance of the Split Personality

This plot twist raises the issue of identify, wherein a good character is threatened by a second personality over which he or she has little control. In "One Life to Live," for instance, Kathy Craig escaped her problems by escaping into the identity of Kitty Mainwaring. Similarly, in the same show, virtuous Vicki Riley has been occasionally taken over by her alter ego Nicki Smith.

The Romeo and Juliet Story

Often a romance blossoms between characters of different backgrounds. Examples include rich Linc Tyler and poor Kitty Shea of "All My Children," Irish Eileen Riley and Jewish David Siegel of "One Life to Live," and the middle-aged Ellen Grant and very young Dale Robinson of "Somerset."

Amnesia

At the drop of a hat, characters can suffer memory loss, a condition that usually serves to convolute time by effectively undoing large portions of the narrative. A good example is from "All My Children," where Donna Beck, a hardened prostitute, spent almost two years of episodes changing into an innocent, reformed young wife. Just as the transformation became complete, a train accident triggered amnesia; when Donna regained consciousness, she thought she was still a prostitute, and the entire process of evolution and transformation had to begin all over again.

Unintentional Bigamy

The most famous soap opera bigamists include Jessie Brewer Taylor of "General Hospital," who was married to Peter Taylor as well as to Phil Brewer; her friend Audrey Baldwin Hardy, who was married to Steve Hardy as well as to Tom Baldwin; and Vicki Burke Riley of "One Life to Live," who was married to Steven Burke and Joe Riley.

Career Strivings

Many soap operas revolve around a company and the various characters who try to get ahead: examples include the Delaney Brands Company in "Somerset," Ewing Oil in "Dallas," and the Frame Enterprises in "Another World." Increasingly, women are insisting on careers too: Nina as a corporate executive in "All My Children."

Romantic and Sexual Adventures

The most obvious (and often convoluted) of the conventional soap opera plots concern love and sex. On "General Hospital," for instance,

Diana loved Phil, who loved Jessie, who was married to Peter, who offered to marry Diana, who was much later jealous of Leslie, who loved Rick, who loved Monica, who was married to Jeff, who became enamored of Diana...and so forth. Human companionship is valuable and difficult to attain; certainly an irony of soap opera is that the characters spend so much of their time chasing after fulfillment with so little success.

Character Types

Characterization and types, comprising the final component of soap opera, tend to be subordinated to plot. Striking in soap opera is the way that characters are isolated from any contemporary context. References to real news are extremely rare; current events are introduced only when they can be used as plot devices.... Soap opera characters do not read books; they do not go to movies; they do not talk about politics; they tend not to have hobbies; they tend not to watch television; and, except for weddings and funerals, they tend not to go to church—in short, when you put them in a room together, they have nothing else to talk about except whether or not they are happy.

Soap opera characters *are* their problems. This decultured context raises the soap opera to the level of myth. When the characters converse, as they do endlessly, it is invariably about tragedy. Because the stories are continuing, almost anything a character says has an ironic horrific subtext relating to some past trauma that has not yet been resolved. Characters imprison themselves in their own past: can they ever forget? Certainly they cannot learn—either from their own experiences or from the experiences of others. Characters generally exhibit a total obliviousness to the implications of the stories in which they are involved and the lessons they should be learning. A good example is from "All My Children," where a major plot line of its first decade revolved around the countless horrible repercussions of having suppressed Little Phil's true paternity. When the situation finally erupted into one overwhelming catastrophe, the character of Anne Tyler reflected on what a horrible decision had been made so many years ago in creating the lie and then blithely attempted, on that very episode, to arrange a similar deception in regard to her own unborn child. Soap opera characters are self-absorbed, clever, stupid, and doomed; like us?

Among the characters, there is, first of all, a distinction between *The Involved* and *The Uninvolved*. Characters in the former category are actively involved in trauma and adventure. Characters in the latter category, in soap opera parlance referred to as tent-pole characters, have few adventures, existing mainly so that the involved can have someone to talk to. The uninvolved keep the tent of the show standing while the others thrash about within it. Jessie Brewer, on "General Hospital," began her soap opera career as one of the most active of the involved characters: for ten years she was intimate with murder, adultery, bigamy, and fatal disease. More recently, as new and younger characters have been introduced, Jessie has been transformed into a tent-pole character without significant problems. For weeks at a time, she may be almost completely written out of the action; when she does participate, it is generally to offer advice, warning, or sympathy. She and the once involved Dr. Steve Hardy of the same show have been transformed into a kind of matriarch and patriarch: fine parent figures, because they keep their advice good and themselves scarce....

The involved characters can themselves be divided into *The Active* and *The Passive*—those who actively break taboos and suffer and those who passively allow fate (and others) to buffet them horrifically. Perhaps the archetypal examples of this dichotomy are Erica and Tara from "All My Children": Erica, the femme fatale, who refuses to allow anything to stand in her way, and Tara, a dishrag heroine, devoted to her child and to anyone with a problem. Each character represents an opposing response to soap opera's unanswering *Weltanschauung*.

Most of the characters on soap opera tend to be middle- or upper-middle-class. They gravitate toward the professions of doctor and lawyer. Other typical occupations include business, journalism, nursing, and writing. Soap operas present a world that is upwardly mobile. Although it is the doctors and lawyers who impress us, it is the working-class characters, trying to escape their class, who most provoke our empathy. Bobbi Spencer, for a while the most neurotic and empathetic villain of "General Hospital," is an orphan and former prostitute determined to succeed no matter what; becoming a nurse was only her first step. The same show's lower-class Heather at one point married for money and then sold her own baby to get ahead. Marco Dane of "One Life to Live," an eternal outsider, tried to succeed through pimping and organized crime; when these schemes failed, he simply adopted the identity of a doctor and went to work in the local hospital, the townspeople almost instantly according him respect because of his title.

Although many critics have objected to soap opera's depiction of the traditional women's roles as mother, daughter, and housewife, the fact remains that soap opera depicts more women and careers than does any other genre. Two leading characters on "General Hospital," Leslie Webber and Monica Webber Quartermaine, are both doctors; on "One Life to Live," the main characters, Vicki Riley and Pat Ashley, are both journalists; and the Coleridge sisters of "Ryan's Hope," Faith and Jill, are, respectively, a doctor and an attorney extraordinaire. Rare is the soap opera female who doesn't also hold down a job outside the home.

Related to upward mobility and the bourgeois values such strivings reflect is the decidedly WASP identity of most soap opera characters. Pioneering work to transcend this orientation was done on Agnes Nixon's "One Life to Live," which introduced ethnic Jews, blacks, and Poles as major characters, as well as on "Ryan's Hope," with its aggressive working-class Irish-Catholic New York milieu and its ethnic Italians and Latinos. There is, nevertheless, a distinction on most soap operas between the upper-middle-class WASP and others; the latter tend to be more colorful and speak in working-class accents, which often seem to parody their class or heritage. Minorities are not always completely assimilated into the soap opera narrative; for example, although there are blacks on "All My Children," they remained tent-pole characters throughout the early years of the series; when, several years ago, Frank and Nancy did acquire a plot of their own, it tended to parallel rather than intersect those of other characters. Only in the last several years have the stories of black characters begun more strikingly to intermesh with the narrative as a whole.

Despite the fact that certain character types recur—such as the perfectly good woman (Jessie) or the all-forgiving, understanding man (the late Pete Taylor of "General Hospital")—soap opera characters are surprisingly three-dimensional. This is in part promoted by certain exigencies of soap opera production: 1) an established soap opera actor is often replaced by another actor to play the same character, 2) each actor, when playing the same role virtually every day for years, cannot help but bring to the performance some of her or his own actual personality, and 3) as writers are replaced, characters and their behavior cannot help but change. Thus while soap opera characters may be basically stock and subservient to the narrative, they become complex as they constantly exhibit paradoxical behavior which is then assimilated into our understanding of their characters.

Concluding Ideas

.... A final, crucial point about soap opera concerns the way the generic material reaches the audience. Although soap operas are televised, it has been noted that audiences do not watch consistently from beginning to end the way they might watch a movie or even a "validated" program like "Hill Street Blues." Since many soap opera watchers are simultaneously cleaning house, studying, or eating, they do not always pay the kind of attention generally afforded other aesthetic creations. In fact, it is not at all unusual for an individual to listen to a soap opera from another room (without seeing the picture) or to watch the picture (with the sound turned off) while talking on the phone; that either the image or sound alone is often sufficient to communicate the genre's essence is testament to the high level of redundancy.

Clearly, the content is significantly more important than the specific form in which that content is embodied. This leads to a crucial fact: that is, it is possible to "watch" television soap opera without even owning a television set. The continuing stories are chronicled in numerous books, many magazines, and syndicated weekly soap opera columns in most big-city newspapers. There is, as well, an ongoing network of soap opera watchers who communicate with each other in person, by phone, and in letter as to the latest development. Many soap opera "watchers" are those who have literally watched the show for a period of their lives and now continue to "watch" them through other means.

The ongoing adventures of Tara and Erica seep, by a kind of cultural osmosis, into our social and psychological world; the evil of J.R. had a meaning even for those who did not watch "Dallas" every week. Soap opera may be television's closest analogue to pure myth, where the created aesthetic experience is less important than the ongoing, hidden mythical structure. Future study of soap opera might well take Claude Lévi-Strauss and structural anthropology as a model and view soap opera as revelatory of our contemporary beliefs and needs. Soap opera invites this kind of analysis—which will surely follow; and indeed, perhaps only then will soap opera achieve the respectability that it so clearly deserves.

Monster Movies: A Sexual Theory

Walter Evans

Whoever fights monsters should see to it that in the process he does not become a monster.
Nietzsche

Our traditional monsters are our creations, but they are also us—*these dark aspects of ourselves which we seek to deny and which, therefore, we must destroy (with silver bullet, stake through the heart, or all-consuming flame). The beast within all humans finds its horrifying face in the gradual (but uncontrollable) transformation of "even a man who is pure at heart" into the Wolfman, the botched electrical experiment which brings a tortured life to the rotting corpses which form Frankenstein's Monster and the suave and seductive Count Dracula whose kiss is passionately deadly.*

Walter Evans argues that the beast exposing its fearsome head in the face of our monsters is primarily a sexual one—the buried, repressed impulses which erupt through the thin pretense of "civilization" in which we wrap ourselves during the light of day. Between the innocence of childhood and the mature romance and marriage of the adult world there is the dark "monstrous" transitional stage of adolescence—when hair really does grow rapidly in new places and uncontrollable urges lead us down dark paths where we have been told never to tread.

Evans' essay is provocative in its thesis and is especially useful in demonstrating how popular culture is able to embody deep-seated psychological forces and enable an audience (through the repetition and meaning offered in popular formulas) to negotiate the boundaries between "the permissible and the forbidden": Evans' monsters both reflect sexual concerns and help to inculcate society's need to accommodate and control those urges. Monsters are destroyed and the lesson of their creation and

Reprinted by permission from the author and the editors, from the *Journal of Popular Film* 4 (1975).

end transforms the normal, daylight world into one which can admit the existence of the beast without being ruled by it.

Evans, however, is writing about a type of Horror which characterized a literary, Victorian-Gothic tradition and found popular expression in America in movies of the 1930s and 1940s. Today's Horror movies are different from "Old Horror" in at least three important ways:

*1) Monsters are not our creations—they are us. Today's monsters are virtually indistinguishable from our friends and neighbors—they are embodied in the faceless mask of Jason (*Friday the 13th*), the blank visage of Michael (*Halloween*) and the scarred, ever-changing face of Freddy Krueger (*Nightmare on Elm Street*). These monsters represent the horror latent in our own hearts and in the hearts of everyone we meet.*

2) Modern Horror takes place in our own backyards. These monsters do not confine themselves to a castle on the hill or the laboratory of a mad scientist. Modern creatures of the night stake the tree-lined Everytown of Elm St., the idyllic rural setting of a summer camp, the house next door where our daughters go to babysit. Nowhere is "safe."

3) The resolutions find Evil undestroyed—temporarily abated, perhaps, but ready to erupt once again the moment we go to sleep (Freddy in your dreams) or stop at that friendly looking country motel (shower, anyone?).

...Yet maybe Evans is still able to help us understand our new monsters as well as our old. Don't adolescents still form the major audience for these films? Aren't there an awful lot of nubile, sexually active teenage girls being chased around by young guys with their phallic knives? And what are all those long tracking shots (in which we share the point of view of an attacking monster) all about if they are not indicative of the way in which we still perhaps identify with the creature, not the victim? The truest monster movie may simply be one yet to be made: Frankenstein Meets Jason—Old Horror with a New Mask.

As has ever been the case, Dracula, Frankenstein, the Wolfman, King Kong and their peers remain shrouded in mystery. Why do American adolescents keep Dracula and his companion monsters of the 1930s and early 1940s alive yet largely ignore much better formula movies of the same period, Westerns (*Stagecoach*), gangster movies (*Little Caesar, Public Enemy*) and others?[1] What is the monster formula's "secret of life"? Is this yet another of the things which "man was not meant to know"?

The formula has inspired a plethora of imaginative theories, including several which attempt to explain the enduring popularity of these movies in terms of: contemporary social prosperity and order;[2] political decay (Alloway 123); the classic American compulsion "to translate and revalue the inherited burden of European culture" (McConnell 26); the public's need for "an acceptance of the natural order of things and an affirmation of man's ability to cope with and even prevail over the evil of life which he can never understand" (Dillard 26); the "ambiguities of repulsion and curiosity" regarding "what happens to flesh,... the fate of being a body";[3] our "fear of the nonhuman" (Thomas 135); the social consequences of "deviance from the norm," particularly physical deviance (Doone 125); and "mankind's hereditary fear of the dark" (Douglas 11).

Dracula, Frankenstein's monster, King Kong and others have been fruitfully approached as cultural symbols, but their power and appeal are finally much more fundamental than class or political consciousness,[4] more basic than abstractions of revolt against societal restrictions, yet more specifically concerned with certain fundamental and identifiable features of human experience than such terms as "darkness" and "evil" seem to suggest. Their power, and that of the other movie monsters is, it seems to me, finally and essentially related to that dark fountainhead which psychically moves those masses in the American film and TV audiences who desperately struggle with the most universal, and in many ways the most horrible of personal trials: the sexual traumas of adolescence. Sex has a central role in many popular formulas,[5] but sexuality in horror movies is uniquely tailored to the psyches of troubled adolescents, whatever their age.

The adolescent finds himself trapped in an unwilled change from a comparatively comprehensible and secure childhood to some mysterious new state which he does not understand, cannot control, and has some reason to fear. Mysterious feelings and urges begin to develop and he finds himself strangely fascinated with disturbing new physical characteristics—emerging hair, budding breasts, and others—which, given the forbidding texture of the X-rated American mentality, he associates with mystery, darkness, secrecy and evil. Similarly, stirred from a childishly perfect state of nature King Kong is forced into danger by his desire for a beautiful young woman, a dark desire which, like the ape himself, must finally be destroyed by a hostile civilization. And so, stirred from innocence and purity (see the Wolfman poem which appears below) by the full moon which has variously symbolized chastity, change, and romance for millennia, the wolfman guiltily wakes to the mystery of horrible alterations in his body, his mind, and his physical desires—alterations which are completely at odds with the formal structures of his society. The mysterious, horrible, physical and psychological change

Bela Lugosi and victim Helen Chandler in *Dracula* (1931).

is equally a feature of Frankenstein, of Dracula's victims, the Mummy and his bride, and countless other standard monster movie characters.

The key to monster movies and the adolescents which understandably dote upon them is the theme of horrible and mysterious psychological and physical change; the most important of these is the monstrous transformation which is directly associated with secondary sexual characteristics and with the onset of aggressive erotic behavior. The Wolfman, for example, sprouts a heavy coat of hair, can hardly be contained within his clothing, and when wholly a wolf is, of course, wholly naked. Comparatively innocent and asexual females become, after contact with a vampire (his kiss redly marked on their necks) or werewolf (as in *Cry of the Werewolf*), quite sexy, aggressive, seductive—literally female "vamps" and "wolves."[6]

As adolescence is defined as "developing from childhood to maturity"[7] so the transformation is cinematically defined as movement from a state of innocence and purity associated with whiteness and clarity to darkness and obscurity associated with evil and threatening physical aggression. In the words of *The Wolfman's* gypsy:

> Even a man who is pure at heart
> And says his prayers by night
> May become a wolf when the wolfbane blooms
> And the moon is full and bright.

The monsters are generally sympathetic, in large part because, as remarked earlier, they themselves suffer the change as unwilling victims, all peace destroyed by the horrible physical and psychological alterations thrust upon them. Even Dracula, in a rare moment of self-revelation, is driven to comment: "To die, to be really dead. That must be glorious.... There are far worse things awaiting man, than death." Much suffering arises from the monster's overwhelming sense of alienation; totally an outcast, he painfully embodies the adolescent's nightmare of being hated and hunted by the society which he so desperately wishes to join.

Various aspects of the monster's attack are clearly sexual. The monster invariably prefers to attack individuals of the opposite sex, to attack them at night, and to attack them in their beds. The attack itself is specifically physical; Dracula, for instance, must be in immediate bodily contact with his victim to effect his perverted kiss; Frankenstein, the Wolfman, the Mummy, King Kong, have no weapons but their bodies. The aspect of the attack most disturbing to the monster, and perhaps most clearly sexual, is the choice of victim: "The werewolf instinctively seeks to kill the thing it loves best" (Dr. Yogami in *The Werewolf of London). Dracula's* Mina Seward must attack her fiance, John. The Mummy must physically possess the body of the woman in whom his spiritual bride has been reincarnated. Even more disturbing are the random threats to children scattered throughout the formula, more disturbing largely because the attacks are so perversely sexual and addressed to beings themselves soon destined for adolescence.

The effects of the attack may be directly related to adolescent sexual experimentation. The aggressor is riddled with shame, guilt, and anguish; the victim, once initiated, is generally transformed into another aggressor.[8] Regaining innocence before death seems, in the best films, almost as inconceivable as retrieving virginity.

Many formulaic elements of the monster movies have affinities with two central features of adolescent sexuality, masturbation and menstruation. From time immemorial underground lore has asserted that masturbation leads to feeblemindedness or mental derangement; the monster's transformation is generally associated with madness; scientists are generally secretive recluses whose private experiments on the human body have driven them mad. Masturbation is also widely (and, of course, fallaciously) associated with "weakness of the spine," a fact which helps explain not only Fritz of *Frankenstein* but the army of feebleminded hunchbacks which pervades the formula. The Wolfmen, and sometimes Dracula, are identifiable (as, according to underground lore, masturbating boys may be identified) by hairy palms.

Ernest Jones explains the vampire myth largely in terms of a mysterious physical and psychological development which startles many adolescents, nocturnal emissions: "A nightly visit from a beautiful or frightful being, who first exhausts the sleeper with passionate embraces and then withdraws from him a vital fluid: all this can point only to a natural and common process, namely to nocturnal emissions accompanied with dreams of a more or less erotic nature. In the unconscious mind blood is commonly an equivalent for semen...."[9] The vampire's bloodletting of women who suddenly enter full sexuality, the werewolf's bloody attacks—which occur regularly every month—are certainly related to the menstrual cycle which suddenly and mysteriously commands the body of every adolescent girl.

Monster movies characteristically involve another highly significant feature which may initially seem irrelevant to the theme of sexual change: the faintly philosophical struggle between reason and the darker emotional truths. Gypsies, superstitious peasants, and others associated with the imagination eternally triumph over smugly conventional rationalists who ignorantly deny the possible existence of walking mummies, stalking vampires, and bloodthirsty werewolves. The audience clearly sympathizes with those who realize the limits of reason, of convention, of security; for the adolescent's experiences with irrational desires, fears, urges which are incomprehensible yet clearly stronger than the barriers erected by reason or by society, are deeper and more painful than adults are likely to realize. Stubborn reason vainly struggles to deny the adolescent's most private experiences, mysterious and dynamic conflicts between normal and abnormal, good and evil, known and unknown.

Two of the most important features normally associated with monster movies are the closely related searches for the "secret of life" and "that which man was not meant to know." Monster movies unconsciously exploit the fact that most adolescents already know the "secret of life" which is, indeed, the "forbidden knowledge" of sex. The driving need to master the "forbidden knowledge" of "the secret of life," a need which seems to increase in importance as the wedding day approaches, is closely related to a major theme of monster movies: marriage.

For the adolescent audience the marriage which looms just beyond the last reel of the finer monster movies is much more than a mindless cliche wrap-up. As the monster's death necessarily precedes marriage and a happy ending, so the adolescent realizes that a kind of peace is to be obtained only with a second transformation. Only marriage can free Henry Frankenstein from his perverted compulsion for private experimentation on the human body; only marriage can save Mina Harker after her dalliance with the count. Only upon the death of adolescence, the mysterious madness which has possessed them, can they enter into a mature state where sexuality is tamed and sanctified by marriage.[10] The marriage theme, and the complex interrelationship of various other formulaic elements, may perhaps be best approached through a close analysis of two seminal classics, *Frankenstein* and *Dracula*.

Two events dominate the movie *Frankenstein* (1931), creation of the monster and celebration of the marriage of Henry Frankenstein and his fiancee Elizabeth. The fact that the first endangers the second provides for most of the conflict throughout the movie, conflict much richer and more powerful, perhaps even profound, when the key thematic relationship between the two is made clear: creation of life. As Frankenstein's perverse nightly experiments on the monstrous body hidden beneath the sheets are centered on the creation of life, so is the marriage, as the old Baron twice makes clear in a toast (once immediately after the monster struggles out of the old mill and begins wandering toward an incredible meeting with Henry's fiance Elizabeth; again, after the monster is destroyed, in the last speech of the film): "Here's to a son to the House of Frankenstein!"[11]

Frankenstein's fatuous father, whose naive declarations are frequently frighteningly prescient (he predicts the dancing peasants will soon be fighting; on seeing a torch in the old mill he asks if Henry is trying to burn it down), declares, when hearing of the extent to which his son's experiments are taking precedence over his fiance: "I understand

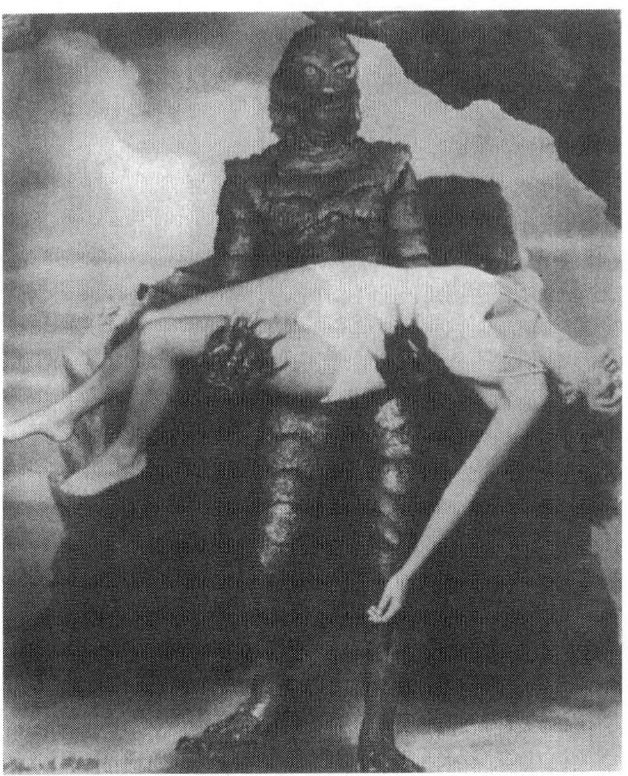

Creature from the Black Lagoon (1954).

perfectly well. Must be another woman. Pretty sort of experiments they must be." Later, after receiving the burgomaster's beaming report on the village's preparations for celebration of the marriage, he again associates his son's experiments with forbidden sexuality: "There is another woman. And I'm going to find her."

There is, of course, no other woman. The movie's horror is fundamentally based on the fact that the monster's life has come without benefit of a mother's womb. At one point Frankenstein madly and pointedly gloats over his solitary, specifically manual, achievements: "the brain of a dead man, ready to live again in a body I made with my hands, my own hands!"

Significantly, a troubled search for the "secret of life" is what keeps Henry Frankenstein separated from his fiance; it literally proves impossible for Henry to provide for "a son to the House of Frankenstein" before he has discovered the "secret of life." Having discovered the "secret of life," he ironically discovers that its embodiment is a frightening monster horrible enough to threaten "normal" relations between himself and Elizabeth. Henry's attempt to lock the monster deep in the mill's nether regions are finally thwarted, and, in a wholly irrational and

A Nightmare on Elm Street: Freddy Krueger is the bogeyman who threatens a teenager and her sexually active friends.

dramatically inexplicable (yet psychologically apt and profound) scene, the monster—a grotesque embodiment of Frankenstein's newly discovered sexuality—begins to move threateningly toward the innocent bride who is bedecked in the purest of white, then quite as irrationally, it withdraws. On his return Henry promises his wildly distracted fiance that there will be no wedding "while this horrible creation of mine is still alive."

The monster is, of course, finally, pitilessly, destroyed,[12] and Henry is only ready for marriage when his own body is horribly battered and weakened, when he is transformed from the vigorous, courageous, inspired hero he represented early in the film to an enervated figure approaching the impotent fatuity of his father and grandfather (there is plenty of fine wine for the wedding feast, Frankenstein's grandmother would never allow grandfather to drink any), prepared to renounce abnormal life as potent as the monster in favor of creating a more normal "son to the House of Frankenstein."

The message is clear. In order to lead a normal, healthy life, Henry Frankenstein must—and can—give up dangerous private experiments on the human body in dark rooms hidden away from family and friends. He must learn to deal safely and normally with the "secret of life," however revolting, however evil, however it might seem to frighten and actually threaten pure, virgin womanhood; only then, in the enervated bosom of normality, is it possible to marry and to produce an acceptable "son to the House of Frankenstein."

Dracula's much more mature approach to womankind is clearly aimed at psyches which have overcome Henry Frankenstein's debilitating problem. *Dracula* (1931), obviously enough, is a seduction fantasy vitally concerned with the conditions and consequences of premarital indulgence in forbidden physical relations with attractive members of the opposite sex.

Of all the movie monsters Dracula seems to be the most attractive to women, and his appeal is not difficult to understand, for he embodies the chief characteristics of the standard Gothic hero: tall, dark, handsome, titled, wealthy, cultured, attentive, mannered, with an air of command, an aura of sin and secret suffering; perhaps most important of all he is invariably impeccably dressed. With such a seductive and eligible male around it is certainly no wonder that somewhere in the translation from fiction to film Dr. Seward has become Mina's father and thus leaves Lucy, who also lost the two other suitors Bram Stoker allowed her, free to accept the Count's attentions. Certainly any woman can sympathize with Lucy's swift infatuation ("Laugh all you like, I think he's fascinating.") and Mina's easy acceptance of Dracula as her friend's suitor ("Countess, I'll leave you to your count, and your ruined abbey.").

Having left three wives behind in Transylvania, Dracula is obviously not one to be sated with his second English conquest (the first was an innocent flower girl, ravaged immediately before he meets Lucy and Mina), and he proceeds to seduce Mina, working a change in her which does not go unnoticed, or unappreciated, by her innocent fiance: "Mina, you're so—like a changed girl. So wonderful—." Mina agrees that indeed she is changed, and, on the romantic terrace, alone with her fiance beneath the moon and stars, begins, one is certain, the first physical aggression of their courtship. John is suitably impressed. "I'm so glad to see you like this!" Discovered and exposed by Professor Van Helsing, Mina can only admit that (having had relations with Dracula and thus become a Vamp) she has, indeed, suffered the proverbial fate worse than death, and shamefully alerts her innocent, naive fiance: "John, you must go away from me."

Only when John and his older, respected helpmate foil the horrible mock elopement—Dracula and Mina are rushing to the abbey preparing to "sleep," he even carries her limp body across the abbey's threshold—only when the castrating stake destroys the seducer and with him the maid's dishonor, is Mina free to return to the honest, innocent, suitor who will accept her past, marry her in the public light of day, and make an honest woman of her.

Lucy, who has no selfless suitor to forgive her, marry her, and make an honest woman of her, is much less successful. When last seen she has become a child molester, a woman of the night who exchanges chocolate for horrible initiations.

The thematic importance of such innocent victims turned monster as Lucy and Mina, Dr. Frankenstein's creation, King Kong, the Wolfman and others points directly to one of the most commonly observed and perhaps least understood phenomena of monster movies, one which has been repeatedly noted in this paper. In those classics which are best loved and closest to true art the audience clearly identifies with the monster. Child, adult or adolescent, in disembodied sympathetic fascination, we all watch the first Karloff Frankenstein who stumbles with adolescent clumsiness, who suffers the savage misunderstanding and rejection of both society and the creator whose name he bears, and whose fumbling and innocent attempts at love with the little girl by the lakeside turn to terrible, bitter, and mysterious tragedy.

Clearly the monster offers the sexually confused adolescent a sympathetic, and at best a tragic, imitation of his life by representing a mysterious and irreversible change which forever isolates him from what he identifies as normality, security, and goodness, a change thrusting him into a world he does not understand, torturing him with desires he cannot satisfy or even admit, a world in which dark psychological and strange physical changes seem to conspire with society to destroy him.

Notes

[1]Though many critics focus on adult themes in monster movies, I believe that adolescents provide the bulk of the audience for such films, particularly the classic films shown on late night television all across America. Adolescents, of course, may be of any age.

[2]Curtis Harrington asserts that such movies are more popular in periods of depression and disorder. See "Ghoulies and Ghosties" in Roy Huss and T.J. Ross, eds. *Focus on the Horror Film* (Englewood Cliffs, New Jersey: Prentice Hall, 1972), 17-18. I should mention one of the finer essays in this fine collection, X.J. Kennedy's "Who Killed King Kong" (106-109.)

[3]Alloway is speaking specifically of the effects of death and decay, 124.

[4]I feel this is clearly true in spite of the more superficial importance of, for instance, the Nazi allusions in such a film as *Return of the Vampire* (1944). The classic monster movies deemphasize such non-essential material.

[5]According to Andrew Sarris, "There are no non-erotic genres any more." The statement was made on "Frame of Reference" following the "Film Odyssey" showing of *The Blue Angel*.

[6]The transformation is less obvious, and perhaps for this reason more powerful, in *King Kong* (1933). Kong himself is safe while hidden deep in the prehistoric depths of Skull Island, but an unappeasable sexual desire (made explicit in the cuts restored in the film's most recent release) turns him into an enemy of civilization until, trapped on

the world's hugest phallic symbol, he is destroyed. The psychological transformation of Ann Darrow (Fay Wray) is much more subtle. While alone immediately after exchanging vows of love with a tough sailor she closes her eyes and, as in a dream vision, above her appears the hideously savage face of a black native who takes possession of her in preparation for the riotous wedding to the great hairy ape. Significantly, only when civilization destroys the fearful, grossly physical beast is she finally able to marry the newly tuxedoed sailor.

[7]*Webster's New World Dictionary of the American Language*, 2nd College Edition (Englewood Cliffs, N.J.: Prentice-Hall, 1970). Interesting, in view of the fiery death of Frankenstein's monster and others, is one of the earlier meanings of the root word: "be kindled, burn."

[8]It is interesting, and perhaps significant, that the taint of vampirism and lycanthropy have an aura of sin and shame not unlike that of VD. The good doctor who traces the taint, communicable only through direct physical contact, back to the original carrier is not unlike a physician fighting VD.

[9]See Ernest Jones, "On the Nightmare of Bloodsucking" in *Focus on the Horror Film*, 59.

[10]In "The Child and the Book," *Only Connect*, Sheila Egoff, ed., G.T. Stubbs, and L.F. Ashley (New York: Oxford UP, 1969) noted psychiatrist Anthony Storr has discussed a precursor of monster movies, fairy tales, in a similar context.

> Why is it that the stories which children enjoy are so often full of horror? We know that from the very beginning of life the child possesses an inner world of fantasy and the fantasies of the child mind are by no means the pretty stories with which the prolific Miss Blyton regales us. They are both richer and more primitive, and the driving forces behind them are those of sexuality and the aggressive urge to power: the forces which ultimately determine the emergence of the individual as a separate entity. For, in the long process of development, the child has two main tasks to preform if he is to reach maturity. He has to prove his strength, and he has to win a mate; and in order to do this he has to overcome the obstacles of his infantile dependency upon, and his infantile erotic attachment to, his parents....The typical fairy story ends with the winning of the princess just as the typical Victorian novel ends with the marriage. It is only at this point that adult sexuality begins....It is not surprising that fairy stories should be both erotic and violent, or that they should appeal so powerfully to children. For the archetyal themes with which they deal mirror the contents of the childish psyche; and the same unconscious source gives origin to both the fairy tale and the fantasy life of the child." (93-4)

[11]The dialogue is followed by a close-up of a painfully embarrassed Henry Frankenstein.

[12]Significantly, the monster himself is pitifully sympathetic, suffering as adolescents believe only they can suffer, from unattractive physical appearance, bodies they don't understand, repulsed attempts at love, general misunderstanding. Though endowed by his single antagonistic parent with a "criminal brain," the monster is clearly guilty of little but ugliness and ignorance, and is by any terms less culpable than the normal human beings surrounding him. He does not so much murder Fritz as attempt to defend himself against completely unwarranted torchings and beatings; he kills Dr. Valdeman only after that worthy believes he has "painlessly destroyed" the monster (a euphemism for murder), and as the doctor is preparing to dissect him; the homicide which propels his destruction, the drowning of the little girl, is certainly the result of clumsiness and ignorance. She had taught him to sail flowers on the lake and, flowers failing, in a visual metaphor

worthy of an Elizabethan courtier, the monster in his ignorant joy had certainly meant only for the girl, the only being who had ever shown him not only love, but even affection, to sail on the lake as had the flowers. His joyful lurch toward her after having sailed his flower is, beyond all doubt, the most pathetic and poignant lurch in the history of film.

Works Cited

Alloway, Lawrence. "Monster Films." *Focus on the Horror Film.* Roy Huss and T.J. Ross, eds., Englewood Cliffs, NJ: Prentice Hall, 1972.

Dillard, R.H.W. "The Pageantry of Death." *Focus on the Horror Film.* Roy Huss and T.J. Ross, eds.

Donne, John D. "Society and the Monster." *Focus on the Horror Film.* Roy Huss and T.J. Ross, eds., Englewood Cliffs, NJ: Prentice Hall, 1972.

Douglas, Drake. *Horror!* New York: Macmillan/Collier Books, 1966.

McConnel, Frank. "Rough Beasts Slouching." *Focus on the Horror Film.* Roy Huss and T.J. Ross, eds. Englewood Cliffs, NJ: Prentice Hall, 1972.

Thomas, John. "Gobble, Gobble...One of Us!" *Focus on the Horror Film.* Roy Huss and T.J. Ross, eds. Englewood Cliffs, NJ: Prentice Hall, 1972.

Magic and Transformation: Relationships in Popular Romance Novels, 1950 to the 1980s

Rita C. Hubbard

The phenomenal continuing success of romance fiction since Harlequin Romances were introduced in the 1950s is a clear indication of how attractive the myth of romantic love is for modern women readers. But does this suggest that the readers of these novels think that only marriage and the love of a strong man will make them happy? Does the popularity of these books hint that a woman can only find happiness by pleasing a man? In the following article, Rita Hubbard argues that although romance novels of the 1950s might have suggested the answers to these questions was an obvious "yes," changing formulaic patterns in Harlequin Romances show a clear move away from women's submissive dependence on men. As women have become more independent and assertive in American culture since the 1960s, the formula of the romance novels has been evolving to keep up with these changes. Love is still important to the women readers of romances (as it is for men) but increasingly, Hubbard shows, love must be present on the heroine's terms if it is to survive.

The serious student of popular culture will want to compare Hubbard's analysis of Harlequin Romances with Crystal Kile's earlier analysis of recent love songs. In many cases it is doubtlessly the case that the same person who reads many romance novels each week is also buying CDs that feature the songs Kile discusses. Yet some of the things Hubbard concludes about recent Harlequins are not necessarily the same conclusions arrived at by Kile. Does this mean that one of these authors must be wrong? Not necessarily. Careful readers of this book will know at this point in their reading that living in the world of popular culture is complicated. Both romance novels and popular love songs verify the

A slightly different version of this essay appeared in *Communication Quarterly* 33 (Spring 1985). Reprinted by permission of the author and *Communication Quarterly*.

myth of romantic love, but the myth takes different forms and the myth may be expressed in contradictory ways. As was discussed in our initial discussion of popular myths, our mindset contains many contradictions. One of the appeals of romances and love songs is that for a short period of time, readers and listeners have these doubts and contradictions resolved. For a few minutes or hours, love is less complicated. No wonder Harlequin Romances sell over 150 million copies every year.

Romance fiction is a publishing phenomenon. While the total number of paperback books sold in the United States in a given year exceeds 575 million, romance novels account for 40% of this total. Inexpensive "brand name" novels, published monthly, with author identification minimized, constitute the largest category of these romance novels. From 1950 to 1979, Harlequin Books was the sole publisher of such novels. In 1979, they sold over 168 million copies in a world-wide market—an average of five books every second—making their line of fiction the most successful ever published. That same year, Simon and Schuster provided competition in the U.S. with Silhouette Books, and since that time new lines have been introduced by various publishers, six of these launched in 1983. More than 100 new category romances, written almost exclusively by women, are published each month.

The American readers of these books, estimated to be 99% female, number in the multi-millions. Marketing researchers report that romances of all types are the first choice of non-college educated women and the second choice among the college-educated.

These romance novels offer dramatic visions of male/female interactions which lead to satisfying and enduring love commitments. Readers do, in fact, read these novels consistently with the average romance reader buying six per month. For them, the novels provide a way of looking at the world, interpretations of gender roles, a set of expectations, and implied guidelines for romantic success.

This study examines formulaic visions of male/female relationship styles in category romances over 40 years, tracing the devleopment of particular fantasy themes and focusing on contemporary attitudes in four specific time periods. Two questions influence choices affecting its development:

1) How are females and males defined in these romances?

2) Have the romances changed their view of male/female relationship styles over a 33-year period?

The analysis is designed to emphasize the definitions of femininity and masculinity and ultimately to identify the images which control such definitions. Femininity and masculinity are cast as variables which can be socially constructed, and they become the factors which signify the changes which have occurred in relationship styles exhibited in the novels. The purpose and effect of romances can be conceived in several ways. They are apparently popular escape novels written to entertain and transport readers from their own humdrum worlds to exciting fictional worlds. Yet they can also reflect recommended and validate specific social orders.

Forty-five novels were chosen for analysis.[1] Since Harlequin Romances were the only existing category romances from 1950 to 1979, they were chosen for the first part of this study which was undertaken in 1980.

The population of Harlequin Romances was defined by three lists of available novels provided by Harlequin Books in September, October, and November of 1980. These lists were used to define the population of Harlequin Romances because: 1) they provide an arbitrary selection of past novels which the readers of these novels are exposed to; 2) Harlequin Books claim approximately equal sales of all novels so that any lists used become acceptable to secure a sample of the population of novels; 3) each list gives roughly equal attention to all three decades.

A random sample of *all* Harlequin Romances was not used because: 1) readers are not exposed to such random choices, and therefore a method was devised which reflected books to which the reader is exposed; 2) not all novels are currently available; 3) no cooperation from the publisher could be obtained to secure a random sample of all books because Harlequin Books reprints on a rotation basis and does not maintain all books as current choices.

Thirty Harlequin Romances were selected randomly from the three lists: ten from the 1950s, ten from the 1960s, and ten from the 1970s. Other publishing houses entered the category romance field beginning in 1979; therefore, 15 novels with 1983 publication dates were selected for the second part of this study. These novels were randomly drawn from Walden Books' 1983 display of category romance novels, namely Harlequin American Romance, Second Chance at Love, Silhouette Desire, Silhouette Intimate Moments, Loveswept, Candlelight Ecstasy Supreme.

Four Formulaic Visions

Vision I, the 1950s: Cinderella as Virgin Earth Mother and the Prince as Benign Dictator

Harlequin Romances of the 1950s extol in their fantasy themes the assumed virtues of the virginal earth mother and the benign male dictator, creating a vision of the rigid male/female relationship which is typical of traditional relations between the sexes in Western culture. In this vision, sexual conservatism is recommended, leading to predefined modes of feeling and action, and the system works to perfection for the instrumental heroes and the expressive heroines.

Without exception, the hero is older than the heroine, masterful, tall, handsome, passionate and powerful, educated, and engaged in a successful career. Thus he can deliver to his chosen heroine all the benefits expected of the ambituous male. His chosen heroine, who fully accepts dominance, is young, small, isolated from family and friends, modestly educated, and low in self-esteem. But she is both willing and able to meet the hero's needs for support, admiration, nurturance, purity, and devotion.

Both find comfort, safety, and a sense of worth in the blending of what are assumed to be their natural competencies. Their arrangement includes divisions of opportunity, responsibility, and privilege. He has a monopoly on formal, overt power, and he assumes his right to rule. She gladly gives obedience in exchange for upward mobility, protection, and enduring love.

At no time in the novels of the 1950s do the heroes and heroines challenge the prevailing symbiosis between men and women. Their posture is accepting and their method of coping with problems is to fit themselves neatly into the societally ordained stereotypes of the decade; their misgivings and reservations are harmlessly ventilated as they grow more and more accepting of their roles which lead them eventually to conjugal happiness.

Love is the sanctioning agent which justifies their motives and actions. It transforms the faults of the hero—moodiness, arrogance, and occasional cruelty—into expressions of caring. Love permits the hero to view the heroine's weakness, ignorance, and capriciousness as endearing qualities. She can accept his past sexual experience and his right to awaken her, knowing that he is dependent on her to control his passionate nature. He can accept her lack of achievement, realizing that his is the role of the risk-taker and doer.

Thus the romance formula vision of the 1950s offers the traditional prescription for a successful male/female relationship style. Woman's role is that of the supportive "Other." Her ultimate security and happiness are to be found in romance, marriage, and the family. Man's role is to rule by his achievement; he is incomplete, however, without the nurturing female to complement him and teach him in the affective domain.

Sweet Waters (Brett 1955) is a typical novel. A plain heroine who is alone in the world is hired by an affluent landowner in Capetown, Africa to care for an orphan boy living with him temporarily. She finds her employer to be cold, sharp, arrogant, and chauvinistic. He orders her about, demands strict obedience, and refuses to teach her or any women to drive because of assumed female incompetence. Yet she falls in love with him, arguing to herself that, "He's perfectly horrid, devastatingly frank and uncaring about other people's feelings, yet there's a charm about him that somehow makes it worthwhile putting up with the brutally calm arrogance." He calls her a doormat, silences her with a raised finger, accepts no "backchat," and declares that "one of these days I'm going to give you all the punishment you deserve."

But love, the agent of forgiveness and understanding, infuses their lives. He finds her tenderness and temerity irresistible and she glories in his masterfulness. In the final pages, he proposes marriage. "I shall be a demanding husband, and I'll never let you forget you're mine." "She thought tremulously that she would never quite believe the miracle of belongling to Nicholas, and for the rest of her life she would strive to deserve it." The plain Cinderella finds validation in the love of a male she considers superior, and he has been assured during the novel of her admiration, acquiescence, nurturance, and purity.

Vision II, the 1960s: Cinderella as Feisty Female and the Prince as Subduer

Of the ten 1960s novels examined, two are similar in vision to those of the 1950s. Eight, however, while containing a formula resembling that of the 1950s books, introduce three new fantasy themes: female rebellion, struggle, and final acquiescence.

The newer heroine has become aware of the social inequality of the sexes and offers feisty but tentative resistance to domination. She challenges the hero by arguing with him and occasionally by her actions. She may choose from among various methods to declare that nature intended her to be more than a docile showpiece, seek a traditional male career, exhibit fearlessness in the face of a gun, venture into the jungle alone and steal a trawler to prove her capability in handling a ship.

Her independence is short-lived, however, because failure is built into the scenario. She is a young women alone without support systems and, if working at all, receives low wages because of her lack of higher education or developed skills. By contrast, the hero against whom she struggles is physically strong, socially and economically secure, and determined to command. He is articulate in argumentation against what he considers her foolish ideas and actions, and he is fully capable of rescuing her from dangers.

The heroine's quest for independence, while it fails, brings her unexpected romantic success because she does not carry her rebellion beyond the bounds of propriety. The hero finds that her spirit excites him and once he has learned to control that spirit, he offers a lifetime of passionate love, marriage, safety and security, sometimes promising to wrap her in cotton wadding or to treat her like a fragile glass bird. His reward, after having aggressively tested her self control, is assurance that his bride-to-be is both pure and awakened by him. He is secure once she has declared that next to being his wife nothing else in the world is of any importance.

In the new plotlines, gender-related values are no longer assumed. The tensions and ambiguities that arose from the new thrust for sexual equality that began in the decade of the 1960s are present, but these tensions and ambiguities are resolved as their heroines come to realize that their challenge for equality can and will be rebuffed at every level by dominant and desirable males, and that the rewards for submissiveness are great. Thus, the novels assimilate in their formulas changes in values, and they likewise offer dramatic evaluations of the new thrust for equality between the sexes which they categorize in their plots as dangerous to female security. Finally in their imaginary worlds, they affirm the interests and attitudes of a majority of society in the 1960s when only a small percentage of women, principally the highly educated, exhibited a strong interest in the new feminism.

In *House of the Winds* (Lane, 1968), we can observe the newer heroine, in this case a small, young orphan who admits that she would have received a fuller education if she had the brains for it. She tricks a big game hunter in Tanzania into taking her on safari into the African bush so that she can photograph wild animals and gain stature in her career. He becomes angry and abusive because he is against taking women on such dangerous trips, and he scoffs at her ambitions. Unlike heroines of the 1950s, this one can drive a car, speak her mind, and brave dangers. As the plot unfolds in the African bush, however, her courage and ambition diminish as the strong, gruff hero rescues her six times from wild animals, the elements, and other threats to her life, each time offering insults as he grabs her roughly out of danger. Finally, he adds to the later rescues his hard kisses which kindle frightening sparks in him and in her. They almost "go too far," but she proves her virtue. She abandons camera and career, promises to be his obedient wife, and to follow him to Nymbaya, even though she does not know what their life will be like there. He promises eternal love, to care for her, and to give her children, as they walk hand in hand toward the "whispering waves."

Vision III, the 1970s: Cinderella as Virgin Temptress and the Prince as Warrior

If equality between the sexes was not possible in the 1970s' real world, nevertheless some women made significant strides toward that goal, and many men and women were converted to being equals in concept if not in action. In Harlequin Romances of the 1970s, this feminism intrudes significantly into the fictional world creating a third formulaic vision with fantasy themes of acknowledged female sexuality, female militancy, and counter-exhibitions of male power. There is, however, in this vision no affirmation of equality as a legitimate goal. In fact, the heroine's militant demands are cast as threats to her own and the hero's happiness and security, and she is confronted and humbled repeatedly until she sees the error of her ways and embraces traditional male/female relationship.

The heroine of the 1970s has increased confidence in her own abilities and exhibits knowingly a powerful sexuality to tempt the hero. But she is led gradually and forcefully by him to the realization that her attempts to assume power and to enjoy sexual freedom will bring about her own ruin. In the end, she not only accepts his domination but rejoices in it. Thus, she reaffirms the old ways dramatically because she has tested equality, even beyond the limits set for the 1960s' heroines, and has found it frightening.

In Harlequin Romances of all three decades, the hero is cast as superior to the heroine in wealth, position, and education. In the 1970s novels he must use these advantages to battle the new feminism and to preserve the old ways. As the militant heroine tests his mettle, he resorts to exhibitions of power. Earlier heroes frequently subdued heroines physically when in the grips of passion, often bruising flesh, and occasionally spanking lightly. The 1970s hero, however, goes further; in his frustrations he may shake the heroine, jerk her out of a seat, threaten to strike her, and even drive his truck within inches of her body. And along with these physical displays, he also educates the heroine with insults, exasperation, and argumentation until she recants. Thus he provides a counter-statement, both verbal and nonverbal, to her liberation rhetoric.

At times he must also preserve her virginity when she is ready to submit to his advances. Although he may be sexually experienced, he has no respect for a permissive woman and holds on to his requirement that his bride be virginal.

The romance formula of the 1970s is one which reflects women's thrust for equality, labels it dangerous, and promises happiness for those who accept the complementary relationship style. It differs significantly from Visions I and II in that the heroines in this vision are permitted to exhibit a strong militancy, to acknowledge their sexuality, and to test the male almost beyond his powers of endurance. As in previous novels, love is the sanctioning agent which transforms behaviors formerly perceived as faults into virtues. The heroine's strong spirit is accepted by the hero once he has channeled it toward his goals. His former threats and abuse are seen finally by the heroine as the results of her not trusting him and his consequent frustration and injured pride.

The Crescent Moon (Hunter 1974) illustrates the changes. A young shorthand-typist meets a famous, wealthy university professor, and though she feels the strong stirrings of passion she cannot accept his chauvinistic attitude. She asserts that she believes in complete equality. And so the sparring begins and continues as he presses his points. "There is no such thing as equality between us." "I don't like ambitious females." "Wouldn't you rather be the chattel of a man than the equal of a mouse?" "You'll find youself a better follower than a leader when we finally do come to terms." And he is right. As he takes an "unhurried toll of her lips" and proposes marriage, she recants:

> In any argument between them he would always win hands down. They both knew that physically he could dominate her any time he chose. If he stopped to ask her, the result would be just the same; he would demand and she would submit and would delight in her own weakness. You could call it chemistry, or the way things were meant to be, but she wouldn't like it at all if it were the other way about.

Vision IV, the 1980s: The Liberated Heroine with Her Man as Equal Partner

Vision IV of the 1980s bears little resemblance to the rhetorical visions of the prior three decades except that love continues to be the sanctioning agent. While Visions II and III were evolutions with variations out of Vision I, Vision IV has a new base of fantasy themes drawn from the feminist perspective: female control, male acceptance of equality between the sexes, and negotiation of relationship terms.

The nature of the heroine shows the most striking changes. She is no longer the standard Cinderella. Instead, she represents many women, all of whom can be heroines. She may be a young woman or as old as 45. She may be small or nearly six feet in height. She may struggle with hardships like divorce, a child born out of wedlock, a troubled husband, but she is not weak or ordinary. She is most often highly skilled, artistic or well-educated, occasionally holding a graduate degree. She may be a concert pianist, head of a construction business, owner of a dance studio, a big animal trainer, president of her own corporation, or independently wealthy. Her energies are devoted to her career and her independence, and she maintains healthy self-esteem. She is situationally nurturing but is not agreeable to the encompassing self-sacrifice of former heroines. She may live alone, but she is not isolated from family and friends. She might be a virgin, but most often she is fully aware of her own sexual needs and, while she is not promiscuous, she is sexually active when she and her hero establish a love commitment.

Further, she does not readily accept a marriage proposal until she is sure that she and her hero can negotiate terms.

Likewise, the 1980s hero is a new man. He might be, like earlier heroes, tall and handsome, affluent, and successful, but these characteristics are not essential. He has become closer in life-size to the men with whom women normally interact. And his situation might even call for a reversal of the Cinderella scenario as he depends on the heroine to help him reach his full potential. However, he has characteristics which were not present in earlier heroes. He is articulate and sensitive in matters of human relations, respecting the ambitions and desires of the heroine and accepting her as an equal partner. He is strong but not overpowering, and he is as caring of the relationship as the heroine is. The arrogant power-bent hero has disappeared from the 1980s romances.

With this new balance of power, the plotlines of the novels show marked changes as the modern heroine is consciously selective in her choices. Does she want a career first and love later? Is love without marriage a better choice? How can she handle a long-distance relationship? Does she dare to love again after a painful divorce? Will the new man in her life be suitable as a father for her children?

The novels' scenes, therefore, shift from the worlds of the heroes into which earlier heroines gained entry to the multi-dimensional worlds of heroines who act, pursuing careers, establishing friendships, dealing with a world in which not only love but success is important to them.

Finally, even love which continues to be at the core of these novels has changed character. The earlier love was an erotic one that fastened on the beauty and perfection of the beloved and changed flaws into virtues. The 1980s novels are sensual and sexual in thrust, and yet erotic love is tempered by pragmatic considerations about whether a permanent relationship will work, whether the parties are compatible, and whether the needs and desires of both participants can be satisfied.

Calculated Risk (Chase 1983) features the newer heroine who must be convinced by an ardent suitor that there is room in her life for a relationship. She is tall and assertive, in her thirties, the self-disciplined president of one of Nashville's most prestigious talent management firms. She drives a blue diesel Mercedes, carries a leather attache case, and has a male secretary. When the hero tries to enter her life, she resists the intrusion and must be persuaded to accept his offer of marriage. In the novel, she acts more than she is acted upon, taking the initiative in working out problems with her suitor's son, setting the conditions of her new relationship, and enjoying a sexual and love commitment without sacrificing hard-won career success. A permanent relationship enriches her life, but it does not change its other dimensions.

Changing Patterns of Formulaic Love

The four rhetorical visions of category romances bear certain similiarities coming out of the very nature of the genre, yet each creates distinct gender definitions which lead to different roles and rules for males and females in each period. They are similar in the set of expectations they provide, expectations consistent with the ideology of heterosexual romantic love which has its roots in the courtly tradition of the Middle Ages. Love between the sexes is an overwhelming passion, inspired by the beauty and character of the loved one, and leading to bliss or misery. Love strikes the hero and heroine almost instantly; often upon merely seeing each other there is a bonding that forecasts a permanent union in which the heroine finds validation for her uniqueness by being singled out from among many women by the hero, and he finds through her the missing key to his happiness.

The outstanding characteristics of this love are magic and transformation. Magic works to solve all problems; neither intellectual activity, the passage of time, frequent interactions, nor hard work are required for the development of a healthy relationship and the blending of personalities. Any problems of character, misunderstanding, or incompatible goals evaporate rapidly in the fire of love over a period of days, weeks, or months. And there are no problems beyond the relational. Economic, political, racial, sociological, or philosophical considerations do not intrude. Romance evolves in a white, heterosexual, middle- or upper-class world.[2]

Love also transforms. A plain heroine can become shining and beautiful when love touches her. A moody, punishing hero can become tender. And love fills them up, permitting them to deny the isolation natural to the human condition because the fusion of their two beings is perfectly accomplished, whether that fusion brings about a complementary relationship as in the first three visions or a symmetrical one as in the fourth vision. So the ultimate promise is sexual and affectional fulfillment in a permanent relationship resulting in happiness-ever-after, even though such promise is incompatible with the facts of human existence.

The distinct gender definitions in each vision, however, lead to different implicit recommendations for relationship styles and relate to changes historically occurring outside the dramas. In Vision I both the female and male are incomplete as individuals. They have different characteristics, separate roles to play, and their complementary relationship is promoted as both natural and good. Dominance is placed at the root of masculinity and nurturance as the core of femininity. While this vision undergoes changes in later category romances, it has continued unchanged in other romance types, among them the novels of Barbara Cartland, who has promoted romantic fantasy for over 50 years. According to Doyle, Cartland consistently defines woman's primary job as providing romance and beauty for men through purity, charm and total devotion to their needs.

The feelings and actions of this vision are not unlike those that predominated in the 1950s. An indication that the particular gender types of these romances and the behaviors which the novels implicitly recommended were standard ideals of the 1950s can be found in Kidd's study of advice articles on interpersonal relations appearing in popular magazines. In these articles, aimed principally at female readers, the rhetorical vision which dominated in the 1950s and early 1960s found virtue in those who made others happy, promoted togetherness, and declared conflict an indication of serious relationship problems. "Females and males were expected to behave according to traditional patterns, and when one did not do so, it was not the pattern but the individual's sexuality that was at fault" (Kidd 33). Career women were faulted for causing their husbands and children psychological damage. Men were described as having a greater sex drive and as needing to have a fragile male ego reinforced with approval and admiration even if this meant, for example, deceiving them during sexual intercourse in order to make them feel kinship with the gods. The meanings of interactions in their articles then were interpreted on a value scale like that in romances of the same period that promoted female nurturance and sacrifice for the good of the relationship and placed men in assertive dominant positions.

But all activity is contextual and all contexts can be broken. There is changeability in social structures as well as in assumptions about gender. Vision II changes somewhat as conflict over gender roles enters the scenarios. The heroine continues to be tender and nurturing but not to the same extent as her 1950s counterpart who seemed to be constantly in the service of children and adults. She has also become articulate and feisty in rebellion. Her occasional actions to assert her independence cause the hero, still superior in strength, status and education, to subdue her, though his job is relatively easy. Her rebellion is cast as a temporary aberration. Thus, the complementary relationship style is only momentarily jarred. Eventual female acquiescence is structured into the novels because the heroine is defined as incapable of independence. Yet the novels' minor changes introduce some of the tensions and ambiguities arising from the new feminism of the late 1960s and suggest female dissatisfaction with the unequal state.

This same female quest for self-fulfillment intensifies in Vision III, as in the 1970s' real world, and so gender definitions and interaction styles change. The female grows in strength and issues militant demands for equality, engaging the hero in a symbolic war. Her consciousness has been raised, her demands are explicit, and her resolve strong. But again, her conviction is not sturdy enough and her capabilities not developed enough to win the war, for the male is defined with even greater strength and he unleashes his full powers of intellect and physical strength to "educate" her and cause her to recant. Thus the novels are tragic-comedies reflecting a social structure in which the female continues to be defined as incapable of the self-determination she desires; therefore, she fails to gain independence but is nevertheless rewarded with fiction's romantic happiness-ever-after when she accepts her inabilities.

Vision IV changes gender definitions radically and promotes a significantly different relationship style that confronts the twin dangers of the human condition, isolation from others and domination by others. Both sexes share certain traits formerly considered gender specific to become equally instrumental and expressive. They reflect feminist ideals of the 1980s as the woman achieves independence and the male accepts sexual equality. There is, however, a special female control fantasy in this vision because the novels concentrate on the heroine's decision-making. She contemplates the male's proposal for a permanent relationship, evaluates the changes of its success, and negotiates its terms just as she negotiates her own career success. She is in total control of her life and fully responsible for all of its dimensions.

This new fantasy theme mirrors to some extent the control fantasy prominent in recent popular self-help books giving advice to women on achieving success as managers. Koester found that most writers depicting the female manager vision show the woman at the doorway or already present in the organization. "In the stock scenarios of the vision the locus of control for the outcome of the scene is placed squarely on the shoulders of the female" (167). Success is possible if she knows how to manipulate events and relationships; the presence of forces and occurrences beyond her control are not considered. So the reversal is complete; the definition of woman has moved from woman incapable to woman in total control.

Over 40 years, the four formulaic visions in category romances have reflected the ongoing changes in social structures and the gradual movement from partiarchy toward equality of the sexes. They have indicated that in fiction as well as in reality conceptual and social frameworks are open to revision; gender definitions are not universally given nor relationship styles unchangeable. But the visions are obviously not authentic reproductions of the real world. By omission and deception they deny the complexity of human relationships and promote impossible dreams. Yet these dreams are so seductive that millions of modern women have made romances a publishing phenomenon.

We cannot assess accurately the degree to which women readers accept the social structure and myths portrayed, but we can note that the novels contain potentially powerful messages related to the nature of the sexes and the recommended repertoire of behaviors which theoretically lead to happiness-ever-after. While romances are generally considered escape entertainments, they can also recommend and validate specific social orders for those caught up in their visions.

Notes

[1]Interested readers are encouraged to contact the author for a complete list of romances analyzed for this study.

[2]Although a few ethnic and homosexual romances have been published, they did not sell well and a recent inquiry indicates that no known publisher has plans for further market experimentation with these.

Works Cited

Brett, R. *Sweet waters.* London: Mills and Boon Limited, 1955.

Chase, E.R. *Calculated Risk.* New York: Simon & Schuster, Inc., 1983.

Doyle, M.V. *The Rhetoric of Romance Fiction: A Fantasy Theme Analysis of Barbara Cartland Novels.* Unpublished Master's Thesis, U of Minnesota, 1978.

Hunter, E. *The Crescent Moon.* London: Mills and Boon Limited, 1974.

Kidd, V.V." Happily Ever After and Other Relationship Styles: Advice on Interpersonal Relations in Popular Magazines, 1951-1972." *Quarterly Journal of Speech,* 61 (1975): 31-39.

Koester, J. "The Machiavellian Princess: Rhetorical Dramas for Women Managers." *Communication* 1982.

Lane, R. *House of the Winds.* London: Mills and Boon Limited, 1968.

Section 8

Thirteenth Generation
Born: 1961-1981

William Strauss
Neil Howe

If you've read this book carefully, hopefully by now, you are getting to know us. You have learned that what we do is mainly determined by what we believe. We tend to share these beliefs with large groups. And a few bedrock beliefs we call myths have a long history and have played an important role in determining the evolution of American life. You have also learned that sometimes beliefs contradict one another. Finally, you have been introduced to the idea that these beliefs are expressed in popular objects, people, rituals and arts—often in subtle, complicated ways. Along the way, you may have concluded that getting to know us was fun, because it uses colorful and familiar elements of your everyday lives in ways you haven't thought of before. But sometimes it is also tough and frustrating because thinking about these elements, so common in your life, is a new and demanding task.

In presenting all these materials, we have dealt tangentially with American sub-groups, but for the most part we have included examples that are popular across a broad spectrum of American societies. So, in all of these familiar but new artifacts, where do you fit in? And what about what is for you a crucial sub-group, your generation of Americans? It is probably quite obvious by now that to answer these questions fully, one or more additional books would be needed (we would like to think that before too long one of our readers will write them). In the meantime, the following article by William Strauss and Neil Howe might prove a handy starting point for you to begin to get to know yourself.

Strauss and Howe describe the values and attitudes of what they term the "thirteenth generation" of Americans, the generation born after the more famous baby boomers and the generation to which most of the readers of this book belong. The two authors employ several different methods in presenting their picture of those born between 1961 and 1981. These include the simple presentation of historical facts and the gathering of a number of provacative statistics. What should interest us here, however, is how much the article uses examples of popular culture materials to reach its conclusions. What your generation sees at the movies, watches on television, listens to on the stereo and buys at the grocery store is all included. And most of the time, in the best popular culture studies tradition, the authors include these examples because they assume they are signs for what your generation believes and values.

You may conclude after reading the article that what Strauss and Howe say about the thirteenth generation doesn't apply to you at all. In this case you'll feel that you've been victimized by a stereotype. For others of you, the article may seem uncanny in its accuracy. In either case, we hope you are convinced by now, that examining the popular materials of your generation will be a valuable help in your getting to know yourself better.

In November of 1979, just after an Iranian mob had swarmed into the U.S. Embassy in Tehran, a University of Georgia student center gave a special screening of the movie *Patton*. The students gave the film a standing ovation, hanged an effigy of the Ayatollah and then ran through the streets chanting anti-Iran slogans. That year, a new breed of college freshman came to America's campuses. Previously, faculty members had lined up to introduce themselves. Suddenly, as a Georgetown campus minister put it, "students began lining up to introduce themselves to us." Meet the smooth opening wedge of the THIRTEENTH GENERATION—what *Washington Post* writer Nancy Smith pointedly calls "the generation after. Born after 1960, after you, after it all happened." These were the babies of 1961, 8-year-olds of Woodstock, 13-year-olds of Watergate, 18-year-old energy crisis and hostage humiliation—and 29-year-olds when a 1990 *Time* cover story defined this generation as post-Boom "twenty-something." In 1979, just as these kids were making life-pivoting decisions about schools and careers, older generations sank into an eighteen-month abyss of national pessimism. For Silent parents, Thinking Small was a midlife tonic. But never having had their own chance to Think Big, the high school class of 1979 saw this grim mood very differently. From the Vietnam hysteria to Nixon's "Christmas Without Lights" to Three Mile Island—at every turn, these kids sensed that adults were simply not in control of themselves or the country.

Unlike the Boomer kids-in-jeans of the 1960s, 13ers present, to elder eyes, a splintered image of brassy sights, caustic sounds and cool manner. Moviegoers know them as Tom Cruise in *Top Gun,* breaking a few rules to win; as *The Breakfast Club,* a film about how teachers try to punish a hopeless and incorrigible "Brat Pack" of teenagers; and as Rob Lowe playing the ultimate *Bad Influence.* In city life, they have become America's kamikaze bicycle messengers, speeding Domino's and Federal Express drivers, murderous inner-city "crack" gangs, computer hackers—guys who, as John Schwartz (author of *Bicycle Days*) puts it, like to "live a little faster." In high schools, 13ers are Asian-American valedictorians and Westinghouse science finalists, more than half of them immigrants or the children of immigrants. Fresh from college, they are the Yale class of 1986, 40 percent of whom applied for investment banking jobs with one company (First Boston)—the lucky ones becoming dealmakers who "age like dogs" in Michael Lewis' game of *Liar's Poker.* In athletics, they are young Olympians leading chants of "U-S-A! U-S-A!", or "Air Jordon" and "Neon Deion" Sanders with their "in-your-face" slam drunks and end-zone spikes, or one-armed Jim Abbott winning against impossible odds. In the army, 13ers are the defenders of Saudi oilfields and the invaders of Panama, whose boom boxes may have helped persuade Manuel Noriega to surrender—one of whom said, on receiving a warm goodbye from the Panamanians, that "to them it's everything to us it's just a battle."

Older generations see them as frenetic, physical, slippery. Like the music many of them listen to, 13ers can appear shocking on the outside, unknowable on the inside. Elders find it hard to suppress feelings of disappointment over how they are turning out—dismissing them as a "lost," "ruined," even "wasted" generation in an unrelenting (and mostly unanswered) flurry of what Ellen Goodman has termed "youth-bashing." Disparaging them as the "dumb" and "numb generation," Russell Baker says "today's youth suffer from herky-jerky brain." Boom evangelists like California's Larry Lea condemn their soullessness and have declared "spiritual warfare" on youth "worship of the devil." Under the headline "Hopes of a Gilded Age: Class of 1987 Bypasses Social Activism to Aim for Million-Dollar Dreams of Life," a *Washington Post* article complains how "the fiery concerns of many of their predecessors over peace and social justice are mementos from a dimming past." Boomers are shocked by the 13er chemical of choice, steroids (which augment the body and dim the mind, just the opposite of Boom-era psychedelics). Sportswriter Bill Mandel contemptuously dismisses baseball slugger Jose Canseco as "the perfect athlete" for his era—"pumped up bigger than a steer and completely oblivious to the vital subtext of his sport." The Boomer media often portray 13ers as driven more by appetites than by ideas—as when Jay Leno tells teenage television viewers why they eat Doritos: "We're not talkin' brain cells here. We're talkin' taste buds." Soft-drink commercials do not show 13ers chanting and swaying on some verdant hillside, but instead careening (like Michael J. Fox for Pepsi) through some hellhouse and winding up on a pile of junk. "What he needs," said a recent Ad Council caption of a confused-looking teenager, "is a good swift kick in the pants." "This is the thought that wakes me up in the middle of the night," says one Boomer teacher in *The Breakfast Club*, "that when I get older, these kids are gonna take care of me." "Don't hold your breath," answers another.

Every year through the 1980s, new reports of their academic scores have triggered harsh elder assessments of their schooling and intelligence. The barrage began in 1983 when *A Nation at Risk* despaired of a "rising tide of mediocrity" emerging from America's schools. Allan Bloom's *The Closing of the American Mind* declared the 13ers' minds quite closed, and Diane Ravitch and Chester Finn's *What Do Seventeen-Year-Olds Know?* answered their own question by saying, in effect, not much. Right or wrong, the message sent to 13ers and their would-be employers is clear: that these kids got an inferior education and are equipped with inferior minds—that they are (to quote one Boomer college president) "junky."

Thirteeners find these criticisms overblown. They look upon themselves as pragmatic, quick, sharp-eyed, able to step outside themselves to understand the game of life as it really gets played. And whatever they are, 13ers insist, they *have* to be. Because of the way they were raised. Because of the world into which they are coming of age. To begin with, 13ers see no welcome mat on their economic future: Since the mid-1970s, while the cost of setting out in life (college tuitions and housing) have raced ahead of inflation, the rewards (salaries and fringe benefits for young workers) have steadily fallen behind. They are suffering what economist Robert Kuttner describes as a "remarkable generational economic disease...a depression of the young" which makes 13ers feel "uniquely thirsty in a sea of affluence." Money isn't everything—but 13ers find themselves both unprepared for and uninvited to most other avenues of social approval. Money means survival, and for a generation whose earliest life experiences have taught them not to trust others, survival must come first.

Older critics seldom acknowledge the odd twists that have so far plagued the 13er lifecycle. In the early 1970s, Norman Lear produced *All in the Family*—style television shows that bred child cynicism about the competence of the adult world—then, in the late 1980s, Lear's "People of the American Way" lobby whipsawed the grown-up kids thus nurtured with a stinging report rebuking their "apathy and disengagement from the political process." When 13ers were entering school, they heard gurus (like Charles Rathbone) say there was "no single indispensable body of knowledge that every child should know," so their schools didn't teach it—then, upon finishing school, they heard new gurus (like E.D. Hirsch, in *Cultural Literacy*) say yes, there was such knowledge, and they hadn't learned it. Thirteeners were told, as Rathbone (and many others) had urged, to be "self-reliant, independent, self-actualizing individuals." So they learned to watch adults carefully and emulate how they behave—collectively resembling Tatum O'Neal in *Paper Moon*, the kind of kids adults have a hard time finding adorable.

Thirteeners, not Boomers, were America's true "children of the 1960s." And, especially, the 1970s. An awakening era that seemed euphoric to young adults was, to them, a nightmare of self-immersed parents, disintegrating homes, schools with conflicting missions, confused leaders, a culture shifting from G to R ratings, new public-health dangers and a "Me Decade" economy that tipped toward the organized old and away from the voiceless young. "Grow up fast" was the adult message. That they did, graduating early to "young adult" realism in literature and film, and turning into what *American Demographics* magazine has termed "proto-adults" in their early teens (where, two decades earlier, Boomers had lingered in "post-adolescence" well into their twenties). At every phase of life, 13ers have encountered a world of more punishing consequence than anything their elders ever knew. Consider the 13ers' matter-of-fact approach to sexuality, yet another trait that has brought adult complaint. First-wavers were just reaching puberty when adults were emitting highly charged sexual signals in all directions. At the time, sex education was unabashedly value-neutral, empty houses provided easy trysting spots, and their parents were, as Ellen Goodman describes them, "equally uncomfortable with notions that sex is evil and sex is groovy." With adults having removed attitudinal barriers against the libido, 13ers have begun re-erecting age-old defense mechanisms: platonic relationships, group dating and a youth culture (reminiscent of Lost-era street life) in which kids watch out for their own safety and for the physical integrity of their own circle of friends. Unlike Boomers, 13ers are coming of age knowing where the youth euphoria of the late 1960s actually led. As Redlands College's Kim Blum puts it, "the sexual revolution is over, and everyone lost."

Thirteeners are growing up in what teacher and author Patrick Welsh describes as "a world of information overload." Hearing others declare everything too complex for yes-or-no answers, 13ers struggle to filter out noise, cut through rhetoric and isolate the handful of practical truths that really matter. Also unlike the homogeneous young Silent, 13ers are coming of age with sharply diverging personal circumstances (what an economist would call a "spreading bell curve") in education, family economics and career opportunities. Where their parents once struggled to break free from a tight generational center of gravity. 13ers wonder if they will ever be able to find one.

Confronted with these facts of life, 13ers have built a powerful survival instinct wrapped around an ethos of personal determinism. In their world, what a person is, what he looks like and whether or not he succeeds depend less on what a person is inside than on how he behaves. Thirteeners are constantly told that whatever bad things strike people their age—from AIDS to drug addiction, from suicides to homicides—are mainly their own fault. In this sort of youth environment, staying alert to the physical is an assertion of virtue. Unlike Boomers at like age, a low-income 13er probably comes from a world of splintered families and general hopelessness—and has little in common with some "Richie Rich" out in the suburbs. And so kids feel obliged to dress up (at an age when most Boomers dressed down) to preserve a sense of personal honor and to avoid being "disrespected" in a real-life game of king of the mountain.

Doing what they feel they must, knowing it brings adult criticism, 13ers have come to accept, even to take a perverse fun in, what a young rapper would call "attitude," in being "BAAAAD." They tend to agree with their elders that probably, they *are* a wasted bunch. From the standpoint of an individual 13er, weak peer competition isn't such bad news. Their own cultural artifacts make half-comic reference to their own garbagey quality. Chris Kreski, the 26-year-old lead writer for *Remote Control,* a 13er-designed TV-quiz-show parody, admits his show is "stupid." (In 13er lingo, words like "stupid," "bad," or "random" are words of praise.) The Bon Jovi song *You Give Love a Bad Name* became an instant hit among the teens of the 1980s. In 1990, when a think tank issued yet another negative report on 13ers (documenting their "massive cheating, resume fraud, assaults on teachers, venereal disease, pregnancies, and materialism"), its authors afterward remarked that 13ers themselves seemed to agree with these findings. In *River's Edge,* a film evoking how many 13ers look at life, one teenager mockingly says to his buddies, "You young people are a disgrace to all living things, to plants even. You shouldn't even be seen in the same room as a cactus."

As they struggle to preserve what optimism and self-esteem they can, 13ers have developed what psychologist David Elkind calls the "patchwork self." Two decades ago, older generations saw great promise in youth. Not now—not these youths, anyway. As first-wavers find themselves elbowed aside by Boomers seemingly at every turn, last-wavers lock their radars onto Nintendo in fantasized quest of fortune or death, or join the Spurtlegurgles in singing the lyric of a missionless childhood ("We're here because we're here because we're here because we're here"). "So many things have already happened in the world that we can't possibly come up with anything else," explains 15-year-old David Peters, a fast-food worker in California. "So why even live?" No other generation in living memory has come of age with such a sense of social distance—of adults doing so little for them and expecting so little from them.

Lacking the ego strength to set agendas for others, 13ers instead react to the world as they find it. They're proud of their ability to poke through the hype and the detail, to understand older people far better (they sense) than older people understand them. They take solace in the privacy that affords them. Many even delight in the most demeaning images of youth ever crafted by the electronic media: Max Headroom, beheaded in an accident, imprisoned within TV sound bites; the Teenage Mutant Ninja Turtles, flushed down the toilet as children, deformed by radiation, nurtured on junk food; and Bart Simpson, the "underachiever" whose creator likens him to everyone's "disgusting little brother"—the "little Spike-Head."

To young Americans uninterested in labels—to those who still remain what Shann Nix calls "the generation with no name"—we assign a number: thirteen. The tag is a little Halloweenish, like the clothes they wear—and slippery, like their culture. It's a name they can see as a gauntlet, a challenge, an obstacle to be overcome. The thirteenth card can be the ace, face down, in a game of highstakes blackjack. Kings and queens, with their pompous poses and fancy curlicues, always lose to the uncluttered ace, going over or going under. The ace—like this generation—is nothing subtle, but it's nice to have around when you're in a jam.

13er Facts

1) Parental divorce has struck 13ers harder than any other American generation. In 1962, half of all adult women believed that parents in bad marriages should stay together for the sake of the children; by 1980, only one in five thought so. A 13er child in the 1980s faced twice the risk of parental divorce as a Boomer child in the mid-1960s—and three times the risk a Silent child faced back in 1950. Four-fifths of today's divorced adults profess to being happier afterward, but a majority of their children feel otherwise.

2) No other American generation has ever grown up in families of such complexity. In 1980, just 56 percent of all dependent children lived with two once-married parents, another 14 percent with at least one previously married parent, 11 percent with a stepparent and 19 percent with one parent. One in five had half siblings.

3) No other child generation has witnessed such a dramatic increase in domestic dissatisfaction (and surge to the workplace) on the part of mothers. Between 1960 and 1980, among mothers with children age 5 or under, the proportion with full- or part-time jobs rose from 20 to 47 percent. Through the 1970s, the number of "latchkey" children under age 14 left alone after school roughly doubled.

4) A late-1980s survey of "teen trendsetters" found 48 percent describing their (mostly Silent) parents as "cool"—versus just 7 percent as "strict" and 1 percent as "nosy." According to youth marketer and pollster Irma Zandl, 13ers associate lack of parental authority with family instability. Observes Zandl, "I've never heard any teenage say, 'I wish my father were more sensitive'."

5) At the ballot-box, first-wave 13ers were the targets of the late-1970s "Proposition 13" school-tax revolts in California and other states.

6) Much like Michael J. Fox in *Family Ties* (the conservative kid of liberal parents), these are by far the most Republican-leaning youths in the sixty-year history of age-based polling. From Boom to 13th, the partisan tone of young voters has shifted strikingly—from roughly a ten-point Democratic advantage to a Republican edge that, in 1985, reached eighteen points (52 percent to 34 percent). In fifteen of sixteen consecutive polls taken between 1981 and 1988, 13ers gave Ronald Reagan a higher approval rating than any other generation—except the Lost.

7) Thirteener teenagers face a much lower risk of dying from disease than did Silent teenagers forty years ago. But this 13er advantage has been almost entirely offset by a much higher risk of dying from accidents, murder, and suicide. Roughly 2,000 minors were murdered in 1988—twice the number killed in 1965 (a year of urban riots when America had 6.5 million more youths under age 18). Homicide is now the dominant cause of youth mortality in America's inner cities. Among black males 15 to 24 years old living in Washington D.C., murder accounted for 47 percent of all deaths in 1987.

8) Fear is a pervasive reality within a generation of urban schoolchildren that brings an estimated 135,000 guns (and six times as many knives) to the classroom each day. Eight percent of urban seventh to twelfth graders say they miss at least one day of school per month because they are physically afraid to go.

9) The decade of the 1970s brought a steep decline in the economic fortunes of children. From the 1950s through the early 1970s, the over-65 age bracket showed the highest poverty rate; since 1974, the under-18 bracket has shown the highest. Thus, the distinction of occupying America's poorest age bracket passed directly from Lost to 13th without ever touching G.I., Silent, or Boom along the way. Roughly one 13er in five now lives in poverty.

10) Through the 1980s, the 13ers' economic distress has moved right up the age ladder with them. In 1967, male wage earners in their early twenties made 74 percent as much as older males; by 1988, that ratio had fallen to 54 percent. Between 1973 and 1988, the median income of households headed by persons under age 25 (adjusted for inflation and family size) fell by 18 percent. The negative trend was not confined

to unmarried 13er mothers; even among married couples with children, the median income fell by 17 percent.

11) From the 1960s to the 1980s, the proportion of household heads age 18 to 24 owning their own homes fell by one-third—the steepest decline for any age bracket. In 1990, three out of four young men that age were still living at home, the largest proportion since the Great Depression.

12) Before 13ers came along, postwar sociologists generally assumed that hardening cynicism was a function of advancing age. No longer. In a late-1980s survey of "Cynical Americans," researchers noted that "the biggest surprise" was how "cynicism now seems to defy the traditional partnership of youth and idealism." Today, cynicism is "hitting hardest among young adolescents—more than half of those age 24 and under...They think it's all bull."

The 13er Lifecycle

Youth: The years of the "Consciousness Revolution" were among the most virulently anti-child periods in American history, producing a childhood world Tom Cruise recalls as "kind of scattered." Sacrificing one's own career or conjugal happiness became passe—even, by the logic of the era, bad for kids themselves. As the 1960s wore on, mothers and fathers increasingly looked at their children as hindrances to self-exploration. By the 1970s, they cast an envious eye at young Boomers—who then mainly looked upon babies like headaches, things you take pills not to have. Adults ranked autos ahead of children as necessary for "the good life," and the cost of raising a child became a hot topic. A flurry of popular books chronicled the resentment, despair and physical discomfort women were said to endure when bearing and raising 13er children. In *Ourselves and Our Children* (whose priorities revealed themselves in the juxtaposition of its title), "consider yourself" was ranked ahead of "benefiting our children" as a principle of sound parenting. Popular parental guides emphasized why-to-dos over what-to-dos, concluding that *doing* the right thing was less important than parent and child each *feeling* the right thing. To accomplish that, authors like Thomas Gordon (in *Parental Effectiveness Training*) advised parents to teach children to understand behavioral consequences at very young ages. Popular books by T. Berry Brazelton and Burton White stressed the determinism of the early childhood years, suggesting that a child's lifetime personality might be substantially sealed by the time he entered school. As Marie Winn would later note, "early-childhood determinism appeared to be a gift from gods" for parents with new wanderlust or careerism who could thereby conclude that their 6- or 10- year-old children could cope with family trauma well enough, given how carefully they had been tended as tots.

Divorce, and its attendant confusion and impoverishment, became the central fear of the 13er childhood world. In *It's Not the End of the World,* Judy Blume offered children the tale of a once-happy family disintegrating amid shouting, slapping and crying. Hearing these messages, even kids in stable families felt vulnerable and reacted by hardening their shells against adversity. While parents tried to persuade themselves (like Kyle Pruett in *The Nurturing Father: Journey Toward the Complete Man*) that family dissolution "freed" parent and child to have "better" and "less constricted" time together, these kids saw things differently. Thirteeners knew that where Boomers had been once worth the parental sacrifice of prolonging an unhappy marriage, they were not. Coping with the debris, America's 1970s-era children went from a family culture of *My Three Sons* to one of *My Two Dads,* encountering step-thises, half-thats, significant others and strangers at the breakfast table beyond what any other child generation ever knew. Reading Norma Klein's *It's OK If You Don't Love Me,* a child could ponder the fate of an adolescent girl who juggled a sex life with two boyfriends while sorting through her feelings about her mother's lover, her mother's former second husband and her father's second wife and their two children.

"The parent is usually a coordinator without voice or authority," observed Kenneth Keniston in 1977, noting how the moms and dads of that decade "hardly ever have...the power to make others listen to them." In homes, schools and courtrooms, America's style of nurturing children completed a two-decade passage from *Father Knows Best* to the tone of self-doubt in Bill Cosby's *Fatherhood:* "Was I making a mistake now? If so, it would just be mistake number nine thousand seven hundred and sixty three." Alvin Poussaint noted the dominant media image of the parent as "pal," who was "always understanding; they never get very angry. There are no boundaries or limits set. Parents are shown as bungling, not in charge, floundering as much as the children." This was not inadvertent. Parents who admit to being "many-dimensioned, imperfect human beings," reassured the authors of *Ourselves and Our Children,* "are able to give children a more realistic picture of what being a person is all about." On the one hand, parents were like Cosby's Cliff Huxtable, gentle and communicative; on the other hand, they expressed ambivalence where children sought clear moral answers, abandoned a positive vision of the future and required children to respond very young to sophisticated real-world problems. Like father and son in *Close Encounters of the Third Kind,* adults became more childlike and children more adultlike.

Through the 1970s, the media reinforced the growing view among children that adults were not especially virtuous, competent, or powerful. Adult life held no secrets. From TV sit-coms to "breakthrough" youth books, older generations made little effort to shield children from any topic, no matter what the effect on a child's sense of security and comfort. "I hate the idea that you should always protect children," wrote Judy Blume in defense of her books. "They live in the same world we do." *Mad* magazine's Al Feldstein put it more bluntly: "We told them there's a lot of garbage out in the world and you've got to be aware of it." One "Self-Care Guide" for latchkey children advised kids of "ways you can protect yourself from mugging and assault: Always pay attention to what is happening around you when you are on the street." And so 13ers were deliberately encouraged to react to life as you would hack through a jungle: Keep your eyes open, expect the worst and handle it on your own.

Approaching Rising Adulthood: Even as first-wavers reach their late twenties, this generation cannot be said to have "come of age." Nothing yet cements them emotionally. To date, the 13th remains a splintery generation; people can (and do) find almost anything they want in these kids. Far more than older generations, 13ers come with myriads of regional subgroups and ethnic minicultures, each thinking its own thoughts, listening to its own music, laying its own plans and paying little heed to each other. Yet the first signs of bonding are beginning to appear—a common *alienation* visible in 13er art and writing and in their growing awareness of their own economic vulnerability. "Sure we're alienated," admits American University student Daniel Ralph. "But who wouldn't be, in our shoes?"

Thirteeners are coming to realize that they bear much of the burden for the Reagan-era prosperity that so enriched the Silent and G.I.s. In inner cities, their impoverishment has caused adult alarm; elsewhere, it has been less noticed, thanks to a veneer of family-subsidized teen affluence. Even in the suburbs, 13ers entering the labor force are bearing much of their nations' new burden of foreign competition and debt. In industries where productivity is stagnant, two-tier wage systems hold elders harmless while making the new hires bear the full cost-cutting burden. Where foreign investors bid up the price of real estate, current homeowners profit, but would-be young homebuyers pay. Even as the 1980s-era spurt of tax reform lowered the tax rate on high-bracket incomes, FICA taxes on after-school wages kept going up.

Spurred by a sense of economic need, youths are working younger, longer, later at night and at more dangerous jobs than any child generation since the Lost. As federal administrators chart the steady rise in child labor law violations, 13ers carefully hone their survivalist ethic. Two-thirds believe they will have to work harder than earlier generations simply to enjoy the same standard of living. After leaving school, 13ers face tough choices made all the more frustrating by the adult wealth they see around them. Scanning her life's options, one Washington, D.C.

youth complained: "The way society presents it, I'll either be strung out on drugs, a manager at McDonald's, or a lawyer."

So far, they have concealed their plight thanks to the distinctly 13er habit of calling as little attention as possible to what they are feeling. In life, as when they walk down the street with their Walkmen and designer shades, they know how to keep others from knowing what they're hearing, watching, or thinking. They leave their troubles behind when they come to work—and take their minds off the job when they leave. Boomer bosses like ad executive Penny Erikson see them as "not driven from within," best suited for "short-term tasks" and in need of "reinforcement from above." Ask 13ers how they're doing, and as long as life stays reasonably patched together, "No problem" is their answer. They have learned to adjust by moving quickly into and (when they see a dead end) out of jobs. They look for quick strikes ahead of long-term promises, the *Wall Street Journal* describing them as "more willing to gamble their careers than...earlier generations." Often, their best chance for success comes from striking out on their own, finding a small market niche and filling it more cheaply and sensibly than older-run businesses. But for every Daryl Strawberry who hits the jackpot, untold others don't. And those who don't run smack into their deterministic ethos—that failure means something must be wrong with *you.* A rising number are masking their economic problems by "boomeranging" back into the parental house after a few years of trying to make it on their own.

Having no place to "boomerang" to, inner-city 13ers inhabit an especially grim world that does not like them, does not want them, and (as they see it) has nothing to offer them. "There's a growing malaise that young people suffer from," observes Victor Herbert, director of New York City high schools. "They feel they're not to be trusted, they're not good people, and they don't have to follow whatever inhibitions have been built up, especially when they're moving in a crowd." Urban kids have begun reacting with a nihilism that older generations consider proof of their worthless ruin. A new, reactionary style of sexism, racism and soulless violence has seeped into 13er-penned song lyrics. As "Ice-T" raps about "bitches," young thugs commit what elders call "hate crimes" targeted against gays, women and high-achieving ethnic groups. A new breed of young criminal shows a remorseless bent toward killing and maiming for no serious reason. Back in the late 1960s, Boomer crime was associated with rage and betrayed expectations; today, the young 13er criminal strikes elders as emotionally detached—even insensible. William Raspberry accuses them of being a "generation of animals," Stanton Samenow of having "the ability to shut off their conscience." The kids themselves invented the word "wilding" to describe their behavior. Asked why his friends go wilding, one New York City youth explained, "Sometimes they do it for fun, sometimes they do it for money, sometimes they just do it."

"We can arrest them, but jail is no deterrent," reports Washington Long, chief of police in Albany, Georgia. "I've had kids tell me. 'Hell, I ain't got nowhere else to go nohow'." "For them, it's just a matter of fact," agrees Washington, D.C. police chief Isaac Fulwood. "Oftentimes, they don't say anything. They just sit there and say, 'Officer, do what you gotta do' "—like the 16-year-old "wilder" Yusef Salaam, who asked his sentencing judge to "Give me the max." (He got it.) As Terry Williams describes it in *Cocaine Kids*, what is new about 13er criminals is their all-business attitude: their use of calculated violence to protect inventory (smugglers), market share (competing gangs), customer service (safe houses), accounts receivable (addicts), employee relations (runners) and risk management (cops). A young drug-runner, says Fulwood, "navigates in a world where most of us couldn't function, a world where you've got to be cunning, slick, and mentally and physically tough." And, of course, a world in which other choices seem even more hopeless. "I got no plans I ain't going nowhere," sings Tracy Chapman, "So take your fast car and keep on driving."

"When you get beneath the surface of their cheerfulness," observes Christopher Lasch, "young people in the suburbs are just as hopeless as those in the ghetto...living in a state of almost unbearable, though mostly inarticulate, agony. They experience the world only as a source of pleasure and pain." Like a whole generation of Breakfast Clubbers, 13ers face a Boom-driven culture quick to criticize or punish them but slow to take the time to find out what's really going on in their lives. By one count, their ranks include a half-million family "throwaways"—a word coined just for them. A generation of self-perceived throwaways might as well take a few risks. Punkers who blast their ears with boom boxes know what they're doing. "They tell me it will hurt me down the line," explains one 20-year-old Ohioan with a deafening sound system in his car, "but I don't care. I'm young and stupid, I guess." Thirteeners know life holds no special favors, for them at least. "I keep hearing this is the best time of our lives," says Harvard student Mandy Silber. "And I wonder—is it all downhill?" Where the earlier generations at like age had every reason to expect someday to nestle into law partnerships, tenured professorships and seats on the stock exchange, 13ers see very clearly the dead-end traps of a "McJobs" economy.

Late in 1989, as East German students poured over the Berlin Wall, a *Washington Post* article described high school kids as "left flat" and "utterly unmoved" by events that brought their teachers tears of joy. The youth attitude that strikes elders as blase is, from the 13er perspective, unflinching and realistic. They have already tramped through the dirty beach where idealism can lead. Remembering how the "freedom" of open classrooms produced noisy chaos and gave them what others constantly tell them was a bad education, they have learned to be skeptical about what happens whenever barriers are broken down. Maybe there will be new wars, maybe bad economic news—at the very least new competition. These kids were less surprised than their teachers when Iraq shattered the post-Cold War peace. American campuses were hardly fazed—Berkeley freshman Charles Connolly speaking for many when he said, "I think we should go in there and take care of it, full throttle." Meanwhile, thousands of Connolly's peers throttled off in uniform to keep oil flowing from Saudi Arabia to the big American homes and cars that so few 13ers can ever imagine buying at the same age their parents did. Where the Korean War once featured hardboiled, Trumanesque elders and sensitive, M*A*S*H*-like juniors, the Persian Gulf crisis features the opposite. Sixty-year-olds assume the complex, polysyllabic tasks: satellite communications, multilateral negotiations, peace-process evaluations. Thirteener 20-year-olds prepare for the brute, one-syllable jobs: sweat, hide, move, hit and kill.

Amid his Silent peers' euphoria over the end of the Cold War, pollster Peter Hart published a highly critical report about "Democracy's Next Generation," noting that only 12 percent of them mentioned voting as an attribute of good citizenship. Then again, 48 percent mentioned personal generosity. Having grown up in an age of anti-institutional feeling, 13ers look at it this way: When you vote, maybe you'll waste your time—or, worse, later feel tricked. But when you do something real, like bringing food to the homeless, you do something that matters, if only on a small scale. The president of MIT has likened the 13er civic attitude to that of the Lone Ranger: Do a good deed, leave a silver bullet and move on.

In *The Disappearance of Childhood,* Neil Postman observes that when 13ers were little, adults gave children "answers to questions they never asked." That problem still plagues this generation—except now the questions are, in effect, what made you the way you are, and how can we fix it? Blue-ribbon committeemen anguish over how to change their attitude about government, and inner-city Boomers "look internally" to understand "how we produced these children." But 13ers consider such efforts a waste of time and energy. Mostly, they figure such talk is pointless—like aspiring opera singer Marie Xaviere, who says that "even if you didn't want us, you made us. But we're here, and we're going to make the best of it." They know they are a generation without an elder-perceived mission. Yet "in spite of all the criticism and generally low expectations," Daniel Ralph insists his generation "will make a difference." What 13ers ask of others, maybe helplessly, is to lend an unjaundiced ear and check out what Nancy Smith calls "our 'attitude', a coolness, a detachment. . . and the way we speak: ironic,